Waste Recycling
and Pollution Control Handbook

Waste Recycling
and Pollution Control Handbook

A. V. Bridgwater
and
C. J. Mumford

George Godwin Limited
The book publishing subsidiary of
The Builder Group

First published in Great Britain 1979 by
George Godwin Limited
The book publishing subsidiary of
The Builder Group
1–3 Pemberton Row, Red Lion Court,
Fleet Street, London EC4P 4HL

British Library Cataloguing in Publication Data

Bridgwater, A V
  Waste recycling and pollution control handbook.
  1. Refuse and refuse disposal
  2. Factory and trade waste
  3. Sewage disposal   4. Waste products
  I. Title   II. Mumford, C J
  628'.44   TD791

  ISBN 0-7114-5306-3

Text set in 11/12 pt Photon Times, printed and bound
in Great Britain at The Pitman Press, Bath

Contents

PART TWO LIQUID WASTE TREATMENT

PART THREE CONTROL OF ATMOSPHERIC EMISSIONS

CONTENTS

PART FOUR   SOLID WASTE DISPOSAL AND RECOVERY PRACTICE

CONTENTS

PART FIVE NOISE ABATEMENT

PART SIX TECHNICAL ADMINISTRATION AND ECONOMICS

Preface

This book gives an overall coverage of practical management of all types of waste to meet the needs of process and plant engineers, managers, chemists, designers, contractors and those concerned with monitoring and enforcing relevant legislation. For the first time the interactions between all forms of pollution are identified and, particularly, the role that recycling has to play, not only in controlling pollution, but often as a significant contribution to controlling costs.

Two factors emerge as being of prime importance—environmental impact considerations reflected by legislation in defining what waste may not be discharged, and economics in defining the best way of handling the waste and assessing the options for recovery.

Since the incentive for effective waste treatment in most industrialised countries is legislative, current and proposed legislation is reviewed. Although this is exemplified by UK law, the principles, their scientific and technological bases and many of the specific constraints are valid internationally.

The incentive for recycling, however, is usually economics. An extensive chapter on technological economics is included which will enable the engineer or manager to evaluate completely not only a possible recycling process, but also the choice of the best waste handling system.

In order to avoid an encyclopaedic approach and to maintain a broad view and conciseness, it has occasionally been necessary to omit detailed descriptions or explanations. However, extensive referencing is included together with sources of more detailed information, with a classified bibliography. SI units have been used throughout, usually with the more commonly accepted industrial alternatives. However, many UK legislative measures are still based on Imperial units and conversion to SI can only, therefore, be regarded as approximate.

Finally, we would like to thank all our friends and colleagues, in the Department and in industry, for helpful discussions and comments during the preparation of the text.

University of Aston in Birmingham　　　　　　　　　　　　　　　　A. V. Bridgwater
June, 1979　　　　　　　　　　　　　　　　　　　　　　　　　　C. J. Mumford

Publisher's Note

While the principles discussed and the details given in this book are the product of careful study, the authors and publisher cannot in any way guarantee the suitability of processes or design solutions to individual problems and they shall not be under any legal liability of any kind in respect of or arising out of the form or contents of this book or any error therein, or the reliance of any person thereon.

Acknowledgements

Published works and sources of industrial information are acknowledged in the text. However, the authors would like to thank in particular Mr R. C. Keen of Bristol Polytechnic, Mr C. Minton of Pollution Control Limited, and our colleagues Dr E. L. Smith and Dr J. K. Maund.

The case studies presented in Chapter 7 are by kind permission of ICI Pollution Control Systems and Pollution Control Limited.

We would also like to thank Bridget Buckley of George Godwin Limited for her patient editing.

A. V. B.
C. J. M.

PART ONE

WASTE MANAGEMENT AND POLLUTION CONTROL

principle, if not in practice, and this is evidenced in the UK by the new integrated recovery/disposal facilities being set up in key locations around the country.

The Waste Producer

The producer of waste materials is primarily concerned with the question, 'What can I do with my waste?'. Unfortunately this often degenerates to 'How easily can I get rid of my waste?', with little regard either to the economics and attractions of the alternatives, or to the consequences. Examples range from the do-it-yourself motorist's dumping of drained sump oil to practices which result in total annual metal losses in the UK of several million tonnes (Chapter 15).

There are a number of legislative constraints within which the producer is obliged to work when disposing of waste. These are discussed in detail in Chapter 4; basically, they impose tight restrictions on gaseous and liquid effluent discharge and disposal of any toxic substance. The effect of these restrictions, for most gaseous and liquid effluents, is to make treatment obligatory to remove or minimise the pollutant before disposal. This often has the effect of concentrating the contaminant into a comparatively small volume, in either the liquid or the solid phase. This occurs, for example, in metal treatment industries when spent plating solutions are neutralised to precipitate toxic metal hydroxides before discharge to the public sewer. The resultant sludge is of considerably less volume than the effluent treated.

The exceptions include biological wastes, for example sewage, when the disposal contractor, i.e. the local authority, is responsible for treatment; again a relatively concentrated waste product, sewage sludge, is obtained. Other exceptions are those methods which destroy waste, such as incineration and cyanide oxidation.

The gaseous and liquid waste producer is thus left with a liquid or solid waste containing at least a relatively high proportion of contaminant. This places him in a similar position to that of the producer of solid waste.

There are several alternatives to the 'easy way out' of disposal and each employs recycling in some form. This may be direct or indirect internal recycling, external recycling to the raw material producer, or sale to a recycling agent (Figure 2.2). Examples of direct internal recycling are process scrap in many industries such as iron and steel, glass, plastics or paper, when offcuts, sprues or damaged materials are fed directly back to the 'melting pot'. Similarly, in refractory brick manufacture a proportion of 'grog', i.e. ground firebrick, is added to virgin clay to improve finished brick properties. Indirect internal recycling includes reprocessing of off-specification materials, again, for example, in metal production industries, or recovery of plating solutions and/or water from effluent treatment plants.

External recycling follows a similar pattern except that the producer may not have the facilities available to reprocess the material, so it is returned to the manufacturer for direct recycling (e.g. glass, damaged pure metal products) or for indirect recycling (e.g. polymeric materials, lubricating oils and damaged alloy metal products). External recycling of metals in small quantities is likely to be handled by scrap merchants as intermediaries: secondary mercury is an interesting example. Sale of waste to be reprocessed includes mainly relatively high-value organic liquids such as solvents and lubricating oil (Chapter 8) and batteries (Chapter 15). The recycling agent usually carries out separation or conversion to produce a saleable product.

Once again, the two main considerations in assessing the alternatives available are technical feasibility and economic viability, and of these it is rarely technical feasibility which is the limiting factor. For example, the separation of almost every combination of metals is possible but not necessarily economic, e.g. lead and antimony in lead–acid batteries (Chapter 15). Polymeric materials are one of the few exceptions but even this is changing (Chapter 16). Almost every problem is resolved, therefore, on its economic merit, although attitude, discussed later, plays a part. In the long term, as resources become depleted, artificial values may be ascribed to some materials to justify recovery.

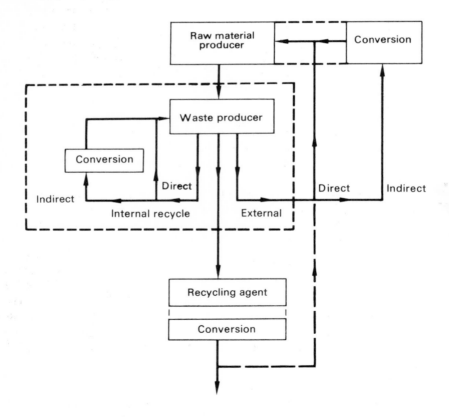

Fig. 2.2 Alternative recycle routes

TABLE 2.1 TECHNICAL AND ECONOMIC FACTORS IN THE SELECTION OF A WASTE-HANDLING SYSTEM

	Technical factors	**Elements of cost**
Direct internal recycling	Purity/contamination of waste Ease of assimilation into raw material feed stream	Cost of internal collection
Indirect internal recycling	Technical constraints of conversion or separation Economy of scale	Cost of internal collection Cost of conversion or separation
External recycling	Characterisation constraints may be applied	Cost of internal collection and storage Possible cost of transport Cost of replacement of lost materials Income or credit (negative cost) from sale.
Sale to recycling agent	Waste may not be saleable Characterisation constraints may be severe Treatment may be necessary to produce saleable materials	Cost of internal collection and storage Possible cost of transport Possible cost of treatment Income (negative cost) from sale
Disposal	Full characterisation may be necessary Pretreatment may be necessary and/or desirable	Cost of internal collection and storage Cost of disposal Cost of replacement of lost materials
General	Size of waste problem Inherent value of waste	Excluding necessary or obligatory costs, e.g. treatment required by law

The waste producer must go through a series of steps or decisions to discover the possibilities, then ascertain the cost of the feasible alternatives. The alternatives are most usefully considered in the following order:

Direct internal recycling
Indirect internal recycling
External recycling to manufacturer
Sale to recycling agent
Disposal

Some of the more important technical factors that require consideration are summarised in Table 2.1. In practice the problem is likely to be more complex, as a waste stream may be divided, perhaps by treatment, with each part following a different route. Furthermore, a reduction in total quantity of scrap or effluent can often result from a critical evaluation of manufacturing quality control procedures.

The next step is to ascertain the total net cost of each system. While specific figures clearly cannot be given, contributory elements to the total net cost for each alternative are included in Table 2.1. For more detail and specific costs, a systems approach to the economics of waste handling which considers unit costs of all steps in recycling or disposal of waste is outlined in Chapter 20. Summation of the elements of cost for each alternative will give a total cost which must include all costs and incomes. This information, together with technical feasibility constraints, will be helpful in deciding on the best course of action, and may be usefully employed in a cost–benefit analysis.

Other factors can also affect the final decision, depending on individual circumstances. For example:

1. Although indirect internal recycling may be an attractive technical and economic proposition, capital may not be available for investment.
2. An internal recycling operation may only prove attractive on a larger scale than is possible within the one organisation. It may be worth while to investigate the possibility of collaboration with another or several other organisations to take advantage of economy of scale. This has already been proposed for hydrochloric acid pickle liquor by a group of users in a small geographical area.
3. For substantial quantities of waste it may be worth while to carry out research into ways of utilising the waste, to reduce costs of disposal or even to turn a cost into a profit. The work of the Building Research Establishment referred to later is one example.
4. It is sometimes necessary to assign artificial costs or values when considering socially desirable waste-handling problems. These are invariably subjective and arbitrary, but without them it is not possible to carry out a useful cost–benefit analysis.

Disposal Contractor

As his name suggests, the disposal contractor is primarily concerned with disposal which, together with transportation or conveyance, constitutes the bulk of his activity. Under some circumstances some or all of the functions of the disposal contractor may be taken over by the waste producer, for example by providing transport or by totally disposing of the waste, as in slags from secondary metal refineries which may be dumped on the smelter's own site, and with gaseous emissions. The disposal contractor may sometimes only provide part of this service, for example specialist transportation, or he may act as an intermediary or agent between the waste producer and the manufacturer or recycling agent. He may carry out this latter function as the agent of the waste producer or manufacturer, or he may act on behalf of the recycler on a contract or free-market basis.

In acting to maximise his return, the scope available to him for optimisation is small due to the considerable legislative pressures recently enacted, which necessitate stricter control over the handling and disposal of many wastes, particularly those that are toxic or hazardous and notifiable.

The range of alternatives available for disposal of gas, liquid or solid wastes may be subdivided into dumping and dilution and then further subdivided by location (Table 2.2). Under some circumstances waste may be dumped in such

TABLE 2.2 WASTE DISPOSAL: DUMPING/DILUTION/DESTRUCTION

(a) *Disposal:* implies irrecoverable loss of waste

Phase	Method	Location	Example
Gas	Dumping Dilution	Underground Land River Sea	Not possible (?)
		Air	Combustion products
Liquid	Dumping	Underground	Industrial effluent to mineshaft
		Sewers	Household and industrial effluent
		Land	Current practice for waste, to gravel pits, brick pits
		River	Treated and untreated industrial waste
		Sea	Raw sewage, industrial waste
		Air	Mist, fog
	Dilution	Underground	Seepage from tips
		Land	Seepage from tips
		River	Treated and untreated effluent
		Sea	Sewage, industrial waste
		Air	Mist, fog
Solid	Dumping	Underground	Spoil, minefill
		Land	Household refuse, filter cake
		River	China clay waste
		Sea	Land reclamation
		Air	As dust and grit in gaseous emissions
	Dilution	All locations	Any waste as small particles will disperse

(b) *Destruction* (partial disposal: the reaction products still require disposal as in (a) above).
Chemical   e.g. cyanide oxidation
Thermal   e.g. incineration

a way that recovery is a practical proposition: it may then be regarded as being stored (Table 2.3). While it is rarely practised deliberately, except for very short-term collection of material for reprocessing, storage clearly has possibilities and is discussed in Chapter 13; it may be regarded as controlled disposal, either to permit future utilisation of the waste or to ensure safety.

Disposal contractors tend to specialise in a few of the wide range of disposal methods available, and the producer therefore chooses the contractor who can handle his particular waste at the lowest cost. It is, of course, possible for a disposal contractor to make use of the facilities offered by competitors but, apart from employment of public/local authority facilities, this is rarely done. The disposal contractor tends to use the cheapest facility possible to maximise his profit.

TABLE 2.3 WASTE DISPOSAL: STORAGE

For future use	Short-term: accumulation of sufficient material to make recovery viable	e.g. solvents
	Long-term, intentional	e.g. metal hydroxide sludge
	Long-term, unintentional	e.g. slag heaps
For safety		e.g. radioactive waste

As well as disposing of waste, the contractor is often in a unique position to bring together a multitude of small waste arisings that separately are impossible to recycle or reuse in any form, but which together offer the possibility of profit. A number of case studies are outlined towards the end of this chapter, one of which is described in greater detail in Chapter 9. This demonstrates an approach to the investigation of the possibilities available for recovery, provides actual results of one investigation, and suggests further ways of increasing the scope and conserving resources. There is no easy way of assessing the possibilities of recovery, but a suggested procedure is given in Table 2.4. One of the biggest problems in any recovery venture is that of reselling the product, so that marketing studies form an important part of the evaluation exercise. The problems are compounded by rapid fluctuations in supply and demand of many wastes and recoverable components. This is illustrated by the waste paper industry over the last few years.

The disposal contractor is thus in a particularly favourable position to become a recycling agent in his own right. One of the disadvantages is that generally only highly contaminated wastes are recycled but these do have a negative cost in that the disposal cost element is removed, and the operation has already made a profit for the contractor. This can open up a wide range of possibilities that offer an attractive return on investment, i.e. greater profits, as well as assuring expansion and growth.

TABLE 2.4 SUGGESTED PROCEDURE FOR EVALUATING POTENTIAL FOR RECOVERY OF
MATERIALS FROM WASTE

1. Calculate total quantity of waste.
2. Analyse waste, for each load if necessary.
3. Calculate total quantity of each material contained in the waste.
4. Calculate total quantity of each material recoverable from the waste.
5. Ascertain or estimate value of each material in steps 3 and 4.
6. Multiply the total quantity of each material by its value. This gives an approximate maximum figure for the income to be achieved by selling that material as not all the material may be recoverable, for example because of dilution.
7. Rank the values (step 5) and the potential maximum incomes (step 6) in descending order.
8. Select the material that has the highest overall ranking of the two lists combined. This will ensure that the highest value material is investigated, which is a useful rule of thumb to follow, and appreciable and economical quantities, which is another useful rule of thumb.
9. Design a process to recover this material. At this stage only an outline flow diagram is required with some essential processing data. It is important to remember that not all the waste may need to be processed.
10. Estimate capital and operating costs (see Chapter 20).
11. Estimate income.
12. Calculate return on investment. This may be on a simple percentage return basis, or may employ a discounting method taking grants and taxes into account. This latter technique is a much more realistic way of assessing the profitability of a project (see Chapter 20).
13. If the return on the investment is sufficiently attractive, this is justification for a more detailed research investigation to confirm the results.
14. The evaluation procedure (steps 8 to 13) should be repeated ideally for all materials but certainly for all materials worth more than £100 per tonne. Below this rough guideline, profitable recovery becomes increasingly less likely as the value falls.

Recycling Agent

As described earlier, there are several mechanisms for recycling waste.

1. Internal recycling is carried out by the waste producer. This is often the most advantageous and economical way of recycling, as the quality of waste/scrap can be controlled.

2. External recycling to the manufacturer is perhaps the next most attractive, if feasible. The manufacturer can usually readily incorporate the waste into his manufacturing process, and is thus able to offer a relatively high price.

3. The external and independent recycling agent is the last alternative available. He can usually take relatively contaminated waste that can only otherwise go for disposal.

External recycling to the manufacturer, directly or via a scrap merchant, is widely practised by the metal processing and fabricating industries, for example. In the case of metals particularly it is sometimes difficult to differentiate between primary and secondary metal producers when the latter may be considered as recycling agents, but both require waste or scrap for operation. The primary producer can only handle metal within specified impurity levels, while the secondary producer can often accept a wide range of metal and metal compounds with relatively high levels of impurities. Other examples of materials that may be recycled to the manufacturer include paper, textiles and glass. The common feature is that the materials may be directly incorporated into the existing manufacturing process with minimum or no additional treatment.

Independent recycling agents form perhaps the smallest and least publicised of the groups identified with waste handling. Due to the importance of marketing both in obtaining waste raw material and selling products, considerable confidentiality tends to surround their operation. Generally they process high-value materials that require simple and/or few steps for separation and purification. Typical examples include non-ferrous metals such as copper, nickel, cadmium and precious metals, solvents, lubricating oils and plastics.

The decision as to which materials to recover is governed by a range of factors including raw material supplies, market requirements, competition, technology and economics, and there are no clear rules or guidelines to follow. In the UK a useful source of information on possible raw materials is contained in the regular bulletin of the Waste Exchange Service. This indicates which waste materials are currently available and which by implication are not therefore being recovered. However, potential recovery agents are more likely to find unexploited raw materials and products by experience, personal contact, good fortune or a systematic study of possibilities.

Attitude

One of the most intangible problems associated with waste recovery is that of attitude, both that of the waste producer and that of the users of recovered materials.

The small- to medium-sized waste producer often wants to be rid of his waste as quickly and easily as possible without considering either the alternatives for disposal or the possibilities of recovery, unless well established and traditional practices exist. Conversely, the largest waste producers such as the Coal Board, the Central Electricity Generating Board and the iron and steel industries produce such large quantities of waste that public and political pressures compel them to dispose of their waste in the most inoffensive and economical way. The size of the problem is such that recovery or reutilisation of even a small part of the waste can produce a significant improvement in terms of cost and public opinion.

Legislation has already produced significant and valuable reductions in levels of atmospheric pollution. To a certain extent this has been a result of public pressure arising from education as to the widespread effects of pollution by gaseous wastes. This has caused the gaseous waste producers to become much more responsible and selfconscious. Unfortunately a similar attitude has yet to be generally adopted by the liquid and solid waste producers and by those waste disposal contractors who are not concerned with gaseous wastes.

The other aspect of the problem of attitude is that of the acceptability of reclaimed materials. Recycled materials have tended to be regarded merely as a stopgap solution to shortages of primary materials, rather than as an alternative, and possibly cheaper, source of supply. In many industries, consumers have preferred primary raw materials, even at considerable price premiums, and as soon as shortages have been alleviated the secondary materials are rejected in favour of the primary source. As a result of this attitude, recycling has so far failed to fulfil its economic promise and will continue to fail until policies and incentives for the use of raw materials are changed.

A variety of reasons are given by consumers for preferring primary raw materials; these are often very subjective and sometimes a result of historical accident. The plastics industry is a good example of the aversion in which consumers hold recycled material. This extends to economics, in that the necessary incentives for industry to overcome its prejudices and accept recycled materials involve price differentials of an irrational size for comparable specification. Consumers can often make a change to recycled materials more easily than they care to admit; an example is the paper and board industry, which for many years would not consider the use of reclaimed raw materials. As supplies have become more scarce and costly, the industry has been using increasing quantities of recycled materials, and even more could be used if the industry had the necessary equipment.

Industry needs sufficient confidence in the reclamation industries to invest money in the necessary equipment on a long-term basis. This supports the case for these industries to be given incentives, perhaps in the form of a straightforward financial contribution which would enable them to invest the necessary capital with confidence without fear of primary materials capturing the market.

Economics and Costs

In some respects the economics of disposal and recovery are simple and straightforward, but in other respects the complexities defy analysis.

It is not unreasonable for the small waste producer to dispose of his waste as cheaply as possible although, as outlined earlier, careful consideration should first be given to recycling. Some form of incentive to recycle, other than mere cost reduction, would be desirable; this incentive should apply also to the disposal alternatives, making the disposal contractor offering a recovery facility cheaper than one who only dumps the waste. Until such a scheme can be devised and implemented there is likely to be little choice available.

Any recycling opportunity needs careful consideration and evaluation. A critical examination of the possibilities may be more rewarding if carried out by an independent specialist with wider experience and a less constricted approach than an in-company examination. Each possibility requires careful technical analysis initially, perhaps followed by an economic evaluation, but this order is not essential and short cuts may be feasible. The science or art of process generation is still in its infancy, but this holds much promise in investigating

TABLE 2.5 ECONOMIC ANALYSIS OF A WASTE RECYCLING PROPOSAL: HYPOTHETICAL AND SIMPLIFIED OUTLINE CASE STUDY (see Figure 2.3)

Data and Cost Estimates

Process: Recovery of 7 tonnes/w dissolved metal from 280 tonnes/w spent electrolyte in a continuous process

Plant capacity	7 tonnes per week
Plant throughput	280 tonnes per week
Estimated total installed capital cost	£900 000
Estimated total operating cost, assumed fixed, including interest, excluding depreciation	£900 per tonne metal
Present value of metal	£1900 per tonne
Projected value of metal assumed increased by £100 per tonne per year (i.e. about 5% per year)	
Time for construction of plant	1 year

Profitability (tax and grant excluded, see chapter 20)

Return on (original) investment, 5 year plant life	31%
Return on (original) investment, 10 year plant life	50%
Payback time	2·21 yrs
Payback time with interest (by NPW at 25%)	3·45 yrs
Net present worth at 25% discount rate	
Net present worth at 5 year plant life	£282 500
Net present worth at 10 year plant life	£824 200
Net present worth at 40% discount rate	
Net present worth at 5 year plant life	£198 000
Net present worth at 10 year plant life	£210 200
Discounted cash flow (DCF) rate of return, 5 year plant life	38%
Discounted cash flow (DCF) rate of return, 10 year plant life	46%

These figures indicate that the proposal is financially attractive, even though tax and grant are ignored.

Uncertainty

Uncertainty may arise in one or more areas of which the following are likely to be most significant:

Capital cost estimates
Operating cost estimates
Realisation for metal product (sales income)
Ability to sell all of the product
Time for plant construction

Sensitivity analysis produces a matrix showing the effect on rate of return of a change for each variable singly and/or in combination. For example:

(a) Base case, 10 year plant life, DCF return = 46%

(b) Capital cost increased by 10%, DCF return = 43%
(c) Operating cost increases by 5% per year, DCF return = 44%
(d) Realisation does not increase but stays constant, DCF return = 34%
(e) Cumulative effect of (b), (c) and (d) together, DCF return = 30%

Risk analysis produces a probability distribution for rate of return or NPW by considering individual probability distributions for each area of uncertainty and approximating the total effect by a Monte Carlo simulation (Figure 2.3).

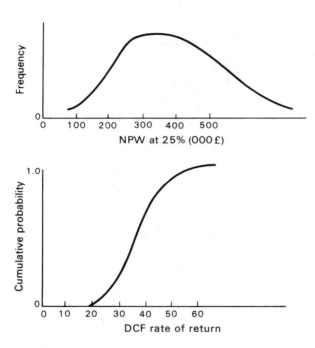

Fig. 2.3 Probability distribution for rate of return on net present worth (Table 2.5)

possible manufacturing processes to make use of waste materials.

Economic analysis of the possibilities may be hindered by lack of information or techniques for estimating capital and operating costs. A number of new
techniques have been developed recently which require minimal information
but which give an acceptable accuracy for preliminary assessment; these are
discussed in more detail in Chapter 20. With these cost estimates, the viability
of any proposal may then be examined by calculating a return on investment,
preferably using a discounting method to account properly for the time value of
money. Under current economic circumstances a return of at least 20–25%
would be required by almost any commercial organisation proposing to invest
in a new venture. For a recycling venture it would not be unreasonable to
expect a return of at least 30–35% after tax.

Accepting that considerable uncertainty exists with any new venture, but particularly in the reclamation industries, it may be useful to take account of uncertainty in the economic analysis. This may be carried out either by sensitivity analysis, where the single and cumulative consequences of small variations in cost and marketing elements are studied by their effect on the rate of return, and/or by risk analysis, which considers the probability of each cost and marketing element and their cumulative effect on the likelihood of achieving an acceptable rate of return on investment.

To illustrate these steps, some figures from a hypothetical case study are given in Table 2.5. The results indicate the information necessary for evaluation of any new proposal. It is unlikely that a situation would arise where sensitivity and risk analyses are necessary, but these techniques are available for identifying and quantifying the risks associated with a new venture.

If recycling or recovery in any form is neither feasible nor economically viable, the alternative is disposal via a disposal contractor. The simplest approach is to obtain quotations against firm specifications and conditions and choose the cheapest. Even here, however, there may be opportunities for cost-saving by installing some pretreatment, such as compaction of waste, to take full advantage of the disposal facility. The cost of the pretreatment operation may be quickly recovered in the reduced disposal costs; a careful study of the possibilities may be rewarding.

An example concerns the sludge produced from metal-plating effluent treatment plant. After sedimentation the sludge contains 95–99% water and may be removed by a disposal contractor in this liquid form. Installation of a filter press to reduce the water content to 75% or less will significantly reduce disposal costs. Typical figures are given in Table 2.6.

Examples

The first two case studies below demonstrate how disposal of waste at small but finite cost can be converted to a profitable recovery operation. The alternative of dumping is clearly hazardous, wasteful and unnecessary. The third case study results from a detailed investigation of the total waste handled by a large disposal contractor in the West Midlands. This is described in more detail later but serves to show some of the possibilities that exist for the disposal contractor.

1. A metal-processing firm was reported to be discharging 1500 litres/h of metal-bearing solution of the following approximate composition and value:

Sulphate	250 g/l	
Nickel	20 g/l corresponding to 240 tonnes p.a.	
	(worth about £400 000 as metal)	
Arsenic	8 g/l corresponding to 96 tonnes p.a.	
Iron	6 g/l corresponding to 72 tonnes p.a.	
Copper	3·5 g/l corresponding to 42 tonnes p.a.	
Zinc	3 g/l corresponding to 36 tonnes p.a.	

TABLE 2.6 EXAMPLE OF THE EFFECT OF PRETREATMENT ON DISPOSAL COSTS

50 tonnes per week liquid sludge requires disposal containing 2·5% solids (97·5% water content).

Cost of disposal is £5 per tonne or £25 per 4·5 m³ (1000 gal):
  Total weekly cost = £250
  Total annual cost = £12 500

Pressing the sludge to 75% water reduces the quantity for disposal to 10 tonnes per week of semi-solid cake. This costs less to dispose of because less specialised transport and disposal techniques are required.

At a disposal cost of £4 per tonne:
  Total weekly cost = £40
  Total annual cost = £2000

Cost of buying and installing filter press = approx. £10 000
Additional cost of discharging (clean) water to sewer (1800 m³ (400 000 gal) p.a.) = about £100 p.a.
Additional labour costs to operate filter press, above that required for sludge disposal = 1/8 man year = about £500 p.a.

Additional maintenance costs on filter press = £400 p.a. (4% on capital cost)

$$\text{Net cost} = £10\ 000 \text{ initially}$$
$$\text{Net annual saving} = £9500$$

The filter press would thus pay for itself in the first year of operation, and thereafter give an annual saving of nearly £10 000.

Preliminary design of a solvent extraction process to recover the nickel indicates that a return on investment of over 200% might be expected, with a payback time of less than six months!

2. An organisation was treating 90 m³ (20 000 gallons) per day of effluent of the following composition (percentage by weight):

Water	95·35
Emulsions	3·00
White spirit	0·60
Greases	0·40
Detergents	0·30
Inorganic salts	0·35
	100·00

Preliminary design of a small plant to recover the white spirit indicated a return on investment of around 40% and a saving for the company of £3300 per year. The attraction of recycling has been enhanced by the increase in crude-oil-based raw material costs.

3. The total waste handled by a waste disposal contractor in the West Midlands was examined and investigated for reclaimable materials. Both hydrochloric acid and zinc oxide appeared to offer attractive returns on invest-

ment in recovery processes: recovery of 2500 tonnes per year hydrochloric acid offered a return of over 50%; recovery of 360 tonnes per year zinc as oxide offered a return of over 25%.

Appreciable quantities of other non-ferrous metals were also present. This evaluation is explained further in Chapter 9. Total metal losses from all sources in the UK are examined in Chapter 15.

CHAPTER 3

Characterisation of Wastes and Pollutants

In order to discuss techniques for the disposal and recovery of wastes it is important to have a clear understanding of the nature of the materials involved. This refers not only to their composition or physical state but also to a complete scheme of characterisation that includes all the information necessary for disposal or recycling. The pattern set out in Chapter 1, classifying waste by phase, is followed in setting out a characterisation scheme. Liquid waste perhaps presents the most varied and inadequately quantified of all waste-handling problems, and this is therefore discussed first. The range of solid and gaseous wastes is more limited and the characterisation used for liquid waste is modified to take account of their greater specificity.

A means of characterising waste is needed by the producer, the disposer and the recycler. Some of the responsibility for safe disposal of waste rests with the producer. He should therefore characterise his waste to comply with legislation and give sufficient information to the disposal contractor to enable him to handle it safely. Experience suggests that the producer often does not have sufficient information, motivation or incentive to carry out this task effectively. This therefore places greater responsibility on the disposal contractor, whose characterisation requirements are probably much more detailed; he accepts a wide variety of wastes some of which are poorly defined. Possibly least is known about the waste processor; he usually operates in a closed and pseudo-traditional market, often buying on long-term contract from the waste producer. Under these conditions the reprocessor's characterisation needs to be most specific, but since his operations are generally in a well defined area the comprehensive scheme described below may be unnecessary.

Characterisation of Liquid Waste

Waste may be characterised according to:

  (a) Origin
  (b) Destination
  (c) Content—phase of liquid and pollutant(s)
  (d) Content—physical nature of pollutant(s)
  (e) Content—chemical nature of pollutant(s)
  (f) Content—quality and concentration of pollutant(s)
  (g) Content—toxicity and hazard
  (h) Treatment method
  (i) Value

It is important to appreciate the limitations under each heading, as it is unlikely that any one method will be sufficient to characterise a waste liquid adequately.

(a) *Origin*

To classify wastes by origin may appear superfluous, since the producer should know where his waste comes from, and the disposal contractor should know where he collects it from. However, neither producer nor contractor may be aware of the alternatives available for treatment or disposal, or of the potential value of the waste if recycled or reused. By itself, a classification by source is not very helpful until it is related to one or more of the other methods of classification. It can then be a useful starting-point for a characterisation scheme and for a discussion of properties, effects or treatment methods.[1-7]

The *Water Treatment Handbook*[2] provides an extensive classification by source, including identification of the multiplicity of waste streams that can arise from each industry and an indication of the contents and requirements for treatment. However, a range of wastes can arise from one industry, each of which requires individual consideration. To be effective, classification either has to become very detailed, and hence unwieldy, or to be simplified.[7-9] The following is a comprehensive but simple and effective list of main sources by type of industry:

  * Sewage
     Metal production (including mining)
     Metal treatment
  * Animal processing
  * Vegetable processing
  * Food processing (if excluded from the above)
     Organic chemical
     Inorganic chemical
  * Agricultural
     Water

When related to type of treatment (q.v.), this list can conveniently be split into wastes normally processed by a biological system (starred) and others. This leads to a simpler classification:

Natural organic wastes (usually water-based)
'Synthetic' organic wastes (usually non-water-based)
Inorganic wastes (usually water-based)

This allows for a multi-effluent industry, but requires additional information in order to be useful. Sources of waste are also discussed in Chapter 6.

Geographical location of the source of waste is also important when considering costs and disposal v. recycling. Transportation, for example, can contribute up to 90% or more of the total cost of waste disposal.

(b) *Destination*

The destination or handling of waste is very much easier to examine and classify than its source (Figure 3.1).

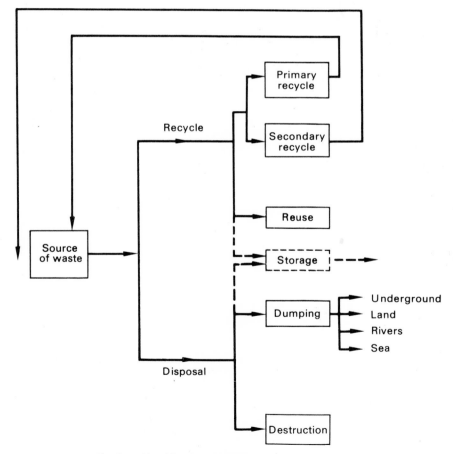

Fig. 3.1 Classification of liquid waste by destination

Recycling may give the primary material for the waste producer to reuse, such as electroplating salts from plating wastes, or a secondary material which is related, such as metal or metal oxides for smelting to metal again from plating wastes. A waste may be reused, rather than recycled, when it is employed for a different purpose: for example, the burning of waste lubricating oils or solvents for their heat content. Further subclassification of primary and secondary recycle and reuse could be by industrial source as under (a) above, but requires an exhaustive analysis of sequential material flows through related industries and a knowledge of marketing factors. Such an exercise is only useful for highly specific materials such as non-ferrous metals (Chapter 15).

Disposal includes dumping on land, underground, to rivers or to the sea; some pretreatment may be necessary to comply with legislation. Destruction, for example by incineration, is also included. Dumping for future recovery is employed in the short term for liquid wastes such as solvents which are accumulated until recovery is practical and viable, but long-term storage has only been seriously proposed for solid wastes,[10] except for radioactive liquid wastes which are a special case. There are, however, a number of examples of dumped waste being reworked as a result of technological progress and rising raw material costs. The disposal alternatives available can only be evaluated with information on liquid composition and costs.

Recent studies of recycling v. disposal include an investigation into the economics of recycling pickle liquor as opposed to neutralisation and disposal,[11] and incineration of pig manure compared with reuse as fertiliser.[12] Other examples are described in Chapter 9.

(c) Content—Phase of Liquid

Waste is most often characterised by content and the plethora of literature on liquid waste is invariably related to treatment of a specific waste, often by a specific method. Probably the simplest and most obvious classification is by phase of liquid, which derives directly from (a) above.

Essentially, two liquid phases may be considered—aqueous and non-aqueous. These may occur together and hence form a third, for example emulsions and oily waste-water from petroleum refining. This is a particularly helpful initial screening test as it differentiates between those wastes where the major constituent, water, may be safely discharged (for example, to rivers), usually after separation of the pollutant, and those wastes which must be totally recycled or disposed of in some other way. This differentiation was recognised in the circular relating to the Deposit of Poisonous Waste Act[13] and also in a related provisional Code of Practice.[14] Subdivisions may be readily formed from any of the other classifications on content, such as identification of the specific pollutant, or origin of waste, as discussed previously, or destination, as shown in Figure 3.2. This classification must be combined into one or more other methods in order to characterise a waste completely.

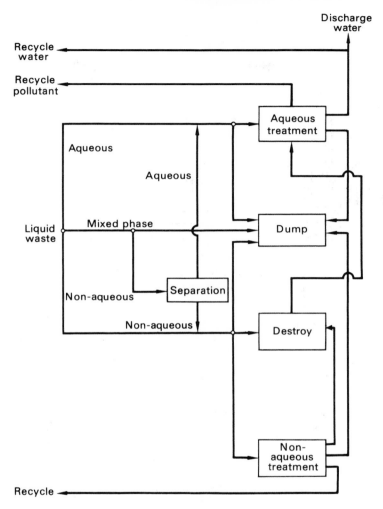

Fig. 3.2 Classification of liquid waste by phase

(d) Content—Physical Nature of Pollutant

Classification by phase differentiates between those effluents which are totally noxious (non-aqueous or 'synthetic' organic wastes), and those effluents from which the pollutant has to be removed or changed to leave an aqueous liquid that is acceptable for discharge. Non-aqueous and mixed wastes that are disposed of need little identification other than that required for safe handling and disposal. Classification in this case is therefore only of academic interest. Further information is necessary, however, for recycling, and sometimes physical characteristics are sufficient. For non-aqueous materials, the physical nature may be classified in two ways—nature of pollutant(s) and conventional physical properties.

The pollutant(s) in either aqueous or non-aqueous wastes may take several forms:

Dissolved gas
Suspended gas
Miscible liquid
Immiscible liquid
Solution of a solid
Suspended solid

Subdivisions may be formed by consideration of multiple-phase contamination and morphology of the contaminative phase, to give the classification shown in

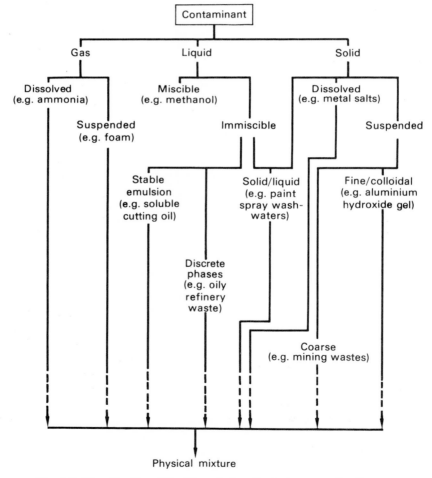

Fig. 3.3 Classification of liquid waste by physical nature of pollutant

Figure 3.3. An alternative, complementary classification is by conventional physical properties. A suggested list for this is given in Table 3.1 for aqueous and non-aqueous wastes. Information on properties of specific chemicals and mixtures is readily available in the literature.[15,16]

TABLE 3.1 PHYSICAL PROPERTIES OF LIQUID WASTES

Aqueous	Non-aqueous
Biological oxygen demand (BOD)	Ash
Colour	Boiling point
Conductivity	Calorific value
Density	Chemical oxygen demand (COD)
pH	Density
Suspended solids	Distillation range
Temperature	Explosive limits
Total dissolved solids	Flashpoint
Viscosity	Odour
	Temperature
	Viscosity
	Volatility

All the above apply also to mixed wastes.

Biodegradable wastes

In addition to the above properties of aqueous waste, the following are also employed:

Ash
COD
Nitrogen content
Odour
Permanganate value
Taste
Turbidity

(e) Content—Chemical Nature of Pollutant

A full chemical analysis is the ultimate and complete classification of waste, but is insufficient by itself to characterise waste adequately. For example, trace quantities of highly toxic materials may be more significant than larger quantities of relatively inert materials. A range of classifications by general chemical action has been employed,[17–21] but none of these appears to cover all types of waste. This may be explained by the tendency to differentiate liquid wastes into sewage and other wastes, probably because identification of pollutants in chemical wastes is easy, whereas among the biodegradeable wastes sewage is particularly difficult to define chemically.

Sewage consists of natural organics (such as protein, fats, carbohydrates) either in solution or suspended, 'synthetic' organics[22] (such as detergents and disinfectants) and various life forms.[20] Painter[23] has reported extensively on the chemical composition of sewage, and other authors have attempted a definition by composition.[24] Apart from sewage, any waste containing organic material may be treated biologically, although this is usually reserved for 'natural' organic wastes which may be conveniently termed biodegradeable.

An initial chemical classification of liquid waste that appears to cover all possibilities is:

Insoluble 'volatile' organics	e.g. hexane
Insoluble nonvolatile organics	e.g. tars
Soluble organics	e.g. acetone
Acids	e.g. sulphuric acid
Alkalis	e.g. caustic soda
Metals in solution	e.g. iron chloride
Metals, suspended	e.g. nickel hydroxide
Cyanide	e.g. copper cyanide solution
Neutral inorganic chemicals	e.g. ammonium sulphate
Natural biodegradeable substances	e.g. potato-processing waste

These classes are not mutually exclusive: a waste may have several of these characteristics, for example alkaline cyanide, or may consist of a mixture, for example suspended metal compounds, alkali and cyanide. Classification may be further expanded into individual chemicals. Chemical analysis will usually give the proportions of each chemical present, except that organics may be characterised by one or more physical properties as listed in Table 3.1. To indicate the scope of identification of individual compounds, a United Nations publication[21] lists 111 inorganic and 328 organic chemicals as examples of products of the basic chemical manufacturing industry. A complete list of chemicals that might be found in waste would be many times larger.

Alternatively the description may be contracted into synthetic organic materials, natural organic materials, and inorganic materials. This abbreviated characteristic corresponds to classification by origin, as in (a) above.

Finally, waste is usually waste because it consists of an unusable and often unpleasant mixture of chemicals.

(f) Content—Quantity and Concentration of Pollutant

Data are required on flow rates of waste and concentration of pollutants, together with variations with time both throughout the day and over the year. This is necessary for design of treatment plant and storage facilities, arrangements for disposal and budgeting. These figures are also needed in order to evaluate the possibility of recycling, either by the producer or by an outside organisation. The information alone is not very helpful, but it complements the other aspects of classification of content of waste. It is, however, possible to estimate the capital cost of a number of processes, including effluent treatment plant, on the basis of capacity only. Techniques available for cost estimation based on minimal information are discussed in Chapter 20.

(g) *Content—Toxicity and Hazard*

Concern at indiscriminate dumping of toxic waste led to the Deposit of Poisonous Waste Act 1972[13] (see Chapter 4) and has been extensively discussed.[14,19,25-32] The Key Report,[19] which preceded the Act, listed a range of chemicals and waste liquids reported to the Committee as toxic (Table 3.2). It is of limited value as complex and vaguely defined wastes, such as kier liquor and alkaloid wastes, are included alongside specific chemicals such as chrome acid and propyl isocyanate. Perhaps an easier approach is a study of exempted materials (Table 3.3).[26,33]

TABLE 3.2 'TOXIC' WASTES DESCRIBED TO THE KEY COMMITTEE

Waste 'chemical' slurry	Highly acid organic residues
Tarry liquids	Sludge from tar distillation
Waste paint	Phenol-formaldehyde sludge
Solid tarry matter	Nicotine waste
Oil-impregnated rubbish	Kier liquor
Arsenic waste	Spent sheep dip
Wastes containing cyanide	Sulphides
Beryllium wastes	Mercaptans
Waste oil	Acid tars
Residues from pesticide formulations	Alkaloid wastes
Photographic waste	Arsenious sulphide
Carbides	Fluorides
Sludges containing copper, zinc, cadmium, nickel, etc. compounds	Plating sludges
	Pickling sludges
Aromatic hydrocarbons	Spent acids
Noxious organic solvents	Sludge from leaded petrol
White spirit	Waste alcohols
Lacquer	Beta-naphthylamine sulphate
Lubricants	Diaminodiphenylmethane
Chrome acid	Propyl isocyanate
Complex cyanides	Sodium acetylide
Water–kerosene mixtures	Chlorphenols
Trichloroethylene	Chlorcresols
Oily slops from petroleum industry	

There is some doubt as to what proportion of industrial waste can be considered deleterious or toxic; the World Health Organisation has estimated 15%, equivalent to about 20 kg per head per year.[34] The actual figure in the UK may be between 2 and 5 million tonnes per year,[35] but there is some confusion as to terminology. Thus, 'toxic' has been considered synonymous with 'poisonous', without specifying toxic concentration. This is discussed further in Chapter 4.

Hazards are more difficult to define. The Key Report[19] simply classified wastes as flammable, acid or caustic, and indisputably toxic. The provisional Code of Practice[14] suggests the adoption of the Blue Book classification,[36]

TABLE 3.3 EXEMPTED WASTES

(1)   Any waste normally arising in the use of premises as an office for any purpose, or as a retail shop (that is to say, a building used for the carrying on of any retail trade or retail business wherein the primary purpose is the selling of goods or services by retail).

(2)   Any waste produced in the course of:
- (i) the construction, repair, maintenance or demolition of plant or of buildings;
- (ii) the laundering or dry cleaning of articles;
- (iii) working mines and quarries, or washing mined or quarried material;
- (iv) the construction or maintenance of highways, whether or not repairable at the public expense;
- (v) the dry cutting, grinding or shaping of metals, or the subjection thereof to other physical or mechanical process;
- (vi) the softening, treatment or other processing of water for the purpose of rendering it suitable for (a) human consumption, (b) the preparation of foods or drinks, (c) any manufacturing or cooling process, or (d) boiler feed;
- (vii) the treatment of sewage;
- (viii) the breeding, rearing or keeping of livestock;
- (ix) brewing;
- (x) any other fermentation process; or
- (xi) the cleansing of intercepting devices designed to prevent the release of oil or grease.

(3)   Any waste (not being waste in any of the foregoing classes) consisting of one or more of the following items whether mixed with water or not:
- (i) paper, cellulose, wood (including sawdust and sanderdust), oiled paper, tarred paper, plasterboard;
- (ii) plastics, including thermoplastics in both the finished and raw states, and thermosetting plastics in the finished state;
- (iii) clays, pottery, china, glass, enamels, ceramics, mica, abrasives;
- (iv) iron, steel, aluminium, brass, copper, tin, zinc;
- (v) coal, coke, carbon, graphite, ash, clinker;
- (vi) slags produced in the manufacture of iron, steel, copper or tin or of mixtures of any of those metals;
- (vii) rubber (whether natural or synthetic);
- (viii) electrical fittings, fixtures and appliances;
- (ix) cosmetics;
- (x) sands (including foundry and moulding sands), silica;
- (xi) shot blasting residues, boiler scale, iron oxides, iron hydroxides;
- (xii) cement, concrete, calcium hydroxide, calcium carbonate, calcium sulphate, calcium chloride, magnesium carbonate, magnesium oxide, zinc oxide, aluminium oxide, titanium oxide, copper oxide, sodium chloride;
- (xiii) cork, ebonite, kapok, kieselguhr, diatomaceous earth;
- (xiv) wool, cotton, linen, hemp, sisal, any other natural fibre, hessian, leather, any man-made fibre, string, rope;
- (xv) soap and other stearates;
- (xvi) food, or any waste produced in the course of the preparation, processing or distribution of food;
- (xvii) vegetable matter;
- (xviii) animal carcases, or parts thereof;
- (xix) excavated material in its natural state;
- (xx) any other substance which is a hard solid and is insoluble in water and in any acid.

which is simplified into the following broad groups:

Explosive
Flammable
Oxidising
Poisonous
Infectious
Corrosive
Radioactive

Information on hazards and precautions to be taken when handling hazardous material is given in the Yellow Book.[37] The Deposit of Poisonous Waste Act 1972[13] requires the producer to know the 'nature' of his waste and to notify the appropriate authority of this;[25] this includes classification by phase, content, proportions of pollutants and such other information as will adequately define the hazards involved in the chosen method of disposal.

Classification of a waste by toxicity and/or hazard is important for safety and to comply with legislation[26-32] (see Chapter 4). In practice, it is better to use the characterisation 'hazardous' and 'non-hazardous' having regard to both toxicity and the environmental implications of the waste on disposal. Therefore the Control of Pollution Act distinguishes waste which is poisonous, noxious or polluting and whose presence on land is likely to give rise to an environmental hazard. The wide scope of this is discussed later, but it also encompasses highly flammable or explosive materials which may have little toxicological significance.

(h) Treatment Method

This is the most common system of classification of waste. A list of methods is given in Table 3.4 together with some examples. The list includes only those operations known to be used in effluent treatment, and has been divided under three main subheadings—chemical, physical and biological. Practically all the listed methods are accepted chemical engineering unit operations or unit processes. Treatment of a waste for recycling, or prior to disposal, may consist of a sequence of operations. A thorough exploration of all the possibilities for a specific problem might use a morphological approach which considers all possible operations, permutes them to give all possible processes, then by application of a number of predetermined criteria reduces the multiplicity of alternatives to a few that may be explored in depth.[38]

Most essential treatment operations prior to disposal have been well documented, and are discussed in Chapters 7 and 8. Recycling processes are either well established and documented, or not practised for any of a number of valid or superficial reasons. A well designed recovery process can not only virtually eliminate a disposal problem but can also significantly reduce disposal costs until they even become negative, i.e. the waste produces an income. There are many areas of waste disposal that would benefit from a careful and thorough examination with this in view.

(i) *Value*

The value of waste material may be found by multiplying the quantity by the concentration and multiplying again by the value of each recoverable component in the waste. Quantity and concentration are discussed under (f) above.

TABLE 3.4 TREATMENT METHODS FOR LIQUID EFFLUENT

Chemical treatment methods	Example
Absorption	Solvent recovery
Cementation	Copper recovery
Chlorination	Cyanide oxidation
Coagulation—see Flocculation	
Demulsification	Soluble oil recovery
Electrolytic processes	Metal recovery
Flocculation	Sewage treatment
Hydrolysis	Cellulose waste
Incineration	Waste oils
Ion exchange	Metal recovery
Leaching	Metal-bearing sludges
Neutralisation	Waste acid
Oxidation	Phenol removal
Ozonisation	Cyanide oxidation
Precipitation	Metals
Reduction	Hexavalent chromium
Thermal decomposition	Recycling hydrochloric acid
Physical treatment methods	
Absorption	Removal of volatile organics
Cooling	Water reuse
Crystallisation	Recovery of inorganic salts
Desorption—see Absorption	
Dewatering—see Filtration	
Dialysis	Desalination
Distillation	Solvent recovery
Drying	Pig manure
Electrodialysis	Desalination
Evaporation	Sulphuric acid recovery
Filtration	Sewage sludge
Flotation	Dairy wastes
Foam fractionation	Metal separation
Fractionation—see Distillation	
Freezing	Desalination
Heating	Demulsification
Phase separation	Oily wastes
Reverse osmosis	Desalination
Screening	Sewage
Sedimentation	Suspended solids removal
Solvent extraction	Metal recovery
Stripping	Ammonia removal
Ultrafiltration—see Dialysis, Reverse osmosis	

Biological treatment methods

Activated sludge	Sewage
Anaerobic digestion	Food wastes
Chemical production	Ethanol
Disinfection	Sewage plant effluent
High-rate filtration	Phenol removal
Oxidation—see Activated sludge,	
High-rate filtration,	
Trickling filter	
Reduction—see Anaerobic digestion	
Single-cell protein production	Organic waste
Trickling filter	Sewage

See also Chapters 7 and 8 for more details and other examples.

Values of chemicals and materials are published regularly in a number of journals which give list prices.[39–41] However, market price may bear no relation to list price and a market research exercise is necessary before embarking on a recovery programme.

Recoverable components identified by analysis may exist in the waste in a different form: metal compounds, for example, are often reported as metal or metal oxide whereas they may exist as acid solutions of metal salts; recovery may be of another metal compound by precipitation, or of the metal itself.

Assessment of the value of the waste or of the recoverable materials it contains is essential for evaluation of a recovery or recycling process. Suggestions for process generation and cost estimation are given in Chapter 20.

In summary, the complete characterisation scheme for liquid waste comprises the following information:

Origin	Where does it come from (type of industry or specific industry)?
Destination	Is it going for disposal, reuse or recycle?
Content	What phase(s) are present in the waste?
	In what form is the pollutant?
	What chemicals form the pollutant?
	What are the physical properties?
	How much is there?
	What is the concentration of the pollutant?
	Is it toxic? If so, to what extent?
	Is it hazardous in any other way (e.g. flammable, explosive)?
	If so, to what extent?
Treatment	How will it be treated, either for disposal or recycle?
Value	Is it worth anything?

To illustrate the application of this scheme, a range of examples is given in Table 3.5, based on extracts from records of a disposal contractor.

TABLE 3.5 EXAMPLES OF CHARACTERISATION OF LIQUID WASTE

Origin	Inorganic, metal treatment	
Destination	Disposal	
Content: phase	Aqueous	
physical nature	Dissolved gases and solids pH 2 Total solids	 11·57%
chemical nature and composition	Acidity as HCl Iron Zinc Lead Cadmium Chromium Nickel	5·81% 1·72% 0·112% 0·024% present present present
quantity	6·8 m³ (1500 gal)	
toxicity and hazards	Poisonous Corrosive	
Method of treatment	None	
Value	None, value of potentially recoverable materials may be calculated[10]	
Origin	Natural organic, cess	
Destination	Disposal	
Content: phase	Aqueous	
physical nature	Solution of solid, suspended solid, pH 8·65 Total solids Suspended matter Ash Flashpoint Electrical conductivity	 0·23% 0·07% 0·678% 110°C 4085 μmhos/cm³
chemical nature and composition	Ether extract	0·31%
quantity	6·8 m³ (1500 gal)	
toxicity and hazards	Bacterial infection	
Method of treatment	None	
Value	None	
Origin	Inorganic, metal treatment	
Destination	Disposal	
Content: phase	Aqueous	
physical nature	Dissolved solids, miscible liquids, pH 0·7 Electrical conductivity Total solids	 178 000 μmhos/cm³ 19·1%

Table 3.5 (*continued*)

chemical nature and composition	Acidity as H_2SO_4	14·5%
	Chromium	6·2%
	Copper	0·46%
	Zinc	0·26%
	Iron	0·51%
quantity	4 m^3 (800 gal)	
toxicity and hazards	Oxidising Poisonous Corrosive	
Method of treatment	None	
Value	None, value of potentially recoverable materials may be calculated[10]	

Origin	Synthetic organic, organic chemical	
Destination	Disposal	
Content: phase	Mixed aqueous–nonaqueous	
physical nature	Suspended solids, immiscible liquid, pH 6·0	
	Total solid matter	37·6%
	Ash	0·62%
	Flashpoint	110°C
chemical nature	Phenol	0·48%
quantity	5·6 m^3 (1250 gal)	
toxicity and hazards	—	
Method of treatment	Demulsification and oil separation	
Value	Small—heat content of oil from burning.	

Characterisation of Solid Waste

The characterisation scheme proposed for liquid waste may be readily adapted to solid waste, where the problem is less as the range is narrower, being restricted mainly to mineral wastes and household refuse about which much is known. Examples of the recycling of process scrap, residues and byproducts, as opposed to waste, are discussed in Part Four.

(a) *Origin*

Solid wastes are inevitably generated in vast quantities by an industrialised society. An estimate of the mass of solid waste generated in the UK in 1973 is given in Table 3.6, from which it is clear that the majority arises from mining and other extractive industries. In the main, such waste materials are inert and are deposited in spoil heaps. However, this leaves approximately 18 million tonnes per annum of household and trade refuse and 23 million tonnes of other industrial wastes to be disposed of or recycled.

TABLE 3.6 SOLID WASTE GENERATION 1973[35]

	Million tonnes	%
Coal mining	58	36
Mining other than coal	3	2
China clay quarrying	22	13
Other quarrying	27	17
Household and trade refuse	18	11
Industrial waste	23	14
Ash and clinker from power stations	12	7
	163	100

Gutt *et al.*[42] have published an exhaustive survey of major industrial solid byproducts and waste materials, including the origins (as in Table 3.6), destinations, content and uses. A list of materials included, their origin and destination is given in Table 3.7.

(b) *Destination*

Most solid wastes are relatively harmless and valueless and are dumped to form, for example, the familiar spoil heaps of the coal mining and china clay industries. However, even these may create a hazard, as for example in the Aberfan disaster when heavy rain caused a tip to slide into a village with great loss of life. There are some examples of reuse (blast furnace slag for roadmaking; red mud from the alumina industry as a pigment), but these tend to be minor. Other than steelmaking slags and copper slags[43] which have a high metal content, there is little recycling of the major industrial byproducts. There are, however, many instances of more specialised recycling, particularly internal recycling of process scrap generally, which most industries carry out, and also of high value materials such as metals, wood and plastics (discussed in Part Four). The pattern of Figure 3.1 is therefore followed for solid wastes, with minor modification to allow for less recycling and the wider range of techniques of disposal shown in Table 3.7.

(c) *Content—Phase*

The question of phase is not generally relevant, although there are many metallurgical or mineralogical phases that may be important in considering reuse. Otherwise wastes are solid, and sometimes 'wet' solid. It is only rarely that solid contaminated with non-aqueous liquid is encountered, as for example in oily swarf. The form of solid may affect 'handle-ability' (e.g. viscous mass or dusty solid).

(d) Content—Physical Nature of Pollutant

The wide range of physical properties that may be attributable to solid waste are listed in Table 3.8. Not all are applicable to every waste, but relevant properties are selected for measurement depending on destination or reuse.

(e) Content—Chemical Nature of Pollutant

A complete chemical analysis provides a certain amount of information. For metals, minerals and metalliferous wastes, however, it will not necessarily describe the chemical compounds present nor the minerals, both of which may have chemical and physical properties very different from those indicated by analysis, which usually reports metal or metal oxide (Table 3.5). Pertinent chemical definition of organic wastes is also difficult because of their biological complexity and also because of the different requirements of the various treatment methods. A simple classification is:

Metals and metalliferous materials
Minerals
Other inorganic materials
Natural organic materials
Synthetic organic materials

This may be supplemented by a complete chemical, mineralogical and biological analysis.

(f) Content—Quantity and Concentration
(g) Content—Toxicity and Hazards

The discussion relating to liquid waste applies equally to solid waste. Some consideration must be given to the effects of mixing materials such as water and metal drosses.

(h) Treatment Method

Many of the methods listed in Table 3.4 for treating liquid wastes may be used to treat solids. Some other techniques are available because of the nature of solids (Table 3.9). Household refuse, in particular, has attracted much attention and this is discussed further in Chapters 14 and 17. Process generation and evaluation are the same for solid waste as for liquid waste.

TABLE 3.7 MAJOR SOLID WASTES: ORIGIN, QUANTITIES AND DESTINATION (adapted from Gutt et al.[42])

Type	Origin	Production (M tonnes/year)	Stockpile (M tonnes)	Method of disposal	Present uses
Colliery spoil	Mining coal	about 50	3000	Mainly tipping on land, some in sea. 7–8 M tonnes/year used	As fill and in manufacture of bricks, cement and lightweight aggregate
China clay waste overburden sand micaceous residue	Quarrying of china clay	22	280	Mainly tipping and in lagoons. About 1 M tonnes/year used	As fine aggregate in concrete, in manufacture of bricks and blocks and as fill
Household refuse	Household	18	Not known	Mainly landfill Some incineration	Resource recovery under investigation
Pulverised fuel ash and furnace bottom ash	Waste from power stations burning pulverised fuel	9.9	Not known	6·3 M tonnes/year used Rest in old workings or artificial lagoons	As fill and in manufacture of cement, concrete blocks, light-weight aggregate, bricks, etc.
Blastfurnace slag	Smelting of iron	9		Nearly all used	As roadstone, railway ballast, filter medium, aggregate for concrete, fertiliser and in manufacture of cement
Trade waste	Industry	6	Not known	Mainly landfill Some incineration	Not known
Steel-making slag	Steel making	4	Not known	2 M tonnes returned to blast-furnaces, rest either dumped or used as fill near steel works or sold	As roadstone
Furnace clinker	Waste from chain grate power stations	2·3		All used	Concrete block making

Material	Source			Current disposal	Uses
Incinerator ash	Residue from the direct incineration	0·6	Not known	Most is dumped. Minor usage	As fill and for covering refuse tips
Byproduct calcium sulphate	Manufacture of phosphoric acid and of hydrofluoric acid	2·1	Not known	Mainly in sea. Some dumped on land. 6000 tonnes/year used	In manufacture of floor screeds
Waste glass	Waste glass within household refuse	About 2	Not known	No utilisation in household refuse	
Slate waste	Mining and quarrying slate	1·2	Over 300	Mainly tipping, some backfilling of old workings. Minor usage	Inert filler, granules, expanded slate aggregate and filter medium, road building
Tin mine tailings	Tin mining	0·46	Not known	Minor utilisation. Tailing lagoons and discharge into sea	Aggregate for concrete
Incinerator ash	Residue from the direct incineration of refuse	0·6	Not known	Most is dumped. Minor usage	As fill and for covering refuse tips
Fluorspar mine tailings	Fluorspar mining	0·23	Not known	Minor utilisation. Tailing lagoons	Aggregate for roadmaking and concrete
Red mud	Production of alumina	0·10	Not known	Minor utilisation, rest in lagoons	Pigment in paints and plastics
Copper slag	Smelting of copper	0·1	Not known	Complete utilisation	Grit blasting
Tin slag	Smelting of tin	0·074	Not known	Major utilisation. Some in tips	Grit blasting and road building
Zinc–lead slags	Smelting of zinc and lead	0·06–0·07	Not known	Stockpiled and used locally	Bulk fill and some in pavement asphalt
Quarry wastes	Quarrying	Not known	Not known	Some utilisation. Rest tipped	Roadmaking, brickmaking

TABLE 3.8 PHYSICAL PROPERTIES OF SOLID WASTE

Absolute density
Angle of repose
Ash
Bulk density
Compressibility
Elasticity
Electrical properties
Hardness
Loss on ignition
Mineralogical composition
Oil content
Particle-size distribution
pH
Physical composition
Solubility
Volatile matter
Water content
Water absorption
Wettability

TABLE 3.9 TREATMENT METHODS FOR SOLID WASTE

Chemical treatment methods	Examples/comments
Calcination	Gypsum
Chlorination	Tin removal
Cooking	Inedible offal
Froth flotation	Coal recovery
	Glass
Hydrolysis	Household refuse
	Vegetable waste
Incineration	Household refuse
Leaching	Gives an aqueous solution which may be treated as a liquid waste (Table 3.4)
Oxidation	Weathering
Pyrolysis	Household refuse
	Polystyrene
Sintering	Colliery spoil
	Millscale
Physical treatment methods	
Adhesion	Household refuse
Agglomeration	Pulverised fuel ash
Ballistic separation	Household refuse
Baling	Cans
Centrifugation	Animal oil separation
	De-oiling swarf
Classification (air)	Household refuse
Classification (wet)	Plastic

Table 3.9 (*continued*)

Comminution	Mining wastes
	Cars
Compaction	Household refuse
Dewatering	Sewage sludge
Dissolution	Forms a liquid waste which
	may be treated as in Table 3.4
Drying	Filter cake
Electrostatic separation	Household refuse
Foaming	Slag
Freezing	Meat products
Granulation	Slag
Impalement	Household refuse
Jigging	Household refuse
Magnetic treatment	Iron removal from slag
	Household refuse
Melting	Selective non-ferrous metal recovery
Pelletisation	Iron and steel fines
Pulverisation	Household refuse
	Swarf
Quenching	Incinerator residues
Screening	Clinker
Settlement	China clay wastes
Shape separation	Household refuse
Sliding separation	Household refuse

Biological treatment methods

Anaerobic digestion	Farm waste
Bacterial leaching	Low-grade copper ore
Composting	Household refuse
Degradation	Plastic
Fermentation	Requires solution or dilute slurry
	—see liquid waste

(i) *Value*

The comments concerning value of liquid wastes apply also to solid wastes.

Characterisation of Gaseous Waste

Gaseous and gasborne wastes are the simplest group to characterise, as the range of common pollutants is more limited and the wastes are inherently difficult to contain. The characterisation scheme proposed for liquid waste is applied here, with comments under each heading to highlight important differences.

(a) *Origin*

Atmospheric pollution by man was preceded by natural pollution from volcanoes and from decay and other biological processes. Today, natural emissions still constitute the major part of atmospheric pollution (Table 3.10).[44] Natural pollution cannot, of course, be avoided and once the pollutants are in the atmosphere man can do little with them. The primary source of artificial or man-generated waste is clearly combustion of coal, wood, oil and similar materials. Chemical reactions, including biological processes, produce most of the remainder.

Gasborne liquid wastes, which are generally insignificant, and gasborne solid wastes constitute about 10% of total gaseous and gasborne wastes.[44] Other than combustion products, which are generally well defined and well documented, classification of waste by source follows the industrial classification set out under liquid waste (page 26). Of these, the metal-producing and chemical industries probably contribute the most, together with non-manufacturing industries such as building, demolition and incineration. Our current technological society has demonstrated a far greater awareness of gaseous wastes than of other types, and has implemented much tighter controls,

TABLE 3.10 SOURCES AND TYPES OF MAJOR ATMOSPHERIC POLLUTANTS[44]

Contaminant	Major manmade sources	Natural sources	Estimated emissions (tonnes/year)	
			Manmade	Natural
SO_2	Combustion of coal and oil	Volcanoes	146×10^6	Negligible
H_2S	Chemical processes Sewage treatment	Volcanoes Biological action in swamp areas	3×10^6	100×10^6
CO	Auto exhaust and other combustion	Forest fires	220×10^6	11×10^6
NO/NO_2	Combustion	Bacterial action in soil	53×10^6	500×10^6
NH_3	Waste treatment	Biological decay	4×10^6	5900×10^6
N_2O	None	Biological action in soil	None	1000×10^6
Hydrocarbons	Combustion exhaust Chemical processes	Biological processes	88×10^6	480×10^6
CO_2	Combustion	Biological decay Release from oceans	$1 \cdot 3 \times 10^{10}$	10^{12}

with the result that they tend to be substantially confined within the producer's plant boundaries. It is therefore the producer who has most need of a characterisation scheme for control, treatment and/or disposal of gaseous wastes.

(b) *Destination*

Either gaseous wastes are disposed of to the atmosphere or the pollutant is removed. There is no choice of disposal site. Treatment requires identification of content and selection of a suitable treatment method. The removal of a pollutant may produce a liquid or solid waste.

(c) *Content—Phase of Pollutant*

The pollutant may be gaseous or may be a suspended liquid or solid. Examples of gaseous waste are given in Table 3.10, which includes sulphur dioxide and carbon monoxide. Other gaseous pollutants have offensive odour, such as mercaptans, some of which are highly toxic. These are discussed in Chapter 10.

Suspended liquid droplets in gaseous wastes are best exemplified by the plumes from cooling towers. Other examples include acid mist from absorption towers and chromic acid mist from chrome plating or anodising processes. Although sometimes troublesome, wastes from such sources are relatively insignificant in terms of volume compared with those containing only gas and suspended solids.

Suspended solids in gas emissions are a common result of most high temperature processes, notably metal production, which is discussed at greater length in Chapter 15. For example, it has been estimated that in 1975 the British Steel Corporation produced nearly 2·5 million tonnes of fumes.[45] These suspended solids may be so valuable—for example, tin[46]—that recovery is essential to the economic viability of the process. Usually, however, they are of low value and removal is practised to meet legal constraints.

(d) *Content—Physical Nature of Pollutant*

A detailed knowledge of the characteristics of a waste is necessary for treatment or recovery. A list of physical properties for gas, liquid and solid-containing gaseous wastes is given in Table 3.11.

(e) *Content—Chemical Nature of Pollutants*

A complete chemical analysis provides most information necessary for characterisation. In many cases the description 'ash' or 'dust' is sufficient if the solid is substantially inert, although even inert particles may create a nuisance.

TABLE 3.11 PHYSICAL PROPERTIES OF GASEOUS WASTE

Gas only	Suspended liquid	Suspended solid
Calorific value	Concentration	Bulk density (settled)
Concentration of pollutant	Density of liquid	Concentration
	Electrical properties	Electrical properties of solid
Density	Flammability and related hazards	Flammability
Explosivity		Hygroscopicity
Flammability	Particle-size distribution	Moisture content
Flashpoint		Particle density
Moisture content	pH	Particle geometry
Odour	Surface tension	Particle-size distribution
Temperature	Viscosity	Solubility
Velocity	(see Table 3.1 also)	Velocity
Viscosity		Wettability
		(see Table 3.8 also)

A simple classification would follow a similar pattern to that for solid wastes:

Metalliferous materials
Other inorganic materials
Organic materials
Inert materials

(f) *Content—Quality and Concentration*
(g) *Content—Toxicity and Hazard*
(i) *Value*

The discussion relating to liquid wastes is equally applicable to gaseous wastes.

(h) *Treatment Method*

The limited range of techniques (some with variations) available for treating gaseous wastes is summarised in Table 3.12. As few chemical and no biological methods are known to be used, the pattern of classification for liquid and solid wastes is not followed here. Invariably the pollutant is relatively dilute and usually one of the purposes of treatment is concentration of the gas, liquid or solid contaminant, the exceptions being in dispersion, incineration, or direct recycling. The concentrated or treated gaseous waste then becomes a liquid or solid waste as characterised in the preceding discussion.

The prevention of air pollution is perhaps the most advanced of the pollution control technologies and there is therefore no shortage of literature on methods of treatment, applications and examples. This is covered in Part Three. The range of methods is narrow; wet and dry methods and their application to the three phases of pollutants are given in Table 3.13.

TABLE 3.12 TREATMENT METHODS FOR GASEOUS WASTE

General methods	Alternatives
Centrifugal techniques	Centrifuge
	Cyclone
Coalescence	
Condensation	
Destruction	Chemical reaction
	Incineration
Direct recycle	
Dispersion	
Electrostatic precipitation	
Filtration	Needle bonded fabric
	Reverse jet
	Reverse pressure
	Shaker type
Gravity settlement	
Total enclosure	
Wet scrubbing	Absorption tower
	Fluidised bed scrubber
	Impingement scrubber
	Irrigated target scrubber
	Pressure spray scrubber
	Rotary scrubber
	Self-induced spray scrubber
	Spray tower
	Venturi scrubber

TABLE 3.13 WASTE GAS TREATMENT SYSTEM

Dry methods	Pollutant	Wet methods
Absorption	*Gas*	Wet scrubbing
Destruction		
Direct recycling		
Dispersion		
Total enclosure		
Destruction	*Liquid*	Centrifugal techniques
		Coalescence
		Destruction
		Gravity settlement
		Total enclosure
		Wet scrubbing
Centrifugal techniques	*Solid*	Electrostatic precipitation
Destruction		Wet scrubbing
Direct recycling		
Electrostatic pre-cipitation		
Filtration		
Gravity settlement		
Total enclosure		

Characterisation of Noise

Clearly, noise cannot be characterised in the same way as gaseous, liquid and solid wastes: it cannot be recycled or reused; it does not accumulate and it cannot be stored; however, it may be regarded as a form of energy pollution, in a rather similar way to radioactive and thermal pollution. All of these decay with time, but the effects may be long-lasting. Noise is perceived as a vibration, usually of air, and it has certain characteristics of frequency, loudness or intensity, and variations of these with time. Frequency is measured in cycles per second (hertz) and the normal range of a healthy young ear is 20 to 18 000 Hz.

TABLE 3.14 TYPICAL SOUND LEVELS (ALL EQUIPMENT UNSILENCED)

Sound pressure (Pa)	Examples in industry	dB(A)	Examples in the living environment	Subjective noise level
200		140		
				Painful
			Jet take-off (60 m)	
20		120		
				Deafening
	Riveting machine Circular saw		Power mower	
2		100		
	Workshop Textile weaving plant Excavator		Tube/subway train Pneumatic drill (15 m)	Very loud
0.2		80		
	Noisy office		Vacuum cleaner (3 m) Motorway/highway (15 m)	Loud
0.02	Average office Large transformer (60 m)	60		
			Light traffic Average house	Moderate
0.002	Computer room Quiet office	40	Public library	
	Broadcasting studio			Faint
0.0002		20	Quiet church	
				Very faint
0.000 02		0	Threshold of hearing	

Loudness or intensity can vary over such a wide range that a logarithmic scale is used as a more manageable measure. The units of this scale are known as decibels and the full range with typical examples is given in Table 3.14. The nature of the relationship between sound levels is such that a doubling of sound intensity is registered as an increase of 3 dB, which is near the lower limit of detection of the human ear, and the threshold of hearing is assigned an arbitrary value of zero. This concept is further complicated in that the ear has different sensitivities to different frequencies: high-frequency sounds are perceived as louder than lower-frequency sounds of the same intensity. In order to measure noise level in a way that reflects the response of the human ear, a system has been devised of weighted frequencies to compensate for this difference, known as the 'A' scale. The recorded noise level, of which the unit is known as the dB(A), then corresponds well to the degree of annoyance. Other decibel scales, not so widely used, known as the 'B', 'C', 'D' and 'N' scales, have different frequency weightings: for example, the 'C' scale gives essentially a measurement of the energy content of the noise, expressed as dB(C).

In most environments the noise level is not constant, but varies with time; the duration of high and low noise levels and their regularity is another significant characteristic. This is known as the noise profile of an environment and is usually expressed in terms of three values: L_{90}, L_{50}, and L_{10} or L_1, where L_{90} is the noise level exceeded 90% of the time which corresponds to the residual or background level of noise; L_{50} is the noise level exceeded 50% of the time and approximates to the average noise level; and L_{10} or L_1 is the noise level exceeded 10% or 1% of the time and represents high-intensity–short-duration sounds. Some typical values are given in Chapter 18.

While these two characteristics, intensity and profile, are the most important indicators of noise nuisance, being relatively easy to measure directly and contributing most to the degree of annoyance, other pertinent considerations are:

1. A method of identifying noise events.
2. A method of measuring the intensity and duration of such noises.
3. A tabulation of the number of events in a given time period.
4. An account of the background noise levels.
5. An account of the variation in intensity of the noise events.
6. Special weighting factors such as season (window open or closed), time of day, type of community, pure tone content of the noise, previous noise exposure of the area.

A number of schemes have been devised which attempt to take such factors into account in measuring or predicting people's reaction to noise. Some of these schemes are listed in Table 3.15 and discussed further in Part Five. None is completely satisfactory, as a wide range of psychological factors also take effect, which are impossible to quantify; L_{eq} is widely held to be one of the most useful.

TABLE 3.15 NOISE PERCEPTION AND PREDICTION SCHEMES

Abbreviation	Scheme	Special features
PNL[47,52]	Perceived noise level (measured in PNdB)	Used in calculation of Composite Noise Rating (CNR) for aircraft noise particularly.
EPNL[47]	Effective perceived noise level (measured in EPNdB)	Corrects PNL for noise due to jet aircraft; used to calculate NEF.
LNP[48–50]	Level of noise pollution	Similar to TNI. $$LNP = L_{eq} + 2 \cdot 56\sigma$$ where σ is the standard deviation noise level with time. For dense traffic this approximates to $$LNP = \frac{L_{50} + (L_{10} - L_{90})^2 + L_{10} - L_{90}}{56}$$
NEF[47]	Noise exposure forecast	Improves CNR by correcting for pure tones and duration; proposed by FAA for prediction of community reaction to airport noise; takes into account factors such as types of aircraft expected to use an airport, subjective noise levels, flight paths, number of flights during day and night periods.
NR[51,52]	Noise rating	Distribution of noise over octave bands between 63 and 8000 Hz.
NC[52]	Noise criterion	Similar to NR.
TNI[48–50]	Traffic noise index	Uses noise climate figures, i.e. noise range recorded for 80% of the time $$TNI = L_{90} + 4(L_{10} - L_{90}) - 30$$
NIL[52]	Noise imission level	Relates noise level to duration $$NIL = L_A + 10 \log \frac{T}{T_o} \text{ dB}$$ where L_A = 'A'-weighted sound level T = duration of exposure T_o = reference duration (e.g. 8 h/day)

Table 3.15 (*continued*)

ECNL[53] L_{eq}[53]	Equivalent continuous noise level	Relates changing noise levels to an equivalent continuous level. Used for monitoring and protection

$$L_{eq} = 10 \log \frac{1}{T_s} \int_0^{T_s} \frac{P_A(t)^2}{P_o^2} \, dt$$

where t = time
T_s = total sampling period
P_A = instantaneous 'A'-weighted sound pressure in pascal or N/m^2
P_o = reference level, i.e. 2×10^{-5} pascal or N/m^2

References

1. *Second International Conference on Waste Water and Wastes,* Stockholm, Institute of Water Pollution Control, February 1975.
2. *Water Treatment Handbook*, Degremont, 1973.
3. LUND, H. F., *Industrial Pollution Control Handbook*, McGraw-Hill, 1971.
4. SOUTHGATE, B. A., *Treatment and Disposal of Industrial Waste Waters*, HMSO, 1948.
5. LINDNER, G. and NYBERG, K., *Environmental Engineering*, Reidel, 1973.
6. CIACCIO, L. L. (Ed.), *Water and Water Pollution Handbook*, Vol. 1, Dekker, 1971.
7. TOMLINSON, T. G., in (2) above.
8. OLDHAM, G. F., in *The Effect of Effluent Restrictions upon Industry*, Symposium, Southampton, Institution of Chemical Engineers, May 1972.
9. BEYCHOK, M. R., *Aqueous Wastes from Petroleum and Petrochemical Plants*, Wiley, 1967.
10. BRIDGWATER, A. V. and GASKARTH, J. W., in *Conservation of Materials*, UKAEA, Harwell, 1974.
11. Institute of Industrial Solid Wastes Management, private communication, 1973.
12. BACKHURST, J. R. and HARKER, J. H., Treatment methods and disposal costs for pig manure, *Environmental Pollution Management*, **4**(5), 221, 1974.
13. Deposit of Poisonous Waste Act, 1972; Control of Pollution Act, 1974.
14. *A Provisional Code of Practice for Disposal of Wastes*, Institution of Chemical Engineers, 1971.
15. *Handbook of Chemistry and Physics*, Chemical Rubber Co., 1976.
16. PERRY, J. H., *Chemical Engineer's Handbook*, McGraw-Hill, 1970.
17. *Refuse Disposal*, HMSO, 1971.
18. BRENDISH, K. R., in (30) below.
19. *Report of the Technical Committee on the Disposal of Solid Toxic Wastes*, HMSO, 1970.
20. NOONAN, J. L., in (5) above.
21. *Economic Aspects of Treatment and Disposal of Certain Industrial Effluents*, United Nations, 1967.
22. MORTENSEN, B. F., in (5) above.
23. PAINTER, H. A., in (6) above.
24. MARSHALL, V. C., *Water Borne Wastes*, Institution of Chemical Engineers, 1974.
25. Department of the Environment, Circular 70/72, *Deposit of Poisonous Waste Act 1972*, HMSO, 1972.
26. MUMFORD, C. J., in (30) below.
27. SCHWER, F. W., *Chemical Engineer*, 91, February 1974.
28. LAVERICK, B., *Industrial Pollution Control Yearbook*, Industrial Newspapers Ltd, 1974.

29. MYERS, S. D. and ISAAC, P. C. G., in (8) above.
30. TEARLE, K. (Ed.), *Industrial Pollution Control,* Business Books, 1973.
31. NEWSOM, G. and SHERRATT, J. G., *Water Pollution,* Sherratt & Sons, 1972.
32. *Deposit of Poisonous Waste,* Symposium, Bristol Polytechnic, July 1973.
33. HIGGINSON, A. E., *Chemical Engineer,* 305, June 1973.
34. Department of the Environment Industrial Waste Survey Unit. *Hazardous Wastes in Great Britain,* HMSO, 1974.
35. Royal Commission on Environmental Pollution, 4th Report. *Pollution Control. Progess and Problems,* HMSO, 1974.
36. *Carriage of Dangerous Goods in Ships ('Blue Book'),* HMSO, 1971.
37. *Dangerous Chemical Substances and Proposals for their Labelling ('Yellow Book'),* HMSO, 1971.
38. BRIDGWATER, A. V., Long range process design and morphological analysis, *Chemical Engineer,* 217, 75, April 1968.
39. *European Chemical News* (UK and Europe) (weekly).
40. *Chemical Marketing Reporter* (USA) (weekly).
41. *Metal Bulletin* (UK) (biweekly).
42. GUTT, W., NIXON, P. J., SMITH, M. A., HARRISON, W. H. and RUSSELL, A. D., *A Survey of the Locations, Disposal and Prospective Uses of the Major Industrial Byproducts and Waste Materials,* Building Research Establishment, 1974.
43. NELMES, W. S., in *The Technology of Reclamation,* University of Birmingham (England), April 1975.
44. HOOG, H., Presidential address to 48th Annual General Meeting, Institution of Chemical Engineers, 1970.
45. TRANCE, F. B., Institute of Metals, Spring Meeting, London, 1973.
46. POCOCK, N. J. B., Institute of Metals, Spring Meeting, London, 1973.
47. REVELLE, C. and REVELLE, P., *Sourcebook on the Environment,* Houghton Mifflin, 1974.
48. WALLIS, A. D., *Environmental Pollution Management,* 5(3), 63, 1975.
49. WEISSBERGER, A. and ROSSITER, B. W., *Techniques of Chemistry,* Vol. 1, *Physical Methods of Chemistry,* Wiley, 1971.
50. KOLTHOFF, I. M., ELVING, P. J. and STROSS, F. H., *Treatise on Analytical Chemistry* Part III, Vol. 2, *Analytical Chemistry in Industry,* Wiley, 1971.
51. Engineering Equipment Users' Association, *Measurement and Control of Noise,* Constable, 1968.
52. RICHINGS, W. V., *Noise Measurement Techniques,* Dawe Instruments Ltd.
53. Department of Employment, *Code of Practice for Reducing the Exposure of Employed Persons to Noise,* HMSO, 1972.

CHAPTER 4

Criteria for Control

Introduction

The criteria for pollution control measures are determined by social and legal considerations which are complementary. Ideally, the aims are to operate any industrial undertaking so as

    (i) to avoid any observable danger to the health of humans or animals;
    (ii) to eliminate, or reduce as far as practicable, damage to the environment;
    (iii) to avoid any creation of nuisance to residents in the vicinity of the operations concerned;
    (iv) to comply with all relevant statutory legislation.

In order to meet these objectives it is necessary to appreciate the quantum, type and potential toxicity and/or objectionable nature of pollutants arising from any given operation or process and the legal constraints that are imposed upon them.

Toxicity

A toxic material is generally understood to be one which may damage health, by interfering with body chemistry, even when it is present in low concentrations. The toxicity of any material can thus be expressed in terms of 'lethal dose 50%' or LD_{50}, i.e. the single dose that will kill 50 per cent of the test population. LD_{50} is generally expressed in milligrams per kilogram body weight (mg/kg) for the species on which it is tested. However, it is affected by the age and sex of the population and by the route of entry to the body. As an example, the LD_{50} of DDT in man is 113 mg per kg body weight if taken orally, but 2510 mg/kg for percutaneous absorption.[1]

Another measure of toxicity, usually applied to aquatic life, is the LC_{50}. Since it would be excessively time-consuming to determine the quantity of any material absorbed by fish from a watercourse under given conditions, it is more convenient to measure the concentration of the substance in the water. LC_{50} is that concentration of a substance which causes death of 50% of a population under prescribed conditions in a prescribed period of time. Thus LC_{50} values are quoted in terms of ppm concentration, the species involved and the exposure time; examples are given later in Table 4.16.

A criterion of toxicity often used with regard to atmospheric pollution of the working environment is the threshold limit value (TLV) (Table 4.1).[2] This expresses the measure of airborne concentration of a substance to which it is believed that nearly all workers may be repeatedly exposed day after day, 7 to 8 hours per day for a 40 hour work-week, without adverse effect. However, it is recognised that, because of wide variation in individual susceptibility, a small percentage of workers may experience discomfort at concentrations at or below the TLV and an even smaller percentage may be affected more seriously. The value is, in fact, intended only as a guide in the practice of industrial hygiene, not as a fine line between safe and dangerous concentrations; it is not recommended for use either in the evaluation of air pollution nuisance or in estimating the toxic potential of continuous uninterrupted exposure.[2]

TABLE 4.1 SELECTED THRESHOLD LIMIT VALUES[2]

	ppm	mg/m³
Sulphur dioxide	5	13
Hydrogen sulphide	10	15
Carbon monoxide	50	55
Lead, inorganic compounds, fumes and dust	—	0·15
Hydrogen fluoride	3	2
Carbon dioxide	5000	9000

There are certain substances for which use of a time-weighted average concentration is inappropriate and these have been assigned a ceiling 'C' limit which should not be exceeded. Examples are hydrogen chloride and nitrogen dioxide, for each of which the ceiling threshold limit value is 5 ppm. When two or more hazardous substances are present it is necessary to consider their combined effect; in the absence of information to the contrary, the effects should be considered as additive.

Threshold limit value–short term exposure limits (TLV–STEL) are also of some relevance to accidental pollution episodes. These represent the maximum concentration to which workers may be exposed for up to 15 minutes continuously, provided that no more than four exposures per day occur, with at least 1 hour between exposures, and provided that the TLV time-weighted average is not exceeded.[2]

Where there is no published TLV for a material it is necessary to refer to other sources of data, for example to the Health and Safety Executive and/or to manufacturers or major users, and to standard reference texts.[3-5] However, tolerable levels of contaminants are continually under review. An extreme example of this concerns VCM (vinyl chloride monomer) which has been recently discovered to cause cancer in animals experimentally and, to date, in a small number of people exposed occupationally. As a result, in the UK the TLV has been revised from 200 ppm to that of a substance with recognised carcinogenic potential awaiting TLV reassignment pending further data acquisition. While it is reassuring that in this case the characteristic disease, angiosarcoma of the liver, is rare in the UK so that a widespread incidence would have readily identified the cause, a carcinogen giving rise to a commoner cancer might have gone undetected for many years.

Environmental Impact

The impact of any industrial undertaking upon its surroundings arises from the total effect of changes in, for example:

(a) Visual amenity
(b) Noise levels
(c) Odour levels
(d) Visibility, e.g. obscuration due to gaseous emissions
(e) Atmospheric pollution, e.g. effects on vegetation or dust deposition
(f) Detectable pollution of natural waters
(g) Detectable land pollution, or dereliction.

With the exception of (a) and to some extent (c), all of these changes can be determined quantitatively using techniques outlined in Chapter 5. Numerical values can therefore be assigned to acceptable base levels for specific cases. This has an important bearing on site selection; for example, it is an important advantage to large process plants to be near the sea so that wastes can be disposed of safely in accordance with legislation, but economically. Similarly, as considered in detail in Chapter 18, processes that are 'noisy' may be at an economic disadvantage if located in residential areas.

Nuisance

A nuisance, in the normal sense of the word rather than the strictly legal interpretation, arises when accepted standards of the factors listed above are noticeably exceeded. In law, nuisance refers to interference with the enjoyment of property, for example land or buildings, or with the comfort of living to a degree which is excessive. The latter is assessed in the light of conditions in the locality and the trades and activities which could reasonably be expected to be followed there. The frequency of the interference is also taken into account.

In general, it should be possible from the information given in the following chapters to foresee the possibility of 'nuisance' arising from a proposed new industrial enterprise, or a change of use of existing premises. However, a number of serious odour and pollution problems have arisen in the past from admixture of wastes and these are discussed later. 'Accidental' pollution, that is the creation of a nuisance or hazard due to plant failure or maloperation, is considered in Chapter 19.

Legislation

Not surprisingly, factors (a) to (g) above are all covered by legislative controls. The extent and administration of these controls vary between countries.

A comprehensive review of legislative controls is beyond the scope of this text; a list of relevant statutes for England and Wales, excluding those dealing generally with road traffic and aviation, is given in Table 4.2 (see also Walker[6]). There is a voluminous amount of subordinate legislation which is also relevant[7] and other legislation covering products.[8]

TABLE 4.2 LEGISLATIVE CONTROLS OVER POLLUTION (ENGLAND AND WALES)

Control of Pollution Act 1974
Highways Act 1959
Local Government Act 1972
London Government Act 1963
Official Secrets Act 1911
Powers of Criminal Courts Act 1973
Public Health Act 1875
Public Health Act 1936
Public Health Act 1961
Royal and Parliamentary Titles Act 1927
Supply of Goods (Implied Terms) Act 1973
Town and Country Planning Act 1971
Trades Description Act 1968
Health and Safety at Work etc. Act 1974

Gaseous Emissions
Control of Pollution Act 1974
Alkali etc. Works Regulation Act 1906
City of London (Various Powers) Act 1971
Clean Air Act 1956
Clean Air Act 1968
Heavy Commercial Vehicles (Control and
　Regulations) Act 1973
Land Compensation Act 1973
London Building (Amendment) Act 1935

Liquids
Seas
Continental Shelf Act 1964
Dumping at Sea Act 1974
Merchant Shipping (Oil Pollution) Act 1971
Petroleum Production Act 1934
Prevention of Oil Pollution Act 1971
Sea Fisheries Regulation Act 1966

Inland
Control of Pollution Act 1974
Clean Rivers (Estuaries and Tidal Waters) Act
1960
Public Health (Drainage of Trade Premises) Act
1937
Rivers (Prevention of Pollution) Act 1951
Rivers (Prevention of Pollution) Act 1961
Salmon and Freshwater Fisheries Act 1923
Water Act 1945
Water Act 1973
Water Resources Act 1963
Waterworks Clauses Act 1847

Solid Waste
Control of Pollution Act 1974
Civic Amenities Act 1967
Dangerous Litter Act 1971
Deposit of Poisonous Wastes Act 1972
Litter Act 1958

Noise
Control of Pollution Act 1974
Land Compensation Act 1973

Nuclear Substances and Installations
Radioactive Substances Act 1948
Radioactive Substances Act 1960
Radiological Protection Act 1970
Electricity Act 1957
Nuclear Installations Act 1965
Radiological Protection Act 1970

Criteria and standards for control are next considered in turn for gaseous, liquid and solid wastes. In practice, however, there is considerable overlap, since the potential nuisance or hazard associated with handling and disposal of a particular waste may have no physical bounds: for example, incineration of a solid waste may result in a potential air pollutant which, on removal by scrubbing, yields a liquid effluent for disposal.

Air Pollutants and their Effects

Combustion processes are the most important source of manmade air pollutants. In combustion, a series of chemical reactions occurs between a fuel and oxygen, derived from air, generally to provide thermal energy. This may be generated in a boiler, to produce steam, or in an oven or furnace for direct heating. In any event, the combustion products are emitted to the atmosphere via a chimney or exhaust vent.

Combustion Products

The normal products of complete combustion of a fossil fuel, e.g. coal, oil or natural gas, are carbon dioxide, water vapour and nitrogen. In practice, however, because of the presence of traces of sulphur and incomplete reaction, combustion results in the emission of carbon monoxide, sulphur oxides, and unburned hydrocarbons and particulates. This problem is common to domestic or industrial combustion equipment and to vehicle emissions. These are sometimes referred to as 'primary pollutants', some of which may take part in reactions in the atmosphere to produce 'secondary pollutants', e.g. photochemical smogs and acid mists.

Carbon dioxide occurs naturally, as a respiratory product from plants and animals and as a byproduct of organic decomposition processes, and is not strictly a pollutant. Conversely, carbon monoxide is highly toxic and undesirable levels may already be attained in areas of high traffic density such as tunnels. The problem must, however, be kept in perspective since traffic fumes are a less significant cause of carbon monoxide poisoning than smoking. Recent research has indeed been interpreted as showing that there would be little value in reducing carbon monoxide pollution from motor cars while so many people still smoke tobacco.[9]

Smoke

One of the commonest air pollutants is smoke, which is a submicron particulate aerosol from a combustion source. Although it generally contains relatively small amounts of particulate matter by weight, it obscures vision because of light-scattering by particles in the range $0 \cdot 3 - 0 \cdot 5$ μm. Thus 'dark smoke' and 'black smoke' are defined by reference to a shade on the British

Standard Ringelmann Chart (see Figure 4.1).

Smoke may significantly affect the microclimate of urban environments by reducing the penetration of sunlight. Apart from its characteristic effect of causing dirt and grime deposition on buildings, precipitation results in retardation of plant growth. The adverse effects of smoke upon a proportion of the exposed population is well established. It is a contributory cause of bronchitis and other respiratory ailments. Furthermore, it tends to increase the effects of other irritants, such as sulphur dioxide.

The main source of smoke in the UK is the domestic open coal fire. However, smoke production has been considerably reduced in recent years, as indicated in Table 4.3,[10] as a result of Clean Air legislation. This has led to improvements in the design and operation of industrial coal-fired equipment and to the increased use of gas or oil firing, together with improvements on the domestic side. The latter include the use of smokeless fuel and central heating.

Sulphur Dioxide

Sulphur dioxide is a damaging pollutant generated mainly from the combustion of fossil fuels, so that the highest concentrations tend to coincide with the highest concentrations of airborne particulates. The extent of the problem is illustrated in Table 4.3. It is interesting to compare the data for 1960 and 1970.[10] The total emission of smoke and the average ground level concentration (glc) fell by about 60% between these years; the total emission of sulphur dioxide increased by 10%, while the average glc fell by about 30%. The reason

TABLE 4.3 SMOKE AND SULPHUR DIOXIDE POLLUTION (ENGLAND AND WALES)

	1950	1960	1970
SO_2: emission (million tonnes/year) Domestic Industrial	0·9 3·9	0·8 4·7	0·5 5·5
Total*	4·8	5·5	6·0
Average glc ($\mu g/m^3$) (urban areas)	†	140	100
SMOKE: total emission (million tonnes/year) Domestic	1·3 1·1	1·2 0·5	0·6 0·1
Industrial*	2·4	1·7	0·7
Average glc ($\mu g/m^3$)	†	140	60

* Including power stations
† Insufficient data for national average before 1958

is that the bulk of the particulate matter is apparently emitted from domestic fires, or small factories, naturally concentrated in urban areas, whereas an increasing proportion of the total sulphur dioxide is emitted from power stations or larger factories. These tend to have high chimneys whereby sulphur dioxide is dispersed over a wide area.

Despite the dramatic improvements exemplified by the data, 'London smog' caused by a combination of fog and pollutants was detected as recently as December 1975.[11]

Another, although more restricted, source of sulphur oxides is chemical works manufacturing sulphuric acid via the contact process. Potential sources of pollutant are

   (i) unreacted sulphur dioxide passing through the absorber tower;
   (ii) unabsorbed sulphur trioxide;
   (iii) particulate acidity leaving the absorber as a fine fume which may coalesce into droplets;
   (iv) leaks.

Sulphur dioxide may also arise locally from acid plant effluents or metallurgical ore sintering operations.

Sulphur dioxide (SO_2) and sulphur trioxide (SO_3) irritate the respiratory tract when inhaled in low concentrations and may contribute to the onset of, or aggravate, asthma, emphysema and bronchial troubles. Furthermore, these oxides combine with moisture in the atmosphere to produce a corrosive sulphuric acid mist which may have a serious effect on vegetation and may damage buildings and structures, particularly those constructed of limestone or dolomite.

Carbon Monoxide

As mentioned earlier, whenever there is incomplete combustion of carbonaceous material, in for example the smelting of iron ore or in internal combustion engines, carbon monoxide is generated. CO is a colourless, odourless gas having almost the same density as air. Its toxic effects are mainly due to interference with the normal transportation of oxygen by the blood to the body tissues. It has an affinity for haemoglobin over 200 times that of oxygen and, by forming carboxyhaemoglobin, decreases the oxygen-carrying capacity of the blood. However, most people experience no ill effects at concentrations of less than 10 ppm.[12] There is evidence that this concentration is exceeded in city streets with a high traffic density[13] and concentrations on Putney Bridge in London have averaged 30 ppm during the working day.[14]

Nitrogen Oxides

The major source of oxides of nitrogen is the internal combustion engine. The oxides of nitrogen comprise nitrous oxide (N_2O), nitric oxide (NO) and nitrogen dioxide (NO_2 and N_2O_4). Nitric oxide, which is colourless, is converted into the dioxide in the presence of moisture and oxygen. The dioxide exists as a reddish-brown vapour and is a highly toxic pulmonary irritant; a dangerous concentration for short-term exposure may arise without warning, since it is only mildly irritating to the eyes and nasal passages. Oxides of nitrogen may also arise from nitric acid production and in the removal of ammonia from coke oven gas by incineration.

Hydrocarbons

Hydrocarbons are the most significant vapour-phase pollutant. The main sources of unburnt hydrocarbons are motor vehicles, but evaporation losses during solvent handling and from processes in which hydrocarbons are used as carriers, for example paint-spraying, make some contribution. While their effects are relatively small when in low concentrations, hydrocarbons may have serious effects when combined with other pollutants, such as oxides of nitrogen.

Dust and Grit

As outlined in Chapter 3, in addition to gaseous pollutants, exhaust gases from industrial processes frequently contain particulate matter. In addition to smoke (a term generally restricted to airborne particles arising from the incomplete combustion of carbonaceous materials) these comprise:

Grit   Hard solid particles 76 μm or greater in diameter
Dust   Solid particles less than 76 μm in diameter
Fumes   Any airborne solid matter smaller than dust resulting
              from chemical reaction or condensation of vapour.
              Classified variously as smaller than 10 μm or than 1 μm.

Any such emissions may constitute a health hazard or be objectionable on aesthetic grounds. Amenities can be affected by

(a) the formation of steamy or coloured plumes (for example due to nitrogen dioxide). These are objectionable both on aesthetic grounds and as giving rise to industrial haze resulting in obscuration of sunlight;
(b) deposition of coarse dust and grit on the ground or on buildings surrounding the source;
(c) build-up of significant ground-level concentrations of fine dust particles which may create a health hazard.

In the absence of any statutory limits, opinions vary as to the acceptability of plumes; a light haze disappearing within about $1\frac{1}{2}$–2 $\times$ chimney height may be regarded as tolerable.[15] As to tolerated dust deposition rates, average figures (1965) for various types of district in the UK given in Table 4.4[16] indicate that exception could not then reasonably be taken to any plant in a rural area whose contribution to deposition was less than 2 mg/m² day, but a plant depositing

TABLE 4.4 DUST DEPOSITION RATES FOR VARIOUS TYPES OF DISTRICT IN THE UK (1965)

Type of district	Total insoluble deposit $(mg/m^2 day)$
Rural	20
Urban	80
Industrial	160
Heavy industrial	> 1000

$20 mg/m^2$ day should be sited in an industrial area. Ground-level concentrations of fine particles, in a normal semi-industrial urban area of the UK, would be expected to be in the range 150–250 $\mu g/m^3$; in a 'smoke-controlled' or semi-rural area, about 50 $\mu g/m^3$.[15]

Control of toxic particulates is more critical and 'dust' hazards should be mentioned here: some dusts, known as 'fibrogenic' dusts, damage the lung tissue directly; others may comprise poisons which are absorbed into the bloodstream and cause other damage to the body. Generally, the most dangerous size of dust particle is between 0·2 and 5·0 μm, since particles greater than 5 μm are unable to penetrate the lung's defences;[17] however, larger particles of some dusts, e.g. asbestos, are also dangerous. Significant airborne concentrations of many of the fibrogenic dusts (i.e. dusts producing characteristic pneumoconioses, such as coal, iron (siderosis), cotton (byssonosis)) would not be tolerated by the general public. In the case of asbestos, however, there is evidence that casual exposure, such as living near a tip containing asbestos waste, can result in the development, possibly years later, of fatal asbestosis.[18] The most dangerous of all metals, so far as effects on the lung are concerned, is beryllium; fatal granuloma of the lung has occurred in persons living in the vicinity of factories using beryllium.[19]

Gas Leaks

Escaping gas may be associated with the storage or processing of volatile materials or with accidents which occur during their handling and transportation. Such gases may be toxic and/or flammable so that large accidental releases create a potential hazard.[20,21] Persistent leaks can in some instances contribute to significant atmospheric pollution phenomena, as in the case of the now almost totally eliminated Teesside mist[22] which, stretching up to 20 miles inland, resulted from reaction of leaks from ammonia plants with sulphur dioxide emissions from boiler plants. When ammonia plant design was improved, and the purging of these plants and urea plants was restricted to a minimum, 95% of ammonia emissions were stopped. Simultaneously there was a change from coal to natural gas fired boilers and a dramatic reduction in sulphur dioxide and dust emissions.

Escaping gases which have given rise to concern are the chlorofluorocarbons which are used in refrigerators and extensively as propellants for aerosol sprays. It has been suggested that following diffusion into the stratosphere these chemicals could cause a reduction in the earth's ozone shield and so more penetration of ultraviolet radiation with unpleasant consequences. However, a proposal for a ban on aerosols containing fluorocarbon propellants to operate in Britain from early 1977 was rejected in view of the uncertainty of current evidence.[23] The latest estimate is that if the 1973 rate of aerosol propellants is continued a maximum depletion of about 8% in the ozone layer will occur in about 100 years resulting in an increase of about 16% in the ultraviolet radiation reaching the ground.[24]

Effects on Vegetation

Air pollutants can have a significant effect upon vegetation. This is of considerable importance since many air pollutants may have an adverse effect on plants at concentrations which human beings tolerate. For example,

TABLE 4.5 EFFECTS OF MAJOR AIR POLLUTANTS

Pollutant	Effects
Carbon dioxide	—
Smoke, dust, grit[28,29,31]	Reduced visibility Deposition on buildings
Sulphur dioxide[29,30,31]	Damage to vegetation Sensory and respiratory irritation Corrosion Discoloration of buildings
Carbon monoxide[12]	Adverse health effects
Oxides of nitrogen[30]	Adverse health effects Damage to vegetation Sensory irritation Reduced visibility following photochemical reaction
Hydrocarbons[30,31]	Damage to vegetation Sensory irritation Reduced visibility following photochemical reaction
Hydrogen sulphide	Odours
Mercaptans	Odours
Lead[32]	Adverse health effects
Hydrogen fluoride	Damage to vegetation Adverse health effects in cattle fed on contaminated crops
Aldehydes	Damage to vegetation Sensory irritation Adverse health effects

hydrofluoric acid can cause damage to susceptible species at airborne concentrations of 0·4 $\mu g/m^3$ averaged over several months, a concentration less than that commonly found in industrial areas.[25] The chief sources of fluoride pollution are potteries and brickworks, cement works, and aluminium, steel, glass-making and phosphate fertiliser works.

Similarly, long-term exposure of plants to levels below 1 ppm of oxides of nitrogen can result in leaf damage and decreased fruit yield. Severe damage to vegetation has been reported in both Europe and North America as a result of heavy sulphur dioxide pollution in and around industrial areas, particularly near large ore-smelting plants. The effect of sulphur dioxide pollution on plants has been studied extensively;[26] it is dependent upon the airborne concentration and length of exposure time, and also on the variable pattern of exposure. Susceptibility varies with species, stage of growth and time of day; environmental factors such as light intensity, water and nutrient supply, and air temperature and humidity are also important. However, it has recently been reported that winter yield of one variety of rye-grass was reduced considerably when plants were exposed to sulphur dioxide at a concentration occurring widely in rural Britain, and that sulphur dioxide pollution may explain the absence of mature and healthy Scots pines in a wide belt of the central Pennines from Manchester to Bradford.[27] More surprisingly, ozone levels at Harwell (Oxfordshire), in central London and elsewhere have been recorded at up to four times the natural background of about 2 ppm in three consecutive summers, and characteristic ozone damage has been recorded on the leaves of an outdoor plant at Ascot (Berkshire).[27]

A summary of the major pollutants, their effects and sources of further information is given in Table 4.5.

Air Pollution Legislation

The Alkali Act—Control of Gaseous Emissions from Specified Industrial Processes

The Alkali Act,[33] as modified by the Clean Air Acts,[34] is concerned with the control of emissions, including smoke, grit and dust from specified chemical and industrial processes. Enforcement is the responsibility of the Alkali Inspectorate. The processes within the scope of this legislation are generally those which give rise to particularly dangerous or offensive emissions or which are technically difficult to control. Under the Act all works listed in Table 4.6 must be registered annually.

The duties placed upon the owner of scheduled works are to use the 'best practicable means'

(a) 'for preventing the escape of noxious or offensive gases by the exit flue of any apparatus used in any process carried on in the work';

TABLE 4.6 WORKS REQUIRING ANNUAL REGISTRATION UNDER THE ALKALI, ETC., WORKS ORDERS

Non-scheduled Works	
Alkali sulphate of soda or potash works: treatment of copper ores by common salt or other chlorides where any sulphate is formed where hydrogen chloride gas is formed	Smelting works in which sulphide ores, including regulus, are calcined or smelted Cement works in which aluminous deposits are used for making cements

Scheduled Works	
Sulphuric acid works	Sulphuric acid (Class II) works
Chemical manure works	Gas liquor works
Nitric acid works	Ammonium sulphate and ammonium chloride works
Chlorine works	Hydrochloric acid works
Sulphide works	Alkali waste works
Venetian red works	Lead deposit works
Arsenic works	Nitrate and chloride of iron works
Bisulphide of iron works	Sulphocyanide works
Picric acid works	Paraffin oil works
Bisulphite works	Tar works
Zinc works	Benzene works
Pyridine works	Bromine works
Hydrofluoric acid works	Cement production works
Lead works	Fluorine works
Acid sludge works	Iron works and steel works
Copper works	Aluminium works
Electricity works (power generation)	Producer gas works
Gas and coke works	Ceramic works
Lime works	Sulphate reduction works
Caustic soda works	Chemical incineration works
Uranium works	Beryllium works
Selenium works	Phosphorous works
Ammonia works	Hydrogen cyanide works
Acetylene works	Amines works
Calcium carbide works	Aldehyde works
Anhydride works	Chromium works
Magnesium works	Cadmium works
Manganese works	Metal recovery works
Petroleum works	Acrylates works
Di-isocyanate works	Mineral works

(b) 'for preventing the discharge, whether directly or indirectly, of such gases into the atmosphere';

(c) 'for rendering such gases where discharged harmless and inoffensive'.

The expression 'noxious or offensive gas' includes the list of gases and fumes

TABLE 4.7 NOXIOUS AND OFFENSIVE GASES

Hydrochloric acid	Fumes from petroleum works
Sulphuric acid and sulphuric anhydride	Fumes containing copper, lead, antimony, arsenic, zinc, aluminium, iron, silicon, calcium, or their compounds
Sulphurous acid and sulphurous anhydride (except those arising solely from the combustion of coal)	Fumes containing chlorine or its compounds
	Smoke, grit and dust
Nitric acid and acid forming oxides of nitrogen	Fumes containing uranium, beryllium, cadmium, selenium, sodium, potassium or their compounds
Chlorine and its acid compounds	Carbon monoxide
Bromine and its acid compounds	Acetic anhydride and acetic acid
Iodine and its acid compounds	Acrylates
Fluorine and its compounds	Aldehydes
Arsenic and its compounds	Amines
Ammonia and its compounds	Di-isocyanates
Cyanogen compounds	Fumes containing chromium, magnesium, manganese, molybdenum, phosphorus, titanium, tungsten, vanadium or their compounds
Pyridine	
Bisulphide of carbon	
Chloride of sulphur	
Acetylene	
Hydrogen sulphide	Maleic anhydride, maleic acid and fumaric acid
Volatile organic sulphur compounds	
Fumes from benzene works	Products containing hydrogen from the partial oxidation of hydrocarbons
Fumes from cement works	
Fumes from tar works	Phthalic anhydride and phthalic acid
Fumes from paraffin oil works	Picolines

given in Table 4.7. The interpretation of the term 'best practicable means' is (Section 27):

> The expression 'best practicable means', where used with respect to the prevention of the escape of noxious or offensive gases, has reference not only to the provision and the efficient maintenance of appliances adequate for preventing such escape, but also to the manner in which such appliances are used and to the proper supervision, by the owner, of any operation in which such gases are evolved.

'Manner of use' in this interpretation is clearly all-embracing and extends to the proper training of operatives. Also, in conjunction with 'supervision of the process', the regular testing and monitoring of emissions is increasingly being considered as one part of 'best practicable means'. In fact, 'practicable' is not defined but, though not binding upon them, the Inspectorate have regard to the definition provided in the Clean Air Act of 1956, namely:

> 'practicable' means reasonably practicable having regard, amongst other things, to local conditions and circumstances, to the financial implications and to the current state of technical knowledge.

Indirect discharges are also subject to control. This includes the regeneration of gases from wet scrubber effluents, escapes from spillage or seepage of process material and any emissions from product storage. However, with regard to both direct or indirect discharges, if 'best practicable means' are used but do not completely prevent the escape or discharge the emission need not unconditionally be rendered 'harmless and inoffensive'. This requirement is also subject to the 'best practicable means' criterion. In practice, the objective is generally met by ensuring that the final discharge is from a vent stack of adequate height. Nevertheless, the objective of rendering emissions harmless and inoffensive is not an alternative to prevention and is accepted only when prevention is technologically impossible or only partially successful.

The Chief Alkali Inspector thus has very considerable powers with which to regulate gaseous emissions from scheduled works. However, unlike many other countries, the general practice in the UK is not to set arbitrary limits for ground-level concentrations (exceptions are certain processes for which upper limits are specified for the concentration of total acidity in effluent gases discharged to the atmosphere (Table 4.8)). In each individual case, the permitted concentration depends on the nature of the discharge, its toxicity or nuisance value, the quantities involved, the proposed method of discharge, the pollutants already present or reasonably likely to be present in the atmosphere, and the effects of synergism or poor atmospheric dispersing conditions. There are however 'presumptive limits' laid down by the Alkali Inspectorate; these have no statutory significance but their attainment is regarded as 'presumptive evidence' that the 'best practicable means' requirement is met. Examples of 'presumptive limits' are given in Table 4.9.

TABLE 4.8 LEGAL LIMITS FOR THE MAXIMUM CONCENTRATION OF SPECIFIC POLLUTANTS IN GASES DISCHARGED FROM WORKS CONTROLLED BY THE ALKALI ACTS

Emission	$g\ m^{-3}$
Hydrogen chloride	$0.46\ HCl$
Sulphuric acid works:*	
chamber plants	9.2 as SO_3
concentration and	
distillation	3.5 as SO_3

* The absence of persistent mist is now required of all acidic emissions, which precludes the emission of all but minor amounts of SO_3.

The first criterion in deciding upon the 'best practicable means' is to ensure that there is no danger to health of residents in the area. One way of estimating a limiting concentration at ground level is to take the threshold limit values (TLV) of the pollutants, divide by a factor of 3 to allow for 24 hour exposure as against the nominal 8 hour day of industrial workers, and then to divide by an arbitrary factor such as 10 to allow for the young, old and infirm in the resident population. Thus,

$$\text{'Acceptable' ground level concentration} \simeq \frac{TLV}{3 \times 10}$$

TABLE 4.9 PRESUMPTIVE LIMITS, AS AT DECEMBER, 1974, FOR WORKS CONTROLLED BY THE ALKALI ACTS

Emission	$g\,m^{-3}$	Notes
(a) *Gaseous*		
Sulphuric acid contact plants	Sulphur emission to atmosphere not to exceed 0·5% of that burned	
Superphosphate works	0·23 as SO_3	Or absorption to be over 99% efficient.
Nitric acid plant tail gas	1·8 as SO_3	Emission to be substantially colourless.
Other emission of NO_x	2·3 as SO_3	No substantial emissions of persistent mist are permitted.
Chlorine	0·23 Cl_2	Complete elimination is normally expected, but an occasional discharge may be permitted during exceptional circumstances.
Hydrofluoric acid	0·23 as SO_3	No substantial emissions of persistent mist are permitted.
Hydrogen sulphide	0·0072	5 ppm by vol. Complete elimination is normally expected, but an occasional discharge may be permitted under exceptional circumstances. Some processes present an intractable problem since it is impracticable to reduce concentrations below 5 ppm, and the waste gases must therefore be discharged from suitable tall chimneys.
From cement works	nil	
(b) *Particulate*		
Arsenic works:		
small	0·115 As_2O_3	these limits also apply to antimony works—as Sb_2O_3
large (emissions greater than 8500 m^3/h	0·046 As_2O_3	
Cadmium works	0·036	Mass emission not to exceed 13·6 kg per week of 168 hours.
Cement works (chimneys):		
small (less than 1500 t/day clinker)	0·46	Based on wet gas sliding scale (also for chimney height) for wet, semi-dry or dry processes; emission velocity to be greater than 16 m/s.
large (1500–3000 t/day clinker)	0·46 to 0·23	
Cement works (low-level emissions)	0·23	
Copper works fumes	0·115	Works for recovering copper and its alloys from scrap must discharge any emissions from tall chimneys whose height is calculated on a sliding scale related to the aggregate rate of working for the whole group of furnaces on the site.

Table 4.9 (*continued*)

Iron and steel:		
sinter plants	0·115	
blast furnace gas		
to atmosphere	0·46	
oxygen-using plant	0·115	
Lead works:		Total allowable mass emission from a works must not exceed:
emission less than 12 000 m³/h	0·115 as Pb	0·27 kg/h
emission 12 000– 24 000 m³/h	0·023 as Pb	2·7 kg/h
emission more than 24 000 m³/h	0·0115 as Pb	5·4 kg/h (this is a target figure;
Phosphorus works	less than 0·046 P_2O_5	compliance with 'best practicable means' requirement is judged on the basis of individual tests).
Power stations:		
built before 1958	0·46	
2000–4000 MW coal fired	0·115	Adjusted to a CO_2 concentration of 12%
Roadstone coating works:		
emission less than 42 000 m³/h	0·46 ⎫	Total particulate dust: permissible emissions
emission greater than 42 000 m³/h	0·23 ⎬	from intermediate size works on sliding scale
Secondary aluminium works	0·115	
Miscellaneous:		
dust (10–75 μm)	0·46	
fume (smaller than 10 μm)	0·115	

However, although it may be that residents in any particular zone are exposed for only 1/20 to 1/80 of the total time (according to variation in wind direction), this approach must be applied cautiously in view of the limitations of threshold limit values outlined earlier. Furthermore, individual air pollutants do not occur in isolation: any atmosphere contains a number of pollutants in varying concentrations, and many of these are synergistic, i.e. the response to one pollutant may be affected by the presence of another. The example of sulphur dioxide being accompanied by smoke was mentioned earlier. Another common example is where hydrocarbons react with oxides of nitrogen in the presence of sunlight to produce photochemical smog. Ozone is a constituent of this smog and has been known to reach a concentration in air of 0·5 ppm in badly affected US cities, a concentration at which it impairs vision, respiration and mental function.

In view of the above, it is considered unrealistic to define a precise safe limit for any pollutant; at best a limit can be defined in terms of a concentration–time relationship at which little or no effect is observed either in isolation or with other pollutants present. The standards for sulphur dioxide and smoke in combination (as distinct from separately) in various countries are summarised in Table 4.10.

TABLE 4.10 AIR QUALITY STANDARDS, SMOKE AND SO_2

Country	SO_2 Standard ($\mu g/m^3$)	SO_2 Duration	Smoke Standard ($\mu g/m^3$)	Smoke Duration
Japan	110	Daily maximum	100	Daily mean
	275	Hourly maximum	200	Hourly maximum
USA	80	Annual mean*	75	Annual geometric mean*
	365	Daily maximum*	260	Daily maximum*
	1300	3 hourly maximum†	60	Annual geometric mean†
			150	Daily maximum†
Canada	30† and 60§	Annual mean	70‡ and 60§	Annual geometric mean
	150‡ and 300§	Daily maximum	120‡	Daily maximum
	450‡ and 900§	Hourly maximum		
Sweden	143	Monthly maximum	100	1 hour maximum
	286	Daily maximum		
	715	99 percentile $\frac{1}{2}$ hourly value		
Netherlands	250	98 percentile daily	90	98 percentile daily mean
	75	50 percentile daily mean	30	50 percentile daily mean
West Germany	140	Annual mean	100	Annual mean
			200	95 percentile $\frac{1}{2}$ hourly } d < 10
	400	95 percentile $\frac{1}{2}$ hourly value	200	Annual mean
			400	95 percentile $\frac{1}{2}$ hourly } d > 10

* Primary standard for the protection of human health
† Secondary standards for the protection of vegetation/wildlife.
‡ Desirable long term goal.
§ Acceptable level for protection of population.

Radioactive Emissions

With regard to radioactive gaseous emissions, the procedure is to reduce the activity as far as is practicable and then to release the gas so as to obtain adequate dispersal. This involves filtration to remove particulate activity, scrubbing to reduce gaseous activity and finally dispersion via a suitable stack. The Radioactive Substances Act requires that emissions be kept to a minimum reasonably practicable.

Clean Air Acts 1956 and 1968

The Clean Air Acts cover a number of specific fuel-burning operations other than those which present special technical difficulties and are registrable under the Alkali Acts. They control the emission of dark smoke, grit and dust either from chimneys or fires in the open.

Control of Smoke

Section 1 of the Clean Air Act 1956 prohibits the emission of dark smoke from a chimney except for permitted periods specified in the Dark Smoke (Permitted Periods) Regulations 1958. 'Smoke' refers to airborne particles resulting from the incomplete combustion of carbonaceous materials and includes soot, ash, grit and gritty substances emitted in smoke. 'Dark smoke' is defined as being as dark as or darker than Shade 2 on the Ringelmann Chart[35] (Figure 4.1) and is permitted for the maximum periods given in Table 4.11. Where a single boiler or unit is fired by more than one furnace discharging into the same chimney, those furnaces are considered to be one furnace. These are aggregate emissions, but the continuous emission of dark smoke otherwise than by soot blowing must not exceed 4 minutes.

There is also a prohibition against the emission of 'black smoke' for more than a total of 2 minutes in any period of 30 minutes. 'Black smoke' here refers to smoke as dark or darker than Ringelmann Shade 4.

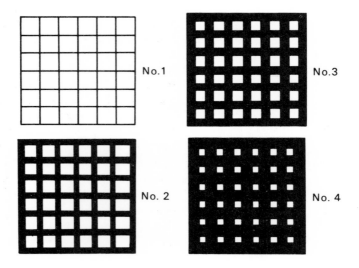

Fig. 4.1 Ringelmann chart for smoke definition: the four shades represent 20%, 40%, 60% and 80% blackness; a 100 mm square is viewed in line with the smoke at about 15 m distance

In the event of legal prosecution in respect of dark/black smoke emission, defences open to the occupier under the Act are (i) that the emission was solely due to lighting up a furnace from cold; or (ii) that there was an unavoidable failure of a furnace or connected apparatus; or (iii) that an unsuitable fuel had

TABLE 4.11 PERMITTED DARK SMOKE EMISSIONS

No. of furnaces served by chimney	Permitted emission of dark smoke in any 8 h period (minutes)	
	Without soot blowing	With soot blowing
1	10	14
2	18	25
3	24	34
⩾ 4	29	41

to be used because suitable fuel was unobtainable; or (iv) a combination of (i)–(iii). However, it must be shown that all practicable steps were taken to avoid or minimise the emission.

Section 3 of the 1956 Act requires that new furnaces must, so far as practicable, be capable of operating continuously without smoke emission when burning fuel of a type for which they were designed. (Domestic boilers with a rating less than 16 120 J/s (55 000 Btu/h) are excluded from this provision.) Any proposed installation of a new furnace must be notified to the local authority; plans and specifications may be submitted for prior confirmation that the proposed furnace meets the requirement.[36] However, the furnace must subsequently be operated properly so as to conform to permissible emissions.

The dark smoke prohibition was extended by Section I of the 1968 Act to premises on which matter is burnt in connection with any industrial or trade waste. This is concerned largely with the prevention of excessive smoke emission from fires in the open. However, subject to certain conditions the Clean Air (Emission of Dark Smoke) (Exemption) Regulations 1969 exempt the emission of dark smoke from the burning of certain materials (Table 4.12).[37]

There is a statutory procedure for notification of a dark smoke offence (S.30, 1956 Act).

Control of Grit and Dust Emissions

Grit is defined as hard, solid particles exceeding 76 μm in diameter.[38] Dust is generally accepted as being solid particles smaller than 76 μm with a lower limit of 1 μm. Anything smaller comprises fumes.

Under Section 2 of the 1968 Act limits may be prescribed on the rate of grit and dust emissions from chimneys of furnaces, excluding domestic boilers of less than 16 120 J/s (55 000 Btu/h) rating; different limits may be prescribed for different cases and circumstances. In the event of legal proceedings in respect of an excessive dust/grit emission it is a defence to show that the 'best practicable means' was used.[39] The Regulations made under this Section, the Clean Air (Emission of Grit and Dust from Furnaces) Regulations 1971, apply to all furnaces; they do not apply to incinerators burning refuse or waste.

TABLE 4.12 EXEMPT CATEGORIES OF MATERIALS AND CONDITIONS UNDER THE CLEAN AIR (EMISSION OF DARK SMOKE) (EXEMPTION) REGULATIONS 1969

Matter burnt	Exemption conditions
Timber and other waste (excluding rubber, flock or feathers) from building demolitions or site clearances	A, B, C
Waste explosives (under the Explosives Act 1875) and matter contaminated by such explosives	A, C
Matter burnt in connection with (a) research into the cause or control of fire, or (b) training in fire fighting	C
Tar, pitch, asphalt and other matter burnt in connection with surfacing (e.g. road works, roof-laying) with any fuel used for such purpose	C
Carcases of diseased animals or poultry	A, C (unless by/on behalf of an inspector; S.84 Diseases of Animals Act 1950.)
Containers (including any sack, box, package or receptacle of any kind) contaminated by pesticides or toxic substances used for veterinary or agricultural purposes	A, B, C

Condition

A   That there is no other reasonably safe method of disposal
B   That the burning is carried out in such a manner as to minimise dark smoke emission
C   That the burning is carried out under the direct and continuous supervision of the occupier of the premises or a person authorised to act on his behalf

Limits are prescribed, in terms of maximum permitted quantities of grit and dust in pounds per hour, for two scheduled classes of furnaces as summarised in Tables 4.13 and 4.14. These limits apply to any period of standard operation of the furnace or any other loading to which it is regularly subjected for a limited time. The proportion of grit in a sample of grit and dust is limited to either 33% or 20% dependent on furnace rating. Each flue of a multi-flue chimney is considered as a separate chimney when computing a permissible emission rate.

Under Section 3 of the 1968 Act, grit- and dust-arresting plant must be provided on new furnaces burning (a) pulverised fuel, (b) other solid matter at a rate greater than 45·36 kg/h (100 lb/h) or (c) liquid or gaseous matter at a rate greater than 366 kJ/s (1·25 × 10⁶ Btu/h). Approval is required from the local authority and there is a right of appeal to the Secretary of State. Section 4 (1) provides for the exemption of prescribed classes of furnace while used for a prescribed purpose. Thus two classes are exempt under the Clean Air (Arrestment Plant) (Exemption) Regulations 1969:[37]

Class 1   Mobile or transportable furnaces used to provide
a temporary source of heat or power (i) in
building or engineering construction,
(ii) for research or (iii) for agricultural purposes.

Class 2   Furnaces in which the matter being heated does
not contribute to the emission of grit and dust
being *either* furnaces burning gas and/or liquid
or certain types of solid fuel fired furnace with
a design rating of up to 1·016 tonne/h (1 ton/h) fuel and
not more than 122·7 kg/m² h (25 lb/ft² h) of grate or
combustion chamber area.

Provision is also made under Section 4(2) for exemption of any specific furnace by the local authority if it is satisfied that the emissions will not be prejudicial to health, or a nuisance.[37]

Chimney Heights
Chimneys of buildings serving processes not involving the combustion of fuel are controlled under Section 10 of the 1956 Act. Local authority approval is required following submission of building plans.

Control under Section 6 of the 1968 Act is applicable to chimneys of furnaces burning pulverised fuel, other solid matter at a rate not less than 45·36 kg/h (100 lb/h) or liquid or gaseous fuel at an equivalent rate not less than 366 kJ/s (1·25 × 10⁶ Btu/h). Approval is necessary when (a) a new chimney is to be erected to serve a new or existing furnace; (b) the combustion space of an existing furnace is to be increased; (c) a furnace served by an existing chimney is removed and replaced by another with a larger combustion space. The preferred form of application is given in the Clean Air (Height of Chimneys) (Prescribed Form) Regulations 1969. The authority then has to consider the chimney's purpose, the position and description of neighbouring buildings, the level of neighbouring ground and other relevant matters. It must not give approval without being satisfied that the proposed height will be sufficient to prevent, so far as is practicable, the smoke, grit, dust, gases and fumes from becoming prejudicial to health or a nuisance. If approval is given, conditions may be attached as to the rate and/or quality of emissions from the chimney. If approval is refused, the authority must state the lowest height that

TABLE 4.13 SCHEDULE 1, FURNACES RATED BY HEAT OUTPUT: STEAM BOILERS
AND INDIRECT HEATING APPLICANCES FOR GAS AND LIQUID

Maximum continuous rating		Maximum permitted quantities of grit and dust			
		Furnaces burning solid matter		Furnaces burning liquid matter	
(J/s)	(Btu/h)	(kg/h)	(lb/h)	(kg/h)	(lb/h)
242	825	0·49	1·10	0·11	0·25
293	1 000	0·60	1·33	0·13	0·28
586	2 000	1·21	2·67	0·25	0·56
829	3 000	1·81	4·00	0·38	0·84
1 172	4 000	2·42	5·33	0·51	1·12
1 465	5 000	3·02	6·67	0·63	1·40
2 198	7 500	3·85	8·50	0·95	2·10
2 930	10 000	4·53	10·00	1·27	2·80
4 395	15 000	6·05	13·33	1·90	4·20
5 860	20 000	7·56	16·67	2·54	5·60
7 325	25 000	9·07	20·00	3·17	7·00
8 793	30 000	10·61	23·40	3·81	8·40
11 724	40 000	13·60	30·00	5·08	11·20
14 655	50 000	16·78	37·00	5·67	12·50
29 310	100 000	29·93	66·00	8·16	18·00
43 965	150 000	42·64	94·00	10·88	24·00
58 620	200 000	55·34	122·00	13·15	29·00
73 275	250 000	67·58	149·00	16·33	36·00
87 930	300 000	78·02	172·00	18·59	41·00
102 585	350 000	88·45	195·00	20·41	45·00
117 240	400 000	98·43	217·00	22·68	50·00
131 895	450 000	108·41	239·00	24·72	54·50
139 222	475 000	113·40	250·00	25·85	57·00

would be approved, with any specified conditions. There is also provision for appeal to the Secretary of State for the Environment.

The Clean Air (Height of Chimneys) (Exemption) Regulations 1969 provide for the exemption of certain types of boiler or industrial plant when used for a prescribed purpose. Approval of chimney height is not necessary[40] for installations used

(a) as a temporary replacement for plant undergoing inspection, maintenance, repair, rebuilding or replacement;
(b) as a temporary source of heat or power for building or engineering construction;
(c) as a temporary source of heat or power for investigation or research;
(d) as auxiliary plant used to bring other plant to an operating temperature; or
(e) as a mobile or transportable source of heat or power for agricultural operations.

TABLE 4.14 SCHEDULE 2, FURNACES RATED BY HEAT OUTPUT: INDIRECT HEATING APPLIANCES AND FURNACES IN WHICH, THOUGH THE COMBUSTION GASES CONTACT THE MATERIAL HEATED, IT DOES NOT CONTRIBUTE TO THE GRIT AND DUST EMISSION

| Heat input | | Maximum permitted quantities of grit and dust | | | |
| | | Furnaces burning solid matter | | Furnaces burning liquid matter | |
$\times 10^6$ (J/s)	$\times 10^6$ (Btu/h)	(kg/h)	(lb/h)	(kg/h)	(lb/h)
0·37	1.25	0·49	1·1	0·13	0·28
0·73	2·50	0·95	2·1	0·25	0·55
1·46	5·0	1·95	4·3	0·49	1·1
2·19	7·5	3·08	6·8	0·77	1·7
2·93	10·0	3·45	7·6	0·99	2·2
4·39	15·0	4·40	9·7	1·49	3·3
5·86	20·0	5·40	11·9	1·99	4·4
7·33	25·0	6·39	14·1	2·49	5·5
8·79	30·0	7·39	16·3	2·99	6·6
10·26	35·0	8·30	18·4	3·49	7·7
11·72	40·0	9·34	20·6	3·99	8·8
13·19	45·0	10·34	22·8	4·44	9·8
14·65	50·0	11·34	25·0	4·94	10·9
29·31	100·0	20·41	45·0	7·26	16·0
58·62	200·0	40·82	90·0	11·79	26·0
87·93	300·0	59·87	132·0	15·87	35·0
117·24	400·0	79·38	175·0	19·95	44·0
146·55	500·0	98·88	218·0	24·49	54·0
168·53	575·0	113·40	250·0	25·85	57·0

Miscellaneous Clean Air Act Provisions
(i) Measurement of Emissions
Provisions for the measurement of grit and dust emissions from furnaces are contained in Section 7 of the 1956 Act as amended by Section 5 of the 1968 Act. These enable a local authority to serve a notice on the owner of a furnace requiring dust and grit emissions to be measured and recorded. The furnaces covered are those burning

(a) pulverised fuel;
(b) other solid fuel at a rate not less than 45·36 kg/h (100 lb/h); or
(c) liquid or gaseous fuel at a rate not less than 366·4 kJ/s ($1·25 \times 10^6$ Btu/h).

In the case of certain furnaces originally outside the scope of the 1956 Act, i.e.

(a) a furnace burning solid fuel, other than pulverised fuel, at up to 1·016 tonnes/h (1 ton/h); or
(b) a furnace burning liquid or gaseous fuel at up to 8207 kJ/s (28×10^6 Btu/h)

the owner may serve a counter notice on the local authority requiring it to measure and record the emissions at its own expense. The administrative procedure is outlined in The Clean Air (Measurement of Grit and Dust) Regulations 1971.

(ii) Smoke Control Areas

Sections 11 and 15 of the 1956 Act, as extended by Sections 8 to 10 of the 1968 Act, provide for the creation of Smoke Control Areas by local authorities. There is provision for the payment of grants in these Areas for the conversion or replacement of domestic appliances to burn smokeless fuels, or use electricity, instead of bituminous coal. It is an offence for the occupier of premises to allow smoke emission from a chimney in a Smoke Control Area, unless the 'fireplace' which the chimney serves is exempt from the local authority's Smoke Control Order or the smoke is not caused by the use of any fuel other than 'authorised fuel'. Authorised fuels[41] comprise:

Anthracite	Fireglo Briquettes
Phurnacite Ovoids	Ancit Briquettes
Coalite, Rexco and Rexco Ovoids	Extracit briquettes
Gloco and gas coke	Syntracite briquettes
Homefire and Roomheat	XL briquettes
Multiheat	Anthracine ovoids
Sunbright and hard coke	Anthrite ovoids
Cosiglow	Gas
Maxiglow	Electricity

Under Section 7 of the 1968 Act the Secretary of State may apply the provisions already described as applicable to grit, dust or smoke under Section 3 of the 1956 Act and Sections 2 and 3 of the 1968 Act to 'fumes'. Fumes are defined as any airborne solid matter smaller than dust.

Under Section 21 of the 1956 Act the local authority may exempt any particular chimney, furnace, boiler, or industrial plant/premises from various provisions for the purpose of investigations or research relevant to the study of air pollution. Under Section 23 a Clean Air Council was set up to review progress in air pollution abatement and to obtain advice from experts on air pollution matters.

The Control of Pollution Act 1974

Miscellaneous provisions relating to air pollution are incorporated in the Control of Pollution Act 1974. Under these provisions:

(a) The Secretary of State is empowered to make regulations controlling the composition of motor fuel and the sulphur content of oil fuel for furnaces or engines. Regulations have in fact been made relating to the lead content of petrol and the sulphur content of gas oils.[42]

(b) Places at which cable burning is to be carried out for recovery of the metal must be registered under the Alkali Act.

(c) Local authorities are empowered to obtain information about air pollution in their areas. This may be by the measurement and recording of the emissions, by an arrangement under which the occupiers carry out the measurements, or by the service of notices requiring occupiers to provide information about emissions. There is provision for appeal to the Secretary of State against the requirement to give information; regulations will be made describing the new powers and grounds for appeal. The local authority will be able to publish material on emissions. There is, however, a prohibition on disclosure of a 'trade secret' without permission, or consent from the Secretary of State.

There are other provisions under which the Secretary of State may direct a local authority to make arrangements for the measurement and recording of air pollution and to pass the information to him, and which increase many of the penalties under earlier statutory legislation on air pollution.

Health and Safety at Work, etc., Act 1974

Under Section 5 of the Health and Safety at Work Act a duty is imposed upon persons controlling prescribed premises to use the 'best practicable means' for preventing the emission into the atmosphere of noxious or offensive substances and for rendering such substances as may be emitted 'harmless and inoffensive'. The means to be used includes reference to the manner in which any pollution control plant is used, and to the supervision of any operation involving the emission of the substances in question.

Effects of Pollutants on Water

River Water

Natural water maintains a wide variety of aquatic life including fish, bacteria, algae and protozoa, all of which are in dynamic equilibrium with the environment. This variety of life is maintained by the relative stability of the temperature and chemical composition (e.g. dissolved salt content) of the water, the presence of sufficient dissolved oxygen, and an essentially neutral pH. The effects of wastes which enter river water vary considerably and may be disastrous. If they noticeably upset the natural chemical and biological equilibrium, the river is termed 'polluted'.

Imbalance may take the form either of damage to one or more species or of the increase of one species at the expense of others—as in eutrophication, where pollution of fresh water by excessive quantities of nutrients, i.e. nitrates and phosphates, results in heavy growths of algae to the exclusion of other species. The resulting mats of blanket weed considerably reduce the on-stream time of waterworks filter plant.

Damage to species may be caused either directly or indirectly. Direct damage occurs when substances accumulate in the water in concentrations toxic to plant and animal life. Significant amounts of this type of pollutant are likely to render the water unfit for use as a water supply, and the destruction of plant and animal life will hinder or prevent natural self-purification.

Toxic Agents

Literature on river pollution is extensive[43,44] and only a brief background review is necessary here. Substances which are toxic at very low concentrations include the following:

(i) *The salts of the heavy metals,* e.g. beryllium, cadmium, lead, mercury, nickel, silver, gold, chromium, zinc and copper. These have total effects on fish at quite low concentrations. For example, in one river only 1–2 ppm of copper was found to have completely exterminated all animal life for 10 miles downstream and decimated the algae concentrations;[45] zinc is fatal to trout at 0·15 ppm and to coarse fish at 1–2 ppm. Generally, fish are less resistant to poisons than are microscopic plants or other animals, and are therefore a good indicator species.

The concentrations of various substances at which toxic effects have been detected in bacteria, algae, crustacea and protozoa in river water of pH 7·5 are summarised in Table 4.15.[46] Substances toxic to fish have been extensively reviewed by Klein.[43] The toxicity of selected metals to rainbow trout is illustrated by Table 4.16; coarse fish are somewhat more resistant.

TABLE 4.15 CONCENTRATIONS (PPM) AT WHICH COMMON MATERIALS SHOW TOXIC EFFECTS IN VARIOUS ORGANISMS

	Bacteria *Escherichia coli*	Green algae *Scenedesmus quadricauda*	*Daphnia magna*	*Protozoa microregma*
Copper (Cu)	0·08	0·15	0·1	0·05
Zinc (Zn)	1·4 to 2·3	1 to 1·4	1·8	0·33
Chromium III(Cr)		4 to 6	42	37
Cyanide (CN⁻)	0·4 to 0·8	0·16	0·8	0·04
Cyanate (CNO⁻)	10	520	23	21
Sulphide (S⁻⁻)	93	40	26	
Phenol		40	16	30
Toluene	200	120	60	
o-Xylene	500	40	16	10
m-Xylene		40	24	70
p-Xylene		40	10	50
Amyl alcohol		280	440	20
Formic acid		100	120	
Butyric acid		200	60	
Butyl acetate		320	44	20
Amyl acetate		180	120	40

An added problem with heavy metals is the facility of certain organisms to concentrate them to a remarkable extent, up to about $\times 10^5$. A dramatic example of this phenomenon occurred in Japan when, between 1953 and 1960, a large number of cases of a neurological disease, over 100 of which were fatal, occurred amongst villagers around Minimata Bay. This was caused by the ingestion of methyl mercury, dumped in chemical waste in the bay and accumulated by fish and shell fish which were then eaten.

(ii) *Cyanides*. These can be fatal to fish at concentrations of much less than 1 mg/litre (1 ppm), e.g. 0·04 mg/l is fatal to trout.

(iii) *Phenols*. These may arise in phenolic wastes from synthetic resin manufacture or from tar distillation. If present in very low concentrations they can be broken down by bacteria, but at concentrations higher than 1–5 mg/litre they may be fatal to bacteria and fish. Phenols also produce objectionable flavours in drinking water, especially when it is chlorinated; about 0·001 ppm of chlorinated phenol is detectable by taste.

(iv) *Other organic chemicals*. Of these, the chlorinated hydrocarbons are especially persistent; since they are broken down only very slowly by natural biochemical processes, they tend to accumulate in the environment. This family includes numerous pesticides, for example DDT, dieldrin, aldrin, endrin and lindane, which are estimated to have a half life of up to 15 years.

TABLE 4.16 TOXIC CONCENTRATIONS OF SOME METALS TO RAINBOW TROUT[47]

Metal	Concentration (mg/l) which kills half the number of exposed fish in 48 hours (LC_{50})	
	Soft water	Hard water
Copper	0·04	0·5
Cadmium	0·05	5·5
Zinc	0·5	3
Lead	1	—
Nickel	15	100

Oxygen Depletion

Indirect damage occurs when substances contribute to the oxygen depletion of the receiving water. This may result from direct consumption of available oxygen by chemical or biochemical means. Chemicals such as sulphides, e.g. from tanning, and ferrous salts tend to oxidise in the water and thus use up oxygen. Biologically labile substances also create an oxygen demand. Examples of organic matter which may enter surface waters and result in such pollution are wastes from soft-drinks factories, breweries, tanneries and slaughter-houses, and sewage or leachings from household refuse. These are discussed in Chapter 7. It has been established that most substances are more toxic in water of reduced oxygen content.

Rivers have a natural ability to recover from this type of pollution since the oxygen required to meet the demand is available via aeration at the surface and, to a smaller extent, from photosynthesis by algae, weeds and similar vegetation. However, if a river is completely deoxygenated, anaerobic conditions result in the production of hydrogen sulphide, methane and other chemicals. It may not then recover until it is mixed with large volumes of

oxygenated water at the sea, in an estuary or on joining a large, relatively unpolluted river.

Because aeration, by dissolution of oxygen at the air–water interface, is
necessary to maintain a satisfactory oxygen concentration in the water, any
substances which interfere with this mechanism have a detrimental effect on
water quality. A layer of grease or oil can have this effect. Oil films exceeding
10^{-3} mm thickness have been demonstrated to have a marked effect on the rate
of oxygen absorption; this is equivalent to an even spread of $2 \cdot 25$ m^3 (500 gal)
per square mile.[48] Oil also tends to coat the gills of fish and affect their utilisation of dissolved oxygen, and to endanger water birds. The commonest types of
pollutant associated with the restriction of oxygen diffusion are, however, the
earlier types of anionic synthetic detergent which may produce large blankets
of froth. This effect is reduced with the more recent biodegradeable detergents.

If present in sufficient quantities, suspended solids may contribute to oxygen
depletion by deposition on, and blanketing of, the river bed. This may cause
destruction of plant and invertebrate life, leading to anaerobic conditions and
the subsequent release of noxious gases. The cloudiness of the water may have
harmful effects on fish and other organisms and significantly reduce photosynthesis.

At 10°C, clean water contains approximately 11 ppm of dissolved oxygen.
Bacterial action on decayable organic matter consumes oxygen. If the dissolved oxygen is used up preferentially by bacterial action, fish and other forms
of life may die; at worst, anaerobic bacteria may take over, resulting in the
production of offensive products with foul odours such as hydrogen sulphide,
ammonia and mercaptans. In the absence of significant concentrations of toxic
materials the water will remain in a healthy condition, and should support life,
if it retains about 40% of saturation, that is 4 ppm dissolved oxygen.

The polluting strength of an effluent is usually expressed as the 5-day
biochemical oxygen demand, (BOD$_5$) (Table 4.17). The effluent is tested at
different dilutions to determine the amount of oxygen consumed during 5 days'
incubation following seeding with micro-organisms. Seeding is usually achieved
by adding sewage effluent to the water for dilution. Substances such as phenol
are biodegradable when diluted but inhibit bacterial action at high concentrations; thus measurement at different dilutions is important.

TABLE 4.17 EXAMPLES OF BOD VALUES

	BOD$_5$ (ppm)
Clean river water	< 3
Well-diluted effluent from sewage works	< 20
Untreated sewage	⩽ 400
Percolate from household refuse landfill sites	Highly variable, e.g. 400 ppm in 1st year; values ⩽ 33 000 ppm have been obtained

Another test, the chemical oxygen demand (COD) test, is quicker and more reproducible than that for BOD but cannot generally be directly related to it. COD may be ascertained under various test conditions, e.g. by oxidation with potassium permanganate or dichromate, but these must be specified since each method gives a different result.

In the UK the Royal Commission Standards recommend 30 ppm BOD and 20 ppm suspended solids for effluents discharged to rivers. This standard has been found adequate for a relatively unpolluted river into which household sewage is discharged with a minimum dilution factor of 8:1.

Effluent Temperature

The temperature of any effluent discharged to a river, or more precisely the resultant temperature of the receiving water, is another important factor. Increased river water temperature can have a deleterious effect on fish life, either indirectly by preventing or discouraging the passage of migratory fish such as the salmon, or as a direct cause of death. For example, the lethal temperature for trout is 25°C; for pike, 30°C.[49] Moreover, a rise in temperature of a river which is already organically polluted will increase the rate of biochemical processes and hence the rate of oxygen consumption. Biological processes accelerate by a factor of 2–3 for every 10°C rise in temperature within the range 5°–40°C. In addition, the solubility of oxygen in water will be reduced. These factors together may cause a serious reduction in oxygen level.

Estuaries and Tidal Waters

The natural processes in these waters can be upset in a similar way to river water. Because of the enormous dilution potential of the open sea, the problem might be expected to be lessened. In fact, estuaries have very complex flow patterns: in some, the water merely moves up and down the estuary with the tidal motion and very slow seaward travel takes place, so that dilution is correspondingly slow.[50]

Very low concentrations of seawater pollutants, for example toxic metals or chlorinated hydrocarbons, may have ill effects due to accumulation. Floating oil is another example of the inability of the large apparent dilution factor to cope with pollution.

Effects of Pollutants on Sewers and Waste Treatment Plant

Limits, or even total prohibition, need to be placed on the discharge of certain substances to municipal sewers in order to avoid danger to sewermen, obstruction to flow, damage to sewage structures or interference with waste treatment processes (see Tables 4.18 and 4.19). Since adequate ventilation of sewers is not easy to maintain, dangerous accumulations of gases or vapours must be avoided. To remove the risk of explosion, petrol and other organic solvents are excluded from sewers. Limits are also placed upon the quantities of cyanides and sulphides which may be discharged to sewers, to prevent formation of toxic gases such as hydrogen cyanide and hydrogen sulphide. Very hot effluents are also excluded since, apart from any hazard to sewermen, they would accelerate chemical degradation and the production of noxious gases.

Obstruction to flow may arise from blockage due to grease, deposition of suspended solids or the trapping of floating materials such as paper or plastics. Abrasive solids (e.g. broken glass) can cause erosion damage or build up to cause silting and eventual blockage. The structure of the sewer may be damaged by a range of substances such as strong mineral acids and alkalis; sulphates may attack concrete sewers. Thus a permissible pH range is usually specified and sulphates and sulphides (which can be converted into sulphates by certain strains of bacteria) are limited.

All sewage plants incorporate a biological oxidation unit, usually of the activated sludge or percolating filter type. The living organisms involved in these processes can only operate within fairly narrow limits of pH, nutrients, temperature and chemical conditions. Any waste which alters these conditions, for example one which contains a significant concentration of any of the biochemical poisons already discussed, may retard or inhibit completely these treatment processes. Therefore it is important to limit pH variations, phenols, cyanides, heavy metals and other toxic materials.[51] An added reason for limiting metal content is that much of it is not removed by biological treatment and is therefore liable to pass into the surface waters receiving the discharge of final effluent.

Water Pollution Legislation

UK law concerning pollution of streams and rivers is in two forms—Common Law and Statute Law.[52,53] The majority of Common Law associated with water pollution concerns the riparian owner's right to abstract water, with certain restrictions, from streams which pass through his land. He has a right to expect the water in the stream or river to enter his land in its natural state, that is without sensible diminution, or increase, and largely unpolluted by anyone upstream.[54] This has been modified in part by the Water Resources Act 1963 in that Water Authorities have control over abstractions. Licences to abstract are issued so as to maintain a minimum acceptable flow in the river.

A riparian owner may commence exercise of his rights at any time and can take action to restrain persons from making discharges which pollute the water in the river. There is no precise definition of pollution but in practice it refers to the addition to a stream of any liquid or substance which reduces its quality or wholesomeness. This includes trade effluents, sewage effluent and cooling water.[55] Action may also be taken by owners of fishing rights, where any discharge acts to the detriment of the fish population. Action may be taken by the Attorney-General in the case of public nuisance.

In practice, to succeed in any action it is necessary for a riparian owner to show that the pollution complained of is, or may in time become, actually damaging. This may not be a simple matter, since any natural water may be polluted to some degree from more than one source. When pollution is proven the Court may award damages and/or grant an injunction preventing the defendant from installing new discharges and imposing a delayed injunction on existing discharges to give time either for necessary remedial measures to be carried out or for alternative arrangements for disposal of effluent to be made. For example, a perpetual Common Law injunction was imposed on one company with a factory discharging to a salmon river, restraining it from discharging effluent which could taint the flesh of salmon, cause tastes or odours in the water, or produce sewage fungus.[56] To obtain damages, the plaintiff must of course prove material loss. Furthermore, if pollution is allowed to continue for twenty years without objection, the polluter will normally have acquired a prescriptive right.

The original legislation relating to water pollution and the discharge of effluents to local authority sewers is extraordinarily complex and to appreciate the present position it is best to review the development.

Rivers (Prevention of Pollution) Acts 1951 and 1961

The 1951 Act set up River Boards to be responsible for the rivers of England and Wales. The Water Resources Act 1963 subsequently transferred responsibility to a reduced number of River Authorities. The 1951 Act gave these Authorities certain powers to control discharges made to non-tidal waters in their care. For the purpose of the Act a stream is any river, watercourse or inland water, whether natural or artificial, except any lake or pond which does not discharge to a stream. Those wishing to discharge through new or altered outlets are required to obtain consent. Agreement may be given subject to the position and design of the outlet conforming to the Authority's specification and to conditions concerning the nature, composition, temperature, total volume and rate of discharge as discussed below. Only limited provision was made for control of discharges made to the non-tidal portions of rivers prior to the Act; this was modified in the 1961 Act. In general there is a prohibition on discharges which could be classed as 'poisonous, noxious or polluting'. Authorities may make bylaws enlarging upon this classification with reference to temperature and colour, albeit with prior notice to affected bodies. In addition, under the Salmon and Freshwater Fisheries Act 1923, it is an offence knowingly to discharge, or permit to be discharged, anything into any fresh water so as to be injurious to fish or fishing.

The 1961 Act extended control to discharges made to non-tidal portions of rivers prior to the 1951 Act.

Clean Rivers (Estuaries and Tidal Waters) Act 1960

This Act extended the jurisdiction of the River Authorities to tidal waters and parts of the sea known as 'controlled waters'. It gave the same powers to impose restrictions on new or altered discharges. At present, only discharges originating after 29 September 1960 are controlled, that is 'existing' discharges are not controlled provided they continue 'unchanged'. 'Change' here refers to a significant increase in total volume or concentration of any pollutant or any other relevant change, such as increase in temperature or alteration in method of discharge. If there is a change, the discharge is 'new' and subject to consent conditions.

Discharge to Underground Strata

The Water Act 1945 made it an offence to cause pollution of a spring or well, the water from which is, or may be, taken for human consumption or for domestic purposes. Any landowner also has a right to redress at Common Law if water drawn from wells on his land is polluted as a result of actions by an identifiable party. Subsequently, the Water Resources Act 1963, referred to earlier, required those who abstracted water from any source of supply to apply for a licence to continue this practice.[55] Thus, since there is also a requirement to maintain a minimum flow of water in a river, the riparian owner no longer has the right to abstract an unlimited supply of water for his own use.

The Water Act 1973

This Act replaced the existing River Authorities by ten much larger Regional Water Authorities with increased responsibilities. These Authorities now both operate the sewage works vested in the local authorities and control the discharges from them. While this results in their setting their own standards of achievement, this is subject to review by the Minister of State and they must account annually for their treatment plant performance. All discharges to the sea within territorial waters are subject to approval by the Water Authority, irrespective of the year they were first made.

The Authorities also have power to control discharges made to underground strata via any pipe, borehole or well. There is a consent procedure similar to that for discharges made to surface waters, that is consent may be refused or granted subject to conditions as to the nature, quality and composition of the effluent and the strata into which it may be discharged. Stipulations may be made regarding measures for the protection of groundwater in strata through which the discharge passes and regarding facilities to be provided for observation of the effects of the discharge on these strata. Allowance is made for appeal to the Minister, and the Authority must keep a register of consents.

Other relevant pieces of legislation are the Oil in Navigable Waters Acts 1955 and 1971 and the Prevention of Oil Pollution Act 1971. While generally applicable to shipping, these make it an offence to discharge an effluent containing oil from a shore establishment or to cause the water or foreshore to be fouled with oil. There is some limited exception for oil refineries. Finally, under the Sea Fisheries Regulation Act 1966, administered by the Ministry of

Agriculture, Fisheries and Food, it is an offence to discharge anything into coastal waters which is harmful to sea fish or sea fishing.

The Control of Pollution Act 1974

This Act extends the existing methods of water pollution control to virtually all inland and coastal waters. New provisions are introduced with regard to accidental pollution. When the whole Act is in force, all of the Rivers (Prevention of Pollution) Act 1951 and the Clean Rivers (Estuaries and Tidal Waters) Act 1960 will be repealed.

Water Authorities keep registers containing information regarding consents, discharges, sampling and analyses and these are available for public examination. Discharges of trade effluents to public sewers are brought under full control.

As to implementation, the system empowering Water Authorities to grant consent for discharges to watercourses was introduced late in 1975. The provisions which make it an offence to discharge without consent were not implemented until mid-1976.[57] The provisions regarding control over trade effluent to sewers and powers and duties of Water Authorities to forestall pollution were introduced during the same period.

Public Health (Drainage of Trade Premises) Act 1937

This Act repealed those sections of the 1936 Act referring to the discharge of trade effluent to local authority sewers. It gave a trader the right to make discharges to these sewers subject to compliance with a set procedure. This procedure and consent conditions are discussed later. Industries discharging to sewers prior to 3 March 1937 were exempted from the consent procedure provided the nature and quantity of the discharge remained substantially the same. This was later modified in the Public Health Act 1961.

Public Health Act 1961

This Act brought under control of the Authorities discharges made to the sewers prior to 3 March 1937, but only in a restricted manner. The local authority may issue a direction which may contain clauses regarding conditions discussed later. Scientific research and experimental establishments were rendered subject to the control of the 1937 Act. While the right of the authority to make byelaws was withdrawn, the scope of the consent conditions was increased.

The Authority may vary the terms of consent but, unless the trader gives his written agreement, this may only be done after a minimum of two years. Information which the Authority is empowered to collect from the trader, as to the plant and effluent from the plant, must be regarded as confidential.

Consent Conditions for Discharge to Public Sewers

By virtue of the Public Health Act 1936, the occupier of any premises is entitled to have connections made to the public sewers solely for the purpose of discharging domestic sewage and surface water. Any material likely to affect the operation of the sewer or the treatment and disposal of its contents, any chemical refuse or waste stream or liquid above 43°C resulting in a hazard or nuisance, or any 'petroleum spirit' or calcium carbide are specifically excluded. However, under the Public Health (Drainage of Trade Premises) Act 1937 as amended by Part V of the Public Health Act 1961, or in Scotland under the Sewerage (Scotland) Act 1968, occupiers of trade premises may discharge effluent into the public sewers provided they comply with certain conditions. In order to do so a Trade Effluent Notice must be served on the authority, stating (a) the nature and composition of the effluent, (b) the maximum quantity which it is proposed to discharge in any one day and (c) the peak rate of discharge.

This notice should normally be served at least two months before it is desired to commence discharging, during which time consent may be given either unconditionally or, more probably, with conditions as to the sewers into which discharge is permitted, the nature and composition of the waste and the maximum daily and the peak rate of discharge, and the periods of day during which the effluent may be discharged. In giving consent for a discharge it is usual to prohibit any substances which, either alone or in combination with any matter in the sewerage system, would give rise to obnoxious, poisonous or inflammable gases, or be deleterious to the sewers, plant or treatment processes.

Typical consent conditions are given in Table 4.18. These limits are likely to apply only in those cases in which the effluent represents a small proportion of the total flow in the sewer. More stringent consent conditions apply when dilution in the sewer is small. The total oxygen load is also commonly limited either in terms of BOD or as a specific permanganate value. Conditions may also be

TABLE 4.18 TYPICAL CONSENT CONDITIONS FOR DISCHARGE TO MUNICIPAL SEWERS

Parameter/substance	Maximum allowed
pH range	6–10 (permitted range)
Sulphate (as SO_3)	500–1000 mg/l
Free ammonia (as NH_3)	500 mg/l
Suspended solids	500–1000 mg/l
Tarry and fatty matter	500 mg/l
Sulphide (as S)	10 mg/l
Cyanide (as CN)	10 mg/l
Immiscible organic solvents	nil
Calcium carbide	nil
Temperature	45°C
Petroleum and petroleum spirit	nil
Total non-ferrous metals	30 mg/l
Soluble non-ferrous metals	10 mg/l
Separable oil and/or grease	300–400 mg/l

imposed regarding the payment of charges and the provision and maintenance of an inspection chamber or manhole, meters to measure the volume and rate of discharge and apparatus for determining the nature and composition of the effluent. Provision is made for the keeping of records and making returns regarding quantity, rate and composition. The trader has the right to appeal to the Minister regarding consent conditions.

When a discharge is of major proportions and special provisions have to be made for its reception and treatment at the sewage works, an agreement may be entered into by the authority and trader regarding a procedure for repayment of the cost of necessary extensions, etc. The waste-waters from food production and fermentation processes and organic compounds from oil refining, carbonisation of coal and chemical syntheses may be amenable to biological treatment similar to that required by sewerage; these may be accepted for discharge at rates calculated to meet the extra costs incurred. Agreement may also be made where the trader wishes the local authority to dispose of sludges resulting from the treatment or pretreatment of wastes at his own premises. In order to ensure compliance with consent conditions, the local authority has the power to enter industrial premises to take samples of effluent.

Charges for Acceptance of Trade Effluent
Policy with regard to charges for the disposal of trade wastes via public sewers may involve:

   (i) no charge at all to traders;
  (ii) a flat rate charge per unit volume of effluent;
 (iii) a scale of charges based upon a formula accounting for certain characteristics of the effluent; or
 (iv) charges similar to (iii) but with a sliding scale.

Method (iii) is being used increasingly and the Mogden formula, or a derivation of it, is commonly applied to relate the charge to the conveyance and treatment costs. The basic formula is

$$C_T = V + B + S$$

where C_T = total cost of treatment per m^3 of effluent
    V = costs related to volume of flow per m^3 of effluent
    B = costs related to aerobic biological treatment per m^3 of effluent
    S = costs related to sludge treatment per m^3 of effluent.

The general formula is

$$C_T = C_v + \frac{O_T\,C_o}{O_M} + \frac{S_T\,C_s}{S_M}$$

where C_T = total cost of treatment per m^3 of trade effluent
    C_V = cost of treatment related to volume only for each m^3 of mixed sewage

C_O = cost of aerobic biological treatment per m^3 of mixed sewage after settlement

C_S = cost of disposal of sludge from each m^3 of mixed sewage

O_T, O_M = oxygen demands of settled trade effluent and settled mixed sewage

S_T, S_M = suspended solids content of trade effluent and mixed sewage.

In this way the cost for any particular trade effluent is weighted according to the difficulty in treating it compared with sewage. An extra charge may also be imposed for toxic metal content.

The methods for assessing oxygen demand, O_T and O_M, may be based on BOD, COD, permanganate value (PV) or McGowan Strength. The last, which is most commonly used, is defined as

$$\text{Strength} = 4 \cdot 5 \text{ (ammoniacal N + organic N)} + 6 \cdot 5 \text{ PV}$$

A joint working party of the CBI and the River Water Authorities has agreed recommended guidelines for charging schemes applicable to industry. This includes the following recommendation: trade effluents should be charged on the following type of formula using average flow conditions:

$$C = R + V + \frac{O_t}{O_s} B + \frac{S_t}{S_s} S$$

where C = total charge per m^3 trade effluent

R = reception and conveyance charge per m^3

V = volumetric and primary treatment cost per m^3

O_t = the COD (mg/1) of the trade effluent after one hour quiescent settlement at pH 7

O_s = the COD (mg/1) of settled sewage.

B = biological oxidation cost per m^3 settled sewage

S_t = total suspended solids in mg/1 of the trade effluent at pH 7

S_s = total suspended solids in mg/1 of crude sewage

S = treatment and disposal costs of primary sludges per m^3 sewage.

Discharge to Rivers

Some indication of the conditions imposed for the discharge of industrial effluents into streams and rivers is given in Table 4.19.[56] Evidently these conditions are intended to protect the receiving waters from the types of pollution discussed earlier.

Each consent is a special case, since the conditions must vary according to the nature and volume of the effluent and the type and condition of the receiving water. With regard to the nature of the effluent, clearly only those pollutants which are, or are likely to be, present determine its effect on the receiving water and the consent conditions are modified accordingly. The

TABLE 4.19 TYPICAL CONSENT CONDITIONS FOR THE DISCHARGE OF INDUSTRIAL EFFLUENT TO RIVERS AND STREAMS

	Maximum allowed
Fishing streams	
BOD (5 days at 20°C)	20 mg/l
Suspended solids	30 mg/l
pH	5 to 9
Sulphide—as S	1 mg/l
Cyanide—as CN	0·1 mg/l
Arsenic, cadmium, chromium, copper, lead, nickel, zinc—either individually or in total	1 mg/l
Free chlorine	0·5 mg/l
Oils and grease	10 mg/l
Temperature	30°C
Non-fishing streams	
BOD (5 days at 20°C)	40 mg/l
Suspended solids	40 mg/l
pH	5 to 9
Transparency of settled sample	not less than 100 mm
Sulphide—as S	1 mg/l
Cyanide—as CN	0·2 mg/l
Oils and grease	10 mg/l
Formaldehyde	1 mg/l
Phenols (as cresols)	1 mg/l
Free chlorine	1 mg/l
Tar	none
Toxic metals—individually or in total	1 mg/l
Soluble solids	7500 mg/l
Temperature	32·5°C
Insecticides or radioactive material	none

polluting effect of an effluent is roughly proportional to the product of its volume and the concentration of pollutant[44] so that discharge may be permitted of a small volume of effluent with a higher BOD or temperature. The physical characteristics of a receiving water, for example a fast-flowing river, the extent to which it is already polluted and its amenity value will affect the consent conditions imposed. Thus, as indicated in Table 4.19, a higher standard of discharge is expected to a fishing stream than to an already polluted stream.

Clearly, consent conditions vary, but they will become more stringent in the future. Limits such as BOD = 10, suspended solids = 15 mg/l and PV = 10 are anticipated. In the past, for an organic effluent somewhat similar to sewage, consent conditions would probably be based on the Royal Commission Standard:[48]

BOD, 5 days at 20°C	20 mg/l
Suspended solids	30 mg/l

The temperature may also be limited, for example to between 30° and 32·5°C.[49] Alternatively, discharges containing heavy metals have limits set on the concentrations of toxic metals allowed (the River Severn has a limit of 0·5 mg/l total toxic metals).[50] The specification for discharge from a metal-finishing works to another river has been quoted[51] as:

Total discharge (in 24 h)	16·4 m³ (3600 gal)
Maximum rate	1·1 m³/h (240 gal/h)
Total heavy metals (Cr, Cd, Cu, Pb, Ni, Zn)	1·0 ppm
Cyanide (as HCN)	0·1 ppm
Suspended solids	60 ppm
pH	6 to 10

In this case, low limits were set on toxic materials (cyanides and heavy metals) but suspended solids were permitted to exceed Royal Commission Standard.

Hazards Associated with Solid Waste Disposal

Potential hazards caused by deposition of wastes on land have generally to be assessed with regard to the risk of injury or impairment of health to persons or animals, or the pollution or contamination of any water supply above or below ground. Although many wastes are inert the widespread variety of toxic wastes is illustrated in Chapter 3, Table 3.5. The detailed potential hazards to the environment from toxic waste deposition may be summarised[58] as:

(a) Physical danger at point of discharge or health risk to operatives arising from:
 (i) handling of toxic, dermatitic, carcinogenic, radioactive or corrosive materials;
 (ii) inhalation of fumes and dust;
 (iii) fires and explosions.
   Note: there are similar dangers to possible trespassers such as totters, children, animals.

(b) Pollution risk:
 (i) air pollution—dust, effluvia, smoke and fume;
 (ii) land pollution—gross amenity damage, undermining of site stability; sterilisation of surrounding land due to heavy metals, pH changes;
 (iii) water pollution—deposited material or percolate escape either through surface run-off or by underground movement threatening streams, rivers, aquifers or even the sea; direct 'poisoning' or eutrophication.

Legislation has been mainly concerned with controlling deposition on land but a combination of the above hazards is present during storage, collection, transportation and disposal by any of the means summarised in Chapter 3. In this respect, the possibilities listed under (b) above exemplify the way in which air, land and water pollution problems are often interrelated.

Waste Disposal Legislation

Under the Deposit of Poisonous Waste Act 1972 it became an offence punishable by heavy penalties to deposit on land any poisonous, noxious or polluting waste so as to give rise to an environmental hazard. Environmental hazard is defined here as 'material risk of death, injury or impairment of health' to persons or animals, or any deposit likely 'to threaten the pollution or contamination (whether on the surface or underground) of any water supply'. Some indication of the types of waste to which this legislation applies is given in Table 3.2 and a list of materials actually deposited on one landfill site is given in Table 13.3. There is a notification procedure under which those concerned are required to inform responsible authorities of the nature and amounts of certain wastes originating, and being deposited, in their areas.

Some of the factors which must be considered in order to comply with the general prohibition of the deposit of hazardous waste on land are (a) the manner of deposition, (b) the quantity of waste, either the single deposit or cumulatively, and (c) the likelihood that children, or others, may tamper with the waste. The fact that a particular waste is in containers is not considered, in itself, to eliminate risk.

Section 2 of the Act emphasises the civil liability of any person for damage ensuing from hazardous waste which they have deposited, or have caused or permitted to be deposited, on land.

Under Section 3 a duty is imposed to notify responsible authorities before any waste is removed from premises for deposit elsewhere, or is deposited on land. The notice must state[59]

  (i) the premises from which the waste is to be removed;

  (ii) the land on which it is to be deposited;

  (iii) its nature and chemical composition (i.e. principal constituents and characteristics, flashpoint and any minor constituents which may be of environmental significance and the concentration of the specified constituents);

  (iv) the quantity and, if the waste is in containers, their number, size and description;

  (v) in the case of a removal, the name of the person who is to undertake removal.

Three clear days' notice must be given before movement; this is required by the local authority and Water Authority for the area in which the waste is to be deposited and also those authorities from whose area the waste is to be removed. Copies must also be given to the person undertaking removal and the operator of the disposal site.

The Deposit of Poisonous Waste (Notification of Removal or Deposit) Regulations 1972 provide exemption for all normal waste from homes, shops or offices, for wastes arising in certain trades or processes, and for materials which are generally not so dangerous that they need to be notified. Provided they do not contain hazardous concentrations of poisonous substances, the wastes listed in Table 4.20 are exempt from notification. Additional exemptions

TABLE 4.20 TYPES OF WASTE FOR WHICH NOTICE OF DISPOSAL IS NOT REQUIRED (PROVIDED THAT IT DOES NOT CONTAIN ANY HAZARDOUS QUANTITY OR HAZARDOUS CONCENTRATION OF ANY POISONOUS, NOXIOUS OR POLLUTING SUBSTANCE)

Class 4

Any waste produced in the course of:

(i) the construction, repair, maintenance or demolition of plant or buildings;

(ii) the laundering or dry cleaning of articles;

(iii) working mines and quarries, or washing mined or quarried material;

(iv) the construction or maintenance of highways, whether or not repairable at the public expense;

(v) the dry cutting, grinding or shaping of metals, or the subjection thereof to other physical or mechanical process;

(vi) the softening, treatment or other processing of water for the purpose of rendering it suitable for (a) human consumption, (b) the preparation of foods or drinks, (c) any manufacturing or cooling process, or (d) boiler feed;

(vii) the treatment of sewage;

(viii) the breeding, rearing or keeping of livestock;

(ix) brewing;

(x) any other fermentation process; or

(xi) the cleansing of intercepting devices designed to prevent the release of oil or grease.

Class 5

Any waste (not being waste in any of the foregoing classes) consisting of one or more of the following items whether mixed with water or not:

(i) Paper, cellulose, wood (including sawdust and sanderdust) oiled paper, tarred paper, plasterboard;

(ii) Plastics, including thermoplastics in both the finished and raw states, and thermosetting plastics in the finished state;

(iii) Clays, pottery, china, glass, enamels, ceramics, mica, abrasives;

(iv) Iron, steel, aluminium, brass, copper, tin, zinc;

(v) Coal, coke, carbon, graphite, ash, clinker;

(vi) Slags produced in the manufacture of iron, steel, copper or tin or of mixtures of any of those metals;

(vii) Rubber (whether natural or synthetic);

(viii) Electrical fittings, fixtures and appliances;

(ix) Cosmetics;

(x) Sands (including foundry and moulding sands), silica;

(xi) Shot blasting residues, boiler scale, iron oxides, iron hydroxides;

(xii) Cement, concrete, calcium hydroxide, calcium carbonate, calcium sulphate, calcium chloride, magnesium carbonate, magnesium oxide, zinc oxide, aluminium oxide, titanium oxide, copper oxide, sodium chloride;

(xiii) Cork, ebonite, kapok, kieselguhr, diatomaceous earth;

(xiv) Wool, cotton, linen, hemp, sisal, any other natural fibre, hessian, leather, any man-made fibre, string, rope;

(xv) Soap and other stearates;

(xvi) Food, or any waste produced in the course of the preparation, processing or distribution of food;

(xvii) Vegetable matter;

(xviii) Animal carcases, or parts thereof;

(xix) Excavated material in its natural state;

(xx) Any other substance which is a hard solid and is insoluble in water and in any acid.

apply to agricultural wastes and to certain deposits allowed under other laws or necessary in emergency and for radioactive wastes. Section 4 of the Act prohibits a tip operator from allowing the deposit of poisonous waste without three days' notice having been received. Following deposition, the operator must notify the authorities within three days.

In order to cut down the clerical work involved in notifications, a 'season ticket' procedure may be introduced. This is not specified under the Act, but where similar consignments of waste are being disposed of regularly it may be permissible: for example, notice may be given that a specified quantity of waste of constant chemical composition is to be deposited on the same tip every week during a twelve-week period. A limit should be set to the period of such a season ticket; in one case, where tipping was controlled within the confines of the site producing the waste, the period covered was twelve months.

The Deposit of Poisonous Waste Act 1972 will be repealed by the Control of Pollution Act 1974 when fully operational. Sections within this Act, together with the enabling power to make regulations, are intended to replace fully the controls and powers outlined above.

Part I of the Control of Pollution Act 1974 revises the law on the collection and disposal of waste by a local authority.[60] The authority must ensure that satisfactory arrangements are made for disposal of all 'controlled' waste in its area, either by itself or by other operators. 'Controlled' waste is household, commercial and industrial waste. If any such waste is difficult or dangerous to dispose of, the Secretary of State has powers to make regulations for the disposal of that special waste.

Disposal authorities will be required to prepare waste disposal plans on the basis of the kind and quantity of controlled wastes involved and the methods, sites and equipment available/required. This includes schemes for reclamation. A licensing system has been introduced by which disposal authorities will regulate disposal; it will be an offence to deposit waste anywhere except on a licensed site in accordance with the conditions of the licence. A licence will also be required for the use of any plant and/or equipment in the disposal of waste. Exemptions may be prescribed in certain circumstances, including cases for which adequate controls are provided by existing legislation, for example incinerators already approved under the Clean Air Acts. Regulations will be made with regard to conditions which may attach to licences, such as the kinds and quantities of wastes which may be disposed of, special precautions necessary, hours of work and any works necessary for satisfactory disposal operations. It is the responsibility of the disposal authority to supervise the licensed activities, including the prevention of environmental pollution. Licensing is not required for the disposal authority's own activities on its own land, but they are required to meet similar standards.

With regard to waste collection, District Councils are required to collect all household wastes in their areas except where the place is isolated or inaccessible, collection costs would be unreasonable and alternative arrangements have been made. They must also collect commercial waste when requested. Collection or disposal authorities may undertake collection of industrial waste. Wastes other than household waste will be subject to reasonable charges based on collection and disposal costs.

EEC Directive on Waste

It is relevant to note that harmonisation of legislation is stressed in the programme of action on the environment of the European Communities.[61] This was one reason behind the recent issue of a Council Directive on waste;[62] what this sets out to achieve, and the way in which it mirrors future legislation, is clear from the Articles reproduced in Table 4.21.

TABLE 4.21 COUNCIL DIRECTIVE OF 15 JULY 1975 ON WASTE (75/442/EEC)

Article 1

For the purposes of this Directive:
(a) 'waste' means any substance or object which the holder disposes of or is required to dispose of pursuant to the provisions of national law in force;
(b) 'disposal' means:
— the collection, sorting, transport and treatment of waste as well as its storage and tipping above or under ground,
— the transformation operations necessary for its re-use, recovery or recycling.

Article 2

1. Without prejudice to this Directive, Member States may adopt specific rules for particular categories of waste.
2. The following shall be excluded from the scope of this Directive:
(a) radioactive waste;
(b) waste resulting from prospecting, extraction, treatment and storage of mineral resources and the working of quarries;
(c) animal carcases and the following agricultural waste: faecal matter and other substances used in farming;
(d) waste waters, with the exception of waste in liquid form;
(e) gaseous effluents emitted into the atmosphere;
(f) waste covered by specific Community rules.

Article 3

1. Member States shall take appropriate steps to encourage the prevention, recycling and processing of waste, the extraction of raw materials and possibly of energy therefrom and any other process for the re-use of waste.
2. They shall inform the Commission in good time of any draft rules to such effect and, in particular, of any draft rule concerning:
(a) the use of products, which might be a source of technical difficulties as regards disposal or lead to excessive disposal costs;
(b) the encouragement of:
— the reduction in the quantities of certain waste,
— the treatment of waste for its recycling and re-use,
— the recovery of raw materials and/or the production of energy from certain waste;
(c) the use of certain natural resources, including energy resources, in applications where they may be replaced by recovered materials.

Article 4

Member States shall take the necessary measures to ensure that waste is disposed of without endangering human health and without harming the environment, and in particular:
— without risk to water, air, soil and plants and animals,

Table 4.21 (*continued*)

— without causing a nuisance through noise or odours,
— without adversely affecting the countryside or places of special interest.

Article 5

Member States shall establish or designate the competent authority or authorities to be responsible, in a given zone, for the planning, organisation, authorisation and supervision of waste disposal operations.

Article 6

The competent authority or authorities referred to in Article 5 shall be required to draw up as soon as possible one or several plans relating to, in particular:
— the type and quantity of waste to be disposed of,
— general technical requirements,
— suitable disposal sites,
— any special arrangements for particular wastes.

The plan or plans may, for example, cover:
— the natural or legal persons empowered to carry out the disposal of waste,
— the estimated costs of the disposal operations,
— appropriate measures to encourage rationalisation, of the collection, sorting and treatment of waste.

Article 7

Member States shall take the necessary measures to ensure that any holder of waste:
— has it handled by a private or public waste collector or by a disposal undertaking,
— or disposes of it himself in accordance with the measures taken pursuant to Article 4.

Article 8

In order to comply with the measures taken pursuant to Article 4 any installation or undertaking treating, storing or tipping waste on behalf of third parties must obtain a permit from the competent authority referred to in Article 5, relating in particular to:
— the type and quantity of waste to be treated,
— general technical requirements,
— precautions to be taken,
— the information to be made available at the request of the competent authority concerning the origin, destination and treatment of waste and the type and quantity of such waste.

Article 9

The installations and undertakings referred to in Article 8 shall be periodically inspected by the competent authority referred to in Article 5 to ensure, in particular, that the conditions of the permit are being fulfilled.

Article 10

Undertakings transporting, collecting, storing, tipping or treating their own waste and those which collect or transport waste on behalf of third parties shall be subject to supervision by the competent authority referred to in Article 5.

Article 11

In accordance with the 'polluter pays' principle, the cost of disposing of waste, less any proceeds derived from treating the waste, shall be borne by:
— the holder who has waste handled by a waste collector or by an undertaking referred to in Article 8;
— and/or the previous holders or the producer of the product from which the waste came.

Article 12

Every three years, Member States shall draw up a situation report on waste disposal in their respective countries and shall forward it to the Commission. To this effect, the installations or undertakings referred to in Articles 8 and 10 must supply the competent authority referred to in Article 5 with the particulars on the disposal of waste. The Commission shall circulate this report to the other Member States.

Table 4.21 (*continued*)

The Commission shall report every three years to the Council and to the European Parliament on the application of this Directive.

Article 13

Member States shall bring into force the measures needed in order to comply with this Directive within 24 months of its notification and shall forthwith inform the Commission thereof.

Article 14

Member States shall communicate to the Commission the texts of the main provisions of national law which they adopt in the field covered by this Directive.

Article 15

This Directive is addressed to the Member States.

This chapter has described why constraints must be applied to the disposal of wastes and outlined the legislative controls currently applied in the UK. The trend is for increased control on waste disposal although all the provisions of the Control of Pollution Act have yet to take effect. Even tighter measures may be anticipated as each community's expectations of its environment increase, and as the economic climate permits. There have been dramatic reductions in ground-level concentrations of the major air pollutants and increased attention is now being focused on solid waste disposal methods.

As described in subsequent chapters, there is adequate existing technology to meet higher pollution control standards and the analytical procedures and instrumentation are available to monitor them. However, a balanced consideration of priorities is essential before introducing further controls. A long-term view favours stricter limitations on those wastes which persist, for example those containing heavy metals, chlorinated hydrocarbons or asbestos, and upon radioactive wastes, rather than expenditure to obtain improvements relating to relatively non-toxic wastes.

References

1. MORAN, J. M., MORGAN, M. D. and WIERSMA, J. H., *An Introduction to Environmental Sciences*, Little, Brown, 1973.
2. *Threshold Limit Values for 1976*, Guidance Note EH 15/76, Health and Safety Executive, 1976.
3. SAX, N., *Dangerous Properties of Industrial Materials*, Reinhold, 1975.
4. BROWNING, E., *Toxicity and Metabolism of Industrial Solvents*, Elsevier, 1965.
5. BROWNING, E., *Toxicity of Metals*, Butterworth, 1961.
6. WALKER, A., *Law of Industrial Pollution Control*, Godwin, 1979.
7. Subordinate legislation having relevance to legislative controls over pollution in England and Wales:

    General Development Order 1963 SI 709
    General Development Order 1973 SI 31
    Town and Country Planning (Erection of Industrial Buildings) Regulations 1966 SI 1034
    Town and Country Planning (Inquiries Procedure) Rules 1969

    Gaseous Emissions
    Alkali etc. Works Order 1966 SI 1143
    Alkali etc. Works Order 1971 SI 960

Building Regulations 1972 SI 317
Clean Air (Arrestment Plant) (Exemptions) Regulations 1969 SI 1262
Clean Air (Emission of Dust from Furnaces) Regulations 1971 SI 162
Clean Air (Measurement of Dust from Furnaces) Regulations 1971 SI 161
Clean Air (Heights of Chimneys) (Exemption) Regulations 1969 SI 411
Dark Smoke (Permitted Periods) Regulations 1958 SI 948
Dark Smoke (Permitted Periods) (Vessels) Regulations 1958 SI 878
ECE Regulation 15
EEC Council Directive 70/156/EEC
EEC Council Directive 70/220/EEC
EEC Council Directive 70/306/EEC

Water (Seas)
Byelaws of:
  Cornwall Sea Fisheries Committee
  Cumberland Sea Fisheries Committee
  Devon Sea Fisheries Committee
  Kent & Essex Sea Fisheries Committee
  Lancashire and Western Sea Fisheries Joint Committee
  South Wales Sea Fisheries Committee
  Southern Sea Fisheries Committee
  Sussex Sea Fisheries Committee
Continental Shelf (Designation of Areas) Order 1964 SI 697
Continental Shelf (Designation of Areas) Order 1965 SI 1531
Continental Shelf (Designation of Areas) Order 1968 SI 891
Merchant Shipping (Oil Pollution) Act 1971 Commencement Order 1971 SI 1423
Petroleum Production Regulations 1966 SI 898
Petroleum Production (Amendment) Regulations 1972 SI 1522
Shellfish Regulations 1915 SRO 125
Shellfish Regulations 1934 SRO 1342

Nuclear Installations
Electricity (Publication of Applications) Regulations 1957 SI 2227
Nuclear Installations Regulations 1971 SI 381
Nuclear Installations (Dangerous Occurrences) Regulations 1965 SI 1824

8. Products—Statutes having relevance to legislative controls over pollution in England and Wales:
Agriculture (Poisonous Substances) Act 1952
Farm and Garden Chemicals Act 1967
Patents Act 1949
Public Health (Regulations as to Food) Act 1907

Subordinate Legislation
Carbon Disulphide (Conveyance by Road) Regulations 1958 SI 313
Carbon Disulphide (Conveyance by Road) Regulations 1962 SI 2527
Compressed Gas Cylinders (Fuel for Motor Vehicles) Regulations 1940 SRO 2009
Corrosive Substances (Conveyance by Road) Regulations 1971 SI 618
Gas Cylinders (Conveyance) Regulations 1931 SRO 675
Gas Cylinders (Conveyance) Regulations 1947 SRO 1594
Gas Cylinders (Conveyance) Regulations 1959 SRO 1919
Inflammable Liquids (Conveyance by Road) Regulations 1971 SI 1061
Inflammable Substances (Conveyance by Road) (Labelling) Regulations 1971 SI 1062
Merchant Shipping (Dangerous Goods) Rules 1961 SI 1067
Merchant Shipping (Dangerous Goods) Rules 1968 SI 332
Merchant Shipping (Dangerous Goods) Rules 1972 SI 666
Petroleum (Carbide of Calcium) Order 1929 SRO 992
Petroleum (Carbide of Calcium) Order 1947 SRO 1442
Petroleum (Carbon Disulphide) Order 1958 SI 257
Petroleum (Carbon Disulphide) Order 1968 SI 572
Petroleum (Carbon Disulphide) (Conveyance by Road) Regulations 1958 SI 313

Petroleum (Carbon Disulphide) (Conveyance by Road) Regulations 1962 SI 2527
Petroleum (Compressed Gases) Order 1930 SRO 34
Petroleum (Corrosive Substances) Order 1970 SI 1945
Petroleum (Inflammable Liquids) Order 1971 SI 1040
Petroleum (Inflammable Liquids and other Dangerous Substances) Order 1947 SRO 1443
Petroleum (Liquid Methane) Order 1957 SI 859
Petroleum (Mixtures) Order 1929 SRO 993
Petroleum (Organic Peroxides) Order 1973 SI 1897
Petroleum Spirit (Conveyance by Road) Regulations 1957 SI 191
Petroleum Spirit (Conveyance by Road) Regulations 1958 SI 962
Petroleum Spirit (Conveyance by Road) (Amendment) Regulations 1966 SI 1190

9. *New Scientist,* **67**(956), 4, 1975.
10. *Protection,* 2, October 1974.
11. *Daily Telegraph* Report, 17 December 1975
12. *Carbon Monoxide Poisoning—Causes and Prevention,* SHW 29, HMSO, 1965.
13. REID, L. E. and TROTT, P. E., *Atmospheric Environment,* **5,** 27, 1971.
14. Scientific Adviser to the GLC. *Report for 1971.*
15. STRAIRMAND, C. J., *Chemical Engineer,* (375), October 1971.
16. STAIRMAND, C. J., *Chemical Engineer,* (310), December 1965.
17. HM Factory Inspectorate, *Health: Dust in Industry,* Technical Data Note 14, Health and Safety Executive, 1970.
18. *Surveyor,* (4353), 2, November 1975.
19. HUNTER, D., *The Diseases of Occupations,* 5th edn., English Universities Press, 1975.
20. *Liquid Chlorine,* HSW 37, HMSO, 1970.
21. *The Bulk Storage of Liquified Petroleum Gas at Factories,* SHW 30, HMSO, 1965.
22. HM Chief Alkali Inspector, *Annual Report,* 1972.
23. *New Scientist,* **67**(961), 336, 1975.
24. *Chlorofluorocarbons and their Effect on Stratospheric Ozone,* Pollution Paper No. 5, HMSO, 1975.
25. Royal Commission on Environmental Pollution, 4th Report, *Pollution Control: Progess and Problems,* HMSO, 1974.
26. *The Effects of Air Pollution on Plants and Soil,* Agricultural Research Council, 1967.
27. *New Scientist,* 189, 23 January 1975.
28. SAUNDERS, P. J. W., *The Estimation of Pollution Damage,* Manchester University Press, 1976.
29. MAGILL, P. L., HOLDEN, F. R. and ACKLEY, C., *Air Pollution Handbook,* McGraw-Hill, 1956.
30. *Medical Aspects of Air Pollution,* Society of Automotive Engineers Inc., New York, 1971.
31. STERN, A. C. (Ed.), *Air Pollution,* Academic Press, 1972.
32. Department of the Environment, *Lead in the Environment and its Significance to Man,* Pollution Paper No. 2, HMSO, 1974.
33. The Alkali, etc., Works Regulation Act 1906 as extended by subsequent Statutory Orders.
34. The Clean Air Acts 1956 and 1968.
35. BS 2742: 1969, *Notes on the Use of the Ringelmann and Miniature Smoke Charts,* British Standards Institution, 1969.
36. *Memorandum on the Miscellaneous Provisions of the 1956 Clean Air Act,* SO 75.50.062.
37. Circular HLG 72/69, Ministry of Housing and Local Government, 1969.
38. Clean Air (Emission of Grit and Dust from Furnaces) Regulations 1971.
39. *Memorandum on the Industrial Provisions of the Clean Air Act 1956,* SO 75.59.
40. Circular HLG 28/69, Ministry of Housing and Local Government, 1969.
41. The Clean Air (Authorised Fuel) Regulations 1956, 1963, 1965, 1969, 1970 (No. 2), 1971, 1971 (No. 2), 1971 (No. 3) and 1971 (No. 4).
42. Motor Fuel (Lead Content of Petrol) Regulations 1976, SI 1966; Motor Fuel (Sulphur Content of Gas Oil) Regulations 1976, SI 1989; Oil Fuel (Sulphur Content of Gas Oil) Regulations 1976, SI 1988.
43. KLEIN, L., *Aspects of River Pollution,* Butterworth, 1957 and *River Pollution 2: Causes and Effects,* Butterworth, 1962.
44. WILBER, G. C. *The Biological Aspects of Water Pollution,* Charles C. Thomas, 1969.
45. BUTCHER, R. W., *Journal of the Institution of Sewage Purification,* **2,** 92, 1946.
46. OLDHAM, G. F., *Chemical Engineer,* (267), CE418, 1972.

47. JACKSON, S., *Chemical Engineer,* (224), CE420, 1968.
48. DOWNING, A. L. and TRUESDALE, G. A., *Journal of Applied Chemistry,* **5**, 570, 1955.
49. PRIESTLEY, J. J., *Process Engineering,* 125, January 1970.
50. Royal Commission on Environmental Pollution, 3rd Report, Cmnd 5054, HMSO, 1972.
51. Ministry of Housing and Local Government, *Standards of Effluents to Rivers with Particular Reference to Industrial Effluents,* HMSO, 1968.
52. WISDOM, A. S., *The Law of the Pollution of Waters,* Shaw & Sons, 1966.
53. MYERS, D. S. and ISAAC, P. C. G., *Chemical Engineer,* (267), CE415, 1972.
54. *Young* v. *Bankier Distillery Co.* (1893).
55. LUMB, C., *Chemical Engineer,* (192), CE248, 1965.
56. ISAAC, P. C. G., *Chemical Engineer,* (239), CE165, 1970.
57. Report of Parliamentary Reply. *Municipal Engineering,* **249,** 7 February 1975.
58. KEEN, R. C., *Deposit of Poisonous Wastes,* Bristol Polytechnic, July 1973.
59. *Disposal of Poisonous Waste Act 1972,* Circular 70/72, Department of the Environment, 19 July 1972.
60. *Municipal Engineering,* 7 February 1975.
61. *Official Journal of the European Communities,* C 112, 3, 20 December 1973.
62. *Official Journal of the European Communities,* L 194, 25 July 1975.

CHAPTER 5

Measurement Techniques

Preceding chapters discuss what needs to be measured for waste treatment, recycle or disposal; but not how to measure it: this chapter briefly describes the
methods available. There is a range of texts devoted entirely to measurement and
analysis;[1-17] an exhaustive review of the subject is beyond the scope of this book. A
summary of the relevant properties requiring measurement and the techniques
available is presented here in tabular form for ready reference. Some tests may be
considered as routine and amenable to automatic control (indicated by 'R' in the
tabular summary), while perhaps the majority are individual tests that only occasionally need to be carried out, when assessing alternative methods of disposal
or evaluating possible recovery processes.

Physical, physico-chemical and chemical properties may require measurement or assessment. Knowledge of these properties is particularly necessary
for the design of suitable disposal, recovery or treatment plant, and in meeting
legislative constraints and controlling hazards. Toxicity is discussed in Chapter
4.

Physical Properties

Table 5.1 shows the large number of physical properties that may require
measurement. With such a wide range, full details of each technique cannot be
supplied; instead, an indication of the relevance of each property, some of the
methods available and references to authoritative texts are provided. In some
cases, where the chemicals or materials may be identified, it is possible to refer
to tabulated data for information. As with any measurement technique, careful
sampling is necessary to ensure that representative waste material is analysed.
Mixed-phase systems are particularly difficult in this respect.

Table 5.1 is based on the characterisation scheme of Chapter 3, and employs the same basic phase classification. This is expanded in the subsequent three

TABLE 5.1 SUMMARY OF PHYSICAL PROPERTIES

Gas (Table 3.11)	Liquid (Table 3.1)	Solid (Table 3.8)
Gas	*Aqueous*	Angle of repose
Calorific value	Ash	Ash
Concentration of pollutant	BOD	Calorific value
Density	COD	Compressibility
Dewpoint	Colour	Density—actual
Explosive limits	Density—bulk	Density—bulk
Flammability	Density—liquid droplet	Elasticity
Ignition temperature	Density—solid particle	Flow rate
Moisture content	Flow rate	Hardness
Odour	Non-aqueous liquid content	Loss on ignition
Pressure	Odour	Mineralogy
Solubility of pollutant	Particle size distribution	Oil content
Temperature	Permanganate value	Particle size distribution
Velocity	pH	pH
Viscosity	Surface tension	Physical composition
	Suspended solids	Porosity
Suspended liquid	Taste	Solubility
Concentration	Temperature	Volatile matter
Density of liquid	Total dissolved solids	Water absorption
Electrical properties	Turbidity	Water content
Flammability and related	Vapour pressure	Wettability
hazards	Viscosity	
Particle size distribution		
pH		
Surface tension	*Non-aqueous*	
Viscosity	Ash	
	BOD	
Suspended solid	Boiling point	
Concentration of pollutant	Calorific value	
Density—bulk (settled)	COD	
Density—particle	Density—bulk	
Electrical properties of	Density—particle	
solid	Distillation range	
Flammability and related	Explosive limits	
hazards	Flammability and related	
Hygroscopicity	hazards	
Particle geometry	Flashpoint	
Particle size distribution	Flow rate	
Solubility	Heat and combustion	
Wettability	Interfacial tension	
	Miscibility with water	
	Odour	
	Suspended solids	
	Temperature	
	Vapour pressure	
	Viscosity	
	Volatility	

tables, which consider gaseous wastes (Table 5.2) subdivided by phase of pollutant, liquid wastes (Table 5.3) subdivided into inorganic and organic liquids, and solid wastes (Table 5.4). These tables should not be regarded as exhaustive or mutually exclusive; they do, however, indicate the extent of information that may be required for treatment, recovery or disposal.

TABLE 5.2 GASEOUS WASTES—MEASUREMENT OF PHYSICAL PROPERTIES

Property	Routine test	Relevance	Methods
A. Gases generally			
Calorific value		Incineration with or without heat recovery	Calculation from published data[18,20,24] Calorimeters[2,24]
Concentration of gaseous pollutant	R	Disposal constraints Design of treatment disposal or recovery plant	Chemical analysis (q.v.) Chromatography[15,19,22]
Density		Dispersion Design of disposal or treatment plant	Chancel flask, or effusiometer—IP S9[18]
Dewpoint		Design of disposal treatment or recovery plant Corrosion Condensation	Tabulated[20] Hygrometer ASTM method[2]
Explosive limits		Fire and explosion hazard Control of combustion	Tabulated[20,24]
Flammability		Fire and explosion hazard Control of combustion	See calorific value and explosive limits ASTM methods[2]
Ignition temperature		Fire and explosion hazard Control of combustion	Adiabatic compression[24] Concentric tube[24] Tabulated[24]
Moisture content Odour		See Dewpoint Potential nuisance Disposal Necessity for treatment	Subjective testing[15,22,23] ASTM methods[2]
Pressure		Design of treatment disposal or recovery plant	Gauges[19,25] Transducer[19,25] Manometer[19,25]

Table 5.2 (*continued*)

Property	Routine test	Relevance	Methods
Solubility of pollutant		Design of separation or treatment plant	Wide range[19] ASTM methods[2] Tabulated[20]
Temperature	R	Corrosion Design of disposal or treatment plant Materials of construction	Thermometer[19,25] Thermocouple[19,25] Resistance treatment[19,25] Pyrometer[19,25] ASTM methods[2]
Velocity		Design of disposal or treatment plant	Pitot tube[21-23] Anemometer[21,22] Orifice, etc.[22,23,25] Rotameters[22] Gas meters[22,25] ASTM method[2]
Viscosity		Design of disposal or treatment plant	Calculated[20] or Tabulated[20]

B. Liquids suspended in gases (see also Table 5.3)

Property	Routine test	Relevance	Methods
Concentration of liquid pollutant	R	Design of treatment or recovery plant Legislation	Sampling and analysis[21]
Density of liquid		Design of treatment or recovery plant	ASTM methods[2] Pyknometer—IP 189, 190[18] Hydrometer—IP 160[18] Relative density balance—IP 59[18]
Electrical properties		Electrostatic precipitation	Tabulated[20] Direct testing[21] Tabulated[20]
Flammability and related properties		Fire, explosion hazard Incineration	See Table 5.3B
Particle size distribution		Design of treatment or recovery plant	Wide range[19,21,23] including: Holography Light scatter ASTM methods[2]
pH		Corrosion	Indicators[19] Test meter[19] pH meter[19]
Surface tension		Coalescence for removal Design of treatment or recovery plant	Tabulated[20] ASTM methods[2]

Table 5.2 (*continued*)

Property	Routine test	Relevance	Methods
Viscosity		Design of treatment plant for removal	ASTM methods[2] Viscometer[24] IP 71[18] Tabulated[20]

C. Solids suspended in gases (see also Table 5.4)

Property	Routine test	Relevance	Methods
Concentration of solid in gas	R	Design of treatment or recovery plant Legislation	Sampling[21,22] Density meter[25]
Density—bulk		Design of treatment or recovery plant and handling equipment	Direct measurement ASTM methods[2]
Density—particle		Design of separation equipment	Displacement—IP 59[18] Pyknometer—IP 190[18] Tabulated[20] ASTM methods[2]
Electrical properties		Electrostatic precipitation	Direct testing[21,22]
Flammability and related properties		Fire and explosion hazard Dust explosion hazard	ASTM methods[2] See Table 5.4
Hygroscopicity		Collection and removal of solid	Direct measurement with exposure ASTM method[2]
Particle geometry		Design of separation equipment Toxic hazard	Observation[22] ASTM method[2]
Particle size distribution	R	Design of separation equipment Toxic hazard	Wide range[2,19,21–23] including Microscopy Holography Light scatter Sieving
Solubility		Suitability for removal by dissolution	Wide range[2,19] Tabulated[20]
Wettability		Suitability for removal by scrubbing	Experimentation ASTM method[2]

TABLE 5.3 LIQUID WASTES—MEASUREMENT OF PHYSICAL PROPERTIES

Property	Routine test	Relevance	Methods
A. Aqueous liquids			
Ash		Incineration	Ignition[2] IP 4, 223[18]
BOD	R	Type of treatment required Legislation and controls	Dilution[15] Manometry[15]
COD		Legislation and controls	Oxidation by acid dichromate[15]
Colour	R	Legislation and controls	Visual comparison[19] IP 17[18] ASTM methods[2]
Density—bulk		Extent of contamination Design of treatment or recovery plant	Hydrometer[2,19] IP 160[18] Pyknometer[2] IP 189, 190[18] Relative density balance—IP 59[18] General[2,19]
Density—liquid droplet		Emulsion breaking Stability Design of treatment or recovery plant	Hydrometer—IP 160[18] Pyknometer—IP 189, 190[18] Relative density balance—IP 59[18] Tabulation[20] ASTM methods[2]
Density—solid particle		Design of treatment or recovery plant	Displacement—IP 59[18] Pyknometer—IP 190[18] Tabulated[20] ASTM methods[2]
Flow rate		Design of treatment or recovery plant	Wide range[25] including: Meters Orifice plates Pitot tubes Venturi meters
Non-aqueous liquid content		Design of treatment or recovery plant	Breaking emulsion—IP 137[18] Solvent extraction[15] ASTM methods[2]
Odour		Legislation and controls	Subjective, empirical[15,22,23]
Particle size distribution		Design of treatment or recovery plant	See Tables 5.2B and 5.2C

Table 5.3 (*continued*)

Property	Routine test	Relevance	Methods
Permanganate value		Legislation and controls	Oxidation with permanganate[15]
pH	R	Corrosion Legislation and controls	Test paper[25] pH meter[19] Titration[19]
Surface tension		Foaming Design of treatment or recovery plant	ASTM methods[2] Tabulated[20] Capillary height[19] Bubble pressure[19] Drop[19]
Suspended solids	R	Design of treatment or recovery plant Legislation and controls	Filtration[10] Centrifuge—IP 316[18] ASTM methods[2] ASTM methods[2]
Taste		Contamination of potable water	Subjective and/or empirical[15] ASTM methods[2]
Temperature	R	Legislation and controls	Thermocouple[19,25] Thermometer[19,25] Resistance thermo-ometers[19,25] ASTM methods[2]
Total dissolved solids	R	Legislation and controls Design or treatment or recovery plant	Evaporation[4,10,15] Electrical conduction[15] ASTM methods[2]
Turbidity		Legislation and controls	ASTM method[2] Turbidity meter[2,4,10,15] See also Suspended solids
Vapour pressure		Fire and explosion hazard	Tabulated[20] See also Table 5.3B
Viscosity		Design of treatment or recovery plant	Viscometer[19] IP 71[18] ASTM methods[2] Tabulated[20]
B. Non-aqueous liquids			
Ash		Incineration with or without heat recovery	Ignition[2] IP 4, 223[18]
Biological oxygen demand		Design of treatment plant Legislation and controls	Dilution[15] Manometry[15] Probe[4]

Table 5.3 (*continued*)

Property	Routine test	Relevance	Methods

Boiling point	R	Design of separation equipment
		Fire and explosion hazard
		Handling and storage
			Wide range[19] including:
			  Conventional boiling point
			  Ebulliometer
			  Ramsay and Young
			  Tabulated[20]
			See also Vapour pressure and distillation range

Calorific value		See Heat of combustion	—
Chemical oxygen demand (COD)		Design of treatment plant Legislation and controls	Oxidation by acid dichromate[2,4,10,15]
Density—bulk		Design of treatment or recovery plant	Hydrometer—IP 160[18] Pyknometer—IP 189, 190[18] Relative density balance—IP 59[18] ASTM methods[2]
Density—particle		Design of treatment or recovery plant	Displacement—IP 59[18] Pyknometer—IP 190[18] Tabulated[20] ASTM methods[2]
Distillation range		Design of recovery plant Incineration	Distillation[25] IP 123, 195, etc.[18] ASTM methods[2]
Explosive limits		Fire and explosion hazard Handling and storage	Tabulated[20]

Flashpoint	R	Fire and explosive hazard
		Handling and storage
			Abel[24,25]
			  IP 33, 170[18]
			Cleveland—IP 36[18]
			Pensky Martin[2,24,25]
			  IP 34, 35[18]
			General[2]
			  IP 303, 304[18]

Flow rate		Design of treatment or recovery plant	See Table 5.3A
Heat of combustion		Incineration with or without heat recovery	Bomb calorimeter[19,24] IP 12[18] Tabulated[20]

Table 5.3 (*continued*)

Property	Routine test	Relevance	Methods
Interfacial tension		Design of treatment or recovery plant	See Surface tension Table 5.3A ASTM methods[2]
Miscibility with water		Design of treatment or recovery plant	Wide range[2,19] including: Hill Hertz Tabulated[20]
Odour		Legislation and controls	Subjective, empirical[15,22,23] ASTM methods[2]
Suspended solids		Design of treatment or recovery plant	Centrifuge—IP 316[18] ASTM methods[2]
Temperature	R	Design of treatment or recovery plant Fire and explosion hazard Handling and storage	Resistance thermometry[19,25] Thermocouple[19,25] Thermometer[19,25] ASTM methods[21]
Vapour pressure	R	Design of treatment or recovery plant Fire and explosion hazards Handling and storage	Isoteriscope[2,19] Micro[2] IP 171[18] Reid[2] IP 69[18] Tabulated[20] See also Boiling point ASTM methods[2]
Viscosity		Design of treatment, disposal or recovery plant	Viscometer[24,25] IP 71, etc.[18] ASTM methods[2] Tabulated[20]
Volatility		Fire and explosion hazard Handling and storage	See Distillation range and Vapour pressure

TABLE 5.4 SOLID WASTES—MEASUREMENT OF PHYSICAL PROPERTIES

Property	Routine test	Relevance	Methods
Angle of repose		Handling and storage Disposal	Direct measurement
Ash		Incineration	ASTM methods[2] Radiation methods[26] See Loss on ignition
Calorific value		Incineration	Bomb calorimeter[24,25] ASTM methods[2]
Compressibility		Disposal	Arbitrary methods relating changes in bulk density ASTM methods[2]
Density—actual		Design of treatment, disposal or recovery plant	Pyknometer—IP 190[18] Displacement—IP 59[18] Tabulated[20] ASTM methods[21]
Density—bulk		Handling and storage Disposal	Direct measurement of weight and volume Bulk density/ash meter[26] ASTM methods[21]
Elasticity		Handling and storage Disposal	Tabulated[20] Experimentation
Flow rate		Design of treatment or recovery plant Handling	Meters[25] Impact flowmeter[26] Radiation[26]
Hardness		Handling Design of treatment or recovery plant	Tabulated[20] ASTM methods[21] Experimentation
Hygroscopicity		Disposal Handling and storage	See Water absorption
Loss on ignition		Incineration	Ignition[25] IP 223[18] ASTM methods[21]
Mineralogy		Disposal Potential reuse	Examination
Oil content		Disposal Incineration Fire and explosion hazard	Extraction with solvent[15]

Table 5.4 (*continued*)

Property	Routine test	Relevance	Methods
Particle size distribution		Handling and storage Disposal Design of treatment or recovery plant	Wide range[21,22] including: Holography Microscopy Sieving ASTM methods[2]
pH		Corrosion Design of treatment or recovery plant	Test paper[19] pH meter[19] Titration[19]
Physical composition		Design of treatment or recovery plant Handling Disposal	Examination and observation
Porosity		Disposal	Calculated from bulk density (q.v.)
Solubility		Design of treatment or recovery plant	Wide range[2,19] including: Campbell Weyl Tabulated[20]
Volatile matter		Fire and explosion hazard Incineration	Heating[4,10,24] ASTM methods[2] See also Distillation range
Water content		Handling and storage Disposal	Drying to constant weight[24,25] BS 1016[27] ASTM methods[2] Range of methods[26] including: Microwave attenuation Capacitance Resistivity Infra-red absorption Neutron moderation
Water absorption		Disposal Handling and storage	Experimentation ASTM methods[2]
Wettability		Design of treatment or recovery plant	Angle of contact related to surface tension[2] (q.v.)

Chemical Analysis

Complete chemical analysis is a highly complex process even with sophisticated modern analytical equipment, and is therefore outside the scope of this book. A list of the techniques available, their application and phase state is given in Table 5.5, and the more common chemicals that may be encountered in waste are listed in Table 5.6, classified by phase and organic

TABLE 5.5 METHODS OF CHEMICAL ANALYSIS

| Method | Application | | | | | | |
| | Metals | Other elements | Inorganic chemicals | Organic chemicals | Phase | | |
					Gas	Liquid	Solid
Amperometry	+	+	(+)	+		+	
Atomic absorption spectrometry	+					+	+
Atomic emission spectrometry	+	(+)	(+)			+	
Atomic fluorescence spectrometry	+	(+)	(+)			+	
Conductometry	+	(+)	+			+	
Coulometry	+	(+)	(+)			+	
Electrogravimetry	(+)					+	
Electrophoresis				+		+	+
Flame photometry	+					+	(+)
Gas chromatography	(+)			+	+	+	(+)
Fluorimetry	(+)			+		+	+
Helium plasma	+	+			+	+	+
Infrared spectrometry			(+)	+	+	+	+
Isotope dilution	+	+			+	+	+
Mass spectrometry				+	+	+	
Nuclear magnetic resonance spectrometry	(+)	+	(+)	+		+	
Polarimetry				+			+
Polarography	+		+	+		+	
Potentiometry	+		+			+	
Radioactivity	+	+			+	+	+
Raman spectroscopy			+	+	+	+	+
Spark (emission) spectrograph		+					+
Specific ion electrode	+	+	+		+	+	+
Thin layer chromatography				+		+	+
Ultra violet spectrometry			(+)	+	+	+	
Visible light spectrometry			+		+	+	
X-ray diffraction spectrometry			+	+			+
X-ray fluorescence spectrometry	+	+					+

nature. Qualitative procedures for identification of chemicals and quantitative analytical methods may be found in the literature.

The origin of the waste often provides a useful indication of what it may contain. The extent and type of analysis is governed by the destination—minimal

TABLE 5.6 MORE COMMON CHEMICALS ARISING IN WASTE AND REQUIRING ANALYSIS

Gas	Liquid	Solid
INORGANIC		
Ammonia	Acids: hydrochloric	Asbestos
Arsine	hydrofluoric	Biocides
Carbon dioxide	nitric	Carbon
Carbon monoxide	phosphoric	Metals, their insoluble
Chlorine	sulphuric	compounds and ores
Hydrogen chloride	Alkalis: ammonia	of:
Hydrogen cyanide	lime	aluminium
Hydrogen sulphide	potassium	arsenic
Nitrogen oxides	hydroxide	cadmium
Phosphine	sodium	calcium
Sulphur dioxide	hydroxide	chromium
Sulphur trioxide	Biocides	cobalt
Volatile metal	Salts: chloride	copper
compounds	cyanide	iron
	fluoride	lead
	nitrate	mercury
	phosphate	nickel
	sulphate	phosphorus
	sulphide	silicon
	Soluble metal	silver
	compounds of:	sulphur
	aluminium	zinc
	arsenic	
	cadmium	
	chromium	
	cobalt	
	copper	
	iron	
	lead	
	mercury	
	nickel	
	silver	
	zinc	
ORGANIC		
Hydrocarbon gases:	Acids	Animal wastes
methane	Alcohols	Biocides
ethane	Aldehydes	Greases
ethylene	Alkanes	Pharmaceuticals
propane	Amines	Plastics
propylene	Animal wastes	Rubbers
butane	Aromatics	Vegetable wastes
etc.	Biocides	Waxes
Mercaptans	Detergents	
Organic liquid vapours,	Ethers	
e.g.:	Paints	
acetone	Pharmaceuticals	
amyl acetate	Solvents	
trichlorethylene	Vegetable wastes	

information is legally required for disposal, but a more complete analysis, including concentrations, is necessary for assessment of potential recovery schemes. Sampling is an important factor, particularly in mixed-phase systems such as slurries and aerosols, and when handling volatile liquids.

Finally, analysis should be confined to what is pertinent: a full analysis should not be demanded if, for example, only the acid concentration is required.

Noise Measurement

An explanation of the nature of noise nuisance and the units of measurement has been given in Chapter 3. Simply, the level of noise may be measured in dB(A) which provides a close approximation to the perceived nuisance level by weighting different frequencies to correspond to the response of the human ear. This is adequate for establishing general levels, monitoring changes and pinpointing hazardous areas. However, to investigate sources of noise and for design of suitable enclosures for noise reduction, analysis of noise into different frequency bands is necessary because of variations in transmission and damping characteristics at different frequencies. For assessment of noise nuisance, for example traffic noise, a noise profile may be measured as dB(A) at L_{90}, L_{50}, and L_{10} or L_1. This provides an indication of maximum or peak noise levels (L_{10} or L_1) against a minimum or background level (L_{90}). To assess nuisance in working environments where noise levels vary, the equivalent continuous noise level (L_{eq}) may be found. Very low frequency noise may be perceived as 'booming' and be felt rather than heard; this can cause extensive structural damage, and is more difficult to identify and measure.

Equipment

A range of equipment is required for noise measurement.[28-30]

(a) *Sound level meter*. The range is from light, portable instruments costing from about £50 upwards to precision sound level meters with inbuilt frequency filters which can cost over £1000. The former are useful for preliminary investigations and the latter more expensive and sophisticated instruments are needed for more accurate assessment including noise profile measurement and frequency spectrum analysis.

The following British Standards specify the characteristics of sound level meters: BS 3489[31] for industrial grade meters having an accuracy of ± 2 dB at 1 kHz in the 'A' filter, decreasing to ± 6 dB at 8 kHz; BS 4197[32] for precision meters having a minimum accuracy of ± 1 dB from 100 to 4 kHz. The taking and interpretation of noise level measurements is covered in BS 4196.[33]

(b) *Microphone*. This is the basic unit common to all sound measurement. Three types are commonly available—capacitor or condenser, moving coil and piezoelectric—all of which are very sensitive and must be protected against humidity, vibration, extremes of temperature, dust, magnetic fields, wind and rain. The microphone used must be compatible with the rest of the equipment.

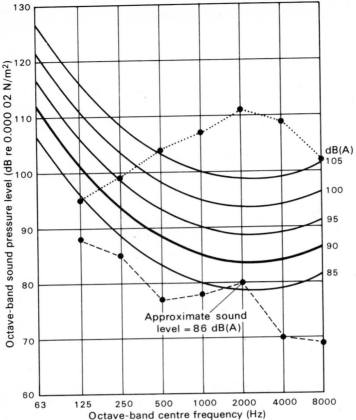

Fig. 5.1 Frequency spectrum of riveting machine
..... measured octave-band levels of machine (measured sound level = 115 dB(A)
− − − assumed octave-band octave-band levels after subtracting the protection of the ear-muffs
Contours indicate approximate sound level (dB(A))

(c) *Calibration equipment.* Calibration of the microphone and sound level meter is essential before and after measurement. This may be carried out with a pistonphone which produces a constant sound-pressure variation at a fixed frequency. Other methods, such as the falling ball, are available.

(d) *Frequency analyser.* Narrow band (octave or ⅓-octave range) analysers are used for frequency spectrum analysis and may be employed with an oscilloscope or recording equipment.

(e) *Noise dose meter.* This simplifies the assessment of fluctuating noise by integrating the sound energy received to give an equivalent continuous noise level, L_{eq}. This is an alternative to (a) and (d).

(f) *Supplementary equipment* for specialist purposes. This includes magnetic tape recorder, level recorder, oscilloscope, random noise generator, impact noise analyser, noise exposure meter and statistical processor.[29,30]

Results

The results of the noise measurement may take several forms.

1. *Simple background and peak noise levels in dB(A).* For example, for lorries travelling along a residential road, say:

background noise level	32–39 dB(A)
lorry noise level	66–85 dB(A)
arithmetical average	78 dB(A)

This method is particularly useful either for preliminary assessment or where noise is continuous and dB(A) levels constant.

2. *Noise profile in dB(A) at L_{90}, L_{50}, L_{10}.* Using the same example:

L_{90}	35 dB(A)
L_{50}	43 dB(A)
L_{10}	77 dB(A)
or L_1	81 dB(A)

The value L_{10} or L_1 gives an indication of the extent of the lorry noise nuisance and will bear a close relationship to the number of vehicles over a given time period (usually taken as 18 hours). This can usefully be broken down into smaller time units to obtain a two-dimensional profile.

Alternatively, these figures may be incorporated into correlations to characterise and quantify the time relationships and variations: two examples are the traffic noise index (TNI) and the level of noise pollution (LNP). For the above example, TNI = 173 and LNP = 33 (see Table 3.15, page 52, for formulae). Both of these indices are difficult to predict and impossible to measure directly, although there are several methods available for measuring L_{10}, L_{50} and/or L_{90}.

Modern computerised equipment can readily derive an index from the above information.

3. *Frequency spectrum.* This is usually applied to continuous and constant noise levels. Intensity is related to frequency, and the result is then compared with the response of the human ear. This is particularly useful in analysing noise from machinery or plant by identifying particular frequencies which are noisy, and this helps in designing the right equipment for attenuation of the noise to an acceptable level. Figure 5.1, the frequency spectrum of a riveting machine, shows the assumed sound level after subtraction of the attenuation provided by ear-muffs. The maximum contour line reached by the attenuated plot is then compared with recommended exposure levels.[28–30,34]

4. *Equivalent continuous noise level (L_{eq}).* This is used in situations where the noise level changes during exposure. Periods of exposure at less than 80 dB(A) may be ignored. Measurement of noise levels and time periods exposed permits calculation of L_{eq}, using either the formula given in Table 3.15 or a nomogram.[30] For example, at levels of 114 dB(A) for 10 minutes, 105 dB(A) for 45 minutes and 92 dB(A) for 5 hours, L_{eq} is calculated as 100 dB(A).[30]

References

1. *Manual of Analytical Methods*, American Conference of Governmental Industrial Hygienists, 1958.
2. *Annual Book of ASTM Methods*, American Society for Testing and Materials, 1975.
3. *Standard Methods for the Examination of Water and Sewage*, Association of Public Health Analysts.
4. *Standard Methods for the Examination of Water and Waste Water*. Association of Public Health Analysts, Federal Water Pollution Control Association, American Water Works Association, 1971.
5. *Official Methods*, Association of Official Analytical Chemists (USA), 1975.
6. *The BDH Spot Outfit Handbook*, British Drug Houses, 1970.
7. CIACCIO, L. L. (Ed.), *Water and Water Pollution Handbook*, Vols I, II, III, IV, Dekker, 1972.
8. COX, G. V., *Industrial Waste Effluent Monitoring*, 54, September/October 1974.
9. Department of the Environment, *Analysis of Raw Potable and Waste Waters*, HMSO, 1972.
10. *Methods for Chemical Analysis of Water and Waste*. Environmental Protection Agency (USA), 1971.
11. HM Factory Inspectorate. *Methods for the Detection of Toxic Substance in Air*, HMSO, 1971 et seq.
12. FEIGL, F., *Spot Tests in Inorganic Analysis*, Elsevier, 1958.
13. HANSON, N. W., *Official Standardised and Recommended Methods of Analysis*, Society for Analytical Chemistry, 1973.
14. *Recommended Analytical Methods for Gas Works and Coke Oven Effluents*, Institution of Gas Engineering, 1971.
15. KOLTHOFF, I. M., ELVING, P. J. and STROSS, F. H., *Treatise on Analytical Chemistry* Part III, Vol. 2, *Analytical Chemistry in Industry*, Wiley, 1971.
16. MCCOY, J. W., *Chemical Analysis of Industrial Water*, Chemical Publishing/Macdonald, 1969.
17. WEISS, F. T., *Determination of Organic Compounds: Methods and Procedures*, Interscience, 1970.
18. *IP Standards for Petroleum and its Products*, Institute of Petroleum, 1975.
19. WEISSBERGER, A. and ROSSITER, B. W., Techniques of Chemistry Series, Vol. I, *Physical Methods of Chemistry*, Wiley, 1971.
20. WEAST, R. C., *Handbook of Chemistry and Physics*, Chemical Rubber Co., 1974.
21. DORMAN, R. G., *Dust Control and Air Cleaning*, Pergamon, 1974.
22. STERN, A. C., *Air Pollution*, Vol. II, *Analysis, Monitoring and Surveying*, Academic Press, 1968.
23. JACOBS, M. B., *The Chemical Analysis of Air Pollutants*, Interscience, 1960.
24. BRAME, J. S. S. and KING, J. G., *Fuel: Solid, Liquid and Gaseous*, E. Arnold, 1967.
25. *The Efficient Use of Fuel*, HMSO, 1958: also *The Efficient Use of Energy*, HMSO, 1974.
26. *Bulk Solids in Transit*, Institution of Mechanical Engineers, 1974.
27. BS 1016: Parts 1–12 (various dates), *Methods for the Analysis and Testing of Coal and Coke*, British Standards Institution.
28. Engineering Equipment Users' Association, *Measurement and Control of Noise*, Constable, 1968.
29. *Noise Control*, Process Plant Association, 1973.
30. Department of Employment, *Code of Practice for Reducing the Exposure of Employed Persons to Noise*, HMSO, 1972.
31. BS 3489: 1962, *Sound Level Meters (Industrial Grade)*, British Standards Institution.
32. BS 4197: 1967, *A Precision Sound Level Meter*, British Standards Institution.
33. BS 4196: 1967, *Guide to the Selection of Methods of Measuring Noise Emitted by Machinery*, British Standards Institution.
34. ANTHROP, D. F., *Noise Pollution*, Lexington, 1973.

CHAPTER 6

Sources of Waste

There are two ways of relating industries and their wastes: Table 6.1 lists industries with the pollutants they produce. Families of compounds are frequently used, particularly for metals, to avoid repetition. Table 6.2 lists pollutants and where they can originate. The lists are not exhaustive but they include most major pollution sources and topical and recent problem areas.

It should be noted that for every chemical, its manufacture and processing are potential sources of pollution. This may arise through entrainment in gas or liquid effluents, spillage, vaporisation, poor housekeeping generally or simply the need to dispose of excess off-specification materials.

In addition to waste, attention must be paid to contaminated receptacles, for example boxes, drums, sacks and bags which may need to be reused or require disposal.

Different wastes may arise from occasional maintenance modifications or rebuilding work, for example asbestos waste from delagging, or cleaning operations, sludges and cleaning solutions, oils and solvents. Non-toxic waste and general factory refuse generation also increases during maintenance or rebuilding. Occasionally liquid or solid wastes are allowed to accumulate or are inherited and special treatment or disposal operations may be required.

TABLE 6.1 INDUSTRIES: TYPE OF WASTE AND ITS PHYSICAL FORM

Key:	G	Pollutant occurs as a gas
	L	Pollutant occurs as a liquid
	S	Pollutant occurs as a solid
	P	Pollutant occurs in particulate form
	A	Pollutant occurs in aqueous solution or suspension

Table 6.1 (*continued*)

Agriculture, Horticulture		
	BOD waste (high and low)	L S A
	Disinfectant	A
	Pesticides, herbicides (see below)	P A
	Fertilisers (see Inorganic chemicals)	A
Cement, Bricks, Lime		
	Chromium	L
	Dust	S
	Fluoride	G
	Sulphur dioxide	G
Coal Distillation, Coal Tar, Coke Ovens		
	Ammonia	G A
	Aromatic hydrocarbons	G L
	Combustion products	G
	Cyanate	A
	Cyanide	G A
	Dust	S P
	Fluoride	G A
	Hydrocarbons (general)	G L A
	Hydrogen sulphide	G
	Phenols	L A
	Polycyclic hydrocarbons	G
	Sulphur dioxide	G
	Tar	G L S
	Thiocyanate	A
Construction, Building, Demolition		
	Combustion products	G P
	Dust	S P
	Metals	S
	Rubble	S
	Timber	S
Electricity Generation		
	Clinker	S
	Combustion products	G
	Cooling water	L
	Pulverised fuel ash	S P
	Sulphur dioxide	G
Fibres, Textiles		
	Bleach	A
	Cyanide	A
	Detergent	A
	Dyestuffs	A
	Grease	L S
	Oil	L A
	Resins	L A
	Silicones	A
	Speciality chemicals for fire-, rot- and waterproofing	LA
	Wax	P A

Table 6.1 (*continued*)

Food Processing		
Animal	Abattoir waste	L S P A
	BOD waste (high and low)	A
	Disinfectants	A
	Grease	S A
	Oil	L A
Beverage	Alkali	A
	BOD waste (low)	A
	Carbon dioxide	G
	Cullet	S
	Detergent	A
Vegetable and fruit	Alkali	A
	Bleach	A
	BOD waste (high and low)	P A
	Oil	L
	Solvent	L A
	Wax	S P A
Inorganic Chemicals		
Chloralkali	Brine	A
	Calcium chloride	A
	Mercury	L
Desalination	Brines	A
Fertiliser	Ammonia	G A
	Nitrates	S
	Oxides of nitrogen	A
	Phosphates	S
Glass and ceramic	Arsenic	A
	Barium	S
	Manganese	S
	Selenium	S
Hydrofluoric acid	Calcium sulphate	P A
Nitric acid	Ammonia	G A
	Oxides of nitrogen	A
Phosphoric acid	Calcium sulphate	P A
	Hydrofluoric acid	A
Pigments	Arsenic	S P
	Barium	S P
	Cadmium	S P
	Cobalt	S P
	Iron	S P A
	Lead	S P
	Manganese	S P
	Selenium	S P
	Titanium	S P
	Zinc	S P
Sulphuric acid	Sulphur dioxide	G P

Table 6.1 (*continued*)

Laundry		
Drycleaning	Chlorinated hydro-carbons	G L
	Hydrocarbon solvents	G L
General	Bleach	A
	Detergent	A
	Phosphate	A
	Sulphate	A
Metals		
Extraction and refining	Acid mine waters	A
	Combustion products	G P
	Carbon monoxide	G
	Chloride	G S P
	Drosses	S
	Dust	S
	Fluoride	G S P
	Glass	S
	Spoil	S
	Sulphides	S P A
	Sulphur dioxide	G
Finishing/surface treatments		
Anodising	Chromium	A
Degreasing	Chlorinated hydro-carbons	G L
	Detergents	A
	Grease	L S
	Solvents	G L
Electroplating	Alkali	A
	Boron	A
	Cadmium	A
	Chromium	P A
	Copper	A
	Cyanide	A
	Detergent	A
	Fluoride	A
	Iron	A
	Nickel	A P
	Organic complexing agents	A
	Phosphate	A
	Precious metals	A
	Silver	A
	Sulphate	A
	Tin	A
	Zinc	A
Foundries	Dust	S P
	Sands	S
Machine shops	Oils	L A
	Oil absorbents	S
	Solvents	L G
	Swarf	S
	Synthetic coolants	L S A

Table 6.1 (*continued*)

Pickling	Acid	A
	Ferrous chloride	A
	Ferrous sulphate	A
	Hydrochloric acid	A
	Hydrofluoric acid	A
	Nitric acid	A
	Phosphoric acid	A
	Sulphuric acid	A
Pigments	See Inorganic chemicals	
Processing/Engineering	Ammonia	G A
	Arsenic	G S A
	Cyanide	S A
	Emulsions	A
	Lubricating oils	L
	Phenols	L S A
	Soluble oils	A
	Thiocyanates	A
Products		
Batteries	Cadmium	S P
	Lead	S P
	Manganese	S
	Mercury	S
	Nickel	S
	Zinc	S
Catalysts	Cobalt	S
	Iron	S
	Manganese	S
	Mercury	S
	Nickel	S
	Organometallics	L S
	Platinum	S
	Silver	S
	Vanadium	S
Mining (excluding metals)	Spoil	S
	Dust	S P
Paint		
	Barium	S
	Cadmium	S
	Chromium	S
	Copper	S
	Lead	S
	Manganese	S
	Mercury	L S
	Selenium	S
	Solvents	G L
	Titanium	S
	Zinc	S

Table 6.1 (*continued*)

Paper, Pulp		
	Bleach	A
	Chlorine	G A
	Copper	A
	Fibres	S P A
	Lignin	A
	Mercury	A
	Methanol	A
	Sulphides	A
	Sulphite liquor	A
	Titanium	S P A
	Wax	S P A
	Zinc	P A
Pesticides, Herbicides		
	Arsenic	S P A
	Carbamates	S P A
	Chlorinated hydrocarbons	L S P A
	Copper	A
	Fluoride	G S A
	Lead	A
	Mercury	L A
	Organophosphorus compounds	P A
	Phenol	S A
	Polychlorinated biphenyls (PCB)	A
	Selenium	S
Petrochemicals		
Detergents	Boric acid	S A
	Phosphates	S A
	Sulphates	S A
Dyestuffs	Aniline	L A
	Chromium	L S P A
	Phenol	A
	Selenium	L S P A
General	Benzene	L
	Boric acid	A
	Chlorocarbons	G L A
	Fluorine	A
	Fluorocarbons	G L A
	Hydrocarbons	G L S P A
	Hydrochloric acid	A
	Hydrofluoric acid	A
	Phenol	L A
	Solvents	L
	Sulphuric acid	A
Miscellaneous	Polychlorinated biphenyls (PCB)	L
	Tetraethyl lead	G L P

Table 6.1 (*continued*)

Polymers, plastics, resins, rubber and fibres	Acid	A
	Alkali	A
	Asbestos	P S
	Cadmium	L S P A
	Cuprammonium compounds	A
	Detergent	A
	Dyestuffs	A
	Fibres	S P
	Formaldehyde	A
	Hydrocarbons	G L A
	Methanol	L A
	Phenols	L S A
	Phthalates	L A
	Polychlorinated byphenyls (PCB)	L A
	Solvents	L A
	Sulphide	A
	Urea	S A
	Wood flour	S P
	Zinc	A
Pharmaceuticals	Drug intermediates and residues	L S A
	Solvents	L A
Refineries	Alkali	A
	BOD waste	L P A
	Combustion products	G
	Emulsions	A
	Hydrocarbons	L A
	Mercaptans	G
	Mineral acids	A
	Phenol	L S P A
	Sulphides	G S P
	Sulphur	S P
	Tar	S P
Sewage Treatment	Purified effluent	L
	Sewage sludge	S A
Tanneries	Arsenic	A
	Chromium	A
	Fibres	S P
	Hair	S P
	Lime	P A
Textiles—See fibres	Sulphides	A
Miscellaneous Electrical, electronics	Copper	S
	Mercury	L
	Precious metals	S
	Selenium	S

Table 6.1 (*continued*)

Explosives, pyrotechnics	Barium	S
	Hydrocarbons	G L A
	Lead	S
	Manganese	S P
	Mercury	L S P
	Nitric acid	A
	Nitroglycerin	L A
	Phenol	S P
	Phosphorus	S
	Solvents	G L
	Strontium	S
	TNT	L A
Motor industry	Chromates	A
	Grease	L S
	Oil	L
	Paint	L S P
	Phosphates	S P A
	Solvents	L
Nuclear fuel and power	Radioactive substances	
	Radioisotopes	
Photography	Alkali	A
	Cyanide	A
	Mercury	A
	Phenols	A
	Silver	P A
	Thiosulphate	A
Vehicle exhaust	Aromatic hydrocarbons	G
	Lead	S P
	Nitrogen oxides	G
Water treatment	Calcium salts	A P
	Filtered solids	L P A

TABLE 6.2 POLLUTANTS AND THEIR SOURCES

Key: G Pollutant occurs as a gas
L Pollutant occurs as a liquid
S Pollutant occurs as a solid
P Pollutant occurs in particulate form
A Pollutant occurs in aqueous solution or suspension

Chemical			Examples	Industrial source
Acid	Mineral	A	Hydrochloric acid	Pickling
			Nitric acid	Chemical reagent
			Sulphuric acid	Byproducts, petrochemicals
	Organic	A	Acetic acid	Petrochemicals
Aldehydes		A	Acetaldyhyde	Photochemical reaction in smog
				Petrochemicals

Table 6.2 (*continued*)

Chemical		Examples	Industrial source
Alkali	P A	Sodium hydroxide Lime	Electroplating Beverage Photography Vegetable and fruit processing
Ammonia	G A	—	Coal distillation Nitric acid Urea and ammonium nitrate works
Aniline and related compounds	L A	—	Dyestuffs
Aromatic hydrocarbons	G L	Benzene Toluene	Coal tar Vehicle exhausts Petrochemicals Pesticides Herbicides

Arsenic	G S P A	Arsine
		Arsenous acid and
		  salts
			Pigment and dye
			Pesticide and herbicide
			Metallurgical processing
			  of other metals
			Glass and ceramic
			Tanneries

Asbestos	S P	Chrysolite Amosite Crocidolite	Equipment and building Insulation Fillers in various industries Motor vehicle assembly Fabric manufacture Polymers, plastics
Carbon dioxide	G A		Combustion Fermentation
Carbon monoxide	G		Coke ovens Incomplete combustion Smelting Vehicle exhausts Metal extraction and refining

Chlorinated
  hydrocarbons
  Chemical
	G L	Trichlorethylene
		1, 1, 1-trichloroethane
			Degreasing (engineering)
			Drycleaning
			Solvents

Pesticidal	L S	D D T BHC Aldrin Dieldrin	Pesticides Wood treatment
Chlorine and chlorides	G S P A		Chlorinated hydrocarbons Chloralkali Paper and pulp Petrochemicals Metal extraction and refining

Table 6.2 (*continued*)

Chemical		Examples	Industrial Source
Chromium and compounds	S P A	Chromic acid Sodium dichromate	Anodising Cement Dyes Electroplating Paint Tanneries
Cobalt and compounds	S P A	Cobalt oxide	Catalysts Fibres Paint Paper and pulp Pickling
Copper and compounds	S P A	Copper sulphate Copper pyrophosphate Cuprammonium compounds	Electroplating Electrical and electronics Etching Pesticides
Cyanate	A		Coal distillation Oxidation of cyanide
Cyanide	S P A	Sodium cyanide Copper cyanide	Heat treatment of metal Photographic Coal distillation Electroplating Synthetic fibre
Disinfectants			Agriculture and horti- culture Food processing
Fluorides	G S P A	Hydrogen fluoride Calcium fluoride	Cement Aluminium
Hydrocarbons, general			Coal distillation Petrochemicals Refineries
Iron and compounds	S P A	Iron oxide Ferrous chloride	Aluminium Electroplating Pickling Pigments Electronics Titanium dioxide

Lead and compounds	S P A	Lead oxide
		Tetraethyl lead
		    (TEL)
			Batteries
			Printing
			Vehicle exhausts
			Explosives and pyro-
			    technics
			Pesticides
			Paint
			Refineries
			Petrochemicals

Manganese and compounds			Catalyst Batteries Glass Paint Pyrotechnics

Table 6.2 (*continued*)

Chemical	Examples		Industrial source
Meat wastes	S A		Meat processing and preparation
			Abattoirs
			Dairies
			Tanneries
Mercaptans	G		Refineries
			Coke ovens
Mercury			Herbicides
Organic	S A	Methyl mercury	Bacterial activity on inorganic mercury
			Pesticides
Inorganic L S A	L S A	Mercurous chloride	Electrical and electronic
			Pesticides
			Explosives
			Batteries
			Photographic
			Scientific instruments
			Chloralkali
			Paints
			Pharmaceuticals
			Paper and pulp
			Catalysts
			Cement
			Combustion of coal and oil
Methanol	L A		Resins
			Paper
Nitrates	S P	Potassium nitrate	Metals heat treatment
			Water treatment
Nitrogen oxides	G	Nitrogen dioxide	Combustion processes
			Electricity generation
Oil and soluble oil	L		Engineering
			Refineries
			Petrochemicals
Paraquat	L S		Herbicide
Pesticides (includes acaricides, avicides, bactericides, insecticides, molluskicides, nematocides, piscicides, rodenticides)		Chlorinated hydrocarbons (q.v.) Carbamates (q.v.) Organophosphorus compounds (q.v.)	
Pharmaceuticals	L S P A	Aspirin Penicillin	Pharmaceutical industry
Phenol and related compounds	S P A	Phenol Cresol	Photographic
			Coal distillation
			Dyestuffs
			Petrochemicals
			Pesticides
			Refineries
			Explosives
			Plastics

Table 6.2 (*continued*)

Chemical		Examples	Industrial source
Phosphorus and compounds	S P A	Phosphoric acid	Detergents Fertilisers Corrosion protection Matches Boiler blowdown Metal finishing
Phthalates	L S P A	Dibutyl phthalate	Plasticiser (polymers)
Platinum and compounds	S P		Catalysts
Polychlorinated biphenyls (PCB)	L S A		Pesticides Plasticiser in paint and polymers Adhesives Lubricants and hydraulic fluids
Silicates	P		Cement Metal extraction and refining
Sulphur oxides	G	Sulphur dioxide Sulphur trioxide	Coal distillation Combustion of coal and heavy fuel oil Electricity generation
Tar	L		Refineries Coal distillation
Thiocyanate	A		Coal distillation
Tin and compounds	G S P A		Tinplating
Titanium and compounds	S P A	Titanium dioxide	Paper Paint Astronautics
Vanadium and compounds	S P		Catalysts
Vegetable waste	L S P A		Natural rubber Starch Breweries Sugar refineries Vegetable and fruit processing and preparation Cattle feed
Wax	S		Paper Refineries Fruit preserving Textiles
Zinc and compounds	G S P A		Synthetic fibres Galvanising Electroplating Paper and pulp

PART TWO

Liquid Waste Treatment

CHAPTER 7

Principles and Design of Aqueous Effluent Treatment Plant

Introduction

The function of effluent treatment is to remove and/or destroy the pollutants present in any liquid stream. Chapters 7 and 8 describe the underlying principles that may be applied and the range of techniques available for the removal or destruction of most common pollutants (see also Further Reading at the end of this chapter). The design and specification of equipment is considered in sufficient detail to assist in a preliminary assessment of treatment requirements, specification of requirements to a contractor, and the checking and evaluation of tenders for equipment or complete installations. The information will also assist in plant operation, maintenance and troubleshooting, but does not form a design manual or replace detailed design procedures: each contractor will have his own expertise in a range of treatment processes.

There are two main types of aqueous waste requiring fundamentally different treatment methods, conveniently referred to as (i) biological and (ii) non-biological or chemical treatment. Biological effluent treatment employs micro-organisms to destroy or convert the pollutants; biodegradeable wastes are therefore almost invariably organic in nature. They may be either naturally derived, such as food industry wastes, or artificially derived, such as petro-chemical wastes. Chemical effluent treatment relies on chemical reactions and physical methods to remove, reduce or destroy the pollutants. A small number of materials, such as cyanide, may be treated by either method. These two basic types of treatment are not completely different, in that many operations, such as filtration, settlement, and pH adjustment, are common to both.

Most biological treatment processes are similar to sewage treatment in process design and identical in principle. Water Authority sewage works have considerable flexibility in operation but cannot always cope with substantial localised industrial loads. The Water Authority may then require the industry to carry out a certain level of treatment before discharge to the sewer. For discharge to a watercourse the conditions are much more stringent, as discussed in Chapter 4, and the degree of processing and purity levels expected are usually at least equal to, or may exceed, those of the Authority's own sewage works discharging into the same water.

Chemical or non-biological treatment, on the other hand, can cover a wide range of different processes; each effluent treatment plant needs individual specification for the best conversion or removal system for its particular pollutants.

Characterisation of the effluent (Chapter 3) is necessary before specification and design of any treatment plant. The basic and essential data are flow rate and composition. Flow rate is represented as the quantity of effluent requiring treatment in a specified time period. For small and/or sporadic quantities of perhaps less than 5 m³ (1000 gal) in a 24 hour period, batch treatment on an occasional basis may be justified. More usually, however, flow rate is expressed as an average hourly or daily flow rate for treatment on a continuous basis. It is also important to have information concerning peak flow rates and their duration, and the plant availability, for example number of hours of operation per day. Similar information is necessary regarding average and peak concentration of each pollutant.

Characterisation of composition is more involved than flow rate and depends on particular circumstances such as type and complexity of effluent and conditions of discharge to sewers or watercourses. The composition will suggest what treatment is necessary. While there are established and popular methods for many common pollutants, a wide choice is sometimes available, dependent on local conditions.

Design Principles

In selecting a waste treatment or recovery method it is as important to consider the overall economics as it is to consider the technology. Other factors also need consideration such as reliability in operation, possible later expansion, flexibility of operation, degree of automation, labour requirements and safety.

In many cases where alternatives are available, the most common or usual method is the cheapest and most effective. In general, 'novel' processes, particularly those only developed to laboratory or pilot plant operation, should be carefully scrutinised as many problems can arise in scale-up. These may be caused by differences in geometry, hydro-dynamics and effluent quality, and deterioration in service. The past performance of a process or item of equipment may therefore assume considerable significance in the choice of a suitable alternative.

In the immediate future energy costs will continue to rise at a greater rate than most other costs, therefore operations which are energy-intensive, such as evaporation, centrifugation or drying, will become increasingly relatively expensive. Processes which produce some return, in the form of recyclable materials or water, will tend to become more attractive. Furthermore, conditions imposed upon effluent discharge will become more strict. All these factors must be balanced, possibly in consultation with a contractor, or local authority, when determining treatment strategy.

It is common experience that effluent treatment plants tend to receive inadequate supervision and scheduled maintenance during routine operation. This should be taken into consideration at the design stage, and subsequently detailed operating instructions and inspection/maintenance schedules should be issued (see Chapter 19).

An overall treatment scheme for handling any effluent is given in Figure 7.1. This includes provision for primary, secondary and tertiary treatment of most constituents of biological and non-biological effluents. When a pollutant is not present, or a treatment is not required, the appropriate stage may be omitted.

Equipment Specification

The sizing of equipment is generally based upon steady-state operation to serve an existing or predicted volumetric throughput of effluent. Consideration must be given to start-up and shutdown of the plant, however; this may require additional surge capacities or recycling provisions. In addition, to benefit from economy of scale (Chapter 20) it is usual to provide over-capacity to cope with any anticipated increase in factory size or variation in flow rate. Alternatively, provision for effluent plant expansion should be allowed in the layout.

Equipment design should be as simple and thus as cheap as is compatible with producing an acceptable effluent or quality of water for recycling. As far as possible, standard equipment should be used; open tanks are often quite adequate. As throughputs increase, greater sophistication is necessary to ensure complete reaction and good flow patterns. Special designs and specifications are often needed for large plant and orthodox chemical engineering practice is invariably followed, taking account of any peculiarities of the system.

It is often cheaper, for small treatment plants of up to 4·5 or even 6·7 m³/h (1000 or 1500 gal/h), to provide an oversize facility employing standard-sized tanks and pumps than to design and construct a 'one-off' plant. Small tanks of up to 2·3 m³ (500 gal) are often of plastic; above this size mild steel or lined steel is more usual. For very large installations, reinforced concrete may be cheaper. Agitators are usually stainless steel; if suitable, low-speed mixing is preferred to reduce maintenance. Piping may often be plastic for low cost and ease of construction. Pumps must be suitable for the conditions and materials being handled but otherwise are largely a matter of personal choice. It is usual to include standby pumps.

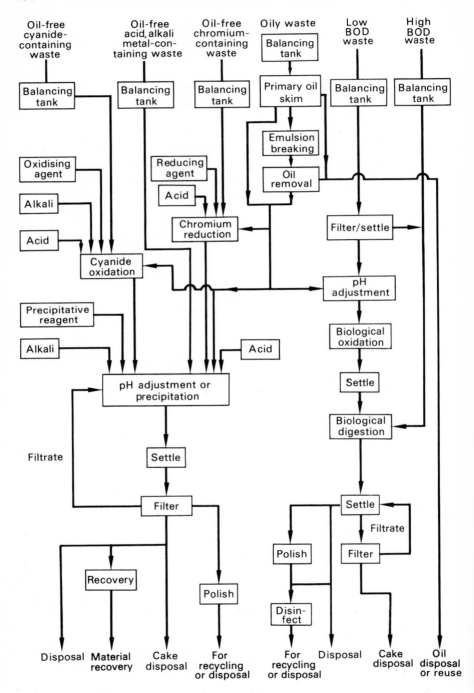

Fig. 7.1. Overall effluent treatment system

When an effluent treatment plant is built to service an existing works, consideration should be given to other related equipment for ease of maintenance and to reduce costs. In particular agitators, pumps and instrumentation should, if possible, be compatible with similar equipment installed by the firm unless there are overriding considerations. A number of special problems can arise: for instance, if aqueous caustic soda is employed, a heated storage vessel and traced heated pipe lines are needed to prevent freezing in cold weather, as concentrated caustic soda solutions can freeze at 15°C.

Materials of Construction

Effluents frequently contain corrosive chemicals and special materials of construction are required. Figure 7.2 provides simple guidelines for most situations. Generally mild steel is adequate for alkaline effluents and rubber/plastic-lined mild steel for acid and chloride effluents, but care is needed to ensure that the construction materials will stand up to all the constituents of the effluent; for instance, for mixed effluents containing corrosive chemicals with solvents (for example hydrofluoric acid and chlorinated hydrocarbons), special metals or alloys or one of the polymer composites might be used. The complete resistance and low risk associated with the use of special metals such as titanium or tantalum may well justify the additional expense, particularly if clad material can be used satisfactorily. Where plastic equipment or piping is used, the layout should be such as to minimise possible mechanical damage.

Instrumentation

The instrumentation in an effluent treatment plant is relatively simple, having two functions, control and alarm, which can be integrated.

Although a choice may often be made between a high level of instrumentation, giving automatic operation, and a less costly low level, the relatively small additional cost of automatic operation is quickly recovered as a result of the much reduced labour requirement and greater consistency of operation. In most situations a well instrumented and automatic plant is to be preferred on overall cost grounds.

The controls usually installed are level controls, pH meters and 'redox' meters (reduction–oxidation) which are linked to effluent or reagent flow via pumps or valves. A flowmeter is normally required on the effluent discharge.

Level controls often consist of a three-probe system operating an on/off mode in which the lowest probe shuts off the pump(s), the middle probe turns on the main pump(s), and the top probe turns on a secondary or standby pump to cope with peak flows. A simpler system would use only two probes and one pump. A visual and/or audible alarm system may readily be provided by means of an additional probe to indicate when overflow is imminent. The action is based on changes in capacitance and almost no maintenance is required. Level controls would be employed in any intermediate storage operation such

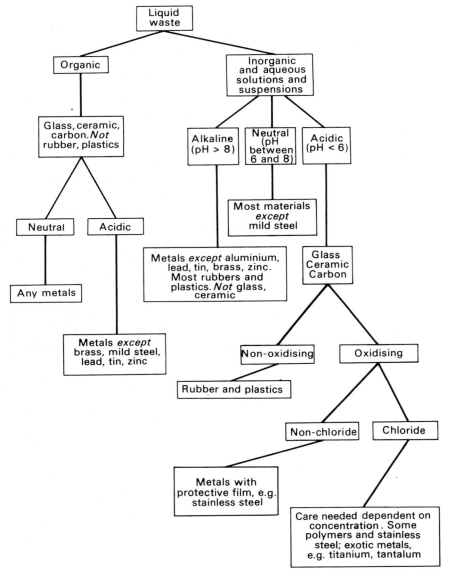

Fig. 7.2 Construction materials for effluent treatment plant

as sumps, reagent make-up, or sludge tank. Very large effluent treatment plants may employ two or three term-control systems providing variable flow rates. Such sophistication is, however, not often required.

pH meters are employed to control the addition of acid or alkali by measuring the pH of the effluent as a potential difference (voltage) across a glass electrode. The potential difference is related to pH and the instrument governs addition of the necessary reagent until the correct value of pH is achieved. The control may be linked to a valve or a pump and may operate on a simple on/off basis for smaller plants, or employ proportional and integral control for more efficient operation and in larger plants. An alarm system is often incorporated to warn if the pH goes outside certain specified limits. A permanent record may also be obtained which is useful, and sometimes necessary, on effluent discharge to sewer or watercourse.

Because of the delicacy of the sensing system, regular cleaning of the electrode is necessary, particularly if lime is employed as the neutralising agent. This cleaning operation may need to be as frequent as every two hours, but every day, or every second day, is usually sufficient. Recalibration is also necessary using standard solutions, perhaps once a month.

pH controls are fitted to any system where acid or alkali needs to be added, as in cyanide oxidation, chrome reduction, neutralisation or pH adjustment. A pH probe and recorder may be required on the final inspection tank prior to discharge to sewer or watercourse. Correct location of the probe in the reactor is very important. It should not be near the effluent or reagent entry point, nor in the path of either stream in the agitation flow pattern. As a general guide, the probe should be near the exit from the reactor.

Redox meters are similar to pH meters in operation and maintenance, except that they control the addition of oxidant (e.g. chlorine or hypochlorite in cyanide oxidation) or reductant (e.g. sulphur dioxide or sodium bisulphite for chrome reduction).

A flow recorder, of which the V-notch weir is a popular example, may be needed at the discharge of treated effluent to sewer or watercourse. A continuous record of flow rate is kept. The total quantity of effluent is also monitored for charging purposes (see Chapter 4).

Other instrumentation and control systems may be incorporated for special purposes: for example, the rate of addition of flocculant or nutrient may be controlled by flow rate or activated by connection to the transfer pumps; suspended solids can be monitored with light transmission meters; total dissolved solids monitored by conductivity meters; water scrubbers linked automatically to related processes. Almost any analytical technique can be incorporated as a monitor/control/alarm instrument in an effluent treatment process if required.

Layout

The basic principles of layout of an effluent treatment plant are to use as little floor area as possible, employ gravity for flows whenever possible, and ensure that any spillage or leakage is contained within the plant and properly collected and recycled for treatment.

A typical layout for the comprehensive pH adjustment/neutralisation scheme shown in Figure 7.3 is given in Figure 7.4. This is largely dependent on site conditions; consideration must also be given to delivery of raw materials

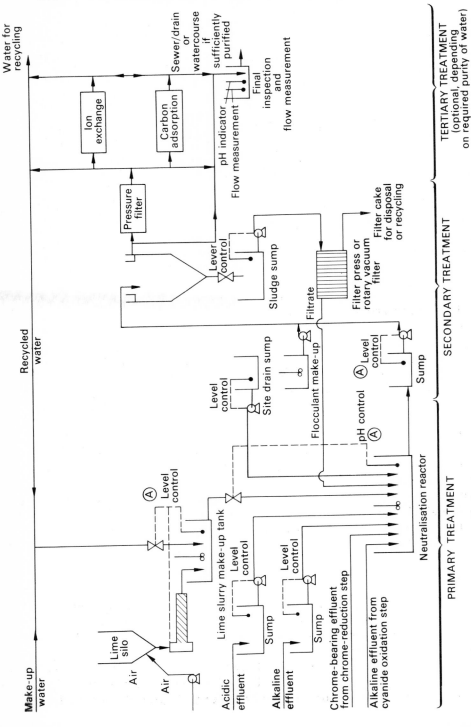

Fig. 7.3 Effluent treatment plant for neutralisation, solids separation and water recycle

A = alarm on instrument

and spares, and removal of waste (filter cake) for disposal without vehicles reversing into the plant area itself. There must be adequate space between plant items for safe passage, and all open vessels less than 1 m above surrounding ground level should be securely fenced. Good access is necessary for maintenance of pumps and probes. Except for good reason, all tanks and equipment should be kept above ground to reduce cost and maintenance requirements, and facilitate inspection of the equipment. Provision should be made for hosing down points. Pumps should be mounted on concrete plinths.

The entire plant should be built on a concrete raft that slopes to a central sump where spillages may be readily collected and returned for treatment. A bund wall is desirable around the perimeter of the plant; the location of this wall should allow for horizontal discharge of any leaks at high level. Unless it is covered by normal factory security, the plant should be fenced off.

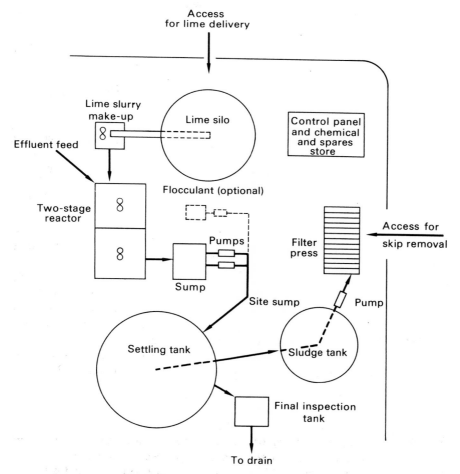

Fig. 7.4 Typical layout of effluent treatment plant shown in Fig. 7.3

Treatment of Individual Pollutants

The more common pollutants of aqueous effluents are discussed in this chapter, together with the range of methods available for treatment. The underlying principle of destruction/conversion or removal applies to all the treatment methods described. Recycling can often be most effective for pollution control, and many of these techniques are applicable to recovery processes. Table 7.1 summarises common pollutants and treatment methods, which are now discussed at greater length in alphabetical order.

Acidic Effluent

For waste containing inorganic or mineral acids such as sulphuric, hydrochloric, nitric or fluoric acids, refer to Mineral acids. If the acids are organic such as acetic acid, refer to Miscible organic compounds.

Alkaline Effluent

Alkaline effluents are usually less of a problem than acidic effluents as most conditions of discharge specify a range of alkalinity/acidity of pH 6 to pH 10 or 12 (pH is defined and explained on page 181).

If an effluent is too alkaline either for discharge or for further treatment, the pH is reduced by acid addition. If other local effluents include acid, mixing is often the most satisfactory way of adjusting pH, although good control may be difficult to obtain. Usually the cheapest acid to add is sulphuric acid, but if there is a restriction on the sulphate content of the resultant treated effluent, say 400 ppm, hydrochloric acid may be employed. Carbon dioxide gas from a nearby boiler installation has been used, as this gives carbonic acid, a weak acid, in contact with water. This can, however, prove an expensive alternative for any but the largest installations.

The equipment for acid neutralisation is simple and consists of an agitated tank with pH control for correct addition of acid and an acid storage tank. The vessels and pipes in contact with acid need to be lined with suitable acid-resistant material. As any acid–alkali reaction is almost instantaneous, the residence time within the reaction tank need be no more than 10 minutes. For concentrated solutions, and/or fine control, a two-stage reaction tank might be specified. Acid requirements are summarised in Table 7.12 on page 183.

Ammonia

Ammonia-bearing wastes may be unacceptable for discharge due to the pH and/or the pungent odour of free ammonia, and because ammonia is highly toxic to fish. Excess waste acid or waste ammonia is often reacted with ammonia or acid respectively to give fertiliser, and this is an accepted recycling

TABLE 7.1 POLLUTANTS OF AQUEOUS EFFLUENTS AND TREATMENT METHODS

Pollutant	Example	Treatment method
Alkali	Sodium hydroxide (caustic soda) Potassium hydroxide (caustic potash) Calcium oxide (lime) Calcium hydroxide Sodium, potassium and calcium carbonates Ammonia (q.v.)	Neutralisation if required— see also Total dissolved solids
Ammonia		Air stripping Incineration Neutralisation Nitrification
Biocides		Incineration
Biodegradeable waste	Sewage Food waste Organic chemicals	Incineration Settlement if necessary, biological oxidation and/or biological reduction, tertiary treatment if necessary
Boron, borates, fluoborates	—	Evaporation Ion exchange
Bromine	—	See Chlorine
Chloride	—	See Total dissolved solids
Chlorine	—	Air stripping Reduction
Chromic acid (hexavalent chromium)	—	Adsorption Cementation Dialysis Freeze concentration Ion exchange Oxidation Precipitation as insoluble salt Precipitation, possibly after neutralisation, using barium salts Reduction to trivalent chromium, then as for metal salts in acid solution Reverse osmosis
Cyanide	Copper cyanide Nickel cyanide Potassium cyanide Silver cyanide Sodium cyanide Zinc cyanide	Biological treatment Carbon adsorption Displacement by acid followed by aeration Electrolysis Evaporation Hydrolysis with steam Ion exchange

Table 7.1 (*continued*)

Pollutant	Example	Treatment method
		Oxidation to cyanate or carbon dioxide and nitrogen
		Precipitation with ferrous sulphate
		Reverse osmosis
		Treatment with hydrogen peroxide and formaldehyde
Emulsified oil	—	Air flotation
		Centrifugation
		Chemical emulsion breaking, then as for oil
		Heating
		Incineration
Fluoride	—	Adsorption on alumina See also Total dissolved solids
		Neutralisation with lime and precipitation
		Precipitation with aluminium sulphate
Fluorine	—	See Chlorine
Metal salts in alkaline solution	Cuprammonium complex	Adsorption
	Nickel and cobalt ammonia complex	Crystallisation
	Cyanides (q.v.)	Destruction or removal of anion, such as cyanide
	Copper pyrophos-phates	Electrodialysis
	Plumbites	Electrolysis
	Zincates	Evaporation
		Freeze separation
		Ion exchange
		Oxidation
		Reverse osmosis
		Solvent extraction
Metal salts in acid solution	Most metals as acid salts, e.g. chloride nitrate sulphate and others	Adsorption
		Cementation
		Crystallisation
		Electrodialysis
		Electrolysis
		Evaporation
		Freeze separation
		Ion exchange
		Neutralisation and precipitation as hydroxide
		Reverse osmosis
		Solvent extraction
Mineral acid	Hydrobromic acid	Neutralisation and possibly precipitation of insoluble salt
	Hydrochloric acid	See also Total dissolved solids
	Hydrofluoric acid	
	Nitric acid	
	Sulphuric acid	

Table 7.1 (*continued*)

Pollutant	Example	Treatment method
Miscible/soluble organic materials	Acetone Alcohol Acetic acid any many more.	Carbon adsorption Desorption by air stripping Incineration—see also Bio- degradeable waste Solvent extraction
Non-metallic inorganic dissolved compounds	Arsenic Selenium	Adsorption Ion exchange Precipitation as insoluble compound
Oil, grease, wax and immiscible organics	Lubricating oil Animal fat Carbon tetrachloride	Air flotation Centrifugation Coalescence if necessary, separation by flotation then aqueous layer to further treat- ment if necessary and oil to incineration or recovery Filtration/adsorption
Organometallic compounds	Tetraethyl lead	Ion exchange
pH	—	Neutralisation
Pharmaceuticals	—	See Biodegradeable waste Incineration
Phenols and related compounds	—	Adsorption on carbon See also Biodegradeable waste Incineration Oxidation Solvent extraction
Phosphate	—	Precipitation as insoluble phosphate See also Total dissolved solids
Sewage	—	See Biodegradeable waste
Sulphate	—	Distillation/evaporation Electrodialysis Ion exchange Precipitation as insoluble sulphate Reverse osmosis See Total dissolved solids
Sulphite liquor	—	See Biodegradeable waste
Suspended particles	—	Centrifugation Filtration Flocculation if possible, settlement/ clarification/sedimentation Hydrocyclone

Table 7.1 (*continued*)

Pollutant	Example	Treatment method
Total dissolved solids	Carbonate Chloride Nitrate Phosphate Sulphate	Distillation Electrodialysis Freezing Ion exchange Reverse osmosis (Desalination)

process to give a useful product. However, it relies on readily available materials as the product is of relatively low value and the economics are marginal.

Removal of ammonia is often carried out by air stripping, in which air flowing countercurrent to the ammonia-bearing liquor under turbulent conditions desorbs the ammonia. If the quantities and/or concentrations are relatively small, the ammonia-laden air may be discharged to atmosphere, otherwise the ammonia is incinerated. An example is the ammonia-bearing liquors from coal distillation. The combustion products are nitrogen oxides and water. Design of the stripping unit and incinerator is complex and dependent on ammonia concentrations and nature of the waste.

Biocides

The term 'biocide' is a generic expression for the range of complex chemicals used to control certain types of organism. Included are insecticides, fungicides, pesticides and herbicides. For small quantities of wastes and/or high concentration of pollutant, incineration is a safe general way of destroying the biocide. Carbon adsorption will give a significant reduction in concentration, but the constraints and the toxic and persistent nature of the chemicals involved necessitate careful examination to ensure satisfactory treatment is effected. Other general removal or destruction methods may be effective but the range of chemical compounds is so large that generalisation is not possible. Each case requires individual study.

Biodegradeable Waste

Biological processes are used for treating industrial wastes containing organic matter and some wastes containing inorganic chemicals such as ammonia and sulphides. Aerobic biochemical oxidation plants are suitable for processing weak liquid wastes with a biological oxygen demand (BOD) content less than about 200 mg/litre. Strong organic wastes and the sludges from aerobic plants are often treated in anaerobic biochemical reduction plants.

The first consideration in assessing the load likely to be imposed on a biological treatment plant is the BOD_5 (Chapter 4). The strengths and pH

TABLE 7.2 EXAMPLES OF ORGANIC TRADE WASTE

Source	BOD₅	pH
Cotton kier liquor	10 000	12–13
Mixed cotton textiles	400	9
Flax retting	2000	5
Wool scouring	5000	—
Rayon	700	10–11
Penicillin	5000	8
Yeast	5000	4–5
Distilling	25 000	4
Vegetable tanning	3000	5–12
Dairies	500	5
Canning	500	6–9
Slaughterhouses	3000	7
Paper mills	200	8
Spent gas liquor	8000	8
Sewage (UK average)	350	7

values of typical organic trade wastes are given in Table 7.2.

A schematic flow diagram of a plant treating weak effluent is shown in Figure 7.5. Balancing or storage tanks may be required if fluctuations occur in waste-water flow or composition. Before the biological treatment step, chemicals such as ammonium salts and phosphates may have to be added to control pH and adjust the BOD: nitrogen: phosphorus ratio to about 100:6:1. Microbial cells are produced during the biochemical oxidation process and these must be separated from the liquid effluent. In many plants part of the microbial sludge or some of the final liquid effluent, or both, are recycled. Depending on the biological treatment used and degree of BOD removal, 0·25 to 0·80 kg of microbial sludge on a dry basis is formed per kg of BOD in the waste-water.

Many methods have been used for dealing with such sludges based on anaerobic biological action (digestion) and physical separation. These methods are also applicable to strong organic wastes containing high concentrations of suspended organic matter, such as vegetable processing wastes. Figure 7.6 shows how the various treatment steps may be combined. The treatment and final disposal of the sludge are important steps in the overall process. Therefore during process design they must not be considered in isolation from the biological treatment step.

Biological Treatment Process

(a) Biological Filters

In biological filtration the waste-water is distributed, for example by rotating distributor arms, over the top surface of a bed of inert material to which air has access. Microbial films build up on the solid support, and the microbes feed on

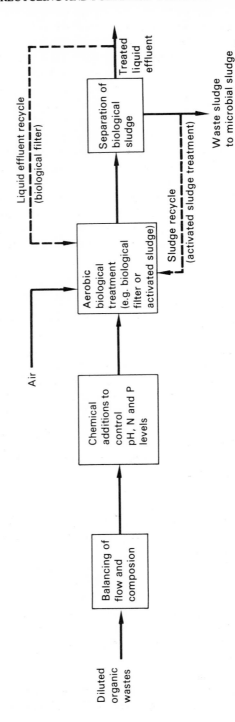

Fig. 7.5 Flow diagram of typical biological oxidation effluent treatment plant

organic pollutants as the waste-water percolates through the bed. Filters as designed for sewage treatment are typically 2·0 m deep and are traditionally packed with broken slag or stone of about 50 mm diameter, although plastic packings are becoming increasingly employed as replacement for stone or slag, and in tall towers operated at high circulation rates. These packings are relatively expensive but their lower density enables cost savings to be made on the containment and support structures, and in the building of taller filters which reduces land requirement. An illustration is given on page 229.

Many variations are used in liquid flow pattern but there are only two basic modes: once-through filtration plants, and recirculation plants which include those used for partial treatment.

There are a number of important design criteria such as BOD loading and throughput per unit area of bed. Table 7.3 summarises performance data for a range of biological filters. Selection of a treatment system is dependent on raw effluent characteristics, the final effluent quality required, and filter capacity required.

(b) Activated Sludge Plants

In the activated sludge process flocculent cultures of micro-organisms are mixed and aerated with waste-water in a tank reactor to maintain a dissolved oxygen content greater than 0·5 mg/l. This is achieved by mechanical aerators, by bubbling air through, or in some recent designs by using pure oxygen rather than air. Following reaction, the suspended flocs are allowed to settle out from the treated liquid and the microbial (or activated) sludge is then returned to the aeration tank. The purification process results in an increase in microbial mass and excess sludge must be removed regularly. In the older activated sludge plants recycled sludge is mixed with the incoming waste-water, and the suspension then passes in plug–flow through the aeration tank. Variations in the method of operation include tapered aeration and incremental feeding of the waste-water.

The completely mixed activated sludge system (see page 228) has been widely used for the treatment of industrial effluents. Since biological oxidation may follow zero-order kinetics, there may be no advantage to be gained in using a plug–flow system. Completely mixed systems are also favoured for the partial but rapid treatment of waste-waters.

There are two further versions of the activated sludge process. One is the contact-stabilisation system, in which the settled sludge is reaerated before being mixed with untreated waste-water. The second is the extended aeration process, which is characterised by aeration times of 24 hours or more: sludge is only removed infrequently and is itself degraded as a result of the long residence time and low BOD:sludge ratio.

Some typical performance figures are given in Table 7.4 for a range of activated sludge processes.

A range of proprietary equipment and processes have been designed to improve the basic processes outlined above. For example, one of these employs

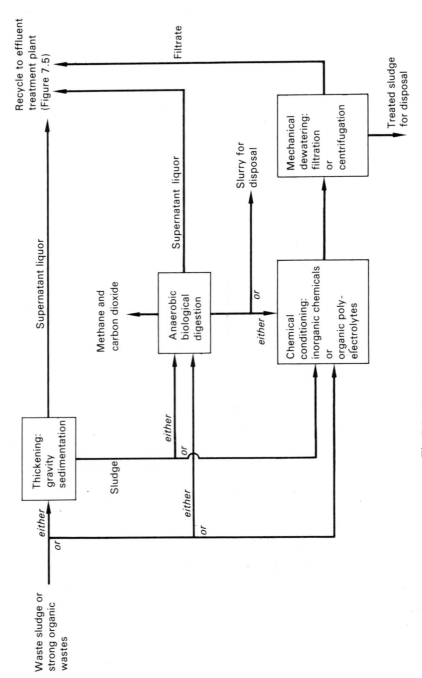

Fig. 7.6 Microbial (anaerobic) sludge treatment

TABLE 7.3 SOME PERFORMANCE DATA FOR BIOLOGICAL FILTERS

Filter type	BOD loading (kg BOD/m³ d)	Hydraulic loading (m³/m² d)	Recirculation ratio	BOD removal (%)	Comments
Conventional media					
Once through, low-rate	0·1	0·8	0	~90	Original BOD < 250 mg/l
Recirculation	0·15	2·4	1:1	~90	Rock or slag media (40–60 mm in size)
High-rate	2·0	20	Between 0·5:1 and 4·0:1, depending on original BOD	~60	Original BOD > 250 mg/l Rock or slag media (100–150 mm in size) Partial treatment only in single-stage unit
Plastic media					
Once through, low-rate	1·0	30	0	~90	Plastic media formed from corrugated PVC or polystyrene sheets ≤7 m deep
Recirculation	4–12	30	Depends on original BOD	~60	

TABLE 7.4 PERFORMANCE DATA FOR ACTIVATED SLUDGE PLANTS

Plant type	BOD loading (kg BOD/m³ d)	BOD loading (kg BOD/MLSS* d)	Aeration period (h)	Sludge concentration (mg/l)	BOD removal (%)
Conventional plug flow	0·48–0·64	0·2–0·4	5–8	1500–3000	95
Completely mixed	0·5–2·0	0·5–1·0	2·5–3·5	4000–5000	85–95
Contact-stabilisation	0·48–0·80	0·2–0·5	6–9 (including sludge aeration of 4–8 h)	2000–6000	85–90
Extended aeration	0·16–0·32	0·05–0·20	20–30	2000–10 000	85–95
Aeration systems					
Air diffusers	1·0 kg BOD/kWh	100 m³ air/ kg BOD			
Surface aerators (mechanical)	1·3 kg BOD/kWh				

* MLSS = mixed liquor suspended solids

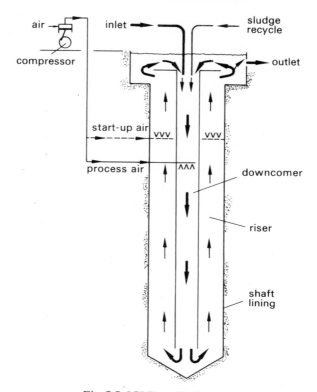

Fig. 7.7 ICI Deep Shaft unit

rotating discs to support a film of microbial growth. High resistance to shock and intermittent loadings is claimed, together with a low retention time and good sludge-settling characteristics.

A more recent proposal is the Deep Shaft process (Figure 7.7), which requires minimal land area and achieves the desired performance by using a high reactor with low cross-sectional area rather than a conventional shallow reactor with a large cross-sectional area. Power requirements are minimised by sinking the reactor into the ground and employing low hydraulic heads to move the effluent through the system.

(c) Anaerobic Sludge Digesters

Strong organic wastes and the sludges obtained from biological filters and activated sludge plants can be digested by micro-organisms under anaerobic conditions. This can reduce the sludge volume by about 65% and the weight of dry solids by about 40%. A well digested sludge can be dewatered more rapidly than the raw sludge and is relatively free from unpleasant odours, which is an important consideration in urban areas. During digestion a mixed population of micro-organisms converts the organics into methane (CH_4) and carbon dioxide (CO_2). About $0 \cdot 5\ m^3$ of gas is produced per kg of volatile solids

TABLE 7.5 SOME PERFORMANCE DATA FOR ANAEROBIC SLUDGE DIGESTERS (BASED ON EXPERIENCE WITH SEWAGE SLUDGES AT 35°C)

	Loading (kg volatile solids/m³ d)	Retention time (d)	Volatile solids reduction (%)	Comments
Standard-rate plant	0·32–0·80	30–90 (digestion period about 25 d)	50–70	Single-stage unit with gravity separation of solids and storage within digester
High-rate plant	1·6–3·2	10–15	50	Complete mixing in 1st stage followed by gravity settling and storage in a 2nd-stage digester

entering the digester, which has an energy content considerably in excess of the energy requirements of the process.

Before disposal, the digested sludge may be consolidated or dewatered as indicated in Figure 7.6. Supernatant or separated liquor is mixed with incoming waste-water or recycled to the biological treatment plant. After dewatering, the cake may be incinerated or dumped as landfill.

Preliminary design information is given in Table 7.5.

Processing of Sludges from Biological Treatment Plants

(a) Sedimentation Tanks

Circular, radial-flow tanks are used for settling suspensions leaving biological treatment plants. In sewage treatment works use is also made of horizontal-flow and upward-flow tanks.

Excess sludge from biological filters and activated sludge plants contains as much as 98–99.5% water. The solids content of sludge from an anaerobic digester is usually higher, typically about 5%. Further thickening of settled sludge may be achieved by leaving it to stand for 24 hours, or by using a secondary settling tank. Operating figures for the main types of sedimentation tank are given in Table 7.6.

(a) Dewatering by Filtration and Centrifugation

The water content of a sludge should be reduced to 96% or less before dewatering. Chemical conditioning is usually necessary with lime and iron or aluminium salts, or with organic polyelectrolytes. The amount of hydrated lime required is about 20% of the dry solids content of the sludge; the dosage of other chemicals is typically 1–2%. Design data for various types of dewatering equipment are listed in Table 7.7.

An overall flow diagram of a typical sewage treatment operation is shown in Figure 7.8. Industrial biodegradeable waste may not require such extensive treatment, for example pretreatment and polishing are unlikely to be needed, and such unnecessary operations may be omitted. A detailed case study is presented later in this chapter.

TABLE 7.6 SOME PERFORMANCE DATA FOR SEDIMENTATION TANKS

Type of tank	Surface loading $(m^3/m^2\ d)$	Retention time (h)	Comments
Rectangular, horizontal flow			Mean horizontal liquid velocity ~ 15 m/h
Upward flow	20–40	2–4	Upward flow velocity ~ 1.5 m/h
Radial flow			Tank fitted with sludge scraper

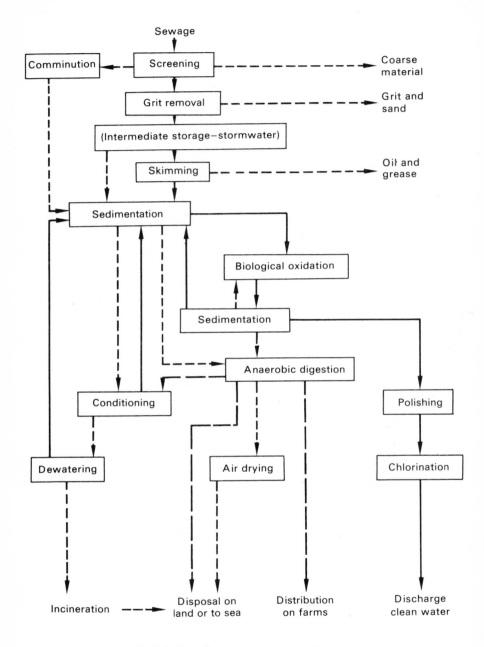

Fig. 7.8 Overall sewage treatment scheme
——— low solids content
– – – intermediate solids content
- - - - high solids content

TABLE 7.7 SOME PERFORMANCE DATA FOR DEWATERING EQUIPMENT

Type of equipment	Solids recovery using conditioners	Moisture content of cake	Output (kg dry solids/m² h)	
Filter press	99	60–75	2–3	(Based on cycle time of about 5 h)
Vacuum filter	95	70–85	10–25	
Centrifuge (continuous solid bowl type)	85–95	65–85	—	

Boron

Boron usually occurs in wastes as boric acid and borates, or fluoborates. Although boron is widely used, little information is available on waste levels, toxicity or treatment processes. The only practical removal methods are reverse osmosis with cellulose acetate membranes at pH 5, or ion exchange with a highly specific resin, for example Amberlite IRA-943. Other common treatment methods, including conventional biological waste treatment, have no effect.

Chlorine

Chlorine, and to a lesser extent bromine and fluorine, are sometimes found in effluent from processes which either produce or use them. All are oxidising agents and may therefore be removed by reaction with a reducing agent. Alternatively, since they are only physically dissolved, air stripping will significantly reduce their concentration.

Little has been published on treatment of dissolved halogen gases. Since they are oxidising agents, treatment may best be effected by reduction. One of the most effective and widely used reducing agents is sulphur dioxide as gas or as a sodium salt such as sodium sulphite, sodium bisulphite or sodium metabisulphite. Sulphur dioxide would react with dissolved chlorine thus:

$$Cl_2 + SO_2 + 2H_2O \rightarrow 2HCl + H_2SO_4$$

and the resultant acids would require neutralisation before discharge.

With sodium sulphite, the reaction is:

$$Cl_2 + Na_2SO_3 + H_2O \rightarrow 2NaCl + H_2SO_4$$

With sodium bisulphite:

$$Cl_2 + NaHSO_3 + H_2O \rightarrow NaCl + HCl + H_2SO_4$$

and with sodium metabisulphite:

$$2Cl_2 + Na_2S_2O_5 + 3H_2O \rightarrow 2\,NaCl + 2\,HCl + 2H_2SO_4$$

The advantages and disadvantages of gaseous and aqueous reagents are discussed under Chromium.

Alternatively, ferrous sulphate is a common, cheap but less effective reducing agent, reacting thus:

$$Cl_2 + 3FeSO_4 \rightarrow FeCl_3 + Fe_2(SO_4)_3$$

The reactions occur rapidly and require a retention time of no more than 10 minutes (ferrous sulphate, however, needs considerably longer). Addition of reagent may be controlled by redox probe—see Figures 7.9 and 10. Careful selection of construction materials is necessary, depending on the concentration of chlorine. Reagent requirements may be calculated on a molecular weight basis: 71 weight units of chlorine require 64 weight units of sulphur dioxide, 126 of sodium sulphite, 104 of sodium bisulphite, and 95 of sodium metabisulphite or 456 of ferrous sulphate. Bromine and fluorine would follow similar reaction mechanisms but probably take longer to react.

Air stripping is also an effective way of removing dissolved gases, but could only be practised on small quantities and concentrations of waste, unless the stripped gas was subsequently recovered. A suitable system would require careful design.

Chromium

Chromium occurs as both hexavalent and trivalent metal in aqueous solution. Most chromium giving rise to pollution is from the metal finishing industry where it occurs in the hexavalent state as chromic acid. The most common method of treating this material is by reduction to trivalent chromium, then precipitation of hydroxide by neutralisation with alkali. A wide range of other methods have been proposed, many associated with recovery of the chromic acid for reuse.

Reduction of Hexavalent Chromium

The extent of the reduction of hexavalent chromium to the trivalent state is dependent on pH, time of reaction, and choice, concentration and degree of excess of reducing agent.

The most common reagents are based on gaseous sulphur dioxide and aqueous sodium salts according to the following reactions:

with sulphur dioxide:
$$2H_2CrO_4 + 3SO_2 \rightarrow Cr_2(SO_4)_3 + 2H_2O$$

with sodium sulphite:
$$2H_2CrO_4 + 3Na_2SO_3 + 3H_2SO_4 \rightarrow Cr_2(SO_4)_3 + 3Na_2SO_4 + 5H_2O$$

with sodium bisulphite:
$$4H_2CrO_4 + 6NaHSO_3 + 3H_2SO_4 \rightarrow 2Cr_2(SO_4)_3 + 3Na_2SO_4 + 1OH_2O$$

with sodium metabisulphite:

$$4H_2CrO_4 + 3Na_2S_2O_5 + 3H_2SO_4 \rightarrow 2Cr_2(SO_4)_3 + 3Na_2SO_4 + 7H_2O$$

The theoretical reagent requirements are listed in Table 7.8, although up to 25% excess may be required. Conditions for satisfactory reduction are pH 2·5 and retention time of 10 to 15 minutes. The pH is critical and should not be allowed to rise above pH 3. It may be necessary to arrange for pH control to be included with acid addition to ensure satisfactory reduction.

Hexavalent chromium levels of 0·1 mg/l (0·1 ppm) may be consistently achieved. Typical flow diagrams are given in Figure 7.9 for gaseous sulphur dioxide and Figure 7.10 for aqueous solutions of sodium sulphite, bisulphite or metabisulphite. Generally sulphur dioxide is preferred for larger treatment plants of above around 9 m³/h (2000 gal/h), when the additional capital cost is outweighed by the cheaper reagent. Comparative reagent costs are given in

TABLE 7.8 THEORETICAL RELATIVE WEIGHTS OF REAGENT AND ACID REQUIRED TO REDUCE UNIT WEIGHT OF CHROMIC ACID OR SODIUM CHROMATE

Reagent	Relative weight to reduce unit weight of:		
	Chromic acid		Sodium dichromate
	as CrO_3	as H_2CrO_4	as $Na_2Cr_2O_7$
Sulphur dioxide SO_2	0·96	0·814	0·733
Sodium sulphite Na_2SO_3	1·89	1·602	1·443
Sodium bisulphite $NaHSO_3$	1·56	1·322	1·191
Sodium metabisulphite $Na_2S_2O_5$	1·43	1·208	1·088
Ferrous sulphate $FeSO_4\,7H_2O$	8·43	7·144	6·40
Ferrous sulphate $FeSO_4$	4·56	3·864	3·47

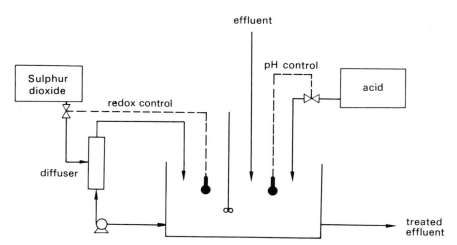

Fig. 7.9 Sulphur dioxide reduction of chromium (the diffuser may be fitted to the incoming effluent stream, but operation is then less controllable)

TABLE 7.9 COMPARATIVE COSTS OF REDUCTION REAGENTS (BULK BUYING ASSUMED)

	Relative reagent cost	Relative equivalent cost of SO_2
Sulphur dioxide	1·0	1·0
Sodium sulphite (25% SO_2)	0·6	2·4
Sodium bisulphite (62% SO_2)	0·75	1·2
Sodium metabisulphite (66% SO_2)	0·8	1·2
Ferrous sulphate	0·15	—

Table 7.9. Sodium chromate and dichromate will behave similarly to chromic acid.

Ferrous sulphate is the traditional alternative to sulphur dioxide. It has the advantages of lower toxicity and lower cost, but the greater disadvantages of a significantly longer reaction time, greater excess of reagent, and the problem of subsequently removing iron by neutralisation and precipitation. The reaction is:

$$2\,H_2CrO_4 + 6\,FeSO_4 + 6\,H_2SO_4 \rightarrow Cr_2(SO_4)_3 + 3Fe_2(SO_4)_3 + 8H_2O$$

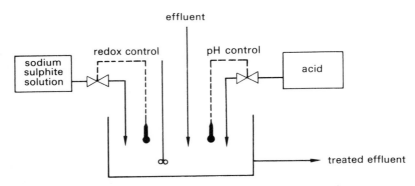

Fig. 7.10 Aqueous sodium sulphite reduction of chromium

Reagent requirements are listed in Table 7.8, but up to 100% excess may be required. Conditions for satisfactory reduction are less well defined compared with sulphur dioxide: a residence time of at least 30 minutes is required, but above pH 3 this increases, as pH increases, to around an hour. Problems can arise with cyanide-bearing wastes due to ferrocyanide complex formation, as well as the problem of subsequent iron removal. Ferrous sulphate is not now widely used.

Other reducing agents that have been proposed but not widely used include scrap iron and steel; this process is sometimes referred to as electrochemical reduction or cementation. This is also pH-dependent, requiring a maximum value of pH 3 to be effective. The reaction is:

$$2\,H_2CrO_4 + 3Fe \rightarrow 6H_2SO_4 \rightarrow Cr_2(SO_4)_3 + 3FeSO_4 + 8H_2O$$

and the resulting ferrous sulphate also reacts according to the reaction given earlier. The time for reaction is variable and dependent on the surface area of iron and steel available and concentration of chromium; it can be as long as several hours. Zinc dust may be employed in a similar way. Hydrazine has been employed in conjunction with sulphite reduction.

Precipitation of Hexavalent Chromium

It is possible to precipitate chromium in the hexavalent state by formation of insoluble barium chromate. This is not widely used as barium salts are too costly, but it is a useful emergency remedy, particularly as treatment is most effective at pH 8–9, i.e. after neutralisation. Lack of treatment may then be more obvious by the yellow colouration of effluent from unreduced chromic acid.

Precipitation of Trivalent Chromium

Chromium may be precipitated as hydroxide when in the trivalent state. This is described under Metal Salts in Acid Solution. No special problems are associated with trivalent chromium.

Removal of Chromium

Ion exchange is one of the more widely employed chromium and chromic acid recovery processes. Cation exchange, although not widely practised, may be employed to recover trivalent chromium ions; anion exchange is employed for hexavalent chromate ions. pH control is necessary to avoid degeneration of the resin. Regenerated solution of up to 6% chromic acid may be achieved. Removal of chromium to less than 1 mg/l (1 ppm) may be consistently achieved. Although ion exchange is particularly suited to low-concentration effluents, recently developed resins are capable of satisfactorily handling relatively concentrated chromic acid solutions. An advantage of ion exchange is its selectivity to specific ions under certain conditions, so that recovery is possible from contaminated waste.

An alternative to ion exchange on uncontaminated rinse or swill solutions of dilute chromic acid is evaporation of water to concentrate the solution. This has the disadvantages of also concentrating any other impurities and possibly accumulating impurities, as well as the high energy cost associated with evaporation.

Other proposals include carbon adsorption, reverse osmosis, freeze concentration and solvent extraction, but none of these is known to have been employed commercially.

Cyanide

Cyanide is probably the best known and most 'emotive' pollutant. The UK cyanide dumping scares of several years ago, resulting in the introduction of the Deposit of Poisonous Waste Act, in fact involved solid cyanide, whereas the subject here is aqueous cyanide in alkaline solution. This can exist as sodium cyanide or a heavy metal cyanide such as nickel, copper, zinc, cadmium or silver. It is the acid gas, hydrocyanic acid (HCN), that is particularly toxic, very small concentrations rapidly causing death on inhalation. Thus acidification of any cyanide compound is highly dangerous. Most treatment methods are devoted to destruction of cyanide by oxidation either partially to cyanate or preferably completely to carbon dioxide and nitrogen. Some recovery methods have been proposed but not widely implemented. A significant proportion of aqueous cyanide waste arises from the electroplating industry, which is currently undergoing considerable change in plating bath compositions, in recycling technology, and in countering a swing away from electroplating.

Oxidation by Chlorination

This is the most popular and widely used method of oxidation. For small installations of up to 9 m^3/h (2000 gal/h) capacity, sodium hypochlorite solution tends to be preferred, while larger plants tend to use gaseous chlorine which costs less but requires a higher initial expenditure. The reactions proceed thus:

With chlorine:

First stage: (a) $NaCN + Cl_2 \rightarrow CNCl + NaCl$
cyanogen
chloride

(b) $CNCl + 2NaOH \rightarrow NaCNO + NaCl + H_2O$
sodium
cyanate

Second stage:
$2NaCNO + 4NaOH + 3Cl_2 \rightarrow 6NaCl + 2CO_2 + N_2 + 2H_2O$

Overall: $2NaCN + 8NaOH \rightarrow N_2 + 2CO_2 + 10NaCl + 4H_2O$

With sodium hypochlorite:

First stage: (a) $NaCN + NaOCl + H_2O \rightarrow CNCl + 2NaOH$

(b) $CNCl + 2NaOH \rightarrow NaCNO + NaCl + H_2O$

Second stage:
$2NaCNO + 3NaOCl + H_2O \rightarrow 2CO_2 + N_2 + 3NaCl + 2NaOH$

Overall:
$2NaCN + 5NaOCl + H_2O \rightarrow 2CO_2 + N_2 + 5NaCl + 2NaOH$

Similar reactions occur with calcium hypochlorite as oxidising agent, and with cyanides of potassium, copper, nickel, zinc, cadmium, tin and silver. The heavy metal cyanides on oxidation give insoluble metal hydroxides which precipitate under the prevalent pH conditions; this is discussed later. Theoretical reagent requirements are listed in Table 7.10.

Conditions for successful oxidation are well defined. pH is critical for both speed of reaction and extent of oxidation, and for most purposes oxidation at pH 10 or above is preferred, when virtually complete reaction should occur in 15 to 20 minutes. At lower pH values, sufficient chlorine (as gas or hypochlorite) must be added to avoid formation of highly toxic free cyanogen chloride. The intermediate cyanate is relatively safe but care needs to be taken that reducing conditions do not occur downstream to reform cyanide. Cyanate may be oxidised by further chlorine addition to carbon dioxide and nitrogen and generally this is preferred, but reaction proceeds more rapidly at lower pH values of between 9 and 10. For all stages of oxidation, excess chlorine is needed to ensure complete reaction and allow for oxidation of any metal ions, e.g. ferrous to ferric. The equipment is similar to that employed for sulphite reduction of chromium (Figures 7.9 and 10), except that acid and/or alkali may be needed for pH control, and a chlorine evaporator is necessary for larger treatment plants to ensure sufficient chlorine is available. Mild steel is usually a satisfactory material for construction. Metal cyanide complexes, in particular nickel, take significantly longer to react and double the suggested contact time is needed. One plant arrangement is shown on page 227.

TABLE 7.10 THEORETICAL REAGENT REQUIREMENTS FOR OXIDATION OF CYANIDE

| | Weight of reagent per unit weight of cyanide as CN for reduction: | |
	to cyanate	to carbon dioxide and nitrogen
Chlorine, Cl_2	2·731	6·827
Sodium hypochlorite, NaOCl	2·865	7·163
Ozone, O_3	1·846	4·615

1 weight unit of cyanide (CN) corresponds to:
  1·885 weight units NaCN
  2·50   .   . KCN
  2·22   .   . $CuCN_2$
  2·13   .   . $NiCN_2$
  6·15   .   . AgCN
  2·26   .   . $ZnCN_2$
  3·14   .   . $CdCN_2$

In addition to the complex stagewise oxidation processes, problems can arise with mixed wastes. For example, excess sulphur-dioxide from a chromium reduction stage might reduce cyanate to cyanide. Similarly, excess oxidising agent from cyanide oxidation might oxidise trivalent chromium back to hexavalent chromium (q.v.). Use of treated alkaline cyanide waste to neutralise or partially neutralise metal-bearing acid waste might also result in stable complex formation such as ferrocyanides. In practice, careful design and supervision can obviate such problems.

Oxidation by Other Methods
(a) Ozonation
This method of oxidising cyanide has attracted much attention due to the low overall cost, complete reaction, and the convenience of the ozone being generated on site. Reactions occur in two stages, as for chlorine oxidation, with cyanate formed as an intermediate:

$$NaCN + O_3 \rightarrow NaCNO + O_2$$
$$2NaCNO + 3\,O_3 + H_2O \rightarrow 2NaOH + 2CO_2 + N_2 + 3\,O_2$$

overall:

$$2\,NaCN + 5\,O_3 + H_2O \rightarrow 2\,NaOH + 2CO_2 + N_2 + 5\,O_2$$

Theoretical reagent requirements are given in Table 7.10, and a slight excess is required for effective oxidation because of ozone's relative instability. The method is suitable for partial or complete oxidation, low or high cyanide concentrations, and any metal cyanides with the possible exception of cobalt cyanide complex. Close pH control is unnecessary as reaction is very rapid between pH 9 and pH 12 and is catalysed by traces of copper if present. Equipment as for sulphur dioxide reduction of chromium is satisfactory, using mild steel but without pH control. Very large installations might justify a packed tower arrangement.

(b) Electrolytic Oxidation
Oxidation by anodic oxidation is particularly suitable for high concentrations of cyanide as the efficiency reduces at lower concentrations, when conventional chlorination oxidation is needed. The action is slow, requiring many hours or even days for adequate cyanide oxidation, but it is effective and valuable for complex cyanides such as nickel, copper and ferro- and ferricyanide complexes. If the solution conductivity is improved by addition of sodium chloride the efficiency at lower cyanide concentrations is improved, and anodic oxidation of chloride to chlorine assists in oxidation of cyanide. This method is not widely used because of the cost of electricity and the slowness of reaction. Steel or carbon electrodes are employed, with air agitation and good venting. A high temperature, around 90°C, is preferred.

(c) Miscellaneous methods
Hydrogen peroxide and formaldehyde can be used to treat cyanide, giving cyanate, ammonia and various organic acids. Zinc and cadmium are also precipitated if present.

Potassium permanganate may be employed as an oxidising agent but its high cost and lack of advantages over other oxidising agents preclude its use.

Biological oxidation is not strictly a 'method' as it is widely employed by nature in effectively destroying very dilute cyanide solutions. There is in addition a specific destructive culture available, but this is not employed industrially.

Almost any oxidising agent may in fact be used, and the following have been suggested but without knowledge of industrial use: permonosulphuric acid, persulphate, polysulphides, hydrogen peroxide, or chromic acid in the presence of copper II, which would require complete enclosure and gas scrubbing equipment.

For difficult wastes and complex mixtures of wastes containing cyanide, such as oily residues, incineration may be a convenient form of oxidation. Careful design and specification is essential to ensure sufficient residence time, and excess air is necessary for complete oxidation. This method may also be useful for sludges, or slurries, either of cyanide or of waste containing cyanide.

Precipitation by Ferrous Sulphate

One of the traditional methods of cyanide removal, reaction with ferrous sulphate to give insoluble complex ferro/ferricyanides is not now practised. This is due to the difficulties in obtaining less than 10 mg/l (10 ppm) cyanide in the treated effluent and in controlling the process, of which the chemistry is not well understood.

Recovery of Cyanide

Evaporative recovery for recycling is an effective treatment method and under some circumstances is economically viable, particularly in very large plating works. The effluent from the first rinse tank after plating is evaporated to give concentrated cyanide for plating bath make-up, and clean water for the last rinse. A closed loop is thus established, but it needs careful control to avoid build-up of impurities.

Cyanide may also be recovered as hydrogen cyanide gas by acidification followed by air stripping. Safety is of critical importance due to the extreme toxicity of hydrogen cyanide. Recovery of cyanide from the effluent gas stream is complicated and costly.

Other Methods of Cyanide Removal

Most chemical engineering unit operations have been applied to the problem of cyanide treatment, particularly ion exchange, reverse osmosis and adsorption, but none has proved viable to date.

Emulsions

Emulsions are physically stable dispersions of small particles of an oily material in an aqueous medium. They may exist naturally, as in milk, be formed accidentally as a result of intimate mixing of oily waste and water, or be produced artificially as in machine cutting 'soluble oils' or suds. Occasionally a water-in-oil emulsion is encountered. Many oily wastes consist of free separated oil as well as emulsion and this free oil (oil being a generalised expression for nonsoluble organic material) must first be removed in a primary separation stage which is described later under Oily Waste. The emulsion is then broken into two discrete phases of oil and water, using one of the secondary treatment methods described below. The resultant oil is then separated.

Emulsions can be broken by chemical, physical and electrical methods, of which chemical methods are most widely used. Precise specification of treatment is impossible due to the very wide range of oily wastes encountered and the presence of other materials such as surfactants and solids which affect emulsion stability. Experimental trials must first be carried out to choose the most suitable system.

Chemical emulsion-breaking consists of adding a highly ionised soluble salt (aluminium and iron salts are particularly effective) or an acid such as sulphuric acid which disturbs the equilibrium of the dispersion and enables the droplets to coalesce. Up to 2% by weight is the usual level required. Alternatively, any emulsifier which maintains the stability of the dispersion may be destroyed by adding a suitable reagent, but the chemicals tend to be very costly and this method is not widely used. Chemical demulsification is sometimes combined with physical or electrolytic methods for enhanced efficiency. Particularly difficult emulsions can be incinerated.

Physical emulsion-breaking includes heating, centrifugation, and precoat filtration, all of which are generally unreliable methods on their own. Electrical methods are rarely employed, and then usually only for high-oil-content wastes.

Once broken, the emulsion has to be separated into oil and aqueous phases; one of the most common methods is by air flotation. Air is dissolved at high pressure in the waste, which is then expanded to atmospheric pressure, releasing many very small air bubbles which preferentially attach themselves to the oil droplets and float them to the surface. This oily froth may be skimmed off; chemical flocculants such as aluminium and iron salts or polyelectrolytes help this process. An alternative for some wastes is coalescence by passing the broken emulsion through a fine fibrous bed, or sometimes just simple sedimentation as for oily wastes.

In practice, it is often difficult to get below 10 ppm oil or achieve better than 90% reduction in oil level, and a biological treatment stage may be needed to produce an acceptable effluent. This has led to the development of various combinations of chemical, physical and biological processes, carefully designed to produce an acceptable effluent from a given waste. Each waste needs careful examination and testing to find the most effective and viable treatment method.

Fluorides

Fluoride-bearing waste streams arise from a variety of chemical processes and often require treatment before discharge. Two main methods are employed: precipitation as an insoluble compound and adsorption with or without chemical reaction. Many of the techniques for reducing total dissolved solids (q.v.) are also effective on fluoride-containing wastes.

The most widely used precipitation reagent is lime, which forms relatively insoluble calcium fluoride. This is employed both on acidic wastes, for pH adjustment or neutralisation as well as precipitation, and also on other fluoridebearing streams. Since the theoretical solubility of calcium fluoride is 8 mg/l (8 ppm), it is usually difficult to reduce fluoride levels to less than about 15 mg/l with conventional treatment equipment and reasonable reaction times. Lower values may be achieved with mixed wastes due to coprecipitation and fluoride ion adsorption. The theoretical reagent requirements of 1·474 weight units of lime as CaO (or 1·947 weight units of hydrated lime as $Ca(OH)_2$) for each unit weight of fluoride as F needs to be increased considerably in practice due to encapsulation of the lime particle with insoluble calcium fluoride. The unreacted centre of the particle is then unable to react and is rendered ineffective. This can mean that up to 70% or 80% of the lime added is not used in extreme cases. Usually 50% utilisation is the best that can be expected. Most fluoridebearing wastes contain other pollutants that require treatment; equipment specification depends on consideration of all factors. Generally, however, a flowsheet similar to that employed for lime neutralisation in pH adjustment is satisfactory (Figures 7.14 and 7.17).

Aluminium sulphate has been used to precipitate fluoride at low concentrations as a coprecipitate. The most effective conditions are pH 7 and between 40 and 200 weight units of aluminium sulphate per unit weight of fluoride, when fluoride levels down to about 3 mg/l (3 ppm) can be achieved. The gelatinous nature of the resulting precipitate can, however, cause problems.

Adsorption of fluoride is particularly suited to low-concentration wastes such as those produced after lime treatments. Hydroxylapatite and alumina have been successfully used in packed beds to reduce fluoride levels to less than 1 mg/l (1 ppm). Ion exchange is also possible but is generally too costly.

Metal Salts in Acid Solution

Most dissolved metals encountered in aqueous waste are in acid solution. The more common metals are:

Aluminium	Mercury
Cadmium	Nickel
Copper	Silver
Iron	Tin
Lead	Zinc
Manganese	

These may exist in solution as salts such as:

Bromide	Nitrate
Chloride	Phosphate
Fluoride	Sulphate

The objectionable constituents are the heavy metals such as those listed above and, to a lesser extent, fluoride, phosphate and sulphate (q.v.). The traditional removal method involves precipitation as insoluble metal hydroxide (or hydrated oxide) by adding a suitable alkali such as caustic soda or lime.

Some typical reactions of metal salts with alkalis are:

Copper sulphate and caustic soda:
$$CuSO_4 + 2NaOH \rightarrow Cu(OH)_2 + Na_2SO_4$$

Nickel chloride and lime:
$$NiCl_2 + CaO + H_2O \rightarrow Ni(OH)_2 + CaCl_2$$

Lead nitrate and soda ash:
$$Pb(NO_3)_2 + Na_2CO_3 \rightarrow PbCO_3 + 2NaNO_3$$

Such reactions are usually very pH-dependent, and there are accepted optimum values for effective reaction and subsequent removal. Unfortunately the optimum pH for a particular metal can be influenced by other metals present, so that the suggested figures in Table 7.11 may need to be adjusted in practice. As a general rule, adjustment to pH 9 will satisfactorily precipitate every metal mentioned above, with the exception of tin where a complex stannate may be formed if caustic soda is employed. Use of lime will overcome this problem.

Reagent requirements need to be individually estimated for each waste, based on analysis of a range of samples. There are too many possible combinations of metal ion, anion, and alkali for a useful reagent requirement

TABLE 7.11 OPTIMUM pH VALUES FOR PRECIPITATION OF METAL HYDROXIDES

Ion	Formula	Optimum pH
Stannic	Sn^{++}	4·0–4·5 (redissolves as pH increases above 7·0)
Aluminium	Al^{+++}	5·0 (redissolves at high pH values)
Plumbic	Pb^{++}	6·0–10·0 (conflicting evidence)
Ferric	Fe^{+++}	7·0
Cuprous	Cu^{+}	7·0–8·0
Chromic	Cr^{+++}	8·0–9·5
Cupric	Cu^{++}	8·5–10·0
Zinc	Zn^{++}	9·0–10·0 (redissolves as pH increases above 11·0)
Cadmium	Cd^{++}	9·5–12·0
Nickel	Ni^{++}	above 10·0
Manganese	Mn^{++}	above 10·0

specification to be tabulated. The requirement may also be complicated when different waste streams are mixed, such as alkaline, treated cyanide waste and acid metal salt. Reaction times are usually rapid, and a nominal 10 or 15 minutes is normally adequate. Equipment is similar to that employed for pH adjustment (q.v.).

The choice of reagent is not easy and depends on:

    capital cost
    operating cost
    efficiency of reaction
    solids separation and disposal cost
    possibility of subsequent metal recovery
    nature of precipitated hydroxide
    composition of effluent.

The usual choice is between caustic soda and lime, as soda ash is difficult to handle and store, evolves carbon dioxide on reaction with acid, and is not usually used unless already available on site.

Caustic soda is more expensive to buy as solid or concentrated liquor, but the effluent plant costs less to install as no solids handling is required. If solid is purchased, dissolution equipment is needed. If concentrated liquor is purchased, heated storage is needed to avoid freezing in winter. The precipitated hydroxides are relatively pure and the solids are not bulked out with unreacted reagent as with lime. A flocculating agent may be necessary with some wastes to aid settlement.

In contrast, lime is cheaper to purchase, particularly in bulk, but requires a more expensive plant for solids handling. The efficiency of reaction is low, and considerable excess can be required if encapsulation occurs. Settlement tends to be more rapid and complete and flocculating agents are rarely required. The high-surface-area particles often tend to adsorb unreacted ions, thus providing a polishing action on the effluent. The solids content of the precipitate can be increased several times over, thus increasing the cost of separation and disposal as well as making metal recovery more difficult. There are various grades of lime, some of which are specially manufactured for effluent treatment.

These points all require careful consideration in choosing an alkali. Generally lime is preferred, particularly for larger plants of throughput greater than $13 \cdot 5$ m³/h (3000 gal/h).

The precipitated metal hydroxide ultimately needs to be separated from the treated effluent. This is usually carried out in two main stages: settlement followed by filtration. Settlement permits the majority of clear treated effluent to be run off leaving all the precipitated hydroxides as a concentrated sludge. Precipitates that are difficult to settle may be aided by adding a flocculant such as an aluminium salt or, more usually, a polyelectrolyte. This is added just before the settling tank stage, using the dosage recommended by the manufacturer. There are no generalisations for usage, except that flocculants are not usually needed with lime neutralisation. While sludge may be directly removed for disposal in the small installations, it is more usually dewatered in a filter press, drum filter, or similar equipment to give a solid cake of up to 75% water and further clear filtrate, which is usually recycled as shown in Figure 7.11 in case of spillage of filter cake when cleaning, or a damaged filter cloth. Smaller plants have conical-bottomed sedimentation tanks with about 5 hours' residence time; larger installations often employ clarifiers. The choice of pressing operation depends on many factors (see pages 200 and 203).

Metal Separation and Recovery

A range of techniques has been applied to remove metals from aqueous solutions, not only in processes to recover metals from waste but also in the wide field of hydrometallurgical processing. Almost every unit operation, unit process or separation method has been examined to determine its relevance to metal recovery, including all the methods listed in Tables 7.1 and 8.1. Only a few have found application in waste treatment and recovery processes, on technical and economic grounds. These include solvent extraction, ion exchange and precipitation, of which the last has already been mentioned. Both solvent extraction and ion exchange are processes for concentration and/or separation of a metal or metals from the solvent (i.e. water), and possibly from other metals.

Solvent extraction is not widely used for small-scale waste treatment because of the high costs involved. The principle is to extract selectively one or more metals from the solution into a suitable organic solvent. The metals are then stripped from the loaded solvent, which is returned to remove more metals. Selectivity is achieved mainly by choice of reagent and pH (Figure 7.12).[1] The principles are outlined on page 225.

Ion exchange is based on a similar principle, except that a solid bed of resin is usually employed to adsorb the metal; the mechanism is more complex in

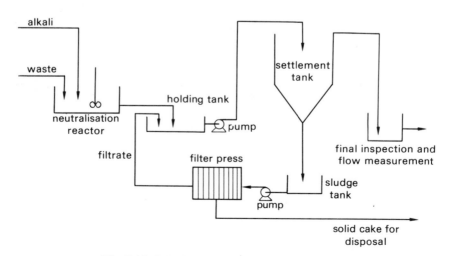

Fig. 7.11 Soluble metal precipitation and removal

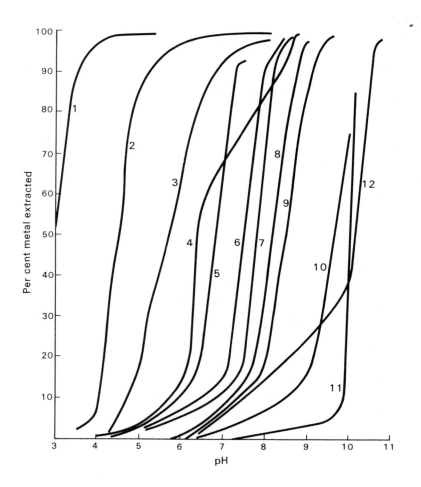

Fig. 7.12 The effect of pH on the extraction of iron, aluminium, zinc, manganese, calcium and magnesium from sulphate solutions by means of naphthenic acid in kerosene[1]

(1) 0·05 M Fe$_2$(SO$_4$)$_3$
(2) 0·05 M Al$_2$(SO$_4$)$_3$
(3) 0·1 M CuSO$_4$
(4) 0·1 M ZnSO$_4$
(5) 0·1 M ZnSO$_4$ + 140 g/1 (NH$_4$)$_2$SO$_4$
(6) 0·1 M NiSO$_4$ + 30 g/1 (NH$_4$)$_2$SO$_4$
(7) 0·1 M CoSO$_4$ + 30 g/1 (NH$_4$)$_2$SO$_4$
(8) 0·1 M FeSO$_4$ + 160 g/1 (NH$_4$)$_2$SO$_4$
(9) 0·1 M MnSO$_4$
(10) 0·1 M MgSO$_4$ + 40 g/1 (NH$_4$)$_2$SO$_4$
(11) 0·1 M MgSO$_4$
(12) 0·1 M CaCl$_2$

that, for every metal cation adsorbed, another cation, usually hydrogen, is released. When the resin is fully loaded, the metal is washed off with strong acid to replace the hydrogen ions and give a concentrated solution. The principle is also applicable to anions and the technique is very suitable for relatively small quantities and the low concentrations of pollutants found in effluents. The resin can be specific or non-specific for total or partial removal of metals.

Cadmium

Most cadmium-bearing effluents may be satisfactorily treated by the cyanide oxidation or hydroxide precipitation processes already described. Precipitation as sulphide has been employed, as well as ion exchange, evaporative recovery and membrane techniques. Recovery could be economically attractive due to the high value of the metal.

Chromium

No treatment methods other than neutralisation or ion exchange are practised for trivalent chromium removal.

Copper

In addition to precipitation of cupric (Cu^{++}) hydroxide by pH adjustment, it is claimed that, if the copper is first reduced to the cuprous form with, for example, hydrazine before precipitation, a more easily settled and handled sludge is obtained. Sulphide is an alternative precipitant, and satisfactory levels of copper in effluent may be achieved at pH 6·5. This method is not widely used outside the mineral and metallurgical industries.

Evaporative recovery has been employed to recycle both copper salts and clean rinsing water. The high cost is often a disadvantage. Ion exchange is also applicable to copper salt recovery.

Copper may be recovered as metal by a variety of methods, particularly by electrolysis, cementation and direct reduction in solution. Electrolytic recovery gives a pure, directly reusable grade of copper, but can only reduce copper down to about 2 g/l (2000 ppm). Fluidised bed electrodes facilitate greater current efficiency and lower ultimate levels but are still not capable of reducing copper to an acceptable level for discharge. Problems can arise with other metals which may co-deposit. Cementation has long been practised to precipitate impure metallic copper from dilute solutions. Iron and steel have been traditionally used and an acceptable effluent copper concentration may readily be achieved. A fixed bed of scrap iron and steel is frequently used, with occasional rousing to knock off cemented copper and expose fresh iron surface. In more sophisticated applications, aluminium has been used to recover copper from spent etchant solution.

Membrane processes, dialysis and reverse osmosis have been successfully used for treating most copper-containing wastes, but the economics are relatively unattractive.

Iron

Iron is one of the less toxic heavy metals and is not usually a problem in effluent treatment. Neutralisation as described above to precipitate hydroxide is usually carried out after oxidation of any ferrous iron to ferric by air oxidation at pH 7.

Pickle liquors resulting from acid treatment of iron and steel to remove oxide scale have attracted considerable attention. Well over 100 different methods have been proposed for treatment, or to recover acid and iron compounds, using most separation methods available (see Further Reading at end of chapter). The traditional pickling acid is sulphuric acid; spent pickle liquor contains up to 10% acid and usually a high concentration of ferrous sulphate. The simplest disposal method is dumping, often by deep well disposal in the USA, although this is not currently practised in the UK. Due to the low cost of sulphuric acid and low value of recovered iron compounds, recovery and recycling processes for waste sulphuric acid pickle liquor have not proved viable.

More recently, however, with the availability of hydrochloric acid in bulk and at relatively low cost, hydrochloric acid pickling has been introduced to the advantage of the iron and steel industry. Spent pickle liquor containing some free acid and a high concentration of ferrous chloride is easily regenerated by hydrolysis of ferrous chloride at elevated temperature, with recycle of both acid and iron oxide, according to the following equation:

$$4\,FeCl_2 + O_2 + 4H_2O \rightarrow 2\,Fe_2O_3 + 8HCl$$

A number of established processes effect this reaction, but tend to be viable only on a large scale. Small-scale proposals need careful evaluation using technical cost–benefit analysis.

Lead

Lead may be precipitated from solutions as hydroxide. It may also be removed by formation of carbonate at pH 8 and 9; by treatment with calcium carbonate, limestone or dolomite; or by formation of insoluble sulphate by addition of a soluble sulphate, e.g. sulphuric acid or sodium sulphate. Precipitation as phosphate above pH 7 is also effective but can give unacceptable levels of phosphate in the effluent.

Lead also arises in suspension, particularly from battery works and battery scrapping areas. It is usually in the form of a suspension of oxide, but some metallic lead is also present. Separation may be readily achieved by settlement, which would precede any other effluent treatment, to give a lead-rich sludge for recycling. A typical residence time of 4 to 5 hours is likely to be sufficient. The resulting sludge is often well compacted and requires digging out or mechanical removal. In larger installations filter pressing is carried out.

Organic lead is usually removed by ion exchange.

Mercury

Precipitative techniques for soluble mercury removal are based on addition of sulphide to form insoluble mercury sulphide. The usual reagent is sodium sulphide under slightly alkaline conditions, when a mercury level of 10–20 μg/1 (0·01–0·02 ppm) is achievable if precipitation is combined with a tertiary polishing stage such as filtration or activated carbon adsorption.

Ion exchange is also practised for mercury removal, mostly on effluents from chloralkali plants which also contain appreciable quantities of chloride. Under these conditions a complex mercuric chloride anion is exchanged after chlorine treatment to oxidise any metallic mercury to chloride. Cation exchange is only satisfactory when chloride levels are low. It is possible to achieve mercury levels down to 2–5 μg/1 (0·002–0·005 ppm).

Coagulation with aluminium sulphate or iron salts has been successfully applied to reduce the mercury content of very dilute waste-water. Dosage is from 50 to 100 mg/1 at neutral pH, when mercury level can be reduced to around 2–3 μg/1.

Carbon adsorption is also effective for further reducing very low concentrations of mercury. Approximately 80% removal or an effluent level of 0·2 μg/1 is achievable.

Several other processes have been employed or proposed, including reduction to metallic mercury for recovery followed by one of the methods described above; solvent extraction; complexation; and adsorption on ground rubber or wool.

Nickel

Precipitative treatment to give hydroxide is a well established method, but if recovery is required the carbonate is preferred using soda ash at pH 7·5 to 8·5. Sulphide precipitation has been used occasionally at an alkaline pH but is not so effective as hydroxide precipitation for reducing nickel levels.

Nickel recovery is attractive in principle because of the high value of the metal. Ion exchange and solvent extraction have been proposed, but only larger plants are likely to be economically viable. Evaporative recovery and reverse osmosis have also been used.

Silver

The main objective of treatment plants for silver-containing wastes is to recover silver rather than prevent pollution. The most common precipitative technique is formation of insoluble silver chloride by adding chloride such as sodium chloride or hydrochloric acid. Separation of silver from mixed wastes is thus relatively easy in acid conditions. Under alkaline conditions when other metal hydroxides are present, these may be dissolved by acidification. Chlorine precipitation will not, however, occur with silver cyanide and the cyanide has to be oxidised first (q.v.). If the oxidant is chlorine-based, the resultant chloride ions will combine with and precipitate the silver. Silver levels down to 1–4 mg/l (1–4 ppm) may be achieved with chloride precipitation under carefully controlled conditions of chloride concentration. Sulphide precipitation has been widely used for reducing soluble silver to very low levels in wastes from the photographic industry. Large-scale application causes problems with solids handling. Other precipitation systems use magnesium sulphate and lime, which is useful for effluents containing high proportions of organic acids; lime and ozone under alkaline pH conditions; and sodium bisulphite, which gives a mixed precipitate of free silver and sulphide.

Ion exchange is also widely used on more dilute waste streams containing silver. Silver recovery is by elution or incineration of resin to give pure silver. Recovery is more difficult with cyanide-bearing wastes.

Cementation is another well established method of precipitating silver from solution. Metallic zinc or iron is used, preferably with a high surface area to give rapid reaction.

Electrolytic recovery is feasible with effluents containing high concentrations of silver, but at low concentrations the efficiency of deposition is considerably reduced and silver levels cannot easily be reduced to less than 200 mg/l (200 ppm).

Zinc

In addition to hydroxide precipitation, sulphide precipitation using sodium sulphide can reduce zinc concentrations to very low levels and is not pH-dependent. Problems can arise in the addition of sulphide to effluent and removal of the zinc sulphide. There is doubt whether this is overall as effective as hydroxide precipitation. The Kastone process for cadmium and zinc cyanide wastes is effective in reducing zinc levels to 1–2 mg/l by precipitation of zinc oxide with hydrogen peroxide and formaldehyde.

Recovery of zinc is not usually a viable proposition because of its relatively low value. The exceptions are large quantities of high-zinc-concentration solutions, as in viscose rayon manufacture, when ion exchange and evaporative recovery may be used. Otherwise ion exchange may be employed as a tertiary treatment or polishing stage. Evaporative recovery in electroplating applications has been reported, but the economics are unlikely to be attractive.

Metal Salts in Alkaline Solution

Relatively few metal compounds that are soluble in alkaline solution arise in waste streams. With metals as cations, the more common are cyanides (of copper, nickel, silver, zinc, cadmium, lead), pyrophosphates (of copper only, usually), and complex ammines (of copper, nickel, cobalt, zinc). Some metals also form complex anions such as zincates, plumbites, aluminates and stannates. Invariably treatment consists of precipitating the metal as an insoluble compound after any other necessary treatment such as cyanide oxidation.

Some individual metals or groups are considered below, but there are some general approaches available for finding a suitable treatment and/or recovery method for metals in alkaline solution. The traditional method of metal removal by insoluble compound formation, with removal by settlement and/or filtration, may be used. A suitable metal compound needs to be identified which is insoluble under the treatment conditions. A suitable reagent must then be found which is effective and cheap, and does not create further pollution problems. Data are available on solubilities of many compounds and reagents (see Further Reading at end of chapter).

An alternative is consideration of the wide range of unit operations which are briefly described in Chapter 8, and which may form the basis of a treatment or recovery method. Similarly, any of the methods for reducing total dissolved solids (q.v.) may be suitable.

Cyanides

Cyanide treatment has already been described. When oxidation is the treatment method, the metal–cyanide bond is destroyed and the metal will usually precipitate as in neutralisation of the relevant acidic metal salt in solution. pH control is important to ensure effective separation, and this is particularly relevant to zinc and lead when soluble anion complexes can be formed at high pH values. If this occurs, double pH adjustment may be needed: acidification to destroy the complex anion such as zincate, followed by alkali addition to the correct pH for zinc hydroxide precipitation. For reasons such as these, together with consideration of economics and the desirability of metal recovery, electrolytic processes may be a realistic alternative, particularly for zinc and nickel. The cyanide is oxidised at the anode and the metal recovered at the cathode. For zinc and cadmium cyanides the hydrogen peroxide system (Kastone) both oxidises the cyanide and precipitates zinc or cadmium oxide. Evaporation for recycling is feasible but is not widely used.

Complex Anions

The more common metal-bearing complex anions are those of zinc as zincate, lead as plumbite, tin as stannate, and alumina as aluminate. The chemistry of the last two compounds is utilised in the purification and recovery of the respective metals. Although these compounds do not occur frequently, their formation can lead to problems in traditional neutralisation and precipitation of metals as hydroxides. If pH control is poor, excessive addition of caustic soda can redissolve these precipitated metals as complex anions, leading to unacceptably high metal content in the final effluent.

The lead in plumbites may be effectively removed by adding sulphuric acid when the anion complex is destroyed and insoluble lead sulphate precipitated. pH adjustment to 8 or 9 with lime and a coagulating agent such as ferrous sulphate is claimed to precipitate lead effectively. Zincates may be removed by pH adjustment to 8 to 9, or acidification to below pH 7 followed by treatment for metal salts in acid solution (q.v.). Aluminates are not usually a problem in effluents as constraints are rarely imposed on aluminium levels. However, if aluminium hydroxide is formed the gelatinous nature of the precipitate may hinder effective settlement of other precipitates.

Stannates tend to be formed under only slightly alkaline conditions and there is perhaps the greatest risk with tin in redissolving precipitated tin hydroxide. Stannate may be hydrolysed by acidification to precipitate stannic hydroxide around pH 5.

Pyrophosphates

Only copper pyrophosphate is widely used, as a substitute for copper cyanide in plating baths. Lime treatment to pH 12 will precipitate calcium pyrophosphate and allow simultaneous co-precipitation of copper hydroxide (see pH adjustment), and although this is a satisfactory method of treatment, considerable excess of lime is required. Conventional pH adjustment will not work, as the solution is already alkaline. An alternative approach is acid hydrolysis of the pyrophosphate to break the complex, followed by conventional pH adjustment to precipitate copper. Treatment to remove phosphate may also be needed. This hydrolysis might be achieved by mixing of suitable waste streams rather than a special acid addition and mixing operation.

Ammonia Complexes

Complex ammines are encountered mainly as copper compounds from ammoniacal leaching operations such as printed circuit manufacture. Some hydrometallurgical processing operations may also produce a metal ammine such as copper, nickel or cobalt. There is also a risk of complex formation if metal-bearing waste streams contact ammonia-bearing waste streams; this must therefore be avoided.

One method of treatment widely practised on cuprammonium complexes from printed-circuit board manufacture is recovery of copper or a copper salt. This is a viable process and there is considerable competition for supplies of this valuable source of copper. Details of the processes are confidential; one involves cementation with aluminium powder to precipitate copper metal. An alum (aluminium ammonium complex) is formed which may itself require treatment before discharge. Electrolysis is another alternative, although little is known about this method in relation to cuprammonium complexes. Copper, nickel and cobalt may be precipitated as metals from such solutions with hydrogen under pressure, but this is too costly as a waste treatment method. Ion exchange is also a possibility but there are no known examples of its use.

Mineral Acids

The mineral acids include hydrobromic, hydrochloric, hydrofluoric, nitric and sulphuric acids. Acidic effluents usually contain other substances in addition to one or more of the above acids and treatment needs to account for all the pollutants.

The acidity is usually reduced to the required level by neutralisation with an alkali such as caustic soda or lime, the reagent requirements and equipment specification for which are discussed under pH control. Other treatment such as precipitation of a metal as an insoluble hydroxide may be carried out concurrent with neutralisation.

Under some circumstances, concentration of acid may be advantageous for recycling, for further reaction elsewhere, or for sale. A variety of techniques is available: see, for instance, Evaporation and Ion Exchange (Chapter 8).

Miscible/Soluble Organic Compounds

A large number of organic chemicals are completely or partially miscible in water and, if present in effluents, may require treatment before discharge. Phenol, which is a special case due to its widespread occurrence and very low permitted levels, is considered separately. Examples of other organic chemicals include alcohols such as methanol and ethanol, ketones such as acetone, aldehydes such as formaldehyde and acetaldehyde, and acids such as acetic acid. They can arise from a range of sources including the chemical, food, and processing industries.

A wide range of treatment methods is available; biodegradation (q.v.) is generally satisfactory, with carbon adsorption for trace concentrations. Difficult wastes may require incineration for complete destruction. Recovery may be effected by solvent extraction, air stripping or steam distillation. Generalisation is difficult because of the wide range of compositions and constituents that may be encountered; the nature of the contaminants must be carefully examined in the context of the treatment methods described above and elsewhere in the book.

Non-metallic Elements and their Compounds (not covered elsewhere)

Few materials can be listed under this heading, and little is known about any of them in the context of effluent treatment. Some of the difficulty arises in the complex chemistry of such elements.

Arsenic

A number of treatment processes are available for arsenic, of which the most common are precipitative. Co-precipitation by addition of a polyvalent coagulent such as ferric sulphate, chloride or hydroxide at neutral pH will give up to 98% removal of arsenic down to 0·05 mg/1 (0·05 ppm), or sometimes less. Up to five times the stoichiometric requirement may be needed. The other main treatment process is formation of insoluble sulphide by addition of sodium or hydrogen sulphide at neutral pH. If arsenite is present this must always be oxidised to arsenate, for example with chlorine.

The most effective, but apparently least used, method is precipitation with lime at around pH 12, when over 90% removal of arsenic may be achieved. Ion exchange is a practical alternative and can also give effluents containing 0·05 mg/1 arsenic or less.

Selenium and Tellurium

Very little is known about removal of these materials from wastes. Activated carbon adsorption, cation exchange and co-precipitation with ferric sulphate all give appreciable removal of selenium. Tellurium behaves very similarly.

Oil, Grease, Wax and Immiscible Organics

An aqueous waste containing immiscible organic material is usually referred to generally as 'oily waste'. There are several stages of treatment: the first or primary treatment stage removes the floating or free oils from the water and emulsified oil; the secondary treatment (discussed earlier under Emulsions) breaks the oil–water emulsion and removes the remaining oil.

Primary treatment uses the difference in specific gravity between oils and water to effect separation. Gravity separation is usually employed by holding the oily waste in a tank and skimming the oil from the surface. Careful design of the tank is necessary to allow sufficient time for separation and avoid any possibility of remixing. The retention or residence time of the holding tank is a function of the oils concerned, in particular their specific gravity, and the degree of separation required. The closer the specific gravity of oil to that of water, the longer the time required for separation. The efficiency or degree of separation tends to be a characteristic of the particular system. Up to 99% separation may be readily achieved with the right design.

The most common oil/water separators are the API separator and the parallel plate interceptor (PPI). The API separator provides for a slow-flowing section of effluent within which oil droplets can rise to the surface for removal by skimming; suspended solids which collect as a sludge at the bottom of the separator can be removed continuously. In the parallel plate interceptor there is a series of longitudinally aligned, inclined plates which allow oil droplets to collect on their underside, coalesce and rise to the surface. In a more recent plate interceptor, the corrugated plate interceptor (CPI), corrugated plates are positioned transversely in the effluent flow.

The PPI is claimed to give 50% better separation than the API separator, but this is not confirmed by other comparative data; the CPI is claimed to give effluents with oil contents less than 20 ppm. The compact design of the API and CPI separators makes it practicable to enclose them, thus minimising odour problems. Such plate separators do not cope with shock oil loadings and they suffer from blockage by waxy deposits. Solutions include the use of an API separator, or an equalisation or surge tank, upstream of the PPI separators. The skimmed oil layer contains a substantial proportion of water and sometimes emulsions, and may be pumped to recovered oil tanks or treated by 'emulsion-breaking'.

The secondary treatment for emulsions described earlier also yields a free-oil-in-water system which may be separated in a similar way. The final waste-water will probably require tertiary treatment, usually biological degradation, or perhaps carbon adsorption.

The separated oil may be recycled, burnt for its heat content, incinerated if it is a difficult waste, or dumped.

There are several ways of handling special wastes where the oil is relatively valuable and/or easily recoverable, and these include solvent extraction into an immiscible solvent, steam distillation, and air stripping of more volatile compounds. It is always worth considering whether recovery or reuse is technically and economically viable.

Organometallics

There are few organometallic compounds that are stable and likely to be found in aqueous effluents. Only tetraethyl lead and mercury compounds such as methyl mercury acetate are known to occur in waste, and methods of treatment are restricted to ion exchange on specific resins. This is a specialised area in which relatively little is known.

A further group of compounds which require special attention are the carbonyls of nickel, iron and cobalt. These are highly toxic and volatile, but their occurrence is rare.

pH Adjustment/Neutralisation

The most widely used form of pH adjustment is neutralisation to remove the undesirable properties of acid or alkaline solutions, but there are many other applications in processes that are pH-dependent. Examples include solvent extraction of metals, biodegradation, chrome reduction and cyanide oxidation (q.v.).

pH, the measure of acidity or alkalinity, is defined in a range from -2 to 15, having a value of 7 for pure water or a neutral solution. It is defined as the negative logarithm to the base 10, $(\log_{10})$, of the hydrogen ion (H^+) concentration in g.ions/l. For example:

(a) For pure water the hydrogen ion concentration is 10^{-7} g.ions/l:

$$\log_{10}(10^{-7}) = -7$$
$$-\log_{10}(10^{-7}) = -(-7) = 7 = pH$$

(b) For hydrochloric acid, the hydrogen ion concentration is found by considering the ionic dissociation of the acid:

$$HCl \rightleftharpoons H^+ + Cl^-$$

1 g.mole HCl gives 1 g.ion H^+ and 1 g.ion Cl^-; or, by molecular weights, $36 \cdot 5$ g HCl gives 1 g.ion H^+ and $35 \cdot 5$ g.ion Cl^-.

Thus $9 \cdot 125$ g/l HCl gives a hydrogen ion concentration of $0 \cdot 25$ g.ions/l and a pH of $-\log_{10}(0 \cdot 25) = 0 \cdot 60$.

(c) For divalent acids such as sulphuric acid, H_2SO_4, each g.mole of acid gives 2 g.ions H^+:

$$H_2SO_4 \rightleftharpoons 2H^+ + SO_4$$

Thus $24 \cdot 5$ g/l H_2SO_4 gives a hydrogen ion concentration of $0 \cdot 5$ g.ions/l and a pH of $-\log(0 \cdot 5) = 0 \cdot 30$, and $9 \cdot 125$ g/l H_2SO_4 gives a hydrogen ion concentration of

$$\frac{9 \cdot 125}{98} \times 2 = 0 \cdot 186 \text{ g.ions/l}$$

and a pH of $-\log(0 \cdot 186) = 0 \cdot 73$.

(d) For alkalis such as caustic soda, NaOH, this dissociates:

$$NaOH \rightleftharpoons Na^+ + OH^-$$

1 g.mole 1 g.ion 1g.ion

and by molecular weights:

40 g   23 g   17 g

As the product of hydrogen ion (H^+) and hydroxyl ion (OH^-) must always be 10^{-14}, a knowledge of the hydroxyl ion concentration enables the hydrogen ion concentration to be calculated, and hence the pH. Thus 10 g/l NaOH gives $4 \cdot 25$ g/l OH^- ions or $0 \cdot 25$ g.ions/l OH^- ions.

Since concentration of OH^- ions $\times$ concentration of H^+ ions $= 10^{-14}$,

$$\text{concentration of } H^+ \text{ ions} = \frac{10^{-14}}{0.25} \text{ g.ions/l}$$

$$= 4 \times 10^{-14} \text{ g.ions/l}$$

and pH $= 13.4$.

Similarly, 1 g/l NaOH gives rise to a hydrogen ion concentration of $10^{-14}/0.025$ g.ions/l $= 4 \times 10^{-13}$ g.ions/l, and pH $= 12.4$.

There is a much less used equivalent measure for hydroxyl ions known as pOH.

pH adjustment is carried out by adding acid to reduce pH or alkali to raise pH. The concept of neutralisation for aqueous effluents ideally refers to adjustment to pH 7, but in practice means bringing the pH to within the range laid down by the conditions of discharge, usually pH 6 to 12, which allows considerable flexibility.

Table 7.12 lists the more common acids and alkalis employed for pH adjustment and gives the theoretical requirements for neutralisation of each chemical quoted.

The choice of reagent for pH adjustment depends on many factors including:

Other pollutants present
Subsequent operations, such as settlement, filtration, solvent extraction
Consent conditions (see Chapter 4)
Costs of reagent
Efficiency of reaction
Capital cost of equipment for effecting treatment

Apart from dealing with acid or alkali present, pH adjustment may be necessary for other treatment: for instance, if metal is to be precipitated, this will determine the controlling pH and the choice of reagent. Subsequent operations may require an absence of certain ions such as sulphate, when lime will be preferred to precipitate sulphate as insoluble calcium sulphate. This reagent will also be chosen if consent conditions are imposed on sulphate. However, the use of lime creates considerably more solids and hence, if settlement follows pH adjustment, greater solids treatment and disposal costs.

Reagent costs are significant, as generally lime is cheaper than caustic soda but requires a greater capital expenditure. Generally, lime is preferred for larger installations of above about 13.5 m³/h (3000 gal/h). Careful evaluation of the trade-off between higher capital cost and lower operating cost is necessary in choosing a system. Efficiency of reaction may also affect the choice between a solid and a liquid reagent; encapsulation of the solid can occur—for example with lime and suphuric acid, when an impervious layer of insoluble calcium sulphate, formed around the outside of the particle, prevents reaction of some of the lime. Reagent utilisation as low as 20% can result, i.e. the theoretical quantity (and thus cost) of reagent is multiplied by 5.

TABLE 7.12 THEORETICAL ACID AND ALKALI REQUIREMENTS FOR NEUTRALISATION

Molecular weight	Pollutant	NaOH	KOH	CaO	Ca(OH)₂	Na₂CO₃	K₂CO₃	CaCO₃	HCl	HBr	HF	HNO₃	H₂SO₄
		Weight unit requirement to neutralise unit weight of pollutant											
40	NaOH	—	—	—	—	—	—	—	0·913	2·025	0·500	1·575	1·225
56	KOH	—	—	—	—	—	—	—	0·652	1·446	0·357	1·125	0·875
56	CaO	—	—	—	—	—	—	—	1·304	2·893	0·714	2·250	1·750
74	Ca(OH)₂	—	—	—	—	—	—	—	0·986	2·189	0·541	1·703	1·324
106	Na₂CO₃	—	—	—	—	—	—	—	0·689	1·528	0·377	1·189	0·925
138	K₂CO₃	—	—	—	—	—	—	—	0·529	1·174	0·290	0·913	0·710
100	CaCO₃	—	—	—	—	—	—	—	0·730	1·620	0·400	1·260	0·980
36·5	HCl	1·096	1·534	0·767	1·014	1·452	1·890	1·370	—	—	—	—	—
81	HBr	0·494	0·691	0·346	0·457	0·654	0·852	0·617	—	—	—	—	—
20	HF	2·000	2·800	1·400	1·850	2·650	3·450	2·500	—	—	—	—	—
63	HNO₃	0·635	0·889	0·444	0·587	0·841	1·095	0·794	—	—	—	—	—
98	H₂SO₄	0·816	1·143	0·571	0·755	1·082	1·408	1·020	—	—	—	—	—

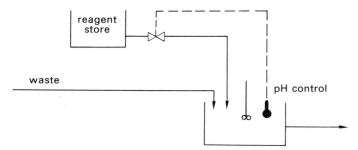

Fig. 7.13 Simple pH adjustment

Equipment requirements are not necessarily sophisticated. A simple tank reactor often suffices, constructed of suitable materials (see page 137) and with pH control on addition of reagent. Figure 7.13 shows equipment for liquid reagents; Figure 7.14, for lime, which is added as a slurry. If concentrated reagents are employed, it is usual to include an intermediate dilution tank, shown as a dotted outline in Figures 7.14 and 15. Fine control of pH is usually carried out in a two-stage process (Figure 7.16). Materials difficult to react, for example where lime is used as the neutralising agent, may be better treated in a multi-stage reactor (Figure 7.17). This is also better for higher throughputs in excess of about 22·5 m³/h (5000 gal/h). 'Tertiary' pH adjustment may be achieved by passing effluent over, or through, a packed bed of limestone. This is useful as a fail-safe device and ensures that the final pH will not fall too low.

Liquid reagents such as caustic soda tend to react quickly and a nominal residence time of 10 minutes is usually sufficient. Solid reagents such as lime may require longer, depending on the reactions occurring; 20 minutes is usually adequate.

There are many possible variations in equipment specification and layout. The comprehensive pH adjustment/neutralisation scheme shown in Figure 7.3 is suitable for all forms of aqueous effluent that can be treated in this way; it provides primary, secondary and, if necessary, tertiary treatment to give discharges to the required standard, with various alternative grades of water for recycling.

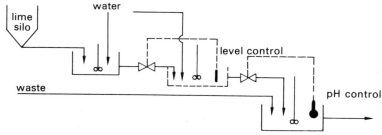

Fig. 7.14 pH adjustment with lime, showing optional additional intermediate reagent dilution

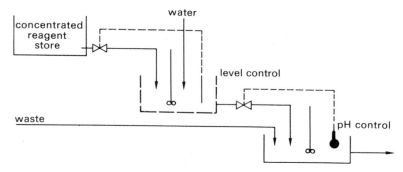

Fig. 7.15 pH adjustment utilising intermediate reagent dilution

Pharmaceuticals

Pharmaceuticals manufacture is a fast-developing industry and one where increasingly stringent health and safety standards are being imposed. Almost all pharmaceutical products are organic and therefore biodegradeable in principle. Biodegradation (q.v.) is one of the main treatment methods for the less noxious waste from this industry. Special problems relate to any potential bactericides in the waste, and the possibility of chemicals passing through the treatment unchanged, only partially treated, or converted to an unacceptable product.

The other main treatment method is incineration, which may be more expensive but does provide total destruction. Careful incinerator design is necessary and effluent gas scrubbing equipment may be needed for removal of hydrogen chloride or sulphur dioxide.

Phenols

Phenol is a particularly noxious organic chemical on account of its low taste-threshold and ready reaction with chlorine to produce an even more unacceptable taste (see page 187). Specification of phenol levels in drinking water are thus severe, and may be as low as 0·01 mg/l(0·01 ppm). A wide variety of processes is

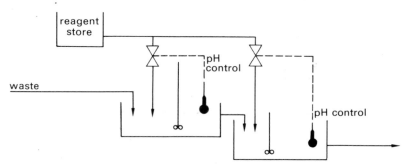

Fig. 7.16 Two-stage pH adjustment giving coarse and fine control

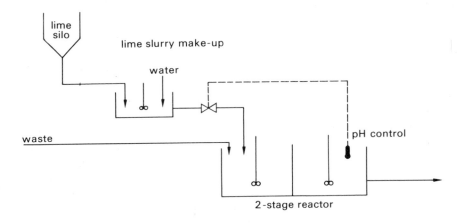

Fig. 7.17 pH adjustment with multi-stage reaction

available to remove or destroy phenol and the range of phenol-like compounds. Generally, recovery is practised in high-concentration wastes of above about 500 ml/l phenol, as this is usually the cheapest treatment method; destruction of phenol is carried out on effluents from such recovery processes and any other wastes of less than around 500 mg/l (500 ppm).

Recovery Processes
Solvent extraction is an attractive method of recovering phenol by absorption in benzene, cumene or similar solvent. The phenol is stripped out with concentrated caustic soda as sodium phenolate. Phenol may be reduced to less than 50 mg/l by this method with up to 99% recovery of phenol. One of the disadvantages, however, is that the solvent may constitute a further pollutant in the effluent.

Steam stripping is applicable to phenol recovery, using counter-current contacting of steam and waste either in a packed tower or, more simply, in a batch still. Phenol content may be reduced to levels comparable to those obtained with solvent extraction. Energy costs are, however, high.

Activated carbon adsorption has also successfully been employed for phenol recovery. Up to 85% recovery has been obtained. The carbon is regenerated by benzene washing (to remove phenol) and steam reactivation. The process suffers from not being continuous and the carbon is easily contaminated beyond use by tars and tar acids.

High-phenol-content wastes with high levels of organic-based contamination may be incinerated, with heat recovery. This may be regarded as reuse rather than recovery.

Destruction Processes

Low concentrations of phenol arising either from recovery processes or elsewhere may be treated in a variety of ways to destroy the phenol, usually by oxidation.

Biological oxidation in a conventional biodegradation process is a proven method of treating wastes containing 50–500 mg/l (50–500 ppm). Greater than 99% reduction in phenol level is attainable, giving effluent concentrations down to 1 mg/l (1 ppm) phenol.

Chemical oxidation of phenol may be carried out with chlorine, chlorine dioxide or ozone. Chlorination with chlorine is not easy, as very high concentrations of chlorine are required to avoid formation of toxic chlorinated byproducts such as chlorphenols, and the reaction is relatively slow. pH and temperature also affect the efficiency of the process, but there is some uncertainty as to optimum pH.

More effective chlorination is achieved with chlorine dioxide, which gives faster reactions and is less sensitive to pH and temperature. Ozonolysis is probably the most effective oxidation process for phenol: complete oxidation is achieved, with no unpleasant byproducts, and the reaction is fast and relatively pH-independent, although a pH of around 12 reduces ozone requirements. The economics, however, may be unfavourable.

All these oxidation processes are capable of reducing phenol down to 0·01 mg/l and may thus be regarded as polishing methods, suitable to follow biodegradation. They are also capable of handling wastes with up to around 500 mg/l phenol and reducing them to acceptable levels at very high conversion efficiencies.

Activated carbon adsorption can efficiently handle any wastes containing up to 500 mg/l phenol, reducing the effluent to around 0·01 mg/l. Multi-stage operation may be necessary if a high inlet concentration has to be reduced to this level.

Phosphorus

Increasing attention is being paid to phosphorus removal as a result of existing and potential problems of over-fertilisation and eutrophication. Precipitative techniques employ salts of aluminium and iron to form insoluble phosphates at around pH 7. Lime is also effective by formation of insoluble calcium hydroxyphosphate. The chemistry of phosphorus is complex and both the formation of precipitates and phosphate ion adsorption contribute to phosphorus removal. Up to 80% or 90% removal of phosphorus may be achieved using simple equipment as described, for example, under pH Adjustment above. Residence times of 10 to 15 minutes are usually adequate, with up to 30% excess of reagents.

Any of the techniques for reducing total dissolved solids (q.v.) are also applicable to phosphate removal.

Sulphate

Some Consents to Discharge impose an upper limit on the sulphate content of effluent, usually because of possible sulphate attack on cements. The most significant source of sulphate is sulphuric acid; if caustic is employed for neutralisation the sulphate level is not affected, as sodium sulphate is soluble.

Treatment with lime is preferred, whereby insoluble calcium sulphate is precipitated. While this effectively controls the sulphate level, the resulting increased solids add to the cost of equipment and disposal. For reduction of total dissolved solids content of water, see page 189.

Suspended Solids

Many treatment methods produce an insoluble precipitate, usually as a very dilute suspension. The more common methods of removing solids are described in Chapter 8. The choice of solids separation system depends on many factors, including:

concentration of solid
density difference between solid and solution
particle size
quantity of suspension
nature of particles in suspension (e.g. electrical and physical characteristics)
economics

The usual method of handling the dilute suspension is by gravity settlement initially, to give a sludge of perhaps up to 5% solids content. This may then be dewatered using one of the filtration devices described later.

There are various types of gravity settling tank. For very small treatment plants a simple tank with a sloping bottom and drain valve is often quite effective. However, a cylindrical conical-bottomed tank is typically employed for flow rates up to about 68 m³/h (15 000 gal/h). As flow rate increases, the method of introduction and distribution of suspension becomes more critical with regard to disturbance of the settling floc. A flocculating agent may be added, before the settling tank stage, to suspensions that are reluctant to settle. A range of proprietary polyelectrolytes is available. With large throughputs, clarifiers are often employed. There are various proprietary designs, which tend to be custom-built and thus adapted to the specific waste involved. Multi-stage gravity settlement, using different designs and specifications for each stage, may give the best results.

The concentrated sludge may be either disposed of directly (which is not usually economical) or dewatered to produce a solid cake of up to 60% or, exceptionally, 70% solids. The usual method is by filter press or rotary filter but, again, a range of proprietary equipment is available, including, for example, belt presses and disc filters. Centrifuges tend to be used only for special applications as a solid cake is difficult to produce, so that the water content of the resulting solids is often unacceptably high.

Total Dissolved Solids

The total dissolved solids content of natural waters includes carbonates, bicarbonates, chlorides, sulphates, phosphates, and nitrates of calcium, sodium and potassium, together with traces of many other elements. Considerable research has been devoted to finding the most economical method of desalination, i.e. of producing potable water from water containing unacceptable levels of these minerals.

The main methods of desalination—distillation, evaporation, ion exchange, reverse osmosis, electrodialysis and freezing—are all applicable to waste treatment, although not generally used; individual viable applications have been found and are described above. Desalination is particularly applicable to integrated waste treatment systems with total recycle of chemicals and water—a concept admired in principle but little practised.

Design Examples

Two case studies illustrate the principles of design and their application to real problems.

Plant 1 Treatment of Effluent from Processing and Dehydration of Potatoes

Effluent from the processing and dehydration of potatoes is first screened to remove gross solids and skins. It is then settled to remove solids, adjusted for pH and treated biologically in two series-operated 'Flocor' filters each filled with 1080 m³ 'Flocor' E plastics filter media. This treatment removes 93% of the BOD load before treatment in an activated sludge plant to produce an effluent of high quality which, after sand filtration and chlorination, is reused in the factory.

The solids from primary sedimentation are dewatered by a centrifuge and those removed from subsequent stages of the process are collected, thickened, conditioned and dewatered on a rotary vacuum filter. An ancillary plant removes grit from the transport water which is then returned to the fluming system. The plant treats up to 2720 m³ of effluent daily.

A flowsheet of the plant is shown in Figure 7.18 and the design details of individual items of plant are shown in Table 7.13.

TABLE 7.13 PLANT 1: SUMMARY OF PLANT AND DESIGN BASIS

1. *Flow*	109 m³/h (24 000 gal/h)
	2610 m³/d (576 000 gal/d)
2. *Composition*	
Suspended solids (crude)	3000 mg/l
BOD (settled)	1000 mg/l
pH	11
Feed to biotowers diluted with Stage 2	
effluent to give feedstock of:	750 mg/l

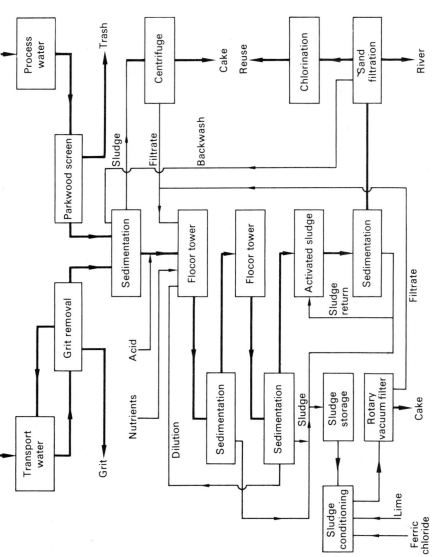

Fig. 7.18 Treatment plant for effluent from potato-processing

Table 7.13 (*continued*)

3. *Design load to biotowers*
   BOD   2778 kg/d (6120 lb/d)

4. *Biotowers*
   2, in series operation, of identical capacity:
   dimensions $12 \times 12 \times 7 \cdot 3$ m ($40 \times 40 \times 24$ ft)
   packed height, 3 lifts each $2 \cdot 44$ m (8 ft)
   'Flocor' total volume   2150 m³ (76 000 ft³)
   circulation   228 m³/h (50 000 gal/h)
   design loading: Stage 1, BOD $2 \cdot 65$ kg/m³ d ($0 \cdot 16$ lb/ft³ d)
                   Stage 2, BOD $1 \cdot 3$ kg/m³ d ($0 \cdot 08$ lb/ft³ d)
   Expected effluent quality, BOD   120 mg/l
   Overall purification efficiency in
     biotower stage   85%

5. *Activated sludge plant*
   Maximum design load, BOD   363 kg/d (800 lb/d)
   Uniformly mixed system of 2 tanks
     capable of series or parallel operation:
   dimensions $9 \cdot 4 \times 9 \cdot 4 \times 3 \cdot 7$ m ($31 \times 31 \times 12$ ft)
   aeration by surface aerators, each $7 \cdot 45$ kW (10 h.p.)
   total capacity   637 m³ (140 000 gal)
   period loading, BOD $0 \cdot 57$ kg/m³ ($5 \cdot 7$ lb/1000 ft³)
   maximum level of solids   2500–4000 mg/l
   sludge recycle $\leqslant 100\%$
   Expected effluent quality
     BOD   15 mg/l
     suspended solids   30 mg/l

6. *Sedimentation tanks*
   Circular tanks
   dimensions: diameter $10 \cdot 3$ m (34 ft)
               sidewall $2 \cdot 75$ m (9 ft)
   surface area   99 m² (910 ft²)
   flow velocity:
     primary settlement u/v $1 \cdot 5$ m/h (5 ft/h)
     biotower settlement u/v $2 \cdot 44$ m/h (8 ft/h)
     activated sludge settlement u/v $1 \cdot 35$ m/h ($4 \cdot 5$ ft/h)
   Sludge removal from primary tank by
     positive displacement pumps and by
     hydrostatic head from others

7. *Solids produced*
   Primary: estimated   4000 kg/d (8750 lb/d)
            at 7% dry solids $56 \cdot 6$ m³/d (12 500 gal/d)
            at 75% moisture $15 \cdot 9$ t/d
   Silt $1 \cdot 53$ t/d
   Biological   1740 kg/d (3580 lb/d)
                                            $1 \cdot 91$ kg/m³ ($0 \cdot 18$ lb/gal d)
   at 4% dry solids after thickening   41 m³/d (9000 gal/d)
   after conditioning, dry solids basis   2272 kg/d (5000 lb/d)
   final sludge at 82% moisture $8 \cdot 3$ t/d

Table 7.13 (*continued*)

Total volume sludge cake for disposal, excluding that in skips in factory	21·5 m³/d (756 ft³/d)

8. *Sludge dewatering*
   Primary: by centrifuge
   Biological: by rotary vacuum filter

face area	11 m² (100 ft²)
conditioning necessary with $FeCl_3$	7 l/m³ (7 gal/1000 gal)
and $Ca(OH)_2$	15 kg/m³ (150 lb/1000 gal)
filtration rate, wet cake	248 kg/m² h (50 lb/ft² h)
operation, daily	8 h

9. *Sand filters*
   4 required

dimensions: diameter	3·05 m (10 ft)
area	7·1 m² (78 ft²)
filter rate	7·5 m³/m² h (150 gal/ft² h)
backwash from elevated storage	20 m³/m² h (400 gal/ft² h)

Plant 2—Treatment of Effluents containing Cyanide and Acid Chrome

Effluents from an electroplating complex consist of a cyanide-bearing stream and an acid chrome stream. The cyanide is oxidised by chlorine gas, and the

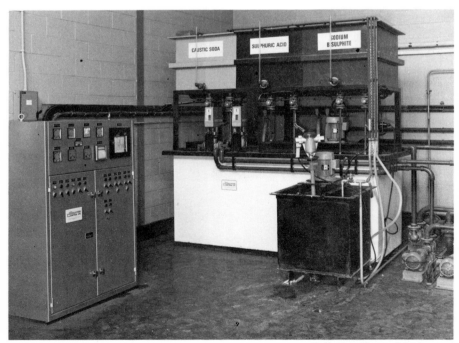

Pollution Control Ltd

Small modular treatment plant for acid chrome effluents, automatically controlled

chrome reduced with sulphur dioxide gas. The two streams meet in the neutralisation tank into which is fed a lime slurry for pH adjustment.

The neutralised effluent is pumped to a settlement tank and the clarified effluent passes through a 20 μm cartridge filter before discharge. The sludge is dewatered in a filter press.

The flow sheet for cyanide oxidation and chrome reduction is given in Figure 7.9 and for pH adjustment in Figures 7.3 and 7.14. Design details of the plant are summarised in Table 7.14.

TABLE 7.14 PLANT 2: SUMMARY OF PLANT AND DESIGN BASIS

1. *Total flow*	22·7 m³/h (5000 gal/h)
2. *Composition*	
2 streams, continuous flow plus concentrates	24 h/d
Stream A, chrome acid, acid bearing	13·5 m³/h (3000 gal/h)
chrome (as CrO_3)	150 ppm
sulphuric acid	300 ppm
hydrochloric acid	50 ppm
iron	100 ppm
nickel	40 ppm
copper	20 ppm
zinc	10 ppm
pH	2·8
temperature	ambient
Stream B, alkaline cyanide	9 m³/h (2000 gal/h)
cyanide (as CN)	120 ppm
alkalinity (as HCO_3)	90 ppm
copper	50 ppm
zinc	50 ppm
oils and greases	30 ppm
pH	10·4
Concentrates	⩽4·5 m³/d (1000 gal/d)
mixed acids (HCl, HNO_3, H_2SO_4), 10–58%	2·27 m³/d (500 gal/d)
alkaline cleaners ($NaOH, NaHCO_3$) plus oils, greases, phosphates, cyanides, gluconates, polyphosphates	2·27 m³/d (500 gal/d)
3. *Equipment*	
(a) Collection system	
The two segregated streams are collected into two collection pits and transferred by pumps	
Stream A, acid chrome	
2 polypropylene/PVC centrifugal sump pumps (@ 6 m (20 ft) TMH)	13·5 m³/h (3000 gal/h)
Stream B, alkaline cyanide	
2 cast iron centrifugal sump pumps (@ 6 m (20 ft) TMH)	9 m³/h (2000 gal/h)
Concentrates: collected locally and slowly bled to appropriate reception sumps	

Table 7.14 (continued)

(b) Treatment

(i) Chrome reduction: effected by direct injection
of sulphur dioxide using a co-current injector:
reaction tank: cubic, open-topped, stirred
by high-speed propeller-type mixer, mild
steel ebonite lined construction   1·68 m (5·5 ft)
pH adjustment for optimum reaction by on/off
control dosing of sulphuric acid (20%);
acid storage in PVC-lined steel tank;
dosing via electric solenoid valve;
acid addition   68 l/h (15 gal/h)
acid hold-up   2·25 m³ (500 gal)
treatment tank retention time   20 min
gas injected periodically under on/off
control of pH meter operating on
predetermined set point   18 kg/h (40 lb/h)
mixer, stainless steel, En58J
Gas injection equipment comprises:
SO$_2$ metering sulphonator;
venturi ejector, polypropylene/ebonised
mild steel;
stainless steel centrifugal pump to drive
motive liquid;
Expected output of chrome   <0·5 ppm

(ii) Cyanide oxidation: effected by direct chlorine
injection in a co-current injector:
reaction tank: cubic, open-topped, stirred
by high-speed propeller-type mixer,
constructed of mild steel, ebonite lined   1·68 m (5·5 ft)
pH adjustment for optimum reaction by on/off
control dosing of sodium hydroxide;
dosing via electric solenoid valve;
rate of addition of sodium hydroxide (20%)   1 l/h (0·4 gal/h)
alkali hold-up, mild steel tank   2·25 m³ (500 gal)
treatment tank retention   20 min
gas injection rate, periodically under
on/off control of pH meter operating on
predetermined set point   22·7 kg/h (50 lb/h)
Gas injection equipment comprises:
chlorine metering chlorinator;
venturi ejector in polypropylene/ebonised
mild steel;
cast iron centrifugal pump to drive motive
fluid;
Expected output of cyanide   <0·5 ppm

(iii) Neutralisation: effected by lime addition
to treated cyanide and chrome waste from Stages
(i) and (ii):
reaction tank: cubic,
open-topped, of ebonite lined mild
steel, stirred by high-speed
propeller-type mixer   1·68 m (5·5 ft)

Table 7.14 (*continued*)

retention time	10 min
pH, adjusted by proportional control—if low (normal), lime is added, if high for any reason, sulphuric acid is added	9·8
lime system: lime mixing tank, cubic, open-topped, with propeller mixer, fed from storage hopper by screw conveyor with linked control to water addition	4·5 m³ (1000 gal)
slurry pumped to feeder box for dosing or recycling;	
final pH	9·8

(iv) Transfer: treated effluent is continuously pumped to settlement tank:
pumps: two
cast iron centrifugal under auto

level control	22·5 m³/h (5000 gal/h)
pressure, head	15 m (50 ft)

(c) Settlement and filtration
(i) Settlement:
settling tank, cylindrical, conical-bottomed with flow directed to top of cone;

diameter	4·7 m (15·5 ft)
settling zone height	6 m (20 ft)
overall height	9·2 m (31 ft)
upward flow rate of clarified liquor	1·2 m/h (4 ft/h)
retention time	5 h
sludge solids concentration	5%
sludge production	1·1 m³/h (250 gal/h)

(ii) Filtration of sludge: sludge from settlement is treated batchwise in filter press:
sludge feed pump, air-operated, diaphragm type;
filter press:

no. of chambers	35
square cross-section	790 mm²
thickness of cake	25 mm
polypropylene filter cloth;	

press discharges from its platform into skip beneath;
filtrate discharged to transfer

((b)(iv) above), initial flow rate	9 m³/h (2000 gal/h)
reducing to	0·45 m³/h (100 gal/h)

(iii) Filtration of clarified effluent: clarified effluent from settlement stage ((c)(i) above) is polished in cartridge filters:

pumps: 2 cast iron centrifugal	22·5 m²/h (5000 gal/h)
head delivery pressure	30 m (100 ft)

filters: 2, 20 μm disposable cartridge filters of 9 elements, with autochange over valve;

effluent content of metal hydroxides	⩽5 ppm

Table 7.14 (*continued*)

(d) Discharge monitoring
pH measurement and recording;
temperature measurement and recording;
flow rate measurement and recording—flume;
total flow measurement and recording—flume

(e) Failsafe: in the event of failure such as power
loss or chemical reagent loss:
all pumps shut down;
treatment continues if and when power
available, with return of discharge liquor
for retreatment;
primary sumps (3(a) above) need to be large
enough for feed storage and recycle

(f) Controls: all controls are housed in a control
panel with motor starters, indicators, recorders and
alarm system. Remote secondary alarm panel, visual and
audible, provided in works laboratory.

References

1. FLETCHER, A. W. and WILSON, J. C., *Transactions of the Institute of Mining and Metallurgy,* **70,** 355, 1961.

Further Reading

Biological Effluent Treatment

BARTLETT, R. E., *Public Health Engineering—Design in Metric: Waste Water Treatment,* Applied Science, 1971.
CIACCIO, L. L. (Ed.), *Water and Water Pollution Handbook,* Vol. 1, Dekker, 1971.
CLARK, J. W., VIEWSSMAN, W. and HAMMER, M. J., *Water Supply and Water Pollution Control,* International Textbook, 1971.
FURNESS, C. D., *Chemical Engineer,* 282, 102, 1974.
MARSHALL, V. C. (Ed.), *Water Borne Waste,* report of a working party on current practice and future developments in the treatment of domestic sewage and industrial effluents, Institution of Chemical Engineers, 1974.
PORTER, K. E., The use of packed beds in water pollution control, *Cebedeau–Decewa,* **398,** 30–42, January 1977.
SIMPSON, J. R. *Process Biochemistry,* **5**(7), 47, 1970.
Water Pollution Control Engineering, HMSO, 1970.

Non-biological Effluent Treatment

BESSELIEVRE, E. B., *The Treatment of Industrial Wastes,* McGraw-Hill, 1969.
ECKENFELDER, W. W., *Industrial Water Pollution Control,* McGraw-Hill, 1966 (also deals with biological treatment).
Economics of Clean Water, US Department of the Interior, Washington, 1970.
GREEN, J. and SMITH, D. H., *Metal Finishing Journal,* 119, 1968.
PATTERSON, J. W., *Waste Water Treatment Technology,* Ann Arbor Science, 1975.

ROSS, R. D., *Industrial Waste Disposal,* Van Nostrand Reinhold, 1968.
ZOJIC, J. E., *Water Pollution, Disposal and Reuse,* Vols 1 and 2, Dekker, 1971.

Solids Separation

PURCHAS, D. B., *Industrial Filtration of Liquids,* Godwin, 1971.
PURCHAS, D. B., *Chemistry and Industry,* 53, 19 January 1974.
RISBY, R. H., *Chemistry and Industry,* 761, 5 October 1974.

Chemical Engineering Unit Operations

COULSON, J. M. and RICHARDSON, J. F., *Chemical Engineering,* Vols 1 and 2, Pergamon, 1955.
GILLILAND, C. S. and ROBINSON, E. R., *Elements of Fractional Distillation,* McGraw-Hill, 1950.
HOLLAND, F. A. and CHAPMAN, F. S., *Liquid Mixing and Processing in Stirred Tanks,* Reinhold, 1966.
TREYBAL, R. E., *Solvent Extraction,* McGraw-Hill, 1963.
WILLIAMS-GARDNER, A., *Industrial Drying,* Godwin, 1971.

CHAPTER 8

Effluent Treatment Operations

The preceding chapter describes methods of treatment for a range of pollutants. These treatment methods, listed in Table 8.1, are all established chemical engineering unit operations or unit processes. They are well documented in the literature and are only briefly described here with particular reference to effluent treatment applications in order to aid process selection, specification and design.

TABLE 8.1 METHODS FOR REMOVAL OF POLLUTANTS FROM AQUEOUS EFFLUENTS

A Suspended or Immiscible Pollutant

Centrifugation	Flotation
Coagulation or flocculation	Gravity settling
Coalescence	Hydrocyclone
Dewatering	Polishing
Emulsion breaking	Screening
Filtration	

B Dissolved Pollutant

Adsorption	Freezing and thawing
Aeration	Heating
Cementation	Hydrolysis
Chemical precipitation, then as A above	Incineration
Chemical reaction	Ion exchange
Crystallisation, then as A above	Liquid–liquid extraction
Desorption/stripping	Neutralisation
Dialysis and electrodialysis	Oxidation
Distillation	pH adjustment
Drying	Reduction
Electrolysis (electrowinning)	Reverse osmosis
Evaporation	

Methods of Separation of Suspended or Immiscible Pollutants

Centrifugation

Materials of similar density are difficult to separate by gravity settling. Centrifugation considerably enhances any small difference in density by artificially increasing gravitational forces. This is achieved by rotating the effluent at very high speed. Separation by the action of centrifugal force is applicable to solid–liquid and immiscible liquid–liquid mixtures. Liquid may be removed from the rotating basket by a skimmer or via perforations. Some characteristics of centrifuges are summarised in Table 8.2.

One application is in the textile industry for the recovery of wool greases and oil. High quality grease from the better types of wool is refined to provide a source of lanolin. The method has also been used for the removal of fat from bone-rendering operations, dewatering of sewage sludges, recovery of oil from waste liquors and recovery of blood from slaughterhouse wastes.

High initial and running costs preclude its use from many operations where filtration or gravity settling are satisfactory alternatives.

Coagulation or Flocculation

Coagulation is used to facilitate the removal of colloidal particles by subsequent physical treatment, for example gravity settling. Very small particles below 10 μm in size cannot be separated simply by sedimentation because of their very low settling velocities. The stability of these fine suspensions is due to electrostatic forces and it is necessary for these to be neutralised to encourage flocculation into assemblages of small particles which will precipitate more readily.

Coagulants are added to neutralise the charges on the particles which then agglomerate to form a floc with improved settling characteristics. Common coagulants are

Aluminium sulphate	$Al_2(SO_4)_3$
Ferrous sulphate (copperas)	$FeSO_4, 7H_2O$
Sodium aluminate	$NaAlO_2$
Ferric chloride	$FeCl_3$
Water-soluble polyelectrolytes	

Other materials, for example clay, lime or silica, may serve as a coagulant aid with low concentrations of suspended material and to improve floc settling.

The floc mass is spongy and, because of its large surface area, adsorbs dissolved matter from solution; therefore it also assists in the removal of colour, turbidity, organic matter and bacteria from solution.

The selection of a suitable coagulant, the correct dosage, and the optimum pH for treatment depend upon several factors such as the effluent requiring treatment, its temperature and other limitations on discharge and also on the

TABLE 8.2 PERFORMANCE AND CHARACTERISTICS OF SOLID–LIQUID SEPARATORS[1]

Equipment	Solids content* for which effective (weight %)	Particle-size range* (µm)	Cake dryness	Relative performance†		
				Cake washing	Filtrate clarity	Crystal breakage
Centrifuges						
Basket	10–50	2–30 000	V	G	A	G
Conical screen (no scroll)	10–40	60–30 000	G	—	A	G
Disc, manual	0.005–0.08	0.1–100	—	—	G	—
Disc, nozzle	0.1–2	0.1–100	A	—	G	—
Disc, self-cleaning	0.08–1	0.1–100	A	—	G	—
Oscillating	40–70	60–30 000	G-V	A	A	A
Scraper	10–50	2–30 000	V	G	A	A
Pusher	20–80	40–70 000	V	A	A	A
Screen-bowl decanter	9–40	30–30 000	G	A	A	A
Scroll decanter	7–60	1–30 000	A	A	A	—
Scroll screen	30–60	100–20 000	V	A	A	A
Gravity filters						
Drum	0.08–0.8	50–6000	G	—	G	—
Flat bed	0.05–5	1–90 000	—	G	V	—
Rotating screen	0.009–0.1	100–10 000	—	—	G	—
Sand	0.002–0.01	0.1–50	—	—	V	—
Table/pan	5–70	50–80 000	A-G	V	G	V
Travelling screen	0.009–0.1	100–10 000	—	—	G	—
Vibrating screen	0.1–1	30–100 000	A	A	G	—
Compression filter						
Automatic filter press	0.2–40	1–200	G	G	G-V	—
Press pan	10–60	1–200	G	G	G-V	—
Screw	1–70	1–200	G	—	—	—

Pressure filters

Cartridge	0·002–0·02	0·6–50	A	G	G-V	V
Drum	0·7–8	5–200	A-G	G	G-V	V
Edge	0·002–0·1	1–200	A	G	G-V	V
Filter press	0·002–30	1–100	G	G	G-V	V
Leaf, horizontal	0·002–0·06	1–100	A	V	V	V
Leaf, vertical	0·008–0·4	1–110	AG	A	G-V	V
Sand	0·002–0·02	0·2–60	—	—	G-V	—
Strainers	0·002–0·02	4–600	—	—	G	—
Tubular element	0·002–0·1	0·5–100	A	G	G-V	V

Vacuum filters

Band/pan	8–50	20–80 000	A-G	V	G	V
Disc	4–40	1–700	B-A	B	G	V
Drum	5–70	1–600	A	G	G-V	V
Leaf	0·07–2	1–500	A	V	G	V
Precoat-drum	0·01–0·1	0·6–100	—	—	V	—
Suction strainers	0·02–0·09	50–200	—	—	G	—
Table/pan	8–50	20–80 000	A-G	V	G	V
Tubular-element	0·08–2	1–150	B-A	—	G	—

* Approximate values.

† A = average; B = below average; G = good; V = very good

equipment available. Alum (aluminium sulphate) is one of the most commonly used coagulants, because of its availability and low cost. Simple laboratory tests are usually sufficient to determine the optimum dosage of coagulant.

A wide range of proprietary polyelectrolytes is also available, which may be required at concentrations as low as 0·5 ppm. Excessive dosing can lead to flotation of the flocs and dosage rates are therefore critical. These coagulents are also susceptible to mechanical damage and should not be added before a pumping stage.

Addition and dispersion of coagulant either may involve a mixing chamber agitated by a high-speed turbine or may be effected at any source of high turbulence such as constrictions or changes of direction in pipelines. An example is included in Figure 7.1 of an application in inorganic and metal-bearing effluent treatment.

Coalescence

Coalescers are used for the separation of liquid–liquid dispersions, which are classified as primary or secondary depending on the drop size of the dispersed phase. Of particular concern are drops in secondary dispersions, or hazes, which are less than about 100 μm in diameter and consequently are not easily separated by gravitational or buoyancy forces.

Primary dispersions are generally separated by gravity forces alone using a simple settler allowing sufficient residence time. However, slight changes in physical properties such as interfacial tension, viscosity, density difference, temperature or the presence of a third component may greatly influence the coalescence characteristics of a particular liquid–liquid system. The presence of impurities or dirt, even as trace amounts, generally aids coalescence and selected solid particles may also produce a similar effect; however, colloidal silica or clay can stablise oil-in-water dispersions. When an impurity is surface active there is invariably a decrease in the rate of coalescence.

Coalescers are usually employed as an alternative to centrifuges, which are very expensive. Numerous coalescing aids have been used to reduce the overall size of gravity settlers; these generally involve an arrangement of baffles or packings. Impingement baffles, possibly with perforations, may be installed in a settler to reduce agitation due to injection of the dispersion. Alternatively the settler may contain Raschig rings or similar packings, pebbles, ballotini or knitted mesh.[2] The standard separators used for oil are described on page 179.

Secondary hazes or dispersions contain drops from 0·1 μm to about 100 μm, which have negligible settling velocities. They may arise from chemical or petrochemical processes, direct contact heat transfer, fuel handling and similar operations. To facilitate coalescence, the drops may be collected by 'interception' methods, such as flotation (q.v.) and fibrous bed coalescence; by methods that enhance the gravitational forces acting on the drops, such as centrifugation (q.v.), flocculation or by addition of chemicals (q.v.); or occasionally by electrically induced settling.

Fibrous bed coalescers are normally limited in use to oil contents less than 8%, in most cases less than 3%, and to mean drop sizes above 1 μm. The fibrous bed may be in the form of a cartridge with inside to outside flow (Figure 8.1), or as a pipeline insert. The range of materials used and typical performance data are summarised in Table 8.3.[3]

TABLE 8.3 PERFORMANCE OF PACKINGS USED IN SECONDARY DISPERSION COALESCENCE

Packing type	Bed thickness (mm)	Max. operating velocity (mm/s)	Pressure drop (bar)
Reticulated ceramic	15	10	0·25
Cotton/glass fibre (cartridge)	50	4·5	0·75
Glass fibre (compressed)	2	20	1·5
Carbon/metal	152	5	0·05
Glass fibre	40	20	0·8
Glass fibre (woven)	3·5	5	0·25
Glass fibre mats	3	15	0·06
Stainless steel meshes	2·5	25	0·08
Fibre diameters	3–35 μm		
Voidages	0·4–0·95		
Phase ratio	0·07–7% v/v		

Dewatering

This is generic expression for any technique that reduces the water content of a liquid–solid system. It commonly implies filtration (q.v.).

Emulsion Breaking

The characteristics of emulsions, their breakdown and subsequent separation are described in Chapter 7. Depending on the nature of the emulsion, coagulation and coalescence principles may also be relevant. To find the best treatment system and optimise the process conditions, it is necessary to experiment with samples of the effluent.

Filtration

Filtration is the removal of particulate solids from a suspension by causing it to flow through a porous medium which retains the solids. (This is a physical separation process and excludes filters in which biological oxidation is carried out.) The suspension may flow under gravity, for example by percolation through a particulate bed, or be pumped under pressure. Filter media, which serve to support the filter cake acting as the filter, may comprise porous solids, granular materials, perforated sheets or woven sheets.

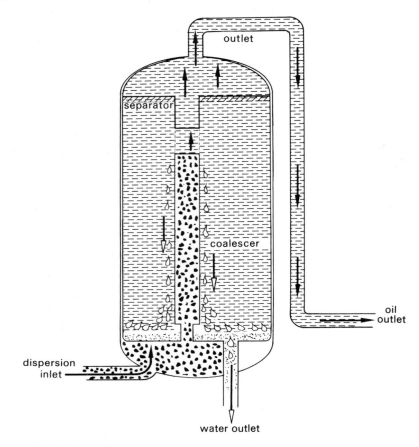

Fig. 8.1 Cartridge coalescer for secondary dispersions—vertical arrangement

A distinction is possible between (a) polishing (q.v.) and clarification, in which very small amounts of solid particles are removed from large volumes of liquid, and (b) cake filtration, involving the recovery of large amounts of solid from reasonably concentrated slurries. In clarification, using for example a sand filter bed, solid particles are deposited throughout part of the bed. Conversely, in cake filtration a thick layer of cake is formed on top of the filter medium.

Pretreatment may be important and may involve, for example, chemical dosing, heating, a freeze/thaw process, or prethickening[4] or precoating of the filter medium.

The filter press is one of the commonest pressure filters and there are numerous designs available. It tends to be restricted to batch operation because of the need for intermittent cake discharge, although semi-continuous operation is possible. As high filtration pressures up to 1830 kN/m^2 (250 psi) can be used, it is applicable to high-resistance filter cakes. However, labour costs can

Fully mechanised filter press with blow-out protection by interlocking guards, suitable for sewage or industrial effluent treatment

Johnson-Progress Ltd

be high and it is generally used when the solids content of the feed is low, or if the cake is of high value.

The vacuum drum filter, or rotary vacuum filter, is an alternative for cake filtration of effluents. This equipment, one arrangement of which is shown in Figure 8.2, comprises a revolving segmented drum covered with filter cloth to which a vacuum of 80–90 kN/m^2 (12 psi) is applied. As the cloth is submerged in slurry a layer of 3–6 mm of sludge is typically allowed to build up. This filter cake is dewatered as the drum revolves and a slight air pressure is subsequently applied to lift the filter cloth and assist cake discharge. The cake is generally removed by an adjustable doctor blade but, for cakes which are difficult to remove, a series of closely spaced strings may be used; the cake becomes embedded in these strings and is released as they pass over rollers at the discharge point. If the filter cake is of value, washing may be incorporated. The drum filter has the advantage of continuous and automatic operation with a minimum of attention. Yields of between 240 and 2400 kg dry solids per m^2 are achievable at a solids content of approximately 25%.

A selection chart in which the relative performance of a range of pressure filters and vacuum filters is compared, and including centrifugal separators mentioned earlier, is reproduced as Table 8.2, page 200. Rotary vacuum filters, belt presses or filter presses are also widely used for dewatering of sludges produced by biological treatment processes.[5]

Paxman Process Plant Division

Paxman rotary vacuum filter, 32·5 m^2 (350 ft^2), fitted with string discharge, operating on effluent sludge from one of the main UK paper mills

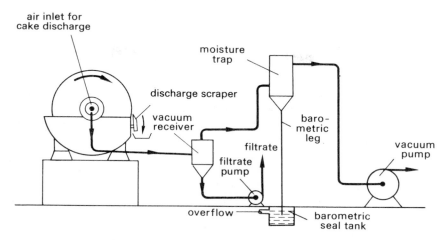

Fig. 8.2 Vacuum drum filter with scraper discharge

Flotation

In air flotation, suspended solid particles or droplets of an immiscible liquid, such as oil, are carried to the surface of the effluent by the action of minute air bubbles. Air is usually dissolved under pressure in the liquid stream to be treated, and when the pressure is reduced the air is released from the super-saturated liquid as extremely small bubbles of about 10–100 μm in diameter. These bubbles collide with, and adhere to, suspended solid or oil particles and, by reducing the particles' apparent density, accelerate their rise velocities. Chemicals may be added to enhance the adherence of gas bubbles, as in mineral benefication. The floating scum or oil formed on the surface is removed by skimming and the clear subnatant liquid is withdrawn from the bottom of the flotation tank.[6] An alternative method of operation is direct injection of bubbles into the tank, but this is usually less effective.

There are three main techniques for air supersaturation of the liquid. In 'direct aeration' the whole of the waste stream is pressurised and hence aerated. Generally, therefore, the separable material must withstand the shear in the pressure pump and release valve or, alternatively, the floc must reform rapidly after pressure release. In one design, however, the waste-water flows down a shaft at the bottom of which air is injected; it then flows up into a flotation tank, bubbles being released as the hydrostatic pressure gradually reduces in the shaft.[7] In partial aeration, which is applicable when the particulates load is small, only part of the effluent stream is pressurised before being fed into the flotation tank; the main stream may be fed in via a flocculant addition tank. With 'effluent recirculation' a side stream of clarified effluent is aerated and cir-culated back to the flotation tank (Figure 8.3). This is used especially when coagulant or flocculant addition (q.v.) is required or the application of shear to the untreated effluent is undesirable.

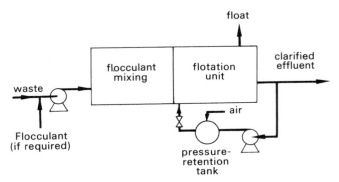

Fig. 8.3 Air flotation using effluent recirculation

Although air flotation is effective for most solids separation applications, if the concentration is less than about 1% it may not be economic compared with other methods because of high energy costs. A major use is in the treatment of oily wastes: for example, in the treatment of oil refinery plant effluents, flocculation followed by air flotation can reduce the oil content to about 15 ppm. Precipitated protein flocculate plus fatty particles have been separated as a sludge with a solids content of 5% to 15% using air flotation. Algae have also been removed by flotation after the addition of aluminium sulphate to effluent in an integrated water reclamation plant. Wastes from potato processing, meat products factories and fruit canneries have also been freed of solids using air flotation; separation is more difficult if there is a high proportion of dense particles such as soil in the stream to be treated.

Electrofiltration, a variation in which bubbles of oxygen and hydrogen are produced from electrode grids in the bottom of a flotation tank using electrolysis, has been used to reduce lead and pigment levels in wash liquor from flexographic ink printing units, to reduce the fat and grease content of effluent from meat preparation and packing, and to treat the effluent from road tanker washings.[7] However, this is a costly process to operate, has some inherent explosion hazard and is not widely used.

Gravity Settling

The separation of solid particles from a suspension by gravity settling is usually termed sedimentation; it may also be referred to as thickening or clarification, when the solids content is relatively high or low respectively. It is applied to the removal of particles of all materials generally in continuous flow but there are practical limitations to minimum particle size below which the settling velocity is too low.[8]

The sedimentation tank is designed to hold the effluent for a sufficient residence time under quiescent or controlled low-velocity flow conditions for the particles to settle to the bottom.

British Steel Corporation (Llanwern Works, Newport)
Large clarifier to recycle water from steel-making fume scrubbing

The settling velocity of discrete particles in a continuum of lower density can be predicted from simple equations depending on whether conditions are laminar or turbulent.[9] However, these equations are not applicable to particles which agglomerate during settling, and hence attain an increased velocity, nor to the hindered settling of concentrated suspensions, when the apparent settling velocity is reduced by upward displacement of liquid. Both flocculant suspensions, for example metal hydroxides, and concentrated suspensions are common industrial effluent treatment problems.

In practice, sedimentation tanks often perform a dual role by both removing solid particles above a characteristic size and thickening the settled sludge, but multi-stage operation is common with high throughputs. Some typical tank arrangements are illustrated in Figure 8.4. The vertical-flow hopper bottom design shown in Figure 8.4a may be operated in water treatment plants with a sludge blanket (Figure 8.4b). This blanket acts as a 'strainer' to remove small particles which would not normally sediment out. Sludge is discharged from the bottom under the hydrostatic head. In the horizontal-flow tank it is necessary for sludge to be collected in the sump by a travelling scraper (Figure 8.4c) or by a continuous conveyor. This is often used to collect grit and sand in sewage treatment. The radial-flow circular tank (Figure 8.4d) provides an increased effluent weir length per unit volume and is simple to construct because the scraper is rotary. This type of tank is generally preferred for large treatment plants with throughputs in excess of 227 m³/h (50 000 gal/h).

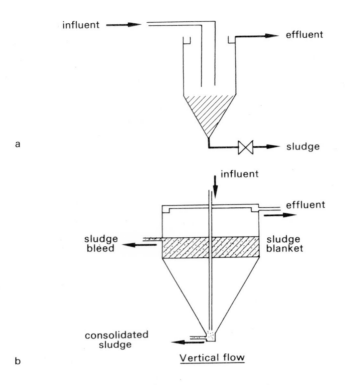

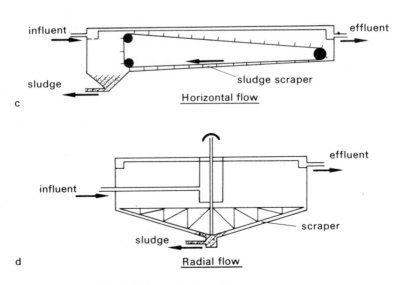

Fig. 8.4 Sedimentation tank arrangements

Hydrocyclone

The hydrocyclone is based on similar principles to the cyclone except that an aqueous rather than gaseous medium is employed. The principle is similar to that of centrifugation except that the energy is supplied to the effluent before it is spun. The liquid stream is fed at high velocity tangentially into a conical-bottomed tank. Particles are spun to the edge of the tank and settle out, while clear effluent leaves via a central dip tube from the top of the hydrocyclone. This method may also be used to classify material by size. Careful design is needed for effective separation which is usually only possible where particle sizes are well defined. This operation is not widely used.

Polishing

Polishing is sometimes necessary to produce an effluent that is particularly free of suspended or dissolved material, for example for discharge directly to a river or for water recycle. If primary and secondary treatment is unable to meet the necessary standards or the requirements are sufficiently stringent, a tertiary treatment or polishing stage is added. It may consist of a filtration unit to remove suspended particles and/or an adsorbent unit to remove dissolved material.

Polishing filtration traditionally consists of a sand filter similar to that employed for potable water treatment. Two units are normally used, one being cleaned by backwash while the other is in operation. Conventional filters (q.v.) may also be employed, although the high initial cost is often a deterrent. Relatively small-scale operations may use disposable cartridge filters. These are popular up to around 45 m³/h (10 000 gal/h) throughput and are typically used on electroplating effluent treatment systems. Suspended solids level may readily be reduced to below 1 ppm.

For dissolved materials, carbon adsorption is an effective and relatively cheap method, particularly for organic materials and heavy metals. Ion exchange is effective on low concentrations of inorganic substances such as chloride, sulphate, and on metals. Total removal of dissolved materials requires a two-stage process of cation and anion exchange (q.v.). Dissolved solids concentrations down to below 1 ppm are not difficult to attain.

Screening

Screening is an operation for the separation of relatively large suspended solids from liquids. The liquid flows under gravity through a filtering medium which has a pore size too small to pass the solids. It is analogous to 'straining', except that this term is usually applied to pumped liquids; unlike true filtration operations, a cake is not required or permitted on the medium.

The screening surface may be stationary, as in bar screens, rotary raking screens and travelling rake screens, or moving, as in travelling band and rotary drum screens.

All types of screens are used in effluent and sewage treatment for coarse solids removal. The solids are retained for subsequent dewatering, disposal or recycle. Vibrating screens are particularly effective. Removal of coarse solids from effluents from slaughterhouses is usually carried out with fine mesh screens which are mechanically vibrated, rotated or cleaned.[10]

The solids need not be particulate, for example screens have been used to remove hair from tanning effluents. The effluents tend to contain lime and lumps of flesh and fat so that screens are subject to blockage: a modified flock-catcher has been developed to overcome this problem.[11]

The majority of effluents from food factories undergo initial screening and efficient self-cleansing is important. Brushed screens, rotating wire mesh screens cleaned by water jets from the reverse side or vibratory screens are used.

Screening to remove paper, rags, faecal matter and any other debris comprises the initial stage in sewage treatment. The sewage first flows, or is pumped, through bar screens, which are coarse screens with spacings of 50–65 mm, and then through fine screens, with spacings of 15–20 mm, before biological treatment.

Methods of Separation of Dissolved Pollutants

Adsorption

Trace impurities can be removed from liquids by contacting them with a solid phase which preferentially retains the impurities on its surface. This is known as adsorption and may be classified as either physical adsorption or chemical adsorption, depending on the nature of the retaining forces. The mechanism is, however, not fully understood.

Adsorption is a potential treatment method for aqueous effluent to remove small quantities of organic compounds, for example surfactants, phenols, pesticides, herbicides and taste- or odour-producing materials. The most common adsorbent is activated carbon in granular form. Powdered carbon has been used for water purification, addition and agitation being followed by a clarification stage, but this is often less convenient for effluent treatment. Effluents may be treated in fixed beds of granular carbon, either in parallel or in series, or in moving beds, as illustrated in Figure 8.5. The bed also tends to filter out suspended solids but, since this is not its primary purpose, their concentration in the inflow should be limited to about 65 mg/1. Higher loadings can result in undesirable pressure losses and require frequent removal of solids by back-flushing. It is considered advisable to remove the bulk of the organics by pretreatment, such as biological or chemical oxidation, if the concentration exceeds 200 ppm.[12] By correct design and operation up to 95%, or even 99%, of organics can be removed. For example, BOD can be reduced from 200 ppm to 1 ppm.[13]

After a certain mass of impurities has been taken up by a bed, a significant concentration of the contaminant remains in the outflowing waste stream. This is termed 'break-through'. Reactivation of the carbon is then necessary. Dependent on the duty, this may be carried out chemically *in-situ* by oxidation of the

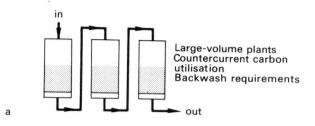

in

Large-volume plants
Countercurrent carbon
utilisation
Backwash requirements

a → out

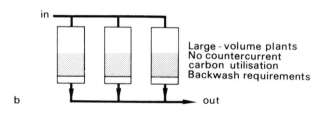

in

Large - volume plants
No countercurrent
carbon utilisation
Backwash requirements

b → out

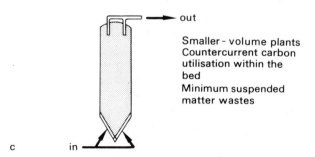

out

Smaller - volume plants
Countercurrent carbon
utilisation within the
bed
Minimum suspended
matter wastes

c   in

Fig. 8.5 Effluent treatment by carbon adsorption:
 a Fixed beds in series
 b Fixed beds in parallel
 c Moving bed

adsorbed organics, as for example with phenols, or the carbon may be removed and reactivated thermally at 870°–980°C. Only on small duties is it economic to discard the spent carbon.

Adsorption has been used to treat coke-oven effluents and to remove complex dyes, hard surfactants and pesticides from aqueous effluents. A common use is to remove odours or tastes from water; it also serves to remove colour. Electroplating solutions frequently contain a variety of proprietary additives, such as gluconates, to improve their performance. These may form complexes with metals so that metal recovery is difficult. Carbon adsorption is an effective polishing treatment in such processes.

Aeration

Aeration involves the intimate contacting of an effluent with air, or sometimes oxygen, to increase the dissolved oxygen content, generally in association with biological treatment processes. Oxygen needs to be distributed throughout the liquid since the efficiency of oxygen transfer is a controlling factor in treatment capacity.

Air–liquid contact may be by forcing air into the base of the vessel via a dome or diffuser plate or by surface agitation using rotating blades, or brushes. Both methods are used in activated sludge plants. Floating surface aerators are used in aerated biological oxidation lagoons and this method has also been used on heavily polluted rivers. An alternative method of aerating effluent by spraying it into the air is not commonly used because of energy costs.

In aeration by gas dispersion, small bubbles are necessary to provide the greatest possible surface area and hence more rapid oxygen transfer. Diffusers of porous material are often removable, to allow dirt to be cleaned from the air side and sediment and deposits from the effluent side.

The rate of oxygen dissolution is considerably increased by using pure oxygen rather than air and some sewage treatment plants utilising oxygen are now marketed. However, the additional cost of oxygen has to be justified economically by the reduction in biological oxidation plant size.

Cementation

Metal may be recovered from aqueous solution by cementation with another metal having a higher standard oxidation potential. Table 8.4 gives the standard oxidation potentials for a range of materials. In general, any metal will tend to precipitate any other metal below it in this table. Thus, metallic iron will displace copper out of solution, and this is probably the best-known example of cementation for metal recovery. Aluminium powder may also be used to displace copper from spent etchant solution. The sacrificial metal must have a lower value than the recovered metal to justify the process. Not every pair of metals will perform in this way, because of the formation of protective films and other barriers.

TABLE 8.4 THE ELECTROCHEMICAL SERIES

Couple	Standard oxidation potential (volts)	
Ca $\rightleftharpoons Ca^{2+} + 2e^-$	2·87	Reducing agents
Na $\rightleftharpoons Na^+ + e^-$	2·71	
Mg $\rightleftharpoons Mg^{2+} + 2e^-$	2·37	
Al $\rightleftharpoons Al^{3+} + 3e^-$	1·66	
Zn $\rightleftharpoons Zn^{2+} + 2e^-$	0·76	
Fe $\rightleftharpoons Fe^{2+} + 2e^-$	0·44	
Ni $\rightleftharpoons Ni^{2+} + 2e^-$	0·25	
Sn $\rightleftharpoons Sn^{2+} + 2e^-$	0·14	
Pb $\rightleftharpoons Pb^{2+} + 2e^-$	0·13	
H_2 $\rightleftharpoons 2H^+ + 2e^-$	0	
Cu $\rightleftharpoons Cu^{2+} + 2e^-$	−0·34	
2Hg $\rightleftharpoons Hg^{2+} + 2e^-$	−0·79	
Ag $\rightleftharpoons Ag^+ + e^-$	−0·80	
$2Cl^-$ $\rightleftharpoons Cl_2 + 2e^-$	−1·36	
Au $\rightleftharpoons Au^{3+} + 3e^-$	−1·50	
$2F^-$ $\rightleftharpoons F_2 + 2e^-$	−2·85	Oxidising agents

Chemical Precipitation

A common method of separating dissolved materials is to render them insoluble by chemical reaction. This is usually achieved by the addition of another chemical which combines with the dissolved material to form an insoluble compound. pH adjustment and temperature adjustment may also produce the same effect. Examples include the precipitation of metal salts in acid or alkaline solution, phosphates and sulphates.

The choice of precipitant depends on availability and cost, and the desired form of the precipitate.

The choice of this method rather than other dissolved-material removal techniques depends on the characterisation of the materials involved including, for example, quantity, concentration, value and chemical characteristics. Equipment design will generally follow the principles set out earlier in this chapter for chemical additions and mixing followed by sedimentation or filtration.

Chemical Reaction

Most effluent treatment involves chemical reaction as a primary stage often followed by separation as the secondary stage.

Reaction may be employed to give a chemical precipitate (q.v.), to destroy a toxic or noxious material as in cyanide oxidation (q.v.) and biological oxidation (q.v.) or to enable further reactions to take place as, for example, in chrome reduction before precipitation (q.v.).

Generalisations are not possible: each problem needs individual and careful attention for the selection of the best reagent and equipment design. (See Further Reading at end of Chapter 7).

Crystallisation

Crystallisation is a potential method for the recovery of dissolved inorganic salts from effluents. It may be performed in equipment operated either batchwise or continuously, taking the form of a simple stirred tank with provision for manual product discharge or a trough or cylindrical shell. Supersaturation leading to crystal formation may be produced by evaporation of liquid, by cooling, or by common ion effect.[14]

This unit operation has been successfully applied to the removal of iron salts from spent pickle liquor and in processes for chemical iron recovery as mentioned in Chapter 9. The majority of the copper sulphate marketed in the UK is produced by crystallisation from copper sulphate liquor obtained from recycled copper.

The initial cost of a crystalliser designed for a specific effluent treatment application is likely to be high and the technique is only economically viable where the crystals have a significant commercial value.

Desorption/Stripping

In stripping, the reverse of physical absorption, a proportion of a soluble gas is removed from a solution by contacting it with an inert carrier gas.

Air blowing has been used to remove volatile organics from aqueous streams to reduce their BOD.[8] Air stripping in a packed tower has also been used to remove ammonia from effluent after adjustment to pH 11 with lime. Ammonia recovery is not normally practised. A 90% reduction in total ammonia may be achieved at reasonable cost. Other examples include dissolved chlorine, bromine and hydrogen cyanide, but care must be taken that the stripped gas does not cause further pollution in its gaseous form.

Stripping is also referred to as the second stage in solvent extraction (q.v.) where solvent is regenerated for recycle.

Dialysis and Electrodialysis

Dialysis is a membrane separation process in which a dissolved material can be removed by contacting the solution with a solvent. The membrane between the solution and solvent is selected to be permeable only to the dissolved material and the solvent. In electrodialysis a voltage is applied across the membrane to assist diffusion of ions.

A wide variety of membranes is used to achieve a balance between the desired properties for a particular application (e.g. high electrical conductivity, high selectivity regarding ions, low permeability to water, good chemical resistance to any corrosive agents and good mechanical strength) and cost.

Electrodialysis has been widely used for the desalting of brackish waters using the arrangement illustrated in Figure 8.6, but it is not applicable to water containing a significant quantity of organic material or to sea water. In effluent treatment it has been used for the recovery of nitric acid and hydrofluoric acid from pickling liquors.

Development is hindered by limitation on the life of membranes, the lack of economy of scale and high energy costs.

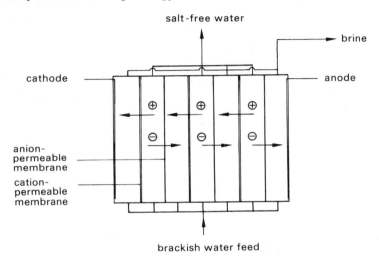

Fig. 8.6 Electrodialysis unit for brackish water treatment

Distillation and Steam Stripping

Distillation achieves separation of a liquid mixture by making use of the differences in volatility between the constituents. Either batch or continuous operation is practised, with plate or packed fractionation columns.

The application of distillation to waste recovery systems is exemplified in Chapter 9 by reference to solvent recovery, which includes an outline description of the various principles involved.

In addition to straightforward distillation, steam stripping is a valuable related procedure for removal and/or recovery of dissolved or suspended contaminants in an aqueous medium; for example, phenol may be stripped from an aqueous effluent by volatilisation of an azeotropic mixture with steam in a continuously operated packed tower. Batchwise operation in a still kettle may be more suitable for low-volume intermittent effluent treatment. In either case the condensate comprises the phenol-rich stream. High recovery levels may be achieved.

Steam stripping is also used to remove ammonia and other contaminants from ammonia plant process condensate. The condensate is saturated with hydrogen, nitrogen, methane, carbon dioxide and residual carbon monoxide; it also contains ammonia, methanol and traces of other organic compounds. A typical analysis is 1000 ppm ammonia, 2000 ppm methanol, 3000 ppm carbon dioxide and 200 ppm other organics.[15] Steam stripping in a packed tower in-

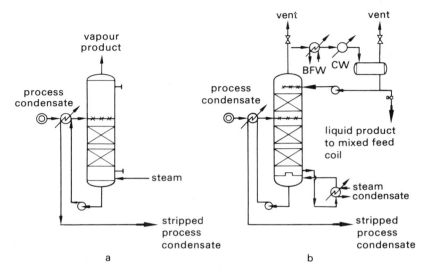

Fig. 8.7 Stripping ammonia plant condensate[15]
        a Vented operation
        b Refluxed operation

jected with live steam and vented to atmosphere results in two streams (Figure 8.7a): the bottoms comprises the bulk of the water from the feed and the overhead product contains most of the contaminants. Unfortunately the latter may result in atmospheric pollution.

An alternative arrangement is with a reboiler, omitting live steam injection (Figure 8.7b). The overhead product is refluxed to produce ammonia and methanol as a concentrated vapour which can be purged and incinerated either in the primary ammonia reformer or a separate unit. The limitation of this arrangement is that burning purge gas with the normal fuel gas results in a considerable increase in NO_x concentration in the reformer stack gases.[15] In a recent development, pollutants are recycled from the reflux drum as a concentrated liquid which is injected back into the process stream to the primary reformer. This gives essentially complete recycling, with the exception of vent gas from the reflux drum which contains 1% of the original ammonia in the feed.

Distillation is not necessarily restricted to conventional packed or plate columns. It has been applied to the recovery of oil from soluble oil emulsions using a Luwa scraped-surface thin film evaporator. The flow diagram is shown in Figure 8.8; the after-treatment stages involving an active carbon filter and pH adjustment are optional to comply with additional constraints on water quality for discharge. The oil concentration in the effluent water is typically 20 ppm and the installation is claimed to cope with a variety of concentrations of different emulsions.

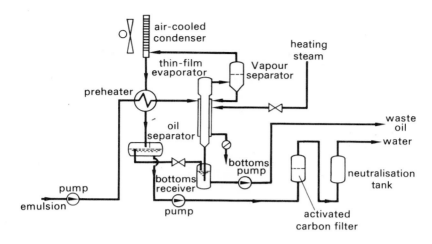

Fig. 8.8 Emulsion cracking by continuous distillation using a thin-film evaporator
(the activated carbon filter and neutralisation are optional after-treatment to
reduce the oil-in-water level to less than 20 ppm)

Drying

Drying refers to the final removal of water from a material. Removal is by
evaporation which can involve a significant latent heat demand. Therefore in
practice drying usually consists of several stages comprising one or more
dewatering operations such as filtration, crystallisation or centrifugation
followed by evaporation of the remainder of the water.

Drying applications in industry arise when moisture may be deleterious to a
product, or if it significantly affects the handling or physical properties, or to
reduce the bulk. Its use in effluent treatment is limited therefore to where there
is a need for a relatively moisture-free, solid product which has sufficient value
to justify the cost of drying.

A common application of drying in waste treatment and disposal is to
sewage sludge, which is 'air-dried' on open beds as an alternative to mechanical
dewatering using filtration, centrifugation or a rotary concentrator. This,
however, relies more upon drainage and decantation than on evaporation. The
process is suited to well digested sludge but occupies a large ground area, is
weather-dependent and may cause offensive odours.[8]

The high cost of drying usually precludes its consideration in waste treatment and disposal although sodium sulphate and thiosulphate from the Holmes
Stretford process are recovered as crystals from a spray-drying operation
before disposal. Drying is more likely to be employed for waste recovery
processes when a significantly higher value may be attributed to a dry product
and/or surplus or waste heat is available.

The types of equipment available are summarised in Table 8.5.

TABLE 8.5 DRYING EQUIPMENT[16]

Material form	Batch operation	Continuous operation
Granules	Tray dryer Shelf dryer	Conveyor dryer Filter dryer Rotary dryer Turbo dryer
Paste	Agitated pan dryer	Flash dryer Screw conveyor dryer Tower dryer
Preformed cakes	Tray dryer Shelf dryer	Tunnel dryer
Solution or slurry	Agitated pan dryer	Spray dryer Rotating drum dryer

Electrolysis

Electrolysis has a range of applications based on reduction at the cathode, and/or oxidation at the anode and/or gas generation.

Metals may be recovered from electroplating solutions by electrolytic reduction, although this is restricted to relatively concentrated solutions.

Cyanide may be oxidised by electrolytic oxidation in relatively concentrated solution above 1000 ppm. Metal recovery may be practised simultaneously. Steel or carbon anodes are employed with the solution at 90°C and air agitation.[17]

Chlorine generation at the anode has been used, rather unsuccessfully, to treat sewage. Some removal of odour, colour and turbidity resulted.

Other applications include gas generation for flotation (q.v.), electrodialysis (q.v.) and ozone generation for oxidation (q.v.).

Evaporation

Concentration of a liquid effluent may be achieved by evaporation. This involves boiling the liquor in an evaporator vessel, and removal and condensation of the vapour. This liquid is then treated separately from the concentrated liquid or solid product. Heat is required, mainly to provide the latent heat of vaporisation, and this is generally supplied by low-pressure steam. Equipment is classified as natural circulation, forced circulation or film-type.

A treatment process based entirely on segregation and evaporation has been described in use at a food factory.[18] It has also been used for the treatment of distillery slop and the recovery and recirculation of spent pickle acid and metal salt solutions for electrolysis.

The production of high-purity water has conventionally involved evaporation and condensation in stills. Plants for the purification of sea water utilise multi-stage flash processing. However, because of the relatively large latent heat of water the energy consumption for evaporation is high; therefore, even with steam from nuclear power stations,[19] evaporation of sea water is only likely to be economic in arid areas. Similar considerations apply to the concentration of aqueous effluents or sewage by evaporation and it is unlikely to be economically viable unless a valuable solid product is recovered.

Freezing and Thawing

Freezing and thawing, i.e. the formation and separation of ice crystals and their subsequent melting, is a potential process for water purification. Either direct or indirect refrigeration may be used to produce an ice slurry containing 30% to 50% of water by weight. However, although this process has been used to purify sea water, there are no known applications to aqueous effluent treatment and in view of the high energy consumption these appear unlikely.

Freezing and thawing has been investigated as a method of conditioning waterworks and sewage sludges. The process breaks down the cell wall in organisms that retain moisture, but with sewage sludge the filtrability deteriorates due to breakdown on shearing and there has been no large-scale application.

Heating

Heating, usually with closed steam, may usefully be applied in effluent treatment operations to reduce the viscosity of the liquid under treatment. This is applied in emulsion breaking. Heating may also serve to accelerate specific chemical reactions, for example oxidation, reduction or neutralisation. It may be used for disinfection of water by boiling or superheating, but it reduces dissolved oxygen and is relatively expensive.

Hydrolysis

Hydrolysis is the reaction of a material with water whereby the water molecule is broken up into a hydroxyl group and hydrogen atom. For example with ferrous chloride and water:

$$FeCl_2 + 2H_2O \rightarrow Fe(OH)_2 + 2HCl$$

or

$$FeCl_2 + H_2O \rightarrow FeO + 2HCl$$

This particular reaction is employed in the treatment of waste hydrochloric acid pickle liquor to recover the acid for further pickling duties and also the dissolved iron (see Chapter 9). Hydrolysis is also employed for treatment of cellulose, as for example in household refuse to give sugars, which may either be recovered or fermented to alcohol, single cell protein or a range of chemicals (see Chapter 17).

The application of hydrolysis to waste treatment and recovery is relatively recent, but it is shown to be a valuable unit process. There are no general rules for selection or specification of hydrolysis as each potential application needs individual attention. Usually hydrolysis requires moderate to extreme reaction conditions, for example of pH, temperature or pressure. Therefore, due to the high processing costs, it tends to be restricted to recovery processes in which the product has a significant value.

Incineration

Incineration of liquid wastes is practicable in specially designed equipment even when they have a substantial water content. The waste is atomised into a combustion chamber fired by an auxiliary fuel, oil or gas. Efficient dispersion is required to provide a large surface area and good mixing with air. The requirement for expensive fuel is reduced if the effluent contains organic materials such as solvents or oil and hence has a significant calorific value. In order to support combustion in air without auxiliary fuel the calorific value must usually be at least $18 \cdot 6 - 23 \cdot 2$ J/kg (8000–10 000 Btu/lb).

Slurries can be incinerated provided no problems arise from blockage of the atomisers. Burners have been designed to handle viscous materials containing particles up to 3 mm in diameter.[20]

Effective destruction depends on all the physical properties affecting combustion (Chapter 3), so usually each incinerator is purpose-built. If chlorinated compounds are present in the waste, resulting in the generation of hydrogen chloride, the exhaust gas requires scrubbing and the resultant liquid effluent may require treatment. Some liquid wastes, such as waste lubricating oils, can be used directly as fuel for a boiler or preheater and thus the waste heat energy is recovered. This is not, however, generally practicable if they contain significant proportions of materials which generate corrosive gases on combustion, such as hydrogen chloride or oxides of sulphur.

An example of a process for 60 tonne/day of aqueous waste from a pharmaceutical plant is shown in Figure 8.9.[21] The water content of the waste is 80–90%; it contains both inorganic and organic impurities and has a high COD value which precludes dumping. The feed is first split into two phases using a fuel-oil-fired concentrator to give a vapour phase containing 75% by weight of the water and some organic solvents, and a smaller liquid phase containing phosphoric acid and hydrochloric acid. Heat recovered from the hot gases is used to generate steam at 1140 kN/m² (150 psi).

The liquid phase from the concentrator is burnt off in a ZTO fuel-oil-fired incinerator from which the gases are cooled and scrubbed in a high-energy venturi to remove inorganic compounds and then in a packed bed for hydrochloric acid removal.

Because it results in thermal destruction, incineration is particularly applicable to many effluents containing toxic or persistent materials although asbestos, heavy metals and similar materials cannot be destroyed. In general,

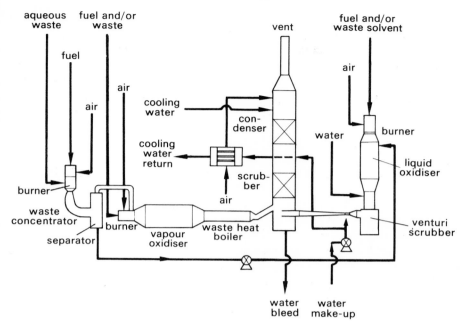

Fig. 8.9 Incineration process for pharmaceutical wastes[21]

however, unless there is a steady supply of high-calorific-value waste of approximately constant properties it is likely to be more expensive than any alternative treatment, even if heat recovery is practised.

Ion Exchange

The function of ion exchange is the removal of dissolved solids in ionic form by exchanging the unwanted ions for less undesirable ions. Ion exchange is used, for example, in the treatment of total effluent from metal finishing processes or for the treatment of individual flows such as chromium wastes. Essentially, all of the cations and anions may be removed from solution by using cation and anion exchangers in series; however, complex cyanides present difficulties and chromium can be present in rinse-waters in both the cationic trivalent form and the anionic hexavalent form. The cations such as iron, chromium and nickel are exchanged for hydrogen ions in the cation exchanger and, when regeneration is performed using hydrochloric or sulphuric acid, they are concentrated in the regenerant solution as chlorides or sulphates respectively. The anion exchanger removes the anions in a similar way, including hexavalent chromium.[22] Regeneration is typically carried out with sodium hydroxide.

Passage of a cyanide-bearing effluent through a cation exchanger results in cation removal and conversion of simple cyanides into hydrogen cyanide. Some complex cyanides are destroyed with the formation of more hydrogen cyanide; the released cation, for example copper, is absorbed. The anion exchanger then absorbs both simple and complex cyanides yielding a non-toxic low-salt-content effluent. Regeneration of the anion exchanger using sodium hydroxide solution removes the majority of the cyanides from the resin but complex cyanides, for example cuprocyanides, are not removed completely. These may be removed at intervals of, for example, three months, using a progressively more highly concentrated sodium hydroxide solution; alternatively, they may be destroyed with sodium hypochlorite solution.[23]

Some of the additives, particularly organic materials such as gluconates used in plating solutions, may have a deleterious effect on the ion exchange resins; therefore an activated carbon column may be installed before the ion exchange columns. Rinses containing other troublesome materials such as oil, grease and chelating agents should also be directed straight to waste.[23] With these precautions the service life of resins may be maintained at about three years.

For large operations two exchanger systems may be installed in parallel, giving continuous steady-state operation with one system on regeneration while the other is operating.

Examples of ion exchange have been described elsewhere; a recent application has been to chromate recovery from cooling tower water blow-down (Figure 8.10). The water is filtered to remove particulates and then dosed with

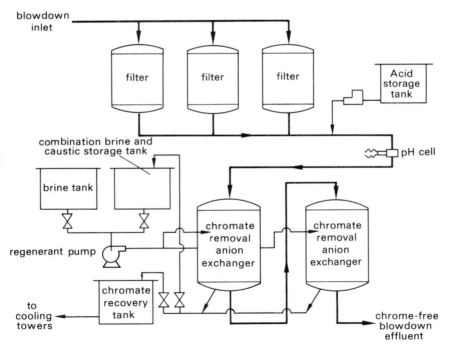

Fig. 8.10 Ion-exchange recovery of chromate corrosion inhibitor from cooling-tower blowdown

an oxidising acid. This ensures that the chromium is in the anion complex form for removal by anion exchange. Regeneration of the resin is achieved with a caustic and salt solution which can be returned with the chrome to the cooling water circuit.

Liquid–Liquid and Solvent Extraction

Solvent extraction is a mass transfer operation in which separation of the constituents of a liquid mixture is achieved by the addition of a solvent which is wholly or partially immiscible with the mixture. It is generally necessary to follow the dissolution process by solute and solvent recovery steps; this may involve distillation, evaporation or stripping, i.e. back-extraction. At its simplest operation may be batchwise, but in practice continuous operation is preferred.

Extraction may be performed in equipment which allows the liquids to be mixed, extracted and separated in discrete stages, for example, mixer–settler cascades. The common form of a mixer–settler is an agitated vessel in series with a larger horizontal settling vessel, in which phase separation may be assisted by baffling or coalescing aids such as knitted mesh packings. Alternatively there may be continuous countercurrent contact in simple spray columns, columns with packed internals or plates of the type described in Chapter 12, in mechanically agitated columns such as the rotating disc contactor, or in centrifugal extractors such as the Podbielniak contactor.[1] In general, equipment with complex internals or perforated plates should be avoided where entrained solids may be present; similarly, excessive agitation is undesirable with systems of low interfacial tension, because of the formation of secondary dispersions.

In practice, application to pollution control has been limited, the technique's main potential lying in the removal of toxic organics from aqueous effluents, e.g. phenols removal.

One example of effluent treatment by solvent extraction is the removal of formic and acetic acids from pyroligneous acid, for which either ether or ethyl acetate may be used as solvent.[24] However, a potential disadvantage with solvent extraction is that saturation of the raffinate (effluent) stream with solvent, or entrainment of fine solvent droplets in it, can substantially increase the BOD.

For the removal of monohydric and higher phenols from effluents from coal distillation plants, creosote oil has been used as solvent in a 5-stage mixer–settler cascade. Removal of 90–93% phenols was achieved, the extract being contacted with 5% sodium hydroxide solution to give sodium phenolate.[25] The use of butyl acetate as solvent in pulsed columns should result in very low phenol levels in the final effluent. Extraction reduced the phenol level of effluent from a phenol-formaldehyde resin plant from 4–6% to 200–500 ppm, using isopropyl ether as solvent.[26] Finally, phenol recovery from an aqueous effluent from catalytic cracking units, plus entrained oil removal, is achieved by extraction using light catalytic cycle oil followed by electrostatic separation.[27]

Solvent extraction is also used to remove grease from wool wastes. For example, a treatment has been described for the recovery of lanolin chlolesterol.[24]

Solvent extraction is now in wide use commercially for the extraction of metals from ores; extraction from an aqueous solution by a solvent is followed by stripping to recover the metal ion. A typical flowsheet for this operation, using a cascade of mixer–settlers, is shown in Figure 8.11. Dissolved metal ions can be removed from effluents in a similar manner, when they otherwise present removal problems or are sufficiently valuable to merit recovery. These include:[28]

Metal ion	Solvent
Zinc	di-2-ethyl hexyl phosphoric acid (EHPA)
Nickel	di-nonyl naphthalene sulphonic acid (DNSA)
Copper	quaternary amines

See also Figure 7.12, page 171.

In summary, solvent extraction is a valuable separation technique for the recovery of materials but capital and operating costs generally preclude its use for waste disposal.

Neutralisation and pH Adjustment

Neutralisation or the adjustment of pH may be practised to bring an effluent into the range for discharge, e.g. pH 6–10, or to facilitate subsequent treatment. A detailed discussion with examples is given in Chapter 7.

Oxidation

Oxidation is a widely used process for destruction of toxic substances such as cyanide and organic materials. Chemical oxidation employs chlorine as gas, chlorine dioxide gas, a solution of hypochlorite, or ozone (an increasingly popular oxidant). These are used for cyanide oxidation (q.v.) and organics oxidation (e.g. phenol, q.v.). Other oxidising agents such as potassium permanganate and nitric acid are rarely employed in effluent treatment. Biological oxidation uses micro-organisms and oxygen from the air to effect oxidation. Incineration may be considered as thermal oxidation (q.v.).

Chlorination

Chlorination is a treatment for odour control as well as being effective in killing bacteria, in cyanide destruction, for the precipitation of minerals and for water

C. W. Cheney Ltd and Pollution Control Ltd

Effluent treatment plant for cyanide oxidation and metal precipitation
Gaseous chlorine is injected into the tank in the right foreground. Oxidised
effluent flows via a weir to the second treatment stage (left foreground) where
neutralisation is effected by addition of acid

treatment. Typical dosage rates of elemental chlorine gas in effluent treatment
applications are given in Table 8.6. Data are for average conditions which may
vary with location.[29]

Ozone Oxidation

Ozone has a high oxidation potential and ozonolysis is used to treat over
455 000 m³/day (100 million gal/day) of household water. Despite this it has
not traditionally been widely used for effluent treatment although it is becoming
more popular. In France it has been applied to remove cyanide from treated
sewage wastes and in Canada as a final 'polishing' agent to remove phenols
from biologically treated effluents.[30] It has been used in the UK to remove
cyanides from industrial waste-water and for colour removal. Ozone is conventionally produced by the passage of a silent electric discharge through dry air,
for which an AC voltage of around 10 kV is required.[31] Feasible applications
for ozonisation, particularly following pretreatment by conventional means, are
the removal of phenols, oils, cyanides, sulphides and sulphites, and detergents.

Biological Oxidation

Biological oxidation involves the utilisation of organic waste, or under some

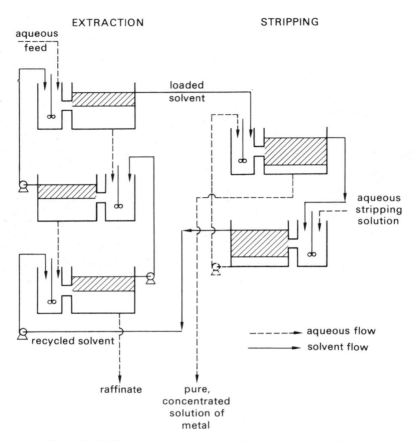

Fig. 8.11 Multi-stage countercurrent solvent extraction and stripping

conditions inorganic waste, by micro-organisms. The microbial mass is subsequently removed from the treated effluent. Percolating filter and activated sludge plants, in which the provision of a large population of micro-organisms as a slime or sludge enables organic materials to be broken down rapidly, are described on page 149.

A conventional percolating filter in which settled sewage is added either continuously or intermittently to the surface by a rotating distributor is illustrated in Figure 8.12. It trickles through the interstices of the angular stone or plastic media and over the slime or film of micro-organisms. The effluent contains a significant concentration of suspended solids, due to film displacement, and passes to a humus tank for sedimentation.

In the activated sludge process a high concentration of microbial sludge in the aerated tank enables organic material to be stabilised rapidly. The mixed liquor from the aeration tank flows through a secondary clarifier and the majority of the solids are then recycled to the aeration tank. The three main arrangements referred to in Chapter 7 are illustrated in Figure 8.13.

Norton Chemical Process Products

Trickling filter employing plastic pall rings

TABLE 8.6 CHLORINATION TREATMENTS

Treatment for	Typical dosage rates (ppm or mg/l)
BOD Reduction	10
Colour (Removal)	Dosage depends upon type and extent of colour removal desired. May vary from 1 to 500 ppm dosage rate.

Cyanide
  Reduction to cyanate
  Complete destruction
	2 times cyanide content
	8·5 times cyanide content

Hydrogen sulphide
  Taste and odour control
  Destruction
	2 times H_2S content
	8·4 times H_2S content

Iron precipitation Manganese precipitation	0·64 times Fe content 1·3 times Mn content
Odour	1–3

Sewage
  Raw sewage
  Trickling filter effluent
  Activated sludge effluent
  Sand filter effluent
	15–20
	
	Average dosage rates 3–8

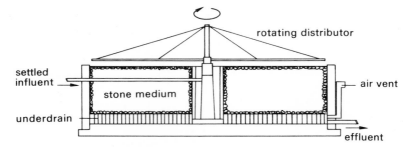

Fig. 8.12 Conventional percolating filter

The conventional plug–flow arrangement may be subject to shock loading on the input side, whereas the completely mixed arrangement approaches steady-state feed conditions. In the contact-stabilisation arrangement, the liquid to be treated is in contact with microbial sludge for a relatively short period prior to flow into the settling tank; the recycled solids are also aerated prior to return to the contact tank. For this reason, a significant proportion of the activated sludge is not exposed to shock-loads on the input side.

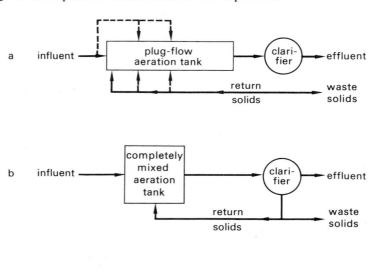

Fig. 8.13 Main activated sludge treatment arrangements
  a Conventional
  b Completely mixed
  c Contact-stabilisation

In warm climates use may also be made of oxidation ponds which comprise shallow lagoons and make use of algae and bacteria. The performance of typical ponds is summarised in Table 8.7.

TABLE 8.7 OXIDATION POND PERFORMANCE

	Aerobic	Facultative	Aerated	Anaerobic
Depth (m)	0·5–1	1–2	2–4	3–5
kg BOD/m² d	0·15	0·05	0·2	0·5
Retention (d)	2–20	5–30	2–10	30–60
% BOD removal	80–95	75–85	50–90	50–70

Reduction

Reduction is essentially the opposite to oxidation. Its major use in effluent treatment is in the conversion of hexavalent chromium to the trivalent state for subsequent separation by precipitation. This is described in Chapter 7 under Chromium.

Reverse Osmosis

In this process pressure is applied to force water through a membrane which is relatively impermeable to dissolved salts and to large un-ionised molecules. However, while the process is mechanically straightforward and can be performed at ambient temperature, the main limitation in the past has been in the development of inexpensive membranes. Reverse osmosis has been used for the separation of toxic ions from plating effluents, acid recovery from pickling effluents, organic removal from vegetable and animal wastes as well as desalination, for which the technique is perhaps best known. It has also been applied to the recovery of cheese whey.[32]

The cost of operation is relatively high since up to 372 kW (0·5 hp) is required per 4·5 m³/day (1000 gal/day) and membrane life is only 6 to 12 months.[8] However, when applied to rinse-waters from nickel plating it has led to 99% recovery of nickel losses for reuse and a waste effluent with only 32 mg/1 nickel.[33] Furthermore, cellulose acetate membranes, which are now available in a spiral-wound modular form, are claimed to have a life expectancy in excess of 3 to 4 years.[34]

References

1. PURCHAS, D. B., *Chemistry and Industry*, 53, 19 January 1974.
2. MUMFORD, C. J., *British Chemical Engineering*, **13**(7), 981, 1968.
3. AUSTIN, D. G., MUMFORD, C. J. and JEFFREYS, G. V., paper presented at Solvent Extraction Meeting, Institution of Chemical Engineers, Newcastle upon Tyne, 7–9 September, 1976.
4. PURCHAS, D. B., *Environmental Pollution Management*, **2**(5), 169, 1972.

5. FURNESS, C. D., Symposium on the Treatment of Aqueous Effluents, Institution of Chemical Engineers, 24 October, 1973.
6. FRANKLIN, J. S., *Effluent and Water Treatment Journal*, 655, October 1973.
7. ICI Ltd, *Microfiltration* (BP 1351882) and *Electrofiltration*, ICI Pollution Control Systems, 1974.
8. MARSHALL, V. C. (Ed.), *Water Borne Waste*, Supplement to *The Chemical Engineer*, October 1974.
9. COULSON, J. M. and RICHARDSON, J. F., *Chemical Engineering*, Vol. 2, Pergamon, 1955.
10. DART, M. C., in *Practical Waste Treatment and Disposal*, DICKINSON, D. (Ed.), Applied Science, 1974, p. 75.
11. WOLSTENHOLME, S., ibid., p. 173.
12. ROSS, R. D., *Industrial Waste Disposal*, Reinhold, 1968.
13. BESSELIEVRE, E. B. AND SCHWARTZ, M., *The Treatment of Industrial Wastes*, 2nd edn, McGraw-Hill, 1976.
14. BAMFORTH, A. W., *Industrial Crystallization*, Godwin, 1965.
15. MARTIN, P. R. and TOWERS, R. G., *Waste in the Process Industries*, Conference Publication, Institution of Mechanical Engineers, 1977, p. 35.
16. WILLIAMS-GARDNER, A., *Industrial Drying*, Godwin, 1971.
17. W. Canning & Co. Ltd, *Handbook on Electroplating*, 20th edn, 1966.
18. CHALMERS, R. K., *Proceedings 22nd Industrial Waste Conference*, Purdue University, Indiana, 1967, p. 866.
19. TEBBUTT, T. H. Y., *Principles of Water Quality Control*, 2nd edn, Pergamon, 1977.
20. DUNN, K. S., *Chemical Engineering* Desk Book Issue, 141, 6 October, 1975.
21. *Process Engineering*, 68, April 1974.
22. ARDEN, T. W., *Water Purification by Ion Exchange*, Butterworth, 1968.
23. VON AMMON, F. K., *Proceedings 22nd Industrial Waste Conference*, Purdue University, Indiana, 1967, p. 788.
24. RICKLES, R.N., *Chemical Engineering*, 72(20), 139, 1965.
25. MURDOCK, D. G. and CUCKNEY, N., *Transactions of the Institution of Chemical Engineers*, **29**, 90, 1946.
26. KIRCHGESSNER, N. H., *Sewage Industry Wastes*, **30**, 191, 1958.
27. LEWIS, W. L. and MARTIN, W. L., *Hydrocarbon Processing*, **42**(2), 131, 1967.
28. DIAMANT, R. M. E., *The Prevention of Pollution*, Pitman, 1974.
29. Capital Controls Co., Colmar, Pennsylvania, USA, Pub. No. 375–1.
30. *Process Engineering*, 104, February 1973.
31. HALL, D. A. and NELLIST, G. R., *Chemical Trade Journal of Chemical Engineering*, (156), 786, 1965.
32. BENNET, G. F. and LASH, L., *Chemical Engineering Progress*, **70**(2), 75, 1954.
33. CHALMERS, R. K., *Applications of New Concepts of Physical–Chemical Waste Water Treatment*, Vol. I, Pergamon, 1972, p. 154.
34. *Process Engineering*, 57, November 1971.

CHAPTER 9

Materials Recovery from Liquid Waste

Many common examples of recycling practice are covered elsewhere in this book. This chapter reviews waste effluents for which material recovery has only recently been proposed, including special examples where 'one man's waste' can be turned into 'another man's profit' by virtue of circumstance, special knowledge or economy of scale.

Table 9.1 illustrates the diversity of recyclable materials from liquid effluents.

Metals

Metal Recovery from Mixed Effluent Treatment Sludges

Considerable quantities of metals are lost annually in aqueous effluent, effluent treatment sludges and filter cakes (see Chapter 15). Attempts have been made to recover the valuable constituents by hydrometallurgical techniques. Figure 9.1[1] shows a typical generalised flowsheet for the separation of all the possible components of an electroplating effluent sludge. Warren Spring Laboratory has applied a range of adaptations of the basic principles in a variety of situations.[1-5] It is, however, exceptional for such recovery processes to be justified economically. A survey of UK non-metallic copper losses[6] concluded that an integrated approach to recovery was not viable.

Metal Recovery from Specific Metal-bearing Wastes

Because of the relatively high value and ease of recovery of metals, there have been many proposals for the reclamation of metals from specific waste solutions: silver and other precious metals recovery from electroplating rinse-waters, copper chemicals from printed circuit board etchant and iron oxides from spent pickle liquor have already been mentioned. Two further examples illustrate the range of operations that may be used in such processes and indicate some of the technical problems.

TABLE 9.1 EXAMPLES OF MATERIALS RECOVERED FROM LIQUID WASTES

Chemical	Example of source
Acetic acid	Paper
Acetone	Petrochemicals
Ammonia	Coke ovens
Ammonium sulphate	Coke ovens
Anthracene	Coal tar
Anthranilic acid	Dyestuffs
Aromatic organics	Coke ovens
Aromatics	Naphtha pyrolysis quench
Benzene	Styrene manufacture
Bromine	Potash
Calcium sulphate	Phosphates
Carboxylic acids	Petrochemicals
Casein	Milk
Chromic acid	Electroplating
Copper salts	Secondary copper
Copper sulphate	Secondary copper
Creosote	Coal tar
Cresol	Coal tar
Ethanol	Cellulose
Ethylbenzene	Styrene manufacture
Ethylene dichloride	Oxychlorination waste-water
Fluorides	Phosphate
Gold cyanide	Electroplating
Hydrochloric acid	Pickle liquor
Hydrofluoric acid	Aluminium
Hydraulic oil	Engineering
Hydrogen	Refineries
Iodine	Saltpetre
Iron oxides	Titanium
Iron sulphates	Pickle liquor
Lubricating oil	Vehicle maintenance
Magnesium chloride	Sea water
Methanol	General purpose solvent
Methylaniline	Dyestuffs
Naphthalene	Coke ovens
Nickel salts	Electroplating
Paint	Automotive
Phenols	Petroleum refineries
Potassium hydroxide	Dyestuffs
Protein	Fermentation
Quench oil	Metal treatment
Silver cyanide	Electroplating
Sodium chloride	Desalination

Table 9.1 (*continued*)

Sodium hydroxide	Dyestuffs
Sodium sulphate	Paper
Sulphur	Desulphurisation processes
Sulphuric acid	Pickling liquor
Sulphur oxides	Ore smelting
Tar	Coke ovens
Toluene	Benzole from coke ovens
Trichlorobenzene	Pigments
Trichloroethylene	Degreasing
White spirit	General-purpose solvent
Xylene	Benzole from coke ovens
Yeast	Brewing
Zinc salts	Rayon

It was discovered several years ago that an aqueous effluent containing up to 300 tonnes of nickel per year, together with other metals and non-metals in solution, was being dumped. At that time the nickel was worth around £250 000 per year as metal, and the current value is around £500 000. Two processes were proposed, one based on solvent extraction to separate the impurities from the nickel followed by electrolysis to recover nickel metal (Figure 9.2) and the other on a series of precipitative reactions to remove the impurities and leave a purified aqueous solution, again followed by electrolysis (Figure 9.3). The capital costs of the two processes were similar. The second system was installed, since equipment was available and the processing methods were familiar. A return on investment of considerably over 100% was estimated, with a payback time of around six months.

Another area which has attracted considerable attention over the last thirty years is the recovery of zinc or zinc chemicals from rayon manufacture. Over twenty processes have been investigated, but most rejected, usually because of poor economics or low quality of product. One recent proposal[7] for recovery of the zinc reviews all the operations that have been tried, and proposes a new approach with evidence of technical feasibility (Figure 9.4). No claims are made for the economic viability of the process, in which there are still a number of technical problems to overcome.

There are, however, probably few such reclaimable wastes still unexploited. About 70 instances of byproduct recovery from aqueous effluent were reported several years ago,[8] including many metals and metal compounds.

Hydrometallurgical Processing

All the examples of metal recovery mentioned are based on hydrometallurgy. There is a rapidly growing interest in hydrometallurgical extraction of metals: that is, extraction, purification and recovery of metals in aqueous solution. The technology, principles and practice are equally applicable to waste metals and alloys. A number of metal scrap problems have recently been investigated and reported, such as nickel/cobalt alloy separation and recovery, cadmium/zinc separation and recovery and bearing metal recovery.[2,9,10] Other examples are

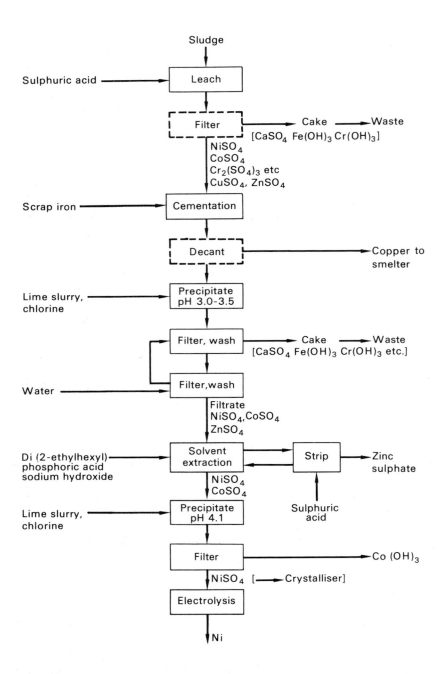

Fig. 9.1 Typical flowsheet for the treatment of a complex effluent sludge[1]

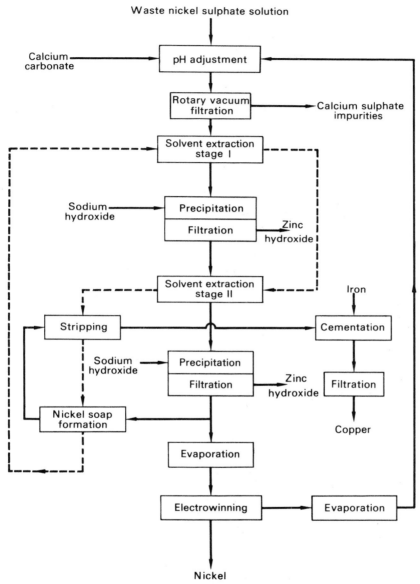

Fig. 9.2 Nickel soap–solvent extraction process for nickel recovery from waste solution

included in Chapter 15. The essential features of a 'wet' process to recover metals are:

(a) Leaching, preferably selective to reduce subsequent purification. Examples include acid leaching, ammoniacal leaching (copper, nickel) and caustic leaching (aluminium, zinc and tin).

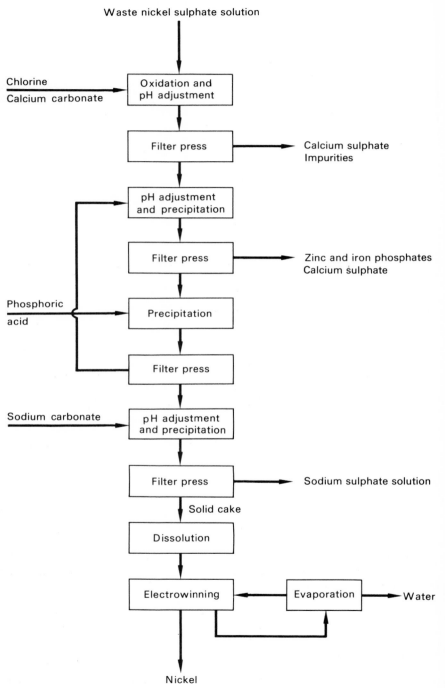

Fig. 9.3 Precipitation process for nickel recovery from waste sulphate solution

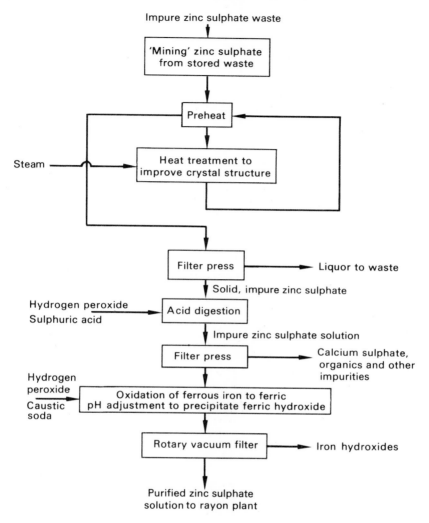

Fig. 9.4 Recycling of zinc sulphate in rayon manufacturing process

(b) Purification, to remove impurities. Examples include most chemical engineering operations, such as ion exchange, solvent extraction and precipitation (Chapter 8).

(c) Reduction, to produce an acceptable metallic product. This final step is unnecessary if metal salts are being produced. Selective reduction is also possible in many cases to further reduce impurities. Examples include electrolysis and hydrogen reduction.

Determination of the best process for a given metal-bearing waste requires careful consideration of a wide range of factors including characterisation of the waste (Chapter 3), economics (Chapter 20) and many aspects of chemical engineering design practice.

Hydrochloric Acid Pickle Liquor

The traditional reagent for descaling or pickling iron and steel products was sulphuric acid. The spent pickle liquor contained up to 20% ferrous sulphate and considerable effort and ingenuity went into the search for viable methods for recovering the acid, but without success. More recently hydrochloric acid pickling has been successfully introduced and, although the acid costs more to purchase, it is more readily recycled than sulphuric acid. A number of processes have been developed, all based on the hydrolysis of ferrous chloride at elevated temperature according to the following equation:

$$4\,FeCl_2 + 4H_2O + \underset{\text{(air)}}{O_2} \rightarrow 2Fe_2O_3 + 8HCl$$

The iron oxide is returned to the iron-making process and the hydrogen

BW Hydrometallurgical Processes Ltd

Plant for the regeneration of hydrochloric acid from ilmenite leach liquors
This recycles acid during titanium dioxide manufacture; a train of spray roasters is shown

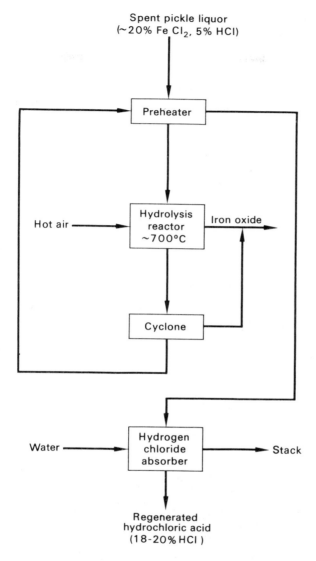

Fig. 9.5 Hydrochloric acid pickle liquor regeneration

chloride gas is condensed to acid and returned to the pickle line (Figure 9.5). The significant advantage of this process is the almost total avoidance of waste, which not only saves the cost of treatment and disposal, but also the cost of buying replacement acid. The same process can be applied to chlorides of aluminium, cobalt, magnesium, manganese and nickel.[11]

Solvents

Solvents are widely used in industry, both in end products and as reagents. While in many uses the solvent is recovered, often product quality begins to be affected or the reagent becomes too contaminated, so that further reuse is undesirable or impossible. The manufacturer may have neither the skill nor the facilities to reprocess this material and thus must dispose of it. As solvents are usually immiscible with water, conventional aqueous treatment is rarely possible and dumping or incineration is necessary. With the considerable overall quantities of solvent-based wastes, their high value and ease of recovery, commercial enterprises now exist to remove or, more usually, purchase such materials in order to recover the solvent.

It is difficult to estimate the quantities of solvents arising in waste, but some indication can be derived from a number of recent surveys, one of which[12] found that in the UK about 130 000 tonnes/year of 'flammable process waste' are produced, which includes all solvents other than chlorinated hydrocarbons or similar, and about 200 000 tonnes/year of 'indisputably toxic waste', which includes the nonflammable solvents. The figures relate to 11 million tonnes of industrial waste produced from 1186 premises. As it has been estimated that about 20 million tonnes per year of trade, commercial and industrial waste (other than spoil, mining and metallurgical waste) are produced annually,[13,14] or even in excess of 30 million,[15] the figures suggested above are probably conservative.

In support of this view, a survey into toxic waste arising in the Greater London Council area[16] suggested that about 5500 tonnes/year of combustible solvents and about 33 tonnes/year of incombustible solvents were disposed of out of a total of 367 000 tonnes/year of toxic waste. Multiplication of these figures by ten will give order of magnitude figures for the UK, i.e. about 60 000 tonnes/year combustible solvents and 400 tonnes/year of incombustible solvents.

These figures are supported by examination of the UK Waste Materials Exchange *Bulletin* (see page 266), which for mid-1976 listed about 26 000 tonnes/year combustible common solvents and about 90 tonnes/year noncombustible common solvents, out of a total waste availability of around 4 million tonnes. There is however some variance in a recent estimate[14] which suggests that only 23 000 tonnes/year of organic wastes arise annually to require disposal. This is believed to be conservative. The 60 000 tonnes/year deduced above is believed to be a fair assessment and does not include wastes which are already internally recycled or externally recycled through a reprocessor. It thus represents the solvent wastes nationally available for recycle.

Some of the more common of the wide range of solvents used industrially are listed in Table 9.2 together with mid-1977 prices. Market forces can raise or depress prices considerably in a short time, but it is clear that many solvents are relatively valuable, particularly if resulting from an extensive processing route for manufacture.

TABLE 9.2 COMMON SOLVENTS, APPROXIMATE MARKET PRICES AND BOILING POINTS

	June 1977 price (£/tonne)	Boiling point (°C)
Acetic acid	220	118
Acetone	200	56·5
Benzene	120	80
Cyclohexanol	520	160
Ethanol (duty-free)	200	78
Ethylene glycol	230	197
Furfural	670	162
Glycerol	650	290
Hexane (normal)	160	69
Isopropanol	210	82·5
Methanol	70	65
Methylethylketone (MEK)	250	80
n-Propanol	340	97
Toluene	100	111
Trichlorethylene	250	87
White spirit	100	155–195

Solvent reclamation is usually based on distillation (see Chapter 8), which relies on differences in volatility to effect separation. Basically, the closer the boiling points the more difficult the separation. In some cases an azeotrope is formed which makes complete separation by simple distillation impossible, and tertiary, azeotropic or extractive distillation has to be carried out with a third component (Fig. 9.6): an example is ethanol and water, when continued distillation will give a product containing 96% ethanol. If high-boiling-point

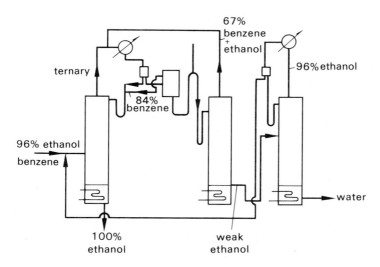

Fig. 9.6 Arrangement of plant for azeotropic distillation of ethanol–water mixtures, using benzene as the extractive agent

materials are involved, vacuum distillation is employed to avoid thermal degradation, as liquids boil at lower temperatures at subambient pressures. Similarly, very low-boiling-point materials might be distilled under pressure, when the boiling point is elevated, to avoid the need for a refrigerated cooling system for the vapour.

Distillation may be carried out continuously when a mixture of solvents can only normally be split into two fractions (Figure 9.7). If there are more than two components to be recovered from the mixture, either additional equipment is needed to give a distillation train (Figure 9.8) or the products must be stored to be redistilled in the same equipment; this technique may be referred to as semi-continuous distillation.

A popular alternative for small quantities is batch distillation, where a number of products are collected sequentially from the top of a column (Figure 9.9). The mixture of solvents is heated in a still at the base of the distillation column, and a fraction rich in the lowest-boiling-point component is first removed from the top of the column and stored. The purity is checked by temperature measurement and analysis such as gas–liquid chromatography. When as much of this first component as possible has been removed, the distillation is continued and the next component is recovered. Small quantities of

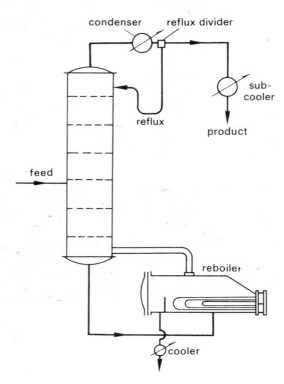

Fig. 9.7 A continuous fractionating column

Sterling Organics Ltd and APV-Mitchell Ltd

Solvent recovery by batch distillation

mixed material recovered between each component are recycled to the next batch. The distillation continues with temperatures increasing until the last solvent is recovered. Careful control is necessary to achieve good separation. High-boiling-point materials can be separated by distillation under partial vacuum or by steam distillation.

The efficiency of separation depends largely on the relative volatilities (or boiling-point differences) and the close contact of vapour and liquid. This contact is effected by ascending vapour continually meeting descending liquid provided by a reflux stream (Figure 9.7), and this is achieved either by regularly spaced trays having a liquid layer through which vapour bubbles, or by a high-surface-area packing giving intimate contact between vapour and liquid. Trays, such as bubble cap or sieve types, tend to be used for larger distillation columns of perhaps more than 1 m diameter, while the various types of packing material tend to be used for smaller columns.

The number of trays or height of packing is a function of duty of the column and, particularly, of the materials to be separated and the desired purity. 'General-purpose' distillation columns are therefore difficult to design, as they are likely to be inadequate for some mixtures and unnecessarily sophisticated for others. A solvent reprocessor is thus likely to need a range of equipment and even then may be restricted in application. Combustible solvents that cannot be separated or recovered, or for which there is no market, can be burnt to provide heat for distillation.

In addition to distillation, a number of other purification steps may be employed, such as washing, neutralisation, carbon adsorption, filtration or solvent extraction, depending on the material and the contamination. In the

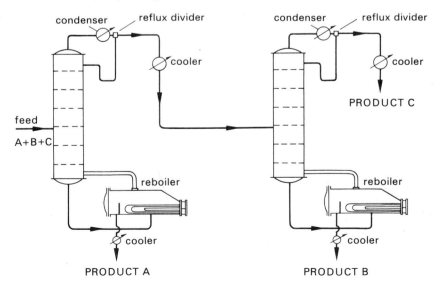

Fig. 9.8 Distillation train to separate a multi-component feed

broader context of organic chemical recycling, any of the chemical engineering unit operations or unit processes briefly described in Chapter 8 may be employed.

Oils

Around one million tonnes (250 million gallons) of lubricating oils and greases are used annually in the UK of which about 50% (475 000 tonnes) is dissipated and irrecoverable. Of the 475 000 tonnes available for recovery, about 75 000 tonnes are so heavily contaminated as to preclude recycling. About 75 000 tonnes/year were being recycled in 1974/75 to give secondary lubricating oil, and a further 110 000 tonnes were reclaimed for blending with fuel oil. This leaves about 215 000 tonnes or 55 million gal/year of recoverable but unexploited oils (Figure 9.10).[17,18,19]

A similar pattern of usage in recoverable fraction and reuseable-recoverable fraction is found throughout the world,[19] with a minimum of 48% non-dissipated waste in Italy and a maximum of 62% in Greece.

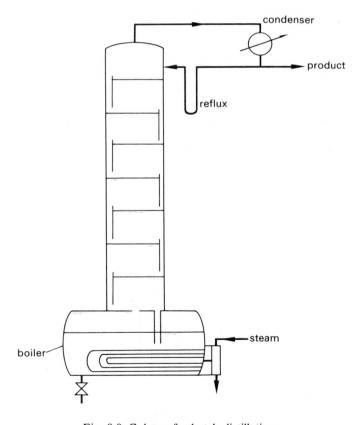

Fig. 9.9 Column for batch distillation

The main problem of recovery is that the waste oil is widely distributed in relatively small quantities. The minimum worthwhile load for a recoverer is about 2·25 m³ (500 gal) and storage facilities for such quantities tend to be restricted to those of large garages, centres such as bus depots and commercial vehicle fleet owners. Moves to rationalise reprocessing have resulted, for example, in the setting up of collection networks[20] and of satellite refineries around the country.[21] The strong competition, however, with about twelve companies actively re-refining oil, acts as a deterrent to more efficient and widespread collection, because of the need to keep costs down. There is considerable interest in recycling relatively high-value oil products such as lubricating oil, where the economic effects of the oil crisis of 1972/3 have been most pronounced. Recycled lubricating oil can be produced at approximately half the cost of virgin oil.

The broad categories of suitable oils for recycling are: used crankcase oils, gear and hydraulic oils, general-purpose lubricating oils and quenching oils. Most lubricating oils are suitable for re-refining provided that they are properly segregated. Generally any oils such as brake fluids or hydraulic oils may be reclaimed more efficiently by being kept separate.

The following contaminants will either impair the efficiency of re-refining, or may completely preclude reprocessing:

Synthetic ester types of lubricants. These are used mainly in turbine engines (aviation, some power stations), also occasionally as gear lubricants. Synthetics have been introduced as crankcase lubricants but the quantities are as yet insignificant.

Glycerides (including animal and vegetable oils and fats). These are found mainly in compounded cutting oils. They are occasionally used in hydraulic brake fluids and EP gear oils but the quantities are usually insignificant.

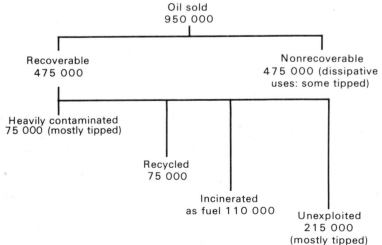

Fig. 9.10 Approximate annual distribution of waste lubricating oil in the UK (tonnes)

Solvents used for industrial cleaning often contain quantities of fatty oils or waxes, for example dry-cleaning fluids. *Cooking fats must* be excluded.

Petroleum jelly or wax. This is not often found in used oil supplies but may be carried in industrial cleaning solvents. Wax also occurs in heavy residual fuel oils.

Heavy fuel oils.

Chlorinated cutting oils.

Soluble oils of all kinds.

Scourable textile oils.

Brake fluids.

Light chlorinated solvents, and *de-greasing fluids* (e.g. perchlorethylene), should be kept to a minimum, but only slightly affect recovery.

Water reduces the efficiency of the process and should be kept to a minimum.

The composition of a typical waste lubricating oil is given in Table 9.3,[18] which illustrates the type of treatment required to provide a base lubricating oil for reblending. Basically, water, light-ends, metals and other solids need to be removed. Segregation of oils by the producer is important; a recent code of practice[22] advocates total segregation if possible, or at least separation into mineral oils, synthetic oils, solvents and general wastes.

A number of processes have been developed for recycling. Published information is not a good guide to current practice, which is highly competitive and usually confidential to the company concerned.

The most widely used process is the acid–clay process, a typical example of which is described and shown in Figure 9.11. The first operation is settling and water drainage. Large particulate solids are then removed by screening and the oil is heated and centrifuged to remove fines down to $2\,\mu m$ and emulsified water. It then passes via a line heater to a flash dehydrator operating at atmospheric pressure and 150°C to separate steam and light hydrocarbons. The dehydrated oil is cooled to 40°C and agitated with 6%–10% by weight of 93–98% sulphuric acid. At the end of the reaction the mixture is settled into two layers, the heavier acid tar being drained off for further treatment, disposal by landfill or incineration. Colour and odour are removed from the oil by clay treatment, which typically consists of mixing with 3%–5% by weight of activated bleaching earth and 0·1%–0·2% alkali, and reacting under vacuum in a stripping tower at about 270°C.[23] The bottoms, comprising SAE 20 and SAE 30 oil and spent earth, are cooled and the earth is removed by filtration for subsequent disposal by landfill or incineration. The tops comprise Derv and SAE 5 or SAE 10 oil.

TABLE 9.3 TYPICAL COMPOSITION OF A WASTE LUBRICATING OIL[18]

Gravity, API at 15·6°C	24·0
Viscosity	99·0 centistokes at 37·8°C
Pour point	−37°C
Flash point	146°C
Heating value	38 230 kJ/kg (16 436 Btu/lb)
Bottom sediment and water	11·0 wt %
Sulphur	0·43 wt %
Ash	2·0 wt %*
Lead	3400 ppm
Zinc	1650 ppm
Phosphorus	1250 ppm
Iron	1025 ppm
Barium	1005 ppm
Calcium	1000 ppm
Magnesium	559 ppm
Copper	177 ppm
Tin	58 ppm
Chromium	29 ppm
Silver	1 ppm

* A figure of 0·8 wt % is quoted[18] but this is incompatible with the metal content as quoted and other data provided.

This comprehensive process may be adapted to a range of feedstocks and different contaminants. Each reprocessing company will also have developed its own variations, depending on the feed-stocks available and products required. It is important to note that reblending is a skilled operation and requires considerable expertise to produce a material of comparable specification to virgin oils. This is particularly true of oils containing additives, for example, for viscosity control or inhibition of corrosion. Thus a battery of quality control tests must be applied to the reprocessed oil.[24] However, there is no objection in principle to continued recycling of recycled oil.

Modifications have been developed to supplement the processes described above. Some are based on solvent extraction, for example with propane[25] or butanol,[26] which is carried out after pretreatment and dehydration and before the acid washing and clay treatment. Other variations employ caustic alkali washing[27] and sodium hydroxide and hydrogen peroxide treatment.[28]

'Suds' oils or emulsified oils in a water base and containing up to 5% oil are generally uneconomic to recycle. This is because the complex composition of current soluble oils, which include emulsifying agents such as petroleum soaps, a coupling agent to make the emulsion stable and often a bactericide, makes reblending a sophisticated control operation only suitable for experienced analysts and blenders. The high cost of transporting large quantities of water is a further disincentive. One example of reuse is where large quantities of spent emulsified oils are brought together for disposal. The emulsion is cracked and an oil-rich layer is produced which is used as a fuel supplement in a local boiler.[29] It is claimed that this pays for the cost of treating the oil and diverting the tankers transporting the waste oils.

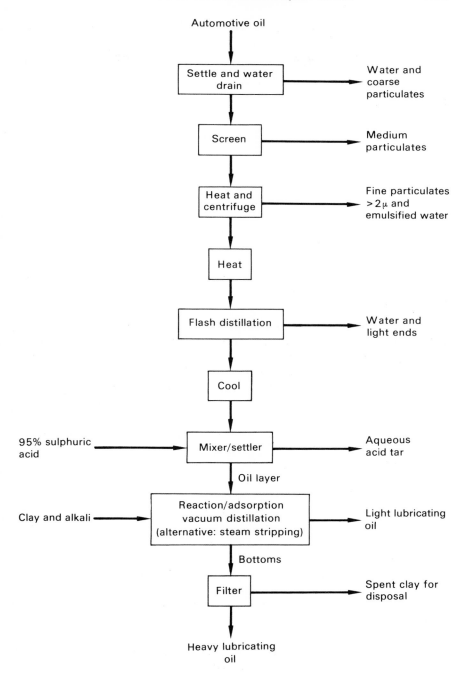

Fig. 9.11 Acid–clay treatment process for recycling lubricating oil

As mentioned in Chapter 13, there is an EEC Directive on the disposal of waste oil.[30] This directs that, as far as possible, disposal shall be by recycling. However, with current transportation and processing costs any significant short-term increase in recycling, as distinct from blending for incineration or to produce a fuel oil, seems unlikely.

Water

The need for water conservation is well understood in most factories since not only is there generally a charge for abstraction or use but costs are also incurred for effluent treatment and discharge, as outlined in Chapters 4 and 7. These can amount to £1 per 4·54 m³ (1000 gal) on an in-and-out basis. The process industries are major users of water (Table 9.4) and can make the greatest economies. In most factories water has two or more types of use with quite different quality requirements. First-grade water, i.e. water fresh from the public supply, is preferred for process uses such as materials transfer, dilution, dissolution and washing. Additional purification, such as softening by ion-exchange, is essential for some processes. Second-grade water, from rivers or private boreholes, may be of adequate purity for non-process applications, for example cooling duties, gas scrubbing and general factory cleaning. If it is to be used for 'intermediate' quality applications, for example as boiler feed water or for raw material fluming, this second-grade water often requires pretreatment. Condensate from steam-raising plant is invariably recycled.

The basic principles of in-factory water conservation are:

(a) to use the minimum water quality acceptable for each specific duty;

(b) to recycle water, or reuse it for a lesser duty, whenever practicable subject to economics;

(c) to monitor consumption regularly and avoid general wastage, for example from overflows or unessential continuous flows;

(d) to use water for washing more efficiently, for example by employing hot water or pressure washing.

TABLE 9.4 COMPARATIVE INDUSTRIAL WATER REQUIREMENTS

	Water consumption		
	m³/tonne	gal/tonne	tonnes/tonne
Woollens	627	138 000	619
Steel	291	64 000	293
Oil refining	19·1	4 200	19
Coke	16·4	3 600	16·2
Milk	3·4	750	3·4
Electricity generation: 0·36 m³ or 80 gal per kWh			

A flow diagram of possible alternatives in factory water supply, usage and disposal is shown in Figure 9.12. A cascade system of water usage is shown for processes I to III: some of the effluent from Process I, which requires pure water, provides part of the water requirements for Process II. Similarly, Process II feeds Process III. A simple treatment such as filtration may be interposed between the processes. This system is limited to some extent by the amount of piping, interstage storage and possibly control instrumentation required. It is more economical if included at the design stage than if modifications to an existing factory have to be financed out of savings in abstraction and effluent disposal charges.

The advantages of designing for water re-use have been demonstrated in an 'instant potato' factory.[31] Potatoes are transported from storage by a fluming water system; grit is removed from this water prior to recycling. The potatoes are treated with caustic soda solution to soften the skins, and the effluent from this process is screened to remove gross solids and skins. Acid is added to this effluent for pH adjustment and, following addition of nutrients, it passes to two high-rate biological filters in series. Following sedimentation and sand filtration, part is discharged to a river and the remainder is chlorinated, mixed with borehole water and reused (see Plant 1, page 189).

The cascade system is common in electroplating works where final rinse-water feeds previous-rinse tanks in such a way that rinse-water flows countercurrent to the material flow and gives most efficient washing for least water consumption. In some installations overflow from the first-rinse tank feeds to the electroplating bath to minimise electroplating solution loss.

Examples of the efficiency of water reuse in various industries in the USA are summarised in Table 9.5.

TABLE 9.5 RECYCLE OF INDUSTRIAL WATER

Source	Recycle ratio
Coal preparation	14·9
Petroleum	7·6
Machinery	5·5
Meat	4·0
Soaps and detergents	3·1
Pulp and paper	3·0
Auto	2·6
Natural gas transmission	2·3
Steel	1·6
Distilling	1·5
Beet sugar	1·5
Textiles	1·3
Corn and wheat milling	1·2
Food processing	1·2
Tanning—leather	1·0

Recycle ratio = $\dfrac{\text{freshwater intake required without recycle}}{\text{actual freshwater intake using recycle}}$

or = average number of times a given volume of water was recycled

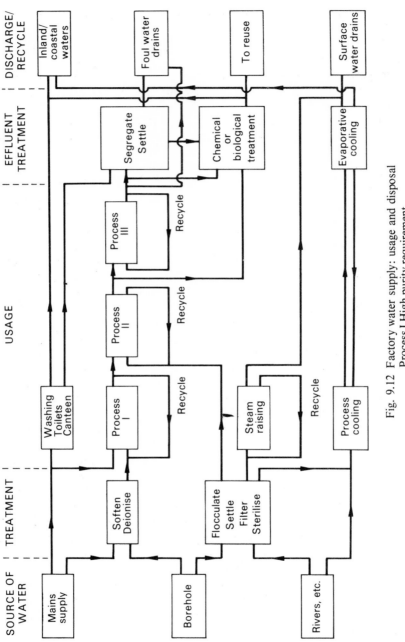

Fig. 9.12 Factory water supply: usage and disposal
Process I High purity requirement
Process II Medium purity requirement
Process III Low purity requirement

Process Water

Water is the most widely used raw material, probably because it is the cheapest to purchase, and for this reason it also tends to be extravagantly used by industry. Water is mostly employed as a general-purpose carrier to support active systems as in electroplating, to remove unwanted materials as in vegetable processing, or to transport materials or energy, for example in cooling-water. The overall effect is generally to downgrade water by adding contaminants or pollutants.

The object of a water recycling system is to remove sufficient contaminants to allow the water to be usefully reused. The treatment should not be designed to produce water of a higher quality than is necessary.

An example of industrial water recycling is the dust-washing system, or basic oxygen steel-making furnace fume extraction system, shown in Figure 9.13. Water is purified only so far as to produce recycle water that will effectively clean the effluent gases for acceptable discharge to atmosphere. The water flow is countercurrent to gas flow in a three-stage washing process whereby the most contaminated water stream washes the most contaminated gas stream. Solids are usually removed in a two-stage process: the first stage gives rapid removal of coarser solids and the second clarifies effluent to remove fine particles. Typical figures for approximate solids contents of the water stream at various points are included in the diagram. A small amount of water make-up is needed to allow for evaporation losses and leaks.

Water recycling has to satisfy much more stringent requirements where a very high level of purity is required by the process conditions. An example is electroplating, where small concentrations of some impurities can seriously impair the quality of the product. After conventional effluent treatment to remove the majority of contaminants (and to satisfy Water Authority requirements where discharge is necessary), tertiary treatment may be needed to ensure removal of all suspended solids, to remove any remaining pollutants in solution and possibly to remove products of the primary effluent treatment process such as cyanates, chlorine, alkali or calcium and sodium salts. Suspended solids can be removed by a polishing operation using, for example, fine-meshed filters for low flow rates or sand filters for high flow rates. Dissolved solids may be removed by a variety of methods, including ion exchange for soluble metals, salts, acids and alkalis, carbon adsorption for organics such as gluconates and detergents and reverse osmosis or dialysis for dissolved materials (see Chapters 7 and 8). The choice of treatment method is dependent on effluent characteristics and process requirements together with economics.

For small plants of less than around $45 \cdot 5$ m³/h (10 000 gal/h) it is doubtful whether water recycling can be economically attractive at present price levels, except in special circumstances of low pollutant levels in effluent and/or low specification for recycled water and/or special problems with water supply. Future costs of water, however, forecast to increase relative to other prices in the short to medium term, may make recycling economically more attractive.

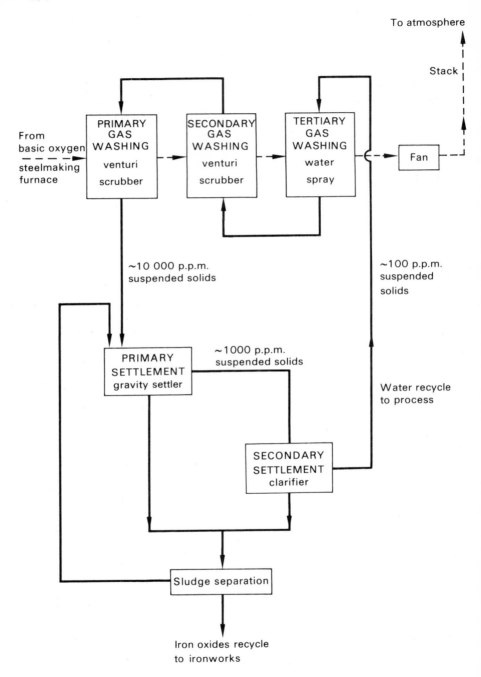

Fig. 9.13 Water recirculation in washing of basic oxygen steelmaking furnace fume

Effluent from biological treatment processes similarly requires tertiary treatment prior to direct recycling. This normally consists of polishing to remove all suspended solids and disinfection or sterilisation to kill all bacteria, at the same time removing trace soluble organics. This tertiary treatment, following on from primary and secondary biological treatment, is practically identical to potable water treatment and with care can produce water of drinking quality standard. It is usual, however, in practice to discharge treated sewage effluent and other treated biological wastes into watercourses for dilution and stabilisation before abstracting a drinking water supply. Particular problems arise with nitrates and phosphates from agricultural and domestic use, and both may require treatment for their removal. Nitrates may be reduced biologically and phosphates are effectively reduced by precipitation of insoluble ferric phosphate by adding ferric chloride solution. These treatments are usually carried out during primary and secondary biological treatment processes.

Cooling-water

Cooling-water is one effluent which can readily be recycled. The pressures to do so are both legislative and economic. Firstly, in the UK the abstraction of water from any source, other than a municipal or statutory supply, requires a licence under the Water Resources Act. Secondly, limitations may be imposed on the temperature at which water may be disposed of and charges may be incurred by its discharge.

Recirculatory cooling-water systems greatly reduce the amount of water used; in fact consumption is limited merely to make-up quantities. Outlet water streams from various process cooling duties are simply pumped to an evaporative cooling unit and the cooled water is recycled. The cooling unit may be a pond, possibly provided with sprays, or a cooling tower.

Ponds

Simple ponds depend upon slow evaporative cooling from the water surface. Their cooling performance is somewhat unpredictable and they are suitable for relatively high temperature water only. If a natural excavation or pond is available, the first cost of this type of facility is low. Otherwise the space requirements and the costs of excavation and lining may render it unattractive. A pond may have some amenity value and may serve as a reservoir for water for fire-fighting.

Spray ponds consist of collecting-basins or ponds over which recycled water is distributed from spray nozzles situated a metre or so above the surface. Since the area for water/air contact is greater, these ponds have a better cooling performance than simple ponds but again require space. To minimise wind loss, either louvres are fitted around the pond or the sprays are situated in the centre of a large reservoir. Since there is a minimum nozzle pressure for effective distribution, pumping costs are higher than for simple ponds. Blockage due to algae formation is sometimes a problem.

Cooling Towers

A cooling tower is simply an enclosed device for the evaporative cooling of water by contact with air. Efficient heat transfer is obtained by exposure of a large water surface area to the air flow, generally by the insertion of baffles or packings.

The principle is that water at elevated temperature is brought into contact with a large volume of air. Some of the cooling (up to one-third) is effected by convection, but the greater part is due to the evaporation of a small amount of water and removal of the latent heat of evaporation. In theory, 1% of the circulation rate is evaporated per 7°C of cooling range; the loss for a typical 10°C differential is therefore 1·5%. Added to this may be a further 1% for purging to avoid solids build-up in the system. The total theoretical consumption is therefore 2·5% of that for a once-through system and practical values of between 3% and 5% of the circulation rate are usual in well-designed towers. Towers are classified as

(a) Natural draught
  (i) Atmospheric type (i.e. frames)
  (ii) Chimney type
(b) Mechanical draught
  (i) Forced draught
  (ii) Induced draught

Natural-draught towers rely upon natural convection to move air through the packing. Atmospheric frames consist of a tall and narrow shell containing a spray system. The long sides are louvred and exposed to prevailing winds so that the air enters and mixes with the water spray. A disadvantage of this design is that thermal performance is dependent not only on air temperature but also on wind velocity and direction. Consequently, water temperatures cannot be controlled with accuracy. Chimney-type towers are characteristically of the concrete hyperbolic type, the alternative timber penthouse type being less common. These towers are inexpensive in operation and are well suited to handling large volumes of water where the cooling range is reasonably high and the required 'approach' to the design air wet bulb temperature (i.e. outlet water temperature less the wet bulb temperature) is only about 10°C. Therefore they are used predominantly in power stations and steel works.

The main disadvantages of natural-draught towers are large diameter, great height compared with conventional industrial towers and very high capital cost. One advantage, however, is that the hot humidified air is discharged at high level so that the plume is less likely to cause a nuisance than that from equivalent mechanical-draught towers.

A mechanical-draught tower is shown diagrammatically in Figure 9.14. A fan is used to provide controlled flow of air through the packing. This enables small compact towers to be constructed, suitable for location on factory roofs or in plant rooms, without consideration of degree of exposure or wind direction. Either induced draught may be used, with the fan driving humidified air

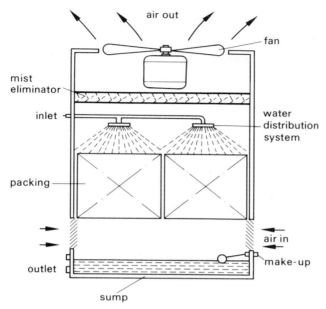

Fig. 9.14 Typical induced-draught cooling tower

out at the top, or forced draught, with the fan located at the bottom. Air velocity and depth of packing can be greater than with a natural-draught system. Problems due to recirculation of humidified air are considerably reduced with induced-draught towers, since the air is expelled at a higher velocity. Performance is dependent on wet-bulb temperature, the 'approach' being about 2°C.

All of these towers are physically very simple in construction and the design principles are well understood.[32,33] The basic design data are:

(i) Total heat dissipation rate and temperature level
(ii) Cooling-water flow rate
(iii) Desirable maximum temperature in summer
(iv) Design (i.e. summer) wet bulb temperature

The duty having been calculated, a size can then be estimated for a given water distribution system, air flow rate and volume and type of packing. Lower recycle temperatures are reflected in decreased heat transfer surface areas within the process being served, i.e. smaller heat exchangers or condensers, with consequent capital savings.[34] Mechanical-draught towers are selected for the majority of industrial cooling-water applications, because of their small space requirement, relatively low capital cost and close 'approach'.

An alternative to water-cooling by evaporation, i.e. by direct contact with air, is indirect cooling using, for example, banks of finned tubes. These are used where water supply is restricted, and have been successfully applied in electricity generating stations as an alternative to conventional water-cooling. Alternatively, direct air-cooling of process streams may be used, for example in petroleum refineries.

As a result of evaporation, mineral salts tend to concentrate in the recirculating water. Since this can result in scale deposits on plant heat-transfer surfaces, it is common practice to bleed off some water and add fresh make-up. Corrosion inhibitors, containing chromates, and biocides may be present in the bleed-off and therefore this requires effluent treatment prior to discharge.

Case Study: Investigation of Waste Recovery Potential

One of the largest waste disposal contractors in the UK, Effluent Disposal Ltd, owns a disused mineshaft in the West Midlands, which up to 1976 served as a depository for around 135 000 m³/year (30 million gal/year) of aqueous effluent. With the cooperation of the company a survey was carried out to determine the quantities and nature of materials dumped and make a preliminary evaluation of the materials that might be recovered.[35]

The procedure for accepting waste (for whatever disposal method) is first outlined, and incidentally exemplifies the precautions taken. Initially, an application is made to the contractor for removal of effluent. The application form gives details of source, quantity and composition of effluent, and is accompanied by a representative sample which is subjected to independent chemical analysis by the Public Analyst to confirm the composition of the effluent and its suitability for discharge down the mineshaft. On receipt of a satisfactory report, arrangements are made for collection and disposal. All materials are discharged directly, except aqueous cyanide solutions which are first oxidised with chlorine. Operation of the site is closely controlled by the local authority, and regular monitoring is undertaken of the liquid level, as well as the atmosphere in the shaft.

Regular pH measurement of the liquid in the mine compared with material discharged suggested that in fact some neutralisation of acids took place in the mine workings, probably by reaction with minerals in the rocks. Laboratory experimentation confirmed this neutralisation effect and also indicated that metals tended to be adsorbed by the rocks.

The results presented below were obtained from the analyses supplied by the analytical laboratory and from quantities recorded on the sales and loading sheets. A twelve-month period in 1971 was covered during which time 135 000 m³ (29·75 million gal) of effluents were discharged to the mineshaft (assuming full tanker loads: although the true figure may be around 10–15% lower, the analysis is based on the quoted figure).

Table 9.6 provides an overall analysis of the effluent received during the twelve-month period and an indication of the total volumes of effluent containing each material. Each tanker load of effluent is a complex mixture of many materials and each load has a different composition. Successive tanker loads might, for example, consist of spent sulphuric acid pickle liquor, emulsified oil, neutralised metal-finishing solution slurry, and stormwater. The volume figures show the materials contained in various proportions of the overall volume of waste. It is estimated that Effluent Disposal Ltd has approximately half of the total market in the West Midlands, which suggests that the total quantities arising in this area are about double those quoted, with the exception of waste hydrochloric acid which is almost exclusively handled by this firm.

TABLE 9.6 ANALYSIS OF EFFLUENT

	Total quantity (tonnes)	Volume (m³)
Sulphuric acid (100%)	3 709	26 500
Iron (as Fe)	1 779	50 500
Hydrochloric acid (100%)	1 266	8 850
Zinc (as Zn)	396	40 000
Nitric acid (100%)	166	1 010
Sodium hydroxide and equivalent	50·6	5 080
Copper (as Cu)	35·7	27 400
Hydrofluoric acid (100%)	28·8	4 870
Chromium (as Cr)	18·3	23 600
Phosphoric acid (100%)	11·4	20
Nickel (as Ni)	10·9	29 800
Cyanide (as CN)	2·4	19 200
Lead (as Pb)	1·4	17 500
Cadmium (as Cd)	0·4	13 500
Oils (including soluble and emulsified)	3 728	6 120
Phenols	36·2	34 800
Total chloride	2 480	—
Total sulphate	4 210	—
Water (by difference)	127 334	
Total approximately	140 000	135 000

Table 9.7 gives quoted list prices at the time of the evaluation[36,37,38] for most of the materials contained in, or capable of being derived from, the effluent. Many of these prices are subject to considerable fluctuations with an overall upward trend.

TABLE 9.7 LIST PRICES OF CHEMICALS AND METALS AT JANUARY 1974

		£/tonne[36]
Sulphuric acid	96%	15·8
	(100% basis	16·5)
Hydrochloric acid	28·5%	16·6
	(100% basis	58·1)
Nitric acid	100%	47·5
Hydrofluoric acid	70%	154
	(100% basis	220)
Phosphoric acid	75% (food grade)	151·6
	(100% basis	202)
Sodium hydroxide (solid)		45·6
Water		0·05

Table 9.7 (*continued*)

	Scrap metal[37]	New metal[37]	Oxide[37]	Sulphate
Iron	8–15	25	8	2[38]
Lead	160	250	230	
Zinc	240–410	580	192[36]	100[36]
Copper	550–650	900		275[38]
Chromium		1030		
Nickel	1100	1500		
Tin		2900		
Cadmium		2500		

Notes
1. Powdered metals command a premium of around £80 per tonne.
2. It should be noted that metal prices, particularly copper and tin, have fluctuated considerably in the last two years, and may not therefore be indicative of future prices.
3. The above are list prices; market prices may vary widely.

Table 9.8 uses the prices quoted in Table 9.7 to give notional values to a range of products that might be recovered from this waste. This aids identification of those materials whose recovery may be economically viable, i.e. the predominant constituents of the waste and the high-value products. The notional minimum and maximum total value of the waste are included to demonstrate the magnitude of material losses in this way: if the most valuable material cannot be recovered economically, it is less likely that recovery of a less valuable material will prove viable.

Hydrochloric acid	1266 tonnes contained in 8850 m^3
Sulphuric acid	3709 tonnes contained in 26 500 m^3
Zinc	396 tonnes contained in 40 000 m^3, of which 360 tonnes contained in approximately 4000 m^3
Copper	35·7 tonnes contained in 27 400 m^3, of which 31·5 tonnes contained in approximately 6500 m^3

A preliminary evaluation of alternatives for recovery of each of the materials in Table 9.8 indicated that hydrochloric acid was probably the most profitable, followed by zinc and other non-ferrous metals. The evaluation procedure considered technical feasibility and economic viability including use of new techniques of process generation and evaluation, and of capital and operating cost estimating as described in Chapter 20.

There were two main sources of hydrochloric acid: (a) zinc processing industries, when the acid was associated with zinc and some iron; (b) iron and steel pickling, when the acid was associated with iron. Acid was also recoverable from the zinc and iron chlorides present in these wastes by high temperature hydrolysis, giving acid and metal oxides. This process is well proven and is widely practised to recover hydrochloric acid in a number of large steel works. The quantities that might be obtained and their notional values are summarised in Table 9.9. Preliminary design studies for recovery of commercial hydrochloric acid based on the hydrolysis process indicated that for acid alone a return of more than 50% might be expected with a payback time of less than two years. For zinc oxide recovery as well, employing elementary chemical technology, the return was estimated at around 25% with a payback time of about three and a half years. The evaluation ignored taxation and possible investment grants (see Chapter 20).

Recovery of any other material could not be economically justified at the scale on which the processes would have to operate, although estimated total

TABLE 9.8 APPROXIMATE VALUE OF RECOVERABLE MATERIALS (1974 PRICES)

		£
Sulphuric acid (commercial, 96%)		61 100
Hydrochloric acid (commercial, 28·5%)		73 500
Nitric acid (100%)		7 900
Water	(process quality)	6 340
	(higher purity)	12 680
Iron	(impure, scrap)	19 600
	(pure)	44 500
	(pure, powder)	142 000
	oxide	20 300
	sulphate (anhydrous)	9 600
Lead	(impure, scrap)	220
	(pure)	350
	oxide	350
Zinc	(impure, scrap)—average	128 000
	(pure)	230 000
	(powder)	255 000
	oxide—average	122 000
	sulphate (anhydrous)	98 000
Copper	(impure, scrap)	21 400
	(pure)	32 100
	(powder)	35 700
	sulphate, anhydrous, technical grade	24 600
	sulphate, anhydrous, high purity	40 500
Hydrofluoric acid (commercial, 70%)		5 750
Chromium (pure)		18 900
Phosphoric acid (commercial, 75%)		2 100
Nickel	(impure, scrap)	11 800
	(pure)	16 500
Cadmium (pure)		1 400
Oil, heat content		1 200

The notional value of the 135 000 m³ (30 million gal) effluent lies between £320 000 and £620 000, depending on whether low-value or high-value materials are recovered.

TABLE 9.9 RECOVERY OF HYDROCHLORIC ACID (1974 PRICES)

(a) *From galvanising and related industries:*	
Zinc	360 tonnes (91% of total zinc present) existing as zinc chloride Value £148 000*
Iron	356 tonnes
Hydrochloric acid	523 tonnes (41% of total hydrochloric acid present) Volume 3500 m³
(b) *From iron and steel pickling industries:*	
Iron	314 tonnes, existing as ferrous chloride
Hydrochloric acid	653 tonnes (51% of total hydrochloric acid present) Volume 4700 m³
(c) *By hydrolysis of zinc and iron chlorides above:*	
Hydrochloric acid	1279 tonnes
Total hydrochloric acid recoverable 2455 tonnes, value £143 000	

* Average value for zinc metal depending on purity (range £86 000 to £209 000); as oxide the approximate value would be £66 000.

metal losses were as summarised in Table 9.10. A number of options were considered deserving of further study. Each had the effect of increasing the quantity of material handled and thus, with economies of scale, might make recovery viable. The possibilities included:

(a) The disposal contractor, in a parallel operation and in common with a number of other organisations, removes relatively high-solids-content sludges and cakes from individual companies own treatment systems and tips them. The total annual quantity of these sludges and cakes is believed to be around 150 000 tonnes in the West Midlands, consisting of around 5% solids. An integrated approach to recovery using these sludges and cakes with the aqueous liquids described above may be much more economically attractive.

(b) A further source of metals is household refuse (see also Chapter 17): the West Midlands produces around 60 000 tonnes/year of metals in household refuse, of which little is recycled. Based on current analysis, this corresponds to:

	Tonnes/year
Iron	64 200
Aluminium	2170
Zinc	1950
Copper	1270
Tin	390
Nickel	25

Metal recycling by hydrometallurgical processing is unlikely to be viable on a small scale but, when reagents and feedstock are free or even at negative cost, at least deserves investigation.

(c) The extensive metal finishing industry in the West Midlands causes trade effluent discharges to have a relatively high metal content. After processing in conventional sewage works the metal is concentrated in the sewage sludge. The levels are sufficiently high to preclude use of the sludge as a fertiliser, and the sewage sludge is now filtered and incinerated. The total metal arisings in the West Midlands from this source is roughly estimated to be:

	Tonnes/year
Iron	7200
Zinc	1560
Copper	830
Chromium	550
Nickel	240
Lead	180
Cadmium	30

Due to the widely variable quality and composition of sewage, and the geographical scatter of sewage works, these figures are very imprecise and do not necessarily represent recoverable quantities.

TABLE 9.10 ESTIMATED CURRENT TOTAL ANNUAL METAL LOSSES IN THE WEST MIDLANDS (TONNES/YEAR)

	Liquid waste	Sludge waste	Municipal refuse	Sewage sludge	Total	Per capita (kg/year)
Iron	2700	2500	64 200	7200	76 600	30
Zinc	600	400	1 950	1560	4 510	1·8
Copper	71	200	1 270	830	2 371	0·95
Aluminium		50	2 170		2 230	0·9
Chromium	37	200		550	787	0·31
Tin		50	390		440	0·18
Nickel	22	100	25	240	387	0·15
Lead	3	50		180	233	0·09
Cadmium	1	50		30	81	0·03

Some of these suggestions are considered over-optimistic; however, if a monetary value were to be placed on conservation, and recycling were financially encouraged, the result would be reduced pollution since recycling is one of the more effective pollution control devices. Much depends, on a national scale, on concerted action by Government and by waste producers, local authorities and disposal authorities.

Relevant developments since the survey (1971) and evaluation (1974) include:

(a) Blockage of the mineshaft in 1976—aqueous waste is now tipped in a near-by disused brickworks; drilling of a test bore into the adjacent colliery within the same fault lines, and planning permission for discharge of waste into these workings.

(b) Increased national awareness of the need to conserve resources and avoid pollution.

(c) The effect of the energy crisis, together with inflation, on transportation costs; these can contribute 90% to the total cost of disposal, and thus discourage integrated treatment.

(d) Greater use of long-term storage of metal-rich sludges in 'ponds' or sealed in blocks of polymerised material, and thus the possibility of their future exploitation.

Waste Exchange

In any attempt to recycle waste or recover materials from it, the most common problem is lack of money, equipment, experience or economy of scale to make recovery technically and economically viable. Recognition of this led to the establishment in 1974 of the UK Waste Materials Exchange, administered by Warren Spring Laboratory, to cover the full range of manufacturing processes except those where satisfactory commercial markets already existed, such as in scrap metals and secondhand equipment.

Quarterly bulletins are issued listing wastes under the two main headings of 'Available' and 'Wanted'. Each section is divided into twelve categories:

Acids and alkalis	Minerals
Catalysts	Miscellaneous
Inorganic chemicals	Oils and waxes
Organic chemicals	Paper and board
Food processing	Rubber and plastics
Metals	Textiles and leather

Each entry comprises a reference number, a brief description, and frequency and quantity of waste arising or requested, and includes a code letter indicating geographical area. The service is free to participants, with the Government currently meeting the full cost.

The scheme has been widely described and discussed:[39–42] up to mid-1976, 1104 items had been listed and 5787 enquiries for 884 of these received. While only 65 transactions were recorded up to early 1976, it is likely that the actual figure was considerably higher. At that time nearly 4 million tonnes of waste per annum were represented in the scheme, which constitutes a significant percentage of total UK waste. Economically, the scheme is more difficult to quantify. The known transactions, representing savings of several hundred thousand pounds overall, are probably less significant to individual participants.

The Waste Materials Exchange Service provides increased opportunity for reusing some of the millions of tonnes of waste that are otherwise discarded or dumped. It also causes firms to look more closely at what they regard as valueless waste and pay closer attention to the possibilities of recycling. Other proposals for local and regional waste exchange services have been reported, but little information is available.

References

1. Warren Spring Laboratory, internal reports and publicity information, 1970–77.
2. FLETCHER, A. W., *Chemistry and Industry,* 5 May 1973.
3. FLETCHER, A. W., in Institution of Chemical Engineers Symposium Series No. 41, T1, 1975.
4. FLETT, D. S. and PEARSON, D. *Chemistry and Industry,* 639, 2 August 1975.
5. JACKSON, D. V., *Metal Finishing Journal,* **18**(211), 235, 1972.
6. Private communication.
7. BOWEN, L. B., MALINSON, J. H. and COSGROVE, J. H., *Chemical Engineering Progress,* 50, May 1977.
8. TEWORTE, W., *Chemistry and Industry,* 565, 3 May 1969.
9. PEARSON, D., *Reclamation Industries,* 31 and 38, September 1971.
10. FLETCHER, A. W., *Industrial Recovery,* **22**(23), 10, 1975.
11. Woodall-Duckham trade literature, *Spray Roasting to Recover Hydrochloric Acid.*
12. Technical Committee on the Disposal of Solid Toxic Wastes, *Disposal of Solid Toxic Wastes,* HMSO, 1970.
13. Working Party on Refuse Disposal, *Refuse Disposal,* HMSO, 1971.
14. Waste Management Advisory Council, *First Report,* HMSO, 1976.
15. *Waste Disposal in the Manchester/Salford Area,* Local Government Operational Research Unit, 1971.
16. HIGGINSON, A. E., *Chemical Engineer,* 305, June 1973.
17. *Mineral Oil Wastes,* Waste Management Paper No. 7, HMSO, 1976.
18. VARTY, K. H., *Birmingham Post,* 27 April 1976.
19. PEARCE, D., *Resources Policy,* 213, June 1975.
20. Beesley, H. and Sons Ltd, trade literature, 1977.
21. HILL, P., *The Engineer,* 1 November 1973.
22. *Code of Practice for the Recovery of Mineral Oils,* Chemical Recovery Association, 1975.
23. *Science Dimension,* **7**(5), 8, 1975.
24. ALLINSON, J. S. (Ed.), *Criteria for Quality of Petroleum Products,* Applied Science, 1973.
25. QANG, V. Q., *Hydrocarbon Processing,* **53**(4), 129, 1974, and *Process Engineering* News Item, 10 May 1974.
26. US Patents 3625881 and 3639229.
27. WHISMAN, M. L., *Waste Lubricating Oil Research,* Report RI 7884, US Bureau of Mines, 1974.
28. US Patent 3620967.
29. Effluent Disposal Ltd, private communication, 1976.
30. Council Directive 75/439/EEC of 16 June 1975, The Disposal of Waste Oils, *Official Journal of the European Communities,* **1**, 194/23, 1975.
31. MCDONALD, D. P., *Process Engineering,* 50, November 1971.
32. JACKSON, J., *Cooling Towers,* Butterworth, 1951.
33. STANFORD, W. and HILL, G. B., *Cooling Towers—Principles and Practice,* Carter Thermal Engineering Ltd, 1966.
34. KERN, D. Q., *Process Heat Transfer,* McGraw-Hill, 1950.
35. BRIDGWATER, A. V. and GASKARTH, J. W., in *Proceedings of Conference on Conservation of Materials,* UKAEA, Harwell, 1974.
36. *European Chemical News* (weekly).
37. *Metal Bulletin* (weekly).
38. Private communication.
39. POLL, A., regular feature in *Quarterly Bulletin of the UK Waste Materials Exchange,* Warren Spring Laboratory.
40. POLL, A., *Process News,* 6, 7 October 1975.

41. POLL, A. and ALLEN, J., *Waste in the Process Industries,* Institution of Mechanical Engineers, 1976.
42. POLL, A. and ALLEN J., *Chemistry and Industry,* 238, 20 March 1976.

PART THREE

CONTROL OF ATMOSPHERIC E[

CHAPTER 10

Control of Dust, Fumes, Mists and Odour from Manufacturing Processes

Gaseous pollutants and contaminants of gas streams were characterised in Chapter 3. They comprise solid or liquid particulate matter in various size ranges, gases and vapours. Engineering aspects of particulate pollutant removal are considered in this chapter together with the removal of low levels of gases or vapours which result in odours, and the recovery of particulate matter.

The design of equipment must take into account all pollutants and the appropriate standards for discharge: selection depends on the nature of other pollutants present—for example, the presence of soot particles may seriously inhibit the operation of a packed absorber. Therefore there is a degree of overlap between the measures discussed in Chapters 10, 11 and 12.

In addition to processes which evolve very low levels of gas contaminants giving rise to odours, there are many which require, for both pollution control and commercial reasons, the removal of a combination of gaseous constituents such as, most commonly, sulphur dioxide, hydrogen sulphide, fluorine and fluorine compounds, chlorine and hydrogen chloride, ammonia and nitrogen compounds. Because of the high solute concentrations, the common methods used involve combustion (either directly or in a catalyst bed), absorption in a liquid or 'scrubbing', adsorption on a solid which may subsequently be regenerated, or condensation. Gaseous pollutants resulting from combustion processes are discussed in Chapter 11. Absorption, adsorption and condensation provide the option of solute recovery and are discussed in Chapter 12.

In general the equipment described below for the control of particulate emissions is applicable to combustion processes provided the materials of construction can withstand the operating temperatures. Additional factors in the control of pollution from combustion processes, for example control of sulphur dioxide emissions, are described in Chapter 11.

A recurring factor in air pollution control is the production of solid or liquid waste streams, depending on the pollutant knock-out or collection system used. These streams must be recovered or disposed of without creating further air, land or water pollution. Therefore in the selection of the optimum gas pollution control system the full costs of operation, including energy costs (which may be particularly significant with, for example, electrostatic precipitation) and solid or liquid waste disposal, must be included. Typical costs are given in Chapter 20. Particular examples of viable recovery operations involving particulates are given in Chapter 12.

Grit, Dust and Fumes

Emissions from manufacturing processes frequently contain solids in the following forms.[1]

(a) Relatively coarse particles, i.e. a substantial proportion in sizes greater than $10 \mu m$: for example, grit and dust from grinding and screening operations, from kilns and calciners and from combustion processes.

(b) A majority of particles between $1 \mu m$ and $10 \mu m$: for example, emissions from steel making and smelting processes and many other industrial emissions contain particles in this range.

(c) True fumes, that is particles less than $1 \mu m$. This range may, either alone or in combination with fogs or other contaminants, cause an industrial haze.

The concentration of dust in the gas stream varies with the source.[2] Dust dispersed from a production process or from mechanical handling systems requires a control system which can handle a high volumetric flow rate of air with a low dust burden. Dust concentration is generally less than $2 g/m^3$. Higher dust concentrations may be present in flue gases from combustion processes, dependent on the air requirements for efficient combustion (see Chapter 11). Higher concentrations may also arise from size-reduction operations, for example grinding, or where the product is essentially dry, for example from industrial dryers. One of the highest dust burdens is associated with pneumatic conveying, up to $20 kg/m^3$.

Separators or collectors for particles fall into four main classes:

Dry inertial separators, e.g. cyclones, baffled settling chambers
Wet de-dusters or scrubbers, e.g. simple spray towers
Fibre and fabric filters, e.g. bag filters
Electrostatic precipitators

Some of the types of equipment, their applications, typical efficiencies and relative costs are given in Table 10.1. However, as discussed later, efficiency of dust-arresting equipment varies significantly with particle-size distribution.

TABLE 10.1 TYPES OF ARRESTMENT PLANT: APPLICATIONS, EFFICIENCIES AND RELATIVE COSTS (BASED ON SUTTON[3])

Type	Application			Efficiency %	Relative total cost of treatment
	Grit > 76 μm	Dust 1–76 μm	Fume < 1 μm		
Medium-efficiency cyclone	S	(S)		60–70	1·0
High-efficiency multi-cyclone	S	S		70–85	1·5
Self-spray separator	S	S	(S)	85–95	2·0
Electro-precipitator	S	S	S	97–99·8	4·0
Bag filter	S	S	S	98–99·8	4·5
Venturi scrubber	S	S	S	98–99·8	5·5

S = suitable; (S) = suitable only under certain circumstances.

Dry Inertial Separators

In settling chambers the gas velocity is reduced so that larger particles separate under gravity. However, since the rate of fall of small particles under gravity is low, they are only practicable for the removal of coarser grits. For such applications they operate at a low pressure drop, e.g. < 0·5 mbar.

Medium-efficiency cyclones of the type illustrated in Figure 10.1 are simple, cheap and robust and the collection efficiency of simple units ranges from 65% upwards. They are most effective for grit removal. Multiple high-efficiency or irrigated cyclones have efficiencies better than 90%. For smaller particle sizes efficiency can be improved by increasing the residence time and angular velocity, i.e. by the use of smaller diameter cyclones of increased length. High-efficiency cyclones comprise nests of small tubular cyclones (Figure 10.1). Efficiency may also be improved by water injection either at the inlet or tangentially at the cyclone walls.

Wet Scrubbers

Wet scrubber designs include simple spray towers, jet-impingement, fluidised-bed scrubbers, self-induced spray de-dusters, venturi and annular-throat scrubbers and disintegrators. These all rely upon the particles being 'wetted' and enlarged by contact with water to allow easier removal from the gas stream. As well as collecting particles, they may also serve to cool gases and hence protect fan, ducting and stack materials.

In the simple spray tower illustrated in Figure 10.2, water sprays are injected into a suitable chamber countercurrent to the flow of polluted gas. The superficial gas velocity is generally between 0·6 and 1·2 m/s (2–4 ft/s) and the droplet diameter must be sufficient to eliminate entrainment. This drop diameter is conventionally in the range 0·1–1 mm. As with other wet

274

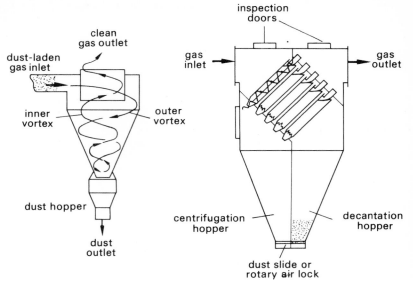

Fig. 10.1 a Medium-efficiency cyclone
b High-efficiency multiple tubular cyclone

Fig. 10.2 Simple spray tower

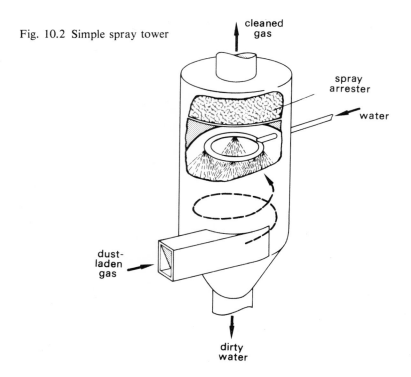

scrubbers, a proportion of the liquid is normally recycled, often after a coarse solids removal stage; the spray nozzles must therefore be resistant to erosion or blockage by suspended solids.

Wetted surfaces in the form of irrigated trays, packings or impingement plates may be included to improve efficiency. However, conventional packed beds employing Raschig ring or saddle-type packing are seldom used because of the possibility of plugging and relatively large gas-pressure drops. A sieve plate column may be used with impingement plates above the orifices; gas velocity through each orifice is about $4 \cdot 5$–$6 \cdot 0$ m/s (15–20 ft/s).

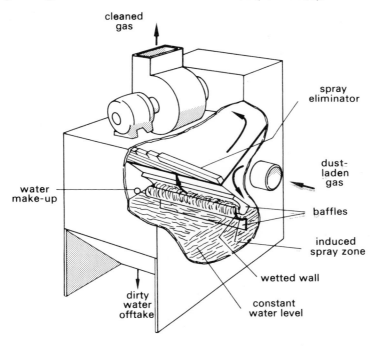

Fig. 10.3 Self-induced spray de-duster

In the self-induced spray de-duster, one design of which is shown in Figure 10.3, the inlet air is passed beneath the constant water level in the chamber and produces a spray for collection; in the jet-impingement scrubber (Figure 10.4) the dust-laden gas is discharged as a jet onto the liquid and then passes via baffles to the discharge stack.

In the fluidised-bed scrubber (Figure 10.5) the dust-laden gas and scrubbing liquid are contacted countercurrently in a bed of spheres·which are fluidised by the gas flow. Fluidisation prevents plugging of the bed and hence this design is applicable to 'sticky' particle collection.

Two designs of venturi scrubber are shown in Figure 10.6.[1] The gas velocity is increased in a venturi and the scrubbing liquid, generally water, is injected radially upstream of the throat section; this results in fine atomisation and good contacting. This type of equipment is often used for cleaning basic oxygen fume, as described in Chapters 9 and 12.

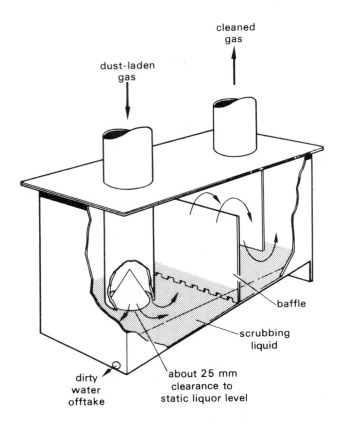

Fig. 10.4 Jet-impingement scrubber

In the disintegrator, water is injected into the gas during passage through alternate rotor and stator blades (Figure 10.7). This produces a very fine dispersion which is more effective in collecting small particles of 1 μm or less, than the relatively coarse dispersions produced in spray or self-induced spray towers. The disintegrator scrubber is relatively compact but operating costs are high due to the power consumption, equivalent to 6·8–8·3 W/m³ s of gas scrubbed. Furthermore, to reduce erosion of the blades some precleaning of the gases may be desirable to remove grit.

A spray eliminator must be incorporated in each of these designs, which are capable of efficiencies better than 99%. In addition, provision must be made for dealing with contaminated water effluent and sludge disposal. They may also

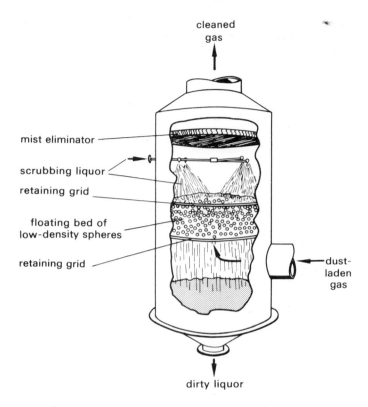

Fig. 10.5 Fluidised-bed scrubber

result in a cold, wet emission to atmosphere which may render the plume more visible and negate the thermal lift available with hot gases. Fan assistance may then be necessary.

Filters

Fibre pads or pleated paper filters may be used to remove relatively low dust concentrations. Bag filters of various types[4] deal with medium-to-high dust concentrations; in these the fabric, of woven or felted cloth, traps the particles but allows the gas to pass through the pores. The mechanisms involved in collection are inertial impaction, interception and diffusion. More efficient collection is therefore provided by fine fibres. Efficiency is also improved by close packing of the fibres, but only at the expense of pressure drop; this may involve a significant increase in fan size and operating costs. The dust cake which accumulates on the upstream side of the filter also serves to increase filtration efficiency.

The fibres, natural or chemical, cellulose or glass, or metal, are spun or woven into cloth or loosely packed or pressed into a felt. The fabric is selected

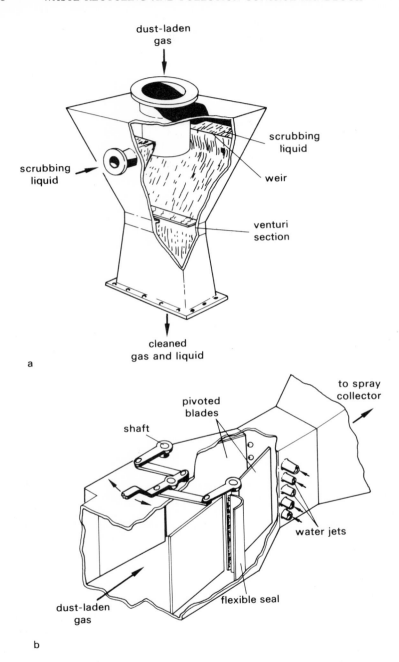

Fig. 10.6 Venturi scrubbers
      a For slurries
      b Incorporating a variable-throat arrangement

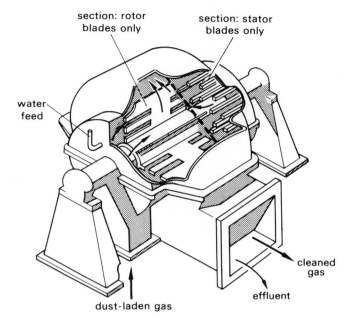

section: rotor
blades only

section: stator
blades only

water
feed

cleaned
gas

effluent

dust-laden gas

Fig. 10.7 Disintegrator scrubber

having regard to collection efficiency, pressure drop, the required strength (determined by the type and frequency of cleaning) and chemical inertness.

The filter fabric is arranged as vertical stockings or bags in a steel-plate chamber so that the particle-laden gas passes upwards through them. For continuous operation the filters are cleaned intermittently either by periodic manual or mechanical shaking or by means of a reverse jet of air; the particles are dislodged into a hopper from which they are discharged by a conveyor or by gravity. A typical arrangement employing mechanical shaking is illustrated in Figure 10.8. Because of the large number of bags, filters require more space than wet scrubbers. Maintenance, involving the location and replacement of split or perforated bags, may be a dirty and difficult operation.

Electrostatic Precipitators

In an electrostatic precipitator the dust-laden gas is passed through a zone containing a high concentration of ions. Dust particles to which the ions become attached hence acquire a charge. This is followed by passage through a collection zone in which the particles move towards, and are deposited on, earthed electrodes.

In the commonest designs the earthed electrodes are vertical plates, with wires suspended between them acting as high-tension discharge electrodes.

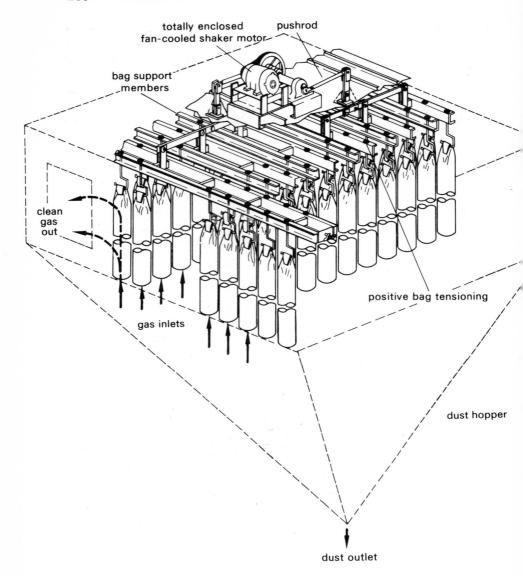

Fig. 10.8 Filter baghouse with mechanical shaking

Dust particles travel to the plates and, following agglomeration and loss of charge, larger particles fall into a hopper beneath. Periodic removal of dust from the plates by vibration, rapping or washing is essential for efficient operation, since build-up of an excessive dust layer will impair the electrical characteristics. One precipitator arrangement employing rappers to dislodge agglomerated dust is shown in Figure 10.9. Wet-wall precipitators are sometimes used, in which a constant flow of water washes away deposited solids.

Electrostatic precipitators find wide application for the cleaning of large-volume gas flows provided the dust does not involve an explosion hazard. Typical uses are for fly ash collection from the exhaust gases from pulverised fuel-fired boilers, the cleaning of exhaust gases from cement manufacture at temperatures of around 350°C, and iron oxide fume removal from large-scale metallurgical operations such as open hearth and electric arc furnaces.

Typical efficiencies of the main types of arrestment equipment are listed in Table 10.2.[1] This serves to illustrate the variation with particle size: the typical sizes of 50, 5 and 1 μm are those responsible for dustfall, dinginess and haze respectively. Relatively simple designs approach 100% efficiency when

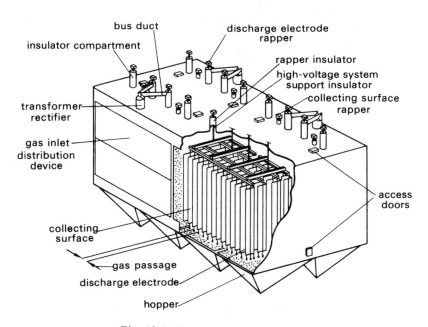

Fig. 10.9 Electrostatic precipitator

arresting 50 μm particles, but more complex equipment is required for efficient collection of smaller particles (Figure 10.10).[5] Consequently, equipment for the reduction of plume appearance or local haze is likely to prove expensive. Furthermore, to obtain a high efficiency over a wide particle size-range two

TABLE 10.2 TYPICAL EFFICIENCIES OR ARRESTMENT PLANT AT VARIOUS PARTICLE SIZES[1]

Equipment	Percentage efficiency at		
	50 μm	5 μm	1 μm
Inertial collector	95	16	3
Medium-efficiency cyclone	94	27	8
Cellular cyclone	98	42	13
High-efficiency cyclone	96	73	27
Tubular cyclones	100	89	40
Jet-impingement scrubber	98	83	40
Irrigated cyclone	100	87	42
Self-induced-spray deduster	100	94	48
Spray tower	99	94	55
Fluidised-bed scrubber	> 99	98	58
Irrigated-target scrubber	100	97	80
Electrostatic precipitator	> 99	99	86
Disintegrator	100	98	91
Irrigated electrostatic precipitator	> 99	98	92
Annular-throat scrubber—low energy	100	>99	96
Venturi-scrubber—medium energy	100	>99	97
Annular-throat scrubber—medium energy	100	>99	97
Venturi-scrubber—high energy	100	>99	98
Shaker-type fabric filter	> 99	>99	99
Low-velocity bag filter	100	>99	99
Reverse-jet fabric filter	100	>99	99

types of collector may be necessary in series, for example a cyclone followed by an electrostatic precipitator.

Given the standardised range of equipment available, it is necessary to select the most effective and cheapest for the duty in question, subject to its being able to stand up to service conditions. The most important of these are:

> Gas: Temperature, composition
> Dust: Toxicity, flammability, 'stickiness'

Blockages may present a major problem in the operation of arrestment plant, for example in packed-tower wet collectors or small-diameter high-efficiency cyclones. Erosion may also be a problem, leading to high maintenance costs, when grit-laden gases are transferred at high velocities. Equipment deterioration due to this or mechanical damage, e.g. perforation of a filter, can result in reduced arrestment efficiencies after a period of satisfactory operation.

In general, inertial collectors are preferred for high-temperature operation and wet de-dusters for the removal of 'sticky' dusts. Electrostatic precipitators can be used with high-temperature gases and, with fabric filters, they are most attractive for fine dust removal. With 'wet' collectors the correct water level must be maintained in the feed tank by metering in make-up water, for example using a constant-head device, to replace the loss in sludge or by evaporation.

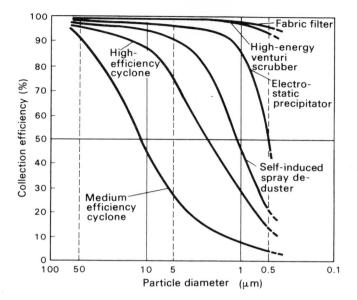

Fig. 10.10 Arrestment efficiencies

Mists Separation

Mists or fogs produced by entrainment of liquid droplets in a gas stream are a common industrial problem in operations involving gas or vapour generation from a liquid, or when a gas is passed through a liquid. This may be in distillation or absorption columns or in evaporators, stills, flash vaporisation tanks and knock-out drums, or in spray cooling. Whenever the exit gas stream is vented to atmosphere without efficient separation of the myriad of drops a visible plume and/or pollution may result.

In addition to the reduction of atmospheric pollution, entrainment separation is often necessary to reduce damage to machinery, as in the case of sprays entering gas turbines, or to avoid carry-over which may affect subsequent gas processing, for example catalyst poisoning or corrosion problems. It may also facilitate recovery of a product, thus increasing overall process efficiency, or reduce liquid losses, e.g. in cooling towers. Some specific uses of entrainment separation are listed in Table 10.3, many of which involve highly corrosive duties.

Normally the droplets to be removed are in the micrometre size-range (Figure 10.11). The primary mechanisms by which such droplets may be collected on a surface have been classified as settling (gravity), centrifugal force, impingement, electrostatic attraction and diffusion.[6] Combinations of these may be used to aid separation (Figure 10.11).

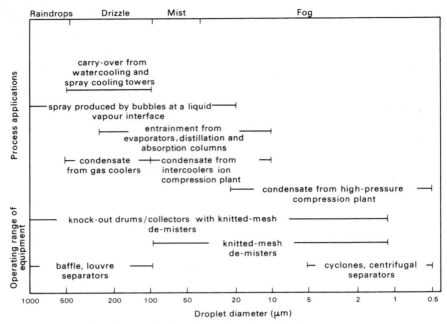

Fig. 10.11 Applications of spray and mist separators

TABLE 10.3 SPECIFIC USES OF ENTRAINMENT SEPARATION

Monoethanolamine from scrubbers
Reduction in air pollution
Air-conditioning spray washers
Sulphuric acid mist
Sulphur from hydrogen sulphide gases
Oil from exhaust steam
Oil and water from gas compressor outlets
Dusts, oils, water, scale from air-tool lines
Placed before jets to reduce erosion, increase vacuum
Chlorinated products from hydrochloric acid gases
Distillery spent mash
Phosphoric acid from phosphorus burners
Oxygen lancing
Tar fogs from furnaces
Acidic mists from enamel smelting furnaces
Removal of sulphuric acid from dried chlorine in elec-
    trolytic caustic manufacture
Removal of liquid chlorine from gaseous chlorine in
    the manufacture of hydrochloric acid

De-misters

For the removal of coarse droplets from a gas stream an entrainment separator, in its simplest form, may consist of a surge drum with interior baffles and provision for liquid drainage. However, the removal of true mists requires the use of an impingement separator which in its common form incorporates simple wire mesh pads. Typical arrangements are shown in Figure 10.12. For spray and coarse mist removal, i.e. droplets in the size range 7–100 μm, a monofilament de-mister pad coalesces the drops so that they drain backwards against the gas flow for collection in a sump. For dispersions containing drops intermediate in size between coarse sprays and fine fumes i.e. 1–10 μm, pads may be used in series; the first pad is chosen to collect and coalesce fine droplets, while the second pad removes larger entrained drops.

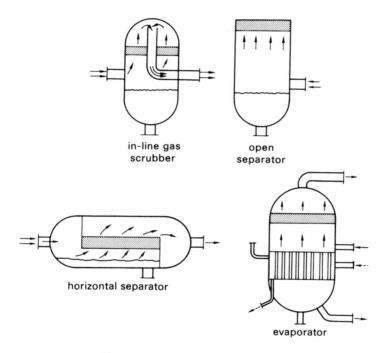

Fig. 10.12 De-mister pad arrangements

Such impingement separators need a large surface area for the droplets to impinge upon, and large free volumes so that the gas or vapour passes through easily. Droplets are momentarily held on the convex wire surface but then flow along to a point where adjacent wires provide capillary space. When this becomes overloaded the liquid flows downwards again. At the lower de-mister surfaces, surface tension retains the liquid until drops are formed. When the drops are sufficiently large for the force of gravity to exceed the combined effects of gas velocity and surface tension, they fall away.[7,8] The de-mister is supported by an open grid which normally rests on a support ring. Free passage through these grids should not be above 90%, otherwise liquid is prevented from draining downwards.

Gas velocity has an important effect on removal efficiency. At high velocities, coalesced droplets may be unable to fall away against the flow; at low velocities, finer drops may drift with the gas without carrying to the impingement target. Empirical expressions based on gas and liquid densities are used to calculate allowable vapour velocity.[9,10]

Under normal operating conditions removal efficiencies of up to 95% can be obtained with knitted-mesh de-misters and this high efficiency is maintained throughout the service life.

The pressure drop across a de-mister is usually less than 25 mm w.g. due to the large free volume, which is usually between 97·5% and 99·0%. A low pressure drop may be particularly important in applications when the prime mover is a blower or fan, i.e. when any increase in back-pressure is accompanied by a reduction in delivered gas volume. The main advantages of de-misters are that installation is inexpensive, operation is continuous and automatic and, since there are no moving parts, very little maintenance is necessary. Consideration has to be given, however, to the presence of solids in the gas stream. If the quantity of solids is small it is generally washed out by the returning liquid;[7] larger quantities may cause blockage with a corresponding increase in pressure drop and a loss of efficiency. In some cases periodic back-washing may prevent blockage.

For the removal of the finest fumes and mists, comprising particles less than 5 μm and largely less than 2 μm, it is necessary to use hydrophobic fibre filters of the type illustrated in Figure 10.13.

Many impingement separator designs will be effective to some extent in removing solid particulates. However, the basic mechanism in a dry packing is filtration, pore size being more significant than fibre or wire diameter. The collected particles will result eventually in increased pressure drop so that some means must be provided for their continuous, or intermittent, removal. This may involve irrigation or intermittent backflushing with gas or liquid, or intermittent vibration.

Cyclonic Separators

Cyclones may be used for droplet collection, in a similar way to their use for dusts, but careful design is necessary to avoid redispersion of the liquid films in the gas exit stream. Internal skirts are introduced to prevent liquid creep. Alternatively, a type of cyclonic spray scrubber design may be used with the tangential gas entry at the base of the tower so that the path of the creeping liquid film is increased.

Electrostatic Precipitators

On a large scale, fine mist removal may be accomplished by electrostatic precipitation. Tar, phosphoric acid and sulphuric acid mists have all been

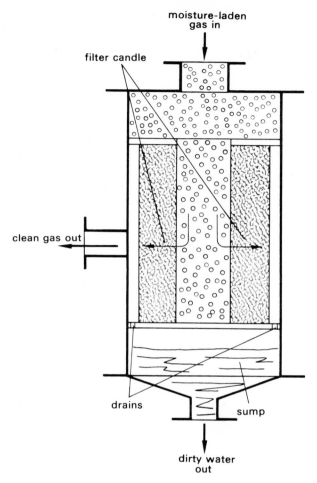

Fig. 10.13 Fibre filter for fine mist or fume removal ($<2\ \mu$m particle size)

treated in this way. For acid mists the chambers may be lead-lined, or constructed of some other suitable corrosion-resistant material.

Odour Control

Certain industrial processes inevitably result in the development of odours, which may cause offence to people either working in the factory concerned or living in the vicinity. Factories engaged in commercial food preparation, animal byproducts manufacture (e.g. glue production), petroleum refining and viscose manufacture as well as sewage works and many other process industries suffer from this problem. Atmospheric conditions, such as humidity and wind intensity and direction, are important factors affecting dilution and dispersion and, by causing odours to accumulate at low levels near their source, increase the nuisance. In the majority of cases the contaminant responsible is organic, often with small proportions of sulphur or nitrogen either alone or in combination. Mercaptans are an example. There are, however, a number of inorganic malodorous compounds.

Each odorant has a concentration in air below which it is undetectable, termed the olfactory or odour threshold. However, this varies from one person to another; moreover, continuous exposure may result in olfactory fatigue, when the odour from a particular substance ceases to be noticed. Commonly occurring compounds known to cause odour in industrial processes at low concentrations are listed in Table 10.4. Of these, the main offenders are probably sulphides and mercaptans. The odour thresholds of certain substances, e.g. butyric acid and methyl mercaptan, may be as low as 0·001 ppm.

TABLE 10.4 COMMON SUBSTANCES WITH OFFENSIVE ODOURS; ODOUR THRESHOLD< 10 PPM (SEE ALSO TABLE 10.5)

Hydrogen sulphide
Mercaptans
Aliphatic or aromatic amines
Fatty acids
Aliphatics with double and triple bonds
Aromatic and aliphatic unsaturated aldehydes
Acrolein, ethyl acrylate
Chloral
Carbon disulphide
Diphenyl ether
Dimethyl sulphide
Unsaturated carbonyl compounds
Nitrobenzene
Hydroxybenzenes
Phosgene
Phosphine
Styrene
Higher aromatics (toluene)
Ring chlorinated hydrocarbons
Hydrogen cyanide

Recognition odour thresholds of a number of substances have been published in the USA by the Manufacturing Chemists Association Inc. (Table 10.5). Attempts at scientific classification of smell have not been very successful. Consequently, its measurement relies upon a trained panel of assessors to whom the odorants are presented in a static air system. In obtaining the data in Table 10.5 the dilution medium was a low-odour background air and the odour threshold was recorded as the lowest concentration at which all members of the panel recognised the odour. In the UK a

TABLE 10.5 RECOGNITION ODOUR THRESHOLDS IN AIR (US MANUFACTURING CHEMISTS ASSOCIATION INC.)

Compound	ppm (volume)	Compound	ppm (volume)
Acetaldehyde	0·21	Ethyl acrylate	0·000 47
Acetic acid	1·0	Ethyl mercaptan	0·001
Acetone	100·0	Formaldehyde	1·0
Acrolein	0·21	Hydrochloric acid gas	10·0
Acrylonitrile	21·4	Methanol	100·0
Allyl chloride	0·47	Methyl chloride	> 10
Amine, dimethyl	0·047	Methylene chloride	214·0
Amine, monomethyl	0·021	Methyl ethyl ketone	10·0
Amine, trimethyl	0·000 21	Methyl isobutyl ketone	0·47
Ammonia	46·8	Methyl mercaptan	0·0021
Aniline	1·0	Methyl methacrylate	0·21
Benzene	4·68	Monochlorobenzene	0·21
Benzyl chloride	0·047	Nitrobenzene	0·0047
Benzyl sulphide	0·0021	Paracresol	0·001
Bromine	0·047	Paraxylene	0·47
Butyric acid	0·001	Perchloroethylene	4·68
Carbon disulphide	0·21	Phenol	0·047
Carbon tetrachloride		Phosgene	1·0
(chlorination of CS_2)	21·4	Phosphine	0·021
Carbon tetrachloride		Pyridine	0·021
(chlorination of CH_4)	100·0	Styrene (inhibited)	0·1
Chloral	0·047	Styrene (uninhibited)	0·047
Chlorine	0·314	Sulphur dichloride	0·001
Dimethylacetamide	46·8	Sulphur dioxide	0·47
Dimethylformamide	100·0	Toluene (from coke)	4·68
Dimethyl sulphide	0·001	Toluene (from petro-	
Diphenyl ether (perfume		leum)	2·14
grade)	0·1	Tolylene diisocyanate	2·14
Diphenyl sulphide	0·0047	Trichloroethylene	21·4
Ethanol (synthetic)	10·0		

Note: Recognition levels in practice may be much lower than the above values, determined in low-odour air. Olfactory fatigue, synergism and the level/type of background odour are important factors.

touring laboratory has been set up by the Department of the Environment, with a panel of six detectors, to establish odour levels in various areas.[11]

Normally, the first step in odour control is to contain the odorous compound by operation within equipment which is, if practicable, sealed and/or located under extraction canopies or in sealed buildings from which air is exhausted by mechanical ventilation via an arrangement of ducts. Several different methods are then available for the treatment of odorous gas streams, dependent upon the type of gas stream, the concentration of the odoriferous compound, its composition and local conditions. Briefly, the main methods, and their advantages and disadvantages are as follows:

Dilution

Dilution of the odorous gas stream, by dispersion from a stack or chimney, is the simplest means of preventing a nuisance from smell. It is feasible provided the odour threshold is fairly high. However, current design techniques for this method are uncertain because dispersion formulae for short sample times are not available.

Neutralisation and Masking

A specially compounded agent may be added to the gas stream to neutralise the odour; to react with it chemically and destroy it; or to combine with it and 'mask' it. In neutralisation the undesirable odour is counteracted by another and in masking it is overridden by a neutral odour; agents of all types are available commercially.

The volatile agent is usually added by spraying. Care is needed in its selection, and in metering the level to match that of the odorous substances. The disadvantage of such treatment is that, under certain atmospheric conditions, separation of the constituents may occur. This is overcome, however, if the constituents react chemically.

Adsorption

Organic odorous substances can be removed by adsorption on to solid packed beds of activated carbon or molecular sieves. The gas stream is simply passed through a tower packed with the adsorbent which is rejected or, preferably, regenerated when it becomes 'saturated'. Difficulties may arise in the use of this process for mercaptans, fatty acids, acrolein and acrylates, oxybenzenes, some phosphorus compounds, higher aromatics and ring-chlorinated hydrocarbons. It is important that regeneration or burning of the adsorbent should not produce a secondary emission problem. There are two types of activated carbon system, deep-bed adsorbers and thin-bed adsorbers.[12] The former are the type conventionally used in solvent recovery plants. Thin-bed adsorbers are preferred for gases, consisting for example of panels 10–20 mm thick arranged to provide a large surface area. These can be used when outside air is brought into, or recirculated within, a space so that the odorous contaminants are reduced to trace quantities. Flow rates with these thin beds vary up to 0·30 m/s (1 ft/s).

Ozone Treatment

Ozonisation, that is oxidation using ozone-enriched air, is useful in odour control when the contaminants have odour thresholds substantially higher than 10 ppm. The main disadvantages are discharge of excess ozone into the atmosphere and slow reaction rate which means that a long contact time is necessary between ozone and odorous gas.

One solution, utilised in the VAR wet oxidation process, involves passing the gas through a chamber into which ozonised water is sprayed.[13] The premises from which the odour is generated are maintained under a slight negative pressure by the extraction of air at 4 to 10 changes per hour, dependent on the intensity of the odour. Some preoxidation is obtained by mixing the foul air with gaseous ozone before it is scrubbed in the chamber. Following moisture separation, the treated air is vented through a stack. This process was developed for sewage treatment plants: only 3·5–5 s contact time is required in the scrubbing chamber compared with about 30 s for comparable reaction with gaseous ozone. The water is recirculated via a contact column fed with fresh ozonised air and the process is automatically controlled; a high-sensitivity ozone concentration meter in the exit stack serves to regulate power supply to the ozoniser so that residual ozone in the exhaust gas is only 0·01–0·04 ppm.

Whatever process is used, it is necessary to restrict carefully the residual ozone concentration, since it is a highly toxic gas having a threshold limit value (see Chapter 4) of only 0·1 ppm in air.

Advantages claimed for the wet oxidation process are its effectiveness, its ability to treat large volumes of air from the surroundings as well as the source of odour and the relatively low running costs. The latter are dependent on ozone dose; for example, a typical dosage for an enclosed sewage works or a meat rendering plant is 10–40 mg ozone per m³ air; total power consumption for air drying, ozone production and injection is 0·5–2·0 kW/m³ × 10³ air per hour.[14]

Absorption (Scrubbing)

Scrubbing of the odorous gas stream with liquid in a spray or packed tower may serve to remove the odour, particularly if physical absorption, due to solubility of the odorous component in the liquid stream, is accompanied by chemical reaction. The wash liquid may be aqueous (water, acid solution or alkali solution) or organic, e.g. amines, dependent on the application. For example, a recirculatory system using sodium carbonate or caustic soda solution is used to scrub out acidic vapours. However, as mentioned earlier, very low concentrations of certain substances can result in unacceptable levels of odour and for these applications scrubbing is unlikely to be economical. Difficulties have arisen with amines, saturated aldehydes, unsaturated carbonyl compounds and phosgene.

Wet scrubbing systems have been applied to odour control of air extracted from animal byproducts plant, either using the scrubber as a condenser or by introduction of a masking or oxidising agent into the scrubbing liquor.[15] In the latter case extracted air is passed through a plate scrubber countercurrent to an aqueous solution of an oxidising agent such as hypochlorite, potassium permanganate or a proprietary disinfectant, or a masking agent. In one proprietary design, ozone is injected into the scrubbing liquid prior to cocurrent and countercurrent spraying into the gas stream via trees of spray nozzles.[16]

Solvent dryer exhausts are generally treated by the condensation process. Odorous vapour is condensed by being passed countercurrent to the scrubbing liquor in an impingement plate column.

High-temperature Incineration

Direct flame incineration, with exit gas temperatures of 650°–800°C, is a common means of odour control. The equipment comprises a combustion chamber with a burner fed by a secondary fuel, generally gas, and provided with an exhaust system for the combustion products.

Temperature and residence times are critical for the destruction of small levels of odorant generally involved. Thus, although the auto-ignition temperature of most common odorants is around 500°C, the destruction rate at this temperature would be too slow, since concentrations are small. Odours from food processing may be eliminated at relatively low temperatures of around 450°–500°C, but it is usually necessary to use temperatures of 600°–750°C, which must be maintained for 0·3–1 s dependent on the odorant and the concentration reduction required.[17]

This kind of incineration, though attractive for relatively high calorific value foul-gas streams, may be costly in terms of secondary fuel; waste heat recovery and/or preheating is desirable, and this is considered economic provided the waste gas flow is above 10 m/s (2 × 10³ ft/min). The hot gases may be used to preheat fresh air, for example for the oven emitting the odorous stream, or to raise the temperature of a heating medium. Alternatively, a heat exchanger may be used to recover up to 70% of the heat content of the incinerated gases by preheating the inlet gases.[17]

Figure 10.14 shows a typical incinerator which can be used for the elimination of fumes and smoke as well as odours from industrial processes.[18] In the combustion chamber the emissions are raised to a predetermined temperature, normally 760°–815°C, with a residence time of approximately 5 seconds. The burner may be fired by gas or oil, or a combination of these. If the fumes contain materials of significant calorific value they are ignited by the burner, which is then automatically throttled back to maintain the preset incineration temperature. This provides maximum efficiency and minimum operating costs. The unit shown in Figure 10.14 is complete with a preheat recuperator, in which the clean, hot exhaust gases are used to preheat the incoming fume-contaminated air stream, and with a heat recovery recuperator from which heated air can be recycled back to the process. Figure 10.15 shows how the unit may be installed.[18]

Catalytic Combustion

Odorous organic substances can be oxidised in combustion reactions in the presence of high activity catalysts. Combustion can proceed at temperatures half those necessary to achieve the same conversion efficiency with straight

Nuway Eclipse Ltd

Gas-fired odour and fume incinerator with heat recovery

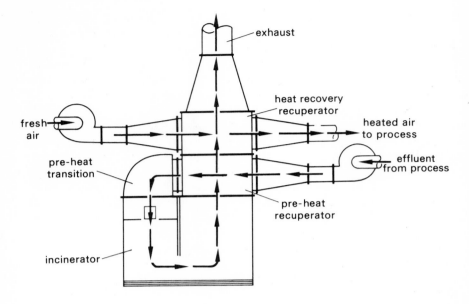

Fig. 10.14 Fume incinerator with pre-heat and heat recovery recuperators

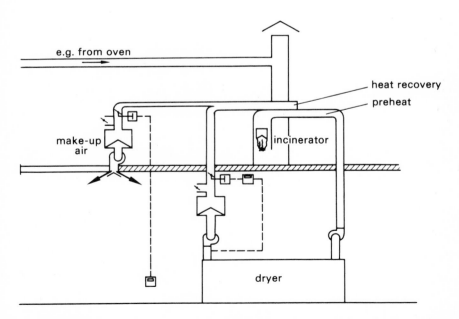

Fig. 10.15 Flow diagram of fume-incineration facility with fume preheat, heat recovery and stack air heat source

thermal incineration.[19] These catalysts are of the surface adsorption type, comprising, for example, active platinum-type metals thinly coated on to a metallic carrier or a ceramic body. Plants based upon this principle have been used for odour control on fish-and-chip frying lines, in animal byproducts manufacture, in paint-drying and paint-coating lines and for solvent incineration on wire enamelling. One problem is the possibility of catalyst poisoning brought about by the irreversible adsorption of contaminant on the surface, which causes a reduction in the 'active' sites; sulphur, chlorinated hydrocarbons and/or traces of heavy metals are particularly poisonous to catalysts. Pilot tests extending over a period of time are therefore desirable before installation of full-scale plant.

A further advantage of on-site trials is that a reduction of 90% in the mass of emissions from a plant will greatly decrease the area around the plant at which the odour is detectable following natural dilution (i.e. that dependent on local climatic conditions), although this reduction may have little discernible effect on the odour of undiluted gases.

One range of catalytic combustion units based upon ceramic honeycombs impregnated with highly active platinum-based catalyst employs the basic design shown in Figure 10.16.[20] These honeycombs have a ratio of surface area to volume of around $1260 \text{ m}^2/\text{m}^3$ ($384 \text{ ft}^2/\text{ft}^3$), thin walls and a pressure drop only 0·05 that of a pelleted bed of similar configuration.[19] In operation, the process gas stream is first preheated by the outgoing deodorised gas stream and then heated to

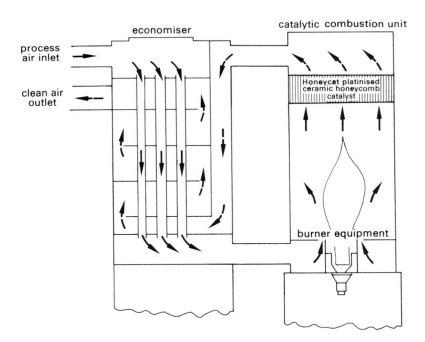

Fig. 10.16 Example of basic design of catalytic incineration unit[20]

ure, e.g. 300°–400°C, in the combustion chamber. A gas- or
electric heater, can be used. Surface reaction occurs on the
d oxygen from the air stream being converted, for example,
water vapour which then desorb from the catalyst surface.
dorous emissions that may be treated by catalytic incinera-
10.6.

TABLE 10.6 PROCESSES FROM WHICH ODOROUS EMISSIONS CAN BE TREATED BY CATALYTIC INCINERATION

Wire and strip enamelling	Core baking
Paint baking	Nitric acid production
Processing, drying and curing of phenol-formaldehyde and cellulose varnishes	Oil refining and petrochemical production
	Blood boiling and drying
Manufacture of glass reinforced plastics	Bone grinding and boiling
	Brewing and distilling
Manufacture of phthalic anhydride, maleic anhydride and ethylene oxide	Fat rendering and extraction
	Glue and size manufacturing
	Fish meal processing
Manufacturing and processing of acrylic plastics	Manufacturing and cutting of PVC and polyurethane
Paper coating	Tanning
Printing and transfer manufacturing	Maggot breeding
	Food manufacturing
Solvent cleaning and storage	Feather burning and hydrolysis
Carbon and graphite baking	Tobacco drying
Production of man-made fibres	Coffee roasting
Manufacturing of tungsten filaments	Manure processing

The removal of particulate matter or odours from a gas stream by the processes described above is common: combustion operations, considered in Chapter 11, are an example. These processes may equally be employed in recovery operations. Some dust, mist and fume treatment processes also reduce gas-phase pollutant concentrations: in wet scrubbing, for instance, dusts are removed and collected in a liquid which may also absorb soluble gases.

An adsorption or scrubbing process for pollutant recovery from a gas stream differs from a similar operation for odour removal only with regard to higher inlet and outlet concentrations and the scale of the operation.

Recovery of Particulate Matter

Particulate matter, once removed from an effluent gas stream, is in theory available for reuse or recycling. Thus, on a small scale, the shot used in the blasting of castings in foundries is separated from the fines of sand and iron, and recirculated to the blasting enclosure. It is common practice in the chemical and metallurgical industries to recycle particulate materials recovered from, for example, crushing, screening, processing, handling, transfer, bulk loading or bagging of powders. On a larger scale, reference is made in Chapter 16 to the potential for reuse of pulverised fuel ash. If recycling is practised, dry collection methods may be preferable to wet scrubbing unless a slurry or sludge is convenient for handling, to avoid a secondary dust problem, or for reprocessing.

Specific examples of in-plant recycling of particulate materials whose emission is unavoidable during manufacturing processes are discussed below.

In-Plant Fines in the Steel Industry

In iron and steel manufacture, in-plant fines are recovered from dust extractors, gas cleaners, scale pits, slag reclamation plants and effluent treatment plants. A summary of the approximate tonnages arising in the British Steel Corporation in 1974 is given in Table 10.7.[21] Of these, some 75% were recycled in the manner illustrated in Figure 10.17. Only the blast furnace wet-collected dusts, arc furnace fume and some of the BOS fume were dumped.

TABLE 10.7 APPROXIMATE TONNAGES OF DUST ARISINGS IN BSC, 1974[21]

Material	'000 tonne	%
Ore preparation plant dusts	300	12·2
Coke oven slurries	63	2·6
Blast furnace dust (dry)	200	8·1
(wet)	183	7·4
Steelmaking fume (electric arc)	39	1·6
(open hearth)	41	1·7
(BOS)	181	7·8
Slag metal recovery (ironmaking)	150	5·0
(steelmaking)	377	15·2
Scales	929	37·2
Acid sludges	28	1·2
TOTAL	2491	100·0

Recommended air pollution control systems for the various processes, for which the technology is highly developed, are listed in Table 10.8.[22] However, the practicability of recycling the various arisings is affected by the chemical analysis, size distribution, physical state and inherent variability of each material. Thus fines are dumped when they contain significant amounts of tramp elements which are undesirable and difficult to remove, for example zinc, lead, sulphur, phosphorus, sodium and potassium. Alternatively, their fineness may render them difficult to handle and to assimilate into the normal production operations.[23] However, the range and tonnage of fines being recycled through existing plants is being increased by the application of new techniques such as high-pressure filtration. A possible long-term solution is to recycle all the wastes through a separate processing plant to produce an acceptable blast furnace burden material. A number of processes are available for this purpose;[21,23] some are blending and agglomeration processes only, but others in-

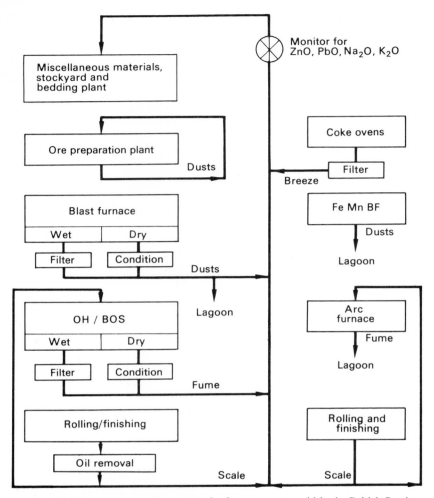

Fig. 10.17 Present recycling routes for ferrous wastes within the British Steel Corporation[21]

volve agglomeration and zinc removal, or zinc removal together with direct reduction or metallizing of the fines. One process is illustrated in Figure 15.13.

Copper Processing

In the working-up of low-grade copper scrap, involving treatment in a blast furnace followed by oxidation and fluxing of impurities in a convertor, a large proportion of tin-bearing or lead-bearing contaminants may be volatilised as an oxides fume[24] (see Chapter 15). After cooling it is economical to remove this fume, generally using a filter bag house. In the manufacture of secondary copper alloy the zinc content of scrap may have to be reduced by blowing air

TABLE 10.8 RECOMMENDED AIR POLLUTION CONTROL SYSTEMS FOR IRON AND STEEL INDUSTRY PROCESSES[22]

Process	Cleaning System	Comments
Sinter Plant	Dry electrostatic precipitators	For both strand and sinter discharge gases
Coke Ovens		
Charging	Smokeless charging car	Considerable development activity,
Discharging	Ensure complete carbonisation	e.g. pipeline charging, enclosed discharging and quenching
Coke quenching	Towers with grid arresters	
Blast Furnaces	3-stage system—Dust catcher, washing tower, wet electrostatic precipitator	For high top-pressure operation, use of high energy wet scrubbers
Steel Furnaces		
Open hearth	Dry electrostatic precipitator	With waste heat boiler
Oxygen converters	Limited combustion of waste gases and high energy wet scrubbers	Possibility of limited combustion with electrostatic precipitator
Electric Arc		
Large furnaces >60 tonnes	Direct or semi-direct extraction with wet EP or high-energy scrubber	Also building extraction through roof
Medium 20–30 tonnes	Direct extraction with high-energy scrubber	
Small <10 tonnes	Semi-direct extraction or roof hoods with bag filters	
In-line Deseamer	Wet electrostatic precipitator	

into the molten metal. On volatilisation the zinc produces dense zinc oxide fumes which, upon recovery by bag filtration, yield zinc oxide of marketable quality.[24]

Cement Manufacture

In cement manufacture the dust produced represents material which has been partly processed. The sources of potential dust emission and the types of dust suppression used on both wet and dry process works are summarised in Table 10.9. Collected dust is invariably returned to that part of the process from which it originates.[25] Wet scrubbers are not widely used for this reason and because of the problem of cement caking. Electrostatic precipitators are used for main exhaust, while low-level emissions from grinding and bagging plants are dealt with by fabric filters.

TABLE 10.9 SOURCES OF POTENTIAL DUST EMISSION AT CEMENT WORKS (BASED ON WARD AND WATSON[25])

Sources of potential emission	Dust	Gas volume flow at temperature (m^3/min)	Gas temperature (approx) (°C)	Inlet dust burden (g/Nm^3)	Types of dust collector*
Quarried material discharge to crusher	Limestone or shale		ambient		H
Raw material milling and drying	Limestone and shale	1300	90	75	C, D, A
Main kiln exhaust, wet process	Dried raw material	8500–11 000	200	9–18	A
Main kiln exhaust, dry process	Mainly dried raw material	4500	140	30–80	A, F
Kiln dust collection hoppers	Mainly dried raw material		100		C
Grate clinker cooler exhaust	Cement clinker	3000–4500	100	4–20	A, B, G
Clinker discharge from cooler	Cement clinker		100		J
Clinker conveyor transfer points	Cement clinker	each point 57	50		C, D, E, H
Clinker store	Cement clinker		30		K, C, E

Table 10.9 (continued)

Cement mill ventilation	Cement	370 (each mill 4474 kW)	80	G followed by A, C, D, E
Cement conveyor transfer points	Cement	each point 57		C, D, E
Clinker loading to ships	Cement clinker			H and C

* Types of dust collector:

A Electrostatic precipitator   F Glass bag filter
B Pebble bed filter   G Cyclones
C Fabric filter, high-pressure reverse jet cleaning   H Dust-suppression sprays
D Fabric filter, low-pressure reverse air cleaning   J Dust-laden air returned to process
E Fabric filter, mechanical shaking to clean   K Total enclosure of source

References

1. STAIRMAND, C. J., *Chemical Engineer*, CE 310, 1965.
2. SWIFT, P., in *Industrial Pollution Control*, TEARLE, K. (Ed.), Business Books, 1973.
3. SUTTON, P., *Chemical and Process Engineering*, 96, 1968.
4. HOPPITT, H. B., *Chemistry and Industry*, 846, 1974.
5. STAIRMAND, C. J., *Chemical Engineer*, 381, 1971.
6. MONTROSE, C., *Chemical Engineering*, **60**(10), 213, 1955.
7. REYNOLDS, S. C., *Petroleum Refiner*, **32**, 138, 1953.
8. YORK, O. H., *Chemical Engineering Progress*, **50**, 421, 1954.
9. YORK, O. H. and POPPELE, E. W., *Chemical Engineering Progess*, **59**(6), 45, 1963.
10. *Demisters and Separators for the Chemical Industry*, Knit Mesh Ltd, Greenfield, Holywell, Clwyd.
11. *New Scientist*, **67**(956), 25, 1975.
12. WALLER, G., *Chemistry and Industry*, 853, 18 November 1974.
13. VAR wet oxidation process, *Process Engineering*, 63, 9 March 1974.
14. ARNOLD, D. B., *Chemistry and Industry*, 899, 18 November 1974.
15. JOHNSTON, J. W., *Chemistry and Industry*, 849, 18 November 1974.
16. Kunststofftechnik Troisdorf, Germany, private communication (Plastic Constructions Ltd, UK).
17. ARNOLD, D. B., *Chemistry and Industry*, 902, 18 November 1974.
18. Incineration and Heat Recovery Equipment, Nu-way Eclipse, Droitwich, UK, private communication.
19. SEARLES, R. A., *Chemistry and Industry*, 895, 18 November 1974.
20. Johnson Matthey Chemicals Ltd, 74 Hatton Garden, London, EC1P 1AE, private communication.
21. TRAICE, F. B., in *Proceedings: The Technology of Reclamation*, University of Birmingham, 7–11 April 1975.
22. SPEIGHT, G. E., *Chemical Engineer*, **271**, 132, March 1973.
23. BRINN, D. G., *A Survey of the Published Literature Dealing with Steel Industry In-plant Fines and their Recycling*, SM/BIB/858, British Steel Corporation, 1974.
24. MANTLE, E. C., *Chemical Engineer*, **272**, 203, April 1973.
25. WARD, P. A. and WATSON, D., *Chemical Engineer*, **271**, 124, March 1973.

CHAPTER 11

Prevention of Pollution from Combustion Processes

Combustion processes in power generation, industrial furnaces and processes, domestic heating, motor vehicle engines and aircraft engines constitute the major man-made contributors to atmospheric pollution. The major pollutants arising from combustion are:

unburnt or partially oxidised particulate matter,
  e.g. smoke, solids such as fly ash;
unburnt or partially oxidised gases,
  e.g. carbon monoxide, incompletely oxidised hydrocarbons;
oxides of nitrogen, NO_x;
sulphur dioxide and sulphur trioxide;

and, to a lesser extent,

lead compounds,
  e.g. from petrol engines;
hydrogen chloride,
  e.g. from the combustion of organic chlorine compounds, as in PVC incineration.

Estimates of smoke and sulphur dioxide emission in the UK related to the various uses of solid and liquid fuels are given in Table 11.1. The data exemplify the improvements brought about in particulate smoke control as a result of the Clean Air Act but sulphur dioxide emissions show an increase largely attributable to industrial applications and power generation. Similar data for oxides of nitrogen (Table 11.2) illustrate the steady increase in low-level and total emissions up to 1970. The largest contribution was from coal-fired power stations. However, over half the total emission is attributed to 'low-level' sources.

In general, pollution from industrial combustion processes must be controlled in the UK to levels discussed in Chapter 4; comparable criteria exist in other countries.

TABLE 11.1 ESTIMATES OF AIR POLLUTION BY SMOKE AND SULPHUR DIOXIDE FROM THE MAIN USES OF FUELS IN GREAT BRITAIN (BASED ON *Combustion Generated Pollution*[1])

		Millions of tonnes		
	Source	1938	1956	1967
Smoke	Coal: Household	1·74	1·28	0·76
	Railways	0·26	0·24	0·02
	Industrial, etc.	0·75	0·76	0·10
	Total smoke	2·75	2·28	0·88
Sulphur dioxide	Coal: Household	1·22	0·91	0·60
	Electricity works	0·40	1·25	1·91
	Railways	0·36	0·33	0·02
	Industrial, etc.	1·68	1·70	0·98
	Coke ovens	0·07	0·11	0·08
	Gas supply	0·14	0·20	0·10
		3·87	4·50	3·69
	Oil: Household	—	—	0·01
	Industrial	0·05	0·48	2·00
	Road and rail transport	0·01	0·03	0·08
	Marine craft	—	0·03	0·04
		0·06	0·54	2·13
	Coke:	0·24	0·35	0·28
	Total sulphur dioxide	4·17	5·39	6·10

Methods available for control are:

(a) The use of tall chimneys to exhaust waste gases and entrained particulates at sufficient height to achieve adequate dispersal and dilution.

(b) Removal of pollutant-forming materials from fuel prior to combustion. The desulphurisation of fuel oils is an example of this approach which may also confer processing advantages, for example in smelting or direct heating applications.

(c) Selection of fuels containing low concentrations of pollutant-forming materials for use in selected areas. Again this is commonly used with regard to sulphur content of solid and liquid fuels.

(d) Removal of pollutants from exhaust waste gases prior to discharge. Arrestment plant of the types described in Chapter 10 is widely used for ash removal.

In numerous processes, for example operation of steel cupolas and cement kilns, the grit and dust burden of the flue gases is, however, increased by entrainment of the materials being processed.

After-burning, or scrubbing as described in Chapter 12, is also practicable.

TABLE 11.2 OVERALL EMISSIONS OF OXIDES OF NITROGEN IN THE UK (BASED ON *Combustion Generated Pollution*[1])

| Source | Thousands of tonnes | | | | | |
	1965	1966	1967	1968	1969	1970
Transport						
Petrol engines	157	166	179	189	194	206
Diesel engines	49	52	55	58	61	63
Railways	2	2	3	4	4	5
	208	220	237	251	259	274
Household						
Coal fires	61	57	52	49	45	40
Smokeless-fuel fires	11	11	11	11	11	10
Gas appliances	8	9	10	12	13	15
Oil-fired central heating	3	3	3	3	3	4
	83	80	76	75	72	69
Commercial, public service, industrial						
Fuel- and gas-oil heating	28	36	41	45	49	54
Coal and coke	286	268	244	232	183	158
Gas	9	10	9	11	12	14
Fuel- and gas-oil, industrial	235	248	263	278	290	304
Incinerators	1	1	1	1	2	2
	559	563	558	567	536	532
Total low-level emissions	850	863	871	893	867	875
Power stations						
Oil-fired	47	53	49	47	57	87
Coal-fired	471	459	482	516	522	522
	518	512	531	563	579	609
Overall total emissions	1368	1375	1402	1456	1446	1484

Control of Combustion Processes

In order to reduce pollution from combustion processes, the processes themselves must be properly controlled to eliminate, as far as is practicable, incomplete combustion of fuel. In combustion, a series of chemical reactions occurs between a fuel (usually a fossil fuel) and oxygen (usually supplied as primary or secondary air). The natural products of combustion are carbon dioxide, water and nitrogen but inevitably other products, e.g. ash and sulphur dioxide, also arise. Combustibles may also be emitted because of failure to burn, or because of incomplete combustion of the carbon and hydrogen in the fuel during the residence time in the combustion chamber.

Incomplete combustion may result from any combination of (i) poor mixing of fuel, air and combustion products, (ii) too low a residence time at high temperature and (iii) insufficient excess air. In the majority of industrial combustion operations the overall rate is controlled mainly by the fuel–air mixing process. If mixing is inefficient, large volumes of excess air are needed to complete combustion; this increases the volume of flue gases discharged and hence results in heat loss. It is also desirable to restrict excess air requirements to minimise formation of sulphur trioxide and oxides of nitrogen. Hence the aerodynamic design of the combustion chamber must achieve a balance between complete combustion with a minimum of excess air, and acceptable pressure drop.

The second requirement for efficient combustion is sufficient residence time at adequate temperature, which involves correct loading of the combustion chamber and control of the rate of heat extraction during combustion to avoid quenching the exhaust gases before reaction is completed. Thus interrelated factors govern combustion appliance design:

Proper apportionment of the fuel and air
Adequate turbulence to ensure thorough mixing
Maintenance of temperature within a certain range
Adequate time for the combustion process to reach completion

The stoichiometric quantity of air can easily be calculated. Some percentage of excess air has then to be added to ensure complete combustion in practice; this amount depends upon the efficiency of mixing and the size of the combustion chamber. Typical values for excess air requirements are given in Table 11.3.

Each individual process has its optimum ratio, deviation from which results in loss of thermal efficiency, often accompanied by increased emission of pollutants. A major shortfall in air supply will result in the emission of pollutants in the form of both unburnt fuel and black smoke, produced by cracking of unburnt fuel under the influence of temperature in the combustion chamber. A less serious shortfall may only result in gas-phase pollutants, e.g. volatiles from solid or liquid fuels and carbon monoxide. The latter may not be visible but can be detected by instruments. Too much air results in poor thermal efficiency. A major excess of cold incoming air may even interfere with the combustion process and also result in the emission of incompletely burnt materials, for example as light coloured smoke. This again can be monitored.

TABLE 11.3 PRACTICAL EXCESS AIR REQUIREMENTS FOR COMBUSTION PROCESSES

Fuel	Method of firing	Level of excess air (%)
Coal	Hand-fired (rare)	100
	Mechanical-fired	30–50
	Pulverised	<20
Oil	—	<15
Gas	—	<10

Formation of Toxic and Corrosive Gases

Carbon monoxide is an essential intermediate product of the combustion of fossil fuels, but forms a stable end-product only where insufficient oxygen is provided. Hence it may result from incorrect control of the combustion process, or if a furnace or engine is operated outside the correct limits. It may also be produced by design where a reducing atmosphere is required as, for example, in metallurgical processes. Normally, with correct design and operation, the concentrations of carbon monoxide in the flue gases from combustion sources are insignificant. Quoted levels[2] are:

	ppm
Gas-fired furnaces	100
Oil-fired furnaces	20
Coal-fired furnaces	200

but these may increase by a factor of 10–100 with poor design or operation. (Petrol engine exhausts contain much higher levels, generally between 4% and 10% by volume.)

Oxides of nitrogen (NO_x) arise in exhaust gases from combustion as a result of the fixation of nitrogen, the reaction between oxygen and nitrogen being promoted by the high flame temperature, and of the oxidation of organic nitrogen-containing compounds in the fuel. Combustion of coal, which contains up to approximately 2·8% nitrogen, and fuel oil, which contains up to approximately 1% nitrogen, results in oxide formation by both mechanisms. Conversely, in combustion of natural gas, which is virtually free of fuel nitrogen, all the oxides arise from thermal fixation.

Nitric oxide (NO) is more stable at high temperatures, which therefore favour the formation of nitric oxide and, following oxidation, nitrogen dioxide (NO_2). The relatively long residence period of combustion products at high flame temperatures in large combustion chambers (e.g. in boilers for power generation) results in nitric oxide formation. Typically lean mixture conditions in furnaces also favour fuel-derived NO formation.

Examples of NO_x emission levels from various combustion processes are given in Table 11.4.

Coal contains sulphur in the form of pyrites, sulphates and organic sulphur. Petroleum oils contain sulphur in the form of mercaptans, thiophenes, polysulphides and sulphides. Typical sulphur contents of a variety of fuels are given in Table 11.5. Combustion of such sulphur-bearing fuels inevitably produces gaseous sulphur dioxide and some sulphur trioxide:

$$S + O_2 \rightarrow SO_2$$

$$2SO_2 + O_2 \rightarrow 2SO_3$$

The maximum concentration of sulphur dioxide in flue gas is around 2000 ppm.[1]

The fraction of sulphur dioxide which reacts to form sulphur trioxide depends upon the temperatures in the combustion and subsequent zones, the amount of excess air and the presence of certain catalysts in flue dust.

Up to about 5% of the sulphur dioxide may be oxidised to sulphur trioxide in boilers, but in some appliances using very low sulphur-content fuels, for example gas-fired domestic water heaters, conversion may exceed 30%.[1] A few parts per million of sulphur trioxide can significantly raise the dewpoint of the flue gas, e.g. from 38°–66°C to 177°C; this is the 'acid dewpoint' at which sulphuric acid begins to condense out, as distinct from the water vapour condensation temperature. This may present a serious corrosion problem in heat exchangers, ducts, stacks and other equipment through which the flue gases pass, since sulphuric acid can condense out on cooler surfaces. Very low concentrations of sulphur trioxide, for example 5 ppm, may also result in stable, persistent plumes from stacks.[1]

Non-combustible Products

Inorganic constituents of fuel are oxidised and, being usually non-volatile, remain in the combustion chamber as ash. Mechanical solid-fuel firing, for example on moving grates, results in the majority of the ash being retained in the furnace, but particulate ash is entrained in the flue gases. The problem is more acute with pulverised coal and atomised oil firing. Hence equipment of the type described in Chapter 10 (in particular electrostatic precipitators) is needed to clean combustion gases prior to discharge to stacks.

Gas cleaning plant for sewage sludge incinerator

Severn–Trent Water Authority

TABLE 11.4 NO$_x$ EMISSIONS FROM A HIGH-INTENSITY COMBUSTOR AND FROM CONVENTIONAL COMBUSTION PLANT[1]

Approx. temperature of flue gas at hottest (°C)	Fuel	N chemically combined in fuel (w/w) (dmmf basis)	Type of plant	Composition of combustion air	NO$_x$ reported in flue gas (ppm v/v) (dry basis)
2300	Coal	1·4%	High intensity combuster	Oxygen-enriched air	10 000–13 000
1500–1700	Coal	Probably 1–2%	A range of coal-fired power station boilers	Air	200–1400
1500–1700	Oil	Not disclosed	A range of oil-fired power station boilers	Air	110–800
1500–1700	Natural gas	Negligible	A range of natural gas-fired power station boilers	Air	50–1500
1500–1700	Cracked residual fuel oil	1·0%	An oil-fired power station boiler	Air	425
1500–1700	Paraffinic fuel oil	0·2%		Air	215

TABLE 11.5 SULPHUR CONTENT OF FUELS[1]

Bituminous coals	1·5–2·5%
Cokes	1·5–2·5%
Gasoline	0·1%
Kerosene	0·1%
Diesel fuel (distillate)	0·3–0·9%*
Fuel oils	0·5–4%*
Purified coal gas	200–500 ppm
Natural gas	Nil (unless added)

*Liable to increase.

Emissions Control

Particulates

The emission of combustible matter from a combustion process depends upon many factors including fuel characteristics, burner and combustion chamber aerodynamics, excess air and the volumetric heat release and absorption rates.

For pulverised-coal firing the important characteristics are fineness of the coal and its volatile content. The manner in which these parameters affect unburnt carbon losses from pulverised-coal-fired boiler furnaces is shown in Table 11.6.[3]

Coarse particulate emissions may result from agglomerates of smoke and fly ash which build up on heat transfer surfaces in boilers. For efficient operation they must be removed intermittently by 'soot-blowing'. The majority of particles are of a size to be efficiently removed by normal dust-collection equipment (Chapter 10).

In oil-firing, particulates emission at a given level of excess air is dependent on the efficiency of atomisation and aerodynamic design of the burner.[1] Operation at low excess air levels, for example less than 2%, acts against the achievement of very low emission levels. Smoke emission reduction by the injection of oil–water emulsions, or steam atomisation, is also practicable. With oil–water droplets, the water is flashed off to steam as the droplets are sprayed into the hot combustion chamber, resulting in secondary atomisation to finer droplets; the water also reduces NO_x formation by cooling the flame. This method has yet to be proved economical, since it increases flue losses and thus may result in decreased thermal efficiency. This is claimed to be offset by a reduction in excess air requirements due to improved combustion characteristics.

Oxides of Nitrogen

Experimental studies are reported to show that NO_x emission levels from flames can be controlled by combustion modifications. Formation of oxides by thermal fixation can be reduced by decreasing the flame temperature; this may

TABLE 11.6 UNBURNT CARBON LOSS—PULVERISED-COAL-FIRED BOILER FURNACES[3]

Heat release rate		Volatile matter in coal* (%)	Coal smaller than 200 mesh (%)	Excess air (%)	Unburnt carbon†			
					Dry-bottom furnaces		Slag-tap furnaces	
(kJ/m³ h × 10⁴)	(Btu/ft² h × 10³)				(kg/10⁶ kJ input)	(lb/10⁶ Btu input)	(kg/10⁶ kJ input)	(lb/10⁶ Btu input)
74·5	20	20	65	10	1·29	3·0	1·29	3·0
74·5	20	48	65	10	0·19	0·3	0·086	0·2
74·5	20	48	80	10	0·026	0·06	0·013	0·03
74·5	20	48	80	40	0·013	0·03	0·008	0·02
149·0	40	20	65	10	2·15	5·0	1·29	3·0
149·0	40	48	65	10	0·26	0·6	0·215	0·5
149·0	40	48	80	10	0·086	0·2	0·086	0·2
149·0	40	48	80	40	0·026	0·06	0·021	0·05

* Dry, ash-free basis.
† Based on 30 478 kJ/kg (13 100 Btu/lb) for coal.

be achieved by dilution with an inert gas, either recirculated flue gas or water vapour. Recirculation of flue gas and mixing with the air supply prior to combustion also assists in the attainment of low smoke levels. Water vapour is used to absorb some of the energy released in combustion, and hence limit the peak flame temperature, in the firing of oil-in-water emulsions referred to above. From the fuel nitrogen levels given in Table 11.4, significant improvement in NO_x emission levels by reductions in flame temperature would be expected only when firing distillate oils or natural gas.

Two-stage combustion reduces oxides formation due to oxidation, by maintaining reducing conditions in the early stages of combustion, and also limits peak flame temperatures. About 80% of the stoichiometric air requirement is fed to the first stage and the remainder to the second stage. Alternatively, oxides formation from organic nitrogen compounds may be reduced in some systems by firing with low excess air levels, albeit with efficient fuel–air mixing which may increase the flame temperature and hence the amounts formed by fixation.

Estimates of the reduction achievable in NO_x emissions from a 1000 MW boiler installation by selected combustion modifications are given in Table 11.7 for both oil and gas firing.[4]

TABLE 11.7   ESTIMATED NO_x REDUCTION FOR A 1000 MW BOILER BY MEANS OF VARIOUS COMBUSTION MODIFICATIONS (BASED ON SALLOJA[4])

Control method	NO_x reduction (%)	
	Gas	Oil
Low excess air	33	33
Two-stage combustion	50	40
Low excess air plus two-stage combustion	90	73
Flue gas recirculation	33	33
Low excess air plus flue gas recirculation	80	70
Water injection	10	10

A fuel-rich afterburner scheme, for use when modifications cannot be made to the furnace itself, is illustrated in Figure 11.1. The fuel-rich first stage serves to destroy the NO_x in the flame gas and, following heat recovery, the second lower-temperature stage removes the combustibles left from the first stage.[1]

Catalytic combustion is applied to the effluent gas stream from nitric acid plants.[5] The gaseous effluent stream from the ammonia oxidation and absorption operations, which produce nitric acid, is predominantly nitrogen but contains residual amounts of NO, NO_2, O_2 and water vapour. The oxides of nitrogen (NO_x) are normally present in concentrations of 1000 to 5000 ppm. The catalytic combustor serves to reduce both the NO_x and NO_2 contents to the levels required by the Alkali Inspectorate and to decolorise the stack emis-

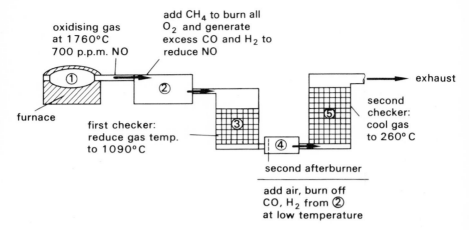

oxidising gas
at 1760°C
700 p.p.m. NO

add CH$_4$ to burn all
O$_2$ and generate
excess CO and H$_2$ to
reduce NO

furnace

first checker:
reduce gas temp.
to 1090°C

second afterburner

add air, burn off
CO, H$_2$ from ②
at low temperature

second
checker:
cool gas
to 260°C

exhaust

Fig. 11.1 Fuel-rich afterburner system for regenerative furnaces

sion. Figure 11.2 is a flow diagram of the two-stage catalytic combustor using noble metal catalysts based on palladium, platinum and rhodium deposited on an inert carrier. The fuel is preferably a hydrogen-rich byproduct gas with an ignition temperature in the range 150°–200°C, a hydrocarbon gas with an ignition temperature in the range of 300°–400°C, or a vaporised liquid fuel with similar characteristics; natural gas is difficult to use because of its higher ignition temperature (480°–520°C) and its susceptibility to carbon deposition. Energy recovery is practised by passing the hot gas through an expander and by generating steam.

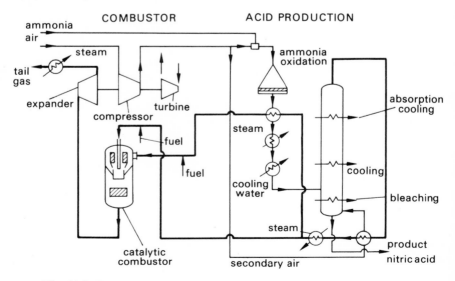

Fig. 11.2 Two-stage catalytic combustor for nitric acid plant effluent gas[5]

Sulphur Dioxide

The control of sulphur dioxide emissions may involve extraction of sulphur from fuels or flue gas desulphurisation. A recent development on a pilot scale has been the use of an SO_2 acceptor material in the combustion zone.

Dispersion from high stacks is the cheapest pollution abatement method but may be used in conjunction with intermittent control. Thus if local climatic conditions are unfavourable for a period, due for example to inversion effects, the load may be reduced or there may be a temporary changeover to a low-sulphur fuel.[6]

Although the concentration of sulphur in fuels is at least ten times higher than in flue gases, fuel cleaning results only in partial removal. Hydro-desulphurisation is widely applied to petroleum-based fuels. This is a high-pressure process involving reaction with hydrogen in the presence of a catalyst to convert organic sulphur compounds into hydrogen sulphide which is either recovered as sulphur or, in limited quantities, disposed of via combustion to sulphur dioxide. About 70–80% of the sulphur present in fuel oils may be removed by hydrodesulphurisation but this is limited generally to low asphaltene oils. Catalytic hydrogenation of coal can remove 75% of the sulphur but is not at present an economic proposition.[7] Dry methods of coal treatment are only capable of 20–30% sulphur removal. The use of sulphur-absorbing additives with the fuel may, for example, be based on the use of finely divided alkaline-earth compounds such as dolomite or limestone to give calcium and magnesium sulphates. These react with the sulphur dioxide and the products can be removed from the waste gas by means of normal gas–solid separators. An overall scheme is shown in Figure 11.3.

Flue gas desulphurisation processes, involving absorption of the sulphur dioxide in liquids or slurries, can achieve greater than 90% removal from the

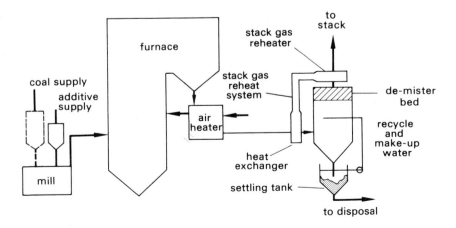

Fig. 11.3 Sulphur dioxide removal based on limestone or dolomite addition

gas stream. Many full-scale plants are in operation in the USA and Japan. The processes involved are discussed in Chapter 12. Various 'dry removal' processes are available relying upon catalytic oxidation of the SO_2.

Some comparative costs for sulphur dioxide elimination are given in Chapter 20.

In summary, established methods for the reduction of sulphur emissions from flue gases involve either scrubbing the flue gases or desulphurisation of the fuel. Scrubbing requires a capital investment equivalent to a significant fraction of the first cost of a power station and reduces operating efficiency. Alternatively, to maintain emissions in Western Europe at 1973 levels was estimated to require a reduction in the average level of sulphur content in fuel oil from 2·6% to 1·0%, with a consequent increase of 25% in fuel costs as at 1974.[8]

The most common methods of combustion control, their applicability and limitations are summarised in Table 11.8.[1]

Chimney Design

Draught[9]

A positive pressure difference is required across any combustion chamber, or furnace, to provide draught so that the requisite amounts of primary and secondary air are available and the combustion products are swept out of the chamber. The draught required depends upon the type of fuel, the method and rate of combustion, and the resistances to flow presented by flues and ancillaries. In addition to pollution control equipment, such as grit arresters or electrostatic precipitators, air preheaters and all waste heat recovery equipment contribute to the frictional resistance to air/flue gas flow.

Mechanical draught by means of fans is preferable on all but small combustion chambers. Centrifugal fans are generally provided. The draught may either be 'forced', with the fan generating sufficient head to force air into the combustion zone but with reliance on natural draught to remove the flue gases, or 'induced', with a large fan located at the base of the chimney assisting or replacing natural draught. Forced draught creates turbulence in the combustion zone and gives improved control; it is used predominantly with oil-fired systems.

Forced and induced draught fans may be used together to provide a 'balanced' draught; with this a small negative pressure, for example 1 mm w.g., is maintained in the combustion chamber. This arrangement allows flexibility in the type of solid fuel used and in the load.

Draught is generally measured by inclined U-tube manometers or diaphragm pressure gauges and is controlled by means of sliding or butterfly dampers.

Dispersal

Flue gases are generally discharged to the base of chimneys at minimum temperatures of 150°–180°C depending on the type of fuel and the combustion application. A chimney serves to achieve dispersal and dilution by simply discharging the flue gases at high level. In so doing it creates a suction at the base, which is made use of in induced draught furnaces.

Figure 11.4 illustrates the principles of dispersion. The plume leaving the chimney at height H_C rises because of the exit momentum of the gases and thermal buoyancy. However, under the influence of wind it bends so that the rise is only H_R. Hence,

$$\text{effective height of discharge, } H_E = H_C + H_R$$

Turbulent diffusion causes the plume to expand and the ground level concentration of any pollutant in the exhaust gases is dependent on the degree of atmospheric turbulence, the wind speed, H_E and the rate of emission. H_R is also variable, depending primarily upon the enthalpy of the gases and wind speed and to a lesser extent upon emission rate, velocity, temperature and other meteorological conditions.

The maximum ground level concentration (glc) associated with any chimney is inversely proportional to H_E and under average conditions arises at a distance of approximately $15\,H_C$ from the chimney. Localised aerodynamic effects due to adjacent buildings or structures within a distance of $10\,H_C$ or high ground may result in increased glc values. The aggregate glc due to emissions from a number of combustion processes can be reduced by the use of a common chimney. In this way the total enthalpy, and therefore the plume rise, is increased. Mere dilution of the gases within a chimney does not, however, reduce the glc of a particular pollutant unless it also serves to increase the total enthalpy of the gases.

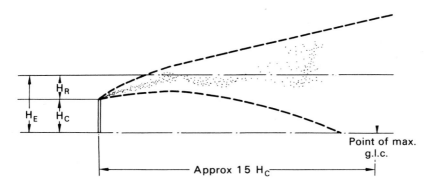

Fig. 11.4 Dispersal from chimney stack
H_C Chimney stack height
H_R Plume rise
H_E Total effective height

TABLE 11.8 COMBUSTION CONTROL METHODS: ADVANTAGES AND DISADVANTAGES (BASED ON *Combustion Generated Pollution*[1])

Method	Advantages	Disadvantages/limitations
Low excess air combustion (*excess air* <2%) Primarily in oil-burning power station boilers.	Low SO_3 concentrations and reduction of low temperature corrosion. Low NO_x emission (only if the flame temperature is not allowed to rise as a result of low excess air).	Requires accurate air/fuel ratio control. Increases combustibles emissions. Requires improved mixing, i.e. better control of burner and combustion chamber aerodynamics.
Flue gas recirculation Power station boilers, industrial processes, domestic combustion appliances.	The peak temperature in a combustor can be controlled by recirculating cooled flue gas to the combustion inlet, and this offers a means of controlling NO_x emission. Soot formation can be suppressed.	Little systematic information exists on the effects of the quantity and temperature of recirculated gases, and on the mode of their introduction into the combustion chamber. Flame stability is adversely affected. The burn-out of carbonaceous residue can be affected, owing to the reduction in residence time. Slagging may result from reducing conditions in parts of the combustion chamber. Engineering problems of ducting and pumping large volumes of flue gas economically.
Staged combustion with heat removal between stages Gas-oil and pulverised fuel (pf) fired power station boilers. Industrial processes.	The peak combustion temperatures are reduced when combustion starts in a fuel-rich zone, and before the rest of the combustion air is introduced, heat is extracted from the primary zone. This reduces emissions of NO_x.	Present application based entirely on empiricism. Fuel-rich regions may be affected by deposit formation because of lower softening temperatures of fuel ash under reducing conditions. Optimisation ought to be based on known temperature history of species concentration in combustion products for minimum emission of NO_x compatible with very low combustible emission for a wide range of turn-down ratios.

Fluidised bed combustion Combustion and gasification of coal and heavy fuel oil with retention of sulphur in the fluid bed. Power generation, steam and gas turbine cycles, industrial and district heating schemes.	Reduced installation costs. Sulphur retention in fluidised bed. Reduced NO_x emission because of lower combustion temperatures. Possibility of combined cycle (steam and gas turbine) operation giving higher thermodynamic efficiency and thus lower pollutant emission.	Scaling up of pilot fluidised bed combusters to power generation unit capacity. The reduction of fuel NO_x formation in the fluidised bed. Gasification combined with solids regeneration.
Gasification of coal and residual fuel oil Power generation, combined process heat and electricity generation.	Gasification of coal or residual fuel oil can be considered as a type of multi-stage combustion. The fuel is gasified to produce a combustible gas which is desulphurised. The sulphur is recovered and the desulphurised gas can be burnt in a gas turbine. The combination of a steam cycle and the gas turbine cycle improves the thermodynamic efficiency of the process and allows economic desulphurisation.	Control of the combined cycle over a load range compatible with the requirements of the gasification and desulphurisation processes. Reduction of the appreciable power requirement (5–8%) of the process. Known gasification processes are of low unit capacity. Up to power station boiler size (660–1300 MW) requires extensive R & D.

Design Factors

The design of any chimney must not impose unacceptable pressure variations on the appliance which it serves. Hence the range of gas flows which can be handled by a chimney of given diameter is limited. Where the appliance is subject to load variations, for example in steam-raising plant, the result may be that only two appliances can be served by a common flue. While this difficulty can be overcome by the provision of an induced-draught fan and pressure control instrumentation, the answer more often is to install a multiflue chimney.

The chimney must also be constructed so that both the gas flue and the structural shell are suited to the particular duty, for example with regard to chemical properties and temperature of the gases and resistance to abrasion. Common constructional materials are listed in Table 11.9. A single-bore chimney may be supported by, or be built into, the building housing the appliances, or it can be free-standing and possibly guyed.

TABLE 11.9 COMMON STRUCTURAL MATERIALS FOR CHIMNEYS

Material	Gas flue	Shell
Brickwork	+	+
Mild steel[6]	+	+
Concrete	+	+
GRP	+	+
Refractory, acid-resisting or insulating brick	+	—
Refractory concrete	+	—
Stainless steel	+	—
Glass-lined mild steel	+	—

The calculation of chimney height for conventional boilers and process heaters using coal- or oil-firing is simplified by use of the Clean Air Act Memorandum on Chimney Heights.[10] Heights of chimneys for gas-fired installations can also be estimated.[11] A greater height than calculated may be necessary with induced-draught systems to ensure that there is sufficient air for complete combustion.[12,13] The UK legislative controls over chimney heights are outlined in Chapter 4.

For electricity generating stations use is made of the principle that the thermal plume rise is a maximum when the flue gases from all the boilers are discharged in one plume.[14] All new coal- and oil-fired stations in the UK have a single chimney in part fulfilment of the 'best practicable means' requirement; multiple flues may be provided to give high efflux velocities when the station is not on full load and to facilitate chimney repairs. 'Basic' chimney heights for power stations, heights for smaller installations in accordance with Alkali Inspectorate requirements, and basic heights calculated from the Memorandum are shown as a function of SO_2 emission in Figure 11.5.[14]

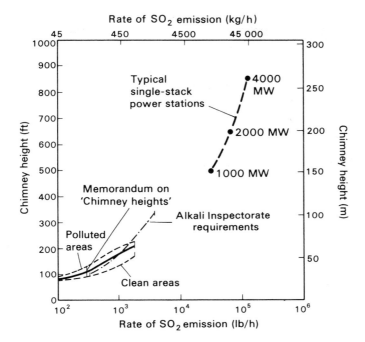

Fig. 11.5 Chimney heights[14]

Problems in Operation

Certain problems are characteristic of chimney underdesign or maloperation. For example, 'downwash' occurs when low-velocity gases from the chimney are pulled down into the low-pressure region on its lee side. This limits dispersal by reducing H_R. 'Inversion' occurs when cold air flows down the inside of the chimney on the windward side; this results in cooling of the flue and gases. Again H_R is reduced, because of the reduction in thermal buoyancy, but in this case there may also be smut formation and acidic condensation within the flue. Smut fall-out occurs when changes in load on a chimney dislodge particulate deposits built up inside the flue as a result of condensation.

To avoid these phenomena the flue gases should be discharged at a velocity at least 1·5 times wind speed; based on a highest common wind speed of 10 m/s, this results in a minimum efflux velocity of 15 m/s for ordinary industrial chimneys up to 4 m in diameter. A compromise is permissible for small installations, for example a minimum of 6 m/s, but the large multiflue chimneys at power stations require higher velocities. The chimney may also be insulated to maintain the waste gas above its dewpoint.

Control of Emissions from Internal Combustion Engines

Of the atmospheric pollutants already described, carbon monoxide, incompletely burnt hydrocarbons, oxides of nitrogen and particulate matter are generally the most significant emissions from internal combustion engines. Sulphur dioxide emissions are negligible as shown in Table 11.1.

The engines are either of the spark ignition type, for example petrol engines, or of the compression ignition type, such as diesel engines. The operating characteristics of the two types of engine, and hence the emissions, differ. However both are predominantly used in 'mobile pollution sources',[2] mainly motor vehicles, railway engines, ships and aircraft, and therefore the problem of pollution control cannot be isolated from considerations such as:

Fuel economy and versatility
Fixed and operating costs
Serviceability
Size and weight
Safety
Noise

Furthermore, control is more difficult than in continuous industrial combustion processes because combustion is a transient, non-steady-state process in a cooled combustion chamber with a large surface-to-volume ratio.

Spark Ignition Engines

In spark ignition engines a controlled proportion of air and petrol is drawn into the combustion chamber, compressed and ignited by an ignition source such as a spark plug. Combustion proceeds via a flame front passing through a homogeneous vapour–air mixture. The major pollutants from spark ignition engines comprise carbon monoxide, oxides of nitrogen, hydrocarbons, polynuclear aromatics, lead and other particulates. By far the major source is the exhaust but small evaporative emissions occur from the fuel tank and carburettor; crankcase emissions of partly or completely burnt gases may also be a problem with old engines but on new designs these are recycled to the engine intake.

Typically, a highly loaded spark ignition engine at constant speed emits concentrations of 1% to 2% carbon monoxide, 2000 ppm to 4000 ppm NO_x and 100 ppm to 200 ppm of hydrocarbons.[1] However, the range of operation in motor vehicles includes steady running, acceleration and deceleration; US emission limits take these into account by means of 'driving cycles'. (Limitations are also placed upon lead content of fuel, those in the US being more stringent than in the UK.)

Excessive exhaust emissions may arise from the causes listed in Table 11.10.

Methods of reducing emissions from spark ignition engines include the use of gas recirculation, thermal reactors and catalytic reactors. Catalytic reactors, in conjunction with improved control over the preparation, metering and distribution of the petrol–air mixture, are considered necessary to meet increasingly stringent US standards.[1]

TABLE 11.10 CAUSES OF EXCESSIVE EMISSIONS FROM SPARK IGNITION ENGINES

Defect	Result
Misfiring of a cylinder	Emission of unburnt petrol
Worn piston rings	Emission of blue smoke due to unburnt lubricating oil
Running with choke left out	Emission of black smoke
Poor adjustment leading to incomplete combustion	Emission of aldehydes, carbon monoxide and hydrocarbons

Compression Ignition Engines

In compression ignition engines air only is drawn into the combustion chamber and highly compressed; fuel is sprayed in as a fine mist via an injector and ignition results from the high temperature of the compressed air. Diesel engines emit smoke intermittently as follows:

White 'smoke'	Generally on cold starting, idling and low loads. Consists of unburnt vaporised fuel plus small proportion of lubricating oil plus, possibly, partial oxidation products.
Blue 'smoke'	Consists of partly vaporised, incompletely burnt lubricating oils.
Black 'smoke'	Consists of particulate carbon plus oily, tarry materials, resulting from incomplete combustion, especially at maximum loads.

The main causes are given in Table 11.11.

Diesel engines also emit noticeable and objectionable odours. Emission is not a predictable function of power but peak power retard has been used to limit both smoke and odours.[2] In general, the reduction of emissions from diesel engines may involve both derating of power output (allowing operation below the smoke point) and good maintenance.

TABLE 11.11 CAUSES OF SMOKE EMISSIONS FROM COMPRESSION IGNITION ENGINES

Defect	Result
Pump defects	Overcharging of cylinders with fuel
Air leakage via pistons and valves	Poor ignition due to reduced compression and cylinder temperature
Dirty injectors	Poor atomisation of fuel
Maloperation of fuel stop	Overcharging of cylinders with fuel

References

1. *Combustion Generated Pollution,* Science Research Council, July 1976.
2. STERN, A. C. (Ed.), *Air Pollution* Vol. IV, *Engineering Control of Air Pollution,* Academic Press, 1977.
3. *The Federal R & D Plan for Air Pollution Control by Combustion Modification,* Battelle Memorial Institute, Colombus, Ohio, 1971.
4. SALOOJA, J., *Journal of Fuel and Heat Technology,* **19**(1), 2–6; (2), 2–7, 1972.
5. FISCHOFF, H., *Chemical Engineer,* (327), 863, 1977.
6. HUGHES, R., *Chemical Engineer,* (315), 754, 1976.
7. *Low Sulphur Fuel Oil from Coal,* PB 203889, US Bureau of Mines, 1971.
8. *Energy and the Environment,* Report of a Working Party—Institute of Fuel/Royal Society of Arts/Committee for Environmental Conservation, 1974.
9. CRESSWELL, C. R., *Notes on Air Pollution Control,* H. K. Lewis, 1974.
10. Clean Air Act Memorandum on Chimney Heights, 1967, 2nd edn, and Circular HLG 69/68, Ministry of Housing and Local Government, 1968.
11. Chimney Design Symposium Conference Publication, CICL, University of Edinburgh, April 1973.
12. *Chimneys for Industrial Oil-Fired Plant,* Shell Marketing Ltd, London, 1973.
13. *Chimney Design Manual,* Brightside Heating and Engineering Co. Ltd, Portsmouth, 1968.
14. CLARKE, A. J., *Chemical Engineer,* (271), 139, March 1973.

CHAPTER 12

Treatment and Recovery Processes for Gaseous Pollutants

In addition to the particulate emissions discussed in Chapter 10, many processes result in the evolution of significant quantities of gases or vapours which may contain or constitute pollutants. These potential pollutants, or derivatives of them, usually require treatment for removal or conversion to a more acceptable form; the treatment can often provide an economical recovery process.

The processes available for the treatment and, if economics are favourable, the recovery of substances evolved as vapour are:

Condensation
Adsorption of the vapour preferentially onto a solid, followed by desorption and recovery
Absorption/dissolution in a solvent or aqueous solution, possibly followed by stripping for recovery

and, less widely applicable,

Chemical conversion by heterogeneous catalysis
Chemical reaction

Some of the principles and applications of these methods are summarised below.

Condensation

'Condensation' refers to the phase change from vapour to liquid consequent upon the cooling and abstraction of the appropriate latent heat of vaporisation.

It is conventionally applied to vapour recovery in chemical and petroleum refining plants, on vapour degreasing and dry-cleaning equipment and in distillation and evaporation plant generally.

On an open vapour-degreasing vat the condenser consists simply of a bank of tubes located around the walls just below the top of the vat. However, the most common type of heat exchanger used for condensation is the shell and tube type illustrated in Figure 12.1. The cooling surface is in the form of a series of tubes sealed into a tube-sheet at either end. The vapour may be condensed either on the outside of the tubes, i.e. on the shell-side, or inside the tubes, and the exchanger may be arranged vertically or horizontally. The area required for heat transfer is calculated from the conventional formula

$$A = \frac{Q}{U_D \Delta T_M}$$

where A is heat transfer area, Q is heat transfer rate, ΔT_M is mean temperature difference and U_D is an overall coefficient for heat transfer given approximately by

$$\frac{1}{U_D} = \frac{1}{h_m} + \frac{1}{h_o} + \frac{x_w}{k_w} + R_D$$

where h_m = mean heat transfer film coefficient for condensing vapour
h_o = forced convective heat transfer film coefficient for the coolant fluid stream
x_w = tube wall thickness
k_w = thermal conductivity of tube wall material
R_D = scale resistance

all in consistent units.

For clean, thin-walled tubes, this reduces to

$$\frac{1}{U_D} = \frac{1}{h_m} + \frac{1}{h_o}$$

These film coefficients are predicted from empirical correlations.

In normal operation the horizontal arrangement is more efficient, since the mean thickness of condensate film on the tubes is less than with vertical tubes. Very low condensing coefficients are associated with the presence of 'non-condensables' such as air or nitrogen in the vapour stream, since the process is then diffusion-controlled. The rate of vapour flow is limited by the permissible pressure drop through the condenser, which may be critical; the coolant fluid side-pressure drop is generally less critical. Both are calculable from empirical correlations.[1,2]

More compact heat exchangers, for example with spiral plates or gasketed flat plates, are also used.[3]

Water is the most common cooling medium, as described in Chapter 9. A chilled solution of brine or glycol, or direct refrigeration, may be used if lower temperatures are necessary. Air cooling is also used, particularly on large in-

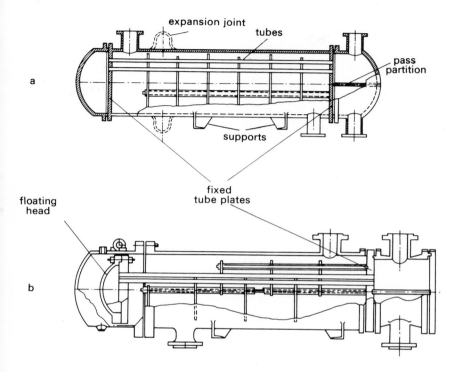

Fig. 12.1 Shell and tube condensers
   a Fixed tube plate
   b Floating-head pull-through type permits expansion/contraction and removal
     of tube bundle for shell-side cleaning

stallations; fins are used on the air side to improve heat transfer to the air which is sucked or blown across the tube bundle.

Direct contact heat exchangers of simple construction may also be used. For example, the spray condenser, in which the hot gas-vapour stream passes through a vessel into which liquid is injected via angled nozzles, is particularly applicable to low-pressure duties. Condensation in this equipment may be combined with scrubbing to remove particulates, or with absorption.

Condensation is an efficient recovery process and some degree of fractionation can be achieved with multi-component vapour streams. There may be potential for recovery of the latent heat of vaporisation, for example by preheating other process streams. However, in many manufacturing operations, e.g. drying, surface coating or spraying, vapours are discharged in air or other inert gas streams at fairly low concentrations and condensation is not then practicable.

Gas Adsorption

In gas adsorption a pollutant is removed from a gas stream by retention on the surface of a porous solid as a result of forces which exist there. The carrier gas passes through the adsorbent bed. After concentration in the adsorbent the pollutant may be recovered, chemically converted to a more readily disposable form with recovery of the adsorbent, or in some cases disposed of with the adsorbent.

Commercial adsorbents are generally in the form of irregular granules, preformed shapes or cartridges and are prepared with a very large ratio of surface area to weight. The porous solids generally used for adsorption are silica gel, activated alumina, activated carbon and molecular sieves. Silica gel and activated alumina are mainly used in gas drying, and as such are not generally applicable to pollution control. Molecular sieves are used in gas drying but can bring about separations of vapour mixtures on the basis of molecular shape and size. Activated carbon preferentially adsorbs organic compounds and is widely used in solvent recovery processes; it also adsorbs sulphur compounds.

Some common applications of activated carbon adsorption in pollution control are summarised in Table 12.1.

TABLE 12.1 APPLICATIONS OF ADSORPTION

Application	Requirement/example
Solvents recovery from air streams in, for example, printing, rubber processing, vapour degreasing, dry-cleaning, surface coating.	Freedom from particulate matter. Inlet vapour concentrations generally $0 \cdot 004 - 0 \cdot 032$ kg/m³ ($0 \cdot 25 - 2$ lb/1000 ft³) and less than 50% of lower explosive limit.[4]
Odour removal, e.g. food processing, chemical manufacture, tanneries, paper and pulp manufacturing.	Refer to Chapter 10.
Removal of sulphur-containing gases (H_2S, SO_2) in combination with catalytic oxidation.	Moving bed of activated carbon with *in-situ* regeneration: the Reinluft process.
Radioactive gases and vapour control.	
Carbon disulphide recovery in the viscose process for rayon	1000 ppm CS_2 and 20–30 ppm H_2S inlet concentrations following bulk H_2S removal by scrubbing with alkaline ferric oxide suspension.[5]

The operation of a carbon bed adsorber involves adsorption of volatile solvent or gas from the gas stream followed by regeneration and recovery. Regeneration generally requires steam to be passed through the carbon bed to displace the adsorbed material which can then be recovered from condensate by either distillation or decantation, dependent on its miscibility with water and relative volatility. Operation may be in either static or fluidised beds. In the more common static bed installations there are two columns, each containing a bed 0·3–0·6 m (1–2 ft) deep, so that while one is in use the other can be regenerated and cooled. Solvent-laden gas passes through the adsorber on stream at superficial velocities of up to 0·3 m/s (1 ft/s). An adsorption efficiency of 99% can normally be obtained with inlet solvent concentrations of 1% solvent.[6] During regeneration, steam is passed through the bed in the opposite direction and, for high recovery efficiencies, the bed may subsequently be cooled and dried with fresh air. Cartridges are seldom used except in special circumstances, because of their high cost. An arrangement of a two-stage regenerative system with deep bed carbon adsorbers for hydrocarbon recovery is shown in Figure 12.2.

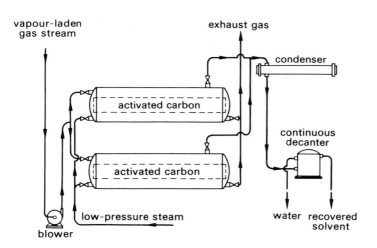

Fig. 12.2 Arrangement of deep-bed adsorbers

The fluidised bed adsorber was introduced for carbon disulphide recovery in viscose rayon manufacture;[5] subsequently it has been applied to acetone recovery to give an outlet concentration of only 100 ppm acetone in air.[7] In operation the carbon is circulated continuously from the adsorber vessel, which contains a number of beds fluidised by the solvent-laden air, to a stripper and then back again. In the adsorber it descends from tray to tray countercurrent to the air flow.

Static beds are generally installed to handle low gas flows or batch processes. Fluidised bed adsorbers are more appropriate for large gas flows when continuous reactivation is required. As illustrated by the data in Table 12.2, fluidised beds have a better steam economy than static beds.[6]

TABLE 12.2 TYPICAL STEAM CONSUMPTION FOR SOLVENT RECOVERY PLANTS[6]

Solvent	Concentration (% vol/vol in air)	Stripping steam/solvent (kg/kg)	
		Fluid bed	Fixed bed
Acetone	1·6	1·5	2·5
Methylene chloride	1·0	1·3	2·4
Toluene	0·9	1·7	3·0
Perchloroethylene	0·2	1·7	Not known
Toluene/ethyl acetate	1·0	1·8	3·0
Toluene/tetrahydrofuran	0·9	1·8	3·0
Ethanol	1·0	1·7	2·8
Solvent heptane	0·8	2·0	4·0

Absorption

In absorption one or more components are separated and recovered from a gaseous mixture by preferential dissolution in a liquid. The solute (the absorbed material) is transferred across the gas–liquid interface and may either dissolve physically in the liquid (the solvent) or react with it. Thus absorption of ammonia in water involves only physical dissolution but absorption of sulphur dioxide into a solution of sodium carbonate also involves chemical reaction, the rate of which can affect the overall rate of absorption.

The driving force for solute transfer is the difference in pressure between the partial pressure associated with the mole fraction in the gas phase and the vapour pressure of the solute in equilibrium with the liquid phase:

$$\Delta P = P_g - P_l$$

where P_g = partial pressure soluble gas in gas phase

P_l = partial pressure soluble gas in equilibrium with liquid phase.

The rate of transfer is directly proportional to the driving force but is restricted by its diffusion rate in both the gas and liquid phases. These restrictions are referred to as the liquid and gas film resistances but they are seldom separated in industrial design practice, and are combined in an overall film resistance:

$$\frac{1}{K_g a} = \frac{1}{k_g a} + \frac{m}{k_l a} \qquad \text{or} \qquad \frac{1}{K_l a} = \frac{1}{k_l a} + \frac{1}{m k_g a}$$

where a = interfacial area

$k_g a$, $K_g a$ = gas film and overall gas mass transfer coefficients (N/m^3)

$k_l a$, $K_l a$ = liquid film and overall liquid mass transfer coefficients (N/m^3)

m = slope of the equilibrium line dy/dx

x, y = mole fractions of solute in liquid and gas.

The overall rate of solute transfer may be expressed by the mass transport equation as:[8]

$$N = K_g a \Delta P$$

where N is in kg mol/s.

The solvent usually flows countercurrent to the gas stream and the operation is conventionally performed in towers. These may comprise simple spray scrubbing towers, similar to the type illustrated earlier in Figure 10.2. More often, packings or plates are incorporated to provide efficient gas–liquid contact as in distillation columns. The liquid flow rate is specific for each duty, dependent on the nature and solubility of the solute to be removed, the inlet and required outlet concentrations, and the gas flow rate.

Packed absorption columns are generally designed using the $K_g a$ coefficient and the transport equation expressed in the form of transfer units using

$$Z = \text{HTU} \times \text{NTU}$$

where Z is the absorber height (m), NTU is the calculated number of transfer units and HTU is the height of a transfer unit (m).

When absorption with chemical reaction is used for more efficient gas removal the mechanism is more complex; the usual effect, except with very slow reactions, is to improve transfer on the liquid side so that the gas film is dominant.

Methods of calculation are given in the standard texts;[8,9] the main problem lies in predicting the mass transfer coefficient. Thus, in the calculation of the height of a packed tower for a specific duty, reliance is generally placed upon empirical correlations of experimental data.

Plate columns are designed on the basis of the 'theoretical plate', assuming that contact between gas and liquid streams is such that they leave in equilibrium with each other. Deviations from this ideal situation are expressed in terms of 'plate efficiency', which may be defined as an overall plate efficiency (ratio of number of theoretical plates to number of actual plates required for a given separation) or as a Murphree plate efficiency for each individual plate.[8]

Equipment

The simplest equipment for absorption is a vessel filled to the requisite level with solvent into which the gas stream is discharged via a sparge pipe near the bottom. The bubble residence time and interfacial area are increased if small bubbles are produced and the vessel is vertical. Variations on this design include mechanical agitation and porous plate sparging. However, unless provision is made for continual make-up and overflow, this method is only suitable for the treatment of intermittent discharges of relatively small volumes of gas. Furthermore, efficiency is low and therefore this method is not commonly used.

The spray tower is useful when solid particles may be present in the gas stream, since it is not prone to blockage. It exhibits a relatively low pressure drop and is therefore applicable to scrubbing at atmospheric pressure; high gas rates can be used provided a mist eliminator is installed at the outlet. However, the spray tower is not suitable for the removal of high solute concentrations because of the limitations on interfacial area and liquid :gas ratio.

Packed columns are most common in pollution control applications, the packing being either individual prefabricated elements, for example rings, or stacked grids or slats. A typical arrangement is shown in Figure 12.3. The packing is required to provide maximum contact area between the phases, with the least possible obstruction to flow: all the packing elements should be covered by a flowing liquid film and there should be even distribution of liquid over the column cross-section throughout the packed height. With the various ring-type packings, random dumping is used up to 50 mm (2 in) diameter; above this, rings are stacked in horizontal rows and elaborate provision has to be made for initial distribution and redistribution of liquid.

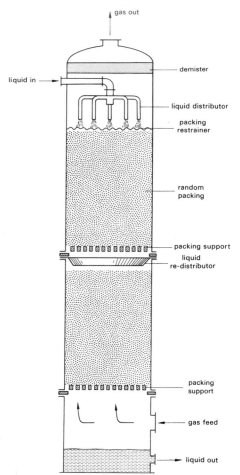

Fig. 12.3
Arrangement
of a packed
absorption tower

The principal requirements of an efficient packing are:

Large surface area
Uniform liquid distribution
Uniform gas distribution
Low density
Low resistance to gas flow
Inertness

Some of the many packing elements available commercially are shown in Figure 12.4. These vary in size between 6 and 50 mm ($\frac{1}{4}$ and 2 in) and are made of glass, ceramic, metal or plastic. Although they are less efficient than the newer types, Raschig rings are the commonest and cheapest. Lessing or cross-partition rings provide increased surface area per unit packed volume but, since the additional surface is in the centre of the ring where wetting is less effective, the efficiency gain is less than might be expected. Berl saddles offer a lower pressure drop, and therefore increased column capacity, compared with rings; the surface-to-volume ratio is higher and wetting characteristics are better. Intalox saddles have largely superseded Berl saddles because they are easier to fabricate. Pall rings are generally considered the most efficient ring packing.

Gauze and multifilament-strand wire packings are also used, both as individual elements (e.g. Dixon rings) and as complete cross-column grids (e.g. Multifil, Hyperfil and Sulzer packing). The separation efficiency of this type of packing is very high at low flow rates, while the pressure drop is very low; however, at high liquid rates the strands become blocked leading to rapid fall in performance. They are available in carbon steel, stainless steel, copper, Monel and nickel.

Efficient liquid distribution, and redistribution at intervals, are particularly important if an ordered arrangement of slats or grids is used, since these have poor 'self-distributing' properties.

A quantitative guide to the performance of different types of packing can be obtained from the value of the mass transfer coefficient $K_g a$, which should be high, and the pressure drop per unit depth of packing and the 'packing factor' (an experimental measure of the capacity of the packing), both of which should be low. Numerous plate column designs are also used for continuous counter-current gas–liquid contacting. Selection may be based on the characteristics of the system:

	Plate column	Packed column
System prone to foaming		+
System containing sludge or solids	+	
Highly corrosive system		+
System with high heat of solution/reaction	+	
Gas phase controlled (low solubility) system		+
Liquid phase controlled (high solubility) system	+	
Flexibility with regard to flow rate	+	

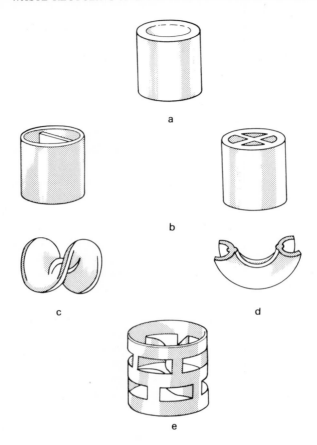

Fig. 12.4 Types of packing
    a Raschig ring
    b Lessing ring; cross-partition ring
    c Berl saddle
    d Intalox saddle
    e Pall ring

Packed columns are generally considered to be more economical and practical up to 0·6 m (2 ft) diameter. Plate columns are usually more economical above 1 m (3 ft 3 in) diameter because of the distributors required in packed columns and because plate cost per unit volume decreases with size, whereas the cost of packing per unit volume remains almost constant.

The internals of plate columns are similar to those of distillation columns but cater for larger liquid:gas ratios. Plate efficiencies tend to be lower than those achieved in distillation practice, generally ranging between 20% and 80%.

Conventional bubble-cap plates are reliable and a standard design procedure is available.[10] However, they are relatively expensive; simple perforated plates with downcomers, although less flexible with regard to variation in operating liquid or gas flow rates, may be preferred. Numerous commercial designs are available including the Flexitray,[11] Turbogrid and Kittel plate.[12]

Absorption Processes

In pollution control applications alkaline solutions of caustic soda, sodium carbonate or calcium hydroxide are often used for treatment of acid gases where physical absorption in water is inadequate. The liquor is normally recirculated, the level of contamination or solute concentration being controlled by a combination of purging via a sidestream and make-up with fresh solution. Automatic pH control may be used to regulate make-up. Purging assists in the removal of particulates, and make-up balances any significant losses due to evaporation. In some cases a reaction product is recovered by absorption in a liquid to yield a marketable product; for example, fertiliser may be recovered by reacting waste ammonia with waste acid. Alternatively, a liquid may be used which can be regenerated, for example ethanolamine solutions are used for hydrogen sulphide absorption and can be recycled following steam regeneration.

Common processes used in the control of major gas-phase pollutants are described below.

Sulphur Dioxide

Sulphur dioxide is generated in considerable quantities during the sintering and smelting of metal ores; the stack gas from smelting/processing sulphide ore may contain up to 8% sulphur dioxide. Several absorption processes have therefore been developed for sulphur dioxide recovery from these gases using alkaline solutions. The gases are available at high temperature and low pressure and contain dust and other contaminants, and the processes are relatively complex. The main incentive for recovery is therefore pollution control, since the products, sulphur and sulphuric acid, are not generally of sufficient value to justify the additional costs incurred in recovery compared with the dumping of sludge.

In the Asarco process (Figure 12.5), gases which have been cleaned by electrostatic precipitation are cooled and then scrubbed with dimethylaniline.[13] This is followed by scrubbing with sodium carbonate solution, to further reduce the sulphur dioxide content and to remove dimethylaniline carry-over, and finally with dilute sulphuric acid to remove traces of dimethylaniline.

Sulphur dioxide is recovered from the solvents by steam stripping and, after scrubbing to ensure freedom from dimethylaniline and drying with sulphuric acid, passes to storage for use in acid manufacture.

The Cominco process (Figure 12.6) recovers sulphur dioxide by absorption in an aqueous solution of ammonium sulphate. Sulphur dioxide is stripped from solution, for use in acid manufacture, by the addition of concentrated sulphuric acid; ammonium sulphate solution is produced as a byproduct for fertiliser manufacture.[4]

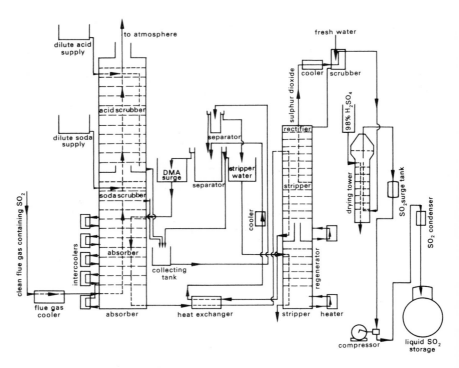

Fig. 12.5 Recovery of sulphur dioxide by absorption in dimethyl aniline solution: Asarco Process[13]

In the Sulphidine process (Figure 12.7), use is made of an equal mixture of xylidine and water.[14] Soda ash solution is added to a second absorber to convert the xylidine sulphate which is formed to sodium sulphate; sulphur dioxide is stripped from the solution using steam. Tail gases are washed with dilute sulphuric acid to recover xylidine vapour.

Numerous similar processes, or modifications of the above, have been developed.[4] In many other cases gas containing a relatively high concentration of sulphur dioxide from smelting operations is fed directly to a sulphuric acid plant. Emissions from contact sulphuric acid plants may themselves be scrubbed with alkaline solutions, for example ammonium, sodium or magnesium sulphate solution, but when the final emissions are cold and wet this may result in persistent visible plumes.[15]

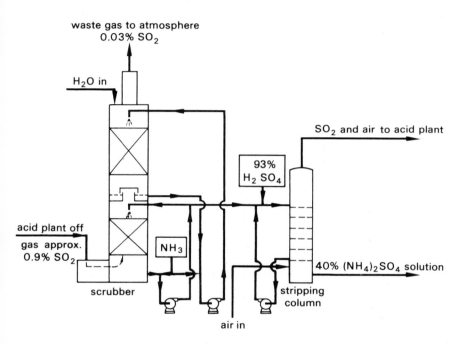

Fig. 12.6 Recovery of sulphur dioxide by absorption in ammonium sulphite solution: Cominco process[4]

The removal of sulphur dioxide from flue gases, particularly those from power stations, has been studied extensively. However, as these usually contain less than 0·5% sulphur dioxide the gas volumes to be processed are very large in relation to the quantity of sulphur recoverable, so that the operation is inevitably expensive. The process applied at the Battersea and Bankside power stations in London used the naturally alkaline river water from the Thames to which was added a small amount of chalk slurry. The flow diagram is shown in Figure 12.8.[4] It achieved SO_2 removal efficiencies of 90% to 95% over many years of operation, but was not held to be the 'best practicable means' for controlling SO_2 emissions from more recent power stations because of the cool, wet chimney plume produced.[16] This occasionally descended near the stations with only minimal dilution, giving rise to complaints. In addition, the liquid effluent discharge, containing mainly calcium sulphate but with some unreacted

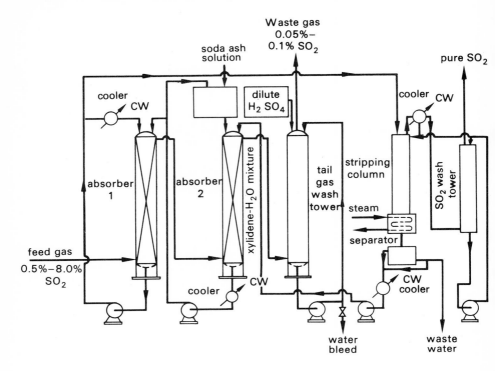

Fig. 12.7 Recovery of sulphur dioxide by absorption in xylidine–water mixture: Sulphidine process[4]

calcium sulphite, imposed an oxygen demand on the river. A major part of the Battersea gas washing plant was therefore closed down in the early 1970s, after which the flue gases were emitted hot and unwashed, as from other UK power stations. No detectable change was subsequently observed in local SO_2 concentrations.[16]

In the cyclic lime process developed by ICI-Howden, a 5% to 10% chalk or lime slurry is recycled after removal of calcium sulphite and calcium sulphate. A flow diagram of this is shown in Figure 12.9. Unfortunately, the calcium sulphite/calcium sulphate is contaminated with fly ash and therefore not marketable. This process was formerly used at Fulham power station (London), with a washing efficiency of greater than 95%, but the operating costs were approximately twice those of the Battersea process and it is no longer used.[17]

In the Fulham–Simon-Carves process, ammoniacal liquor from gas works or coke ovens may be used, with the eventual production of sulphur and ammonium sulphate.[18] This process was tested at Nottingham, but there were corrosion problems and operating costs were relatively high.[17]

In the United States there is greater commitment to flue gas desulphurisation, with particular emphasis on fossil-fuel-fired power plants. Once-through alkaline solution scrubbing processes are favoured, the majority of plants using an aqueous slurry of lime or limestone and producing calcium sulphate/calcium sulphite for disposal.[19] In an alternative process, magnesium oxide slurry is used; the magnesium sulphate/magnesium sulphite is reprocessed to yield a 10% to 15% sulphur dioxide gas stream, for sulphur or sulphuric acid manufacture, and regenerated magnesium oxide. When this process is applied to solid-fuel-fired installations, efficient particulates removal is necessary to avoid accumulation in the recycled slurry. A sodium sulphate process is also used; this makes provision for regeneration and produces an SO_2 concentration of 20% which may be used directly in an acid plant.[20] There are also double-alkali scrubbing processes in which the absorbent, a solution of sodium or ammonium salts, is regenerated by treatment with lime or limestone. In Japan, the gypsum produced by this process has been marketed.[19]

In the USA in 1976 more than 90% of the 12 000 MW of coal-fired utility boiler sulphur dioxide control systems in use or under construction were of the type that produces solid waste calcium salts for disposal. This proportion will be maintained for the estimated 100 000 MW to be controlled by 1985.[21] The US preferences in disposal processes are based upon more favourable economics and greater operating experience. Processes which produce sulphuric acid require a reliable local market for it, since it is expensive to store in quantity or to transport over large distances. Scrubbing of flue gases from power stations is not currently practised in the UK.

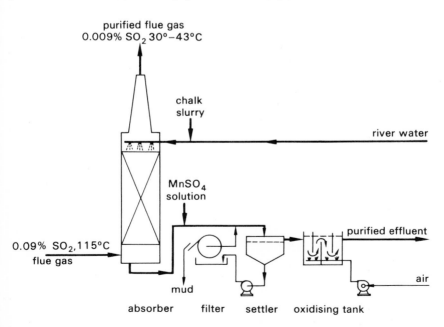

Fig. 12.8 Removal of sulphur dioxide from flue gas by scrubbing with alkaline river water: Battersea process[4]

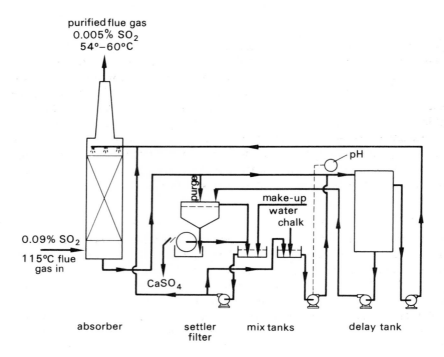

purified flue gas
0.005% SO_2
54°–60°C

pH

purge

make-up
water
chalk

0.09% SO_2

115°C flue
gas in

$CaSO_4$

absorber   settler   mix tanks   delay tank
             filter

Fig. 12.9 Cyclic line process for sulphur dioxide absorption: ICI–Howden process

Hydrogen Chloride

Hydrogen chloride is very soluble in water and absorption in a packed tower containing stoneware packing is the conventional removal process. Because of the high heat of solution, cooling may be necessary; the corrosivity of the resulting solution and, if recovery is not viable, its disposal produce the only difficulties.

Incineration of plastic waste containing polyvinyl chloride (PVC), or cable-burning to remove PVC insulation from electric cables, results in the generation of hydrogen chloride. Depending on the scale and concentration, this may be removed by absorption in water or a recycled alkaline solution, but particulates require separation and acid recovery is not practicable.

On a large scale, hydrogen chloride is produced as a byproduct of processes for the chlorination of organic chemicals. It is recovered by scrubbing with water or weak acid produced *in situ*, to yield marketable hydrochloric acid. The exit gases from conventional plants manufacturing hydrochloric acid are also scrubbed with water. Resultant dilute streams are generally neutralised and disposed of, since the energy requirements for concentration to a marketable grade are uneconomic.

Chlorine

Chlorine evolved in vent gases, during its manufacture by electrolysis of a chloride salt, is recovered by absorption in water or carbon tetrachloride when the concentration is about 10% or more. The chlorine is then recovered by distillation.[14] Recovery of 97% can be achieved, with less than 0·5% chlorine in the exit gas stream. Recovery from vent gas streams containing less than 1% chlorine, or occasional discharges (for example, from tanker unloading operations on delivery to users), is not economic; the chlorine is removed by scrubbing with sodium hydroxide or lime solution in conventional absorption towers. Absorption efficiencies of these units may approach 99·9% and result in exit concentrations of less than 10 ppm chlorine.

Fluorides

Hydrogen fluoride and silicon tetrafluoride are emitted from plants producing aluminium and phosphoric acid or phosphate fertiliser, as well as from the fluorine industry. These gases are readily soluble in water and the concentration of fluorides in the waste gases is reduced to acceptable levels by scrubbing, usually in spray columns or packed columns with open-grid packing since large volumes of low-pressure gas are involved. The acids are not generally economic to recover but are recycled to build up concentration and precipitated by lime treatment for disposal.

Hydrogen Sulphide

Processes are available for the removal of hydrogen sulphide from gas streams based upon absorption in an aqueous ethanolamine solution. Processes which generate hydrogen sulphide as a pollutant are very limited, for example the evaporation of kraft paper pulping liquors and some metal smelting operations. However the removal of hydrogen sulphide from fuel and refinery gas streams in hydrodesulphurisation operations is extremely important commercially to reduce subsequent odour, corrosion and other problems during processing or use. It also provides a major source of sulphur.

The Girbitol process for hydrogen sulphide removal makes use of ethanolamines, generally either monoethanolamine or diethanolamine, to sweeten gases which contain hydrogen sulphide, carbon dioxide and traces of other sulphides such as mercaptans. Absorption in a plate tower is followed by stripping to regenerate the ethanolamine and release the acid gases for reprocessing. Hydrogen sulphide is usually partially oxidised to water and sulphur, with recovery of the latter as a valuable byproduct.

Catalytic Conversion

Chemical reactions, in particular oxidation, can be carried out on the surface of solid catalysts. Application of this technique to produce valuable products is practised in conventional chemical manufacturing but it is not widely used to produce recycle streams for recovery in pollution control. However, important applications of catalytic combustion, in which low levels of pollutants can be destroyed by oxidation at temperatures well below their autogenous ignition temperatures, were referred to in Chapter 10 for odours and in Chapter 11 for oxides of nitrogen.

One example of catalytic conversion is shown in Figure 12.10. Flue gas from power generation plants can be desulphurised, following particulates removal, by passage with air through a fixed catalyst bed at approximately 455°C. The sulphur dioxide is converted to sulphur trioxide which is absorbed in sulphuric acid, as in conventional acid manufacture.

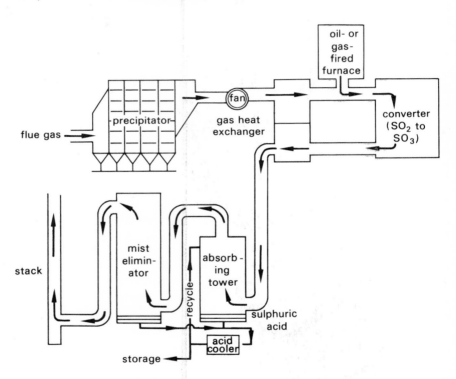

Fig. 12.10 Desulphurisation of flue gas by catalytic oxidation, with reheat

The predominant methods proposed for the control of emissions from internal combustion engines are based upon catalytic reaction. Noble metal oxidation catalysts are in use for the oxidation of carbon monoxide and hydrocarbons in the USA. Reduction catalyst reactors are proposed for the reduction of oxides of nitrogen. Various arrangements are proposed using either two reactors in series, the reduction process preceding the oxidation process, or dual catalysts.

Chemical Reaction

Chemical reactions following adsorption on to surfaces may be applied to the control of gaseous pollutants.

Although not applied directly to exhaust gases, dry oxidation processes have been conventionally applied to the removal of sulphur compounds from fuel gases. Finely divided ferric oxide serves to convert hydrogen sulphide to iron sulphide: for example, under moist, alkaline conditions at about 40°C:

$$6H_2S + 2Fe_2O_3 \rightarrow 2Fe_2S_3 + 6H_2O$$

The iron oxide is subsequently regenerated, yielding sulphur which may be recovered either by solvent extraction or by combustion to give sulphur dioxide for acid manufacture. A variety of processes are available, all based on iron oxide under different conditions.[4] Zinc oxide may also be effectively employed for sulphur and sulphide removal.

An active form of alumina has been used to remove gaseous fluorides from the emissions arising in primary aluminium production. Fabric filters are coated with alumina injected into the gas stream. After reaction with the fluorides, the alumina is returned to the manufacturing process; the fabric of the filter also serves to remove particulate matter.

Energy Recovery

Effluent gas streams at elevated temperatures can be subjected to waste heat recovery in heat exchangers. The outlet temperature is dependent on natural draught and thermal plume rise requirements.

Waste gases from which energy recovery involving combustion is practicable include coke-oven gas, refinery tail gases, blast-furnace gas, hydrogen and carbon monoxide. The outputs tend to be variable, but these gases may be burnt directly in boilers which can also burn auxiliary fuel to make up the shortfall from the total process energy requirement. Gas streams which are diluted with inerts and hence of low calorific value, or multi-waste gases, may require multi-port burners. These may incorporate auxiliary fuel burners and refractory chambers with waste heat recovery systems.

The methane generated during anaerobic sludge treatment is a valuable source of energy. Generally it comprises 70% CH_4 and 30% CO_2, and has a calorific value of 23·5 MJ/m^3. On combustion it provides power for the sewage works and waste heat is used to raise the temperature of the digestion tanks. This process is discussed further in Chapter 17.

References

1. KERN, D. Q., *Process Heat Transfer*, McGraw-Hill, 1950.
2. BUTTERWORTH, D., *Introduction to Heat Transfer*, Oxford University Press, 1977.
3. *Thermal Handbook*, Alfa Laval, 1969.

4. KOHL, A. and RIESENFELD, F., *Gas purification*, 2nd edn, Gulf Publishing, 1974.
5. ROWSON, H. M., *British Chemical Engineering*, **8**, 180, 1963.
6. AVERY, D. A. and BOISTON, D. A., *Chemical Engineer*, (225), 8, 1969.
7. *Chemical Age*, 611, 23 October 1965.
8. SHERWOOD, T. K. and PIGFORD, R. L., *Absorption and Extraction*, 2nd edn, McGraw-Hill, 1952.
9. NONHEBEL, G., *Gas Purification Processes for Air Pollution Control*, 2nd edn, Newnes-Butterworth, 1972.
10. *Bubble Tray Design Manual*, American Institute of Chemical Engineers, 1959.
11. THRIFT, G. C., *Chemical Engineering*, **61**, 177, 1954.
12. PFEIFFENBERGER, C. A., *Chemical Engineering*, **60**, 242, 1953.
13. FLEMING, E. P. and FITT, T. C., *Industrial and Engineering Chemistry*, **42**, 2253, 1950.
14. STRAUSS, W., *Industrial Gas Cleaning*, Vol. 8, Pergamon, 1974.
15. IRELAND, F. E., *Chemical Engineer*, (221), 261, 1968.
16. CLARKE, A. J., *Chemical Engineer*, (272), 139, 1973.
17. CRESSWELL, C. R., *Notes on Air Pollution Control*, H. K. Lewis, 1974.
18. REES, R. L., *Journal of the Institute of Fuel*, **25**, 350, 1953.
19. STERN, A. C. (Ed.), *Air Pollution*, Vol. VI, 3rd edn, Academic Press, 1977.
20. BETTLEHEIM, J. and BILLINGE, A., paper presented to 2nd International Symposium on the Control of Gaseous Sulphur and Nitrogen Compound Emissions, University of Salford, April 1976.
21. LAMANTIA, C. R. and LUNT, R. R., paper presented to World Congress on Chemical Engineering, Amsterdam, 28 June 1976.

PART FOUR

SOLID WASTE DISPOSAL AND RECOVERY PRACTICE

CHAPTER 13

Industrial Waste Disposal

Introduction

The treatment and disposal or recovery of non-gaseous effluent wastes is described in Chapters 7–9. This chapter is concerned with methods for the treatment and disposal of other wastes, either liquids or solids, which are not normally discharged via sewerage systems or into natural waters. As discussed in Chapter 3, a large proportion of these wastes are 'non-hazardous', but stringent controls are applicable to the remainder. Household and trade refuse, which arises in large tonnages and is heterogeneous in nature, is considered separately in Chapter 14, together with other special wastes which, by reason of their toxicity or persistence, call for special measures.

The two principal methods of disposal are surface tipping (landfill) and incineration. Disposal at sea is practised for special materials for which surface tipping is inappropriate. Certain wastes may also be disposed of by special burial. There is considerable scope for recovery and recycling of materials; this is discussed separately in Chapters 15–17.

The percentages of combined industrial and household refuse disposed of by various methods in Western Europe are given in Table 13.1.[1] Composting, that is biochemical degradation of organic matter in a process involving preparation, digestion, curing and finishing to produce a humus-like material (see Chapter 17), is rarely applicable to industrial waste.

Whatever the method of disposal adopted it may be necessary for wastes to be segregated, collected, transported and possibly processed prior to disposal. A *Provisional Code of Practice for the Disposal of Wastes* has been drawn up which emphasises the need for liaison between the two or more parties involved.[2] Although this is concerned mainly with deposition on land, the

TABLE 13.1 WASTE DISPOSAL METHODS USED IN WESTERN EUROPE:[1] ESTIMATED % OF COLLECTED DOMESTIC AND COMMERCIAL WASTES PROCESSED BY EACH METHOD

Method	United Kingdom	France	The Netherlands	Federal Republic of Germany	Switzerland	Italy
Incineration	15	20	23	20	53	13
Composting	1	10	16	2	13	1
Landfill:						
controlled	60	7	12	16	4	6
uncontrolled	24 84	63 70	49 61	62 78	30 34	80 86
	100	100	100	100	100	100
Estimated % of total wastes collected for disposal	88	80	87	90	90	70

requirements regarding identification and handling of wastes are of general application. Firstly, the waste producer should classify the various wastes and certify their contents. Any known hazards should be disclosed. Identification is first made in terms of physical states:

> Liquids
> Slurries
> Sludges
> Thixotropic solids
> Solids

and then as to hazard, using the Blue Book scheme mentioned in Chapters 3 and 12 (Table 13.2). Whenever reasonably possible, wastes of different classes or of different content should be segregated to allow for separate collection, transportation and disposal; alternatively, the classes and content of the mixture should be certified. The producer should make sure that his own employees, and those of any carrier employed on waste collection and transportation, conform to the code of practice. The carrier's responsibilities should include the provision of equipment, containers and vehicles which are of suitable design and condition, the instruction and training of his own employees, and a system of work to ensure that suitable waste-handling equipment and protective clothing are used when necessary. He should also plan the routes of vehicles; with 'hazardous' wastes, personnel should be provided with written instructions. Appropriate emergency services should be advised of the journey. The vehicles or containers should carry bold markings and relevant safety information. The movement, storage and labelling of petroleum spirit, petroleum mixtures, calcium carbide and carbon disulphide is in fact regulated by the Petroleum (Consolidation) Act 1928. This has been extended to cover about

TABLE 13.2 PROPOSED CLASSIFICATION FOR HAZARDOUS WASTES[2]

Class 1	Explosives
Class 2	Gases; compressed, liquefied or dissolved under pressure
Class 3	Inflammable liquids
Class 4(a)	Inflammable solids
Class 4(b)	Inflammable solids or substances liable to spontaneous combustion
Class 4(c)	Inflammable solids or substances which in contact with water emit inflammable gases
Class 5(a)	Oxidising substances
Class 5(b)	Organic peroxides
Class 6(a)	Poisonous (toxic) substances
Class 6(b)	Infectious substances
Class 7	Radioactive substances
Class 8	Corrosives
Class 9	Miscellaneous dangerous substances, that is any other substance which experience has shown, or may show, to be of such a dangerous character that these Rules should apply to it
Class 10	Dangerous chemicals in limited quantities.

200 flammable substances and about 120 corrosive materials.[3,4] Some form of Transport Emergency Card should be carried on the vehicle: 'Tremcards', for example, carry the following information:

Names and synonyms of the material
Summary of its principal hazards
Appropriate protective equipment
General emergency procedures
Detailed advice on the treatment of spillages and fires
    and first aid treatment of casualties
An emergency telephone number for obtaining expert advice on the material.

However, a pilot survey in the UK in 1974 showed the identification of wastes to be seldom comprehensive and safety measures to be generally inadequate.[5]

The site operator should arrange for geophysical surveys of the site. With regard to site selection, 'good practice' is held to be adequate to cope with surface run-off. Comprehensive requirements are laid down with regard to prevention of nuisance arising from the site, and detailed records should be maintained (the recognised principles for controlled tipping are discussed in Chapter 14). Comprehensive arrangements should be made to deal with health, safety and security on the site.

The site operator should supply to the other parties a list of pertinent site information, including details of acceptable wastes, capacity and rate-of-deposit data, a plan and geological data relating to the site, and details of safety, health and security controls.

No site should be used for the deposition of wastes which include listed materials (Table 13.3) unless the permeability of the ground is such that leakages to underground water supplies will not occur within 250 years. Some wastes pose special problems for land disposal and may need to be processed:[6] oily sludge is one example of a material which cannot be satisfactorily buried because it persists for years almost unchanged and can migrate.

TABLE 13.3 MATERIALS DIFFICULT TO DISPOSE OF SAFELY ON LAND

1. Non-biodegradeable hazardous materials Chlorinated hydrocarbons Slowly degradeable materials Mineral oils, greases 2. Poisonous or persistent materials, including heavy metals Phenols Cyanides, including metal-cyanide complexes Drug residues Chromium, cadmium, lead, mercury, nickel, copper, zinc Rodenticide and pesticide residues	3. Strongly acid or alkaline materials in quantities which would disturb the neutrality of the landfill Hydrochloric, sulphuric, nitric, phosphoric, chromic, or hydrofluoric acid Sodium hydroxide 4. Non-aqueous liquid wastes where these would dissolve material used in sealing a site

Landfill

Just how much hazardous waste is disposed of annually in the UK, and what proportion is deposited as landfill, is not clear. However, one estimate[7] gives 88% of toxic waste disposed of on land, of which 82% is flammable, 72% acid or caustic and 96% indisputably toxic. Another estimate[8] quotes 90% landfill disposal from which a figure of 2·4 million tonnes annual deposition has been calculated. The potential environmental problems associated with the deposition on land of hazardous wastes was discussed in Chapter 4. However, some indication of the wide variety of materials still disposed of by this method is given by Table 13.4, which lists some of the materials notified for deposit on one landfill site during one year.[9] In fact, objections raised against certain of these materials prevented their deposit on the site.

Sites which accept toxic wastes might be expected to be located near to those areas in which the materials are generated. In fact, however, the lack of suitable sites or their unacceptability (from, for example, hydrogeological considerations) has resulted in increased carrying distances; this applies particularly to toxic wastes transported by contractors, which may be transported up to 320 km.

There may be some 500 landfill sites accepting toxic waste in England alone, but over half of these probably receive less than 10 tonnes per week and only 1% receive in excess of 2000 tonnes.[9] Thus only a relatively small number of sites specialise in toxic waste disposal; a greater number accept an amount which, on an individual site basis, is very small and relatively insignificant. The physical size of the site is no criterion; some large local authority sites do not accept toxic waste while, conversely, the intake to a contractor's site of less than 100 ha may be mainly toxic wastes, other waste being accepted merely to provide cover material.[9]

Sites are not evenly distributed around the country. Some are in the centre of industrial and residential areas and others deep in rural areas; a few are located on the coast. It has been reported that nearly 30% of all toxic waste travels over 50 km before disposal and over 13% travels 150 km.[8]

Site areas are typically below the level of the surrounding land, either natural depressions or excavations from extractive operations. Clay pits are useful since the excavation then has an impervious lining. In some instances—for example, on sites located on estuaries—artificial mounds of waste are created to build the land up above its original level. In any event, toxic waste disposal as landfill should always involve the adoption of techniques for rapid covering of deposited material if solid or, if liquid, for safe absorption of waste into previously deposited innocuous waste.[10] Soakage trenches are used for this purpose.

Control Procedures and Site Features

Every producer has an obligation to provide, on a notification form that complies

TABLE 13.4 ABRIDGED LIST OF MATERIALS NOTIFIED FOR DEPOSIT ON ONE LANDFILL SITE IN ONE YEAR (objections prevented the deposit of some materials)

Acetate
Acetone
Acid tars
Adhesives
Alkaline wash fluid
Alkali sludge
Aliphatic amines
Aluminium fluoride
Aluminium hydroxide
Ammonia
Ammonium hydroxide
Asbestos dust

Barium chloride
Behenic acid
Benzene
Benzole sludge
Bisulphite of lime
Butyl acetate

Cadmium
Calcium chlorate
Calcium fluoride
Calcium sulphate sludge
Carbon black
Caustic cleaning solution
Cetyl stearyl acid
Chrome
Chromic acid
Chromic trioxide
Chromium hydroxide
Cider
Copper
Copper hydroxide
Cyanide

Detergent
Diatomaceous earth
Dibutyl phthalate
Dyestuffs

Enamel
Esters
Ethanol
Ethyl benzoate
Ethylene glycol
Ethylene oxide

Fats
Fatty acid and solids
Filter cake

Fluoroboric acid
Formaldehyde
Formic acid
Foundry slag
Glue

Hexavalent chromium salts
Hydrocarbons
Hydrochloric acid
Hydrofluoric acid

Ink, ink sludge
Insecticide
Iron hydroxide
Iron oxide
Isocyanates
Isopropyl acetate resins

Kerosenes
Ketones

Lacquers
Latex
Lead

Magnesium oxide
Magnesium salt
Mallic acid
Mercury
Methanol
Methyl ethyl ketone
Methylated spirits
Methylene chloride

Naphthalene
Nickel
Nickel chromium
Nickel hydroxide
Nitric acid
Nitrocellulose

Oil and grease (various)

Paint stripper and solvent
Paint thinner and waste
Paraffin
Petroleum ether and waste
Phenol
Phenol formaldehyde
Phenol methanol
Phosphoric acid
Polyacrylic acid size

Polyamide
Polyester
Polystyrene
Polyurethane
Polyvinylacetate
Potassium chloride
Prepolymer
Propyl alcohol
Propylene oxide
PVC

Red oxide paint
Resin
Rubber

Sewage sludge
Silica alumina
Silicone catalyst
Soap
Soda ash
Sodium
Sodium chloride
Sodium hydroxide
Sodium hypochlorite
Sodium nitrate
Sodium oxalate
Solvents
Soot
Starch
Stearic acid
Steroids
Styrene
Sulphuric acid

Tallow and wax
Tar emulsion
Tin salts
Titanium oxide
Toluene
Trichloroethylene

Vanadium
Vanadium oxide

Xylene

Zinc dialkyl
Zinc hydroxide
Zinc oxide
Zinc phosphate
Zinc sulphite

with the requirements of the 1972 Act and/or Control of Pollution Act 1974, information regarding the nature and quantity of wastes to be disposed of and their chemical composition; provision is made for the report of an analytical chemist and for the use of a numerical coding system. A representative sample of the waste accompanies the report to the analytical laboratory. Identification of the risks, the best practicable means of disposal and authorisation for such disposal are recorded on the form. A copy of the form must be carried by the driver of the vehicle used to transport the waste to its disposal point and is a condition for entry to the site. Cope et al.[11] suggest a suitable design for such a form.

Desirable features of disposal sites are set out in Table 13.5. Analysis of wastes is an essential part of any control procedure. The methods described in Chapter 5 may be necessary, or for simple hazard identification a test kit may be used.

A code of minimum acceptable standards of operation for the collection, transportation and disposal of waste has been published by the National Association of Waste Disposal Contractors.[13] Contractors are advised to ensure that the producer declares all relevant details of the chemical and physical nature of the waste, its quality, rate of arising and any special properties. Where possible there should be regular inspection of waste arisings; consideration should be given to any hazards anticipated in loading, transporting, unloading, disposal and/or treatment of the waste before removal is undertaken. Admixture of wastes during transport or disposal should be avoided, unless technical evidence shows that no environmental or personnel hazard will be created. Personnel engaged on disposal should be intelligent, medically fit and properly trained.

Guidelines are given for the safe loading and unloading of wastes. Firstly the waste must be categorised and certified by the producer, and checked by the contractor who should advise on segregation and storage prior to collection. The correct type of container or tanker should be selected, and loose waste or containers should be adequately sheeted and secured during transportation. Appropriate protective clothing/equipment should be provided for, and worn by, personnel where necessary. A check-list is provided to ensure that physical, chemical and fire hazards are avoided during loading and unloading. Guidelines are also given for the safe transportation of waste by road and sea.

Incineration

The object of incineration is to control combustion of the waste to produce a residue which is not degradeable and contains no combustible material, and gaseous combustion products. The residue then requires disposal and the gases require treatment, for example to remove entrained particulates, using the methods described in Chapter 10.

It has been estimated that in 1972 only some 10%–15% of industrial combustible waste was disposed of by incineration. It has traditionally been used for

TABLE 13.5 DESIRABLE FEATURES OF DISPOSAL SITES (based on COPE *et al.*[11])

All sites (landfill, processing, incineration)	Object
Security fence and locked gate	Prevention of unauthorised access
Facility for sampling incoming waste and spot checks to compare consignment with notification details Facility for recording data on incoming wastes in a register Facility for segregation of wastes	Safety Selection of treatment process Compliance with Deposit of Poisonous Waste Act 1972
Emergency equipment, e.g. fire-fighting, gas-detection, first aid equipment; antidotes; breathing equipment, respirators, dustmasks; telephone connection to fire, ambulance, police and other emergency services	Safety and loss prevention Compliance with Health and Safety at Work Act 1974

Landfill sites

Impervious continuous boundary beneath the deposit, $\geqslant 15$ m thick[12]

Freedom from naturally occurring surface waters, streams or rivers

Nearest waters at risk $\geqslant 2$ km away[12]

Series of boreholes permitting sampling of the aqueous strata at different depths beneath the deposit in the direction of the aquifer(s)

Sufficient covering material to ensure that each day's deposits are covered with $\geqslant 150$ mm of inert compacted material so as to limit the working face of the tip to $\leqslant 15$ m

Sites for waste-processing plants

Facility for the collection, segregation and analysis of rainwater collecting on the site before ultimate disposal

Facility for the monitoring of gaseous and liquid discharges from the site to comply with established standards

Facility for the segregation and analysis of any solid residues left from the process before ultimate disposal

Management control methods to log the above data in a register

---

the disposal of some wastes, for example bagasse (the residue after leaching sugar cane), where incineration produces process steam in sugar refineries. General application has been comparatively neglected until recently.

Incineration becomes a viable alternative where land for surface tipping is not available within reasonable distance, and for toxic wastes. The main disadvantage is the high capital investment required not only for the incinerator itself but for ancillaries including fans, lifting gear, instruments, pollution control provisions and residue treatment plant. Provision for waste heat recovery involves an extra capital cost which is rarely justified economically. Operating costs are generally significantly higher than for disposal on land, when transportation is excluded.

Incineration substantially reduces the bulk of a waste which is an advantage in landfill disposal where tipping facilities are restricted; in some cases it also destroys dangerous substances. A less common application of incineration is to concentrate an inert component by burning away combustible material, so assisting recovery. Copper salts adsorbed on carbon at 2–3%, for catalytic applications, can produce material with a 50% copper content on incineration.[14]

The combustion of waste is generally an exothermic process, water being driven off prior to the thermal decomposition. Some wastes, however, will not support combustion continuously and a secondary fuel, usually oil or gas, is required throughout incineration. This may significantly reduce the economic viability of the process, although admixture of wastes may be practised to avoid or reduce the additional expense.

Equipment

Since wastes vary in physical form, flammability and calorific value there is a wide variety of incinerator types. Some indication of the range available is given by Table 13.6. The multicell and rotary designs are most flexible for a range of applications.

TABLE 13.6 SUITABILITY OF THE MAIN GENERAL TYPES OF INCINERATOR FOR DIFFERENT WASTES

Liquids
- Multicell
- Submerged combustors (for concentration of waste-waters)
- Vortex

Liquids and sludges
- Multicell
- Rotary

Sludges
- Multicell (with lagoon hearths and sludge burners)
- Rotary (for de-watered sludges)
- Multiple hearth

Solids
- Single-cell
- Multicell
- Rotary drum
- Fluidised bed
- Multiple hearth

Drummed wastes
- Multicell (with added drum cell)

In general, liquid waste which may be sprayed into the incinerator in a similar way to fuel oil, and can be supplemented by oil, creates less handling problems than solid waste which may require some form of grate. Whether the form be liquid or solid, for complete, controlled combustion the design/operating parameters vary for each waste. They include the waste characteristics and calorific value, combustion time and temperature, proportion of secondary fuel consumed, air-supply provisions and the degree of turbulence required for mixing the waste with air.

Basic design data include the mass and volume to be incinerated daily, the proposed methods of handling and feeding the waste, whether operation is to be batchwise or continuous, and the firing period. The means of ignition and afterburning, the extent of gas cleaning required and the viability of waste heat recovery are other factors.[15]

The requisite combustion time is obtained by controlling the rate at which the waste travels through the combustion zone. For solids, a grate system generally serves to retain the waste through the consecutive drying, ignition and combustion processes. Temperatures in the combustion zone are generally about 900°–1100°C for complete combustion. Secondary fuel assists in heating the incinerator during start-up and in primary combustion for wastes of high moisture content; it may also be necessary for secondary combustion, as described in Chapter 11, to minimise smoke and odour production. Primary air is supplied from beneath the fire bed, for the combustion process, and secondary air within the furnace to control temperature and promote turbulence. Natural draught may or may not need to be augmented by means of fans. Some designs of solid waste incinerators use baffles or mechanical agitation of the waste on the grate to promote turbulent mixing of the waste and air.

A further design consideration is whether the gaseous products of combustion need to be scrubbed. Thus, while a variety of wastes can be destroyed in one unit, using secondary fuel for ignition and afterburning, it may be more realistic to limit the acceptable range at the design stage.

In multicell units the products of combustion in one cell can be used to raise successive cells to the required temperature. Figure 13.1 shows a two-cell design in use for a combination of granulator residues, carbon cake, general

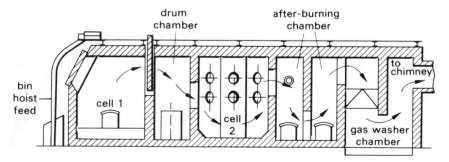

Fig. 13.1 Diagrammatic representation of chemical waste incinerator[16]

Lyon and Pye Ltd

Solids incineration unit for disposal of 300 kg/h paper and plastic waste
Right, feed storage; centre, incinerator and acoustic enclosure for fans; top
left, multiple cyclones; left, wet scrubber and chimney

waste and liquid residues comprising diphenyl, glycol, methyl benzoate and dimethyl terephthalate and, in another installation, for succinic acid and heavy oil. Solid waste is incinerated in the first cell which is connected via a primary flue chamber, which can be used for burning out small drums, to the second cell provided for liquid wastes. Gases pass subsequently into an oil-fired after-burning combustion chamber; the burner in this chamber is controlled to fire only at temperatures below 800°C, for fuel economy.

The rotary drum furnace (Figure 13.2) comprises a refractory lined drum inclined at an angle to the horizontal and rotated slowly about its axis; waste is metered into the higher end and ash removed from the opposite end. Nozzles may be provided at the feed end to disperse liquid wastes into the furnace. The angle of inclination may be variable between 2° and 5° and the speed of rotation, generally about 5 rpm, is also variable so that the retention time of waste can be controlled for efficient combustion. After-burning provisions may be incorporated in a separate chamber.

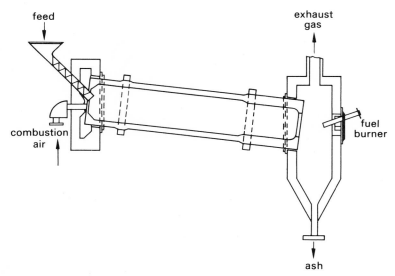

Fig. 13.2 Rotary-drum incinerator

Fluidised-bed incinerators have been used in the refinery and paper industries where waste-heat recovery makes them viable despite the high first cost. Sand is used as the bed medium, at temperatures not exceeding 1090°C. Complete combustion can be ensured but solid waste must be broken up prior to feeding to the bed. Limestone may be added to the bed to eliminate hydrogen chloride and sulphur dioxide emission by formation of non-volatile calcium chloride and calcium sulphate.[15] A fluidised-bed furnace used to dispose of refinery sludges is shown in Figure 13.3.

The multiple-hearth incinerator comprises a number of hearths stacked vertically. Waste fed into the top of the unit is moved around by means of rabble arms rotated by a centrally driven shaft. Figure 13.4 shows a multiple-hearth incinerator used for sewage sludge cake. Liquefied petroleum gas is used as a supplementary fuel to warm up the furnace and to maintain burning of difficult sludges. The incinerator shown is 15 m high with 7 hearths and is capable of continuously incinerating 5905 kg/h of sludge in the form of a 65% moisture-content cake. In the upper hearths the hot exhaust gases serve to dry the sludge cake before combustion at 900°C in the middle hearths. The ash cools down in the lower hearths and preheats the incoming air. This type of furnace has also been used for oily waste disposal.

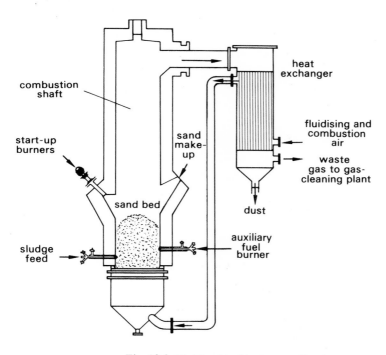

Fig. 13.3 Fluidised-bed incinerator[17]

A submerged combustion incinerator of the type shown in Figure 13.5 is used as an evaporator to concentrate waste liquors prior to their atomisation and incineration, with supplemental fuel gas if necessary. It has been used for incineration of chlorinated hydrocarbon wastes in conjunction with an absorber to recover 15–18% hydrochloric acid.[16]

Incineration is a disposal method requiring a substantial capital investment. In addition to the furnace and associated charging hoppers and grates, some or all of the following ancillaries and provisions are required.

1. A tipping/unloading bay or area sufficient to accommodate the range of sizes and designs of lorry used in collection.

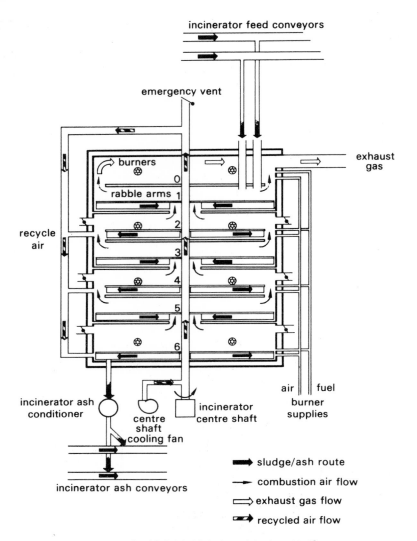

Fig. 13.4 Multiple-hearth incinerator[18]

2. Storage facilities for incoming waste. These may include tanks, pits, open ground or a covered area for drums and bales.
3. Suitable lifting gear, e.g. cranes with grab buckets, is required in both areas.
4. Scales to weigh, and apportion, waste.
5. Enclosure of the areas assists pollution control, by reducing the emission of noise, odour, fumes and dust, as well as limiting moisture take-up by the waste.
6. Provision for residue removal and subsequent disposal. Generally residues amount to 15–25% of the initial input volume of waste. In addition to

materials handling equipment, scales may be required for weighing outgoing residues.
7. Pollution control plant. Gaseous emissions require treatment as outlined in Chapter 10 and 12, depending on the waste incinerated.
8. Analytical and quality control laboratory.

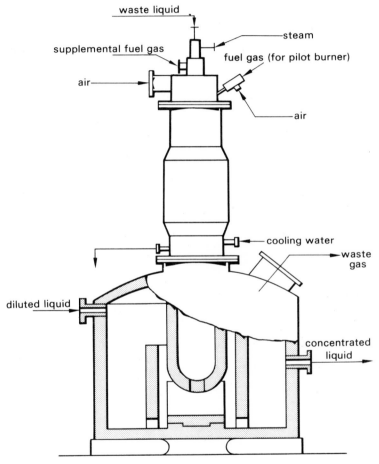

Fig. 13.5 Submerged combustion incinerator[16]

Special Applications

In general there is a wide range of incinerator capacities and degrees of integration into general waste-processing facilities. For example, solvents and still residues from a photographic film factory are incinerated in a unit with a capacity of up to 1·36 m³/h (300 gal/h).[19] Waste calorific value ranges from 4652 to 51 170 kJ/kg (2000–22 000 Btu/lb) and natural gas is used as the support fuel. Heat recovery supplies 6350 kg/h (14 000 lb/h) of steam for process heating.

The incineration of rubber waste in the form of scrap tyres is an operation requiring a carefully designed incinerator and gas cleaning plant in order to comply with statutory limits on dust and smoke emissions. One design, with for example a capacity of 80 car tyres or 0·5 tonnes/h, employs a cyclonic incinerator; this is a cylindrical grateless furnace with pressurised air injection.[20] It is gas-fired and the air is applied tangentially to the combustion chamber, producing a swirl so that the combustion gases pass through by a cyclonic action. This increases both the turbulence and the flow path and hence ensures almost complete combustion. The tyres are introduced tangentially into the furnace on a flat belt conveyer via a water-cooled throat which prevents premature firing through radiant heat. Temperatures in the furnace are sufficiently high to destroy the tyres completely; the metal bead wires form molten globules which are removed with the ash. The gases pass to a waste heat boiler and then to an irrigated electrostatic precipitator in which the electrodes are maintained at a DC voltage of -150 kV; negatively charged particles are thus attracted to the water film on the wall of the tower and washed to a settling tank at the base.

Heenan Environmental Systems Ltd

Tyre incineration plant: vertical cyclonic unit with horizontal tyre feed

One general-purpose custom-built incinerator[21] with a total capacity of 2 tonnes/h of material, having a calorific value of 29 075 kJ/kg (12 500 Btu/lb), is designed for the incineration of organic wastes including solvents, lacquers, oils and chlorinated cleaning fluids, with provision for combustion of liquids and sludges, solids, general refuse and drummed material in four separate chambers. Materials are delivered from storage to give the required blend in terms of viscosity, water content, calorific value and material types. Blended liquid waste is passed to the incinerator feed systems and ignited in the appropriate chambers; solid wastes are introduced separately by mechanical handling according to loading schedules. The temperature in the incinerator chambers is controlled to 1200°C to avoid damage to the refractories. Combustion gases pass through an after-burner chamber, to ensure complete combustion; they are then scrubbed by passage through a gas-wash chamber containing water sprays, which is designed to remove both acid gases, such as hydrogen chloride evolved from chlorinated plastics or solvents, and particulates before the gases are dispersed via the stack. The incinerator is provided with automatic fail-safe devices so that malfunction of a burner in any chamber results in immediate shutdown; this prevents accidental emission of smoke or partially incinerated material.

Other Processes and Combined Facilities

A process is now available to convert hazardous wastes in solid, liquid or sludge form into a hard polymer.[22] The wastes are conveyed to a series of containers fitted with high-speed disintegrators for the purpose of dissolution and dispersion; chemical pretreatment may be applied to some wastes. Polymerisation is initiated by the addition of special reagents to produce polymer in slurry form. This is pumped to an adjacent disused marl-clay pit where it sets in three days to give a hard, rock-like solid. No gases or liquid effluents are produced. A wide variety of wastes can apparently be treated,[23] but not combustible or flammable wastes. Polymerised wastes are claimed to have low permeability, good resistance to leaching by water and good physical strength, and to be non-biodegradeable.

Because of the wide variety of hazardous wastes, a logical step has been the construction of waste-processing centres to provide a comprehensive service for chemical processing of inorganic or organic wastes, recovery from either type of waste, and incineration of organic wastes.[21] Material is received in bulk road tanker or in packaged lots, i.e. any combination of 0·023, 0·045 or 0·20 m³ (5, 10 or 45 gal) containers. The inorganic wastes processed are those that are essentially incombustible; after laboratory analysis they are chemically treated batchwise to produce either insoluble precipitates, which are separated, or innocuous water-soluble derivatives. For example, cyanides are converted to cyanates by treatment with either chlorine or sodium hypochlorite, as discussed in Chapter 7. Fumes from the processing vats are extracted and passed to the incinerator. The end-product is either reclaimed product or treated material suitable for direct disposal.

Recovery operations at one site include recovery of 10 tonnes/week of copper, in the form of copper or copper hydroxide, from various solutions, and recovery of lesser quantities of nickel, cadmium, tin, cobalt and lead. Some organic wastes are destroyed by high-temperature incineration. On an integrated plant contaminated gas-washing liquor can be pumped across to the inorganic chemical treatment area for reprocessing. Furthermore, air is extracted from both the drum opening area and from certain storage tanks and fed to the incinerator to prevent odours within the confines of the site. Inert residues are removed from the incinerator into waste storage bins for disposal as landfill.

Effluent Disposal by Pipeline to Tidal Waters

Numerous considerations arise in the satisfactory use of tidal waters for disposal of wastes, notably those of public amenity, in the water and on the shore; conservation of flora and fauna; and commercial navigation and fishing. The disposal system must not be subject to damage by shipping, weather or vandalism and consideration has to be given to the possible long-term effects of silting and erosion.[24] Consent for discharge is required from the Water Authority or River Purification Board; planning and other considerations involve the local authority. These and other authorities to be consulted require information as to the location and condition of the area into which discharge is proposed, its present and future use, and the properties of the effluent. A summary of the criteria relating to effluent properties is given in Table 13.7.

The tidal water outfall should be designed to give the required primary dilution at the outfall. A suitable diffuser device such as a blank-ended sparge pipe may be provided for this purpose. With buried effluent pipes the sparge pipe can be extended above the sea-bed level; it may be 100 m or more in length.[25] The density of the effluent determines whether it is located on the sea bed, as is more usual, or above it.[26]

Location of the outfall should give adequate further dispersion to allow the concentration of any persistent materials to approach the background levels and to give time for natural treatment. A study of the hydrology of the sea area is required in selection of outfall position for good secondary dilution, so as to make full use of tidal movement. Alternatively, tidal discharge may be used, the effluent being stored in lagoons or tanks on shore and discharged on the ebb immediately after high tide.[24]

Deep Sea Disposal

From the early 1960s a voluntary consent scheme operated in the UK under which wastes disposed of by dumping at sea were notified to the Ministry of Agriculture, Fisheries and Food, with the objective of preventing undesirable

TABLE 13.7 CRITERIA FOR EFFLUENT IN TIDAL WATER DISCHARGE SYSTEMS[24]

Property	Criteria
Volume	No significant reduction in salinity Relevant to load of constituents
Temperature	No significant effect on normal temperature regime Not critical except for some large cooling-water discharges
pH	No toxic effects, e.g. pH 6–10 at point discharge Neutralising effect of sea allows effluent discharge at pH 1–13
Oxygen demand (BOD)	No significant reduction in dissolved oxygen that would affect marine life Not critical for open sea
Dissolved solids	No physical effect (see below for toxicity) Quite uncritical
Water/immiscible liquid	No visible effect Limit concentration in effluent to a few ppm
Persistent floatable solid	No visible effect in tidal waters or on beach Eliminate from effluent unless can macerate to degradeable form
Dense suspended solid	No accumulation or blanketing of sea bed Normally up to 300 ppm in effluent
Persistent toxins	No acute toxicity at outfall No sub-acute effects in area No bio-accumulation in area Primary dilution to maintain below 96 h LD_{50} at outfall Regular ecological monitoring Limit concentrations and loads in effluent as necessary
Non-persistent toxins	No acute toxicity at outfall Check that degradation is not to persistent toxin Primary dilution as persistent toxin Regular ecological monitoring Limit concentrations and loads in effluent as necessary
Nutrients	No eutrophic effects (unlikely to be critical for UK sea areas)

pollution of sea areas inhabited by fish stocks and minimising entry of undesirable chemicals into food chains.[27] Disposal is now covered by two international conventions, the Oslo convention,[28] now ratified, and the London convention.[29] The Oslo convention is limited in application to certain sea areas but the London convention will cover all areas; both require signatory countries to enact legislation to control the disposal of wastes at sea. In the UK the relevant legislation is the Dumping at Sea Act 1974, which replaces the earlier voluntary scheme.

Under the Dumping at Sea Act a licence is necessary for any sea-disposal operation. The licensing authority must have regard to the need to protect the marine environment, and the living resources which it supports, from any adverse consequences of dumping the substance(s) covered by a licence. Appropriate conditions must be included in the licence to protect the environment. In practice, materials listed in Table 13.8 are banned from sea disposal except

TABLE 13.8 ANNEX I TO THE OSLO CONVENTION: MATERIALS BANNED FROM SEA DISPOSAL

The following substances are listed for the purpose of Article 5 of the Convention:

1. Organohalogen compounds and compounds which may form such substances in the marine environment, excluding those which are non-toxic, or which are rapidly converted in the sea into substances which are biologically harmless.
2. Organosilicon compounds and compounds which may form such substances in the marine environment, excluding those which are non-toxic, or which are rapidly converted in the sea into substances which are biologically harmless.
3. Substances which have been agreed between the contracting parties to be likely to be carcinogenic under the conditions of disposal.
4. Mercury and mercury compounds.
5. Cadmium and cadmium compounds.
6. Persistent plastics and other persistent synthetic materials which may float or remain in suspension in the sea, and which may seriously interfere with fishing or navigation, reduce amenities, or interfere with other legitimate uses of the sea.

---

in trace quantities. Materials listed in Table 13.9 require special care in disposal. Other properties of the waste have then to be evaluated prior to approval. The criteria are that the material should not be disposed of as liquid (i.e. adsorption into inert material should be practised), it should be packaged to avoid release during descent and in certain instances it should reach the sea bed intact. Generally, licence conditions require disposal into waters at least 2000 m deep, at least 240 km from the nearest coast, away from sea-routes, and possibly in a specified area.

Underground Disposal

In addition to surface tipping in old quarries or other landfill sites, waste may be disposed of in boreholes and disused mine-workings. Provided they are carefully selected, mineshafts may shield the dumped material from contact with circulating waters, thus protecting the environment from contamination. Pumping of liquids under pressure into porous and permeable rocks at depth is widely practised in the USA, although not yet in the UK.

TABLE 13.9 ANNEX II TO THE OSLO CONVENTION: MATERIALS REQUIRING SPECIAL CARE IN SEA DISPOSAL

---

1. The following substances and materials requiring special care are listed for the purposes of Article 6:
   (a) Arsenic, lead, copper, zinc and their compounds; cyanides and fluorides, and pesticides and their byproducts not covered by the provisions of Annex I.
   (b) Containers, scrap metal, tar-like substances liable to sink to the sea bottom and other bulky wastes which may present a serious obstacle to fishing or navigation.
   (c) Substances which, though of a non-toxic nature, may become harmful due to the quantities in which they are dumped, or which are liable to seriously reduce amenities.
2. The substances and materials listed under paragraph 1(b) above should always be deposited in deep water.
3. In the issuance of permits or approvals for the dumping of large quantities of acids and alkalis, consideration should be given to the possible presence in such wastes of the substances listed in paragraph 1 above.
4. When, in the application of the provisions of Annexes II and III, it is considered necessary to deposit waste in deep water, this should be done only when the following two conditions are both fulfilled:
   (a) that the depth is not less than 2000 metres,
   (b) that the distance from the nearest land is not less than 150 nautical miles.

However, many wastes disposed of in this way irreversibly pollute the rocks and may thus form an environmental hazard. The use of old quarries may endanger groundwater sources where the enclosing rocks are both porous and permeable, but quarries in mudstone sequences, such as the old brick pits of the West Midlands, effectively seal toxic material from surrounding rock. Landfill sites and old quarries used as soakaways which, for the safeguarding of surrounding groundwater, rely on either dilution of toxic material by ground and meteoric waters or adsorption of the metals in them by clay minerals, are in many instances potentially dangerous.

Selection of subsurface disposal sites requires careful consideration of the hydrogeological conditions in the area and stringent controls must be exercised. In the same way, when a site is considered for surface disposal, long- and short-term risks of pollution must be assessed. Monitoring controls must be developed to detect and assess movement of effluents in the subsurface so that pollution risks are minimised and potable water sources, both present and future, are protected.[30]

Case Study

Until recently, the largest underground disposal facility in the UK was receiving 135 000 m³ (30 million gal) per year of aqueous waste. Although this was closed down in late 1977 because of blockage, a new shaft is being sunk into the same workings to utilise the voids available.

Although this is currently unique in the UK it has much potential, and a

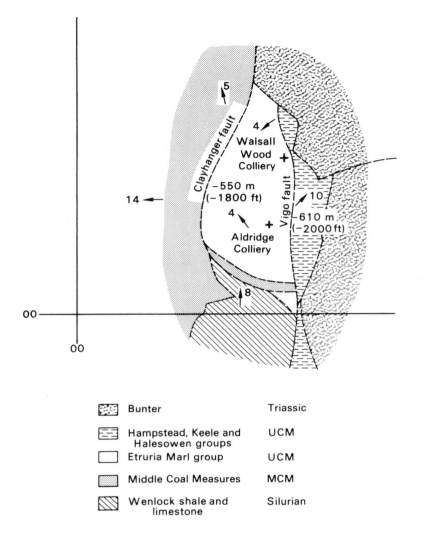

Fig. 13.6 General geology of the Walsall Wood area

description of the facility and the safeguards operated is included, not only to stress the safety of such disposal but also to identify the features of a suitable site.

The underground receptacle is a disused coal mine, i.e. the void space available in open roadways, the collapsed areas of the seam workings, and the zone of increased permeability of the rocks above the mined areas formed as a result of subsidence fracturing. Although the majority of the aqueous effluent received is discharged directly, some wastes are chemically treated prior to disposal. Quantities, concentration and analysis of the waste are given in Chapter 9.

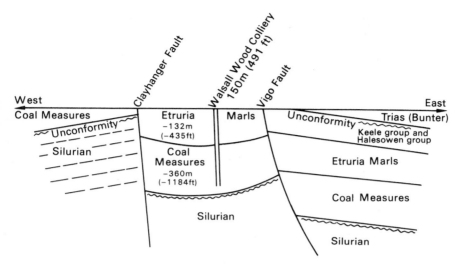

Fig. 13.7 East–West cross-section showing geology of the down-faulted block

This mine is regarded as a 'safe' facility since it is located in a down-faulted block which is separated from the rest of the South Staffordshire Coalfield by two major pre-Triassic normal faults: the Clayhanger Fault in the west, with a down-throw to the east of approximately 549 m (1800 ft), and the Vigo Fault in the east, with a down-throw in the same direction of considerably more than 610 m (2000 ft) (Figures 13.6–8). The disposal shaft at Walsall Wood is approximately 518 m (1700 ft) deep with the top of the shaft at +150 m (+491 ft) OD (Ordnance datum). Coals were worked in this colliery in a total of nine

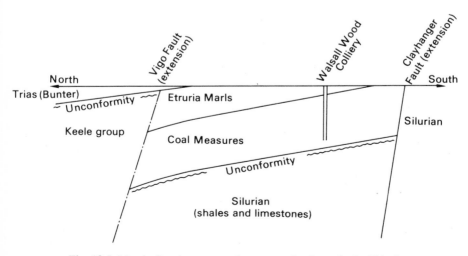

Fig. 13.8 North–South cross-section across the down-faulted block

seams in the Middle Coal Measures. The uppermost seam worked is the Bottom Robins Seam at $-177\cdot8$ m (-583 ft) OD and the lowest is the Deep Seam at -361 m (-1187 ft) OD.

The uppermost rocks of the fault block form part of the Etruria Marl Series of the Upper Coal Measures, which have a measured thickness of some 282 m (924 ft) in this shaft. These rocks consist of a sequence of red mudstones and sandstones/conglomerates with a clay matrix, which acts as an effective upper seal to the liquids. The Middle Coal Measures are approximately 305 m (1000 ft) thick in this area and unconformably overlie rocks of the Silurian Wenlock Series. There is, therefore, a considerable thickness of Coal Measures rocks below the lowest worked seam and these probably act as a lower seal to the liquids (Figures 13.7 and 8).

The faults contain a considerable thickness of clay-rich material so that they act as effective lateral seals, along with unmined Coal Measures rocks near them. The effluent disposal area is thus effectively isolated from surrounding rock.

The above features, together with the dryness of the mine, satisfy criteria for 'safe' long-term disposal.

Consent for use of the mine for disposal, given in 1965, stipulated that liquid effluent was not to rise above -152 m (-500 ft) OD in the shaft and that the shaft was to be sealed at this level when use of the facility ceased. The considerable thickness of clay/shale material at this level in the rock sequence allows permanent sealing. Furthermore, lateral movement of effluents below this level, if the liquids penetrated the lateral seals (boundary faults), would not contaminate any permeable rocks in the Upper Coal Measures outside the area.

Calculation of available void space, based on approximately 10% of the mined volume, gave the facility a life of between 30 and 60 years if all available space could be filled and no sealing of parts of the mine occurred as a result of floor heave, lubrication of the seat earths and shales, deposition of various precipitates from the wastes, or airlocks in the system—any of which problems may have contributed to or caused the blockage.

The new shaft is being sunk up-dip from the Walsall Wood Colliery, in the abandoned Aldridge Colliery in the same fault block (Figure 13.8). The workings of the two collieries are connected at three levels, but liquids in the new shaft will not fill this space as most of the Aldridge workings are above the -152 m OD level prescribed in the original licence. Vertical and lateral sealing characteristics are similar to those at Walsall Wood, as, apparently, will be the available volume of void space and thus the life expectancy, provided the licence conditions allow filling above the original -152 m OD level in both collieries; this would be considered acceptable as long as permanent sealing was still possible.

Although, since it is difficult to monitor what happens underground, doubts about mineshaft disposal cannot be entirely allayed by such exhaustive surveys, the method is attractive for intractable wastes and more use may be expected to be made of it in the future.

References

1. JACKSON, F. R., *Recovery of Energy from Waste*, Noyes Data Corporation, 1975.
2. *A Provisional Code of Practice for Disposal of Wastes*, Institution of Chemical Engineers, 1972.
3. Petroleum (Inflammable Liquids) Order 1971; Inflammable Liquids (Conveyance by Road) Regulations 1971; Inflammable Substances (Conveyance by Road, Labelling) Regulations 1971.
4. Petroleum (Corrosive Substances) Order 1970; Corrosive Substances (Conveyance by Road) Regulations 1971.
5. KEEN, R. C., *Hazards of Toxic Waste Disposal Operators on Landfill Sites*, University of Aston, 1974.
6. MUMFORD, C. J., in *Industrial Pollution Control*, TEARLE, K. (Ed.), Business Books, 1973.
7. *Disposal of Solid Toxic Wastes*, HMSO, 1970.
8. Industrial Waste Survey Unit, *Hazardous Wastes in Great Britain*, Harwell Hazardous Wastes Service, 1974.
9. KEEN, R. C., *Solid Wastes*, 101, March 1975.
10. KEEN, R. C., *Deposit of Poisonous Waste*, Bristol Polytechnic, 1973.
11. COPE, C. B., CHAPPELL, C. L. and KEEN, R. C., *Municipal Engineering*, 46, 9 January 1976.
12. GRAY, D. A., MATHER, J. D. and HARRISON, I. B., *Quarterly Journal of Engineering Geology*, 7, 181, 1974.
13. *Code of Practice*, National Association of Waste Disposal Contractors, 1976.
14. BENTLEY, J., *Deposit of Poisonous Wastes*, Course Proceedings, Bristol Polytechnic, 1973, p. 28.
15. DUNN, K. S., *Chemical Engineer*, 141, 6 October 1975.
16. *Process Engineering*, 76, February 1973.
17. *Process Biochemistry*, 28, July 1968.
18. Severn-Trent Water Authority, *Coleshill Sewage Sludge Incineration Plant*.
19. *Process Engineering*, 7, May 1974.
20. Redman Heenan Froude Ltd, Publ. No. 2 M 1172 EW 8319.
21. COLEMAN, A. K., *Chemistry and Industry*, 534, 5 July 1975.
22. *Surveyor*, 35, 1 November 1974.
23. Polymeric Treatments Ltd, Brownhills, Staffordshire, information bulletins.
24. MOSS, A., Paper 31, Eurochem Conference —*Chemical Engineering in a Hostile World*, National Exhibition Centre, Birmingham, UK, 20 June, Clapp & Poliak, 1977.
25. CARTER, L. and MOSS, A., *Chemical Engineer*, 97, February, 1975.
26. CARTER, L., *Chemistry and Industry*, 825, 2 October 1976.
27. PEARCE, K., Paper 32, Eurochem Conference—*Chemical Engineering in a Hostile World*, National Exhibition Centre, Birmingham, UK, 20 June, Clapp & Poliak, 1977.
28. *Convention for the Prevention of Marine Pollution by Dumping from Ships and Aircraft*, CMND 4984, HMSO, 1972.
29. *Convention on the Prevention of Marine Pollution by Dumping of Wastes and Other Matters*, HMSO, December 1972.
30. MATHER, J. D., Hydrogeological survey techniques, *Surveyor*, 26, 1 June 1973.

CHAPTER 14

Disposal of Household and Other Special Wastes

Household Refuse

Increased amounts of household refuse are produced each year. Furthermore, the bulk density of collected refuse has decreased sharply, so that total volume has increased substantially. These trends, exemplified by the data given in Table 14.1, arise from the increased use of disposable packaging, the improvement in general living standards and the change in methods of domestic heating. The average analysis of refuse and the changes which have occurred in composition are shown in Table 14.2.

TABLE 14.1 VARIATION IN TONNAGE AND DENSITY OF REFUSE COLLECTED, CITY OF BIRMINGHAM, UK[1]

Year	Population	Tonnes	Density (kg/m³)	(cwt/yd³)	Volume (m³)	(yd³)
1934	1 002 600	246 942	382·8	5·76	645 183	843 900
1960	1 090 500	318 280	252·5	3·80	1 260 550	1 648 800
1970	1 084 180	294 429	146·2	2·20	2 014 144	2 634 500

Methods of household refuse disposal and their attendant advantages and disadvantages are summarised in Table 14.3. Controlled tipping and incineration are the principal methods in the UK, the emphasis at present being on land reclamation which allows scope for the deposition of some industrial waste alongside household refuse. A very small percentage may be composted, but this is not a complete means of disposal by itself.[3] A limited amount of recycling, for example of metals, is carried out in conjunction with tipping and incineration (see Chapter 17).

TABLE 14.2 ANALYSIS OF REFUSE BY WEIGHT (PER CENT), CITY OF BIRMINGHAM, UK[1]

Type of refuse	1934	1960	1970
Dust and cinder	75·03	49·72	15·91
Vegetable and putrescible	6·09	11·56	13·23
Paper and cardboard	7·71	20·48	51·42
Metal	3·31	6·44	6·41
Rags	1·51	1·39	2·42
Glass	1·15	7·26	6·45
Plastic	—	—	1·14
Unclassified debris	3·20	3·15	3·02
Total	100·00	100·00	100·00

Controlled tipping, which accounts for about 90% of the total refuse, is based on well established principles.[4] These seek to avoid nuisance from pests or from pollution of aquifers or watercourses, smell, fire or windblown materials, and to provide adequate physical control resulting in even settlement and biological breakdown of the organic fraction. Tipping is generally the cheapest disposal method.[5]

TABLE 14.3 METHODS OF HOUSEHOLD REFUSE TREATMENT AND DISPOSAL (adapted from GUTT et al.[2])

Method	Advantages	Disadvantages
Controlled tipping	Provides means of land reclamation	May involve increased transportation Amenity damage
Pulverisation before controlled tipping	Higher density in tip Less subsequent settlement Less top covering required More acceptable near housing Recovery of metals possible	Additional processing plant required Odour nuisance Higher cost
Refuse baling before controlled tipping	As for pulverisation— maximum use of tipping space	As for pulverisation
Separation (see Chapter 17)	Recovers many values such as metals, glass and refuse-derived fuels (RDF) Products relatively clean Maximised resource conservation	High cost Suitable outlets needed

Table 14.3(*continued*)

Method	Advantages	Disadvantages
Direct incineration (see Chapter 17)	Large reduction in volume Limited energy (fuel) requirement Ferrous metal extraction possible from clinker Further extraction of aluminium and copper possible Allows use of waste heat Mixed refuse and sewage sludge can be treated	High installation and maintenance costs Pockets of unmixed trade wastes in the fire-bed disrupt burning control Expensive flue gas cleaning necessary Recovery limited to non-combustibles Corrosion problems with waste heat utilisation
Composting (see Chapter 17)	Refuse can be composted with sewage sludge Attractive in areas where soil humus is depleted	Expensive, and leaves a proportion to be tipped Metal content of compost may limit its use
Pyrolysis (see Chapter 17)	No air pollution Greater recycling of waste Metal extraction processes applicable Gaseous, liquid and solid byproduct fuels produced in excess of process requirement Other chemical byproducts available from condensate	High installation cost Special site requirements Viable byproduct outlets needed
Hydrolysis (see Chapter 17)	Suitable for refuse with high paper content, producing sugars, protein, yeast, etc., for recovery	Only theoretical exercises and small pilot projects on special trade wastes at present

Pulverisation may be carried out prior to tipping for land reclamation, as part of transfer loading or prior to incineration. However, only about 4% of refuse is currently pulverised, although the advantages, in the case of tipping, include:[6]

  (i) easier conformance with the Code of Practice;[4]
 (ii) more even and greater initial settlement of refuse because of its increased homogeneity;
(iii) greater speed in reclaiming land (and making it available for building, where this is practised);
 (iv) reclamation of smaller areas of land which would be unsuitable for crude refuse tipping.

Pulverisation can also be used at transfer stations to increase the bulk density of the refuse and so improve the vehicle payload. Direct compression may also be used for this purpose.

The considerable increase in the percentage of refuse incinerated, expected by the late 1970s, has been slow to materialise. Incineration provides a method of effectively burning the combustible components of refuse to reduce the volume of material so that it may be disposed of in the form of a relatively innocuous residue. It results in a reduction of 90% by volume and 60% by weight of the original. The residual material must be chemically and physically stable and should not change on exposure to air. No significant proportion of putrescible material should be left in the resultant ash so that it can be disposed of without nuisance, and be useful for infill. Even for tipping, a sterile residue is desirable to avoid leaching-out of pollutants into the soil or groundwater.

In 1977 a survey was made of reclamation and disposal programmes among 548 local councils in the UK, to ascertain practice with regard to collection, reclamation and the ultimate disposal of household refuse.[7] Based on a response of just under 25%, the general pattern of disposal is given in Table 14.4. This confirms the popularity of landfill disposal as shown in the following figures relating to UK practice:[4]

Direct tipping or landfill	90·4%
Incineration with some separation	7·6%
Direct incineration	0·7%
Pulverisation and landfill	1·0%
Composting	0·3%

TABLE 14.4 REPORTED METHODS OF HOUSEHOLD WASTE DISPOSAL

Method	%
Controlled tipping	33
Crude tipping	3
Landfill	18
Composting	0
Incineration	4
Pulverisation	4
More than one method used	28
Unspecified	10
	100

Transfer Stations

A transfer station is an installation for handling solid waste which provides for transfer from collection vehicles of limited capacity, operating over a limited area, into high-capacity trailers which then transport the compacted waste over longer distances to the disposal site. Because transportation is such a major cost item in collection and disposal, transfer stations help to reduce costs. They also allow a wider area to be served by a centrally located disposal facility of large capacity.

A transfer station should be located near the centre of the weighted collection area which it serves (the term 'weighted' refers here to a collection area analysed with respect to both geographic form and population/refuse distribution[8]). It must also be designed and located in such a way that it does not create a nuisance and/or give cause for complaints by neighbours, and is convenient for road and possibly rail transportation.

For the volume of waste handled by smaller towns or private hauliers a transfer station may have a holding capacity of $76 \cdot 5 \, m^3$ ($100 \, yd^3$) and a $4 \cdot 82 \, m^3$ ($6 \cdot 3 \, yd^3$) transfer compactor. Such a compactor is also able to pack into large-capacity ($50–57 \, m^3$ ($65–75 \, yd^3$)) long-haul trailers or large-capacity containers handled by tilt-frame trucks. For large-scale operations the station may have a push-pit of $122 \, m^3$ ($160 \, yd^3$) holding capacity and an $8 \cdot 5 \, m^3$ ($11 \, yd^3$) transfer compactor. This larger station allows up to four local collection vehicles to discharge simultaneously and compacts the refuse into long-haul trailers of 46 and $57 \cdot 3 \, m^3$ (60 and $75 \, yd^3$).[9]

The Brentford Refuse Transfer Station serves three London boroughs and exemplifies a large-scale operation.[10] Refuse collection vehicles and open 3 tonne tipper lorries report to a weighbridge where the weights are recorded. The vehicles then proceed on a one-way circulatory system through a traffic-light controlled access point where they may be held until a tipping hopper is free. There are ten compactors and each vehicle is efficiently directed to whichever bay is free at an operational compactor. Refuse is compacted by means of a ram into $6 \times 2 \cdot 4 \, m$ ($20 \times 8 \, ft$) square containers located on special trailers. This is automatically controlled and one container caters for $2 \cdot 7$ to $3 \cdot 1$ vehicle loads. Each container is weighed and then removed from its trailer by a $20 \cdot 3$ tonne capacity fork-lift truck. The containers may be stacked, or loaded onto a waiting railway wagon. A train of 20 wagons, with three containers per wagon and an average load of 600 to 700 tonnes, transports the refuse to a site in Oxfordshire. Here the containers are off-loaded at the railway sidings by a travelling gantry and transported by lorry for disposal in a gravel pit.[11]

Tipping of Crude Refuse

Tipping is economical because it requires a minimum of physical plant and has relatively low labour costs. Sanitary landfill, i.e. excavation followed by backfilling with refuse, is practised in some countries but is not popular in the UK, where the emphasis is on reclamation of existing voids, e.g. exhausted quarries, or low-lying land such as estuaries.

Standard construction equipment may be used for excavation and earthmoving and for refuse handling, replacement and compaction. Purpose-built landfill compactors with steel wheels that chop and compact the refuse are finding increased application. However, several disadvantages may be associated with tipping of untreated refuse having a composition similar to that given in the last column of Table 14.2. Firstly, the wide variation in physical character of the crude material means that it cannot be fully compacted on tipping. This results in uneven settlement during subsequent years.

Uneven settlement can be overcome by piling or by building on rafts, but methane and carbon dioxide gas generation generally preclude the use of landfill sites for building in the UK; therefore they are predominantly reserved for amenity space or agricultural use.

Vegetable and putrescible matter, i.e. the organic content of the refuse, must decay by biochemical action. This depends upon the action of aerobic and anaerobic bacteria, but when the material is 'sealed' in the ground aerobic biochemical processes are inhibited. The anaerobic condition results in noxious smells, an extended period of decay before a stable tip is obtained and a highly polluted leachate. For example, the percolate may be 20–30 times as strong, with regard to BOD, as average settled sewage.[12] A ready source of food may be provided for rats, and a breeding ground for flies, but good practice can minimise these problems. Birds, especially seagulls, are becoming an increasing nuisance.

Biological degradation commences and raises the temperature of tipped refuse almost immediately it is deposited. The temperature may reach 65°C in four to six weeks,[13] followed by a slow fall to soil temperature after up to two years; this is dependent upon the amount of organic matter, degree of compaction and access of air and water.

In refuse tipping, consideration must be given to the 'secondary wastes' produced, namely gases (generally over 90% of which are carbon dioxide and methane) and leachate. Although methane is flammable in the range 5% to 15% in air, insufficient oxygen is left in a landfill when the lower limit is reached, so that no danger of explosion exists[14] except in excavations and drains serving the site. Such excavations are not uncommon on landfill sites for the disposal of, for example, liquid wastes or low-level radioactive material. Lateral movement of gases depends on the nature of the surrounding soil and the cover and can be controlled by installing vents of permeable material or sealants, with pumping where appropriate. The carbon dioxide tends to move down to the lower parts of the landfill, and eventually the underlying strata, to reach the groundwater. By increasing water acidity this may result in an increase in hardness and mineral content. Leachate from rainfall and inflowing groundwater also tends to seep down to underground strata. The sealant most commonly used to control gas and leachate movement is compacted clay in a continuous layer $0 \cdot 15$–$1 \cdot 2$ m deep. Provision may be made for leachate to be pumped off from the bottom of the fill.

The high paper and cardboard content of refuse, now exceeding 50%, can create problems. Paper salvaging, since it only applies to unsoiled paper, only reduces the paper content at the tip by about 10%. Voids, formed mainly by cardboard boxes and likely to harbour tip vermin, may be avoided by the use of modern equipment which can achieve a high degree of compaction. Windblown paper and plastic can cause a nuisance during the tipping operation, and high combustibility can lead to tip fires.

In order to minimise such nuisances it is essential to provide good tip management and to follow the established practices of controlled tipping. Layers of deposited refuse should be restricted in depth to 2·5 m. At the end of the working day a 0·23 m (9 in) layer of soil, or any other suitable inert material, should be placed over each layer of refuse and the tip face. This seal controls odour emission, prevents light litter from being blown about, reduces fires and prevents the emergence of fly larvae. However, tipping of untreated refuse according to these principles can result in up to 20% loss in effective tip capacity.

With proper management, as briefly outlined above, the quality of the environment need not be seriously impaired by landfill operations, although the heavy traffic generated may cause some loss of amenity in the immediate vicinity.

Pulverisation and Tipping

Pulverisation serves to reduce the particle size of the refuse. This results in maximum exposure of surface area for biochemical action and gives better compaction on tipping. The end product is also thoroughly mixed, i.e. of uni-

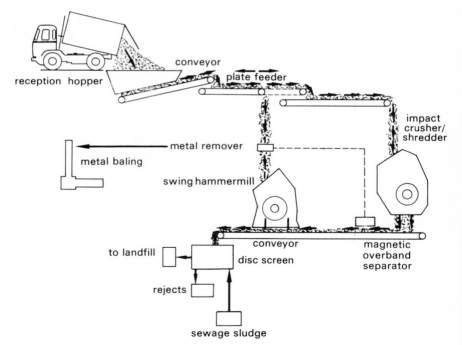

Fig. 14.1 Pulverisation plant with provision for metal recovery (either a hammermill or an impact crusher/shredder may be used alone)

form and homogeneous character. The two basic methods involve either dry processing or wet processing. In the dry process, hammermills are used to reduce the particle size of refuse in a dry condition. The power consumption and maintenance costs of dry pulverisation are high because of the high operating speeds and abrasive nature of the refuse.

Figure 14.1 is a schematic diagram of a pulverisation plant incorporating both a swing-hammermill, for example a single rotor machine giving a high degree of reduction, and a heavy-duty crusher which will handle bulk and household refuse without pre-separation.[9] The swing-hammermill is capable of producing a pulverised waste containing at least 85% in the -50 mm $(-2$ in) size-range from household refuse and trade waste; typical capacities range from 5 to 30 tonnes/h. A typical impact crusher/shredder can produce a waste of up to 60% in the -50 mm size-range, suitable for controlled tipping.

British Jeffrey Diamond

Hammers and hammer pin extractor for 1750 × 2250 mm refuse pulveriser

In wet pulverisation a controlled amount of water is added to the refuse, which is tumbled in high-capacity drums. The water serves to reduce the strength of the paper-based constituents and 'self-pulverisation' is produced by the tins, bottles and other solid objects. The capital cost of wet pulverisation plant is higher than for the dry process but operating costs can be less.

However, wet pulverisation suffers from several serious disadvantages. A 'sausage' of unpulverisable waste, comprising for example carpets and textiles, may have to be removed daily from the machine. Furthermore, the waste decomposes rapidly as a result of its high surface area and high moisture content, and hence high biological activity, and can create an odour nuisance necessitating odour 'masking' on some tips.

British Jeffrey Diamond

1500 × 2250 mm refuse pulveriser plant

High-density Baling

High-density baling is an alternative method for reduction of waste volume. The average density of baled waste is estimated at 1040 kg/m³ (65 lb/ft³), i.e. an improvement of 5 or 6:1 compared with crude refuse. Figure 14.2 shows a typical flow diagram, including provision for metal separation. The waste may be compressed into bales measuring 1·2 × 1·1 × 0·6 m (48 × 45 × 24 in); two bales strapped for loading have a combined weight of 1905 kg (4200 lb).

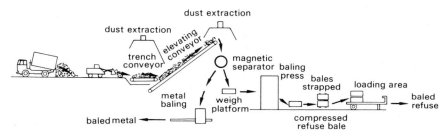

Fig. 14.2 Flow diagram of a typical high-density baling plant

High-density baling plants with capacities in excess of 1000 tonnes per day are in operation in the USA. The first plant is Europe came into use at the Polmadie Works in Glasgow in 1976. The press there accepts untreated household refuse, trade waste and bulky refuse via a 2·4 m (8 ft) wide inclined plate conveyor. Vehicle body shells and bulky waste of similar type may be loaded directly into the press charge box. The average charge of refuse is approximately 1·27 tonnes and, with final baling forces of about 18 890 kN/m², the reduction for household refuse is to one-sixth of original volume. For less dense, bulky refuse such as furniture this may increase to one-fifteenth. At maximum throughput the press produces 38 bales per hour which, with an average bale weight of 1·27 tonnes, is equivalent to approximately 41–51 tonnes of refuse per hour. The ejected bales measure approximately 1·2 × 0·9 m square and are of sufficient mechanical strength to retain their uniformity in handling without strapping or wiring. They are pushed in pairs onto an articulated flat-bottomed trailer for transport to the landfill site. Each trailer has a capacity of 14 bales or approximately 17·8 tonnes.

Incineration

Household refuse is mostly carbonaceous, the combustibles being mainly cellulose and hydrocarbons with traces of sulphur (small compared with fossil fuels). The overall average moisture content is between 20% and 25%. Thus refuse incinerator chimney emissions contain, in addition to dust and grit, nitrogen, carbon dioxide, oxygen, moisture, sulphur dioxide, hydrogen chloride and oxides of nitrogen. However, in the volumes produced with the dilution by excess air they do not result in pollution problems provided the proportions of refuse constituents are balanced.[13] Conversely, the surreptitious burning of waste material on open bonfires causes atmospheric pollution even when the materials themselves are relatively inert, for example packaging materials, wool, paper, textiles and rubber.

Incineration technology has changed considerably in recent years, for example, in the design of furnace grates, auxiliaries, refractories and mechanical handling and in allowable throughputs. There has been a switch to direct and continuous incinerators in place of the batch-fed type used in the past, sometimes with pre-separation of values. The changes are a result of the alteration in refuse composition already referred to, i.e. the sharp increase in packaging materials (paper, cardboard, bottles, plastic containers, cans, foils, etc.) and the reduction in mineral content (fine ash and cinder from solid fuel fires) (see Table 14.5).

TABLE 14.5 SOME PROJECTED CHANGES IN DOMESTIC REFUSE TO 1985 (see also Figure 17.1)

Constituent	% by weight		
	1975	1980	1985
Metal	9	9	8
Glass	10	9	9
Paper	41	43	46
Rag	3	3	3
Vegetable and putrescible	15	17	16
Plastics	2	5	7
Dust and cinder	17	12	9
Unclassified debris	3	2	2

The extent to which incineration is applied to refuse disposal in Europe is illustrated in Table 14.6; it is not yet a popular method in the UK.

TABLE 14.6 REFUSE INCINERATION IN WESTERN EUROPE—1975 ESTIMATES[15]

	Population (millions)	Household and trade refuse (million tonnes/ year)	Amount incinerated		% of total refuse fired in energy recovery plants	Number of incinerator plants	
			(%)	(million tonnes/ year)		With energy recovery	Without energy recovery
UK	56·5	18·0	15	2·7	3·4	5	29
France	53·0	15·0	20	3·0	10·4	23	45
Germany	63·0	20·0	23	4·6	22·0	33	7
Switzerland	6·7	1·9	80	1·5	52·0	17	37
Belgium	10·3	3·2	19	0·6	9·6	5	9
Netherlands	13·9	4·2	23	1·0	20·0	7	3

systems (Figure 14.3c) provides more flexibility with improved overall efficiency.

A number of alternative combinations are possible, but with the limitation that disposal is a continuous operation irrespective of seasonal changes in energy demand. An advanced incineration application for district heating and cooling in the USA is illustrated in Figure 14.4. This produces 5°C chilled water for cooling and saturated steam at $1 \cdot 03 \ kN/m^2$ for heating; package boilers are on standby to cope with peak steam demands and a condenser to deal with any steam surplus to requirements.[18]

Recycling

Many of the constituents of refuse can be recycled (see Chapter 17). Considerable quantities of refuse arise every year and local authorities are encouraged to increase their recycling activities. Metals and paper are currently the most widely salvaged materials. However, because of the thoroughly heterogeneous composition of waste (see Table 17.2, page 500), sorting processes are complex and for many components the cost of separation exceeds their value.

Other Special Wastes

A variety of wastes are highly toxic or persist in the environment. Additional control measures and precautions, beyond those described in Chapter 13, are called for in their disposal. Some examples of UK practice follow, from which it is clear that wastes with a high toxicity, or which may generate toxic compounds if allowed to mix and react with other wastes or moisture, require very special care in disposal. This applies particularly to wastes that persist because they are resistant to biodegradation, such as mercury- and cadmium-bearing wastes, certain metal drosses, biocides and pharmaceutical wastes (see also Table 13.3).

As more becomes known about the potential long-term effects of relatively low levels of toxic materials in the environment, however remote the risk, even more stringent control measures may be required for such wastes. Disposal procedures involving analysis, segregation, treatment and final disposal will then become increasingly elaborate; contractors may be more reluctant to deal with the wastes or disposal may become prohibitively expensive. A result may be that measures for waste reduction and recycling become more attractive.

Radioactive Waste

'Radioactive waste' comprises any substance which constitutes scrap material, or an effluent, or other unwanted surplus substance arising from the application of any process involving radioactive materials.[19] This also includes any substance or article which requires to be disposed of as being broken, worn, contaminated or

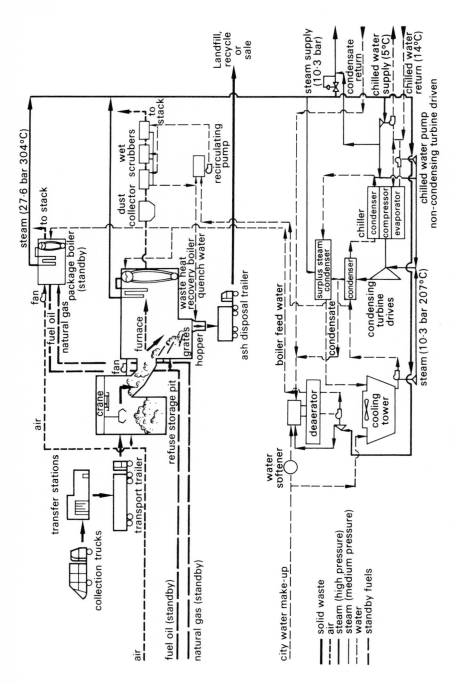

Fig. 14.4 Flow diagram of district heating and cooling facility based on refuse incineration[18]

otherwise spoilt. The position in the UK is simplified in that the majority of waste from the major users of radioactive materials, nuclear power stations, is returned to British Nuclear Fuels Ltd at Windscale for reprocessing and extraction of various nuclides.[20] Furthermore, a large number of sealed radioactive sources are returned directly to the supplier, generally the Radiochemical Centre Ltd at Amersham, and are excluded from the provisions of the Radioactive Substances Act as far as authorisation for disposal is concerned.

In general, this Act controls the disposal and accumulation of radioactive wastes and provides for the registration of users of radioactive materials and mobile radioactive apparatus. It prohibits accumulation or disposal of radioactive waste except as authorised by the Secretary of State. Disposal facilities and the inspection of premises are also covered. The United Kingdom Atomic Energy Authority is exempted from the Act, as are establishments subject to the Nuclear Installations Act[21] where accumulation of waste takes place on site. Disposal of waste from licensed sites, e.g. to the sea, is covered by the Act; by administrative agreement, similar standards are applied to UKAEA premises.

At present, the most important industrial applications of unsealed radioactive substances and those giving rise to the greatest volume of waste materials are:[22]

The manufacture and processing of nuclear reactor fuel
Luminising
Extraction of thorium from various ores
Manufacture of gas mantles
Manufacture of electronic devices/sealed tubes containing radioactive gases.

Of these, nuclear reactors are most important, accounting for several thousand million curies of activity and creating the greatest waste disposal problem.

Although radioactivity eventually decays, it is not always feasible to await decay before dispersal because many radio nuclides have half lives in excess of hundreds or thousands of years. The basic principles applied are therefore (i) delay and decay, (ii) concentrate and store or (iii) dilute and disperse.[20] Selection is dependent on many factors including the quantity and type of radioactivity, the physical and chemical form of the waste, and the geographical location.

Solid Waste
The main very-high-activity solid waste (above 1600 curies) consists of the used fuel elements from nuclear power stations. Some 1422 tonnes of these rods are returned annually, in special road transport flasks, for reprocessing at Windscale. The other main methods of solid waste disposal comprise:

(a) Storage in special facilities, i.e. 'active waste' stores at all nuclear power stations and most licensed nuclear sites.[20]

(b) Burial: generally this is restricted to low-activity waste and the licence is subject to conditions relating to the coverage of the material in pits and total activity in surface dose rates.[23] The major burial site is at Drigg in Cumberland where 13 809 m³ and 2981 m³ of solid wastes were buried in 1973 and 1974 respectively.[20] Burial is also practised by smaller users of radioactive materials where the waste is disposed of with normal trade waste. This relies upon dilution: special approval is required, since limits are imposed on the activity per package and the total activity which may be disposed of.[24] Items of higher activity require special disposal arrangements via the National Disposal Service.

(c) Sea dumping: this has been used to a moderate extent in the UK and may become more important, e.g. very large quantities of waste with total beta/gamma activity of 10⁴ curies per year, excluding tritium, may be dumped in the North Atlantic deeps.[25]

The volume of solid waste may be reduced by compression or incineration. There are active waste incinerators at three power stations in the UK; the flue gases from these are scrubbed and filtered. Most power stations also have incinerators for very low-activity waste. Segregation into combustible or non-combustible and high-level or low-level activity is an important measure.[20]

Liquid Waste

Liquid waste with an activity greater than 100 curies per litre is concentrated by evaporation, chemical treatment or ion exchange.[26] The effluent is then treated as low-level waste, i.e. having an activity of less than a fraction of a micro-curie per litre. The residue, or sludge, is dealt with as described for solid waste.

Low-level effluent may be disposed of via sewers or directly into rivers, but these methods have limited application. Relatively large quantities of radioactive effluent are discharged into the sea, generally via pipeline into deep water.

Asbestos Waste

Table 14.7 shows the wide variety of industrial activities which may involve the use of asbestos, other than asbestos factories themselves. The dust from asbestos can cause serious damage to health if inhaled. The diseases that may result are a specific pneumoconiosis (asbestosis), lung cancer and mesothelioma. Crocidolite (blue asbestos) presents the most serious health hazard. The commercially important grades of asbestos are chrysotile, crocidolite and amosite, but, except for small specialised applications, imports of crocidolite ceased in 1970. Consumption in the UK now averages about 173 000 tonnes a year.

About 99% of all asbestos waste is disposed of by landfill operations. The cumulative total of waste disposed of by three major manufacturers in 1974 was 63 030 tonnes. In addition there is about 10 200 tonnes per year of stripped insulation material.[26] Detailed recommendations relating to the disposal of asbestos residue, and waste materials containing asbestos, have been published as a code of practice.[28]

TABLE 14.7 INDUSTRIAL ACTIVITIES WHICH MAY INVOLVE ASBESTOS[27]

Factories in which asbestos and its products are used:

Electricity generating	lagging and de-lagging
Steel	lagging and de-lagging
Heavy engineering	furnace insulation
Loco building	
Railway carriage building	heat and sound insulation
Boiler making	heat insulation
Paper	manufacture of filter papers and grinding of rollers
Linoleum	
Floor tiles	
Rubber	
Paints	used as a filler
Plastics	
Adhesives	
Roofing compounds	
Motor assembly	incidental grinding in assembly of brake and clutch parts
Motor vehicle repair	repairs to brake and clutch parts
Building trades	trimming of asbestos/cement sheets and insulation boards; asbestos spraying
Scientific	insulation
Light engineering	making of asbestos washers and gaskets
Electrical engineering	insulation systems

Contractors carrying out work involving use of asbestos may be found in:

Dockyards
Shipbuilding
Ship repairing
Generating stations
Installation of plant in heavy industries e.g. steel
Large building projects—industrial and domestic—
 on insulation and repair of heating apparatus e.g. in schools

Other asbestos exposures may occur in:

Certain aircraft maintenance activities
Disposal of asbestos/cement waste which may be used e.g. as
 hard standing in car parks
Car body underseals
Asbestos/asphalt mixes for road surfacings

The common categories of asbestos waste are fine dust; loose fibre, swarf, small offcuts and floor sweepings; waste from fixing or stripping of insulation; offcuts and broken pieces from friable materials; offcuts, broken pieces and reject material from high-density products (e.g. asbestos cement); and empty sacks or bags which have contained loose asbestos fibre mixtures. Fine dust from, for example, sanding or machining operations should be bagged off into polythene sacks of adequate strength which can be tightly sealed. Loose fibre should be handled in a similar way but, in the case of material collected by vacuum cleaning, disposable paper bags may be used. Waste insulation material can be collected on polythene sheeting which is then folded to form a sealed container. Automatic collection into disposable receptacles is desirable for broken pieces and rejects of friable material. A mechanical plant for dealing with waste material has been described which is almost entirely free of dust apart from that associated with the handling of filled bags. In operation, an unopened paper sack is slipped onto a nozzle; this ejects waste into the sack, which is distended only by the incoming waste so that there is no displacement of air or leakage of dust on filling. Sacks or bags emptied of waste should be bundled and sealed in an impermeable bag.

All the above operations are regulated under the Asbestos Regulations 1969 and require, for example, adequate provisions for dust extraction and the provision of approved respirators and protective clothing for all employees engaged on the work. Furthermore, under these Regulations no asbestos wastes should be despatched from a factory except in suitable closed receptacles which prevent the escape of asbestos dust; if they contain crocidolite they must be marked with a specific warning.[29] Waste which is sealed in bags or receptacles needs no special transport but special containers are available which can be removed direct to a disposal tip by specially fitted road vehicles. Wet waste should be transported in suitable vehicles, such as sludge tankers. Empty containers or vehicles should be cleared of loose fibre or dust by, for example, vacuum cleaning. The action necessary in the event of spillage during transport ranges from rapid re-collection in the original receptacle by the driver to the summoning of assistance and rapid containment by covering and/or wetting, followed by controlled removal, dependent upon the quantity spilled. Written instructions should be issued to drivers.

At the tip there should be vehicular access for the waste to be deposited at the face itself, which should not exceed 1·8 m (6 ft). Vehicles should have a low discharge point and waste should be deposited at the foot of the face. Alternatively, if waste has to be deposited over the tip face, care is necessary during tipping and formation of the tip to avoid spillage from receptacles. Deposited material should be covered with at least 230 mm (9 in) of consolidated earth, or other dry wastes, to form a seal. This should be done promptly and coverage should be complete at the end of the day. In the case of crocidolite waste, covering should be immediate. Disposal of limited quantities of wet waste is acceptable on a dry tip but it must be covered to eliminate dust escape on subsequent drying-out.

Waste from high-density material is unlikely to produce a dust hazard on tipping but may do so if subjected to pounding by lorries or dumper trucks.[30] Disposal should be as already described, but with covering as soon as practicable rather than daily. High-density waste may also be disposed of in wet pits containing sufficient water to maintain coverage.

In a recent survey of eight sites,[31] each taking between 200 and 32 500 tonnes a year of asbestos waste, no serious operator hazards were found; however, closer conformance with the Code of Practice was recommended.

Polychlorinated Biphenyl (PCB) Wastes

Polychlorinated biphenyls are mixtures of chlorinated biphenyls which are excellent dielectrics, stable to chemical, biological and thermal degradation and fire-resistant. Their widespread detection in the environment, for example in predatory birds which feed on aquatic organisms, together with an incident in Japan involving ingestion of PCB-contaminated rice, led to OECD agreement in 1973 on a recommendation that the use of PCBs in open systems and dispersive uses should be discontinued and their use limited to closed systems where they are recoverable, where non-flammability is an overriding consideration, or where no adequate substitute is available. Since 1971 commercial sales in the UK have been restricted voluntarily to dielectric applications and research. Future use is confined to controllable closed systems, i.e. power correction capacitors and transformers.

A Code of Practice has been introduced in the UK with the aims of restricting PCB levels in human foods to the lowest practicable and reducing levels in the environment by all practicable measures.[32] This is applicable to all wastes containing greater than 0·1% PCBs. Strict personnel safety precautions are required during transfer. Transfers should preferably be undertaken on hard, undrained, bunded surfaces; spills should be absorbed at once in a flammable absorbent and care taken to avoid ingress into sewers or watercourses.

Liquid wastes should be removed from large equipment as completely as practicable; they should be transported in labelled, heavy-duty, specially secured containers. Disposal should be by reclamation, or by destruction in incinerators fitted with gas scrubbing devices and operating at temperatures greater than 1100°C. Mean residence time should not be less than 2 s and excess oxygen content not less than 3%; the stack gases and scrubber liquids should be sampled to an agreed schedule. Manufacturing wastes and contaminated solid wastes should be similarly incinerated. Special precautions are not required for the disposal of small capacitors unless the concentration at any particular landfill site or recovery facility exceeds one capacitor per tonne of refuse. In this eventuality the reason should be ascertained and disposal arranged to reach an average concentration of one capacitor per 7 tonnes of refuse. Other wastes should be recovered where possible, or destroyed by incineration or, as a last resort, buried at low concentration in landfill.

Mineral Oil Wastes

Mineral oil wastes arise inevitably from the handling and refining of petroleum and in the chemical processing of oil-based products. Further wastes arise during transportation and distribution, in usage (e.g. as lubricants) and in spent oils reclamation.

Waste-waters containing oil from refining and petrochemical plants can normally be treated for discharge to sewers or watercourses, as described in Chapter 7. Other classes of waste comprise:[33]

(i) Oily wastes and sludges as tank bottoms, separator bottom sludge and flocculation sludge. These contain (depending on source) oil, water, oil degradation and corrosion products and additives.

(ii) Spent lubricating oils containing volatile soluble and insoluble contaminants; spent 'suds', i.e. emulsions, containing up to 8% oil plus additives such as emulsifiers and biocides, metal swarf and 'tramp' oil.

(iii) Oil-containing residues: acid tar sludges containing sulphuric acid; oil additives and hydrocarbon products; spent clays with up to 40% oil content plus oil-related impurities; distillation bottoms containing high-boiling non-volatile residues from oil reclamation.

These wastes should be reclaimed as lubricant or, where practicable, recovered for fuel use as discussed in Chapter 9. Non-recoverable wastes should preferably be incinerated in a unit of appropriate design or landfilled under suitable conditions. The selection of a landfill site involves hydrogeological and amenity considerations and the volume of waste for disposal should be minimised as far as practicable, e.g. by water removal. Aqueous waste should be dispersed in other wastes as far as is practicable. Crude recovery is recommended, as is chemical solidification of oil sludges to yield solid material for landfill. Acid tars should be neutralised with alkaline materials and/or mixed with refuse, and covered without delay. Spent clays should be steamed, to reduce the oil content, prior to landfill. Oil-additive manufacturing wastes should be damped to reduce any tendency to self-ignition. The depth of the deposit should be such as to avoid contamination of the soil overlay if it is subsequently disturbed. Covering should be effected expeditiously.

Sludge from leaded gasoline storage tanks requires special treatment and, according to the recommendations of the UK manufacturer of leaded additives,[34] should be mixed into concrete, incinerated or weathered and the treated residues disposed of as landfill. The disposal of spent quench oil from metal-hardening applications, which is liable to contain cyanide or sodium nitrate/nitrite, involves filtering and careful incineration. Recycling can be a viable method of disposal.

The 'best practicable means' are recommended to avoid accidental/careless release of wastes to the environment. This may warrant a monitoring system to detect sources of oil leakage and the installation of interceptors on surface water drains.[33] A high standard of personal hygiene is essential when handling mineral oil wastes because of the potential health hazards. In general, mineral oil can affect the skin, depending on extent and duration of exposure, to cause dermatitis or, on long-term exposure, ulceration which may undergo malignant change.[35] Adequate personal protection and good washing facilities are essential.[36]

The Council of the EEC recently issued a directive on the disposal of waste oils to be implemented within two years of notification.[37] Member States are required to take the necessary measures to ensure the safe collection and disposal of waste oils. Under Article 4, measures shall be taken to prohibit:

> any discharge of waste oils into internal surface waters,
>   groundwater, coastal waters and drainage systems;
> any deposit and/or discharge of waste oils harmful to the soil
>   and any uncontrolled discharge of residues resulting from the
>   processing of waste oils; and
> any processing of waste oils causing air pollution which exceeds
>   the level prescribed by existing provisions.

Where the above aims cannot otherwise be achieved, measures must be taken to ensure that undertakings carry out the collection and/or disposal of the products offered to them by holders in an assigned zone. Any undertaking which disposes of waste oils must obtain a permit from the authorities. Any holder of waste oils unable to comply with the measures to meet Article 4 must place the oils with the disposal undertakings. Holders of certain quantities of waste oils containing impurities in excess of percentages, yet to be fixed by the authorities, must handle and stock them separately. Undertakings that collect and dispose of waste oils must do so with no avoidable risk of water, air or soil pollution.

Any establishment, collecting and/or disposing of more than a specific quantity (> 500 litres) of waste oils per annum must keep a record of their quantity, quality, origin, location, receipt and despatch, and/or convey this information to the authorities on request. Similarly, any undertaking involved in disposal must supply any information regarding disposal/deposit requested by the authorities and is to be inspected periodically to ensure compliance with permit conditions.

Indemnities may be granted to collection/disposal undertakings for the service rendered but these must not exceed annual 'uncovered' costs taking into account a reasonable profit. One suggested method of financing these indemnities is by a charge imposed on products which after use are transformed into waste oils, or on waste oils themselves. In any event, financing and indemnities must be on the principle of 'the polluter pays'.

Unstable and Potentially Explosive Chemicals

A service for the disposal of unstable and potentially explosive chemicals is available from the Chemical Emergency Centre, Harwell.[38] Such chemicals may have become hazardous through age: for example, ethers, which tend to form peroxides on prolonged storage; or monomers, which are liable to spontaneous polymerisation. The service also covers the disposal of gas cylinders which have suffered from corrosion and neglect; these cylinders are often not suitable for reuse and may present a serious hazard if attempts are made to discharge the contents.

Heat Treatment Salts

One leading supplier of heat treatment salts undertakes, for a charge, the disposal of residues arising from their use.[39] These residues may contain sodium cyanide and the conditions under which drums are accepted therefore serve as an example for other toxic wastes. Only original salt drums of a specific size may be used and these must be sound and in good condition. Drums for disposal must contain solid only, be effectively sealed to prevent leakage and be marked with the weight and a Ministry dumping number. They must then be kept dry and in a clean condition pending collection. The subsequent disposal procedure involves delivery to a UK port, loading on to a charter vessel and dumping in mid-Atlantic to a depth exceeding 3657 m (2000 fathoms) subject to conditions agreed by the Ministry of Agriculture, Fisheries and Food. Sea disposal is governed by specific authorisations granted under the Dumping at Sea Act 1974.

There is a published code of practice for heat treatment cyanide and related wastes.[40] Cyanide-containing molten salt wastes arise from their use in baths for the treatment of metal components and to improve zinc adhesion in galvanising. Wastes, which arise at about 200 factories throughout the UK, contain about 600 tonnes of cyanide annually, divided almost equally between solid salt wastes and aqueous effluents. The total arisings of solid heat treatment residues have been estimated as 2000 tonnes. Table 14.8 lists sources of 'cyanide' wastes and the usual recommended disposal methods.

TABLE 14.8 CYANIDE-CONTAINING WASTES

Source	Disposal method
Ladled-out or discarded bath contents (may also contain barium, lead, nitrates and other salts)	Sea-dumping or chemical oxidation*
Cyanide spills	Sea dumping or chemical oxidation*
Baths, apparatus, utensils containing salt residues	Sea dumping or chemical oxidation* or landfill after any necessary treatment
Contaminated building materials	Landfill after any necessary treatment
Vent dusts and floor sweepings	Sea dumping or chemical treatment or landfill—depends on composition
Quench oils	Incineration
Waste-waters	Chemical oxidation*
Oily solid (from the bottom of salt baths)	Incineration or, if separated from oil, as bath contents

* Chemical oxidation is carried out after aqueous dissolution (see Chapter 7).

The salt waste should be accumulated in steel drums which, together with other waste of high cyanide content, should be labelled 'cyanide waste' and stored in a safe location. Suitable personnel training and protection are essential.

Although dilute aqueous cyanide tends to be biologically oxidised in the environment, recommendations with regard to landfill give the following guidelines:[40]

> (i) Where sites provide a significant element of containment the cyanide waste should contain not more than 1000 g/m^3 cyanide as CN, the average over the site being not more than 10 g/m^3 cyanide as CN.
> (ii) Where underlying strata allow only slow leachate migration, the corresponding figures are 10 and 1 g/m^3.
> (iii) Where underlying strata allow rapid leachate migration, the cyanide waste should not contain more than 1 g/m^3 cyanide as CN.

The upper-level cyanide wastes should be covered soon after deposit; acid disposal at the same location must be avoided.

Halogenated Hydrocarbon Solvent Wastes

Aliphatic halogenated solvents find widespread applications in the metal cleaning, textile, leather and dry-cleaning industries. They are efficient oil, fat and grease solvents, hence their use for cleaning and de-oiling. The common materials go under a variety of trade names but are in fact one or more of the chemicals trichloroethylene, perchloroethylene, 1,1,1-trichloroethane and 1,1,2-trichloro-1,2,2-trifluoroethane. Limited quantities of methylene chloride are used in paint strippers. These solvents are toxic at high vapour in air concentrations, for example threshold limit values of trichloroethylene and 1,1,1-trichloroethane are currently 100 ppm and 350 ppm respectively[41] (see Chapter 4), and can cause dermatitis on prolonged exposure. Above certain concentrations they may also inhibit anaerobic digestion at sewage treatment works.[42] About one-third of the total consumption is for dry-cleaning.[42]

Most of these solvents are ultimately lost by evaporation into the atmosphere, i.e. only a few per cent is 'waste' with other general dirt and water from the specific cleaning processes. Some 6000 to 10 000 tonnes/year of dry-cleaning waste arises in the UK, of which solvent constitutes 1000 to 2500 tonnes. Most is disposed of by landfill. Still residues and cartridge filters are disposed of separately.

Oily waste from the use of perchloroethylene, and some trichloroethylene, in degreasing and de-oiling in the textile and leather industries consists mainly of spinning oils and knitting lubricants which have been efficiently solvent stripped. The complexity of the mixture and the presence of detergents generally makes oil recovery impracticable so that disposal is usually by landfill. Use as fuel and incineration are other possibilities.

Almost two-thirds of the total consumption of halogenated hydrocarbon solvents is in metal cleaning, in either 'cold cleaning' or 'vapour degreasing'. 1,1,1-trichloroethane is generally used in cold cleaning, because of its relatively lower toxicity, and is ultimately lost by evaporation. Trichloroethylene is mainly used in vapour cleaning and waste arises as sump residue with a solvent content of 50% to 80%. The residue may be processed in a recovery still yielding waste with 30% to 50% solvent content. It has been estimated that 9000 tonnes/year of sludge containing between 3000 and 7000 tonnes of trichloroethylene in admixture with metal fines, cutting and lubricating oils and factory dirt arises in the UK each year. Most is disposed of on land but reprocessing is also undertaken by specialist companies.

According to the Code of Practice,[42] if recovery as discussed in Chapter 9 is not feasible,[43] consideration should be given to the use of any wastes containing halogenated hydrocarbon solvents as a fuel, or to their disposal by incineration. Incineration facilities which incorporate gas scrubbers can handle wastes with halogen contents of less than 25% to 30%; other facilities are restricted to wastes containing less than 1% because of the controls outlined in Chapter 4. Subject to licensing, incineration may be carried out at sea to avoid the necessity of scrubbing of stack gases.

Solvent wastes should be segregated and should not be disposed of to foul or surface water sewers without specific permission from the appropriate authority. Normal waste arising from dry-cleaning may be disposed of by landfill without special precautions on the site; liquid wastes should be handled separately.

However, landfill disposal of wastes with a high solvent content, for example metal cleaning wastes, should normally only take place on sites with a significant degree of leachate and waste containment with respect to sensitive waters and where there are no nearby dwellings.

Generally, tanker discharges, or disposal of waste in $0 \cdot 2$ m^3 (45 gal) drums or other containers, should be at the foot of the working face not less than 2 m from the surface of the landfill and not less than 2 m from the flanks. Two persons should be present, upwind and 'well away' from the tanker, during discharge. Disposed containers should only be opened by a competent, fully informed person.

Lead-containing Wastes

Some guidance relating to the disposal of waste materials containing lead is included in the *Code of Practice for Health Precautions* prepared with particular reference to the smelting and refining and the lead accumulator industries.[44] Silicate slags from smelting plants, though characterised as poisonous waste, present little hazard when damp and can be disposed of on approved tips. This is permissible because they are insoluble in water and dilute mineral acids. Conversely, soda slags disintegrate on exposure to moisture and soluble constituents such as sodium chloride and sodium carbonate can be leached out; thus although the lead content is small, for which reason further processing is not a viable proposition, some may dissolve out. Nevertheless disposal is permitted to suitable tips.

Care should be exercised in the disposal of steel drums or wooden cases used for the transportation of drosses and residues. Wooden cases should be incinerated on site, under controlled conditions so as not to contaminate the atmosphere, and the ashes resmelted for lead recovery. Steel drums may be disposed of to scrap merchants provided they are first cleaned, preferably by washing. Lead drosses and other residues which have to go to other smelters should be damped, and conveyed in closed containers or covered lorries, to prevent dust dispersion.

It is recommended that battery cases be washed free from lead-containing materials before disposal. Otherwise they should be disposed of as poisonous waste. They should not be burned under uncontrolled conditions on domestic fires.[45]

References

1. HARVEY, K., *Chemical Engineer*, (270), 65, 1973.
2. GUTT, W., NIXON, P. J., SMITH, M. A., HARRISON, W. H. and RUSSELL, A. D., Building Research Establishment CP19/74, 1974.
3. BIDDLESTONE, A. J. and GRAY, K. R., *Chemical Engineer*, (270), 76, 1973.
4. Working Party on Refuse Disposal, Department of the Environment, *Refuse Disposal*, HMSO, 1971.
5. BRIDGWATER, A. V., GREGORY, S. A., MUMFORD, C. J. and SMITH, E. L., *Resource Recovery and Conservation*, **1**, 3, 1975.
6. SKITT, J., *Chemical Engineer*, (270), 55, 1973.
7. *Local Authority Refuse Collection and Disposal*, survey for the International Reclamation and Disposal Exhibition, National Exhibition Centre, Birmingham, UK, 12–16 September 1977.
8. HAGERTY, D. J., PAVONI, J. L. and HEER, J. E., *Solid Waste Management*, Van Nostrand Reinhold, 1973.
9. Peabody Holmes Ltd, Publ. No. 65, 3M/12/76.
10. KEEN, R. C., private communication, 1977.
11. *A.R.C. News*, June, Amey Roadstone Co., 1977.
12. Ministry of Housing and Local Government, *Pollution of Water by Tipped Refuse*, HMSO, 1961.
13. HIGGINSON, A. E., *Chemical Engineer*, 217, April 1974.
14. TCHOBANGLOUS, G., THEISEN, H. and ELIASSEN, R., *Solid Wastes—Engineering Principles and Management Issues*, McGraw-Hill, 1977.
15. MARX, A., *Chemical Engineer*, 601, September 1976.
16. Bechtel Corporation, San Francisco, report for Electric Power Research Institute, USA, 1975.
17. PORTEOUS, A., *Resources Policy*, **1**, 284, 1974.
18. *Power*, 18 December 1974.
19. Radioactive Substances Act 1960, Section 19.
20. KINSEY, J. S., MSc Thesis, University of Aston in Birmingham, 1975.
21. The Nuclear Installations (Licensing and Insurance) Act 1965, 1969.
22. *The Control of Radioactive Wastes*, Cmnd. 884, HMSO, 1959.
23. UKAEA Health and Safety Branch, *Environmental Monitoring Associated with Discharges of Radioactive Waste during 1964 from UKAEA Establishments*, ASHB (RP) R66, UKAEA, Harwell, 1965.
24. MARTIN, A., and HERBISON, A., *Introduction to Radiation Protection*, Chapman & Hall, 1972.
25. WEBB, E. A. M. and MORLEY, F., *A Model for the Evaluation of the Deep Ocean Disposal of Radio-active Waste*. National Radiological Protection Board, NRPB R14, Harwell, June 1973.
26. GLUECKAUF, E. (Ed.), *Atomic Energy Waste*, Butterworth, 1961.
27. *Asbestos: Health Precautions in Industry*, HSW 44, HMSO, 1970.

28. *Recommended Code of Practice for the Handling and Disposal of Asbestos Waste Materials,* revised edn, Asbestos Research Council, March 1973.
29. Asbestos Regulations, 1969.
30. KEEN, R. C. and MUMFORD, C. J. *Annals of Occupational Hygiene,* **18,** 213, 1975.
31. KINSEY, J. S., KEEN, R. C. and MUMFORD, C. J., *Annals of Occupational Hygiene,* **20,** 85, 1977.
32. Department of the Environment, *Polychlorinated Biphenyl (PCB) Wastes,* Waste Management Paper No. 6, HMSO, 1976.
33. Department of the Environment *Mineral Oil Wastes,* Waste Management Paper No. 7, HMSO, 1976.
34. *Leaded Gasoline Tank Cleaning and Disposal of Sludge,* Booklet 27173, Associated Octel Co. Ltd.
35. KIPLING, M. D., in *Annual Report of HM Chief Inspector of Factories,* 1967, p. 105.
36. *Effects on the Skin of Mineral Oil,* SHW 397, HMSO, 1965.
37. Council Directive 75/439/EEC of 16 June 1975, The Disposal of Waste Oils, *Official Journal of the European Communities,* **1,** 194/23, 1975.
38. Chemical Emergency Centre, Atomic Energy Research Establishment, Harwell, Didcot, Oxfordshire.
39. Cassel Heat Treatment Service, Mond Division, ICI Ltd.
40. Department of the Environment, *Heat Treatment of Cyanide Wastes: A Technical Memorandum on Arisings, Treatment and Disposal including a Code of Practice,* Waste Management Paper No. 8, HMSO, 1976.
41. *Threshold Limit Values for 1976,* Technical Data Note 2/76, Health and Safety Executive, 1976.
42. Department of the Environment, *Halogenated Hydrocarbon Solvent Wastes from Cleaning Processes,* Waste Management Paper No. 9, HMSO, 1976.
43. *Code of Practice for the Recover of Chlorinated Solvents and Other Halogenated Organic Compounds,* Chemical Recovery Association, 1976.
44. HM Factory Inspectorate. *Lead—Code of Practice for Health Precautions,* Department of Employment, August 1973.
45. Department of the Environment, *Lead in the Environment and its Significance to Man,* Pollution Paper No. 2, HMSO, 1974.

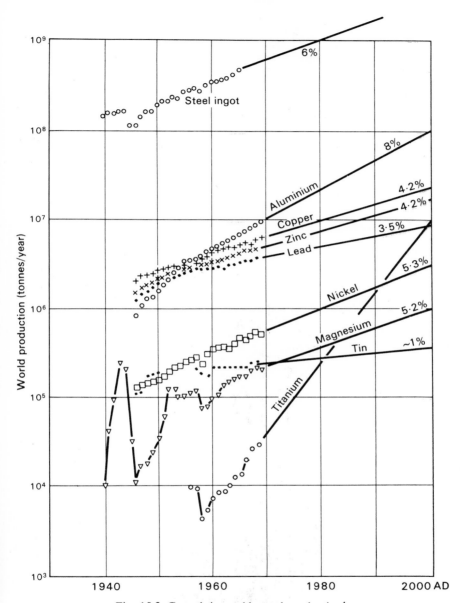

Fig. 15.2 Growth in world metal production[4]

In industrial societies, a general pattern of usage is followed (Figure 15.4[6]). An established recycle system feeds the secondary metal industries. Further avoidable losses result from inefficient collection and sorting, and unavoidable losses where metals go to dissipative or sacrificial uses such as lead in petrol or paint. Statistics on some scrap metals and metal-bearing wastes are

TABLE 15.3 FORECAST OF TIME TO DEPLETION BASED ON EXPONENTIAL RESERVE INDEX (ERI)[3]

Item	Lowest projected yearly growth rate (%)	Reserves (millions of tonnes)	ERI (how many years left)	1 × reserves low growth rate no recycling	10 × reserves low growth rate no recycling	10 × reserves low growth rate 50% recycling	10 × reserves low growth rate 100% recycling beginning 1990
Iron	1·3	100 000	109	109	267	319	598
Aluminium (bauxite)	5·1	1170	35	35	77	91	135
Copper	3·4	308	24	24	76	95	170
Zinc	2·5	123	18	18	76	101	212
Molybdenum	4·0	5·4	336	336	87	104	165
Silver	1·5	0·2	14	14	82	117	328
Chromium	2·0	775	112	112	222	256	416
Titanium	2·7	147	51	51	127	152	255
Uranium	10·6	4·9	44	44	66	—	—

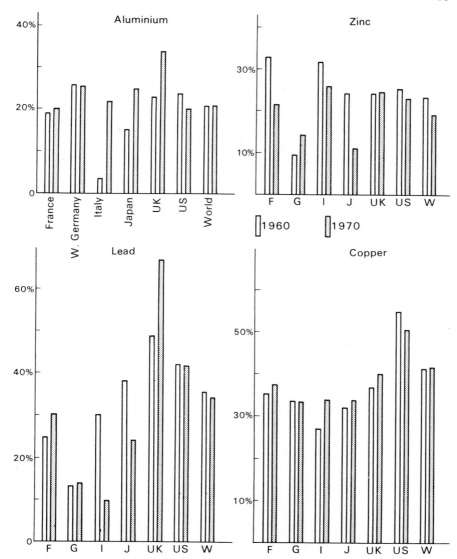

Fig. 15.3 Domestically supplied scrap as percentage of consumption for selected countries, 1960 and 1970[5]

scarce but an estimate has been derived of total UK metal losses in chemical wastes and sewage (Table 15.4). Not all of these metalliferous chemical wastes are recoverable, because of the methods of disposal and dilution; in the table an overall figure for percentage recoverable is suggested for each type of waste. Moreover, there is a lack of information on sources: it is likely, for example, that of the metals present in sewage sludge only a minority is from the metal finishing industries.

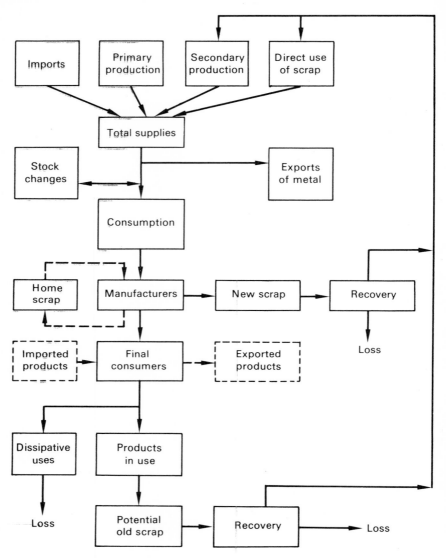

Fig. 15.4 Flow of metal in an industrial economy[6]

In addition to chemical wastes, substantial quantities of scrap metals are believed to be available but not recovered or exploited and thus can be considered as a loss or lost opportunity. An example is household refuse (Table 15.5). Other considerable quantities of metals are lost, but comprehensive data are only known to be available for the USA. Most reported work on non-ferrous metals[12,13] is based on a US survey in 1969 by the Battelle Institute[14] and, for iron and steel in the USA for 1970, on a report by an EPA sponsored

TABLE 15.4 ESTIMATED ANNUAL UK METAL LOSSES FROM CHEMICAL WASTE

Tonnes in:	Chemical liquid waste	Chemical sludge waste	Sewage waste	Total sludge
Aluminium	—	250	—	250
Cadmium	5	250	80	335
Chromium	130	1 000	1 350	2 480
Copper	210	1 000	2 000	3 210
Iron	10 800	12 500	50 200	73 500
Lead	10	250	760	1 020
Nickel	60	500	340	900
Tin	—	250	—	250
Zinc	2 400	2 000	9 090	13 490
Approximate percentage recoverable	20%	50%	20%	

Figures derived and extrapolated by scaling up data for West Midlands[7,8,9,10] and allowing for regional industries.

project.[15] The essential results from this work are given in Table 15.6 together with some comparable data for the UK. From this information and other data in the references several other relationships may be developed to predict the total annual losses and recoverable losses as fractions of recycled scrap.

The 'available potential' is estimated by assuming average life cycles of major classes of products and using consumption data for the beginning of each life cycle. 'Available metals' thus represents an idealised metal arising for the year being studied, and this is then related to the actual recovery of scrap in that year. Any metal not recovered may be regarded as either lost or contributing to an accumulating pool of obsolete material. In either case it can be regarded

TABLE 15.5 METAL CONTENT OF UK HOUSEHOLD REFUSE[11]

	Quantity (tonnes/ year)	Percentage of domestic refuse	Percentage of total metals	Percentage of non-ferrous metals
Ferrous	1 284 000	7·34%	91·7%	
Non-ferrous	(116 000)	(0·66%)	(8·3%)	(100%)
Aluminium	43 300	0·25%	3·1%	37%
Copper	25 400	0·15%	1·8%	22%
Nickel	500	—	—	—
Tin	7 800	0·04%	0·6%	7%
Zinc	39 000	0·22%	2·8%	34%
Total	1 400 000	8%	100·0%	100%

TABLE 15.6 RECYCLED METALS AS A FRACTION OF AVAILABLE POTENTIAL IN THE UK AND USA

	(a) Fraction recycled of total available	(b) Fraction unexploited or lost	(c) Fraction of losses (b) theoretically recoverable	(d) Fraction of losses (b) not recoverable	(e) Fraction of existing recycle lost = (b)/(a)	(f) Fraction of existing recycle (a) recoverable but lost = [(b) × (c)]/(a)
Aluminium (USA, 1969)[12,14]	0.48	0.52	0.8(?)	0.2(?)	1.08	0.87
(UK, 1974)[16,17]	0.60	0.40	0.45 (excl. packaging) 0.8 (incl. packaging)	0.55 0.2	0.67	0.3 0.53
Copper (1969)[12,14]	0.61	0.39	0.6	0.4	0.64	0.58
Lead (1969)[12,14]	0.42	0.58	0.4	0.6	1.38	0.55
Zinc (1969)[12,14]	0.14	0.86	no data	no data	(6.14)	—
Iron and steel (1970)[15]	0.58	0.42	0.58	0.42	0.72	0.42
Stainless steel (1969)[12,14]	0.88	0.12	no data	no data	0.14	—

as a lost opportunity. Some uses of metals are dissipative and they are thus unrecoverable; this distinction is made in Table 15.6. The metal content of household refuse is included in these data.

Data for current aluminium usage and losses in the UK agree well with US figures for other non-ferrous metals—the reduction in aluminium losses may be explained by improved recycling technologies. From this information it is possible to estimate both total and recoverable losses or non-exploited scrap resources (Table 15.7). These are rough approximations: comparisons between the UK and USA may not be entirely valid, but they provide some indication of the extent of the problem. Other current research suggests that these figures may be a little high, but are not unreasonable.

Table 15.8 summarises the conclusions of Tables 15.4 and 15.7 and assigns early 1977 values to each metal (as for newly produced material). The value of the metals as scrap is very roughly half the virgin material value, but chemical wastes have a significantly lower value because of the need for costly concentration and purification. Although the detailed figures of Table 15.8 may be viewed with scepticism, there is undoubtedly considerable scope for improved recovery of metals.

As in primary metal production, the cost of extraction increases as grade of ore (metal content) decreases. Thus, while Tables 15.4 to 15.6 distinguish between 'losses' and 'recoverable losses' (i.e. unexploited scrap and arisings), the definition of 'recoverable' depends on economic rather than technical considerations. The search for new ways of recovering metal values from what is currently discarded or not collected is hampered not by lack of technology but by lack of a technology that is viable. This is why most attempts to recover metals from chemical wastes have proved unsuccessful and economically acceptable solutions have only been found in special situations.[7]

Future development of the secondary metal industries depends on:

More efficient and more thorough reclamation of scrap
More technically efficient recycling processes
Product design with a view to recycling
Economic optimisation of alternative recycling technologies.

To these must be added factors such as the political considerations and changes in industrial and consumer attitudes referred to earlier.

Progress has already been made with the invention and development of a wide range of physical separation methods for household refuse (Chapter 17), and shredded vehicle scrap (q.v.), while, with the growth of hydrometallurgy for primary metal extraction, a number of operations and complete processes have been developed for the chemical processing of scrap and metal-bearing materials.

One proposal to recover a metal by hydrometallurgical processing rather than by physical separation/concentration and pyrometallurgical (high-temperature) processing is outlined under 'Copper' later in this chapter. Many such proposals have been made for metal recovery from scrap and wastes:

TABLE 15.7 ESTIMATED ANNUAL TOTAL AND RECOVERABLE SCRAP METAL 'LOSSES' IN THE UK

	1974 Scrap metal recovery[18] (tonnes)	Fraction of existing recycle lost in total (Table 15.6)	Total 'losses' (tonnes)	Fraction of existing recycle 'lost' but recoverable (Table 15.6)	Recoverable 'losses' (i.e. unexploited) (tonnes)
Aluminium	215 600	0·67	144 500	0·53	114 300
Copper	254 000	0·64	162 600	0·58	147 300
Lead	199 000	1·38	274 600	0·55	109 500
Zinc	85 000	(6·14)	—	0·5 (assumed)	42 500
Iron and steel	12 000 000 (1972)	0·72	8 600 000	0·42	5 000 000

examples include iron and steel (q.v.) for which over thirty chemical production methods have been seriously proposed; recycling of steel pickle liquor to recover iron and regenerate acid (well over 100 different methods);[19,20] and reclamation of high-value non-ferrous metals from effluent treatment residues (see Chapter 9). For the present, however, the secondary metal industries rely almost exclusively on traditional pyrometallurgy for separation and purification.

Aluminium

Aluminium, of all the non-ferrous metals, offers the greatest inducement for recycling. The growth rate for aluminium over the last ten years is around 9% per annum[21] and this trend is expected to continue to the end of the century. In comparison, the growth rates for most other non-ferrous metals have been around 4% to 5% per annum, while for lead and tin there has been very little growth; this trend is also expected to continue. The second important inducement to recycle is the fact that the energy required to recycle aluminium and alloys is only 5% of that required to produce virgin metal.[22] As the energy cost is particularly high for aluminium production from ores, this saving not only offers considerable economic advantage but aids conservation of energy.

On a worldwide basis, 27% of aluminium produced is from recycled scrap, whereas in the UK the figure is nearer 40%.[21] This difference is not unique to aluminium and may be explained by several factors including greater efficiency, UK traditions of recycling, absence until recently of primary production facilities, scrap import/export imbalance, greater emphasis on manufacturing with consequent scrap generation, and slower growth rate of the UK economy resulting in a greater proportion of old or obsolete scrap. Currently around 500 000 tonnes of aluminium and alloys are produced annually in the UK of which about 200 000 tonnes is from reclaimed scrap. The organisation of the industry is set out in Figure 15.5.

The two basic sources of secondary material are classified as essentially new scrap, arising from manufacturing processes or operations, and old scrap, arising from obsolete products. In the UK, new and old scrap arise in roughly equal proportions. In addition, some in-plant scrap may be recycled internally and not enter the external market. The secondary aluminium industry is shown in more detail in Figure 15.6, which also outlines the main end uses of the aluminium produced. The estimated lives of some aluminium products are given in Table 15.9.

Since a considerable proportion of the aluminium produced is used in the form of a wide range of alloys, the impurities and alloying elements play a significant role in the secondary metal industry, most of whose output is in the form of alloys. Various types of scrap and the contaminants are shown in Table 15.10.

TABLE 15.8 SUMMARY AND IDEALISED VALUES OF ANNUAL TOTAL AND RECOVERABLE UNEXPLOITED ('LOST') METALS IN THE UK (from Tables 15.4–15.7)

	Approximate value early 1977 virgin metal (£/tonne)	Total losses				Recoverable losses			
		Table 15.4 (tonnes)	Table 15.7 (tonnes)	Total (tonnes)	Value as new metal (£ million)	Table 15.3 (tonnes)	Table 15.6 (tonnes)	Total (tonnes)	Value as new metal (£ million)
Aluminium	600	250	144 500	144 750	87	125	114 300	114 425	69
Copper	800	3 210	162 600	165 810	133	942	147 300	148 242	119
Iron/steel	70	73 500	8 600 000	8 670 000	607	18 810	5 000 000	5 020 000	351
Lead	400	1 020	274 600	275 620	110	279	109 500	109 500	44
Zinc	400	13 490	(521 200)	(534 690)	(214)	3 298	42 500	45 798	19
Total value as new metal, £ Millions					1151				602
Total value as scrap metal, £ Millions (approximately)					570				300

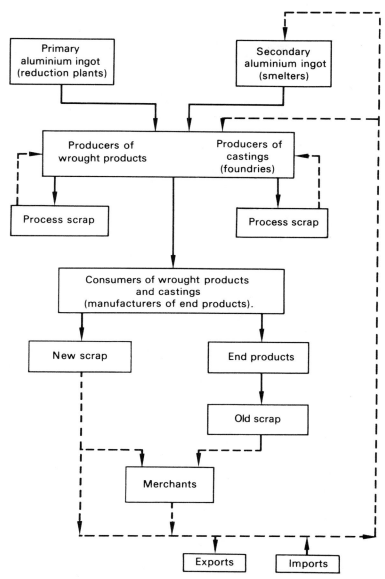

Fig. 15.5 Flow of aluminium scrap

Recycling Technology

The wide range of compositions and large number of aluminium alloys require a detailed classification system. There are eight main groups covering well over a hundred different specifications. Ideally the raw material would be uncontaminated scrap of one alloy only, but this is impractical and groups of alloys

TABLE 15.9 USES AND AVERAGE LIFE OF THE MAJOR ALUMINIUM PRODUCTS

	Estimated life (years)
Cars	11
Buses and coaches	15
Land Rovers	15
Goods vehicles	8
Rail	30
Marine	25
Aircraft	15
Freight containers	10
Caravans	20
Other transport	15
Building	20
Foil	< 1
Other packaging	< 1
Household, office and medical	15
Hollow-ware	15
Litho sheet	< 1
Other engineering and industrial plant	30
Beer barrels	15
Other chemical and food plant	25
Electrical equipment	30
Defence	25
Miscellaneous	15
Unidentified	15

TABLE 15.10 TYPES OF ALUMINIUM SCRAP AND TYPICAL CONTAMINANTS

Description	Major alloy type	Typical contaminants
Old scrap		
Castings, automobile pistons, engine parts	Casting alloys	Steel, brass, zinc, magnesium, paint, oil, grease
Building scrap	Wrought alloys	Steel, copper wire, paint, plastics, rubber
Cables, domestic utensils	Pure Al	Steel core wires, handles
Vehicle bodies	Al-Mn, Al-Mg-Si	Rivets, bolts, paint, plastic
Packaging material	Pure Al, Al-Mn or Al-Mg	Lead and tin foil, paper, plastic, lacquer
General engineering scrap	All alloys	Any of above
New scrap		
Sheet cuttings, trimmings	Wrought alloys	Steel, stainless steel
Extrusions, discards	Wrought alloys	Lubricants
Turnings, millings, borings	Cast or wrought alloys	Steel, brass, titanium, magnesium, lubricants
Castings, pistons	Casting alloys	Steel, brass inserts
Drosses	Cast or wrought alloys	Oxides, sand, fluxes

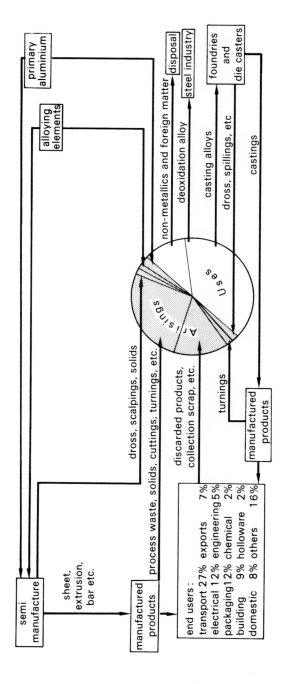

Fig. 15.6 Aluminium uses and recycling

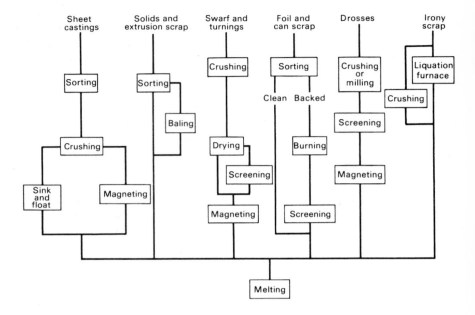

Fig. 15.7 Types of aluminium scrap and treatment processes

tend to be treated together and refined to give a desired product. Scrap therefore requires sorting and some pretreatment to prepare the metal in a form suitable for charging to the smelter. A summary of the main types of scrap and pretreatment processes is given in Figure 15.7.

There are two basic types of refining operation: removal of non-metallic contamination, mainly aluminium oxide and hydrogen from moisture; and removal of undesired alloyed elements, such as magnesium particularly and also sodium and calcium.

Aluminium oxide forms immediately when metal contacts air and the thickness of the film increases as the temperature increases. Smelting of scrap metal must, therefore, be carried out with the minimum of contact with air, particularly for scrap of small particle size and/or large surface area. Molten salt fluxes are normally used; the oxide collects in the flux and increases its viscosity, so that regular replacement of the molten salts is necessary, depending on the oxide content of the scrap. Hydrogen is removed as a consequence of fluxing and magnesium removal and no special treatment is necessary.

Magnesium is removed as oxide, chloride or fluoride. Oxide formation by addition of air is cheap but inefficient and chloride or fluoride processes are orthodox practice. The chloride process uses aluminium chloride or direct injection of chlorine gas and the fluoride process uses aluminium fluoride, or sometimes cryolite or sodium silicofluoride. In all cases magnesium chloride or fluoride is formed, which combines with the flux. None of the reactions is very efficient, particularly at low magnesium levels; various devices are included to improve both rate and extent of reaction, including rotation, mechanical agitation and nitrogen gas bubbling.

There are three main types of furnace, rotary, well and electric induction. The rotary furnace is popular because of its efficiency. Capacity is from 1 to 10 or exceptionally 20 tonnes. Operation is by melting the flux, adding the aluminium-containing material and proceeding with contaminant removal until an acceptable level is attained. Alloying elements are then added to the required specification and the melt is cast. The well furnace is widely used in North America and has capacities from 10 to 100 tonnes. It has the advantage not only of larger batches but also of a lower surface area and lower operating temperature, which reduces flux and energy requirements. Operation is otherwise similar to the rotary furnace. The induction furnace is the most recent introduction and is more flexible in operation.

Environmental Effects

From the outline description of the smelting processes, it is apparent that pollution control is a serious problem. Control of fume from degreasing and de-oiling of swarf is achieved by an after-burner. Provision may also be made for grit removal and dust cleaning equipment.

Salt fume is removed by filters, electrostatic separators or wet scrubbers. Magnesium removal by chlorine addition causes fume that is most efficiently removed by scrubbing with aqueous caustic soda to remove both chlorine and magnesium chloride. This produces a wet effluent which also requires satisfactory disposal. This can be avoided with the new fumeless methods that have been developed.

Solid waste is also produced in the slags, spent fluxes and drosses. Some fluxes and drosses can be recycled after processing, but some solid waste remains to be disposed of. This has traditionally been tipped, but in the UK recent legislation has necessitated re-examination of the problem.

The severity of the pollution prevention requirements is illustrated by the fact that the cost of pollution control can be about 75% of the cost of the basic smelting plant.

Copper

Copper, one of the oldest known metals, has been recycled since the Bronze Age. It combines valuable mechanical and electrical properties with unique aesthetic appeal. The predicted growth rate in copper for the next 30 years is around 4·2% per annum, the current 40% contribution of scrap to total copper

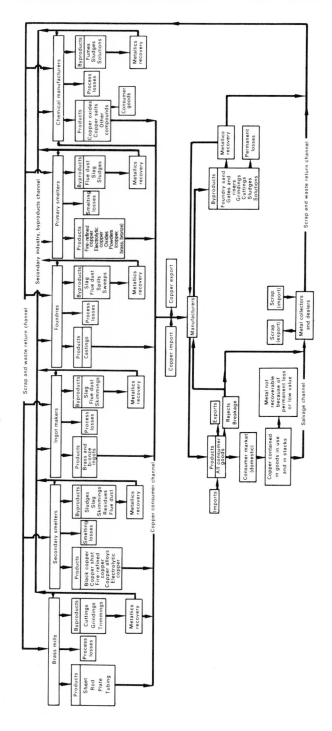

Fig. 15.8 Flow of copper-base alloy scrap to consumers

production increasing as virgin supplies diminish. Alternatively, costs and scarcity may lead to increased substitution.

There is a wide variety of copper-bearing wastes and scrap, ranging from high-grade electrolytic scrap that only requires remelting or electrolysis to produce top-grade copper, down to low-grade drosses and chemicals which require a full smelting and refining operation (Table 15.11). About half of all copper produced goes to the electrical industry, and insulated cable is the largest single source of secondary copper. Secondary alloys such as brasses, bronzes and gun metal are also significant, as are copper products from the transport and building industries. A complete list of sources would be very extensive, but scrap can be simply classified as (i) new or process scrap arising from offcuts, punchings, swarf and (ii) old scrap arising from building demolition and automobile scrapping. These arise in roughly equal proportions.

TABLE 15.11 SOURCES OF SECONDARY COPPER

	New scrap	Old scrap
Copper (high-grade; greater than 90% copper)	Offcuts, trimmings, punchings, swarf	Water tanks, water supply pipes, copper boilers
Alloys	Offcuts, trimmings, punchings, swarf	Industrial scrap, e.g. heat exchangers, valves, marine scrap
Cable and other electrical	Rejects, damaged products	Overhead conductors, cable
Mixed (40–75% copper)	Rich drosses and skimmings	Mixed scrap, unsortable scrap, electronic scrap
Low-grade (12–30% copper)	Skimmings, ashes, residues, dross	Copper-clad steel, automobile radiators
Wastes	Miscellaneous processing waste	Electroplating sludges, contaminated chemicals, catalysts, some clad materials

The copper industry is significantly affected by material substitution resulting from unpredictability of supply and price fluctuation in the primary industry. Examples include the use of aluminium cables for power transmission, printed circuits and miniaturisation in electronic fields; stainless steel and aluminium piping; polyester-impregnated glass-fibre-moulded hot-water tanks in domestic water-supply systems. Secondary copper industry prices closely follow movements in the primary industry, but also vary with supply and demand and with quality. The scrap merchant may be just a collector of scrap, a dealer or intermediary, or he may offer a comprehensive service of collection, buying, sorting, classifying and selling. (Scrap merchants usually handle all scrap metal, both ferrous and non-ferrous, although there is probably a tendency for specialisation.)

Recycling Technology

Pyrometallurgical Processes

The secondary copper industry relies mainly on pyrometallurgical processes to smelt and refine the metal and alloys. In the UK there are four or five major secondary refiners who can handle most copper-bearing materials and process them in economically sized equipment to give a copper product. In addition there are many more ingot producers who mainly remelt and refine copper alloy scrap to a specified ingot composition. This is essentially a jobbing operation in a free market and is carried out on a much smaller scale of 10 tonne lots down to $\frac{1}{2}$ tonne or even less.

Some materials require pretreatment after sorting. The most important example is cable: the two main processes used to separate copper from the covering material are burning, which is relatively cheap but results in air pollution (smoke and hydrogen chloride from PVC), and the more recently introduced granulation or shredding with subsequent mechanical separation. Cryogenic shredding, molten salt baths and organic solvent leaching have also been proposed, but not practised. In addition to hand sorting, more use is now made of mechanical separation methods such as air classification, eddy current separation, heavy media separation and pinched sluice separation (see Chapter 17).

The principles of secondary copper and alloy refining are shown in Figure 15.9 and a flow sheet of a secondary copper refinery in Figure 15.10. The first and fundamental operation is reduction of copper oxides to copper, together with removal of impurities such as iron, zinc, aluminium and magnesium as a slag. Reduction is effected in a blast furnace by adding coke, forming iron which acts as a reductant; slag formation is achieved by adding sandstone and some limestone to give an iron silicate slag. The 'black' copper produced is very impure and is typically 74% copper, 8% tin, 7% zinc, 8% iron and 3% nickel. The slag has a very low copper content and, after water shotting, has proved very suitable shot-blasting material.

The impure copper is refined in a convertor based on oxidation of impurities. Some scrap is often added together with coke to maintain the temperature. Zinc, some tin and some lead is volatilised and carried out to be recovered from the gas stream. The rest of the tin accumulates in the slag, which is also high in copper, and is returned to the blast furnace. Other impurities, such as arsenic, antimony, remaining lead and some nickel, can be removed by specialised treatments in the convertor. There are two main types of convertor, based on side-blowing and top-blowing, and the latter may also rotate.

The converted copper is about 98–99% pure, the main impurities being nickel, lead, tin and antimony. The metal is cast into anodes and electrolytically refined to pure copper. Nickel is recovered from the electrolyte as nickel sulphate, and the anode slimes are sold for their precious-metal content. Some copper scrap can be directly electrolysed, but control of impurity levels may be very difficult.

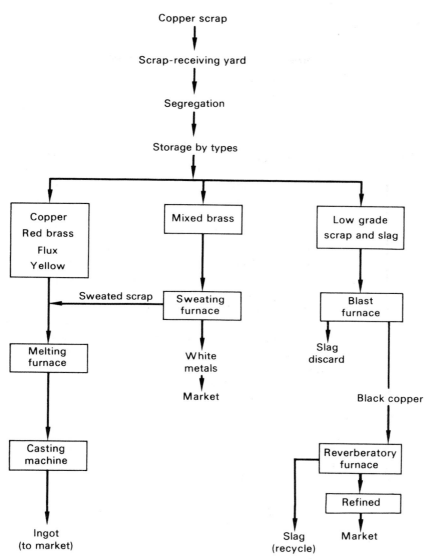

Fig. 15.9 Processing of secondary copper

The ingot producer often employs a reverberatory furnace as this is the most flexible, able to handle a wide feed size-range as well as low grades of scrap. Impurities are removed by oxidation and slag formation with added flux. The actual conditions of operation depend on the feed composition and the product required. Oxygen-assisted melting has been introduced recently with qualified success. Other types of furnace used include the rotary, with lower cost and flexibility, electric induction furnaces for high-grade alloys (particularly bronzes) and a range of specialised rocking and crucible furnaces.

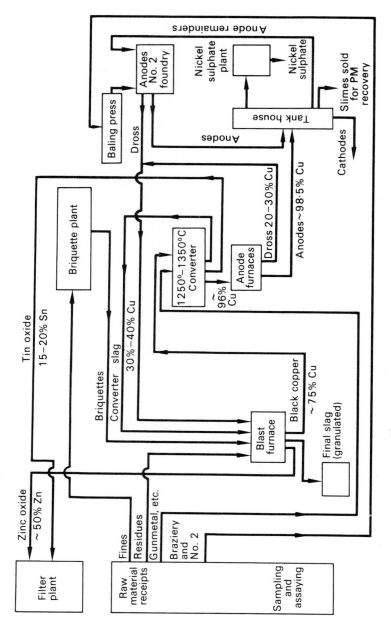

Fig. 15.10 Flowsheet of UK secondary copper refinery

Hydrometallurgical Processes

Aqueous dissolution to separate and recover copper from copper-bearing materials such as sludge, slag, dross as well as metal scrap is an established technology. The last ten to fifteen years have seen a great many new proposals for hydrometallurgical extraction, purification and recovery of copper as well as other metals. The attraction of aqueous processing is that highly selective leaching agents may be used and recovery is relatively easy and virtually complete. The possibilities are wide-ranging (see Further Reading).

Basically, leaching may be carried out with any of the mineral acids to give an acid salt solution or with ammonia to give a complex ammine, which is more selective. Pressure leaching may also be used with either system to improve the reaction rate and make the dissolution more selective, for example with complex copper–nickel–zinc scrap. Other possibilities include cyanidation to give an alkaline aqueous solution, and ammonium sulphate with chromic acid. In all leaching reactions it is possible in principle to dissolve either the copper or the impurities.

Once copper is in solution, a large number of separation methods are available for purification, if necessary, and recovery. The more common purification processes include solvent extraction, ion exchange and precipitation. If the initial dissolution is sufficiently selective, purification is unnecessary and the copper can be recovered by reduction. The traditional method of reduction is by cementation on scrap or sponge iron, but this gives an impure copper powder that has to be smelted.

Electrowinning is another method which incorporates a measure of separation and can give a high-grade metal product. The newest technique is hydrogen pressure precipitation which gives a consistent high-quality copper powder suitable for direct use.[23] This technology was developed for nickel and copper recovery from sulphide ores, but is applied instead to a metallic feedstock (Figure 15.11). The hydrometallurgy of copper ammine complexes is well known. This has been developed to recover pure copper from copper-bearing scrap by atmospheric ammonium carbonate leaching in air.[24] The soluble copper ammonium carbonate solution is purified and the copper recovered as powder by pressure hydrogen precipitation. Such processes are applicable to secondary copper but not yet widely used. Separation tends to be more complete than by pyrometallurgical recovery and costs are roughly comparable, but tight profit margins and the conservatism of the industry are likely to delay introduction of the new methods.

Modern technology produces wastes that the traditional secondary industry cannot easily handle, such as the spent etchant from manufacture of printed circuit boards which can either be acid or ammoniacal and is usually quite rich in copper. Recovery may be by cementation or electrowinning; alternatively, if a suitable market is available, copper chemicals may be produced. Another example is the recovery of copper and other metals from plating wastes (Chapters 7 and 9).

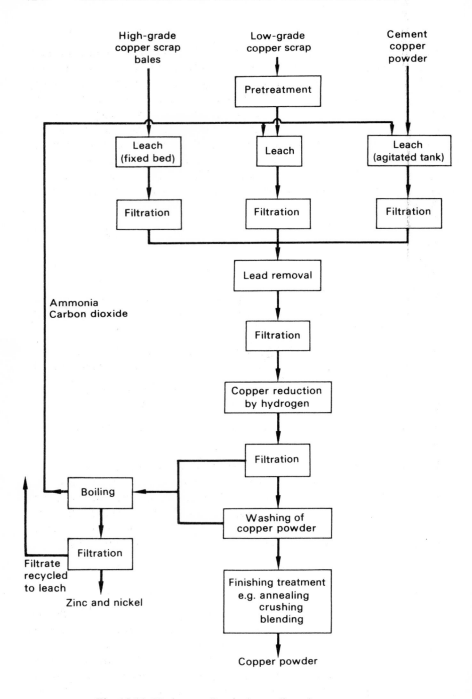

Fig. 15.11 Hydrometallurgical recycling of copper

Environmental Effects

Traditional pyrometallurgical smelting and refining produce mainly gaseous wastes as furnace fume: about 15 tonnes of waste gas are generated per tonne of anode copper; under some circumstances, 40 tonnes gas per tonne copper.

The gases are first cooled to allow filtration to be carried out. Heat recovery causes too many problems of corrosion, deposits and blockage and is not usually practised. Simple, easily maintained air- or water-irrigated coolers are usually used. Filtration is often by cyclone and bag filters. A wide variety of materials is likely to be present and may cause corrosion or form deposits that prevent effective pollution control; these include zinc, zinc oxide, zinc oxychloride; tin, tin oxide; lead, lead oxides; antimony; arsenic; cadmium; chlorine; hydrogen chloride; sulphur oxides.

Iron and Steel

In the UK about 52% of all iron and steel produced is derived from scrap; in 1977 this amounted to about 12 million tonnes per year, but demand is currently lower. There are three main categories of scrap:

Internal (home, in-house, circulating, revert)	Scrap that never leaves the works, such as offcuts, damaged and off-specification material
Process (new, prompt, industrial)	Scrap that is waste or reject material from fabricators and other users
Capital (old, obsolete, post-consumer)	Scrap that has finished its working life, such as cars, industrial machinery, ships

There are many grades of scrap with an established price structure that is subject to market fluctuation. Top-grade scrap is known as heavy scrap; the lowest, known as destructor scrap, is often baled, can have a very low iron content and may contain a high level of tramp elements which are difficult or impossible to remove from the recycled steel, as well as non-metallics such as glass, paper or rubble. A list of the main grades is given in Table 15.12.

Recycling Technology

Almost all scrap iron and steel is reprocessed pyrometallurgically although serious attempts have been made to employ hydrometallurgy. Modern basic oxygen steelmaking technology requires a certain level of scrap for cooling during oxygen-blowing at a level of about 30% of the molten iron charge. As each batch is carefully controlled for a specific end use, careful control of the scrap is also necessary to avoid contamination with tramp elements that are impossible or difficult to remove. Other processes producing steel from molten

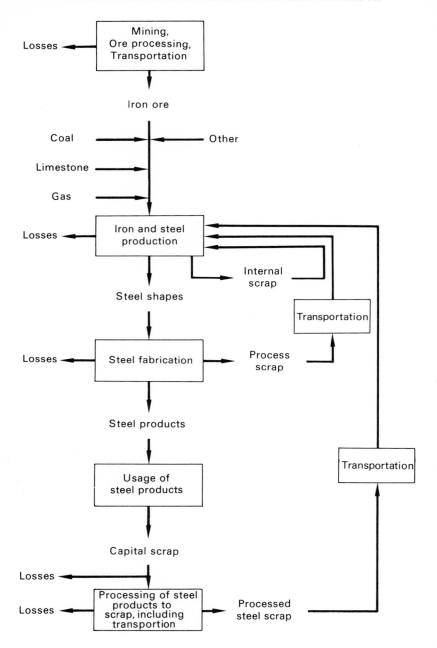

Fig. 15.12 Simplified flow diagram of steel supply system showing major recycle loops

TABLE 15.12 UK IRON- AND STEEL-MAKING SCRAP SPECIFICATIONS

1   **Heavy steel scrap** (but excluding box sections and hollow material) not less than 10 mm thick, in sizes not exceeding (a) 1·50 m × 0·5 m, (b) 1·10 m, or (c) 0·60 m × 0·50 m, free from wrought iron, alloy and all deleterious material.

2   **Heavy wrought iron and steel scrap,** in sizes not exceeding (a) 1·50 m × 0·5 m, (b) 1·10 m × 0·50 m, or (c) 0·60 m × 0·50 m (but may include properly cut heavy motor chassis frames), free from alloy, cast iron and all deleterious material.

3   **Medium wrought iron and steel scrap,** not less than 3 mm thick, in sizes not exceeding 0·80 m × 0·50 m (including any sheared piping) free from all deleterious material.

4   **Compressed new steel,** in works furnace sizes, free from coated, tinned, galvanised and all deleterious material.

5   **Compressed old wrought iron and steel,** in works furnace sizes, free from coated, tinned, galvanised, enamelled and all deleterious material.

6   **Old light wrought iron and steel,** suitable for pressing; free from coated, tinned, enamelled, galvanised and all deleterious material.

7   **Short, heavy or crushed steel turnings,** free from bushy, alloy and non-ferrous metal.

8   **New loose lightsteel cuttings,** suitable for pressing; free from coated, tinned, galvanised and all deleterious material.

9   **Heavy cast iron scrap,** not less than 13 mm thick, in works furnace sizes, free from burnt.

10   **Light cast iron scrap,** in works furnace sizes, free from burnt.

11   **Cast iron borings,** free from corroded lumps.

12(a) **New production steel scrap,** 1·50 m including cut structural scrap, billet ends, bar ends, etc., not less than 6 mm thick, in sizes not exceeding 1·50 m × 0·60 m and free from alloy and all deleterious material.

12(b) **New production steel scrap,** as 12(a), not exceeding 1·10 m × 0·50 m.

12(c) **New production steel scrap,** as 12(a), not exceeding 0·60 m × 0·30 m.

12(d) **New production clean shovellable steel scrap,** not exceeding 150 mm in any dimension, including new factory sheet clippings, punchings, stampings, etc.

13(a) **Fragmentised scrap—old wrought iron and steel scrap,** fragmentised into pieces, approx. 150 mm max, free of dirt, grindings, swarf, turnings and borings, non-ferrous metals or foreign materials of any kind which adversely affects the performance in respect of the undernoted limits:

     Density—960 kg/m³ minimum

     Metallic yield—minimum 92·0%

Tin content (Sn)	maximum 0·05%
Copper content (Cu)	maximum 0·30%
Sulphur and phosphorus	maximum 0·04% each

13(b) **Fragmentised scrap.** As Spec. 13(a), *except* Density—1040 kg/m³ minimum.

13(c) **Fragmentised scrap.** As Spec. 13(a), *except* Density—1120 kg/m³ minimum.

13(d) **Fragmentised scrap.** As Spec. 13(a), *except* Copper content (Cu)—0·25% maximum.

13(e) **Fragmentised scrap.** As Spec. 13(d), *except* Density—1040 kg/m³ minimum, Copper content (Cu)—0·25% maximum.

13(f) **Fragmentised scrap.** As Spec. 13(d), *except* Density—1120 kg/m³ minimum, Copper content (Cu)—0·25% maximum.

iron and scrap, such as the open hearth, are being phased out. The other significant scrap-processing operation is the electric arc furnace which uses a 100% scrap feed. Again, careful control of the feed materials is essential to produce an acceptable product. This is achieved partly by pre-sorting of the scrap, both by the scrap merchant to maximise his income and also by the steelworks.

The technology and chemistry of steelmaking is complex and relies on thermodynamic equilibria of a range of oxidation and sometimes reduction reactions to convert impurities into insoluble, fusible and less dense compounds known as slag. This floats and may be removed by decantation before or after the metal is poured. Some elements are relatively easy to remove and present few problems in refining, while others are difficult and sometimes impossible to remove by orthodox practice (Table 15.13). It is very important that those impurities that are retained (copper, tin, etc.) should be carefully controlled as, once present in the melt, they cannot be removed, only diluted with uncontaminated molten iron or scrap. There appears to be a risk that the only source of tramp-element-free iron and steel will be from iron ore, since metals such as copper will continue to build up as scrap continues to be recycled. This is likely to lead to increasing stocks of lower-grade scrap as modern design specifies increasingly complex and sophisticated mixtures of metals. There are several ways of overcoming such problems, including good design for recycling and alternative recycling technology.

TABLE 15.13 MOVEMENT OF ELEMENTAL IMPURITIES IN STEELMAKING

Mostly retained in steel	Partially retained in steel	Mostly eliminated from steel
Antimony	Carbon	Aluminium
Arsenic	Chromium	Calcium
Cobalt	Hydrogen	Magnesium
Copper	Lead	Silicon
Molybdenum	Manganese	Titanium
Nickel	Nitrogen	Zinc
Tin	Phosphorus	Zirconium
Tungsten	Sulphur	
	Vanadium	

Alternative Recycling Technology

A considerable amount of research effort has been put into alternative iron and steelmaking processes,[25] which fall into three main groups:

(i) Hydrometallurgical, where the iron-bearing material is dissolved in a mineral acid—hydrochloric, nitric or sulphuric acid.

(ii) Electrolytic, where an oxidation-reduction closed cycle is set up, usually employing ferrous–ferric chloride.

(iii) Vapometallurgical, where a volatile compound of iron, usually the chloride or carbonyl, is vaporised.

Each of these methods is currently used to a limited extent in specialised applications, but not for large-scale production.

A serious attempt to use one of the advanced hydrometallurgical processes was made in the late 1960s when iron powder was in vogue. Peace River Mining and Smelting and the Research Council of Alberta, Canada, put forward a proposal to dissolve iron-bearing material in hydrochloric acid, purify the solution by crystallisation of ferrous chloride and reduce this with hydrogen.[26] A 50 000 tonne/year plant was built at Windsor to take steel scrap from Detroit, just across the Canada/USA border, and process it (Figure 15.13). The plant was never operated and was dismantled shortly afterwards for reasons probably associated with marketing the product, since the processing technology was proven.

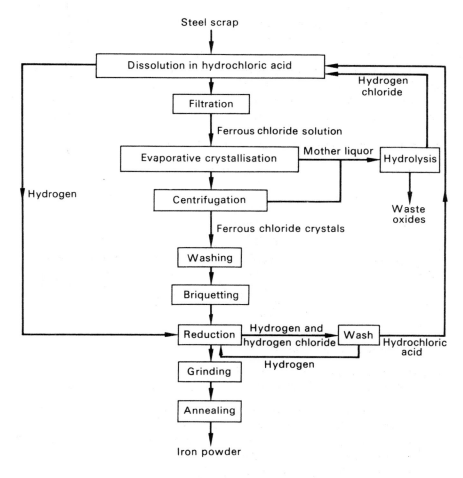

Fig. 15.13 RCA process flow diagram[26]

The principle of chemical recovery of metals is attractive as good separation may readily be obtained, low-grade and low-cost scrap may be employed, high purity of products is usually obtained, and energy consumption can be significantly less than with conventional methods.

Electrolytic recovery of iron has not been seriously promoted since the early part of the century when a series of basically simple processes were tried out as outlined in Figure 15.14.[25] The advantage of electrolytic iron is its high purity and thus greater resistance to corrosion. There are, however, problems of energy cost and economies of scale, but possibilities exist for more specialised products such as high-speed continuous production of iron foil.

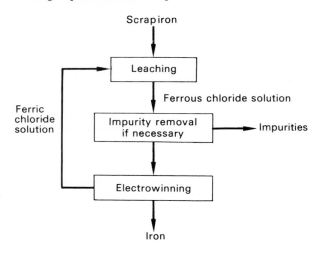

Fig. 15.14 Electrolytic recovery of iron

Ferric chloride has attracted much attention as it has the lowest vaporising/subliming temperature of all the metal chlorides. Many processes based on vaporisation of ferric chloride using chlorine or hydrogen chloride have been proposed and developed to pilot-plant scale.[25] The technology is largely proven. The gaseous ferric chloride may be oxidised or hydrolysed to ferric oxide and chlorine or hydrogen chloride respectively. Alternatively, it may be directly reduced to iron although little work has been carried out on this. The possibilities for iron recovery from low-grade scrap and metal separation from mixed metal waste deserves re-examination.

Iron powder produced by decomposition of iron carbonyl is currently manufactured in small quantities. Costs are very high, and serious technical and safety problems would arise in large-scale operation.[25]

Environmental Effects

Much of the air pollution arising from iron and steel reprocessing occurs as dust and fume. Removal of gas-borne solids is by conventional means:

cyclones, electrostatic precipitators or wet scrubbers are commonly used. The separated dust and fume is largely iron oxide and therefore may be recycled. In an iron and steelworks employing an ore feedstock these solids may be returned via the sinter strand; an electric arc facility cannot recycle the fume so directly, and disposal or sale to an ore-processing works is necessary. Several recovery processes have recently been suggested,[27] such as that shown in Figure 15.15, but few have been installed because of doubtful economic viability. With an electric arc furnace, and to a lesser extent with a steelmaking furnace, any zinc in the scrap, for example as galvanised steel, tends to be vaporised and collects in the dust and fume. Zinc losses in this way have been estimated at around 25 000 tonnes per year; not only is this significant as a loss, but the zinc-laden air is difficult to recycle in iron and steelmaking. This problem is discussed later.

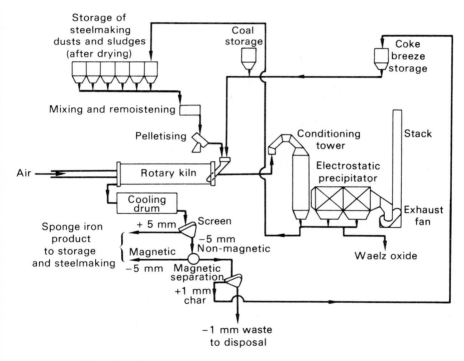

Fig. 15.15 Waelz recycling process for steelmaking dust wastes

Lead

Lead rates fifth in terms of metal consumption in the UK although its growth potential to the end of the century is among the lowest at around 3·5%. The changes in use between 1965 and 1973 are shown in Table 15.14. The most significant product is currently storage batteries, which is seen as a major growth area for

TABLE 15.14 UK LEAD CONSUMPTION (TONNES)

Use	1965	%	1973	%
Cable	132 610	31	45 831	13
Batteries—as metal	42 161	10	54 188	15
Battery—oxides	42 743	10	52 343	14
Tetraethyl lead	36 136	8	54 370	15
Other oxides and compounds	26 731	6	37 129	10
White lead	4 174	1	1 711	<1
Shot	5 817	1	7 411	2
Sheet and pipe	69 069	16	55 312	15
Foil and collapsible tubes	3 700	1	1 521	<1
Other rolled and extruded	5 539	1	863	<1
Solder	15 655	4	16 438	5
Alloys	23 561	6	18 613	5
Miscellaneous	20 351	5	18 391	5
Totals	428 247		364 121	
Of which:				
Imported lead and lead bullion	193 211		160 332	
Scrap lead	235 036		203 789	
% recycled	55%		56%	

lead as a viable alternative is most unlikely to appear for at least 15 to 20 years. This growth is offset by the reduction in use for cables, building, plumbing and fabrication.

The proportion of lead produced from recycled material consistently ran at 55–60% from 1965 to 1973, and is the highest of the more common metals. The extent of recycling for each category of lead identified in Table 15.14 may be roughly estimated as:

Battery lead (total)
Sheet and pipe
} 90–100%

Cable
Foil and tubes
Other rolled and extruded
} around 50%

Tetraethyl lead, etc.
Other oxides and compounds
White lead
Shot
Solder
Alloys
Miscellaneous
} probably ⩽ 10%

Batteries have a high level of recycling and a relatively short life compared with other recoverable lead products. The lead–acid storage battery is currently predicted to have considerable growth potential with the advent of a wide range of prototype electric vehicles. About 80% of all batteries produced are for cars.

Between 5 and 6 million batteries enter the UK market each year either as original equipment on new cars, or as replacements. The average life of a car battery is currently estimated to be 3 years (33 to 39 months) and thus between 1·5 and 2 million batteries are scrapped each year.

The well established secondary lead industry competes little with the primary lead industry as it almost exclusively handles soft and light alloyed lead. This is because a substantial proportion of the output from secondary lead smelters consists of lead and lead alloy approximating to the requirements of battery makers. The price at which lead alloy is sold, which is lower than the value of equivalent virgin elements, maintains the closed market but the difference is insufficient to make separation into components an economically attractive proposition. The whole market moves with changes in primary metal prices, but the margins remain constant. When necessary virgin metals are bought in to supplement the recycled material.

The metallic lead used in a battery is usually an alloy of lead and antimony with traces of arsenic and tin. The antimony content can range from 0% to 15%, depending on the price of antimony and the physical properties required, which vary for different parts of the battery.

Recycling Technology

Battery Lead

Batteries and other lead scrap are usually handled and sorted by scrap merchants before forwarding to the secondary metal smelters for refining. Batteries are usually treated separately by specialist firms for a number of reasons including the size of the market, handling problems of breaking up battery cases and separating metals from non-metals, the complex chemical nature of the lead and lead-containing materials in the battery, and the need to produce both soft lead and an alloy product of specific chemical and physical properties for the battery manufacturer.

The first stage is the breaking up of the battery to discard as much of the waste as possible. In spite of the development of reliable industrial processes to break batteries, traditional handbreaking by scrap merchants continues as fill-in work for quiet periods. Smelters tend to prefer such pre-treated scrap and thus avoid the problem of disposing of the waste and acid that even 'drained' batteries contain. When purchasing whole batteries, the smelter bases his estimate of lead and antimony content of mixed battery scrap on experience.

The range of direct and indirect processes to recover lead for batteries is summarised in Figure 15.16. The Stolberg and Tonolli processes are the most important. Whatever the method of breaking, the collected lead values are smelted in a two-stage process to yield crude soft lead and crude antimonial lead (Figure 15.17). Smaller works employ a rotary furnace to first produce soft lead directly, leaving antimonial slag behind for later reduction with coke or

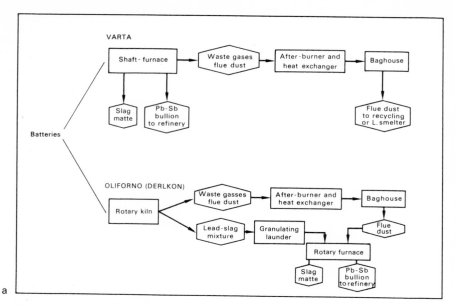

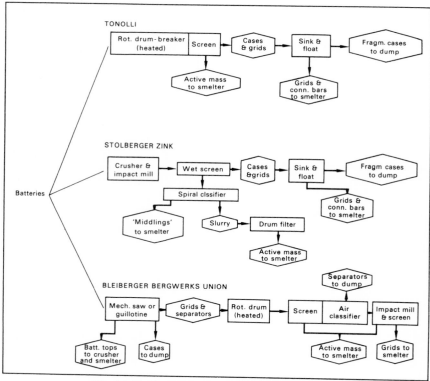

Fig. 15.16 Recovery of lead from batteries
a Direct process
b Indirect process

anthracite fires to give antimonial lead. Greater flexibility is, however, obtained by using two furnaces, a reverberatory to produce soft lead and antimonial slag and a blast furnace to reduce the latter. Both soft lead and antimonial lead require refining to remove copper (by adding sulphur), arsenic and tin (by adding caustic soda) and antimony from soft lead (by blowing in air) (Figure 15.17).

Other Lead Recycling Processes

Soft lead is relatively easy to melt and refine. Copper, zinc, and cadmium are removed by adding sulphur to form a dross. Copper dross is particularly valued, since copper is much more valuable than lead and can represent a

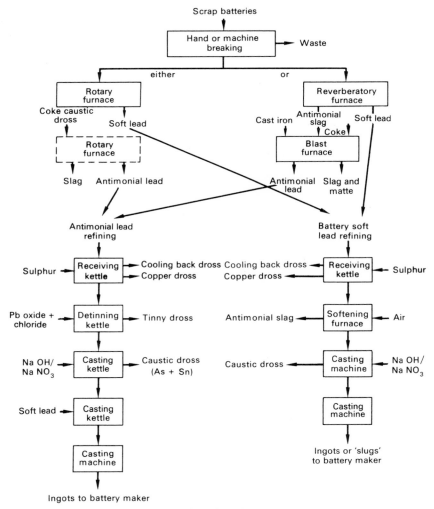

Fig. 15.17 Smelting of battery lead

TABLE 15.15 TYPICAL LEAD–ACID CAR BATTERY COMPOSITION

	Plastic case			Hard rubber case		
	(wt kg)		(wt %)	(wt kg)		(wt %)
Case and lid		0·8	5		7·5	31
Separators and splash guards		0·3	2		0·3	1
Metal: total		11·1	64		11·1	47
grids	3·7		21	3·7		16
paste as metal	3·7		21	3·7		16
paste as oxide	3·2		19	3·2		13
connectors	0·5		3	0·5		2
sulphate*	(1·7)		—	(1·7)		—
Electrolyte		5	29		5	21
		17·2	100		23·9	100

* Sulphation in a spent battery varies considerably: a typical figure is around 15% of total metal content. This is not included in the above analysis.

useful bonus. Tin, arsenic and antimony are removed by preferential oxidation using caustic soda.

Lead–tin alloys are widely used for solder and printing metal. Compositions are complex and this branch of the industry tends to be versatile, working in small lots and with a quick turnover. This practice provides the necessary versatility. Contaminant metals are removed by the methods outlined above but on a small scale, using simple kettles and furnaces.

Antimony supply is erratic and prices can change dramatically: leady antimony recycling is a source of antimony for alloying and refinement is either by oxidation of antimonial lead, to give a high antimony slag for subsequent reduction, or by carefully controlled crystallisation of a leady antimony eutectic.

Tin

The consumption of tin is largely controlled by its greatest single outlet as tinplated steel. Nearly half of all tin production is to meet this demand, while much of the remainder is used for alloys (Table 15.16). Statistics suggest that only about 5% of tin production worldwide is from recycled metal. The forecast growth in tin consumption over the next 30 years is minimal, perhaps reaching 1% per annum.

The thickness of tin coating on steel has been progressively reduced: the tin content of tinplated steel is now only about 0·5–0·6%. At these levels, not only is there reduced economic incentive to recover the tin, but the technical problems increase. Recovery is still practised in the UK, mainly on new process scrap from the tin-can producing industry. However, use of all-aluminium cans is increasing. An additional incentive to de-tin steel is that steel producers will only permit very low levels of tin in scrap steel: steel containing tin suffers a price disadvantage of around £5 per tonne.

TABLE 15.16 USES AND DISTRIBUTION OF TIN IN THE UK (1975)

	%
Tinplate	39·5
Tinned copper wire	3·0
Other tinning application	5·5
Solder	7·5
Alloy (white metal, bronze, gunmetal, other)	35·5
Wrought tin	1·0
Chemical and other	8·0

Almost all secondary tin is consumed by tin–lead alloy producers, of whom the most important are the solder producers. It can be seen from Table 15.17 that a wide variety of impurities must be tolerated both in the metallic and oxidised states. The secondary tin industry is also one of the most complex in material flows, as it is based almost entirely on alloys and interacts closely with the lead and copper industries.

TABLE 15.17 SOURCES OF SECONDARY TIN

Source	Contaminants
Tinned steel: mainly offcuts from tinplate and coin production (used coins usually too soiled)	Iron, non-metallics
Solder: slag, drosses, grindings, electronic scrap, old radiators	Lead, antimony, chloride fluxes
Bronze: direct recasting	Copper
Secondary copper smelters: slags	Copper, lead, nickel
fume	Zinc, lead
Bearing metal: used and rejected components, machinings	Lead, antimony, copper, aluminium
Tinned copper wire: drosses from tinning pots	Copper, chloride flux, non-metallics
Type metal: currently recycled in-situ, mainly drosses	Lead, antimony
Secondary lead smelter: drosses from tin separation process	Lead, organic
Precious metal scrap	Precious metals
Tin chemicals: spent catalysts, wastes, contaminated chemicals (care needed with highly toxic organotin compounds)	Wide range including precious metals

Recycling Technology

The processes involved are complex, various and not well documented (see Further Reading).

There are essentially two types of operation: (i) smelting, in which oxidised material is reduced by carbon to give liquid slag and metal; (ii) melting metal, in which some separation may be obtained by selective melting. Rotary furnaces are most widely used for their versatility, although reverberatory furnaces, blast furnaces and electric furnaces are also employed. Selective melting is traditionally carried out on a gently sloping hearth furnace, the molten tin being allowed to drain away. The ash or residue is high in tin and is smelted. A highly-skilled alternative metal-refining process is selective solidification, partly by means of the formation of complex alloys and crystal structures. The equipment is based on hearth furnaces or iron kettles but there is a wide variety to suit, for example, different feedstocks and product specifications.

Zinc and cadmium are removed by selective oxidation or by adding chlorine as gas or chloride salts. Arsenic is removed with molten caustic soda. Bismuth and lead may be removed by vacuum distillation, although this process has not been widely adopted. In all cases the impurities are removed as liquid slags from the surface of molten metal.

An alternative method of refining is by electrolysis which yields a tin–lead alloy very largely free from both metallic and non-metallic impurities. Both simple and complex aqueous and molten salt baths have been successfully used. Electrowinning is also used to reclaim tin from the aqueous solutions produced by leaching tin-plate with caustic soda.

TABLE 15.18 REPORTED UK ZINC CONSUMPTION (1971) (thousands of tonnes)

Use	Virgin zinc	Secondary zinc	Total
Galvanising	96·5	2·1	98·6
Alloys: brass	56·4	39·7	96·1
die-casting	67·4	2·0	69·4
	123·8	41·7	165·5
Chemicals: zinc dust	3·4	12·2	15·6
oxide	21·0	14·3	35·3
other	2·9	10·5	13·4
	27·3	37·0	64·3
Semi-fabrications	26·1	0·3	26·4
Total	273·7	81·1 (= 23% of total consumption)	354·8

Zinc

Zinc is perhaps best known as a sacrificial metal in protecting iron and steel from corrosion, although its major use is in the production of alloys as shown in Table 15.18. Also shown are the other main uses and the balance between the consumption of secondary and primary metal, giving an overall figure of around 23% for the contribution of secondary zinc to total zinc production. Predicted zinc consumption to the end of the century is estimated to follow copper closely at around 4% per annum.

Only a relatively small fraction of zinc is used in semi-fabricated forms, unlike copper and lead, and a correspondingly small quantity of scrap is available. Much of the secondary zinc available is consumed without conversion to high-grade metal, for example as brass, oxide and other chemicals.

Secondary zinc arises in several main forms:

Metal and oxide dust or fume from other non-ferrous and ferrous metal smelting and refining operations.
Drosses, skimmings, ashes, blowings from galvanising.
Galvanised steel scrap as new clippings or old scrap.
Alloys, mainly brass.
Chemical residues, including oxide, chloride and sulphate.

Other than brass, which accounts for around half of recycled zinc, the main use is for zinc chemicals. Most of the remainder is converted to zinc dust, zinc oxide, chloride or sulphate. Diecasting alloys may not be recycled outside the diecasting plant and the small extent of recycling is entirely internal. Semi-fabrications go to three main outlets: dry battery cans, and architectural and printing applications. There is some internal recycling in all these fields. Little information is available on old and process scrap arisings in this area but they are believed to be insignificant.

Recycling Technology

Recycling of zinc centres on the manufacture of a relatively small range of chemicals (Figure 15.18). Zinc dust is manufactured by vaporising zinc in a closed system. High metallic zinc content dross from galvanisation is often used. Around 80% of zinc dust is produced from secondary zinc.

Oxide may be produced in three ways. The 'direct' method reduces crude oxide, such as ashes from galvanising, in a furnace which is subject to an air blast. The zinc is reduced, oxidised and carried out of the furnace to be recovered in a bag filter. Purity is not as high as with the other processes. The 'indirect' process starts with metallic zinc which is vaporised, oxidised in the vapour phase and collected. Purity and quality are controlled by selection of raw material and conditions of operation. Zinc oxide may also be produced chemically by precipitation from aqueous solution as the hydroxide or basic carbonate. The precipitate is filtered and calcined to oxide. All the zinc oxide produced is used in a wide variety of irrecoverable applications such as paint.

Chloride is manufactured by dissolution of low-grade residues such as ashes and skimmings in hydrochloric acid. After filtration the solution is evaporated to the required strength and is marketed as solution, owing to the deliquescent nature of zinc chloride. Sulphate is produced in an analogous way using sulphuric acid. Purity can be a problem due to the frequent presence of chloride fluxes in the raw material which give rise to chloride contamination.

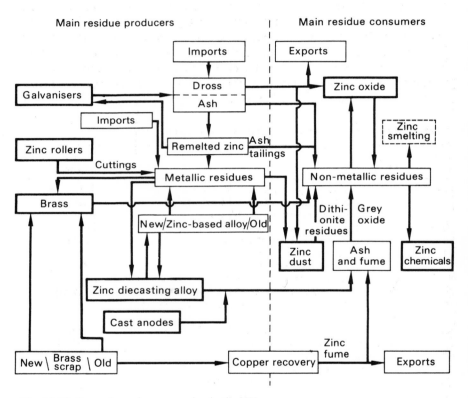

Fig. 15.18 Secondary zinc processing in the UK
        Boxes in heavy outline indicate main sources of secondary zinc and zinc residues in the UK

The recent attention paid to physical sorting systems for household refuse and scrapped vehicles is likely to produce a new zinc-rich fraction for recycling. This may be a mixture of metals or a concentrate from which zinc can be recovered by volatilisation as metal or oxide, or by melting. A recent development, still at the demonstration stage, is a proposal to recover zinc from electric arc furnace fume by hydrometallurgical extraction with sodium hydroxide.[28]

Other Metals

All metals are recycled to a certain extent. In general, the more valuable a metal, the greater the degree of recycling. In the precious metal industry, for example, it can be worthwhile to launder overalls and door mats to recover metals. Since dissipative usage as in paints, additives, insecticides, or preservatives makes reclamation impossible, the most expensive metals such as beryllium and tantalum tend to be used in reclaimable products. Table 15.19 lists some other metals with brief comments on uses and level of recycling. Each metal and sometimes each industry has its own technology for recycling, which can be very specific. The techniques are often confidential and economics dictate what and how much is reclaimed. Almost 100% recycling is obligatory in certain specialist applications involving radioactive substances. Good recovery is also desirable of those metals which are particularly toxic, for example antimony, arsenic, beryllium, cadmium and mercury.

TABLE 15.19 LESS COMMON METALS: USES AND RECYCLING

Metal	Use	Proportion recycled
Antimony	Alloyed with lead in lead–acid batteries	Very high
	Alloyed with lead and tin in tin type metal	Very high
	Paints; flameproofing compounds	nil
Arsenic	Alloyed with lead in lead–acid batteries	High
	Miscellaneous alloys where special properties are required	Moderate
	Insecticides; preservatives	nil
Barium	Pyrotechnics; pigment; medical	nil
Beryllium	Nuclear industry; special alloys both ferrous and non-ferrous in aerospace and specialised industries	Very high
Bismuth	Alloys with steel and aluminium	Moderate
	Low-melting-point alloys, e.g. fire-protection devices	Moderate
	Pharmaceuticals	nil
Cadmium	Batteries; electroplating for corrosion protection; alloys in bearings	High
	Paints	nil
Chromium	Alloying metal, particularly stainless steel	High
	Electroplating	Low
Cobalt	Special alloys, ferrous and non-ferrous	Very high
	Pigment	nil
Columbium (niobium)	Low-level alloying element	Low (due to dissipation)
Gold	Wide range of industrial applications, many electronic	Very high
	Jewellery	Minimum
	In-plant scrap and residues	Maximum
Indium	Low-melting-point alloys; special steels; electronics	High

TABLE 15.19(*Cont'd*)

Metal	Use	Proportion recycled
Magnesium	Alloys with aluminium and other non-ferrous metals	High
	Galvanic anticorrosion applications	nil
Manganese	Alloying metal for ferrous and non-ferrous metals, widely used	Low
Mercury	Scientific instruments; electrical switchgear	High
	Paints; insecticides	nil
Molybdenum	Alloying metal widely used in high-strength, high-temperature applications	High
Nickel	Alloying material in ferrous and non-ferrous applications; electroplating; catalysts	High
Palladium	Electronics; catalysts	Very high
Platinum	Electronics; catalysts; corrosion-resistance equipment	Very high
Plutonium	Nuclear industry	Maximum
Rhodium	Electronics; scientific instruments; decorative uses	Low
Silver	Photographic film and papers; electronics; jewellery; catalysts; electroplating	High
Tantalum	Corrosion-resistant equipment—often cladding; electronics	Very high
Tellurium	Low-level alloy in ferrous and non-ferrous applications; electronics	Low
Thallium	Scientific instruments	Low
Titanium	Corrosion-resistant alloys	High
	Pigment; paint; paper; plastics	Minimal
Tungsten	Light bulbs; electronics; cutting tools; dies; special steel alloys	Moderate to high
Uranium	Nuclear industry	Maximum
Vanadium	Alloy in special steels	Moderate to high
Zirconium	Nuclear industry	High

Recycling Vehicles

Over a million cars, nearly as many as are put on the road, are scrapped each year in the UK. This represents a significant part of the steel production cycle. In addition to the basic ferrous metal, metals such as lead, copper and aluminium are recycled as well as spare parts.

A scrapped vehicle may go to a scrap yard for recovery of spare parts and preliminary sorting into ferrous and non-ferrous materials and thence to a scrap merchant. Alternatively it may go directly to a scrap merchant for breaking and sorting into ferrous material, non-ferrous metal, and waste such as tyres, upholstery and windows. At any one time there are probably around a million vehicles, or a year's supply, being held, stored or processed.

British Jeffrey Diamond

BJD 789 Autoshredder Plant shreds scrapped cars and separates them into ferrous and non-ferrous fractions

The scrap merchant may be able to handle all the ferrous and non-ferrous materials and sell them to the steel works and secondary metal refineries. Alternatively he may only carry out a preliminary sorting and pass the metals on to more specialised merchants. The ferrous part of the car is usually compressed into bales of low-grade scrap for subsequent smelting. The level of impurities is highly dependent on the degree of separation carried out by merchant and scrap yard and the practical limitation imposed by current automobile design and construction. At worst, the bales comprise a complete car without any separation of non-ferrous metals and include, for example, battery, wiring and possibly aluminium cylinder head.

One survey of bales showed that on average the ferrous content was 86%, ranging from 64 to 90%, and copper 0·48%, ranging from 0 to 2·4%. The variability and unpredictability of these tramp elements reduce the value of the scrap and limit its market. The composition of a typical car reaching the scrapyards and of the non-ferrous fraction separated after shredding are shown in Table 15.20.

TABLE 15.20 COMPOSITION OF A TYPICAL CAR

	kg	%
Steel	540	63·0
Cast iron	140	16·0
Aluminium	13	1·0
Copper	11	1·0
Zinc	6	0·5
Lead	5	0·5
Rubber	71	8·0
Glass	28	3·0
Plastic	48	5·0
Miscellaneous	10	1·0
Non-ferrous fraction after shredding and magnetic separation		
Copper		3·5
Zinc		13·0
Aluminium		4·0
Lead		1·5
Iron		12·0
Stainless steel		present
Rubber and other combustibles		24·0
Glass and other combustibles		42·0

There is wide variation with type and make of car and country of origin.

The most significant method of handling scrapped vehicles is the shredder, which can reduce a car to fist-sized lumps of metal in 30–60 seconds. The products are magnetically separated to produce (a) high-ferrous-content scrap and (b) non-ferrous and non-metallic scrap. The former is more consistent and of a higher grade than is obtained by traditional methods and the latter provides a more easily sortable non-ferrous fraction.

Until recently the non-ferrous metal has been hand-sorted, but more efficient recovery has resulted from the development of separation processes based on the different physical properties of materials (see Chapter 17).

An alternative process employs cryogenic embrittlement in liquid nitrogen. At temperatures of around −200°C steel and zinc become very brittle while copper and aluminium are not so affected. This allows baled or compressed scrap to be reduced in size much more readily with less expenditure of mechanical energy. Although of doubtful economic viability, the principle may perhaps be applicable to non-ferrous concentrates or other difficult scrap materials such as insulated cables and complex articles.

References

1. MEADOWS, D. H., MEADOWS, D. L., RANDERS, J. and BEHRENS, W. W. III, *The Limits to Growth*, Earth Island, 1972.
2. DUNHAM, K., *Conservation of Materials*, UKAEA, Harwell, 1974.
3. TIEN, J. K., ARONS, R. M. and CLARK, R. W., *Journal of Metals*, 26, December 1976.
4. CROWTHER, J., *Availability of Metals in the Next Thirty Years*, Conference, Birmingham, Institution of Chemical Engineers, 1972.
5. CLAY, J. A., *Future Developments—A Primary View of the Secondary Non-Ferrous Scrap Industry*, Spring Meeting, Institute of Metals, 1973.
6. CHAPMAN, P. F., in *Conservation of Materials*, UKAEA, Harwell, 1974, p. 125.
7. BRIDGWATER, A. V., *Resource Recovery and Conservation*, 1(2), 115, 1976.
8. BODEN, P. J., *Conservation and Recycling*, 1(1), 119, 1976.
9. Severn-Trent Water Authority, private communication, 1974.
10. CANNING, W., private communication, 1977.
11. FLETCHER, A. W., *Chemistry and Industry*, 414, 5 May 1973.
12. BEVER, M. B., *Conservation and Recycling*, 1(1), 137, 1976.
13. KELLOGG, H. H., *Journal of Metals*, 29, December 1976.
14. Battelle Memorial Institute, *A Study to Identify Opportunities for Increased Solid Waste Utilisation*, National Technical Information Service PB 212730, 1972.
15. REGAN, W. J., JAMES, R. W. and MCLEER, T. J., USEPA Report EPA-SW-45D-72, Environmental Protection Agency, Washington, 1972.
16. PITCHER, D. E., *The Reclamation and Recycling of Aluminium and its Alloys*, University of Nottingham, 1976.
17. WALL, J., Aluminium Federation Committee Paper AS36, December 1975.
18. EVANS, D. B., World Bureau of Metal Statistics, private communication.
19. SWINDIN, N., *Transactions of the Institution of Chemical Engineers*, **22**, 56, 1944.
20. HODGE, W. W., in *Proceedings of the 15th Annual Water Conference of the Engineers' Society of Western Pennsylvania*, 1954, p. 33.
21. *Aluminium—the Recyclable Metal*, Association of Light Alloy Refiners Ltd, 1975.
22. CHAPMAN, P. F., *Metals and Materials*, **8**(2), 107; (6), 311, 1974.
23. BOLDT, J. R., *The Winning of Nickel*, Methuen, 1967.
24. KUNDA, W., VELTMANN, H. and EVANS, D. J. I., in *Copper Metallurgy*, Ehrlich, R. P., (Ed.), AIMM, 1970.
25. BRIDGWATER, A. V., Chemical alternatives to the conventional manufacture of iron and steel, *Symposium on Chemical Engineering in the Iron and Steel Industry, Swansea*, Institution of Chemical Engineers, 1968.
26. GRAVENOR, C. P., GOVETT, G. J. and RIGG, T., *Canadian Institute of Mining Bulletin*, **57**, 421, 1964.
27. TRAICE, F. B., in Proceedings, *The Technology of Reclamation*, Birmingham University, 1975.
28. Cardiff University Industry Centre, private communication, 1977.

Further Reading

Aluminium

BOURCIER, G. F., DALE, K. H. and TESTIN, R. F., recovery of aluminium from solid waste, *Proceedings of the 3rd Mineral Waste Utilisation Symposium*, US Bureau of Mines, 14–16 March 1972.

CHAPMAN, P. F., in *Conservation of Materials*, UKAEA, Harwell, 1974.

DEAN, K. C., VALDEZ, E. G. and BILBREY, J. H., *Recovery of Aluminium from Shredded Municipal and Automotive Wastes*, TMS Paper No. A74–91, Metallurgical Society of AIME, 1974.

EDWARDS, J. D., FRACY, F. C. and JEFFREIES, Z., *Aluminium and its Production*, Vols. I and II, McGraw-Hill, 1930.

PITCHER, D. E., *The Reclamation and Recycling of Aluminium and its Alloys*, University of Nottingham, 1976.

SIEBERT, D. L., *Impact of Technology on the Commercial Secondary Aluminium Industry*, Information Circular 8445, US Bureau of Mines, 1970.

SMITH, F. H., The recovery of aluminium from waste products, in *Disposal of Waste Materials*, Society of Chemical Industry, 1972.

WALL, J., Committee Paper AS 36, Aluminium Federation, 1975.

WINTER, D. G., *Current Industrial Practice in the Recycling of Aluminium in the UK*, Report LR 234, Warren Spring Laboratory, 1976.

WOOD, D., Aluminium, Spring Meeting, Institute of Metals, 1973.

Copper

BISWAS, A. K. and DAVENPORT, W. G., *Extractive Metallurgy of Copper*, Pergamon, 1976.

BOLDT, J. R., *The Winning of Nickel*, Methuen, 1967.

BUTTS, A., *Copper*, Reinhold, 1954.

CHAPMAN, P. F., in *Conservation of Materials*, UKAEA, Harwell, 1974.

COOPER, J. B., *Generation, Collection and Merchanting of Scrap*, Spring Meeting, Institute of Metals, 1973.

EHRLICH, R. P., *Copper Metallurgy*, Extractive Metallurgy Division of the Metallurgical Society of AIME, 1970.

FARTHING, T. W. and LEEDHAM, M. J., Spring Meeting, Institute of Metals, 1973.

JACOBI, J. S., *Reclamation and Recycling of Copper and its Alloys*, Nottingham University, 1976.

SPENDLOVE, M. J., *Methods for Producing Secondary Copper*, Information Circular 8002, US Bureau of Mines, 1961.

Lead

COOPER, J. B., *Generation, Collection and Merchanting of Scrap*, Spring Meeting, Institute of Metals, 1973.

Lead 65, Proceedings of Second International Conference on Lead, Pergamon, 1965.

Lead 68, Proceedings of Third International Conference on Lead, Pergamon, 1968.

Lead 71, Proceedings of Fourth International Conference on Lead, Lead Development Association, 1971.

PEASE, M. E., *Secondary Lead Alloys*, Paper A10, London Chemical Engineering Congress, Institution of Chemical Engineers, 1974.

Various authors, *Lead and Zinc Symposium*, New York, AIME, 1970.

Tin

JACKSON, D. A., *Recovery of Tin and Tin Alloys from Certain Secondary Materials*, AIME Meeting, Dallas, 1963.

MANTELL, C. L., *Tin*, Reinhold, 1949.

POCOCK, M. J. B., *Secondary Tin*, Spring Meeting, Institute of Metals, 1973.

TABLE 16.4 PLASTICS CONSUMPTION BY COUNTRY IN 1974[3]

	Production ('000 tonnes)		Consumption ('000 tonnes)		Consumption (kg/capita)	
	1971	1972	1972	1973	1972	1973
USA	9626	11 784	11 172	12 703	53·10	60·38
Japan	5282	5 766	4 413	5 688	41·28	53·20
West Germany	4837	5 603	4 278	4 928	71·14	81·96
France	1677	2 134	2 198	2 515	42·20	48·29
Italy	1920	2 158	1 758	1 931	31·99	35·13
UK	1605	1 634	1 660	1 859	29·41	32·62

Disposal and treatment methods are summarised in Table 16.5.

The range of alternatives—together with the advantages, disadvantages and costs, when available, is summarised in Table 16.9. An attempt has been made in this table to rank the alternatives on the basis of resource conservation and viability, to obtain a qualitative determination of the most attractive method of handling.

Dumping

Plastic and plastic-containing wastes are traditionally dumped.[10] As all material values are thus lost, the cost of replacing materials should be added to the cost of dumping in order to arrive at a true total cost. The actual cost of

TABLE 16.5 ALTERNATIVES FOR HANDLING PLASTIC WASTE

Disposal:
>   Direct by dumping.
>   By biological degradation.
>   By irradiation degradation.

Reuse:
>   Pyrolysis to gas, oil or waxes.
>   Incineration to heat.
>   Biological degradation to protein.
>   Chemical reaction to oil.
>   Chemical degradation followed by fermentation to protein.

Recovery of:
>   Monomer: pyrolysis
>   Polymer: direct internal
>   direct by sale to recycling agency
>   by compatibilising
>   by extraction
>   Additives: by extraction
>   by chemical reaction.

dumping (about £2/tonne in 1977[11]) is relatively high because of the low bulk density and hence high volume of the waste. Transport costs add a further £10–£20 per tonne (1977[11]) depending on quantity and distance.

Biological Methods

Disposal

The digestive action of a variety of micro-organisms which can attack and degrade many plastics in commercial use offers a means of disposal. Efforts directed towards preventing such attack[5,12,13] have been reversed in an attempt to meet the problem of plastic wastes disposal by developing highly resistant strains of the organisms[14] and also by increasing the susceptibility of the plastic product. This is achieved, in principle, by modifying the structure of the plastic so that, while under normal storage conditions and shelf life it retains its properties, it is rapidly broken down under the moist and acid conditions of a tip. One way of achieving this is by incorporating starch as a filler. The cost of the plastic is thus higher and the disposal costs not significantly reduced. In the longer term, however, greater consolidation of the tip can be expected, with improved fertility.

Reuse

Research has also been carried out on conversion of plastic waste to protein or foodstuffs.[12,15,16,17] Chemical oxidation is required before fermentation to improve the efficiency of the process, which has only been developed to pilot scale. The value of the product is unlikely to exceed about £200 per tonne compared with about £500 per tonne for a typical virgin thermoplastic (1978 prices), and the conversion costs will probably offset a major proportion of this value. A significant capital investment would be required because of the nature of the biological process, which is relatively slow and needs extensive support.

Irradiation

The effect of ultra-violet radiation on thermoplastics is well known and is reponsible for the ageing and allied degradative processes associated with scission of the polymer chain. Thus reversal of the protection afforded by current technology is a logical method of promoting the disposal and dispersal of plastic waste by utilising natural radiation. There has been much research in this area and literature dealing with all types of radiation is extensive, including X-rays, gamma-rays, alpha particles, UV radiation, microwaves and lasers.[5,10,18]

However, no values are recovered with these techniques, and their economic performance is poor. The cost can vary from a small positive advantage of omitting anti-oxidants, etc., to the high cost of incorporating in the product sophisticated accelerators and 'chemical clocks'. An added complication is the variable susceptibility of different plastics to radiation. On the positive side is the socio-environmental benefit of a reduced litter problem, which is impossible to quantify.

Pyrolysis

Thermal degradation of plastic waste, which yields a mixture of hydrocarbon gases, oils and waxes,[19,20] has been widely researched, and a number of commercial plants have been built (Figure 16.1). Most interest is centred in Japan, where the level of plastic waste arisings is high. Individual and mixed plastics

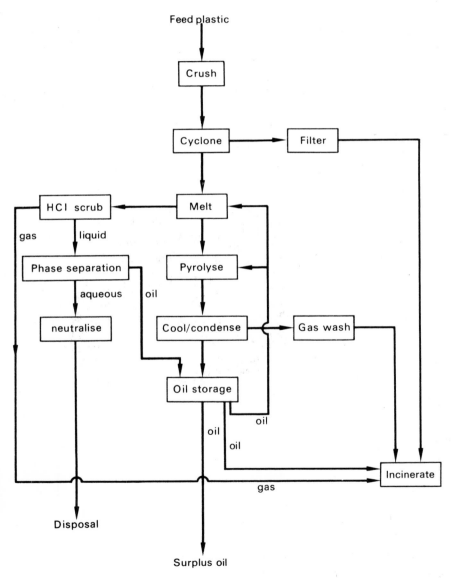

Fig. 16.1 Gifu plant for plastics pyrolysis (Sanyo Electric Co., Japan[20])

have been pyrolysed under a variety of conditions of temperature, pressure and atmosphere, and in a range of reactor types including fixed beds, fluidised beds, molten salts and rotating kilns.[18-22] Some examples of the pyrolysis products of plastics are given in Table 16.6. It is possible to obtain up to 90% liquid yield or complete gasification by altering the reaction conditions. Higher temperatures favour gas production.

TABLE 16.6 THERMAL DEGRADATION OF PLASTICS[25]

Converted to: (wt % based on feed)	Polystyrene at 740°C under 'cracker gas'	Polyethylene at 740°C under 'cracker gas'	Polyethylene at 740°C under N_2
Hydrogen	—	0·5	0·3
Methane	0·3	16·2	7·0
Ethylene	0·5	25·5	35·1
Ethane	—	5·4	3·6
Propylene	—	9·4	22·6
Isobutane	—	1·1	8·7
1:3-Butadiene	—	2·8	10·3
Benzene	2·1	12·2	—
Toluene	4·5	3·6	—
Xylene	1·2	1·1	—
Styrene	71·6	1·1	—
Indene	1·4	0·3	—
Naphthalene	0·8	8·7	—
Residue	Balance	Balance	Balance

The advantages are that a heterogeneous and variable feedstock may be used and a useful proportion of values contained in the scrap may be recovered although the value of the recovered materials cannot be readily quantified. Possible major disadvantages are the need for operation at high throughputs of 500 tonnes per day or more to be viable,[23] and the necessity for specialised facilities for handling the mixed hydrocarbon product. The economics are however claimed to be improving[24] and have now reached break-even. A process employing only a mixed plastic waste feed has been developed in Japan,[5,20] which gives an oil yield of 90% at a throughput of 36 tonnes per day. A disadvantage of such processes is the need to segregate the plastic from mixed waste.

Recovery

The alternative to partial degradation to a mixed hydrocarbon product is depolymerisation; however, this is only effective for polystyrene. Table 16.6 gives typical figures for recovery of monomer in fluidised bed pyrolysis for polystyrene and polyethylene. It may be advantageous to separate polystyrene from mixed waste (which would necessitate development of a segregation technique: see, for example, Figure 16.2) or to restrict feed materials.

Incineration

Because of the secondary pollution resulting from incineration and the low combustibility of some plastics, widespread use of this method is restricted to refuse disposal, where plastic is a minor proportion of total waste handled (although forming a significant proportion of total plastic waste arisings). Calorific values of a range of materials are given in Table 16.7 for comparison.[7,26]

The economics are currently considered advantageous compared with dumping in that some value may be recovered as heat, disposal costs are lower because of the considerable reduction in weight and volume and there is less environmental nuisance. There is still total loss of plastic which needs replacement with virgin materials and this alternative is therefore little better than dumping in terms of resource conservation. The cost of incineration is about £5–£7 per tonne (1978), ignoring credits.

TABLE 16.7 COMPARATIVE CALORIFIC VALUES[7]

	kJ/kg	Btu/lb
Polyethylene	46 520	20 000
Polypropylene	46 520	20 000
Polystyrene	41 565	17 870
PVC	17 955	7 720
Polyurethane	23 680	10 180
GRS rubber	44 220	19 010
Polyester	29 800	12 810
Paper	17 655	7 590
Natural gas	52 800	22 700
Bituminous coal	35 305	15 178
Lignite	25 780	11 084
Wood	20 550	8 835

Chemical Reaction and Extraction

Disposal

Direct or indirect disposal by chemical reaction, except incineration, does not appear to be employed or to have been seriously proposed.

Reuse

Most chemical reaction methods are based on alternatives to pyrolysis whereby the polymer chain is cracked by reaction rather than heat to give a mixture of hydrocarbons.[27] Unlike pyrolysis, these high-temperature and/or high-pressure processes tend to require relatively pure feedstocks and to give more specific products. Because of the specialised nature of the processes, capital costs tend to be high.[27]

Recovery

A range of solvent extraction processes has been developed whereby the plastic is recovered by dissolution in solvents and by cryogenic techniques.[28] Similar methods may be employed for the additives.[29,30] Other specialised methods have been proposed,[10] such as hydrolysis[31] and distillation of oxidation products.[32] Chemical oxidation is also employed to break the polymer chains prior to biological conversion to foodstuffs[33] or other more specific hydrocarbon products. Nitric acid is often employed as the oxidant and long reaction times are necessary.

The disadvantages of such methods are high capital and operating costs and low-volume operating levels. Viability thus depends on value of product, process efficiency and economies of scale.

Compatibilisation

Normally a basic incompatibility exists between different plastics and with aged material that prevents their being directly mixed and reused for high-specification products. Additives ('compatibilisers') have been developed that eliminate this incompatibility and permit alloying of different plastic wastes; current work includes investigation of ethylene vinyl acetate copolymer (EVA)[32] and chlorinated polyethylene (CPE).[34,35]

It is claimed that homogeneous mixtures of compatibilised plastics have specifications at least equal to those of virgin materials, and that specifications may be readily controlled (Table 16.8, page 458).

The technology is simple although not yet fully developed, and relatively cheap as the compatibilisers are believed to cost about 30% more than virgin plastics.[10,31] The method of recycling may be applied to a single waste plastic or mixture of any of the common plastics that arise in scrap and is not restricted to a single recycle. This approach seems to offer most promise in conserving resources although a number of other problems remain such as segregation of plastic from mixed waste such as refuse.

Direct Recycling

Process plastic waste is generated on an in-plant basis as sprues and trimmings from injection moulding processes, etc. Techniques for recycling this waste are well developed and very efficient.[7] In general, thermoplastic waste has a recycle potential inversely proportional to its age so that newly generated scrap can be reground and incorporated in the next batch of mouldings without detriment.

As the cost of raw materials increases, more manufacturers are attempting to economise by introducing a low level of 'external' material from other sources into their product. Introduction of aged waste lowers the specification of the final product unless a compatibiliser is employed, but this need not be a problem with low-specification products. A further limitation is that the external waste must be pure and clean.

External Reprocessing

The problems of recycling commonly available plastic waste have led to development of a number of processes which treat a heterogeneous feedstock as a polymer 'alloy' and use this directly to manufacture products.

The need also arises to separate plastics from other materials and a number of processes have been developed for this. One process, illustrated in Figure 16.2, is designed especially for plastics recovery.[20] Processes are also available to separate different plastics; one example is shown in Figure 16.3.[36] There are numerous alternative processes which employ the separation stages discussed in Chapter 17. These are used in appropriate combination, according to the waste involved, to give complete separation.

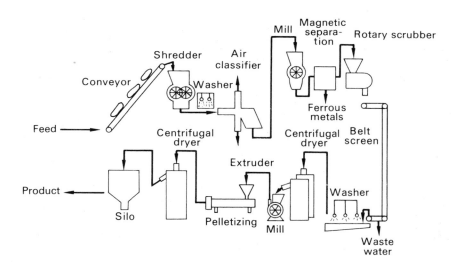

Fig. 16.2 Process for the separation of refuse and recovery of plastics[20]

Although this type of recycling initially produced very low-specification materials and is still mainly used for this purpose, recent commercial processes such as the Regal.[22,31] Reverzer,[20,31] and Remaker[5] have shown much improvement. These feature new handling and extrusion techniques and can accept even highly contaminated feedstocks for conversion to an alloy product with a range of specifications, currently employed for low-specification products such as pallets, fencing, guttering and flowerpots. The market has thus opened up to a limited extent for scrap plastics and, to date, low-grade products. It is controlled by the product quality and marketing restrictions discussed later. Similar processes have also been developed using a filler such as wood.[5]

TABLE 16.8 EXAMPLE OF EFFECT OF COMPATIBILISERS ON PLASTIC ALLOY PROPERTIES[34]

50% binary mixtures	Tensile strength				Impact strength			
	without CPE		with CPE		without CPE		with CPE	
	(kN/m^2)	(psi)	(kN/m^2)	(psi)	(J/m^2)	(ft lb/ in²)	(J/m^2)	(ft lb/ in²)
ABS/PS	6 074	881	19 002	2756	0	0	2 732	1·3
ABS/LDPE	6 212	901	9 515	1380	2732	1·3	15 131	7·2
ABS/HDPE	5 143	746	12 742	1848	0	0	9 247	4·4
ABS/PVC	44 436	6445	21 774	3158	7145	3·4	45 602	21·7
PS/HDPE	4 744	688	16 079	2332	1471	0·7	2 732	1·3
PS/LDPE	8 485	1230	7 777	1128	2101	1·0	2 732	1·3
PS/PVC	2 220	322	14 141	2051	1261	0·6	2 522	1·2
PVC/LDPE	6 964	1010	8 729	1266	1051	0·5	10 297	4·9
PVC/HDPE	—	—	10 542	1529	1891	0·9	8 196	3·9

CPE = chlorinated polyethylene.

Summary of Alternatives

The range of techniques available for handling plastic waste described above is summarised in Table 16.9 with the main advantages and disadvantages of each. An attempt has been made to rank techniques in terms of resource conservation, overall viability and general applicability to plastic waste, with a 'best' score of 1. Summing the scores gives a qualitative assessment and suggests which methods are most attractive for handling the increasing quantities of plastic waste. This technique is not new and to be effective requires a more exhaustive, and perhaps a weighted, list of criteria. The simple scheme used in the table suggests that attention should be directed to total recycling/reuse to recover the maximum amount of material with highest value.

Marketing

The introduction of what is essentially an alternative source of feedstock material into an already well-defined market will cause certain problems, particularly since there is a general reluctance within industry to accept reprocessed material. As Milgram[37] points out, the necessary incentives for industry to overcome its prejudices and accept recycled material involve price differentials of an irrational size for comparative specifications. It is technologically proven that recycled polymers can meet many duties and satisfactorily replace virgin materials, but little short of legislative pressure, such as a tax upon virgin material usage, is likely to influence the aversion in which industry holds this secondary resource.

Processes of the Regal and Reverzer type could easily be adapted to

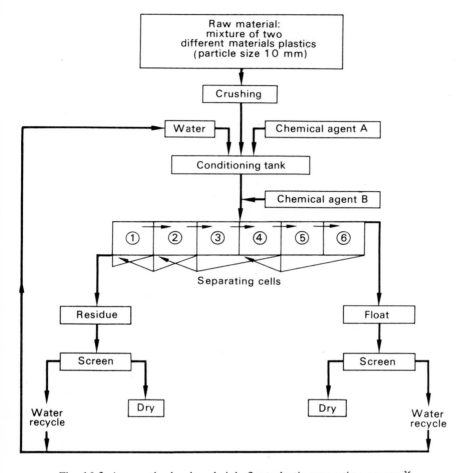

Fig. 16.3 A recently developed sink–float plastic separation process[36]

manufacture a wide range of conventional plastic products. These have the facility to use almost any quality of input waste material in a highly contaminated condition, but are restricted to the manufacture of paving stones, shoe heels, garden furniture and industrial pallets. These products are all in a low-tolerance, low-value and high-volume market.

The problem is essentially twofold in that the industry must first be convinced of the ability of the recycled product to meet the essential specifications of the original material; it must then be convinced of the economic viability of such a process. An example of the most promising area for immediate exploitation is the relatively small-scale user of plastics who uses them as an integral part of his product. Under certain circumstances it is possible to arrange for return of his products on a trade-in basis, so that he guarantees a market for

TABLE 16.9 COMPARISON OF DISPOSAL AND TREATMENT METHODS FOR PLASTIC WASTES.
RANKING: A = RESOURCE CONSERVATION, B = OVERALL VIABILITY, C = OVERALL APPLICABILITY TO PLASTIC WASTE

	Advantages	Disadvantages	Ranking			
			A	B	C	Total
Disposal: Dumping	Easy Low capital cost Accepts any waste	No recovery Environmental problems	14	12	1	27
Biological	Degrades when dumped	No recovery Not fully developed Higher cost	12	13	6	31
Irradiation	Less environmental problems	No recovery High cost Poor control	12	13	6	31
Reuse: Pyrolysis	Partial recovery of values Accepts wide range of feedstock Technically developed	Requires high throughput Product processing facilities needed	5	5	2	12
Incineration	Reduction in waste quantity Heat recovery Handles heterogeneous waste	Recovers low-value product only Limitations in furnace design Generates pollution Viability questionable	11	11	3	25
Biological	Partial recycle achieved Helps solve 'food crisis'	Requires prior chemical treatment High capital and conversion cost Will not accept heterogeneous waste Low capacity	9	10	9	28
Chemical reaction	Recovers selected materials	High specificity to feed and product High cost	10	6	11	27

Recovery:

	Advantages	Disadvantages			
Monomer: Pyrolysis	Gives good yield of monomer Repolymerisation overcomes most recycling problems	Only applicable to styrene Possibly unnecessary and uneconomic compared with other methods	4	4	10	18
Polymer: Direct internal	Reduces operating costs	Application limited to in-plant waste	3	1	8	12
Direct external	Technology developed Insensitive to contamination High degree of recycle	Marketing problem Low value product Low specification product	2	2	5	9
Compatibilising	Accepts mixed wastes Gives high-specification product Technology simple Low capital cost	Not fully developed Compatibilisers expensive (at present)	1	3	4	8
Extraction	Selective	Not fully developed High cost	6	6	11	23
Additives: Extraction	Selective	Not fully developed Only partial recovery of values High cost: loss may exceed gain	7	6	11	24
Chemical reaction	Selective	High specificity to feed and product High cost: loss may exceed gain Low operating levels Partial recovery of values	7	6	11	24

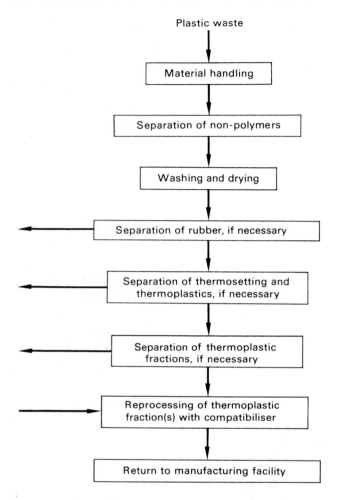

Fig. 16.4 General flowsheet of plastics reprocessing

his finished product and also a feedstock of known quality and quantity. This gives the recycle operation economic appeal as well as promoting resource conservation.

Economics

Assessment of technical viability is not difficult. Unfortunately, other non-quantifiable and often subjective considerations, including public opinion, prejudice, environmental issues and present and planned legislation affect the overall assessment of any proposal.

A process was designed to accept a heavily contaminated feedstock and produce 1500 tonnes per year compatibilised polyolefins containing 23% CPE as compatibiliser. The outline flow sheet is given in Figure 16.4. It was proposed that the system be set up as a closed-loop. Capital and operating costs were estimated which enabled a DCF rate of return to be calculated (see Chapter 20) as 50% after grant and tax, with a payback time of 1·6 years. This assumed a pessimistic feedstock cost and ascribed the same value to the product as virgin plastic. By fixing the return at 25% it was calculated that the product value could be reduced by 40%, or the feedstock cost reduced to an insignificant level. The economics are clearly attractive even from a commercial viewpoint without considering the loss of resources and the cost and disadvantages of the alternative—dumping. However, some of the 'social' factors mentioned above were found to weigh against the proposal.

Rubber

The largest single application of rubber is for vehicle tyres: the total weight is about the same as for all other applications put together at about 220 000 tonnes per year in the UK.[38,39] The other main categories of usage are cables, hose and tubing, belting, footwear, cellular products, and a wide range of minor uses. All except tyres are referred to as general rubber products, none of which individually presents a disposal problem or has significant potential for recovery, except for new scrap and in-plant recycling.

The disposal options for tyres, of which 24 million are scrapped every year in the UK, are shown in Figure 16.5.[40] Table 16.10 shows the variety of materials in a

TABLE 16.10 ANALYSIS OF TYPICAL CAR TYRE[38]

		Cross-ply or textile radial	Steel radial
Rubber compound		74% wt	74% wt
Rubber polymer	51		
Carbon black	26		
Process oils	13		
Sulphur	1		
Zinc oxide	2		
Others	7		
	100		
Wire: bead		3% wt	3% wt
Wire: belt		—	13% wt
Fabric (e.g. rayon, nylon polyester)		23% wt	10% wt
		100% wt	100% wt
Typical weight		6·75 kg	

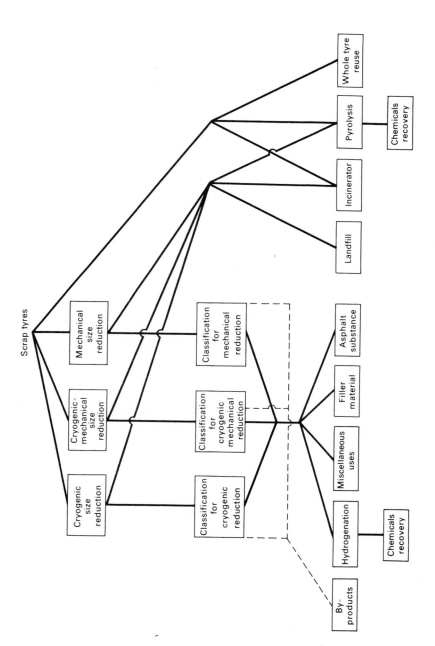

Fig. 16.5 Scrap tyre disposal system

tyre, all of which are chemically or physically modified during manufacture so that reclamation is difficult. Figure 16.6 shows the tyre cycle[38] in which retreading plays a significant role. Retreading scrap tyres is a useful and profitable recycling operation: unfortunately, very few tyres can be retreaded more than once, so the total number requiring disposal is largely unaffected.

Two products may be obtained from scrapped tyres by physical treatment: 'crumb' and 'reclaim'. Crumb is a granular material produced from the peripheral surface of the tyre during buffing to prepare a clean straight surface to receive the new tread. Around 18 000 tonnes per year are produced which can be reincorporated into new rubber compound up to about 10%. Crumb has the advantage of being uncontaminated with the other materials involved in tyre construction such as wire and fabric. It may also be manufactured by grinding the tread from a 'scalped' tyre when this method is used to prepare a retread.

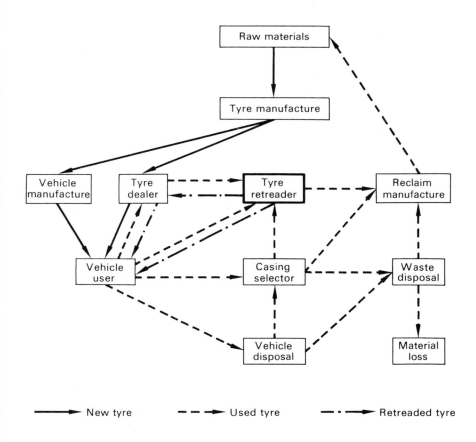

Fig. 16.6 Rubber tyre cycle

Reclaim is essentially devulcanised rubber and is processed and sold in sheet form. A flow diagram of a popular process is shown in Figure 16.7.[38,41] Before being processed, the tyre must be reduced to a uniform particle-size and the wire and fabric reinforcements separated using sieving and air flotation. After blending and mixing the reclaim rubber sheet is suitable for blending with new rubber up to 30% or 40% by weight, giving a product containing up to about 25% of reclaim. The advantage lies mainly in the economics as reclaim costs

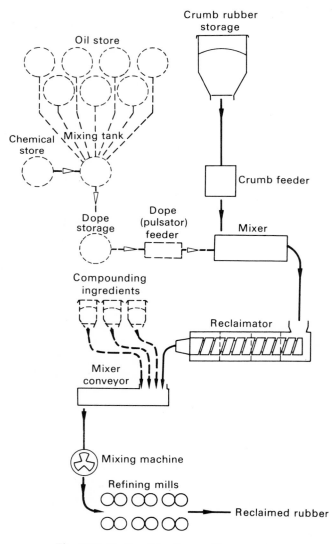

Fig. 16.7 Reclamation from rubber crumb

only about half the price of new rubber. The separated fabric or lint is too contaminated for reuse and is dumped, and the steel is sold as low-grade scrap metal. The initial particle-size reduction is the most difficult step in the process and a variety of methods have been used or suggested.[40] The energy consumption and maintenance costs of mechanical size-reduction are high. Cryogenic processing may be used to change the physical properties to obtain more efficient mechanical disintegration.[40,42]

Thermal methods of treating scrapped tyres have also been assessed for resource recovery and for disposal. Incineration not only gives effective disposal of scrap tyres but can provide heat for recovery and allow carbon black, zinc oxide and steel to be reclaimed. Most incinerators, however, serve only as an efficient method of disposal. Careful design and control is needed to ensure complete combustion (Chapter 13).

Pyrolysis potentially produces a greater proportion of recovered materials.[38,43] Three main products are recovered: solid char containing essentially carbon with some tars, a liquid fraction containing a wide range of organic compounds and a gas which may be employed for in-plant heat supply. Temperature, rate of heating and method of operation are important in determining the products. Low-temperature pyrolysis (around 500°C) tends to give greatest liquid yield. Typical product proportions for medium-temperature operation of up to 700°C are 36% solid, 55% liquid and 9% gas.[38,39] If the heating rate is increased the proportions change to 41:44:15; low-temperature operation using recycled gas gives 36:35:29;[38,43] high-temperature operation at around 900°C gives 55:20:25.[38] One of the first commercial pyrolysis plants to be installed is the Goodyear/TOSCO process[44] (Figure 16.8). Others are

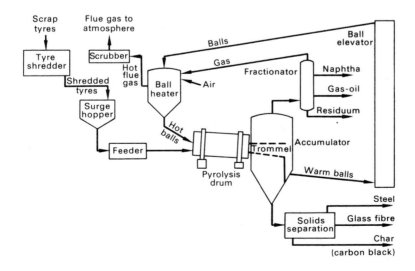

Fig. 16.8 Goodyear/Tosco pyrolysis process for rubber tyres[44]

being considered. The products are of inherently low value, and such processes may prove to be viable only in the long term.

A variation on pyrolysis is hydrogenation, in which pyrolysis takes place in a hydrogen atmosphere: as a result, unsaturated compounds in the rubber are saturated, and this is accompanied by thermal degradation at high temperature (Figure 16.9).[40] The products and behaviour are similar to those of straight-forward pyrolysis. The requirement of a hydrogen supply is a commercial disadvantage.

Other possibilities for reuse of tyres include recreational land and sea reclamation;[40] many others are listed in a comprehensive RAPRA report.[38] Proposals have been made for the use of recycled tyre rubber particles, and of mixtures of these particles with wood fine wastes, as sorbent material for oil-spill recovery.[45] Economics remains the greatest single obstacle to the many possibilities for reuse.

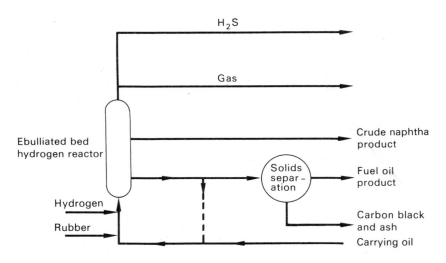

Fig. 16.9 Conceptual H-rubber plant[40]

Textiles

Recycling, reprocessing and reuse of fibre wastes are traditional in the UK textile industry. However, the relatively simple operation when only natural fibres were present in wastes, and could be reprocessed and blended directly with virgin fibres for reuse, has become complicated by the increased use of natural/manmade fibre blends. Together with the contraction of the textile industry, this has led to a decline in the reclamation industry.

Reclamation is also affected by fashion trends in colour with regard to market outlets, since it is uneconomic to over-dye unfashionable colours and they may not be easily blended.[46] Another factor is that textile sorting by hand is expensive and only economic with high-value fibres, like wool, or if large quantities are available. Mixed fibre wastes are exported in quantity for sorting and reprocessing where labour costs are low.

Arisings

Total fibres used in the UK textile industry include 65–70% of manmade fibres, which comprise about 65% synthetics, such as polyamide, polyester, acrylic and polyolefin fibres. The remainder are mainly cellulosics such as viscose, cellulose acetate and cellulose triacetate. Sources comprise:[40]

(i) Manmade fibre manufacture. This waste is identifiable by type and most easily recycled. About 10% of fibre waste occurs at the filament fibre stage of which half is reprocessed for reuse or recycled internally. About 4% wastage occurs at the staple fibre stage. A relatively small loss occurs at the pre-filament stage.

(ii) Textile manufacture. This waste is more varied. About 1·5% arises in the fibre-to-fabric manufacturing processes, i.e. spinning, weaving, knitting, dyeing and finishing.[47] Over 7500 tonnes of fabric is wasted annually during making-up.[47]

(iii) Post-consumer. This source, comprising used products, is the largest but the waste is heterogeneous and hence most difficult to recycle. Mixed textile waste in UK household refuse is currently estimated to amount to 500 000 tonnes per year.

Recovery

Wastes are collected from the main source by a network of merchants, and pass to reprocessors. Processing reduces the waste to fibres which are blended with virgin fibres, carded and spun into threads and yarn.

Essentially, the wastes are sorted by hand according to the shade and type, or the majority fibres in blends. They are then 'opened', that is reduced to fibres by a rag-pulling machine. The fibres may be further opened or 'garnetted' on a different machine to produce a fine 'felt' for dyeing, blending, carding and spinning. Manmade fibres that are identifiable by type and uncontaminated can be reprocessed for higher-grade applications such as clothing and furnishings. Alternatively they find lower-grade applications such as fillings, felts and wipers. Provided they are uncontaminated, the thermoplastic manmade fibres (nylon, polyester and the polyolefins) can be recovered by melt processing.

Some other separation processes are summarised in Table 16.11. Developments have also been made in identification of fibres by fluorescence of bleach in synthetics under ultra-violet light, and by spectroscopy, as a basis for separation processes.

TABLE 16.11 SEPARATION PROCESSES FOR TEXTILE FIBRES (based on BROMLEY and DUNSTAN[46])

Process	Use
Carbonising	Removal of cellulosic fibres from animal fibres by carbonisation with hydrogen chloride gas (dry process) or sulphuric acid (wet process).
Solvent separation	Recovery of cellulose acetate and polyester fibre from cotton/polyester blends. Cellulosic fibres are removed by catalysed hydrolysis in dilute acid solution.
Electrostatic separation	Separation of wool/polyester blends on the basis of the fibres accepting different electrostatic charges.

Paper

It has been suggested that of all materials presently discarded, recovery of paper can offer the greatest economic savings. The UK consumes between 7 and 8 million tonnes of paper per year, valued at £250 per tonne as sheet or reel or £500 per tonne on average as finished products (1974 prices). Paper arisings for 1974,[48] a time of high demand, and for 1976[49] suggest that the quantity of recycled paper tends to remain fairly constant, changes in demand being satisfied by varying import levels of paper and pulp (Table 16.12). The potential recycling routes and byproducts of wood utilisation and paper production are illustrated in Figure 16.10.

TABLE 16.12 SOURCES OF PAPER PRODUCTION

	1974 (million tonnes/year)	1974 (%)		1976 (million tonnes/year)	1976 (%)
Imported paper	3·5	44		3·1	46
Imported pulp	2·5	31		1·7	25
Waste overall	2·0	25		2·0	29
Process waste from the paper industry		13			
Waste paper merchants associated with paper mills		33			
Independent merchants		28			
Local authorities		21			
Imports		5			
Total	8·0	100	100	6·8	100

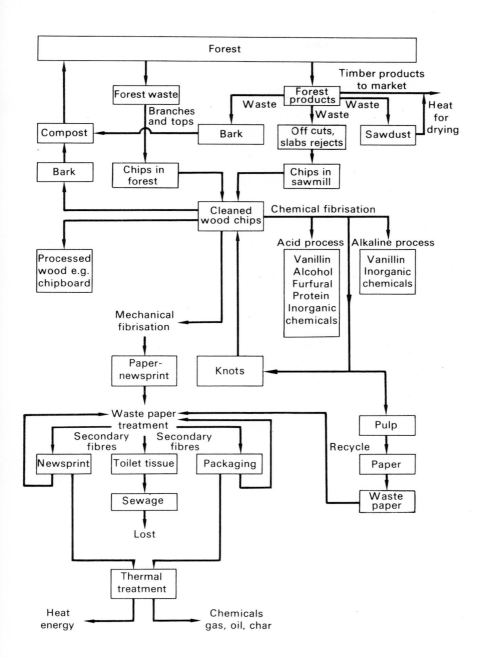

Fig. 16.10 Existing and potential recycling in pulp and paper production (based on Dewhirst[50])

Forestry Practice

Paper is primarily derived from the cellulose contained in wood. There are two main products from the forestry industries: wood for constructional timber and wood for papermaking. With improved forestry practice, sawmill systems have been modified (with the object of maximum wood utilisation) to provide the approximately 50% non-timber product in a more usable form for paper pulp or byproducts. Sawmill chips have thus become a valuable byproduct. Bark and sawdust remain after sawmilling and pulpwood production. Chips from the sawmill may be used in pulpmaking provided the two plants are located together; the bark and sawdust are burnt to provide steam and power. Sawdust may also be pulped and mixed with other fibres to produce packaging or printing papers. Mulched bark may be reused as humus (transport costs are a limiting factor here). Even tree roots may be pulped or used in, for example, particle board production; this is practised in the USA.[50]

Chemical Recycling and Byproduct Recovery in Pulping Processes

Wood is essentially a complex mixture of cellulose and lignin. Pulping is the preparation process to separate the lignin and free the cellulose fibres. The main processes are based on chemical dissolution of lignin, leaving relatively pure cellulose for production of higher-grade papers.

The main pulping process utilises an alkaline solution of sodium sulphide and sodium bicarbonate; this is known as the kraft process. The waste liquors are concentrated, the dissolved organics burnt out by incineration, and the inorganic smelt dissolved. Causticising with slaked lime provides recycle delignification liquor. Steam and power are generated by the waste incineration operation, the only problem being the potential for odour generation due to hydrogen sulphide and mercaptans. Tall oil, a black viscous liquid containing resins, fatty acids and methanol, is recovered as a byproduct from the digestion process. This process gives the longest fibres and hence the strongest paper.

Of secondary importance is the acid process based on sulphur dioxide. The original acid process used calcium bisulphite and chemical recycling was impracticable.[50] The high-BOD waste liquors, containing all the dissolved organic materials from hydrolysis and reaction of lignin, constituted a serious disposal problem and were sprayed on country roads as a binder; some are currently spray-dried to produce limited quantities of lignosulphates binders. A change was made to soluble sulphites, of either sodium, magnesium or ammonium, to facilitate recovery of the digestion solution by incineration of the spent liquor.

In the process based on sodium bisulphite, delignification involves two stages using (i) a mixture of sodium mono- and bi-sulphites and (ii) liquid sulphur dioxide. Chemicals recovery involves incineration of the concentrated waste liquors in a steam-raising boiler and dissolution of the inorganic smelt in a solution of sodium bicarbonate and sodium sulphide. Reaction of this solution with sulphur dioxide and carbon dioxide yields sodium monosulphite, which is

successful that chips are now produced specially for it. It is also practicable for sawdust or wood chips to be converted to fermentable sugars by hydrolysis, as described for refuse in Chapter 17, but this is unlikely to be economic in the short term.

Future and Potential for Recycling

The forecast growth in the UK paper industry is around 3% per year giving a demand in 1980 of about 8·5 million tonnes, although the growth is not distributed equally among the sectors (Table 16.13).[48,51] Good predictive models have been obtained which relate both total waste paper arisings and individual sector requirements to gross domestic product.[51] These forecasts suggest a waste paper demand of around 2·0 million tonnes per year in 1980 and 2·4 million tonnes per year in 1985, but do not consider any changes in economic incentives or political considerations.

TABLE 16.13 PAPER PRODUCTION BREAKDOWN AND FORECASTS OF GROWTH

	Paper and board production, 1973 (% share of market)	Forecast annual growth rate to 1980 (%)
Newsprint	9·5	1·9
Other printings	28·0	2·7
Corrugated board	18·0	6·8
Packaging paper	7·5	3·2
Boards	25·5	Negligible
Other	11·5	Negligible

It has already been suggested that the total potential for waste paper recycling is about 80% of consumption but only about 25–30% is recovered. Since merchants already recover all the waste paper that is economically viable from non-household sources, it is from household and small trader waste sources that extra supplies must be obtained. The grade composition of this waste should correspond to that of expected increases in demand but the downgrading of waste paper on recycling due to technical limitations, such as shortening of the fibre and mechanical damage, creates a problem. Hence the importance of fibre upgrading by the de-inking, cooking and bleaching methods referred to earlier.

It has been estimated that of the approximately 7 million tonnes per annum of paper waste in the household and commercial waste in the UK, about 200 000 tonnes is reclaimed annually by local authorities. Assuming a 25% recycling rate,[54] about 1·7 million tonnes of extra waste paper is considered likely to be available for recycling;[51] however, there is in principle no reason for this to be seen as an upper limit. With the increasing paper content of refuse (see Chapter 17) at least 2 million tonnes per annum of extra waste paper should become available by 1980. The likely grade-composition of waste derived from household and small trades sources is predominantly low-grade paper residuals[51] (Table 16.14).

TABLE 16.14 COMPOSITION OF WASTE PAPER FROM HOUSEHOLD AND SMALL TRADE SOURCES IN THE EEC[54]

	Estimated (%)	Forecast quantity (tonnes) 1980	Forecast quantity (tonnes) Material balance approach (1980)
Newsprint, magazines, brochures	36	720 000	410 000
Corrugated and kraft waste	46	920 000	520 000
Mixed papers	18	360 000	200 000

The problems lie in several interrelated areas:

1. *Attitude.* Segregation at source gives a cleaner product that is more easily recycled. Attitude, and lack of incentive, have already been shown to prevent this approach.

2. *Technology.* Segregation from other refuse is possible but is not very efficient, although there is considerable research in this area as described in Chapter 17.

3. *Economics of operation.* In addition to the poor economics of separation from mixed waste, there is the collection and transportation cost of a segregation-at-source exercise, even if this could be adopted. Such costs are likely to equal or exceed the value of waste paper collected.

4. *Economics of investment.* The paper industry is capital intensive and, even if all the above obstacles could be overcome, the problem would remain of financing the necessary investment. This is complicated by the heavy commitments of larger paper companies in forestry and pulp production. A fairly rapid changeover to higher waste paper utilisation at the expense of pulp production is therefore a sensitive issue.

5. *Incentive.* As with any resource conservation proposals, fiscal incentives could radically affect status. In the short term, however, reliance will probably be placed on developing changes in attitude by encouraging charity collections. This may be viewed as an indirect fiscal incentive and does overcome some of the technological, economic and attitude obstacles mentioned above.[53]

Glass

About 2·5 million tonnes of glass are produced annually in the UK and about 1·6 million tonnes of this are used in the manufacture of containers. Most glass containers are used for food and drink, and most container glass is disposed of in household and trade refuse; at present, it constitutes about 9% by weight of this waste. The weight of glass disposed of in other forms, for example plate glass, is relatively small.

The main recycle route for glass is in broken or crushed form, i.e. as 'cullet'. About 16% of the glass industry's total output is returnable. Surprisingly, over 80% of glass containers are non-returnable though the returnable bottle predominates in soft/alcoholic beverage and milk marketing.[55] Preference for one-trip containers arises from increasing consumer affluence and the unsatisfactory economics associated with handling 'empties', unless a bulk delivery and collection service is well established. Thus a 1974 survey found that a UK national recovery scheme for bottles would cost £15 M to £20 M to set up and yield reusable bottles at 4p to 5½p each compared with 3p to 4p for new bottles.

The Glass Container Manufacturer's Institute has a research programme, one aim of which is the increased reuse of glass in raw glass manufacture. However, the various disincentives mentioned in Chapter 2 have the result that, while bottle manufacturers use up to 30% of in-works cullet, there has been a slump in clear cullet trading.

Recovery Schemes

The majority of glass containers end their useful life in the home (consumer cullet), on catering or licensed premises (catering cullet) or at the factories of food/beverages/household products manufacturers (process cullet).[56] Consumer cullet is the largest potential source, but as the weekly quantity per household averages only about 2 kg there is a problem of collection. Cullet from factories, arising from rejects or breakages on filling lines, is generally contaminated and the quantities involved do not appear to justify collection and cleaning.[56] The amount of cullet from catering is not great and, since it is widely dispersed, is not currently collected.

In an attempt to stimulate recycling, a directory has been published listing manufacturers and merchants prepared to purchase cullet from the public.[57] However, cullet fetches a relatively low price of £5–£10 per tonne (1974), with a minimum quantity of one tonne. The results of a study involving 1000 households in York suggested that the cost of collection and recycle of non-returnable glass bottles was likely to exceed that of making new ones.[58] Nevertheless, one major glass container manufacturer has considered it commercially attractive to institute a bottle-recovery scheme covering 22 000 households around its works. This is based upon regular collection of white flint glass bottles from which all lids are removed.

A glass reclamation scheme involving the location of specially modified containers ('Bottle Banks') in car parks was recently introduced in Oxford. The recovered glass is stored in council premises until a full load has been collected for transportation to a glass manufacturer.[59] Trial schemes are now operating in other towns in the UK. The success of any such venture for recycling low-value products depends upon the availability of central collection points and a favourable public attitude. Charities, where collection is necessarily free and voluntary, probably have the best chance of success.[56]

It is interesting that separate glass collection continues successfully in Jersey, although the necessity has been removed with the recent closure of the refuse-composting plant (see page 551).

Separation Methods

As an alternative to separate collection, cullet can be removed from household refuse. The Garrett process for glass recovery from household refuse treats an underflow fraction from an air classifier[62] (Chapter 17). The principle is applicable to any feed with a high glass fraction.

The material is first ground to − 32 + 200 mesh size, repulped and conditioned with proprietary glass-selective reagents, and the glass is separated from impurities by froth flotation. The mixed colour, sand-size glass product, claimed to be of exceptional purity, melts to give a glass free of stones and similar materials. A flow diagram of one arrangement is shown in Figure 16.13. Glass reclamation is also an integral part of the Black-Clawson process (Chapters 17 and 19). However, due to the low value of the recovered glass, economic viability of such processes is doubtful.

Cullet may be hand-picked and passed under a magnetic separator, washed and possibly subjected to air blowing, before being crushed and intermixed with other raw materials for remelting. It has been estimated that the cost of crushing and cleaning cullet is about 25% of its value[56] but the extent of cleaning needed is clearly dependent on the source. If the cullet is of the same composition as the parent glass, quality control is obviously simpler. Mixed coloured cullet can be used for green glass manufacture. However the main market, amounting in the UK to about 75% of the total,[56] is for clear (flint) glass, so for optimum utilisation waste glass should be colour sorted.

In equipment now available for glass sorting, separation is based on either transparency or colour sensing.[60] Cullet, which must be clean and dry, has first to be reduced to size grades of 6–20 mm and 20–40 mm. It is then hopper-fed into a vibrating tray and thence by inclined chute to the inspection unit. The results of optical inspection by means of a light source and optical sensor are evaluated electronically to trigger an air blast each time a predetermined type of particle is detected. This blast deflects the selected particles from the main product stream. Transparency sorting allows glass to be identified irrespective of colour and facilitates separation from opaque 'contaminants' such as bottle-tops, corks, ceramics and stones. Colour sorting allows flint glass to be separated from mixed coloured glass; a typical performance at 1·5 tonnes/h throughput is 95% flint glass recovery with a 1·5% contamination of mixed coloured particles. The mixed coloured glass can also be separated, usually into amber and green fractions, to meet a specification of 10% contamination of each colour in the other.

An electronic optical sorter of this type (see Figure 17.13) has been used to recover flint glass concentrates from mixed glass products, namely glass recovered from raw urban refuse or residues from incineration.[61] For example, a glass concentrate containing 83% flint glass was obtained from a presorted refuse feed containing 55% flint glass with a 64% recovery. Poorer-quality products reclaimed from incinerator residues would be unsuitable for direct reuse without further upgrading, which would be uneconomic.

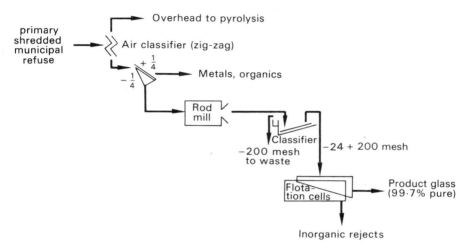

Fig. 16.13 Garrett process for glass recovery from refuse[62]

Problems in Reuse

Internal recycling is normal in glassworks: containers which fail to meet quality control standards are crushed and remixed with the basic raw materials (sand, soda ash and lime/limestone) in predetermined quantities. Recycling of internal cullet may range from 10–30%, or even 50%[63] and glass can be remelted many times without suffering degradation. It is usually passed under an electromagnet to ensure that no ferrous metal contaminants enter the melting furnace. The advantages of cullet reuse are that it melts at a lower temperature than the basic raw materials, aids their mixing, saves energy costs and reduces furnace wear.

External cullet is not so readily used since it may have originated from other manufacturers, or other countries, to different specifications. A greater problem is the presence of contaminants such as ceramics, aluminium or other metals which may interfere with furnace operation and result in flaws in the finished containers. Aluminium, for example, reduces the silica to silicon giving opaque intrusions; bottles manufactured from glass contaminated in this way are mechanically weak. Since it is likely to be uneconomic to sort out all 'faulty' products, in such an eventuality the complete batch of bottles would probably be discarded as landfill.

Alternative Uses

One recycle route for non-returnable bottles is as glass fibre; one UK manufacturer uses up to 18 000 tonnes per year.[64] The bottles, which must be all of the same density and colour, are melted in a gas-fired furnace and the glass is extruded as a continuous, relatively coarse fibre for use as insulation. In addition there are possible outlets for glass waste in building and thermal insulation products. Some recent developments,[65] are the following:

Bricks (94% glass with 6% bonding material)
Insulating wool
Lightweight aggregate
Road surfacing material (i.e. replacing crushed limestone in asphalt)
Concrete bricks containing glass aggregate
Tiles, based on a high proportion of selectively graded glass set in either cement or polymeric resins[66]
Decorative panels, for use as dividing screens or roof lights[66]

It has been shown to be technically feasible to produce an inexpensive insulation material by foaming waste glass.[67] Waste glass, which has not been colour-sorted, cleaned or sized, is crushed and milled. A foaming agent, either water or calcium carbonate, is then added and the mixture is reheated to about 750°C.

Despite these developments, reuse of glass in either glass manufacture or glass fibre manufacture are considered the most likely future outlets.[65]

Mineral Wastes

Very large tonnages of mineral wastes arise in the UK every year. The type, origins and destinations of these are summarised in Table 3.7. The major arisings in Great Britain,[65] in millions of tonnes per annum, are:

Colliery spoil	51·0
China clay waste	22·0
Slate waste	1·2
Pulverised fuel ash and furnace bottom ash	0·9
Furnace clinker	2·3
Calcium sulphate	2·1
Blast-furnace slag	9·0
Steel-making slag	4·0

Although these are generally of low intrinsic value, many have potential for reuse in the building and construction industries.

Colliery Spoil

Approximately half of the material extracted in coalmining is waste or spoil, most of which is disposed of by dumping in heaps. Small quantities are dumped at other inland sites such as quarries and about 10% into the sea.[65] Waste was formerly loose-tipped on heaps, resulting in 'burnt-out' spoil; more recent heaps which are layered and compacted by earthmoving machines contain unburnt spoil or 'minestone'. Minerals present in coal spoil comprise quartz, the clay minerals, pyrites, and magnesium, iron and calcium carbonates. Burning reduces the content of combustible material and, apart from increasing the undesirable sulphate content, results in greater stability.

The quantities of colliery spoil which are available could make a significant impact on aggregate supply in the future.[68] At present about 7·8 million tonnes per annum is used as fill in road embankments and building sites; with certain exceptions, burnt spoil has been preferred. Lightweight aggregate is made from unburnt spoil, mainly for use in the manufacture of precast concrete blocks. A process is, however, under development for the production of dense aggregate which would find wider application, for example in road construction.[68]

China Clay

China clay, composed mainly of kaolinite ($Al_4Si_4O_{10}(OH)_8$), is won from granite rock for use as paper filler and in the ceramic industry. Quartz and mica are also present in the rock and extraction and separation involves the production of an aqueous slurry. About 80–90% of the extracted rock is spoil so that the waste produced[65] for every 1 tonne of china clay is typically:

Overburden	2·0 tonnes
Micaceous residue	0·9 tonnes
Waste rock	2·0 tonnes
Coarse sand	3·7 tonnes

The bulk of these materials is dumped, resulting in the white heaps characteristic of the landscape around St Austell in Cornwall. At present, 10 million tonnes of coarse sand are produced annually in the UK, of which about one-tenth is used as bulk fill in road construction or in the manufacture of building materials, e.g. calcium silicate bricks. About 2 million tonnes of micaceous residue and 10 million tonnes of overburden and waste rock are also produced which are tipped, occupying 800 hectares of land. Numerous outlets have been examined for china clay wastes[65] but transport costs tend to be restrictive due to the remoteness of the industry from South East England and other centres where demand for aggregate is great. Some consideration has been given to bulk transport to special depots in such areas.[68]

Slate Waste

About 90% of the 1·2 million tonnes output from slate quarries accumulates in mountains of inert but unsightly loose-tipped waste. Ground slate is used as an inert filler in, for example, plastic and rubber products and as granules on roofing felt. Lightweight aggregates can be produced which have the advantage that the processing costs are lower than for any other synthetic aggregate.[68] There should be few pollution problems but the major problem in utilisation is the remoteness of the waste deposits at quarries in Wales, the Lake District, Devon and Cornwall.[68]

Pulverised Fuel Ash

Pulverised fuel ash (PFA) is a finely divided ash produced from the widely used process of pulverised fuel firing of industrial plants. In the period 1971–72 about 9·5 million tonnes were produced in the UK of which 5·4 million tonnes, or 57%, was sold for various uses.[65]

The Central Electricity Generating Board has found it impracticable to utilise a higher proportion to date because of the remote location of many power stations, the cost of alterations to older stations to facilitate vehicle loading and the unsuitable quality of some ash. The major uses of PFA are summarised in Table 16.15.[65] The predominant use is as backfill, for which PFA has the advantages of low density and, when moistened and compacted, self-hardening properties. Until recently economic haulage distances were around 20 miles but for use on ground of poor bearing capacity this has now increased to 100 miles.[69]

Feasibility studies have been reported on proposals for total utilisation of PFA.[70] One proposed flow system (Figure 16.14) is based on an existing commercial process for the production of iron oxide, carbon pozzolan and lightweight aggregate. Some of the beneficiated pozzolan or aggregate streams are diverted into production of alumina, regulated-set cement, and Portland cement. There are also proposals to utilise waste silico-fluorides from superphosphate fertiliser production.

TABLE 16.15 UTILISATION OF PFA, 1971–72

	Thousands of tonnes	%
Fill, roads and building sites	3571	66·7
Concrete blocks	1202	22·4
Precast concrete	67	1·3
Lightweight aggregate	244	4·5
Grouting	66	1·2
Cement manufacture	64	1·2
Fired clay bricks	27	0·5
Cement-stabilised soil	48	0·9
Industrial filler	8	0·2
Concrete-mortar	15	0·3
All other uses	43	0·8
	5355	100·0

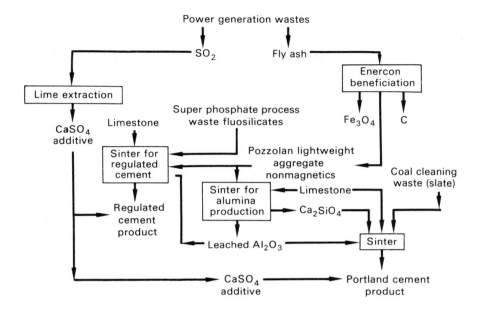

Fig. 16.14 Proposal for total utilisation of PFA

Calcium Sulphate

Calcium sulphate is produced as a byproduct of industrial processes, notably phosphate and phosphoric acid manufacture, hydrofluoric acid manufacture and to a lesser extent the neutralisation of waste sulphuric acid.[65] Approximately two million tonnes per year of this chemical are produced, some of which is reclaimed. However, the majority is disposed of by dumping on land or to sea.

The major outlet for calcium sulphate is as Plaster of Paris in the building industry. The recovery problems are mainly economic since, even after dewatering, the calcium sulphate needs to be dried which can be expensive for a relatively low-priced material. The other serious disadvantage is the level of impurities such as acid which can be neutralised, phosphate, iron, aluminium and fluoride. All of these affect important characteristics of the final product, such as rate of setting, workability and subsequent strength, by changing the calcium sulphate crystal structure. This process is not well understood, and methods of impurity removal would probably prove uneconomic. With the introduction of new building techniques and the current availability of large quantities of artificial calcium sulphate, it may be possible to utilise its peculiar properties. Other uses for waste calcium sulphate are as a filler for polymeric materials, as a soil conditioner and as a source of sulphate for sulphuric acid or ammonium sulphate manufacture.

Blast-furnace Slag

Blast-furnace slag, a byproduct of iron manufacture, is an example of waste which is well established as a construction material: the 9 million tonnes produced in 1971 was all reused.[68]

Selective cooling results in the production of three different types of slag:[71,72]

(a) A crystalline product resembling igneous rock produced by slow cooling in air. This is suitable for use as roadstone or dense aggregate for concrete.

(b) A lightweight aggregate produced by foaming molten slag with a limited amount of water. This is used for blockmaking, for roof and floor screeds and for structural reinforced concrete.

(c) Quench glass, produced by rapid cooling and used in the manufacture of slag cements.

In addition, small amounts are converted into a synthetic fibre for slag wool.

Steelmaking slag

The refining of pig iron into steel requires controlled adjustment of the various impurities. The main process in use is the basic oxygen process and the pig iron is fused with a limestone flux under oxidising conditions. The slag, produced by passage of phosphorus, sulphur, silica, manganese and carbon into the limestone, is of variable composition, but consists mainly of calcium silicates, free lime and mixed oxides.[65] It is unsuitable for use as aggregate for concrete, because metastable compounds are present.[68] High-phosphate slags are valuable as fertilisers and low-phosphate slags find use as roadstone.

Red Mud

The alkaline extraction of alumina produces large quantities of ferruginous residues. These are termed 'red mud' because of their brick red colour due to iron oxide. The quantity of residue varies according to the grade and composition of ore, but typically ranges from 0·5 to 1 tonne of waste on a dry basis per tonne of alumina produced. Around one-third of this waste consists of ferric oxide.

Considerable research has been carried out with the aim of recovering the iron and some of the other consitituents of the residue, or using the material in some other way.[73] The iron recovery processes are mostly based on a complex multi-stage smelting procedure, sometimes including recovery of other materials from slags. None appears to have been economically viable. Chemical separation of the iron by acidification with waste sulphur dioxide gases gives an iron oxide concentrate which can be converted to pigment or smelted. Processes to recover titanium and alumina by chemical processing also appear to have been unsuccessful.

The red mud has also been used in clay products, both as a colouring agent

Iron and steel-making slag processing plant

and as a replacement material. It is an efficient adsorbent for sulphur compounds in stack gases and effluent treatment. The high soda content can be of assistance in both cases. It may also be used as fill, for soil stabilisation, as a catalyst for coal hydrogenation, and to produce a chloride-resistant cement.

Many potential applications have been found for this waste material but few, if any, have been successfully exploited. Therefore most red mud continues to be dumped.

Miscellaneous Wastes

There are many other wastes, both organic and inorganic, for which recycling of some proportion is an economic proposition. Only a few are considered here in some detail to exemplify the general approach.

As a general rule, material which is not over-degraded in the manufacturing process may either be directly recycled or reused in-house for a product of different specification. For example, pottery waste can often be reground and reused for a lower-specification product as an alternative to disposal by landfill: waste sanitary porcelain can be reused in ceramic tile manufacture. Depending on economics, the material may undergo a significant amount of reprocessing before reuse. The flux salts used in secondary aluminium smelting serve as an example: the sodium and potassium salts which become contaminated during smelting are recovered by dissolution in water, filtration to remove impurities, evaporative crystallisation and finally drying.

For inert inorganic solids there may be an outlet as a filler, for example in resin-bonded formulations or cements. A common problem, however, is the cost of transport from the producer to the consumer. Apart from those already discussed, some metallurgical slags have special properties and are reused in limited quantities: for example, copper blast-furnace slag is a valuable grit-blasting material; reject tin slags, which are glassy and stable, are used either for road-making or grit-blasting[65] (see Chapter 15).

Organic wastes invariably have the potential for thermal treatment to produce energy, or fuel and organic chemicals, but in general the economics currently tend to be unfavourable.

Food-processing waste may form a valuable source of animal feedstuffs. They may be recycled directly, for example as pig food, or indirectly following drying and possibly reinforcement with protein and vitamins, as for example with sugar beet waste, described below. In some cases, as discussed in Chapter 1, there is no clear distinction between byproducts and waste. Thus, in the extraction of vegetable oils from nuts and seeds the residual solids have traditionally been blended for animal food. Both the hulls and the meal (i.e. cake from which the oil has been extracted) may be utilised in this way. Alternatively, food waste can be hydrolysed and fermented to produce alcohols. A less valuable product may be produced by composting.

Iron Oxide Pigments

There is a relatively small but established market for inorganic pigments. Various forms of waste or byproduct ferrous materials are readily converted to a small number of useful pigments, particularly brown, red and black, which may be incorporated in, for example, cements.

Brown iron oxide is derived from BOS (basic oxygen steelmaking) fume formed by oxidation of iron during steelmaking. A description of the scrubbing process for removal of this fume is given in Chapter 9. The fume contains impurities such as zinc oxide, fluorides and other non-ferrous metals. Processing is necessary to remove any impurities which affect the setting characteristics of the cement, such as the zinc oxide and fluorides. Comminution and classification are also necessary for production of a consistent and acceptable product. Quality, and particularly colour consistency, is very important and a thorough understanding of the latter characteristic is essential for successful marketing of any pigment.[74]

Red iron oxide is formed from the oxidation product of the hydrolysis of spent hydrochloric acid pickle liquor. The principles of this process have been described in Chapter 12. As with brown oxide, both chemical and physical processing are necessary to remove contaminants such as iron chlorides and oxychlorides and to produce a consistent product. In addition to in-plant treatment of spent pickle liquor, at least one firm in the UK takes in spent acid and successfully markets a red iron oxide pigment in addition to regenerating the acid.

Black iron oxide is derived from red or brown oxide by partial reduction to the black, magnetic form which is then processed to give an acceptable pigment.

A yellow oxide can be formed from spent sulphuric acid pickle liquor, but the process is complicated and therefore probably uneconomic.[74]

While it is unlikely that a sufficient demand for iron oxide pigments exists to justify conversion of more than a small fraction of waste, the processes illustrate that relatively high-value materials can be successfully produced from low-value wastes.

Sugar Beet

Approximately half the refined sugar consumed in the UK comes from the indigenous sugar beet industry. The proportion is significantly higher in Western Europe and the long-term plans for the EEC are to make the community more self-sufficient in sugar.

The sugar beet extraction and refining industry (Figure 16.15) is notable for the reutilisation of wastes, which include soil which is sold to farmers and horticulturists, stones which are sold for road making and concrete, lime-rich filter cake which is sold as a soil conditioner for acidity adjustment, and sugar/molasses-rich beet residue which is sold as cattle food. There is a net surplus of water which requires biological treatment to reduce the sugar content before discharge.

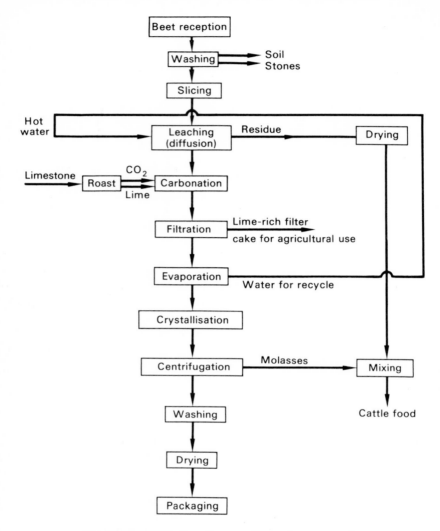

Fig. 16.15 Outline flow diagram of sugar beet processing

Corn Waste

In the production of corn (maize) in the USA, 2·75 tonnes of stalks, leaves and cobs are produced per tonne of corn. The extent of the waste amounts to nearly 80 million tonnes of stalks per year and 28 million tonnes of cobs. Some of the possibilities of reusing this waste are summarised in Table 16.16, which shows the effort and thought that have been put into trying to reuse over 100 million tonnes per year of waste from just one product. Few of the applications have been successful, mostly due to unfavourable economics.

TABLE 16.16 REUSE OF CORN (MAIZE) STALKS AND COBS[75]

Stalks

Paper	Earliest attempt 1802. Many proposals since then, but none currently commercial. Some quality problems exist but are not insurmountable.
Insulating board	Acceptable products may be formed. Commercial exploitation successful around 1930, but died due to cost of harvesting stalk and transportion costs.
Acoustical board	Research only.
Hardboard	Successful product but not exploited commercially.
Moulded fibre products	Possible for a range of products such as window frames. No commercial development.
Xylose	Hydrolysis of xylan, a pentosan, present to about 20% in corn stalks. Problems with purification.
Maizolith	Continuous pulping gives a jelly-like material that dries to a hard, dense compound like vulcanised fibre and may be machined. Drying is difficult and properties cannot compete with modern polymers.
Fuel gas	Fermentation of corn stalks and sewage gives a fuel gas containing 64% methane.
Composting	Possible but not yet attempted. Slow deterioration a problem.
Incineration	Field burning practised for disposal. No exploitation planned.

Cobs

Furfural	Hydrolysis of pentosans gives pentoses which may be further reacted to give furfural (or 2-furaldehyde). Commercially exploited to produce significant quantities of furfural, which is used directly as a solvent and as a precursor for many other chemicals. Other pentosan-containing materials can also be used.
Xylose	Hydrolysis of xylan gives xylose (a pentose) which can be crystallised and used, or converted to furfural. Pentoses may be fermented to acetone, butanol and ethanol.
Dextrose	Dextrose may also be recovered from cellulose residue from above by further hydrolysis.
Lignin	Remains in cobs after above processing. Recoverable but uneconomic.
Plastics	Thermosetting resins may be produced by adding hexamethylene tetramine. Products compare favourably with current marketed products, but there has been no exploitation.

TABLE 16.16 (*Cont'd*)

Board	Insulating board and hardboard, as from stalks, cannot be made because of short fibre length. Fire-resistant board has been successfully made.
Fuel gas	Destructive distillation (pyrolysis) of cobs gives similar products as wood. Not economic. Fermentation with sewage gives gas with a good heating value but the process is complicated and has not been developed.
Cleaning	Shotblasting with ground cobs and rice hulls has been found to be very effective and is employed where suitable.
Oxalic acid	Chemical oxidation with strong nitric acid gives oxalic acid which can be purified by crystallisation. Not exploited. Fusing cobs with three times their weight of sodium hydroxide gives a mixture of oxalic and acetic acids with a yield of 35% and 20% respectively. Not exploited.
Concrete	Ground, dried cobs can be incorporated in concrete to give low-density high-insulating-property material.
Adhesive extender	Ground cobs as flour are incorporated into adhesives to improve spreading and other properties.
Abrasives in soap	Ground cobs can be incorporated up to 60% by weight.
Dynamite	Used as substitute for wood flour.
Lightweight bricks	Incorporation of ground cobs gives a porous product after firing when the cob particles burn away.
Floor-sweeping compound	Ground cobs may be substituted for sawdust.
Dry-cleaning compound	Incorporated as a dirt absorbent to be brushed off.

Diatomaceous Earth

Diatomaceous earth is widely used as a filter aid in the filtration of beverages and oils. A process has now been developed for the recovery of spent filter aids of this type based on the flow process shown in Figure 16.16.[76] Spent filter aid as a slurry or wet cake may either be filtered and fed to a rotary kiln, as in this diagram, or be dried prior to calcination. Calcination takes place at 1000°–1300°C and after cooling the regenerated diatomite product is lightly crushed. The product is finally classified into selected particle size-ranges for blending, grading and reuse.

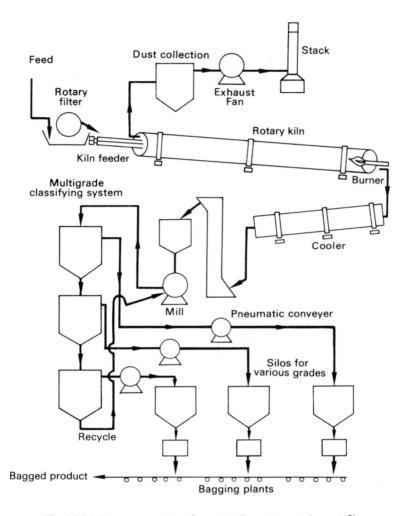

Fig. 16.16 Recovery process for spent diatomaceous filter aid[76]

Sewage Sludge

Sewage sludge, of which an estimated 3 million tonnes of dry solids arise in the UK each year, has a number of potential uses as alternatives to disposal by landfill. These are to produce alcohol or animal feedstuffs by hydrolysis and fermentation, to produce fuel by pyrolysis or to generate heat on incineration. It may also be used as a fertiliser. Limitations are imposed by any significant accumulation of heavy metals in the sludge.

References

1. *Europlastics Yearbook,* IPC, 1974.
2. *Chemical Marketing Reporter,* 17 June 1974.
3. *Japan Plastics Industry Annual,* Plastics Age, 1975.
4. REUBEN, B. G. and BURSTALL, M. L., *The Chemical Economy,* Longman, 1973.
5. STAUDINGER, J. J. P., *Plastics and the Environment,* Hutchinson, 1974.
6. *European Plastics News,* 3 October 1974.
7. PAGET, R., *Polymers, Paint and Colour Journal,* 652, 31 July, 1974.
8. *Chemical Week,* 5, 6 November 1974.
9. *Chemical Week,* 29, 27 November 1974
10. BESSANT, J. R., Design study, Department of Chemical Engineering, University of Aston, 1975.
11. BRIDGWATER, A. V., GREGORY, S. A., MUMFORD, C. J. and SMITH, E. L., *Resource Recovery and Conservation,* 1(1), 3, 1975.
12. EGGINS, H. O. W., MILLS, J., HOLT, A. and SCOTT, G., *Microbial Aspects of Pollution,* Academic Press, 1971, p. 269.
13. SYBERG, A. La dégradation biologique des produits a base de hauts polymers, *Tribune Cebedeau,* 18(265), 588, 1965.
14. DOLEZEL, J., *British Plastics,* 105, October 1967.
15. BROWN, B. S. and MILLS, J., *Campus scientifica,* 1(2), 1973.
16. KULKHARNI, M., *Polymer Engineering and Science,* 5(4), 227, 1965.
17. *Chemical Engineering News,* 50(37), 37, 1972.
18. JACKSON, H. R., *Recycling and Reclaiming of Municipal Solid Wastes,* Noyes Data Corporation, 1975.
19. ZERLAUT, G. A. and STAKE, A. M., *Recycling and Disposal of Solid Wastes,* Illinois Institute of Technology, 1974.
20. KAMINSKY, W., MENZEL, J. and SINN, H., *Conservation and Recycling,* 1(1), 91, 1977.
21. BAUM, B. and PARKER, C. H., *Society of Plastics Engineers Journal,* 29(5), 41, 1973.
22. BAUM, B. and PARKER, C. H., *Plastics Waste Disposal Practices in Landfill, Incineration, Pyrolysis and Recycle,* Manufacturing Chemists Association, 1973.
23. DARNEY, T., *Recycling Assessment and Prospects for Success,* US Government Report PB213961, 1972.
24. *Chemical Week,* 53, 11 December 1974.
25. *Chemical Industry,* 559, June 1973.
26. BALL, G. L. and WEISE, B., *Combustion Products from Incineration of Plastics,* Final Report, EPA/670/2–73–049, PB222001, US Environmental Protection Agency, 1973.
27. BARBOUR, D. et al., *The Chemical Conversion of Solid Wastes to Useful Products,* US Government Report PB233178, 1974.
28. Mitsubishi Heavy Industries Ltd, Japanese Patent JA 4934576, 1974.
29. *Environmental Science and Technology,* 135, February 1974.
30. Kanebo Ltd, Japanese Patent JA 49 41330 Appl. No. 83070 (52755U), 1972.
31. *Modern Plastics International,* 36, February 1974.
32. DRECHSEL, W. and KAHMANN, L., *Plaste und Kautschuk,* 21(8), 578, 1974.
33. BROWN, B. S., *Nature,* 161, 12 July 1974.
34. SCHRAMM, J. M. and BLANCHARD, R. R., SPE Regional Technical Conference on Plastics as Ecology, New Jersey, October 1970.
35. SCHRAMM, J. M. and BLANCHARD, R. R., US Patent 368783, 1972.
36. SAITOH, K., NAGANO, I. and IZUMI, S., *Resource Recovery and Conservation,* 2, 127, 1976.
37. MILGRAM, T., *Incentives for Recycling and Reuse of Plastics,* US Government Report PB214045, 1974.
38. *A Study of the Reclamation and Reuse of Waste Tyres,* Rubber and Plastics Research Association of Great Britain, 1976.
39. CHEATER, G. *Chemistry and Industry,* 569, 16 June 1973.
40. SEARCH, W. J. and CTVRTNICEK, T. E., *Resource Recovery and Conservation,* 2, 159, 1976.
41. US Rubber Reclaiming Company, US Patents 2653348, 2653349, 1946; also *Environmental Pollution Management,* 74, May/June 1975.
42. BIDDULPH, M. W., *Conservation and Recycling,* 1(2), 169, 1977.
43. DOUGLAS, E., WEBB, M. and DABORN, G. R., Symposium on Treatment and Recycling of Solid Waste, Manchester, Institute of Solid Waste Management, 1974.

44. RICCI, L. J., *Chemical Engineering*, 52, 2 August 1976.
45. KOUTSKY, J., CLARK, G. and KLOTZ, D., *Conservation and Recycling*, 1(2), 231, 1977.
46. BROMLEY, J. and DUNSTAN, R., *Proceedings First World Recycling Congress*, Basle, 7–9 March 1978.
47. LUND, G., *R & D Management*, 5(2), 167, 1975.
48. BRIDGE, N. K., in *Waste in the Process Industries*, Institution of Mechanical Engineers, 1976, p. 23.
49. *Waste Paper*, Newsheet 4H7, British Paper and Board Industry Federation, 1977.
50. DEWHIRST, L., *Chemistry and Industry*, 721, September 1976.
51. TURNER, K. R. and GRACE, R. P., *Conservation and Recycling*, 1(2), 179, 1977.
52. Newell Dunford Engineering Ltd, publicity material, 1977.
53. POLLITT, M., *Recycling and Waste Disposal*, 12, February 1977.
54. MASSUS, M., *Waste Paper in the EEC*, Report to the European Commission, 1974.
55. HENDER, V. C., Conference on Packaging and Litter, Department of the Environment, March 1973.
56. *Proceedings First World Recycling Congress*, Basle, Exhibitions for Industry, 7–9 March 1978.
57. Glass Manufacturers Federation, Portland Place, London.
58. GOODING, K., *Financial Times*, 29 July 1974.
59. *National Association of Waste Disposal Contractors News*, 13, October 1977.
60. Gunson's Sortex Ltd, London.
61. PALUMBO, N. J., *Proceedings of the 3rd Mineral Waste Utilization Symposium*, Chicago, Illinois Institute of Technology, 14–16 March 1972, p. 311.
62. MALLAN, G. M. and FINNEY, C. S., 73rd National Meeting, American Institute of Chemical Engineers, Minneapolis, 1972, p. 27.
63. WILLERUP, O. E., *Conservation and Recycling*, 1(1), 149, 1976.
64. Versil Ltd, Raynor Mills, Liversedge, Yorkshire.
65. GUTT, W., NIXON, P. J., SMITH, M. A., HARRISON, W. H. and RUSSELL, A. D., *A Survey of the Locations, Disposal and Prospective Uses of the Major Industrial By-Products and Waste Materials*, CP19/74, Building Research Station, Department of the Environment, 1974.
66. BREAKSPERE, R. J., HEATH, P. J. and MORGAN, R. J., *Proceedings of the First World Recycling Congress*, Basle, Exhibitions for Industry, March 1978.
67. CAAHON, H. P. and CUTLER, I. V., *Proceedings of the 3rd Mineral Waste Utilization Symposium*, Chicago, Illinois Institute of Technology, 14–16 March 1972, p. 353.
68. GUTT, W. *Resources Policy*, 1(1), 29, 1974.
69. BARBER, E. G., in *Pollution Control Yearbook*, Fuel and Metallurgical Journals, 1974, p. 245.
70. JACKSON, J., *Proceedings of the 3rd Mineral Waste Utilization Symposium, Chicago*, Illinois Institute of Technology, 14–16 March 1972, p. 85.
71. GUTT, W., *Chemistry and Industry*, 7, 189, 1971.
72. GUTT, W., *Chemistry and Industry*, 439, 3 June 1972.
73. MOODIE, S. P. and HANSEN, R., in *Treatment, Recycle and Disposal of Wastes*, 3rd National Chemical Engineering Conference, Mildura, Victoria, 20–23 August, Institution of Chemical Engineers, 1975.
74. MC. G. TEGORT, W. J. and MOWAT, G., in *Treatment, Recycle and Disposal of Wastes*, 3rd National Chemical Engineering Conference, Mildura, Victoria, 20–23 August, Institution of Chemical Engineers, 1975.
75. MANTELL, C. L., *Solid Wastes*, Witney, 1975.
76. Newell Dunford Engineering Ltd, Surbiton, UK, Publication DSE4.

CHAPTER 17

Recovery of Materials from Household Refuse

Introduction

Within the last ten years there have been moves to exploit the materials contained in refuse, several of which, notably metals, are of high intrinsic value. Both the fuel crisis and the concern over resources in the early 1970s provided new incentives to attempt to reuse refuse rather than throw it away.

A difficulty arises in the design of recovery systems in that the contents of refuse vary widely with time, both long-term and seasonally, and also geographically. The basic composition is often taken to be that given officially[1] as the UK average, reproduced in Table 17.1. Figure 17.1 shows the composition has changed since 1936 and the projected changes to 2000.[1,2] Table 17.1 also gives analyses of refuse arising in individual locations in the UK and the variation for one source. There is a pattern in the composition, but surprising local differences.

In the UK the total quantity of household refuse is currently approximately 18 million tonnes per year: estimates range from 15 to over 20 million tonnes. One estimated figure for 1980 is nearly 24 million tonnes and for 2000 around 33 million tonnes.[2] The problem of disposal is thus likely to increase, particularly as landfill will become more expensive and difficult as suitable sites, including those made accessible by transfer loading, are used up.

As outlined in Chapter 14, over 90% of refuse in the UK is currently disposed of by tipping.[1] In industrial conurbations incineration tends to be more widely used. The only materials currently recovered are ferrous metals which are readily separable by magnetic separators, but only a small fraction is recovered nationally. Recently a scheme was installed for burning Birmingham refuse to supplement coal in a boiler installation at IMI Witton (Figure 17.2)[8,9,10] ;

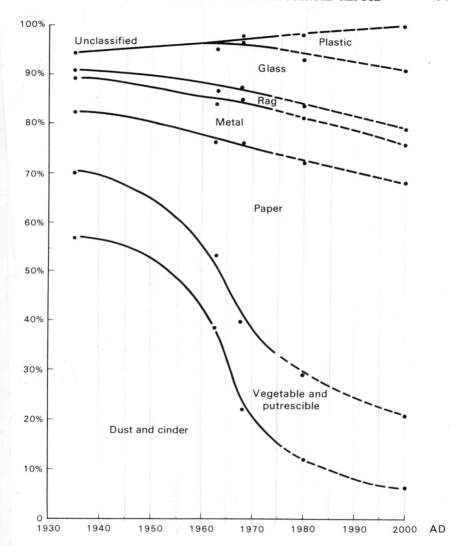

Fig. 17.1 Projected changes in composition of domestic refuse in the UK

60 000 tonnes per year refuse are handled, giving 3500 tonnes per year ferrous metals and replacing 25 000 tonnes per year coal. Separation of non-combustibles other than ferrous metal, to raise the calorific value of the fuel, was rejected as being uneconomic. Although other sorting and separation processes have been carried out as pilot operations, financed by government, and a number of proposals are currently being implemented, this is believed to be the first commercial use of household refuse in the UK.

Several assessments of the various disposal and recovery alternatives[10] confirm

TABLE 17.1 HOUSEHOLD REFUSE COMPOSITION, PERCENTAGE BY WEIGHT

A. UK/USA

	UK (average) 1968	London[3] 1967 Mean	London[3] 1967 Range	Stevenage[4] 1975	West Midlands[5] 1975	USA (typical)[6] 1971
Dust and cinder	21·9	19·7	4–43	25	20	5
Vegetable and putrescible	17·6	19·5	9–31	16	18	14
Paper	36·9	32·9	20–48	32	30	55
Metal	8·9	10·7	5–17	9	6	9
Rag and textiles	2·4	2·7	1–6	5	7	4
Glass	9·1	10·6	6–16	6	7	9
Plastics	1·1	1·3	1–3	5	3	1
Unclassified	2·1	2·6	0–13	2	9	3
	100·0	100·0		100	100	100

B. Europe/USA (1974)[7]

	UK	France	Netherlands	W Germany	Switzerland	Italy	USA
Organic	27·0	22	21	15	20	25	12
Paper	38·0	34	25	28	45	20	50
Fines	11·0	20	20	28	20	25	7
Metal	9·0	8	3	7	5	3	9
Glass	9·0	8	10	9	5	7	9
Plastics	2·5	4	4	3	3	5	5
Miscellaneous	3·5	4	17	10	2	15	8
	100·0	100	100	100	100	100	100
Average water content (%)	25	35	25	35	35	30	25
Heat energy content (kJ/kg)	9770	9300	8370	8370	10 000	7000	11 600
Generation (kg/cap/yr)	317	272	206	349	250	210	816

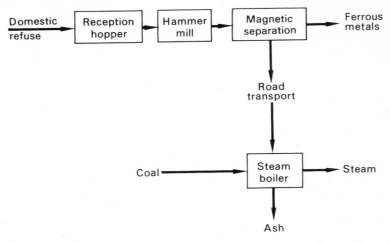

Fig. 17.2 IMI Witton refuse burning scheme (West Midlands County Council)

the view that landfill is the cheapest method overall and also that straight incineration and recovery of a refuse-derived fuel share second place. Recovery of energy as steam or electricity from incineration, or fuel from pyrolysis, is generally expensive. The added value of sorted or derived products does not justify the cost of gaining them.

TABLE 17.2 DETAILED QUALITATIVE COMPOSITION OF HOUSEHOLD REFUSE

Dust and cinder:
    Ash; soil; stones; sweepings; crockery; glass; dust.

Vegetable and Putrescible:
    Fruit and vegetable waste; meat waste; bones; garden waste; wood.

Paper:
    Newsprint; magazines; books; cardboard; waxed board; packaging.

Metal:
    Food and beverage cans and part cans; bottle tops; foil; foil containers; toys; discarded household items; electrical discards; discarded consumer durables; batteries; car spares; wire; nails; screws; nuts and bolts.

Rag and textile:
    Clothing of natural or synthetic fibre; carpet and sweepings; rags; leather.

Glass:
    Whole bottles; broken glass; white, brown or green glass; discarded household items, usually broken.

Plastic:
    Film packaging; containers; sponges; buttons; toys; consumer durables; household items; clothing; footwear; rubber.

Alternatives Available for Recovery

Before investigating ways of recovering valuable materials, it is necessary to have some idea as to what is available for recovery. There are two broad categories: material and energy.

Of the categories given in Table 17.1, each comprises a wide range of different items of which a selection is given in Table 17.2 to illustrate the variety. Many refuse components contain a number of different materials, e.g. tin cans contaminated with food, metal staples in paper, and many household items which are complex mixtures of metals, plastics and other materials. Separation is therefore difficult. A preliminary distinction may be made between inorganic and organic wastes, as many components of the former can be directly recycled while the latter has other properties which can be exploited in addition to the possibilities for recycling.

Many waste constituents, particularly the organic components, have a high calorific value (Table 17.3) giving an overall heat content for refuse of around 10 MJ/kg (4000 Btu/lb). This energy may be released by burning directly in an incinerator, when the heat released may be recovered (Chapter 14). Alternatively, the refuse may be first treated by pyrolysis to give a higher-value fuel product which can be used more effectively as a fuel or provide a source of chemicals.

TABLE 17.3 HEAT CONTENT OF HOUSEHOLD REFUSE

	Heat energy content		Typical % of refuse	Contribution to total refuse heat value	
	(MJ/kg)	(Btu/lb)		(MJ/kg)	(Btu/lb)
Dust and cinder	7·0	3 000	22	1·54	660
Vegetable and putrescible	5·8	2 500	18	1·04	450
Paper	14·5	6 250	35	5·08	2190
Rag and textile	15·8	6 800	6	0·95	410
Plastics	37·2	16 000	3	1·12	480
				9·73	4190

Heat energy content of 1 tonne refuse = 9730 MJ or $9 \cdot 22 \times 10^6$ Btu

The alternatives listed in Table 17.4 are derived from a number of sources[7,10,11,12] et al. and illustrate the effort and ingenuity that have been devoted to resource recovery from household refuse. This chapter deals mainly with current practice and research, and the basic technology involved in implementing resource recovery proposals.

TABLE 17.4 ALTERNATIVES AVAILABLE FOR RESOURCE RECOVERY FROM HOUSEHOLD REFUSE

Alternative	Methods
A (Unprocessed waste)	Energy recovery (followed by D) Direct by incineration Indirect by pyrolysis to a gas, liquid and solid fuel Indirect by landfill to give methane by anaerobic decomposition
B Primary physical separation into organic (C, E, F, G) and inorganic (D) fractions	Dry separation (followed by C and D): organic fraction used as refuse derived fuel (followed by E) Wet separation (followed by C and D)
C Secondary physical separation of organic fraction	Paper fibre recovery Composting to give humus Plastics recovery
D Secondary physical separation of inorganic fraction	Ferrous metal recovery Non-ferrous metal recovery; total and individual, copper, aluminium, zinc Glass recovery, total and by colour— clear, green, brown
E Thermal processing of organic fraction	Incineration for heat recovery Use as coal substitute—RDF (refuse derived fuel) Pyrolysis to gas, liquid and solid fuel/chemicals
F Chemical processing of organic fraction	Hydrogenation: pyrolysis in a hydrogen atmosphere Gasification by partial oxidation or stream reforming; adaptation of pyrolysis and town gas manufacture Oxidation in aqueous medium to organic acids Hydrolysis to sugars
G Biological processing of organic fraction	Hydrolysis and fermentation to ethanol Hydrolysis and fermentation to yeast—single-cell protein Anaerobic digestion to methane

Physical Separation Processes

Refuse is essentially a physical mixture of components, and it might be assumed that physical separation would provide the individual components in a more or less acceptable state, but this would be unduly optimistic in view of the technological and economic limitations—and there is the further problem of reusing the components once recovered. Cans, for example, are contaminated with paper wrappings or printed with paint and lacquered, they are increasingly fitted with aluminium ends, and in addition may be contaminated with food which may have dried on. While this is partly a technical and partly a marketing problem, it is an essential consideration in evaluating a resource recovery proposal: for instance, should tin cans be recovered whole or shredded, clean or dirty, hollow or crushed, wet or dry?

Most physical properties of materials have been utilised in attempts to effect separation. A comprehensive list of physical separation techniques is given in Table 17.5, showing the properties exploited. The majority are based on fundamental and simple properties such as density, size/shape, and electromagnetic properties, which are utilised in variations of classification, screening/sieving, and magnetic/electromagnetic separation respectively (Table 17.6). Dry operation tends to be preferred generally to wet operation which presents problems of dirty water disposal and contamination of products.

TABLE 17.5 PHYSICAL SEPARATION TECHNIQUES AND PROPERTIES UTILISED
(Compiled from many sources; particularly, DOUGLAS and BIRCH[13])

Separator	Properties exploited
Air classifier (see Horizontal, Rotating cylinder, Three-stage aspirator, Vertical, Zigzag)	
Ballistic separator	Aerodynamic drag, density, size, shape
Cryogenic separator	Glass point
Cyclone	Density, size, shape, drag
Electrodynamic separator (Eddy current separator)	Eddy current forces, density, size, shape, friction
Electrostatic precipitator	Electrical conductivity, induced charges
Elutriation (wet)	Density, drag, size, shape
Ferro-fluid separator (see Magnetic fluid separator)	
Fluidised bed	Density
Froth flotation	Physico-chemical
Hand sorting	
High-tension separator (see Electrostatic precipitator)	
Horizontal air classifier	Density, size, shape, drag
Hydrocyclone (see Cyclone)	
Hydropulper	Density, size, shape, drag, wet strength, rigidity

TABLE 17.5 (*Cont'd*)

Separator	Properties exploited
Impalement separator (see Selective impalement)	
Inclined conveyor separator (see Ballistic separator)	
Inertial separator (see Ballistic and Thrower Separators)	
Jigging	Density
Linear induction motor eddy current separator (see Electrodynamic separator)	
Magnetic drum	Magnetism
Magnetic fluid separator	Density
Metal detector (see also Sortex-type separator)	Electrical properties
Optical sorting (see Hand sorting and Sortex-type separator)	
Multimagnetic belt	Magnetism
Permanent magnet eddy current separator (see Electrodynamic separator)	
Rising current separator	Density, drag, size, shape
Rotary screen	Size, shape
Rotating cylinder air classifier	Density, size, shape, drag
Secator separator (see Ballistic separator)	
Selective comminution (see Selective pulverising classifier)	
Selective adhesion	Melting point
Selective impalement	Strength, hardness
Selective pulping (see also Hydropulper)	Wet strength
Selective pulverising classifier	Brittleness, strength, hardness
Shape separator	Shape
Sifting screen	Size, shape
Sink–float	Density
Spiral classifier	Size, shape
Sortex-type separator	Colour, opacity, reflectance
Sweating furnace	Melting point
Tabling	Density, friction, shape
Three-stage aspirator	Density, size, shape
Thrower separator	Elasticity, drag, friction
Trommel (see also Rotary screen)	Size, shape
Vertical air classifier	Density, size, shape
Vibrating elutriator	Density, size, shape
Vibratory screen	Size, shape
Vortex classifier (see Rotating cylinder air classifier)	
Wemco RC Separator (see Rising current separator)	
Winnowing (see air classifiers— Horizontal, Rotating, Cylinder, Vertical)	
Zigzag air classifier	Density, size, shape

TABLE 17.6 PHYSICAL SEPARATION METHODS (SEE ALSO FIGURES 17.3–15)

	Dry	Wet
Classification	Ballistic separator	Elutriator
	Cyclone	Fluidised bed
	Ferrofluid separator	Hydrocyclone
	Fluidised bed	Jigging
	Horizontal air classifier	Rising current separator
	Inertial separator	Sink–float
	Magnetic fluid separator	Tabling
	Rotating cylinder air classifier	
	Spiral classifier	
	Three stage aspirator	
	Vertical air classifier	
	Vibrating elutriator	
	Vortex classifier	
	Winnowing	
	Zig-zag air classifier	
Screening	Rotary screen	
	Sifting screen	
	Trommel	
	Vibratory screen	
Magnetic-electro-magnetic	Eddy current separator	
	Electrodynamic separator	
	Electrostatic separator	
	Linear induction motor eddy current separator	
	Magnetic drum	
	Metal detector	
	Multimagnetic belt	
	Permanent magnet eddy current separator	
Miscellaneous	Cryogenic separator	Froth flotation
	Hand sorting	Hydropulper
	Impalement separator	Selective pulping
	Optical sorting	Tabling
	Selective adhesion	
	Selective comminution	
	Selective impalement	
	Selective pulverising classifier	
	Shape separator	
	Sortex-type separator	
	Sweating furnace	
	Thrower separator	

Newell Dunford Engineering Ltd

End view of rotary air classifier in operation

Most of the equipment designed for physical separation is based on traditional chemical engineering and scientific principles but a fair amount of ingenuity is required to apply these successfully to such a thoroughly heterogeneous feedstock as household refuse. Even after extensive development work, design is still essentially by trial and error and improvements are constantly being made. Figures 17.3–15 show some of the best known and, by inference, more successful equipment of the wide range that has been developed.

As well as for household refuse separation, such equipment is widely used for in-factory treatment of waste; examples include air blowing to remove aluminium foil bottle-tops from recycled cullet at glassworks; cryogenic metal scrap treatment; sweating furnace for non-ferrous metal separation; and jigging and tabling in the mineral processing industries. In fact many of the separation methods applied to refuse have been derived from existing applications.

Size-reduction is subsidiary to separation but essential for efficient operation. Equipment ranges from applications of traditional techniques such as the hammermill (Figure 17.16) to new developments of special application to household refuse such as the Liberator developed by Warren Spring Laboratory to handle refuse packed in large plastic sacks (Figure 17.17), in which the sacks are torn apart in the machine to release the contents for further processing. Table 17.7 (page 517) lists types of equipment and applications.

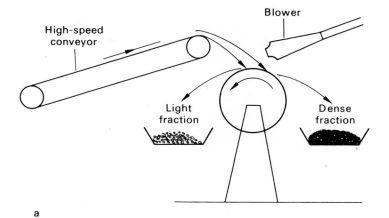

a

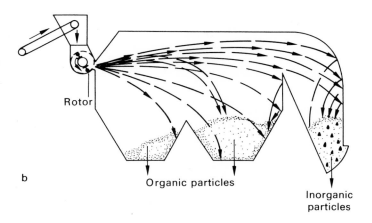

b

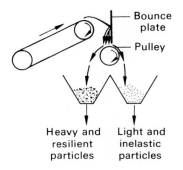

c

Fig. 17.3 Types of inertial separator
  a Ballistic separator (Warren Spring Laboratory)
  b Ballistic separator
  c Secator

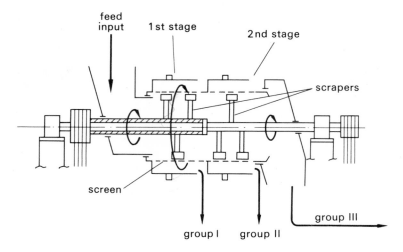

Fig. 17.4 Selective pulverising classifier
        Group I: glass, dirt, ceramics, food waste, brittle materials
        Group II: paper-rich fraction
        Group III: plastics, textiles, leather, metals, ductile materials

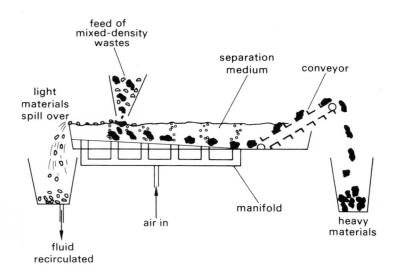

Fig. 17.5 Dry fluid bed separator

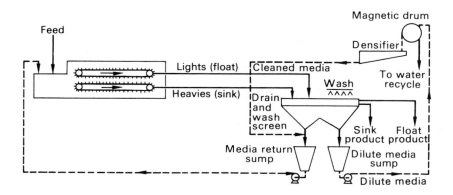

Fig. 17.6 Heavy media separator

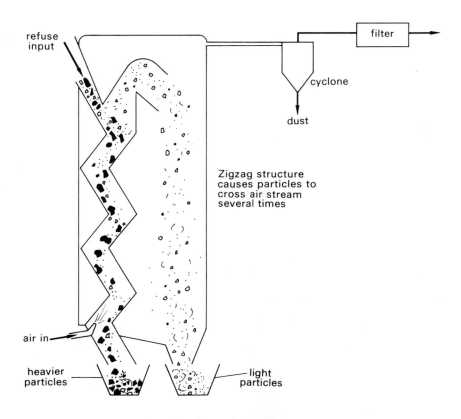

Fig. 17.7 Zigzag air classifier

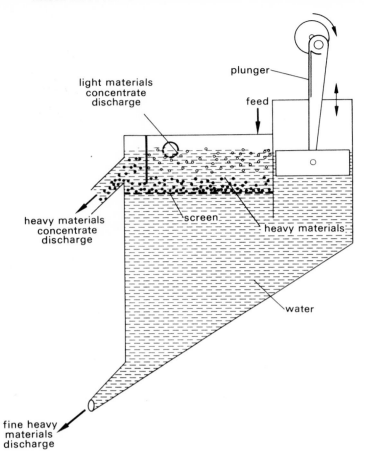

Fig. 17.8 Fixed screen jig

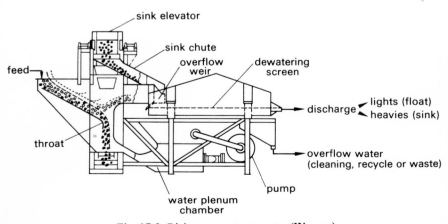

Fig. 17.9 Rising-current separator (Wemco)

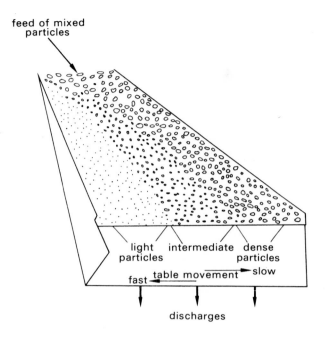

feed of mixed
particles

light
particles

intermediate

dense
particles

fast — table movement → slow

discharges

Fig. 17.10 Vibrating-table separator
The table slopes from the input end down to the output end. A lateral
slow–fast stroke separates particles of different inertia

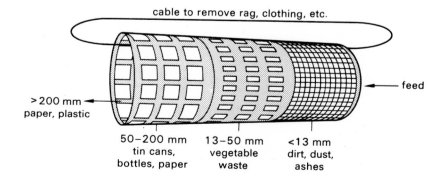

cable to remove rag, clothing, etc.

feed

>200 mm
paper, plastic

50–200 mm
tin cans,
bottles, paper

13–50 mm
vegetable
waste

<13 mm
dirt, dust,
ashes

Fig. 17.11 Rotary screen or trommel

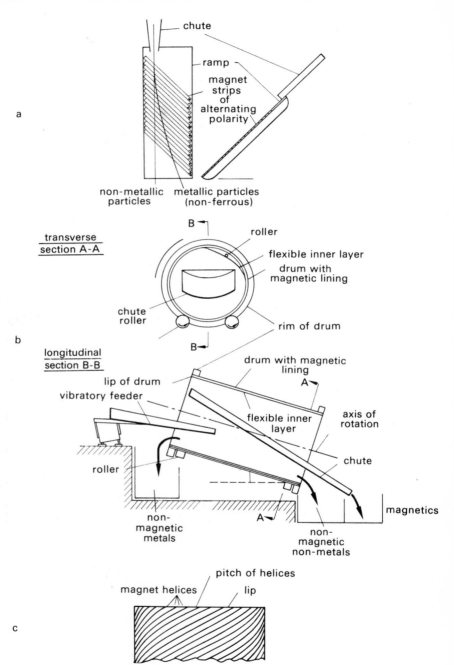

Fig. 17.12 Permanent magnet non-ferrous metal separators
      a Schematic diagram of ramp metal separator in frontal view (left) and side
         view (right)

Peabody Holmes Ltd

Aerodynamic separator

b Schematic diagram of rotary-drum metal separator: the lower portion is a
longitudinal cross-section B-B taken parallel to the axis of drum rotation; the
upper portion is a transverse section A-A taken perpendicular to the axis of
drum rotation
c Permanent magnet array on the interior surface of the drum

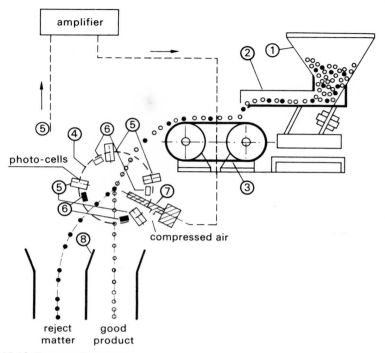

Fig. 17.13 Sortex colour separator
Commodities to be separated are:
(1) Fed from the *hopper*
(2) by means of a *vibrating chute*
(3) aligning themselves on a *grooved belt*
(4) They are then projected in single file into the *optical box*
(5) and inspected by six *photo-cells* (four for shade and two for colour)
(6) against *coloured backgrounds*
(7) Any discoloured items are deflected from the main stream by an *air jet*
(8) to the other side of a *dividing edge* for separate collection

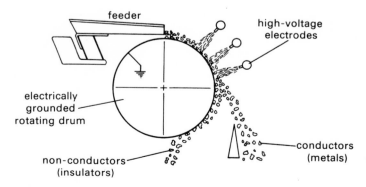

Fig. 17.14 High-tension separator
Non-conductors: glass, plastics, rubber, bone, wood, textiles, ceramics
Conductors: metals, paper

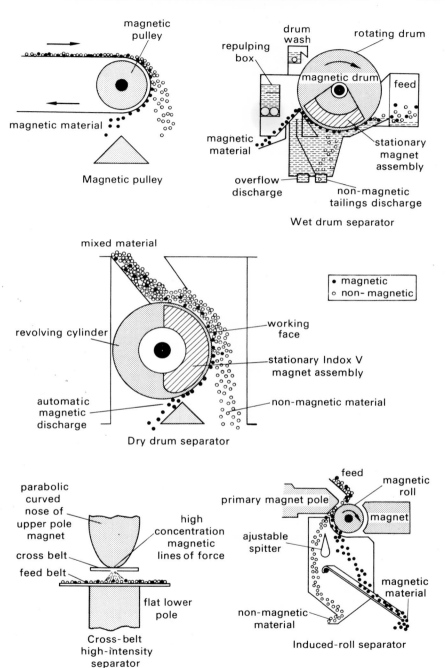

Fig. 17.15 Magnetic separators

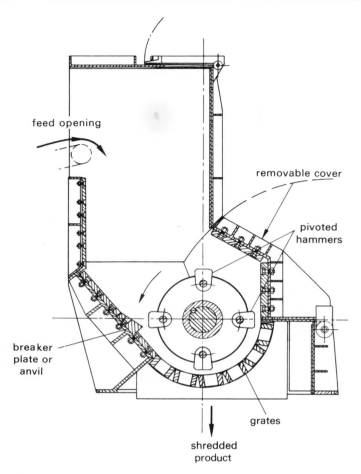

feed opening

removable cover

pivoted
hammers

breaker
plate or
anvil

grates

shredded
product

Fig. 17.16 Hammermill

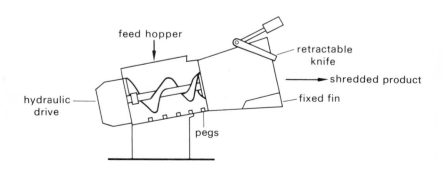

feed hopper

retractable
knife

shredded product

hydraulic
drive

fixed fin

pegs

Fig. 17.17 Liberator (Warren Spring Laboratory)

TABLE 17.7 SIZE-REDUCTION EQUIPMENT

Equipment	Application
Ball mills and rod mills	Fine grinding
Cage disintegrators	Brittle or friable material Also aids disentanglement
Crushers: (a) Impact, e.g. hammermill (b) Jaw, gyratory, roll	Primary application to brittle or friable material
Disc mills	Special operations
Hammermills: Crusher impact	
Shears	Metal, wood
Shredders: (a) Pierce and tear, e.g. Liberator (b) Cutting	Plastic bags, paper and board Paper and board
Wet pulpers/pulverisers	Secondary operation on pulpable materials such as paper

Integrated Recovery Schemes

Fourteen integrated recovery schemes were reported in the USA in 1974[12] and 25 processes were reported in 1977[10] solely for producing refuse-derived fuel (RDF). In addition to extensive activity in the USA and the work of Warren Spring Laboratory in the UK, serious investigations have been carried out in Sweden, Spain, Italy, Germany, France, Denmark, Holland and Japan. Production of RDF for use as a coal substitute, with metal as an added bonus, appears to be currently the most favoured system. Two demonstration plants are under construction in the UK, and a number of plants are nearing completion in other parts of the world. Figures 17.18–23 show some proposed processes and illustrate how the various separation methods may be integrated.

Selective Separation Processes

A range of processes for selective separation of one or more components of refuse is shown in Figures 17.24–28. Figures 17.24 and 17.25 show practical applications; conceptual approaches are illustrated in Figures 17.26–28. There is no 'best' method; alternative methods and configurations are continuously being devised and tested to improve separation efficiency, reduce costs and/or produce a more useful material. The methods and principles are also employed in 'back end' systems to recover values after thermal treatment (discussed later). Other applications include separation of scrap metals into different fractions such as ferrous/non-ferrous/non-metallics from shredded automobile scrap (Chapter 15). Non-ferrous metal concentrates can be segregated, and also different grades of the same metal.

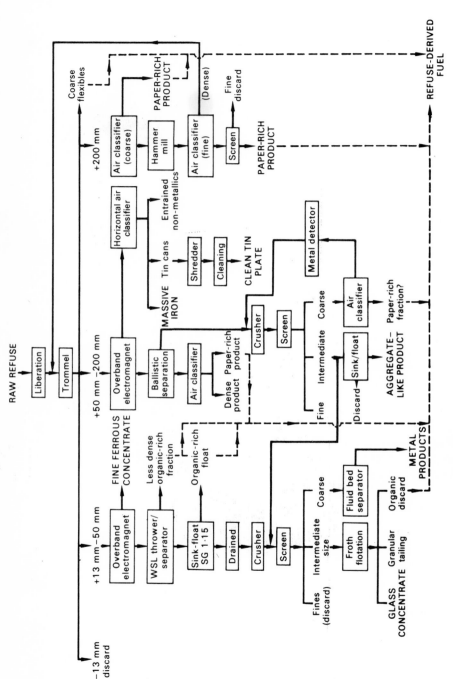

Fig. 17.18 Raw refuse processing circuit (Warren Spring Laboratory): a proposed total separation system with most stages technically proven

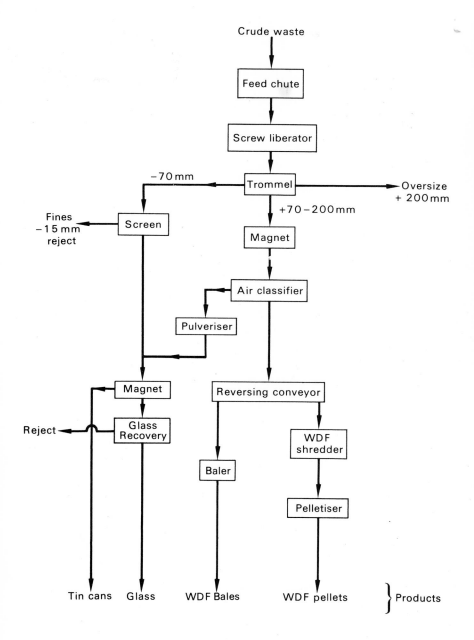

Fig. 17.19 Waste-sorting plant, Doncaster (South Yorkshire County Council)[14]
Feed waste analysis similar to the Byker plant (Figure 17.20)

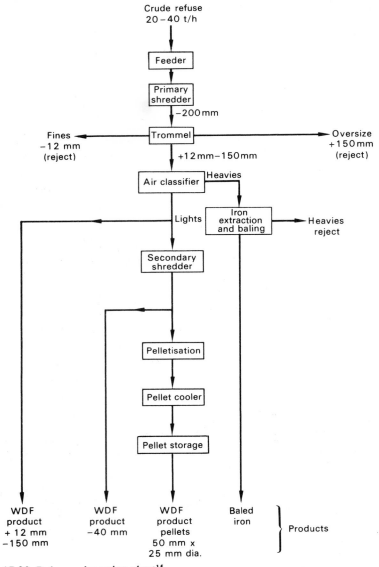

Fig. 17.20 Byker reclamation plant[15]

Waste feed analysis	(% w/w)		
Screenings below 12 mm	10–15	Glass	8–10
Paper/cardboard	30–40	Unclassified	3–5
Vegetable/putrescible	15–25	Moisture average	20–30
Textiles/rags	3–5		
Plastics/rubber	4–8	*Objective characteristics of WDF*	
Wood	1–2	Calorific value (gross)	> 14 MJ/kg
Ferrous metals	8–10		(6000 Btu/lb)
Non-ferrous metals	1–2	Moisture content	⩽ 20% wt
		Non-combustible material	⩽ 5% wt

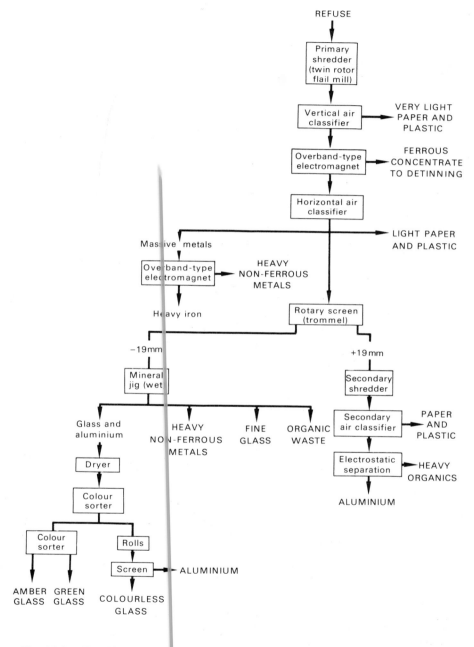

Fig. 17.21 Simplified flowsheet of US Bureau of Mines raw refuse separation plant, giving complete separation process as in the Warren Spring process

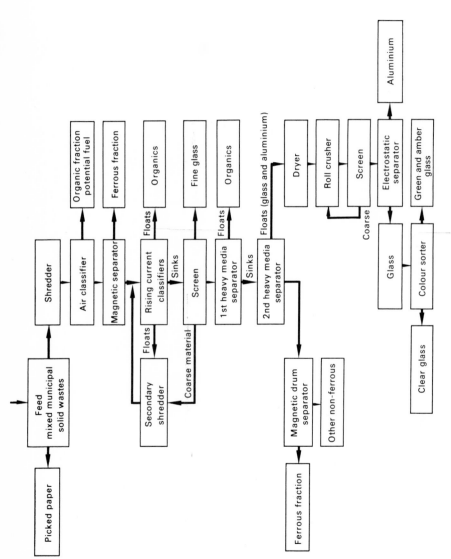

Fig. 17.22 NCRR processing scheme for separating materials from mixed refuse, adapted for the City of New Orleans solid waste disposal

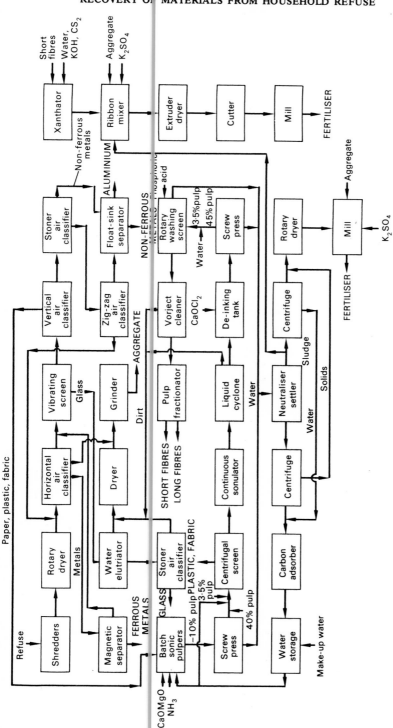

Fig. 17.23 The Biocel process and products: although perhaps impractical and uneconomic, this system produces no waste at all. It is the result of considerable ingenuity and illustrates what is technically possible[17]—product distribution is shown on page 524

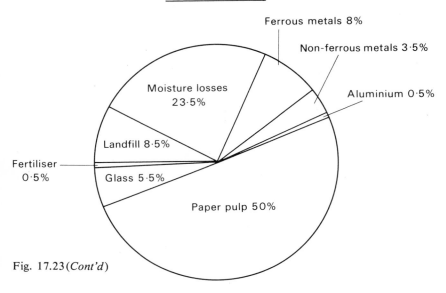

Product distribution

Fig. 17.23 (*Cont'd*)

Fig. 17.24 (*opposite*) The Ames resource recovery system, one of the few operational dry separation systems, recovers metals and a solid-fuel-type product (RDF).[18] A number of others are being installed, but were not in operation in early 1978

Future Development of Refuse-sorting

The primary objective of current research is cheaper household refuse disposal, taking into account current disposal costs, effect of new legislation and consequent increased costs, together with the additional costs of a resource recovery process and the revenues from recovered materials to offset against current costs. Resource conservation is regarded as an added bonus. The problems in optimisation lie mainly in not knowing the cost of a new recovery process until it is built and operational, nor the potential income until the products are marketed. The technology largely exists and may be expected to develop for many years. Current effort appears to be directed to studying the payoff between a complex process having high capital and operating costs but giving a high-value product, and a relatively simple process with low costs producing a lower-value product. Perhaps the most difficult area is marketing the products, which are often unfamiliar to processors; special techniques may need to be developed to reprocess them efficiently. Until these new reclaimed materials are available in sufficiently large quantities to make a new reprocessing technology viable, assessment of market value and size is difficult.

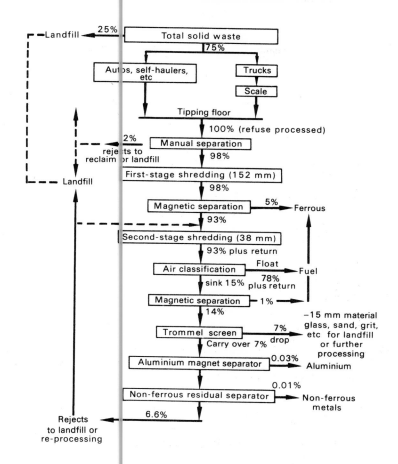

Table 17.1 identified the main components of household refuse as

    Metal, ferrous/non-ferrous
    Paper
    Plastic
    Vegetable and putrescible   }   Forms basis of RDF
    Rag and textile
    Glass
    Dust and cinder

Early efforts were directed towards segregation either into individual components or into the more valuable and/or easily separable components such as metals, paper and glass. The main materials that may be expected to be reclaimed are listed in Table 17.8. Many uses for the concentrates have been proposed. Most seem to be technically feasible but few have been found both economically viable and acceptable. However, it now seems to be accepted that complete separation is uneconomic and processes attempt to recover as much as possible in two main fractions—metals and RDF. Efforts are being directed towards producing more compact and easily handled RDF by compaction and extrusion, for example as pelletised fuel known as densified refuse-derived fuel (dRDF).

Of the respondents to a survey of local authorities in the UK,[22] nearly half practised no reclamation at all. Of those reclaiming some materials, the most

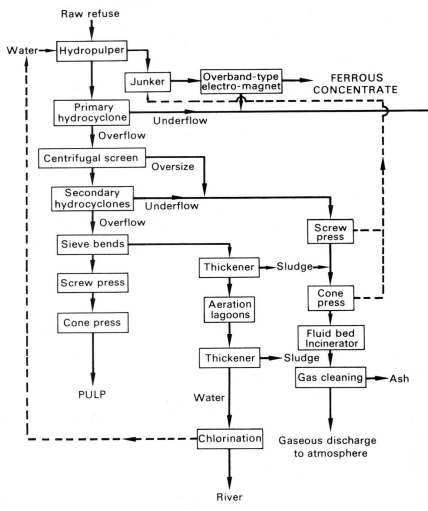

Fig. 17.25 Simplified flowsheet of the refuse-processing plant, Franklin, Ohio (Black-Clawson process)—one of the few wet processing systems to have been proven on pilot scale.[19] Wet processing has the advantage of giving a cleaner product, but as the product is wet there is the additional problem of waste-water disposal

popular was paper, followed by metals (Table 17.9).

In determining a specification for a marketable recovered material it is necessary to consider quality control, delivery schedules and price structures in the light of current technological possibilities. Pricing policy is also important in marketing, as this is the most sensitive factor in determining profitability. The price must take account of the saving in disposal cost, the inherent value, and the market forces relating to the recovered material. Guaranteed flow and/or

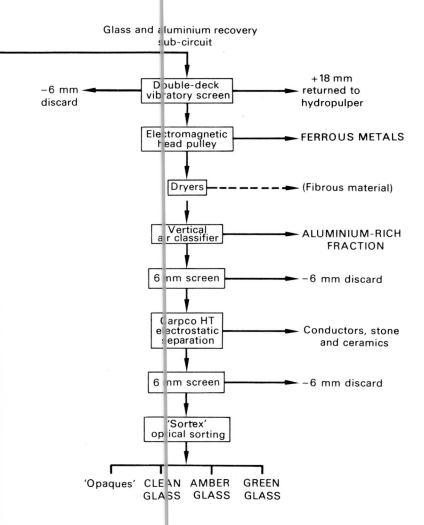

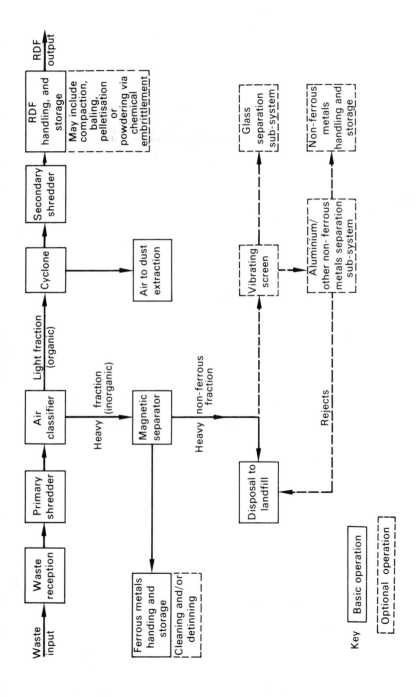

Fig. 17.26 Typical RDF-system flowsheet based on dry separation of the inorganic and organic fractions.[10]

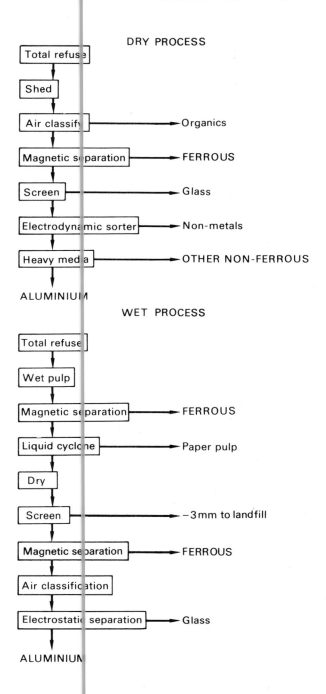

Fig. 17.27 Typical outline flowsheets for metal recovery by dry and wet processing[16]

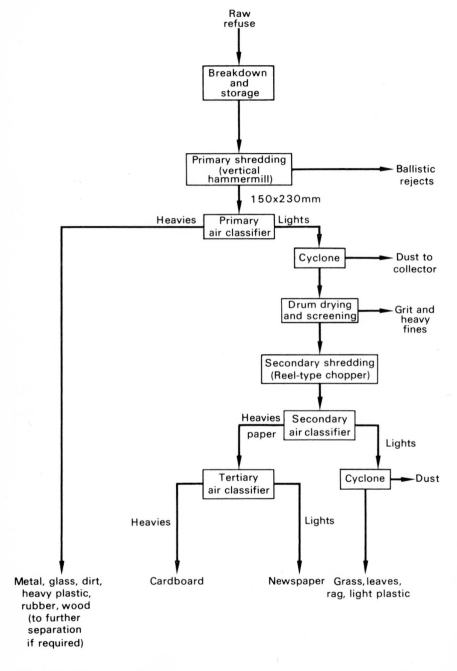

Fig. 17.28 EPA air-classification of solid wastes: schematic flow diagram of process for waste-paper recovery from municipal refuse[20]

minimum prices would be expected. In the survey referred to above, local authorities were found to prefer the security of long-term contracts. It was also confirmed that simple economics of cost versus profit was the largest single factor in deterring or encouraging councils to reclaim. Of those local authorities handling trade waste, most separated and/or reclaimed materials, presumably at a profit.

Energy Recovery from Refuse

The 18 million tonnes per year of refuse arising in the UK contain sufficient energy to supply around 5% of UK requirements. This potential, together with forecasted depletion of non-renewable fossil fuel reserves, has led to a considerable amount of research throughout the world into possibilities for energy recovery. By current economic criteria such operations are expected to pay for themselves, and the overall economic objective is thus to reduce disposal costs.

Table 17.10 lists the seven main ways of utilising the heat content. Incineration produces heat and/or electricity, while pyrolysis, digestion, fermentation

TABLE 17.8 RECOVERABLE COMPONENTS FROM HOUSEHOLD REFUSE

	Approximate efficiency of recovery of component
Combustibles (65%)	
Paper fraction (32%) Paper, plastic	90%
Putrescibles (22%)	80%
Other combustibles (11%)	
Metals (8%)	90% overall
Ferrous (7%): Tinplate (6%)	90%
Massive iron, steel (1%)	
Non-ferrous (1%): Aluminium	70%
Other non-ferrous, mainly copper, zinc	60%
Glass (7%)	70% overall
Colourless	50%
Amber	50%
Green	50%
Miscellaneous (20%)	
Dust, dirt, ash, grit (17%)	
Larger inert materials (3%)	

Typical dry weight percentage of feed is given in brackets.[13,21] Each component is a rich fraction containing up to 90% of the stated material.

TABLE 17.9 IRDE LOCAL AUTHORITY QUESTIONNAIRE ANALYSIS—1977[22]

Number of questionnaires issued	548	
Number returned	135 (24·6% response)	
Refusal to complete (of those returned)	17	

		% of positive response (118)
No reclamation of any kind	56	47·5
Paper and cardboard only	31	26·3
Metals only	7*	5·9
Paper, metals	8	6·8
Paper, textiles	1	0·8
Paper, textiles, metals	7	5·9
Paper, metals, glass	2	1·7
Metals, oil	1	0·8
Metals, textiles, compost	1	0·8
Paper, metals, textiles, oil, compost	1	0·8
Paper, metals, textiles, bones, cinders, glass	1	0·8
Paper, plastic, metals, glass, heat	1	0·8
Paper, metals, textiles, glass	1	0·8

* Ferrous only, 5; ferrous and non-ferrous, 2.

and separation produce a notionally storable fuel. Incineration has the disadvantage that unless the heat produced can be used immediately, it must be converted into another energy form; alternatively, electricity is generated for which many cheaper sources are available. A storable fuel (or chemical feedstock) in gas, liquid or solid form is more attractive in the long term. Gases have a high volume-to-weight ratio and are relatively expensive to store and transport, but give cleaner and more efficient combustion. Liquid fuels are easier to store and transport but can cause greater pollution. Solids present the general problem of handling in transport, storage and use, in addition to increased pollution in handling and burning.

Thermal Processing

Incineration
Incineration is a popular and useful method of refuse disposal in large urban areas where landfill is remote and expensive (see Chapters 13 and 14). The major disadvantage is economic: incineration costs approximately three times as much as landfill, and attempts to recover thermal energy have not generally proved economically viable. Recovery of heat as steam/hot water for use locally cannot usually be economically justified, whether the heat is used domestically or industrially. The problem of seasonal loading may be overcome by provision of an air-conditioning system with appropriate heating and cooling,[12] but again economic viability is questionable. The difficulties largely

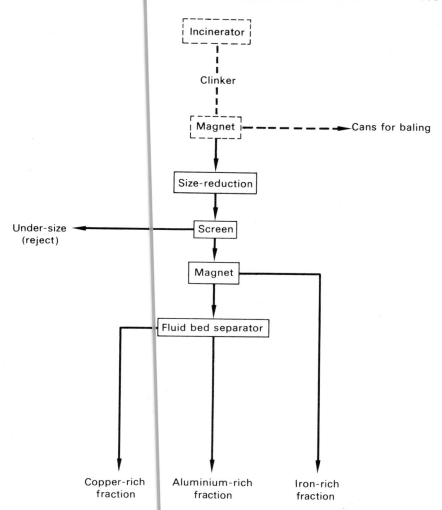

Fig. 17.29 Metal recovery from incinerator clinker (Warren Spring Laboratory)

lie in distribution, availability, grade of heat and size and proximity of customer. While UK experience seems firmly against energy recovery, there is greater optimism in the USA where a large number of possibilities are currently being explored practically and theoretically. Conversion of thermal energy to electricity to overcome some of these difficulties is uneconomic and is generally regarded as the most expensive option for solid waste treatment.

However, with increased use of incinerators for waste disposal some attention has been paid to the possibility of resource recovery after incineration, directed primarily at metals, both ferrous and non-ferrous, which tend to be relatively unaffected. Proposed processes by Warren Spring Laboratory and the US Bureau of Mines are shown in Figures 17.29 and 17.30.

TABLE 17.10 ENERGY RECOVERY FROM REFUSE

	Advantages	Disadvantages
(a) Incineration with heat recovery	Good method for district heating Higher burn-out efficiencies can be expected with prepared fuel (RDF) than with unprepared refuse Commercially available plant Can be developed to air conditioning system High volume-reduction of refuse Sterile char	Corrosion of boiler tubes at high steam temperatures Steam flow not sufficiently dependable to run power plant auxiliary systems High initial costs Slagging of heat exchange surface can give high cleaning costs and downtime Pollution problems
(b) Incineration with electricity generation	Total electric power production package available Good overall system efficiency Possible revenue from material recovery High volume-reduction of refuse Sterile char	Serious technical problems with gas clean-up before turbine New electrical generation equipment required Very high initial and running costs Other problems as (a)
(c) Pyrolysis to give oil, gas and char	Oil can be used in conventional boiler with minor modifications Existing power plant can be used Higher-value products than incineration Front- or back-end resource recovery options may be included High volume-reduction of refuse and sterile char Overall disposal cost claimed to be less than landfill	Technology unproven Problems with corrosiveness and storability of pyrolytic oil High initial and operating costs Costly feed preparation Waste-water disposal problem
(d) Pyrolysis to give gas and char/slag (gasification)	Produces low to medium heating-value gas Feed preparation not essential, although preferred Existing power plant can be used Fairly high overall system efficiency Higher-value products than with incineration	Potential plugging of slag Fuel gas not compatible with natural gas without additional processing/expenditure Storage of fuel not viable High initial and operating cost Unproven viability Waste-water disposal problem Low heating value of gas necessitates local use

TABLE 17.10 (*Cont'd*)

	Advantages	Disadvantages
	Fuel gas usable in most boiler types Technology more advanced than (c) Front- or back-end resource recovery options may be included Gas may be employed as chemical feedstock High volume-reduction and sterile char	
(e) Solid fuel preparation as RDF	Gaining acceptance by manufacturers and users Existing facilities can be used with minor modification to generate steam or electricity Revenue from other recovered materials High overall system efficiency Relatively low costs dRDF improves storage and handling Largely proven technology Plant available commercially	Low bulk density of unprepared refuse makes storage difficult Potential increase in particulate loading and pollution Densifying/pelletising equipment still presents problems High costs and unproven viability
(f) Anaerobic digestion to give methane	Existing steam or electricity generation plant can be used Revenue from other recovered materials possible Product compatible with SNG after carbon dioxide removal	Sensitive to moisture and oxygen environment Very low overall system efficiency Product contaminated with carbon dioxide which requires separation Reaction rates very low, requiring large reactors and long residence times Residue disposal problem unless landfill is employed
(g) Fermentation to chemicals	Revenue from other recovered materials possible Technology well developed High-value products recovered	Sensitive to contamination High energy costs in purification from an aqueous base High costs Residue disposal problem Viability doubtful

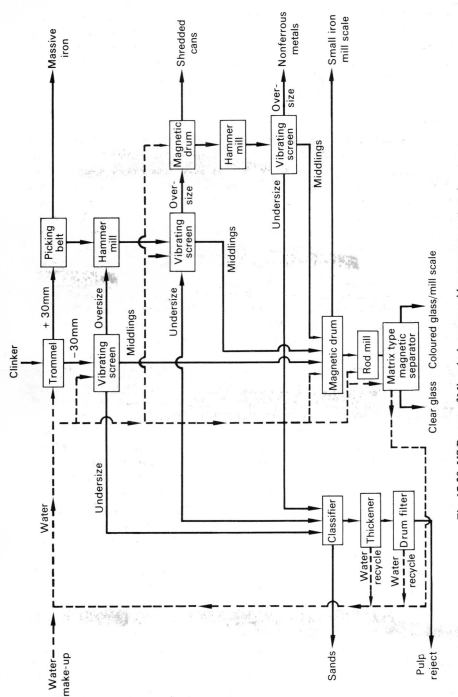

Fig. 17.30 US Bureau of Mines incinerator residue recovery system

Post-incineration or back-end treatment is useful to add on to existing incinerators but the product oxidation and contamination probably make it less valuable than that recovered before incineration. Both the recovery processes illustrated and others proposed employ the principles and operations described earlier under physical separation methods. The overall objective is to obtain as pure a product as possible with the minimum number of steps.

Pyrolysis

Pyrolysis is, in principle, thermal treatment in the absence, or with a limited supply, of air or oxygen; it results not in combustion or oxidation but in a complex series of chemical reactions producing a mixture of gas, liquid and solid residues, which may be utilised as fuel or raw material for the chemical industry. Heat must be supplied to the process and this may be effected by external application, internal hot gases. circulating hot solids, or partial oxidation or combustion. It is usual to separate out inert materials such as metals, glass, dust and stones prior to pyrolysis to avoid product contamination, and increase throughput. The remaining organic fraction, consisting mainly of paper and board, plastics, putrescibles and rag, is effectively RDF and may conveniently be approximated to cellulose in chemical composition, since cellulose is the principal ingredient of paper and putrescibles which together form the bulk of the organic fraction. This material can be treated as a basic raw material for a range of processes of which pyrolysis is but one.[7,23,24,25] Others are described later.

At high temperature the cellulosic organic materials break down into four main products: fuel gas, pyrolytic oil, aqueous condensate and a carbonaceous solid residue. The proportion and composition of the products are affected by pyrolysis temperature, method of heating, rate of heating, contact time, recirculation, secondary processing, drying, type of equipment, catalysts, pressure and chemical additions such as oxygen, air, water, hydrogen, carbon monoxide or carbon dioxide. Information on the effects of these variables is still being gathered and a surprisingly small amount of coherent data is available although pyrolysis has been practised since before 1800 to produce gas from coal.

There are two main types of pyrolysis process. High-temperature or slagging pyrolysis ('gasification') usually involves addition of some air or oxygen to achieve a temperature of around 1500°–1600°C and gives mainly gaseous products and a liquid slag (see Purox and Andco-Torrax processes, described later). Low-temperature or simple pyrolysis can be operated to give gas and liquid or gas only (see Occidental/Garrett process and Warren Spring/Foster Wheeler cross-flow system).

Generally pyrolysis temperature is one of the most important variables in controlling the proportion of the four products. Pyrolysis begins at around 250°C and becomes significant above 300°C. As temperature increases, greater proportions of gas are formed and less liquid distillate and solid char. Some typical figures of product composition are shown in Figure 17.31. These assume that no products are recycled internally or externally. The effect of rate of heating is also shown, high heating rates favouring oil production. The liquid portion comprises two separate fractions—oil (known as pyrolytic oil) and water containing a variety of mostly soluble organic chemicals. The heating value of the gas ranges from around 240 kJ/kg (100 Btu/lb) when contaminated with nitrogen (from partial oxidation with air) and carbon dioxide, to around 2100 kJ/kg (900 Btu/lb) when no nitrogen is present and carbon dioxide is removed. The Occidental/Garrett process is one of the few to achieve demonstration status of 180 tonnes/day refuse input and produce a significant proportion of liquid oil (Table 17.11).

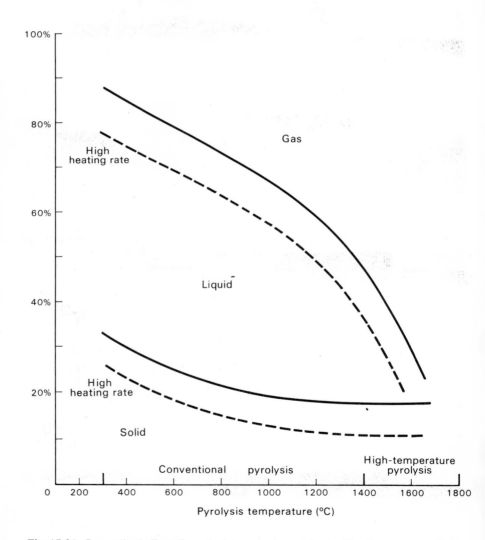

Fig. 17.31 Generalised effect of pyrolysis temperature and rate of heating on proportions of products

The basic chemical reaction may be represented by the degradation of cellulose in the following approximation:

$$10C_6H_{10}O_5 \rightarrow 13C + 10C_4H_9O_3 + \underbrace{4CO + 3CO_2 + H_2} + 5H_2O$$

$\qquad$ cellulose $\qquad$ solid $\qquad$ pyrolytic $\qquad\qquad$ gas $\qquad\qquad$ water
$\qquad\qquad\qquad$ char $\qquad$ oil

Other reactions can also occur, depending on conditions and additions:

Partial oxidation

$$C_6H_{10}O_5 + \tfrac{1}{2}O_2 \rightarrow 6CO + 5H_2$$

Reforming

$$C_6H_{10}O_5 + H_2O \xrightarrow{\text{heat}} 6CO + 6H_2$$

Hydrogenation

$$C_6H_{10}O_5 + H_2 \xrightarrow[\text{low temperature}]{\text{pressure}} \text{oil} + H_2O$$

Hydrogasification

$$C_6H_{10}O_5 + 12H_2 \xrightarrow[\text{high temperature}]{\text{pressure}} 6CH_4 + 5H_2O$$

Hydro-oxynation

$$C_6H_{10}O_5 + CO + H_2O \xrightarrow[\text{low temperature}]{\text{pressure}} \text{oil}$$

Shift

$$CO + H_2O \rightleftharpoons CO_2 + H_2$$

Although many variations have been proposed employing the above simple pyrolysis reaction with one or more of the other reactions mentioned, most schemes are based either on simple thermal pyrolysis or, sometimes, on pyrolysis with partial oxidation. With as yet unproven economic viability, the added cost of a pressure system and a hydrogen supply for the hydrogenation methods is probably difficult to justify.

Pretreatment of waste is usually preferred, to recover other values, reduce reactor size and give greater reaction control, and to avoid relegation of the solid char to the category of a waste product by the inclusion of a high proportion of inert material. Although resource recovery can be practised on this solid residue, less efficient operation usually results, giving a less marketable product. Drying is also beneficial to reduce the quantity of aqueous effluent requiring treatment and reduce possible undesirable side reactions.

Some of the earliest work on household refuse was carried out in the late 1960s,[27,28] particularly in Denmark. Since then pyrolysis has been extensively researched throughout the world, notably by Warren Spring Laboratory in the UK[27] and by a number of US EPA-sponsored projects with research and

TABLE 17.11 CHARACTERISTICS OF TYPICAL PYROLYSIS PRODUCTS OF OCCIDENTAL PROCESS[26]

Fraction	Char	Pyrolytic oil	Gas	Water
Yield (weight %)	20	40	27	13
Composition	Weight (%)	Weight (%)	Volume (%)	Weight of condensible organics (%)
Carbon	48·8	57·5	Water 0·1	Acetaldehyde 13·0
Hydrogen	3·9	7·6	Carbon monoxide 42·0	Acetone 18·0
Nitrogen	1·1	0·9	Carbon dixoide 27·0	Methanol 20·6
Sulphur	0·3	0·1	Hydrogen 10·5	Chloroform 1·0
Ash	31·8	0·2	Methyl chloride 0·1	Toluene 1·3
Chlorine	0·2	0·3	Methane 5·9	Formic acid 14·4
Oxygen (by diff.)	13·9	33·4	Ethane 4·5	Furfural 7·2
			C_3 to C_7 hydrocarbons 8·9	Acetic acid 1·3
	100·0	100·0		Methylfurfural 6·9
				Naphthalene 1·6
				Methylnaphthalene 1·3
				Phenol 6·5
				Cresol 2·6
				100·0
Heating value, kJ/kg (Btu/lb)	21 000 (9000)	24 400 (10 500)	Gross heating value, kJ/Nm³ 99·0 (Btu/scf) = 21 500 (550)	Water ~5% ~8% 13%

commercial organisations in the USA.[7,10,12,23,24,25] Over 150 processes have been researched, but few have been developed to demonstration plant scale or to a point where commercial plants may be offered. The processes shown in Figures 17.32–37 represent the most advanced currently available.

Warren Spring Laboratory produced the Cross-Flow reactor system (Figure 17.32) which is currently being developed and marketed by Foster Wheeler Power Products for tyre pyrolysis. This system was developed after research on laboratory scale retort pyrolysis and induction heating with circulating steel balls. To obtain better heat transfer to the refuse (one of the more serious

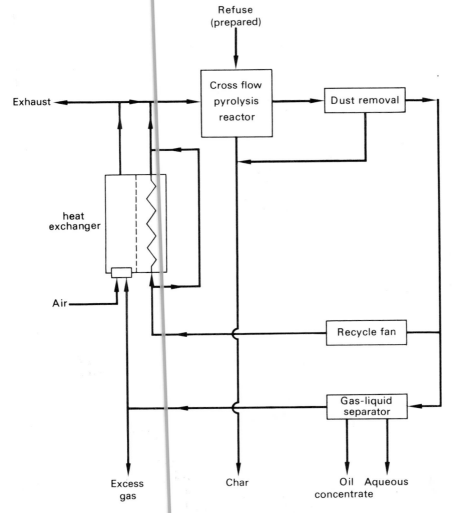

Fig. 17.32 Pyrolysis by hot product gas recycling—cross-flow system (Warren Spring Laboratory/Foster Wheeler Power Products)

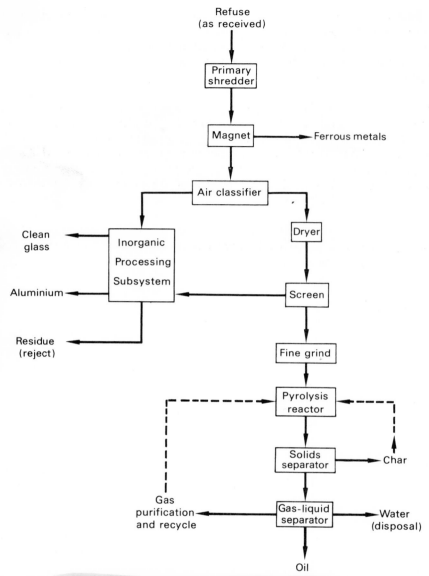

Fig. 17.33 Occidental resource recovery and pyrolysis process (formerly Garrett Process)

problems), some of the gas produced is recycled, with preheating, to provide a heat transfer medium. Char is removed from the pyrolysis reactor and oil and aqueous fractions are condensed out. While some of the gas is used for recycling and predrying the feed material, at least 50% should be available surplus to in-plant requirements. Resource recovery could be practised before or after pyrolysis.

The Occidental (formerly Garrett) process employs a front-end separation system to recover metals and glass and remove other inerts (Figure 17.33). The refuse then has to be ground very small before pyrolysis in a gas transfer reactor, and the cost of grinding contributes significantly to the doubtful economic viability. A significant proportion (40%) of pyrolytic oil is formed in the process together with high-grade gas (27%) and solid char (20%) (see Table 17.11). Of particular interest is the high quality of products and the low proportion of aqueous phase (13%). These characteristics are achieved in the design of the process, which is a low-temperature pyrolysis reaction at 480°C and employs rapid or flash heating of a finely shredded feed using recycled hot char to supply heat. The most important aspect of this process is the significant quantity of liquid oil produced, which is the most useful and valuable product: nearly 1 tonne of oil is produced for each 5 tonnes of refuse processed.[12,26,29] The oil is claimed to be compatible but immiscible with No. 6 fuel oil; it is known to be corrosive and it readily polymerises on storage. In spite of the wide publicity this process has received and the advantages of producing a liquid product, its future appears uncertain and these are no plans for commercial exploitation.

The Destrugas (Karl Kroyer) system (Figure 17.34) is one of the earliest pyrolysis systems using household refuse as feedstock and employs indirect heating to 1000°C in a vertical retort. One of the main problems is heat transfer from the reactor wall to the refuse bulk which imposes design and throughput limitations of about 1·25 tonnes/hour/reactor.[27,28,30] Resource recovery does not appear in the flow sheets but may be incorporated as a front-end or back-end system. The demonstration pilot plant in Denmark on which much of the experimental work was carried out is now believed to have been dismantled, although a replacement is operating in Japan. Plans for commercial application are still under consideration but have not yet been realised.

The Landgard process (Monsanto Envirochem Systems) produces gas and char only in an oil-fired horizontal rotary kiln at a maximum temperature of 980°C (Figure 17.35). The gas is normally burnt to raise steam, although it could be otherwise used. The only pretreatment is shredding; some post-pyrolysis treatment is practised to recover ferrous metals, carbon char and glassy aggregate.[12,31] Oil production is minimal by design, in that any oil formed is thermally decomposed to gas. This is one of the few refuse pyrolysis systems to be installed in a 'live' situation, in Baltimore. Although Monsanto appear to have relinquished their interest, the system is understood to be operated very satisfactorily by the City of Baltimore, at about half design capacity. To meet air pollution requirements, additional gas-cleaning equipment is necessary. The process is being operated as an incinerator, but the gas could be used elsewhere.

The Purox (Union Carbide) process is one of the most widely publicised (Figure 17.36). This employs pyrolysis and partial oxidation in a vertical shaft furnace, using pure oxygen rather than air to avoid dilution of the pyrolysis gas with nitrogen. The process differs from those previously described in that a slag is formed which is run off to a water quench. The maximum temperature is

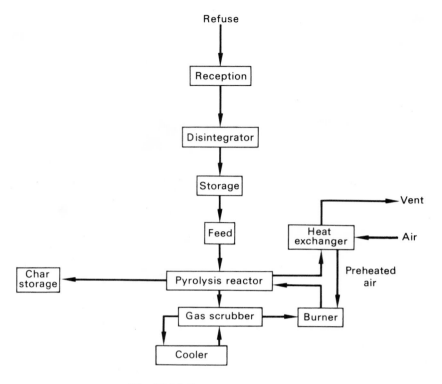

Fig. 17.34 Destrugas system

1600°C and only two products are formed—gas and solid. The small amount of oil formed is returned to the reactor. The gas represents over 80% of the fuel value of the incoming refuse and, even after deducting in-plant requirements, about 70% is available as surplus.[12,32] Resource recovery may be carried out as a pretreatment operation or on the solid product to recover metals and glass. Although this is a well developed and technically attractive process, the very high initial costs are precluding commercial development. A plant of capacity around 1000 tonnes/day would cost nearly £30 million (1978). Recent studies suggest that the UK is not yet ready for a process of this size or cost.[33]

The Andco-Torrax (Carborundum) process (Figure 17.37) is a high-temperature (1650°C) slagging system (like Purox) and uses all the gas, either in-plant or to export energy (like Landgard), rather than exporting surplus gas. Pyrolysis is based on partial oxidation with air, giving a relatively low-grade fuel gas product. This avoids the need for expensive oxygen generation, but at the cost of producing a less valuable product.[12] One plant is already in operation in Luxembourg with two further plants planned for Grasse (France) and Frankfurt. As this is essentially a two-stage incineration process it is difficult to understand its adoption in Europe where air pollution standards tend to be less severe than in the USA.

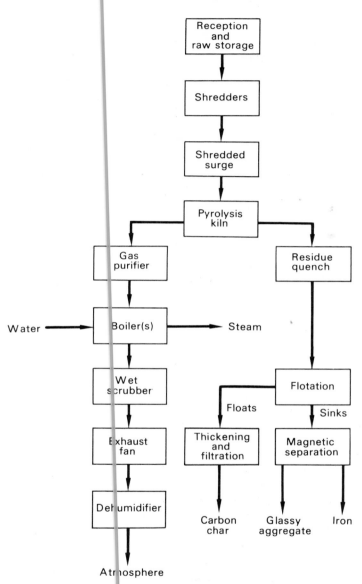

Fig. 17.35   Landgard (Monsanto–Envirochem) resource recovery and pyrolysis system

Many other systems have been proposed and devised, for example, based on fluidised beds or molten salts to effect good heat transfer. In addition to pyrolysis of refuse, many of the ideas and research efforts have been applied to other organic wastes such as rubber, plastic and sewage, including mixtures of these with refuse. The Andco-Torrax process, for example, has been fed with sewage sludge, waste oil, tyres and polyvinyl chloride together with refuse.

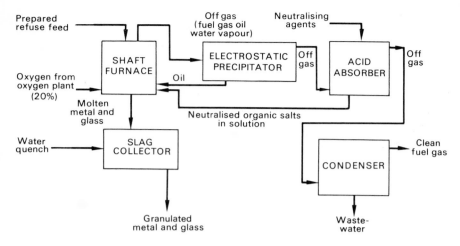

Fig. 17.36 Purox (Union Carbide) pyrolysis process

The current view is that pyrolysis is still an expensive alternative to conventional waste disposal. It is capital intensive in that a very large capital outlay has to be made before recovering any money, and is unlikely to be adopted as a refuse disposal alternative by local authorities in the short term. There are few areas of the UK where waste arises in sufficient quantity at one site to justify installation of such a process; probably only the London, West Midlands, North West and Central Scottish conurbations could justify such a process. Capital-intensive industries generally exploit economy of scale by building plants as large as possible, and this is seen as a serious handicap for pyrolysis processes in the UK.

In the longer term, however, pyrolysis must be seriously considered as a fuel source. As oil and gas supplies become more scarce and consequently more expensive, coal will assume a greater significance; already considerable effort has been expended in developing the necessary technology for coal gasification and liquefaction. The UK has extensive coal reserves, but other countries will need to develop alternative feedstocks, e.g. cellulose in the form of trees. There is also the opportunity to combine refuse with coal or other biomass. The UK, rather than relying on one fuel feedstock, may develop an alternative technology, perhaps based on biomass conversion. Pyrolysis of refuse and/or other organic material may then change from an expensive disposal option to a primary fuel/chemical feedstock provider. The alternative for this role, biological fermentation, is in fact being pursued in Brazil where an ethanol-based fuel and chemical industry is being developed.

Considerably more work is needed on basic research, technical feasibility and economic viability to assess pyrolysis both as a disposal option and as a fuel supply process for the future.

Biological Conversion Processes

The range of biological processes devised and developed to convert the organic portion of refuse to a useful product includes:

Composting to give a humus-rich soil additive
Digestion to methane
Fermentation to single-cell protein
Fermentation to alcohol
Enzymic conversion to glucose
Hydrolysis to sugars (as a pretreatment for fermentation)

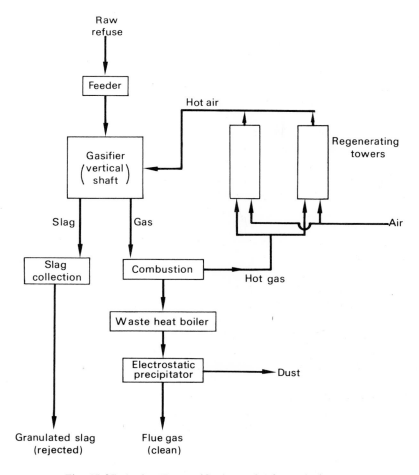

Fig. 17.37 Andco-Torrax (Carborundum) pyrolysis system

Composting

Composting—natural biodegradation of organic material—is commonly practised in the garden compost heap in which waste is rotted down and reincorporated into the garden, often for the following year's crop. This process has
been developed into an industry to convert the organic fraction of household
refuse and other wastes such as sewage sludge into a useful product, humus,
which can be sold. While not widely practised in the UK or Europe, this is an
acceptable method of disposal.[13,34] US practice, however, does not appear to
have found much commercial success and interest seems to be waning, with
most plants now closed down.[7,23]

There are three basic operations: refuse preparation, aerobic digestion, and
upgrading of final product. Preparation usually consists of a front-end separation system to remove biologically inert materials such as metal, glass and ash,
and comminute the refuse. Very small particle sizes of less than 20 mm are
preferred and secondary grinding to this size is usually carried out after the
separation steps. It may be necessary to include additives such as moisture to
increase the water content to around 50%, nutrients such as ammonium nitrate
to raise the carbon/nitrogen ratio to between 30 and 40 and the car-
bon/phosphorus ratio to between 80 and 130, and possibly acids or alkalis to
maintain pH at between about 5 and 9.[23,35]

General Engineering Co. (Radcliffe) Ltd

Dano refuse composting plant

Aerobic digestion may be carried out by the traditional winnowing method where material is left for about 5 weeks, being turned every 3 or 4 days, or in purpose-built digesters where the time necessary is reduced to about 4 or 5 days. A popular mechanised digester is a drum slowly revolving at $\frac{1}{2}$–1 rpm and heated to about 60°C to optimise the process. Typical dimensions are 2·7–3·7 m (9–12 ft) diameter and 18·3 m (60 ft) long. Other types of equipment have been proposed based on pits, heaps, cells, bins, silos and tanks and employing a variety of aeration devices. While the mechanised process described above uses more costly equipment, there is considerable saving in land and operating costs which usually more than compensates for the additional initial equipment costs.

After digestion, further grinding and screening may take place with the oversize being returned to the process. Curing by storing for 10–30 days, which is necessary to stabilise the humus, gives darker colour and shorter fibre length which improve the marketability of the product. Further grinding and screening may be employed and sometimes pelletisation, granulation, drying and magnetic separation. A flow diagram of a typical process is shown in Figure 17.38.

It is possible to incorporate other wastes such as organic industrial waste and sewage sludge into an overall process (Figure 17.39). Such centralised treatment takes advantage of economy of scale, and reduces disposal problems for a range of wastes.

Digestion to Methane
Biological degradation of any organic material may be carried out under controlled conditions to recover the degradation products. Examples are ethanol, single-cell protein (SCP) and other organic chemicals mentioned later. Biodegradation occurs in anaerobic conditions both industrially, as in ethanol production and sewage digestion, and naturally, for example in marshes giving rise to methane formation. This latter phenomenon may be utilised to convert the organic fraction of refuse to methane for use as a fuel gas. The overall reaction may be represented by:

$$C_6H_{12}O_6 \rightarrow 3CO_2 + 3CH_4 + \text{heat}$$

cellulose   carbon   methane
dioxide

The reaction proceeds via a number of intermediate stages which involve formation of ethanol, acetic acid and other chemicals.

A number of ways have been proposed of utilising this process, based on principles similar to those of composting except that air is excluded and the gases formed are collected. As both carbon dioxide and methane are generated in approximately equal proportions, most of the carbon dioxide has to be removed to give a fuel gas product. Work is continuing to obtain information for process design[7,23–25,36,37] in order to optimise the system variables and thus minimise cost; experience with sewage sludge digestion is already available.

Sewage or sewage sludge is often used to innoculate the refuse with bacteria,

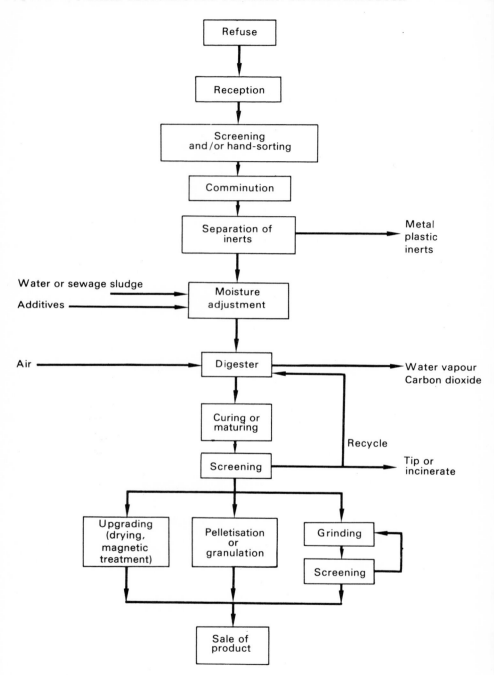

Fig. 17.38 Compost production process

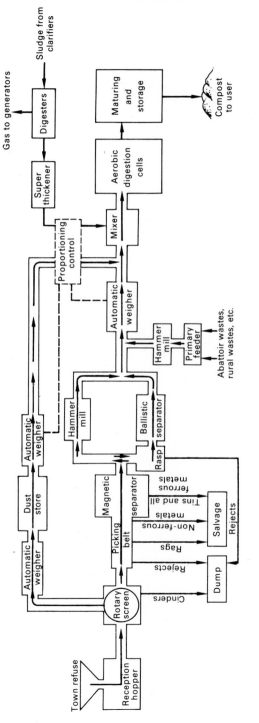

Fig. 17.39 Composting plant (Jersey, CI)

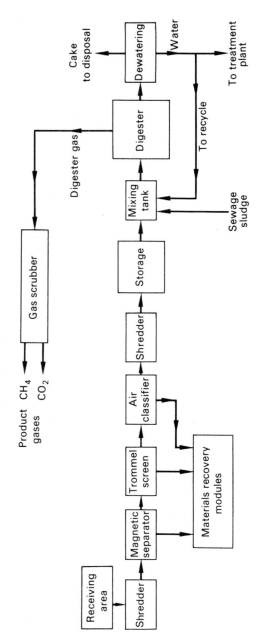

Fig. 17.40 Anaerobic digestion process for solid waste utilisation

thereby also solving another disposal problem. The process currently appears to be rather slow, maximum production of methane reaching typically about 0·17 m³/kg refuse (2·7 ft³/lb refuse) after 6 months at 37°C.[38,39] Another study[7,40] demonstrated the improvement with increased temperature as well as time, giving a maximum yield of 0·17 m³ methane per kg refuse after 30 days at 60°C. However, the proportion of methane decreases with increased temperature and retention time. The digester stage is the most critical in view of the high residence time for useful gas production, and it is to this area that most attention is being directed.[41,42] The process is carried out in an aqueous medium. There is considerable advantage in operating at high solids content to reduce the quantity of water being held in the reactor and hence the size and cost of the necessary equipment. An upper limit appears to be 50% solids. One process is outlined in Figure 17.40,[40] while another[38] advocates modified landfill with gas collection. The technology for carbon dioxide separation is available and proven, based on absorption in suitable solvents such as amines.

This method of conversion of solid waste to fuel gas has the advantage of relatively low-level technology compared with pyrolysis, but insufficient work has been carried out to be able to comment usefully on the economics. It is well suited to small-scale applications.

Fermentation

The fermentation of organic constituents of waste must be carried out via conversion of the cellulose and carbohydrates to sugars. This pretreatment may be carried out chemically with acid or alkali (described later), biologically or enzymically, or by irradiation with electrons, microwaves, light or laser.[43] It is possible to carry out the pretreatment at the same time as fermentation but the reaction rate and yield are adversely affected.

The basic process is outlined in Figure 17.41. Depending on conditions and design, products may be obtained from one extreme of nearly all ethanol with some single-cell protein (SCP) as byproduct, through a range of combinations to nearly all SCP. Recovery of SCP is by thorough washing of the yeast, filtration to reduce the water content and final concentration to a solid product by spray drying or drum drying. Ethanol is recovered by simple distillation to give a 96% ethanol azeotrope with water. This is satisfactory for many purposes but, for 100% material, azeotropic distillation with a third component is necessary (see Chapter 8). The basic process can be applied to a wide range of feedstocks such as agricultural/horticultural wastes, paper industry wastes, oil or, in principle, any organic material.

The products that can be derived include SCP[43] as a food supplement, for which a good future seems assured; ethanol as a product and as raw material for the chemical industry; and other organic chemicals such as acetone, butanol, isopropanol, lactic acid, butyric acid, acetic acid, glycerol, and erythritol.[44]

The state of the art is not yet well advanced for treatment of refuse, but considerable experience has been obtained for many other applications including production of SCP and ethanol from other resources.

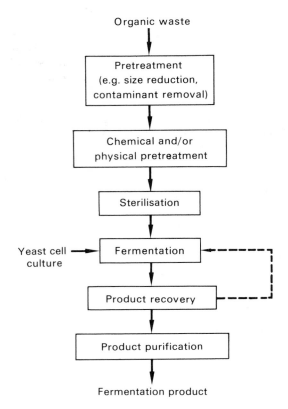

Fig. 17.41 Basic fermentation process

Enzymic Conversion

There is considerable interest in the application of enzyme technology to effect reactions that are too difficult or costly by other means. Attention is also being paid to the possible substitution of enzymic processes for more costly operations. In the application to refuse recovery, a process to convert the cellulose content to glucose by enzymic hydrolysis has been proposed.[45] An outline flow diagram is shown in Figure 17.42. Advantages claimed for this process include high specificity towards cellulose (thus absence of reaction with other impurities present) and good yields of 40–50% from newspaper. Relatively high concentrations of glucose of up to 10% are obtainable. Currently only pilot plant operation is practised, but it is claimed that full-scale operation will be technically feasible and practically achievable by 1980.

Chemical Conversion Processes

This is perhaps the least developed approach to the recycling of household refuse. One of the few serious studies on chemical processing, as opposed to thermal, biological or physical processing, has been the development of a process to hydrolyse the cellulose to fermentable sugars[44] either as a product or as a first stage in the production of ethanol, protein or other organic products. A flow diagram of the overall hydrolysis/ethanol fermentation process is shown in Figure 17.43. This typically employs up to 1% sulphuric acid at high temperature. Although the sugars may be recovered it is more advantageous to employ the aqueous solution as a raw material for a variety of fermentations to produce, for example, alcohol, acetone, lactic acid and a number of other organic chemicals.[44] An investigation into the feasibility of producing methanol or ammonia from solid household waste[46] has received little attention.

Chemical oxidation has been proposed as an alternative to biological oxidation.[24] A pulped slurry of waste is heated to 160°–320°C at 70–140 bar under a high oxygen partial pressure. Carbon monoxide, carbon dioxide, organic acids and a fibrous sludge are obtained. The gases can be utilised for energy generation via a turbine, and heat economy is achieved by preheating the feed with hot product.

Chemical treatment of separated refuse fractions is often essential for effective recycling, as in the case of metals where complex pyrometallurgical or hydrometallurgical processing is necessary to produce new metal (Chapter 15).

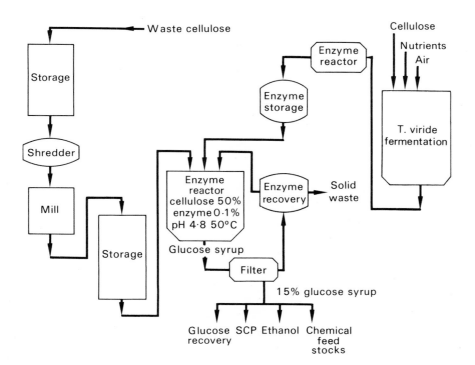

Fig. 17.42 Enzymatic conversion of waste cellulose

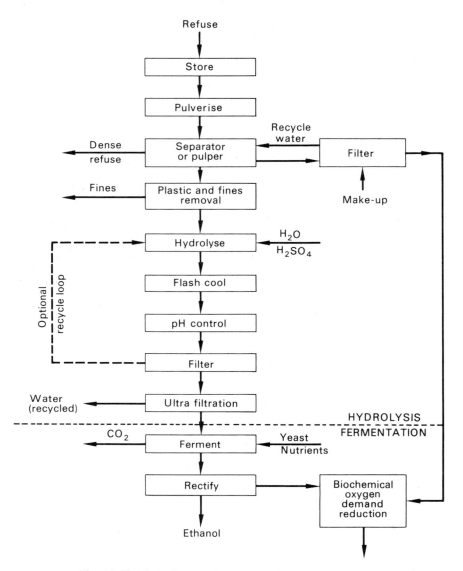

Fig. 17.43 Flow diagram for obtaining ethanol from refuse

An interesting but improbable process for reclaiming metals from incinerator residue, based on hydrochloric acid leaching, is shown in Figure 17.44.

Cellulose may theoretically be converted into a wide range of products either based on cellulose or derived from it. Some of the possibilities are listed in Table 17.12.[24,44]

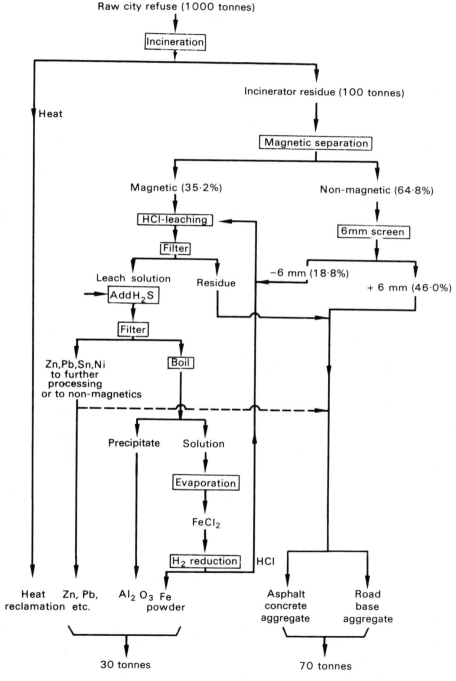

Fig. 17.44 Useful product recovery from raw city refuse[47]

TABLE 17.12 CELLULOSE PRODUCTS AND DERIVATIVES[24,44]

Cellulose compounds	Use
Benzyl cellulose	Lacquers, plastics
Cellulose acetates	Plastics, textiles, film
Cellulose esters	—
Cellulose ethers	—
Cellulose nitrate	Explosives, plastics, lacquer
Cellulose xanthate	Plastics, film, fibre
Ethyl cellulose	Adhesives, plastics, varnishes
Ethyl hydroxyethyl cellulose	Emulsifier, thickener
Methyl cellulose	Adhesives, latexes, foods, cosmetics, pharmaceuticals
Sodium carboxymethyl cellulose	Thickener
Sodium cellulose sulphate	Paints, textiles, paper, adhesives

Cellulose derivatives	Mechanism of formation
Acetic acid	Alkaline degradation
	Thermal degradation
Acetone	Thermal degradation via glucose
Arabitol	Via glucose
Butyl alcohol	Via glucose
Butyric acid	Via glucose
Carbon	Thermal or chemical degradation
Carbon dioxide	Thermal, chemical or biological degradation
Carbon monoxide	Thermal, chemical or biological degradation
Citric acid	Via glucose
Ethanol	Via glucose
Erythritol	Via glucose
Ethylene	Thermal degradation
Formic acid	Thermal degradation
	Alkaline degradation via glucose
Formaldehyde	Thermal degradation
Furfural	Thermal degradation
Glucose	Hydrolysis
Glycolic acid	Alkaline degradation
Hexane	Via glucose
Hydroxymethylfurfural	Thermal degradation
Isopropyl alcohol	Via glucose
Lactic acid	Alkaline degradation
Levulinic acid	Via glucose
Methane	Thermal degradation
	Biological degradation
Oxalic acid	Alkaline or acid oxidation
Single-cell protein (SCP)	Via glucose
Sorbitol	Via glucose

The possibilities for chemical processing of refuse or refuse fractions may be extensive, but the economics are very unlikely to be attractive or even to compare with other processing methods. This is due to the more complex and hence more costly process requirements resulting largely from contaminated and heterogeneous feed.

References

1. *Refuse Disposal*, HMSO, 1971.
2. FLINTHOFF, F. L. D., *The Disposal of Solid Waste*, British Plastics Federation, 1973.
3. DOUGLAS, E. and JACKSON, D. V., in *Environmental Engineering Aspects of Pollution Control*, Society of Environmental Engineers, 1971.
4. *The New Prospectors*, Warren Spring Laboratory, 1976.
5. West Midlands County Council, private communication.
6. ABERT, J. G., ALTER, H. and BERNHEISEL, J. F., *Science*, **183**, 1052, 1974.
7. PAVONI, J. L., HEER, J. E. and HAGERTY, D. J., *Handbook of Solid Waste Disposal—Material and Energy Recovery*, Van Nostrand Reinhold, 1975.
8. MARSHALL, J. E. and HARVEY, K., Paper 24(2) in *Public Works Congress, Birmingham*, Institute of Solid Wastes Management, 1976.
9. Imperial Metal Industries, publicity, 1976.
10. WILSON, D. C., *Engineering and Process Economics*, **3**(1), 35, 1978.
11. National Centre for Resource Recovery, *Resource Recovery from Municipal Solid Waste*, Lexington, 1974.
12. WEINSTEIN, N. J. and TORO, R. F., *Thermal Processing of Municipal Solid Waste for Resource and Energy Recovery*, Ann Arbor, 1976.
13. DOUGLAS, E. and BIRCH, P. R., *Resource Recovery and Conservation*, **1**(4), 319, 1976.
14. *The Doncaster Project*, South Yorkshire County Council, 1977.
15. SINGH, R., *Municipal Engineering*, **156**(23), 1037, 1976.
16. ALTER, H. and HOROWITZ, E., *Resource Recovery and Utilisation*, ASTM, 1974.
17. *An Analysis of Solid Waste Proposals for the Hackensack Meadowlands Commission*, Fairleigh Dickinson University and Stevens Institute of Technology, 1973, (See also (24) below).
18. FUNK, H. D. and RUSSELL, S. H., in *Proceedings of 5th Mineral Waste Utilization Symposium Chicago*, US Bureau of Mines and Illinois Institute of Technology, 1976.
19. HERBERT, W., in *Proceedings of 3rd Mineral Waste Utilization Symposium, Chicago*, Illinois Institute of Technology, 1972.
20. BOETTCHER, R. A., Report SW–30c, US Environmental Protection Agency, 1972.
21. ABERT, J. G. and ZUSMAN, M., *Journal of the American Institution of Chemical Engineers*, **18**(6), 1089, 1972.
22. *Local Authority Refuse Collection and Disposal Survey*, International Reclamation and Disposal Exhibition, 1977.
23. MANTELL, C. L., *Solid Wastes*, Wiley, 1975.
24. JACKSON, F. R., *Recycling and Reclaiming of Municipal Solid Waste*, Noyes Data Corporation, 1975.
25. HAGERTY, D. J., PAVONI, J. L. and HEER, J. E., *Solid Waste Management*, Van Nostrand Reinhold, 1973.
26. MALLAN, G. M. and TITLOW, E. I., *Energy and Resource Recovery from Solid Waste*, Washington Academy of Sciences, 1975; see also MALLAN, G. M. and FINNEY, C. S., *73rd National Meeting, Minneapolis*, American Institute of Civil Engineers, 1972, and MALLAN, G. M., *7th National Meeting, Atlantic City*, American Institute of Chemical Engineers, 1971.
27. DOUGLAS, E., WEBB, M. and DABORN, G. R., in *Symposium on Treatment and Recycling of Solid Waste, Manchester*, Institute of Solid Wastes Management, 1974.
28. KROYER, K., *Pyrolysis of Waste*, Stads-og Hauneingeniren, 1970.
29. LEVY, S. J., Report SW–80d2, US Environmental Protection Agency, 1975.
30. THEL, A., *Municipal Engineering*, 26 October 1974.
31. SUSSMAN, D. A., Report SW–75d1, US Environmental Protection Agency, 1975.
32. FISHER, T. F., KASBOHM, M. L. and RIVERO, J. R., *Chemical Engineering Progress*, 75, October 1976.
33. MILLBANK, P., *Surveyor*, 19, 21 January 1977.
34. BIDDLESTONE, A. J. and GRAY, K. R., *Chemical Engineer*, 76, February 1973.
35. GRAY, K. R. and BIDDLESTONE, A. J., *Chemical Engineer*, 71, February 1973.
36. KISPERT, R. G., SADEK, S. E. and WISE, D. L., *Resource Recovery and Conservation*, **1**, 95, 1976.
37. Idem, ibid., **1**, 245, 1976.
38. AUGENSTEIN, D. C., WISE, D. L and COONEY, C. L., ibid., **2**, 257, 1977.
39. AUGENSTEIN, D. C., WISE, D. L., WENTWORTH, R. L. and COONEY, C. L., ibid., **2**, 103, 1977.

40. PFEFFER, J. T. and LIEBMAN, J. C., ibid., **1**, 295, 1976.
41. JEWELL, W. J. *et al., Bioconversion of Agricultural Wastes for Pollution Control and Energy Conservation,* Cornell University, 1976.
42. JEWELL, W. J., *Energy, Agriculture and Waste Management,* Ann Arbor, 1975.
43. ROGERS, C. J., *Resource Recovery and Conservation,* 1(3), 271, 1976.
44. PORTEUS, A., Paper A25, *London Chemical Engineering Congress Proceedings,* Institution of Chemical Engineers, 1974.
45. SPANO, L. A., MEDEIROS, J. and MANDELS, M., *Resource Recovery and Conservation,* **1**(3), 279, 1976.
46. Mathematical Sciences Northwest Inc., *Feasibility Study of Conversion of Solid Waste to Methanol or Ammonia,* prepared for City of Seattle, 1974.

PART FIVE

NOISE ABATEMENT

CHAPTER 18

Noise Control

Source of Noise

As outlined in Chapter 3, noise is unwanted sound. It may be tolerated by the persons involved in generating it but may cause annoyance when heard by an outsider sensitive to his surroundings. Objections are more likely if the noise has some characteristic causing it to be recognised above the general background of sound. The longer term effects can be quite serious to persons and property.

The human ear is more sensitive to high- than to low-pitched sounds so that most offence tends to be caused by easily attributable high-frequency noise. This is especially the case if the sound contains a pure note. Noise generated at night is more likely to cause annoyance because of the absence of 'masking' by non-attributable or background noises.

Industrial noise is produced as a consequence of rapid energy dissipation. Typical causes are:

Direct air disturbance, for example by rotating fans and compressors;
Friction between moving parts, for example an object and a cutter blade, rotating shafts in bearings, grinding wheels;
Release of gas or vapour under pressure, for example steam from relief valves or puffs of gas from engine exhausts;
Impact between moving bodies, for example with reciprocating hammers or presses, during riveting or from gear trains.

Noise sources in process plants which are likely to contribute significantly to community noise are listed in Figure 18.1.[1] To these must be added noise sources associated with materials handling, such as vehicles, and stockyards. Generally acceptable levels of noise are discussed later.

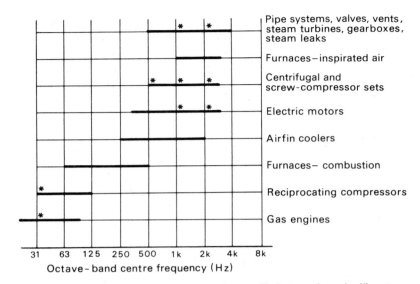

Fig. 18.1 Chemical and petroleum process equipment likely to make a significant contribution to community noise[1]
        * Frequency at which throb or pure tone is likely to be significant

Flow noise is generated in piping at points where pressure reductions occur. Control valves radiate noise directly and also via pipe walls. Many valve suppliers manufacture low-noise varieties and prediction methods for their noise generation are accurate to within ±5 dB.[2] Steam turbines produce tonal noise which can be in the range 85–95 dB(A) at 1 m distance.[2] Gearboxes produce tonal noise at tooth-meshing frequency and harmonics. Steam leaks are a major source of high-frequency noise and may produce well over 90 dB(A) within a radius of several metres.

The terms used to describe the noise transmission from a source are 'sound power level' (L_w or PWL) and 'sound pressure level' (L_p or SPL). PWL is the power emitted by the source independent of its environment. SPL is related to the PWL of the source, and the distance between it and a receiver and the effects of screening and attenuation. A practical relationship is

$$SPL = PWL - 20 \log r - A - B - C \pm D$$

where r = distance between receiver and source
        A = atmospheric attenuation
        B = ground cover attenuation
        C = screening attenuation by intervening objects
        D = diffusivity index of the source in the specific radiation direction.

Standardised practical values are available for A, B and C.[2]

The sound power level of any furnace is related to its heat release (Figure 18.2). Large box-type furnaces emit high-frequency noise from burners and low-frequency noise from their panels. Naturally aspirated vertical cylindrical furnaces emit noise from their burners and air inlets. Forced-draught furnaces may produce less burner noise since they are enclosed in plenum chambers but the associated fans, drive motors and gear boxes add to the overall noise. Similarly, with boilers the total noise level comprises that from combustion noise, air fans plus drives and steam leaks.

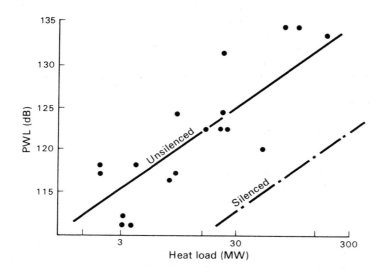

Fig. 18.2 Furnace noise

High-speed reciprocating compressors may generate mid- and high-frequency noise in the range 85–105 dB(A) close to the equipment. Large low-speed reciprocating compressors produce some high-frequency mechanical noise, low-frequency noise from their air inlets, plus noise from the drive motor; if uncontrolled these may result in noise levels of 85–95 dB(A).[2]

Noise from individual electric motors up to 745 kW (1000 hp) is unlikely to be troublesome but the aggregate noise may be.[1] There are wide differences in noise generation between motors of different types; the cooling fan is the predominant source. The SPL at 3 m of unsilenced, totally enclosed fan-cooled motors, or CACA motors, can be estimated approximately from Figure 18.3.[2] Most manufacturers can supply small and medium-sized motors with reduced noise outputs. Centrifugal and screw compressors are inherently noisy; the problem is accentuated since the noise consists of a series of penetrating tones. Noise at the compressor piping interface can radiate from the piping and as a result of vibration transmission.

A summary of other typical noise levels associated with engineering processes is reproduced in Table 18.1.

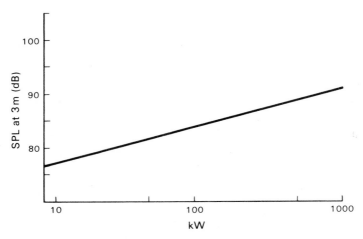

Fig. 18.3 Noise from totally enclosed fan-cooled electric motors

TABLE 18.1 TYPICAL NOISE LEVELS ASSOCIATED WITH ENGINEERING PROCESSES

Machine shops: range 84–101 dB(A)	
General m/c tool noise	85–97
Capstans and autos	84–94
Slotters and thread-rollers	88–96
Cold-heading machines	93–101
Foundries: range 83–110 dB(A)	
Furnaces and cupolas	83–95
Moulding machines	95–103
Casting shake-out	95–107
Chipping and fettling	93–110
Forging and forming: range 88–113 dB(A)	
Small presses	88–98
Cropping and blanking	89–99
Hot-forging presses	96–108
Forging hammers	99–113
Finishing processes: range 84–98 dB(A)	
Assembly line	84–94
Polishing and grinding	84–96
Barrelling	87–97
Shot-blasting	84–98

Effects of Noise

A summary of the general effects of noise on health was given by the Wilson Committee.[3] These include the prevention of sleep, induction of stress, hearing loss, annoyance, interference with communication, disturbance of concentration and hence working efficiency and personal safety.

Hearing Loss

It is well established that loss of hearing may follow exposure to high levels of noise. The damage may be sudden in onset and temporary or permanent in effect, or gradual in onset and permanent in effect.

One effect may be a temporary threshold shift (TTS), i.e. a reduction in the threshold of sensitivity of hearing which passes off after a period of minutes or months. A second effect is a permanent threshold shift (PTS). In some cases it has proved difficult to identify the loss due to noise because of other factors, e.g. presbycusis—deterioration due to age. The perception of sound at high frequencies, particularly around 4000 Hz, is most sensitive to damage; the most critical range is that involved in hearing speech, that is 600–2400 Hz.[4]

Noise levels of over 90 dB in the vicinity of a worker require control since permanent damage to hearing is likely if exposure continues over a period of years. Pain may result from exposure to a noise level of 125 dB or above. Maximum limits for noise level at work were published in a 1972 code of practice.[5] This is based on a total power concept equivalent to a maximum continuous level of 90 dB(A) over 8 hours at the place of employment. Allowance is made for continuous exposure to higher sound-pressure levels for shorter periods.[6] The code also provides guidance for calculating the equivalent level when levels vary over measurable periods. An overriding condition imposed upon the A-weighted sound levels is that the unprotected ear should not be exposed to a sound-pressure level greater than 135 dB or, in the case of impulse noise, an instantaneous sound pressure greater than 150 dB.

Interference with Communication

Speech is the simplest and most versatile method of communication and understanding it depends upon frequencies in the range 600–2400 Hz. Interference is produced particularly by high-intensity pure tones of 300 Hz or low-intensity pure tones of 500 Hz.[4] A speech interference level (SIL) criterion gives permissible noise levels in octave bands for communication over different distances.

Annoyance

The two effects mentioned above are generally restricted to occupational exposure to noise although there is evidence that general urban noise reduces hearing capacity.[4] Conversely, annoyance is more likely to arise away from work. Sensitivity to noise appears to depend upon both the personality and the age of the individual, the age-group between 25 and 40 years being most sensitive. Recurrent interference with sleep is injurious to health but there is no evidence to suggest that moderate noise can cause mental illness.[7] However there is a wide variation between individuals in the amount of noise that they will tolerate and adapt to.[4]

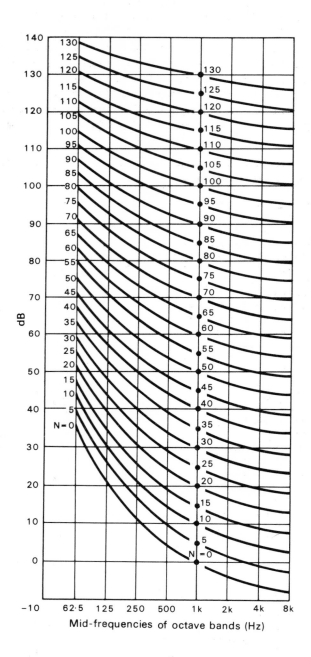

Mid-frequencies of octave bands (Hz)

The degree of annoyance caused by noise depends upon its intensity, frequency, impulsive nature and persistence. For example, the noise of machinery is usually a broad-band sound, i.e. it covers a wide range of frequencies, and for a similar energy output more annoyance is caused by a near-pure tone sound. Although high frequencies are generally more annoying than low frequencies,[8] the place in which noise is experienced and the time of day and year are relevant. An attempt has been made to evaluate such factors in terms of noise ratings with curves relating noise to its 'acceptability'; an example is given in Figure 18.4. Other noise assessment and prediction schemes are described in Chapters 3 and 5.

Fig. 18.4 (*opposite*) Noise-relating curves

Criterion	dB
Broadcasting studio	15
Concert hall, legitimate theatre 500 seats	20
Class room, music room, TV studio, conference room 50 seats	25
Bedroom (see corrections below)	25
Conference room 20 seats or with public address system, cinema, hospital, church, courtroom, library	30
Living room (see corrections below)	30
Private office	40
Restaurant	45
Gymnasium	50
Office (typewriters)	55
Workshop	65
Corrections for dwellings	
Pure tone easily perceptable	−5
Impulsive noise, i.e. irregular duration and/or intervals	−5
Noise only during working hours	+5
Noise during 25% of time	+5
6·0%	+10
1·5%	+15
0·5%	+20
0·1%	+25
0·02%	+30
Economic tie	+5
Very quiet suburban	−5
Suburban	0
Residential urban	+5
Urban near some industry	+10
Area of heavy industry	+15

Criteria for Control

Under English common law any industrial enterprise must avoid material interference with the comfort of its neighbours, or their enjoyment of property. Therefore any local resident can bring a civil action for 'nuisance' at common law. It is no defence to show that the 'best practicable means' are in use, i.e. that the noise is unavoidable. Nor is it generally a defence to show that the plaintiff moved to the 'nuisance', i.e. that the noise existed before the plaintiff moved to the locality.

Local authorities have powers to control the noise from industrial installations under the Control of Pollution Act 1974. Noise abatement zones may be created in industrial areas in which noise is likely to affect local communities. Registered noise levels will be established by measurements taken around the zone; such registered levels may not be exceeded without permission during a holding period. Subsequently the authority will decide whether an order is to be made requiring the noise to be reduced. However, any noise reductions deemed necessary must be discussed with the factory occupier having regard to the technical and economic feasibility of achieving them.

Local authorities will have powers, either on their own initiative or on that of a contractor, to specify noise-level control requirements for construction works. Controls will enable the authority to deal with the general level of noise emanating from the site.

With regard to places of work, the Health and Safety at Work Act 1974 empowers the appropriate minister to make orders regulating noise levels. The existing Code of Practice[5] sets a limit, as already described, for exposure without ear-protection. One approach is to reduce the levels in areas regularly visited to 90 dB(A) or below, but to leave without control areas which are not normally visited, marking them as 'noise-hazardous' areas in which ear-protection is obligatory.

An attempt was made by the Wilson Committee to establish levels above which a community nuisance could be expected, as follows:[3]

1. A basic level of 50 dB(A) for new factories, or factories or processes modified in such a way as to increase noise radiated outwards.
2. A basic level of 55 dB(A) for old factories not typical of the area.
3. A basic level of 60 dB(A) for old factories in keeping with the area.

Allowances are made as follows:

1. If the noise is pure tone, i.e. a whine, hiss, screech, squeal or noticeable humming noise, subtract 5 dB(A).
2. If irregular impulsive noise, e.g. bangs, clanks, thumps, hammering or riveting, or if noise is irregular enough to be noticed, subtract 5 dB(A).
3. If the noise occurs on:

Weekdays only 8 am–6 pm	add 5 dB(A)	the lowest appropriate one of these to be applied
Evenings up to 10 pm	add 0 dB(A)	
Weekends	add 0 dB(A)	
Night time 10 pm–7 am	subtract 5 dB(A)	

4. Type of district:
   (a) Rural (residential)   subtract 5 dB(A)
   (b) Suburban or urban,
       no road traffic   add 0 dB(A)
   (c) Residential urban   add 5 dB(A)
   (d) Urban with light industry
       or main roads   add 10 dB(A)   } Select one only
   (e) General industrial area   add 15 dB(A)
   (f) Heavy industrial area   add 20 dB(A)

5. In some cases the noise from the process is not constant, but significantly louder noises occur at intervals, say for less than half the time. When these louder noises occur during the day the following allowances may also be made to determine an intermittent limiting level:

Noise occurring approximately 15 min/h	add 5 dB(A)
Noise occurring approximately 5 min/h	add 10 dB(A)
Noise occurring approximately 1 min/h	add 15 dB(A)
Noise occurring approximately 1 min/half day	add 20 dB(A)

Note: This allowance is not applicable to noises occurring during the evening or at night.

These criteria make allowances for pitch, irregularity, pure tones, time of day or night, duration, and familiarity and may be computed for any particular series of circumstances.

It has been found preferable in practice to work to a level 5 dB(A) below the calculated level allowable outside the nearest house.[1]

Subsequently BS 4142:1967 was published for the rating of industrial noise.[9] This is based upon a comparison of the measured noise level, corrected to take account of its character and duration—termed the CNL—with the actual background level. The principle applied is that, except at high noise levels, annoyance appears to depend upon differences in level: e.g. the difference between a general background level accepted in an area and a disturbing noise level which tends to increase the background. Two methods of assessment are in fact given. The preferred method is based on the existing background noise levels. The alternative method uses an assumed base level of 50 dB(A) modified according to circumstances. While the use of measured background noise levels is more accurate, experience with petroleum plants is that the 50 dB(A) level method enables a reasonable prediction to be made of likely complaints.[2] A proposal for rating community noise given in an ISO Recommendation[10] indicates that a given level of complaint will result from lower noise levels.

Where a minimum of community noise intrusion will be tolerated, the noise from the factory should not exceed the existing background noise so that the total noise level increases by no more than 3 dB(A).[2] It follows from earlier discussion that easily distinguished noises such as whines and hisses should be eliminated.

Recommendations have been made for maximum levels for noise from building sites.[11] For sites in rural, suburban and urban areas away from main road traffic and industrial noise a maximum level of 70 dB(A) is recommended, measured outside the nearest window of the occupied room nearest the site boundary. A maximum level of 75 dB(A) is proposed for sites in urban areas near main roads and in heavy industrial areas. (See Chapters 3 and 5.)

Noise Control Technology

Industrial noise requires control to limit its effect both with regard to occupational safety and health, i.e. to minimise its effect upon the workforce, and to avoid community nuisance. As with all pollution control measures, consideration should be given to noise abatement at the equipment and factory design stage. It is a problem equally of town planning and of engineering, and to implement noise control measures on an existing plant may be very expensive and indeed sometimes impractical. For example, since the human ear responds logarithmically to sound-pressure fluctuations, silencing measures which result in a reduction of one-half in noise energy are only just recognisable; subjectively worth-while reductions involve a tenfold reduction.[8]

The options available for noise control are the following:

(a) *Reduction at source.* This includes the specification of limits on noise when purchasing new equipment and the substitution of equipment, or processes, by less noisy alternatives.

It is recommended that the equipment supplier incorporates the best practicable means for noise control and furnishes full information on the sound level likely to be produced.[5]

(b) *Reduction by enclosure.* This involves preventing noise radiation by the construction of a heavy enclosure around the source such that sound is reflected inward from the inner surfaces. Problems may arise from the need for access and ventilation.

(c) *Reduction by the use of silencers or filters.* This method is applicable to the control of noise from ducts, exhausts or conveyor systems, the ends of which must be open to the atmosphere.

(d) *Vibration damping and isolation.* This attempts to reduce vibration, for example by the application of a layer of damping material, or to isolate machine vibration from a surrounding structure by mounting it on resilient supports.

A thorough noise survey should precede any programme for noise control. An appropriate combination of these methods can then be selected.

Reduction at Source

A fundamental method of reducing noise emission from an equipment or process is by substitution. This simply entails the use of a less noisy alternative, any excess cost being balanced against the reduced provisions for noise control under (b) to (d) above.

The fundamental mechanisms of noise generation are not considered here.[8] However, there are several basic control principles. Firstly, noise levels increase rapidly in relation to speed: hence, for example, the noise from gears is proportional to approximately the square of the speed of rotation; the noise from a fan is proportional to approximately the tip speed to the sixth power.[12] Therefore the speed of moving machinery should preferably be the minimum practicable. Secondly, impact noise can be reduced by cushioning, or the peak level at least reduced by making use of lesser force applied over a longer period of time. Thirdly, consideration should be given to avoiding resonance, that is the condition when the natural frequency of vibration of a machine casing or other surface coincides with the exciting vibrations of the machine, since this will result in the greatest total noise emission. Finally, consideration should be given to the dynamic balancing of machinery and accuracy of manufacture, for example reduction of clearances in bearings.

British Steel Corporation (Llanwern Works, Newport)

Resonator cavities on sinter plant exhaust main, which control the low-frequency sound

TABLE 18.2 EXAMPLES OF NOISE REDUCTION BY SUBSTITUTION

Potentially noisy operation	Possible alternative
Manufacturing	
Riveting	Welding
Rolling/forging	Pressing
Cold working	Hot working
Machinery	
Vibratory conveyors	Belt conveyors, bucket elevators, etc.
Mechanical presses/hammers	Hydraulic presses
Metal gears	Plastic or fibre gears
Gears	Belt drives
Small, fast machines	Larger, slower machines

The fundamentals of machinery noise reduction by design have been reviewed in a fully referenced publication by HM Factory Inspectorate.[13] As far as substitution is concerned, some alternatives are given in Table 18.2.

With certain operations it is common experience that more sound is emitted in some directions than in others. Clearly the juxtaposition of working and residential areas needs to be taken into account when installing such equipment.

Reduction by Enclosure

Enclosures are fabricated from sound-insulating sheets lined internally with sound-absorbent material. A typical arrangement of a machine and drive motor enclosure is shown in Figure 18.5. The sheets should be of impervious high-density material, e.g. sheet steel; the insulation value increases with increasing weight. Sound-absorbent material should be porous; fibrous glass or mineral wool is commonly used. An efficient lightweight enclosure which provides an attenuation of 20 dB(A) is illustrated in Figure 18.6.[14]

The enclosed machine can be mounted on vibration isolators. In any event,

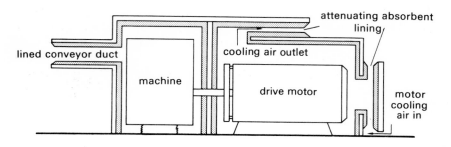

Fig. 18.5 Reduction by enclosure—typical arrangement

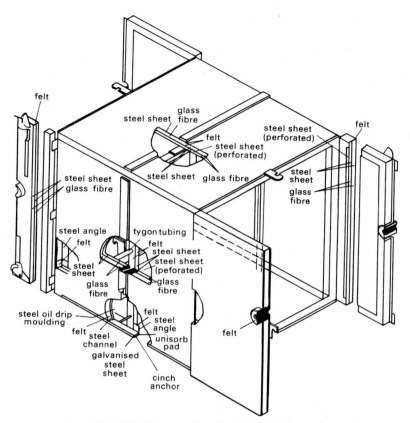

Fig. 18.6 Construction of a noise-reducing enclosure

any pipes or conduits passing through the enclosure should be isolated from the outer sheet structure.

The insulation potential of enclosures is severely limited by any leaks or gaps. For example, in the case of an enclosure designed to give a 40 dB(A) reduction the noise radiation from the outer casing is $10^{-4} \times$ that impinging upon the inside; a similar amount of sound would escape through a hole $10^{-4} \times$ the area of the enclosure walls.[8] The loss of soundproofing associated with leaks of various sizes is illustrated in Figure 18.7.[8] Hence, transfer of material to or from an enclosed machine should, if practicable, be effected via ducts or chutes lined with sound-absorbent material. To allow observation of operations within the enclosure, double-glazed windows and internal illumination may be required.

Silencers or Filters

Filters, or reactive silencers, reduce noise transmission by reflecting sound within a given frequency range, generally at low frequencies. Typical

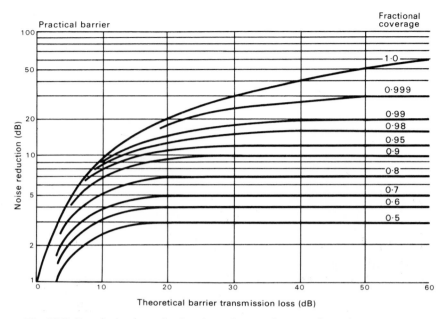

Fig. 18.7 Practical noise reduction through an enclosure—dependence on gap size

applications to compressor outlets give attenuations of up to 25 dB, depending on design.

Absorptive silencers depend upon sound absorption by suitable fibrous materials placed along the walls of a transmission duct. Glass wool or mineral wool is commonly used, and may be covered with a sheet of perforated metal for mechanical protection. This control method is particularly applicable to the process industries where noise generation occurs in a duct or boiler with one end unrestricted and open to atmosphere. The noise emanating under these circumstances depends upon sound absorption along the duct.

While lining the duct with fibrous material is very effective for high-frequency noise, its performance is poor with low-frequency noise. This is demonstrated by Table 18.3 which gives the extent of various types of duct treatment necessary to achieve a given attenuation for different sound frequencies.[8] Typical applications are to the inlets/outlets of fans, blowers and gas turbines and on gas vents generally.

Vibration Damping and Isolation

Application of a layer of damping material such as foam or flexible rubber to a noise-producing structure can reduce the radiated noise energy. The principle applied is that high internal energy losses in the damping material result in the conversion of vibrational energy into heat. This method is particularly applicable to sheet metal panels, chutes, bins and ducts.

An adequate thickness of damping material needs to be bonded to the panel;

TABLE 18.3 MINIMUM MUFFLER LENGTHS (METRES) FOR 20 dB(A) ATTENUATION[8]

Muffler	Frequency (Hz)			
	50	200	800	3200
Lined duct (2 sides) 710 mm wide	∞	4·9	2·4	5·5
Lined duct (2 sides) 710 mm wide, spaced lining	8·3	2·1	18·3	∞
Lined duct (4 sides) 1·2 × 1·2 m interior dimensions, spaced lining	7·6	4·9	7·6	∞
Parallel baffles 100 mm thick, 304 mm on centres	30·5	4·3	1·5	1·8
Maxim silencer, 144-72VP	9·1	8·8	9·1	12·2
Haydite blocks	9·8	5·8	4·6	2·4
Pydee array	27·3	5·5	3·6	3·6
Soundstream absorber, 8H4B2C	8·2	3·0	2·4	2·7
Soundstream absorber, 8Q2A1A	7·0	2·7	2·1	2·7
Acou-Stack staggered baffles	13·4	4·0	2·4	2·7
Thick wavy baffles	8·5	3·4	3·0	3·6
Helix mufflers	∞	4·9	4·9	4·6

this thickness may, for example, be equal to that of the panel itself.[13] Application may be by spraying as a liquid, trowelling on as a mastic or sticking on in the form of a preformed sheet or felt.

Some degree of damping is provided by bolted or riveted joints within a structure. In addition, certain structural materials possess a relatively large inherent damping capacity, for example some forms of cast iron, plastics such as nylon and some bonded laminated sheets.

Structure-borne vibration can be reduced by isolation of the vibration source. This may involve supporting a vibrating machine such as a conveyor or sieve, or a power press or drop hammer, upon resilient mountings. Individual components of a machine, e.g. a prime mover, may also be supported on resilient mountings. The objective is not to prevent vibration but to limit its transmission through a rigid structure to some remote surface from which it may radiate as noise.

Satisfactory results may sometimes be obtained using simple metal or rubber springs but often damping is also required, to avoid low-frequency oscillation of the isolated source. Proprietary resilient mountings comprising either compact lightweight rubber mouldings, metal springs, or pads of various materials such as felt, cork, sponge rubber, are then more convenient.[13] Care is required in their selection so as to combine effective isolation with sufficient rigidity to support the machine in a 'fixed' position. Since the effectiveness of a resilient mounting depends upon the mass and resilience of the supporting structure, it should be attached to a heavy, firm base. Machinery which generates heavy impact forces, e.g. power presses and guillotines, should always be provided with resilient mountings but special foundations may be necessary.[15]

Typical costs, features and applications of a selection of relevant noise-control measures are summarised in Table 18.4.[16] Further information is available in the literature referred to here and in the Bibliography (Chapter 21).

TABLE 18.4 NOISE CONTROL METHODS: COMPARISON AND COSTS[16]

Type of noise reduction	Description of method used	Typical application	Advantages
Noise reduction at source	(a) Replace with quieter machine process (b) Modification of existing process (c) Better maintenance—reduction of clearances, balancing	Replace hammer with a press. Use non-vibrating conveyors Re-shaping cam profiles Machine tools. Gearboxes	A permanent solution. 15 dB(A) reduction sometimes achieved Can improve machine as a whole Increases machine life
Enclosure	(a) Total enclosure of machine by a well-sealed box of sufficient mass (b) Partial enclosure—only noisiest parts of machine enclosed	Automatic machine tools e.g. cold header. Generators Power pack of hydraulic operated machine	20 dB(A) attenuation often easily obtainable Better access, etc.
Plant layout for low noise exposure	Separate noisy machines into one area—partition off	Moving the one noisy machine out of an otherwise quiet area	New layouts can be planned for low noise
Noise refuges	Enclosed control room or rest area	Control room in a compressor house Shop floor office	20 dB(A) easily obtainable
Damping treatment	Apply viscous damping materials or deadened structures	Circular saw blade. Job chute, conveyors, stillages	Usually only small areas of metal need treatment
Impact surface treatment	Surfaces where impacts of hard objects occur covered with soft material	Rubber-lining a steel hopper or bowl feeder	15 dB(A) reduction often obtainable
Air silencers	(a) Exhaust silencer (b) Duct silencers—used to reduce noise carried in cooling and air distribution systems (c) Reactive silencers	Press clutch, air tools, internal combustion engine Fans, cooling towers, vents in enclosures Reciprocating compressor intakes	20 dB(A) reduction usually obtainable Usually 20 dB attenuation of medium and high frequency noise Suitable for low-frequency noise
Screens, barriers and curtains	Movable screens (say 2 m high) arranged around noisy area	Screening fettling areas Screening typing areas	Easily installed
Anti-vibration mounts	'Soft' mounting isolates vibrating structure from its foundation	Decoupling hydraulic pump from oil tank	Can be usefully applied to some machine components
Sound absorptive room treatment	Sound absorptive material (e.g. glass fibre) prevents sound reflection from hard surfaces	Office ceiling	Can reduce background noise in a large office

Disadvantages	Typical time scale for installation	Cost effectiveness	Typical costs (UK, 1976)	Comments
uieter machine/process may lower production rate	Medium-long	Variable	Variable	Ultimately, noise reduction at source will usually be the best solution, but this may take many years
ngineering development work often required	Long	Medium-high	Variable	
ypical noise reduction only 4 dB(A). Personnel may require training	Medium-continuing	Low-medium	Variable	
ccess to machine restricted. Cooling extra space required	Short-medium	Medium	£20–80 per m² of enclosure	A quicker solution, but requires care-full design to make it acceptable to operators
laximum noise reduction often 10 dB(A) or less	Short	Medium	£30–90 per m² of partial enclosure	
hanging existing layout can be inconvenient	Medium-long	Variable	Variable	Should be con-sidered with all new plant layouts
lan being protected will usually spend part of the day outside the refuge	Short	Medium	£1200 for small refuge	Enclosing the man instead of the machine
laterials can be temperature-sensitive	Short	High	£2 per m² treated	Only effective on a limited range of structures
/ear can be reduced by a mild steel sheet. Destroy-ed by high temperatures	Short	High	Rubber/plastic sheet £20 per m²	Many applications in reducing component fall noise
ncreased back-pressure. lay require periodic treatment	Short	High	£3–£30 for medium sized silencer	Special equipment which must be accurately specified
oor low-frequency attentuation	Short	Medium	£60 for silencing 3400 m³/h (2000 cfm) fan duct	
lay only give about 12 dB(A) attenuation	Short	Medium	£300 for a 1700 m³/h (1000 cfm) compressor	
ow attenuation—about 5 dB(A) usually	Short	Low-medium	£10 per m²	Work in progress can sometimes be used as a screen
nti-vibration mounting a whole machine will seldom decrease its noise	Short	Variable	£40 for 4 medium-sized mounts	Floor-transmitted vibration is seldom significant industrial noise source
/ill not improve noise environment of people close to a noise source	Short	Very low for existing buildings, medium for new ones	£2 per m² of room surface treated	Unlikely to find application in workshops

References

1. SUTTON, P., *Chemical Engineer*, (227), CE119, 1969.
2. MIDDLETON, A. H., *Chemical Engineer*, (306), 115, 1976.
3. WILSON, B., *Committee on the Problem of Noise—Final Report*, HMSO, 1969.
4. COATES, T., *Chemical Engineer*, (227), CE112, 1969.
5. Department of Employment, *Code of Practice for Reducing the Exposure of Employed Persons to Noise*, HMSO, 1972.
6. Department of Employment, *Noise and the Worker*, HSW 25, 3rd edn, HMSO, 1971.
7. KNIGHT, J. J., *Chemical Engineer*, (227), CE108, 1969.
8. RICHARDS, E. J., *Chemical Engineer*, (229), CE223, 1969.
9. BS 4142: 1967, *Method of Rating Industrial Noise Affecting Mixed Residential and Industrial Areas*, British Standards Institution, 1967.
10. Recommendation R 1996, International Standards Organisation, 1971.
11. Ministry of Public Building and Works, *Noise Control on Building Sites*, Advisory Leaflet No. 72, HMSO, 1969.
12. *Noise Control*, Process Plant Association, October 1973.
13. *Notes for the Guidance of Designers on the Reduction of Machinery Noise*, Technical Data Note No. 12, Health and Safety Executive, 1975.
14. RICHARDS, E. J., *Proceedings of the Institution of Mechanical Engineers*, **180**(1), 1099, 1965–66.
15. HARRIS, C. M. and CREDE, C. C., *Shock and Vibration Handbook*, McGraw-Hill, 1961.
16. HAY, A., Paper 6B–3, *Plant Engineering and Maintenance Engineering Conference, Birmingham*, 1976.

PART SIX

TECHNICAL ADMINISTRATION AND ECONOMICS

CHAPTER 19

Organisation and Procedures

The technology of waste treatment and pollution control practice has been covered in earlier chapters. The responsibilities of management, and the way in which these responsibilities may be discharged, are now discussed.

Minimisation and/or recovery of waste, in addition to being sound manufacturing practice, is a primary step in pollution control and resource conservation. However, it must be backed up by an established organisation. The methods of disposal, if this is chosen, and plant associated with them should be regularly monitored. Management should in addition keep the potential for recovery continually under review as an alternative to disposal.

Increased attention is currently focused on safety, both with regard to occupational hazards and to the possibility and consequences of accidental spillages or emissions, and these are therefore considered separately. Finally, modelling is introduced as a useful aid to the prediction and correlation of the effects and costs of management decisions.

Management Responsibilities

The aims of management in handling waste and pollution control are generally, within financial and technological constraints:

(i) to avoid any potential risk to human or animal health;
(ii) to minimise damage to the natural environment and annoyance to neighbours;
(iii) to meet appropriate statutory obligations.

It is a prerequisite of modern process plants that performance is achieved without hazard to either employees or the surrounding population. This is part of a broader consideration of the minimum 'disamenity' which is economically viable for any new product or process. The manner in which any accepted risk imposes costs on society either through the producer, the consumer or the environment is shown in Figure 19.1. The outer arrows represent the manner in which the hazards are evaluated by management, by comparison with internal and statutory controls. Criteria and procedures are then established for 'safe' manufacturing and products.

As far as legal requirements in the UK are concerned, it is the responsibility of the factory occupier to determine in detail the controls applicable to his own particular site and operations. Some indication of the possible implications have been given in Chapters 4 and 18; in each case it is necessary to refer to details of legislation[2] and to seek advice from specialists or, for example in the case of works registered under the Alkali Act, from the Inspectorate.

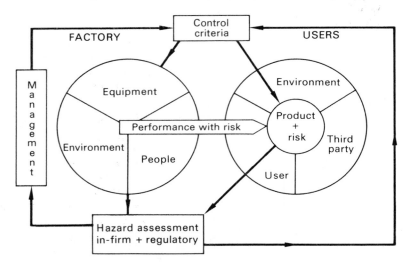

Fig. 19.1 Environmental impact of process plants (based on Fishlock[1]): effect of manufacturing (left) on the factory and its environment and (right) on product users, third parties and their environment

Common experience is that consultation with the various regulatory authorities can be most helpful if begun at the pre-design stage of a factory. However, this is not always possible when changes occur in legislative controls, or in ownership or use of a factory. Whatever the situation, pollution control and waste treatment are unfortunately too often considered as expensive constraints on profitable manufacturing so that legal obligations are just met but not improved upon. Inadequate initial planning, and piecemeal additions or modifications to plant, militate against integration of waste reduction and treatment to achieve the most economical system.

For the future it is relevant to note that recommendations are to be made to the EEC regarding a requirement for an 'environmental impact study' for any proposal or programme for urban or industrial development which, by reason of its scale or its effects on the natural environment, may have a harmful effect on the latter.[3] Such a study is intended to be carried out before the proposal/programme is finally settled and is likely to include:

(a) an analysis of the original state of the environment which may be harmed by the programme or proposal;
(b) an explanation of the reasons behind the choice of site;
(c) foreseeable effects of implementation of the proposal or programme on the natural environment and, in particular,
  direct and indirect effects
  short- and long-term effects
  temporary and permanent effects;
(d) description of measures to be taken in order to reduce or eliminate unfavourable effects on the environment;
(e) description of the alternatives to the programme or proposal or to certain of its elements or to the proposed location (including maintenance of the status quo). The foreseeable effects on the environment need analysis in each case;
(f) proposals concerning inspection procedures to be carried out;
(g) a short summary of the impact study capable of being understood by the non-specialist.

Waste Reduction

Attempts to reduce the amounts of waste produced during manufacturing must begin at the process and product design stages. Within the overriding financial constraints considered in detail in Chapter 20, all alternative processing routes can then be considered.

Once the factory is in operation, in-plant materials control and quality control procedures are of prime importance.

Part of the materials-control function, within the overall factory efficiency-control function, is a continuing analysis of materials consumption compared with planned figures. This applies to direct materials, that is materials used directly in manufacture; to indirect materials, such as items for factory maintenance and cleaning; and to utilities, i.e. fuels, steam, process water, cooling water, electricity, compressed air and possibly special gases. At steady state, when there is no accumulation in the system, increased consumption of direct or indirect materials and utilities (except electricity and compressed air) compared with the planned figures for a given production level must, from simple mass and energy balance considerations, result in an increase in gaseous, liquid and/or solid waste generation. Apart from the direct effects of this on profitability, increased costs will therefore be incurred in waste treatment or disposal, or in recycling.

The considerations arising in the establishment and operation of materials control systems are outside the scope of this text. However, provided that transmission lags are minimised, control information can provide 'early warning' of excessive waste-generation and of which production processes within the factory are the causes.

Common sources of waste arisings include:

Raw materials damaged or off-specification on receipt.
Materials damaged or contaminated in storage.
Process losses from, for example,
   leaks or spillages
   production of off-specification materials
   low yields
   maloperation
Equipment cleaning.
Damage to, or contamination of, materials in transfer between operations.
Damage to, or contamination of, products in storage.
Leaks and spillages.
Miscellaneous losses from drain points, vents, sampling points, overflows.

The major functions of quality control are to determine the levels of quality of raw materials, materials in process and finished product, to compare existing qualities with established specifications and to initiate remedial action if and when deviations occur. The specification for standard quality may include relevant physical and chemical data, limits of composition on all impurities, dimensional limits and other quantifiable criteria relevant to the suitability of the material or product for its intended use.

The application of quality control thus involves sampling and analysis and/or testing and/or inspection of all materials, products or wastes for comparison with these standards (Figure 19.2). It is on such bases that primary or secondary recycled materials are accepted or rejected for use in manufacturing, and that in-process material or products are recycled or sent for disposal.

The later in the process that off-specification material is produced, the greater the financial loss; return of material from the consumer and return due to failure in use are the most serious. The feasibility of recycling may also be reduced after a critical stage in the manufacturing process, for example after packaging, or some irreversible physical change, or painting/dyeing.

Both quantity and value of waste generated can often be reduced by the application of control earlier, at more stages, or more frequently during manufacturing operations, but this may be limited by economic factors or by the fact that analysis involves the destruction or degradation of material. In the process industries the samples analysed may therefore represent only $10^{-5} \times$ total production. Automatic sampling and analysis are being used increasingly in continuous production, for example in petrochemicals manufacture, to reduce lags in the control system and enable remedial action to be taken more rapidly.

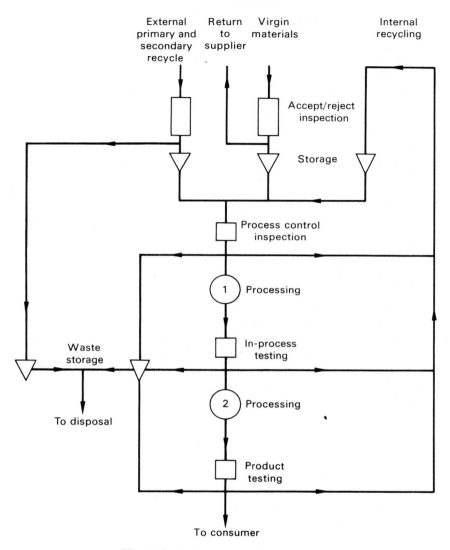

Fig. 19.2 Quality control and recycle system

The manner in which efficient materials and quality control act together to reduce 'controllable' waste, possibly by demonstrating the need for modified plant or operating procedures, depends largely on the particular factory, the scale of operation and whether production is batchwise or continuous.

Water conservation is a problem common to many industrial enterprises and serves to exemplify some of management's options. In all cases, as with the minimisation of general 'wastes' production, measures aimed at improved water economy should be instituted, wherever possible, at the design stage. For existing facilities, critical examination of water requirements may be based on Table 19.1.

The three major uses of water are as a process material, as a means of transportation and as a heat-exchange medium. Consumption is particularly high in the process industries: e.g. a pulp mill consumes 227–250 m³ (50 000–55 000 gal) per tonne of product; a paper mill, 31·8–54·5 m³ (7000–12 000 gal) per tonne of paper. Therefore considerable efforts are made to recycle water in such operations.

Process water is likely to be the most heavily polluted stream since it has been used as a vehicle for chemical or physical changes in the manufacturing process, or for the scrubbing or leaching-out of impurities from process materials. The nature and level of the pollutants will vary with the process. The effluent may also be raised in temperature. However, process water discharge is generally less in volume than water from other uses.

TABLE 19.1 EXAMINATION OF WATER REQUIREMENTS AND ECONOMY MEASURES (based on CHALMERS[4])

---

1. Construct a water 'balance sheet' for the factory. Relate input flows to output and to need.
   Record water intake with all taps closed.
2. Exclude cooling and uncontaminated waters from direct discharge to drain. Initiate or extend reuse and recycle. Examine bleed-off rates.
3. Examine timing on automatic flushing systems, and spring-loaded taps or pedal controls for domestic supplies.
4. Compare day and night flows (differences arise from higher night pressure in mains).
5. Stop rinse flows when no work is present.
   (a) On/off pedals at tanks with hand-operated processes.
   (b) Mechanical linkages controlling water supply against plant cycles on automatic plants. Incorporate time-delay if required.
   (c) Conductivity controllers.
6. Examine efficiency of water use.
   (a) Avoid short-circuiting in rinse tanks.
   (b) Use air agitation whenever possible.
   (c) Counter-current rinsing.
7. Determine precisely the water flow needed to maintain the required quality in each rinse tank. Control the maximum flow by pipeline restrictors.

Water is used for transportation in diverse processes such as papermaking, coal-washing, fruit and vegetable processing, molten phosphorus transfer, disposal of boiler ash and recovery of battery lead. This water becomes contaminated by matter dissolved or entrained from the material being conveyed and, since treatment is required before discharge, recycling should be maximised.

Water may be used for cooling purposes either in a once-through system or in a closed-circuit recirculatory system which relies upon evaporative cooling. Water from a once-through system should create no disposal problem if its temperature is below 25°C, unless a leak develops in a heat exchanger or similar equipment, when it may be contaminated by process materials. However, once-through systems are only economic in special locations. Water from a recirculatory system is seldom heavily polluted, but any purge stream produced by 'blowing-down' is likely to have a higher solids concentration.

The existence within most manufacturing plants of different grades of wastewater, so that recycling opportunities vary with the grade and degree of contamination of the stream, serves as a starting-point for management to examine the technical feasibility of a water recovery or recycling scheme. A mass balance based on a flow diagram (such as Figure 9.12, page 254) can be drawn. Each and every proposal in the overall recycling/recovery scheme must, however, be examined in detail, and justified in terms of economics using the techniques described in Chapter 20.

Integrated Design

Some consideration should be given to integration of waste treatment facilities, taking account of the interrelationship of gaseous, liquid and solid wastes stressed earlier. In the simplest form this may only involve, for example, neutralisation of one effluent stream by another or adsorption of a liquid in a solid waste. More complex arrangements involving recovery of valuable metals or other materials have been discussed in earlier chapters.

A prime example of what is technically possible in integrated waste treatment is the plant designed by the Black Clawson Company for Franklin, Ohio (see Figure 17.25).[5] The facility takes in domestic refuse and sewage, and processes them to yield saleable materials such as ferrous metal, glass, fibres and aluminium. The final liquid effluent is of an acceptable quality for discharge to a river.

In all cases, however, management must only invest in complex schemes after a full and realistic assessment of the costs, and any profits, involved. How this may be done is described in Chapter 20.

Plant Manning and Activities

Waste treatment and recovery operations have tended to be allocated low priority compared with manufacturing and this, together with unpleasant working conditions associated with some activities, has resulted in recruitment problems. Often the importance of the operations, and the problems created if they are not performed properly, have not been recognised: where they are labour-intensive, unskilled operatives are often used, particularly in solid waste disposal by landfill or to 'mind' rudimentary effluent treatment plants.

However, increased legislation and the advances in technology which are being introduced in, for example, toxic waste incineration and the recovery of materials from liquid effluents result in a need for trained and/or qualified operators. Technical control may require a chemical technologist with support from a control laboratory. The increased emphasis on recovery and recycling also requires personnel to operate efficient materials and cost control systems.

Waste treatment plants generally are increasing in complexity and capacity to comply with stringent legislative controls; they are also handling a wider variety of heterogeneous wastes. These changes are reflected in the increased quality of management required in waste treatment operations. In some cases, for example with a plant of the complexity of that shown in Figure 17.25, they exercise all the usual functions of production managers of process plants (Table 19.2). In these activities the amount of assistance available from specialists depends upon the scale and degree of sophistication of the operation. However, as already indicated, where recovery is involved procedures must be established for the control of materials, quality and costs if the venture is to be successful. Furthermore, with the increase in plant complexity and instrumentation for monitoring, particularly with continuous operation, the scheduling of maintenance becomes more important.

TABLE 19.2 MANAGEMENT ACTIVITIES IN WASTE TREATMENT PLANT OPERATION

Operation planning:
  (a) Medium-term
       Based on estimates of supply/demand and costs
       Concerned with availability of plant, materials and labour
       Contingency plans—breakdowns, stoppages
  (b) Short-term
       To attain targets set in (a) above
       Concerned with start-up, shutdown and throughputs
       Objects are best utilisation of plant, labour, direct materials and utilities, etc.

In-plant control:
  (a) Operational and process control
  (b) Control of operating efficiency
       Concerned with efficient use of direct and indirect materials, direct and indirect labour, utilities, plant, transport, etc.
  (c) Control of plant efficiency
       Maintenance of plant (prevention, turn-around and breakdown maintenance)
       Attainment of specified plant and equipment performances
  (d) In-plant material control
  (e) Control of personnel
  (f) Quality control of products/wastes
  (g) Attainment of established safety standards

Contingency planning is particularly necessary with regard to the services provided by public authorities, i.e. the collection and disposal of household refuse and the treatment of sewage, which can be seriously disrupted by labour disputes.[6] For example, temporary measures for refuse collection may involve making available ample tipping space within reasonable distance, allocation of sites for local dumps, a large stock of sacks and tentative arrangements for their distribution.

In addition to the functions outlined in Table 19.2, the management of a waste treatment facility needs to give more than average attention to public relations. The suspicion aroused by 'waste' in any form, and the connotation with pollution and amenity damage discussed in Chapter 1, means that a waste pyrolysis plant or solid waste transfer station may engender more local hostility and be more closely watched than a manufacturing plant of similar pollution potential. Therefore as well as providing, and operating continuously, appropriate site pollution control measures it may be necessary for management to go out of its way to advertise that this is being done. The impact of the plant on its immediate environment should be minimised in every way possible, for example by screening with trees, providing for adequate and if possible unobtrusive access to the site and avoiding traffic congestion.

Pollution Control and Monitoring

Management control involves setting objectives and then monitoring, either continually or periodically, how closely they are attained. An initial audit defines the general aims and identifies those areas in which performance needs assessment: air pollution, water pollution, waste disposal, noise, potential material recovery. Less quantifiable areas, such as the visual impact of the factory, or the consequential effects of transportation of materials to and products from it, may also be included.

It is important to note the different criteria for air pollutants: it is recognised, for example, that fixed levels for sulphur dioxide do not take into account the fluctuations that occur or their impact, in the short or long term, on the acute or chronic medical effects. Unfortunately there appears to be little reliable data on what constitutes an appropriate standard for exposure of the public to a specific pollutant or mixture of pollutants. The limitations of using fractions of threshold limit values were described in Chapter 4 and are exemplified by Table 19.3.

In order to monitor emissions, discharges or other disposal methods it is first necessary to compile a comprehensive list. Thus all effluent discharges, their frequency, flow rates and relevant composition/concentration data must be collated. A block diagram of similar form to Figure 9.12 (page 254) may be used. A similar exercise must be followed for gaseous emissions, whether they are continuous, intermittent or arise only in case of emergency or plant breakdown (Table 19.4).

Specific levels of control should then be laid down for each disposal route in terms of quantity and quality, measured in terms of the parameters described in Chapter 3. In doing this a balance must be struck between ideal levels and what is practicable. Possible future changes in legal limits and foreseeable

TABLE 19.3 EXPOSURE AND EFFECTS OF AIR POLLUTANTS (based on CHANLETT[7])

	Population exposed	Exposure profile Period of exposure	Type of pollutant Dust, fume, gas, vapour, mist (noise)	Level of pollutant	Possible results or effects
Occupational exposure	Adults (16–65) Mainly male Fit for work (health possibly monitored)	Basic working week e.g. 40 hr/wk, 48 wk/yr + overtime (therefore intermittent elimination and recovery times)	Generally single pollutants Known origin Hazards known Recognised problem Personal protection provided Probably freshly formed/released	Possible measurable fractions of Threshold Limit Values which are recognised criteria	Specific effects e.g. pneumoconiosis, hearing loss Increased costs (accident rate, compensation, retraining) and lowered efficiency
Environmental exposure	All, including infants aged and infirm	Continual unless area vacated (therefore elimination and recovery depend on irregular periods of low/zero concentrations)	Mixture of primary pollutants, from different sources, and secondary pollutants Origins may be difficult to prove Hazards not quantified Exposure unheeded	Normally very low At limits of analytical/ instrumental sensitivity ($\mu g/m^3$)	Decreased well-being Non-specific respiratory troubles Irritation of eyes, nose and throat Damage to property and vegetation Injury to animals Decrease in 'amenity' Long-term ecological effects

modifications in plant reliability or operating procedures should also be taken into account.

The type of monitoring for a specific site depends on the quantity and nature of the discharges: the following serves as general guidance.

TABLE 19.4 EXAMPLES OF SOURCES OF CONTINUOUS OR INTERMITTENT ATMOSPHERIC EMISSIONS

High level

Routine:	Vents	General ventilation (factory atmosphere)
		Local extraction (dust and fumes)
		Process equipment
	Flare stacks	
	Chimneys	
Irregular:	Plant maloperation	Process plant
		Extraction plant
	Flare stacks	
	Plant failure	Process plant
		Extraction/collection plant (scrubbers, filters, cyclones, precipitators)

Low level

Routine:	Process equipment, cleaning or steaming
	Materials handling (discharge, conveying, bagging)
	Waste handling/deposition on land
Irregular:	Plant maloperation (e.g. unauthorised venting)
	Plant failure
	Start-up/shutdown
	Dismantling/demolition (and transportation)
	Unauthorised waste incineration

Gaseous Emissions

A variety of means is available to monitor stack emissions (Chapter 5). Typical examples are:

Combustible gas monitors to indicate or record organic content of flue gases
Television cameras to record smoke and visible vapour plumes
Oxygen or carbon dioxide meters for flue gas analysis.

In addition to monitoring emissions, these are aids to efficient plant operation: on combustion processes, for example, gas analyses provide information on quantity of excess air and efficiency of combustion.

A strict monitoring programme may be necessary where fine particulates are emitted in any of the ways listed in Table 19.4, for example in iron and steel foundries, cement works and power stations. Measurement of sulphur dioxide levels is also required in power stations.

Liquid Wastes

Standards for effluent discharge in the UK are specified in Consents for Discharge; these must be taken as maxima rather than target figures. Instrumentation for the monitoring of liquid compositions is summarised in Chapter 5 and flows must be metered. Where monitoring instrumentation performs a control function it should be robust and arranged to 'fail-safe', preferably with an alarm system (Chapter 7).

Solid Wastes

The criteria to be applied when monitoring solid waste disposal were outlined in Chapter 4 and analytical methods in Chapter 5. The major difficulty which arises is that of obtaining a representative sample from heterogeneous waste for economical analysis so that, on every occasion, it can be segregated and disposed of by the most appropriate route.

Changes in production processes, maloperation or admixture of wastes can result in unpredictable changes in waste composition. Therefore laxity must not be allowed to arise in the certification of compositions of waste for disposal. Notification procedures, where applicable, and the codes of practice referred to in Chapters 13 and 14 should be complied with whenever practicable.

The minimum analysis for each sample of waste received as an 'unknown' is summarised in Table 19.5. A battery of tests has been developed on this basis as an aid to rapid identification of hazardous wastes.[9] This is considerably less costly, but may not entirely replace a systematic analysis.

TABLE 19.5 MINIMUM ANALYSIS FOR WASTE SAMPLES[8]

	Minimum necessary wastes analysis	
For inorganic wastes	Reaction with water ⎫ Reaction with acids ⎪ Identification Reaction with alkalis ⎬ of any gases Effect of heat ⎭ evolved pH, total solids Presence of sulphides, total cyanide, ammonium compounds Concentration of metals, particularly Pb, Zn, Cd, Hg, Sn, As, Cu, Cr, Ni	For mixtures of inorganic and organic wastes all these analyses should be completed
For organic wastes	Calorific value Flash point Miscibility with water (or other wastes) Viscosity at various temperatures Halogen, sulphur, nitrogen content Ash content Analysis of ash Organic content by BOD, COD, PV or total carbon methods	

Where effective control is based upon instrument monitoring, two important precautions must be observed: firstly, the instruments must be kept in operation, whether used intermittently or continuously, and must be regularly maintained and recalibrated when necessary. For complex instruments this may involve a service contract with the suppliers. Secondly, even if the instrument is part of an automatic control system, for example pH control of effluent discharge, management must compare the measurements obtained with the established criteria and take appropriate action when deviations appear. The measurements are more likely to be heeded if they are all relayed back to a centralised bank of recorders, possibly in a control room. Complex installations may require the use of data-logging and computers.

Whenever materials which are significantly toxic are disposed of, whether as gas, liquid or solid, it is prudent to reinforce the monitoring required by law. Any data collection programme should be supplemented by a 'walk-around' survey at suitable intervals. This should result in the early detection of any change in visual impact, deterioration of amenities or damage to vegetation and wild life before they become the subject of complaints from neighbours or the authorities.

Case Study: Analysis and Segregation before Determination of Disposal

A company in the UK has recently acquired an old factory previously sublet to a number of small firms. A tour of the site reveals an accumulation of 'wastes' of the four main categories A, B, C and D described below, for the safe disposal of which a stepwise procedure is required.

A. 75 drums brown viscous liquid (colour variation between drums).
   Miscellany of drum labels including:

> 'Corvic'
> 'Genklene'
> 'Do not use, 10/9/73'
> 'Scrap'
> 'U/S'

B. 125 corroded drums with removable lids, mostly without labels, apparently factory refuse, plus some empty drums labelled 'Cassell Heat Treatment Salt'.

C. 50 drums with removable lids.
   Off-white, partly agglomerated crystalline powder.
   No labels, drums corroded.

D. About 1¼ tonnes fibrous white material in a single pile, wet and 'self-thatched' on top.

Procedure

The first step is to secure the storage area and the second is to attempt to identify the wastes. An approach may be made to the previous occupiers for this purpose; if this is unsuccessful, enquiries as to the nature of the businesses may indicate likely constituents of the waste. (For examples, refer to Chapters 3 and 6.) Visual examination and analysis is then necessary; a full analysis would be expensive and superfluous but important chemical and physical properties must be determined. (For examples refer to Chapters 3 and 5.) Every drum should be checked with complete disregard to the names painted on them or to temporary labels, since such drums are commonly reused.

Analyses
  A. Discarded lubricating oil.
     Segregated by grades in different drums.
     No unexpected chemical contaminants or solvents present.
  B. 'Factory refuse'.
     94 drums — floor sweepings, sawdust.
     Oily rags.
     Wooden lathes covered with plaster.
     31 drums — washed sodium cyanide containers.
  C. Soda ash.
     Uncontaminated but containing moisture.
  D. Chrysotile asbestos.
     Matted on surface, dry interior.

Alternatives for Treatment/Use/Disposal
The waste material in leaking or potentially unsound drums should be redrummed or put into other suitable receptacles as necessary and be labelled. For waste D, approved handling procedures must be followed before disposal.[10]

Waste A may be used as fuel for boilers or sent for recovery, or be disposed of other than by landfill. Notification is necessary under the Deposit of Poisonous Waste Act 1972.

Waste B may be disposed of by landfill or incineration. It would be prudent to first check the 'floor sweepings' for cyanide contamination. The 'clean' sodium cyanide containers must be checked for trace residues; prior to disposal they may be pierced to prevent reuse, and the name overprinted to avoid confusion.

Waste C may be kept for neutralisation of spillages if acid is to be used on the premises, or sold via the Waste Materials Exchange (Chapter 9) or, if these methods are uneconomic, disposed of by landfill.

Waste D should be notified to the appropriate authorities and to HM Factory Inspectorate, and be disposed of strictly in accordance with the Code of Practice referred to in Chapter 14.[11]

Occupational Safety and Health

In providing plant and establishing a system of work for waste disposal it is important that operator safety is not overlooked. In the UK the requirements of relevant parts of the Health and Safety at Work, etc., Act 1974, which applies to all people at work, impose duties on the employer:[12]

(a) To ensure, so far as is reasonably practicable, the health, safety and welfare at work of all his employees.
(b) To provide and maintain plant and systems of work that are, so far as is reasonably practicable, safe and without risks to health.
(c) To make arrangements for ensuring, so far as is reasonably practicable, safety and absence of risks to health in connection with the use, storage and transport of articles and substances.
(d) To provide information, instruction, supervision and training to ensure the health and safety at work of his employees.
(e) So far as is reasonably practicable to maintain the works in a condition that is safe and without risks to health and to maintain means of access and egress that are safe and without risks.
(f) To provide and maintain a working environment that is, so far as is reasonably practicable, safe and without risks to health and adequate as regards facilities for welfare at work.

Within factories[13] these requirements served to extend existing legislation, whereas landfill sites were not previously covered. Thus a survey commenced in 1974[14,15] found that facilities on typical landfill sites accepting toxic waste tended to be rudimentary, possibly lacking even basic amenities such as water supply, sewer connection, telephone and electricity supply. Some sites were completely unfenced and unmanned, though typically they had a gateman and one or two bulldozer drivers. Since 80% of the total disposal cost for landfilling is transportation, many contractors were originally hauliers and scant attention was found to have been given to technical aspects of waste handling and, in general, to operator safety.

In order to handle a waste safely it is necessary to know, at least in general terms, its toxicity, dermatitic properties, flammability, stability, corrosiveness and any other hazards. Contractors handling many and varied wastes tend to be at a disadvantage in this respect, particularly if transportation is by a third party. Proper notification of wastes as described in Chapter 13 is therefore essential. Potential operator hazards on waste disposal sites include the following.

Toxic Hazards

(a) *Inhalation of dust or fumes.* Exposure may arise in the open air during the tipping or disturbance of a waste, or by the wetting of a reactive waste, for example metal drosses,[16] or by the mixing of incompatible materials such as bleaching powder (hypochlorites) or sulphides and acids. Exposure may also arise in entering confined spaces for cleaning or inspection, for example soakage trenches, excavations, road tanker barrels. Toxic products, e.g. carbon monoxide, hydrogen chloride, hydrogen cyanide, may be produced during accidental or unauthorised waste combustion.

(b) *Absorption.* Ingress of toxic materials via the skin or mucous membranes is possible with some materials likely to be offered for disposal. These include certain solvents, alkaloids, aniline, mercury and phosphorus compounds.

(c) *Ingestion.* Intake of toxic materials via the digestive system is not usually a major problem in industry, largely because regulations prohibit eating and drinking in specific work areas and lay down minimum requirements for washing facilities.[17] On a site lacking these provisions, heavy metals, classic poisons (e.g. arsenic, cyanide and strychnine), dangerous drugs and synthetic poisons (e.g. acaricides, fungicides, insecticides, rodenticides) can create a hazard.

Corrosive/Dermatitic Hazards

The possibility of eye or skin injury may arise when handling corrosive materials such as acids, alkalis, phenols and cresols. The dermatitic hazard associated with prolonged/intermittent exposure to many chemicals is less appreciated:[18] for example, a large proportion of the materials listed in Table 13.4 (page 352) can act as dermatitic agents.

Physical Hazards

Noise may present an occupational hazard to landfill machine operators; bulldozers in particular are a major problem,[19] and to a lesser extent scrapers and cranes.

Fires are common on landfill sites but the danger to operators is probably minimal because operations are in the open air. Accidents have, however, arisen in using landfill machinery to control burning material by smothering or isolation.

Mechanical Hazards

Vehicle accidents are a real hazard wherever heavy plant is used and bulldozers and compactors present a significant overturning risk. Primary entanglement with machinery is a hazard of some operations, as in removing material fouling the drive on bulldozers or forcing jammed skips. Because of the isolation of many sites, machinery maintenance may be carried out under rudimentary conditions, and without proper facilities for machinery decontamination. In addition to 'normal' slips and falls, the untidy state of some landfill sites may create a particular hazard of simple accidents.

Infective Hazards

Infectious diseases such as anthrax and tetanus must be considered. Leather, wool and bonemeal wastes are potential carriers of anthrax.[20] Slaughterhouse and hospital wastes and sewage sludge may contain pathogenic organisms which are harmful via skin contact. Gastro-intestinal infections can result from neglect of personal hygiene.

As with other industrial activities, the Health and Safety at Work Act requires that operators of waste treatment or pollution control plant should provide a safe place of work, safe plant and appliances and a safe system of work. Some of the treatment and recovery processes described earlier amount to chemical plants of varying degrees of complexity. To ensure safety in operation, some permutation or combination of the measures summarised in Table 19.6 is required; it is assumed that proper safety practice has been followed in process development, plant design, construction and commissioning. Many of the measures listed are covered in the UK by the Factories Act 1961, or regulations made under it, or by the Highly Flammable Liquids and Liquefied Petroleum Gases Regulations 1972 and similar legislation.

TABLE 19.6 SUMMARY OF SAFETY MEASURES

Access	Control of access to plant, e.g. against trespass by children Security of fencing Designation of restricted areas, e.g. containing flammable materials, 'eye-protection' zones, 'hearing-protection' zones Freedom from obstruction of roads, access ways, escape routes
Alterations	Formal approval for plant or process changes Hazard and operability study prior to implementation: repeat when in use Updating of all operating instructions, notices, procedures Removal/isolation of obsolete plant or lines
Cleaning procedures	Vacuum cleaning/wet scrubbing where appropriate (e.g. asbestos, toxic dusts) Discourage use of compressed air for 'blowing' or 'dusting down' Procedures for rapid neutralisation, treatment, cleaning up of spillage

Communication systems	Adequate log books, recipe sheets, batch sheets
	Identification of vessels, lines, valves, e.g. by code numbers
	Inter-shift communication and records
	System for reporting and follow-up of:
	    Plant defects
	    Process deviations
	    Hazardous occurrences, e.g. leaks, spillages, overpressure relief
	    Accidents: minor/major injury and/or material loss
	Warnings, notices:
	    Statutory notices
	    Notices relating to specific hazards
	    Notices relating to temporary hazards (and their subsequent removal)
	Identification of materials
	See also Permit-to-work systems, Operating procedures

Table 19.6(*Cont'd*)

Contractors	Familiarisation with plant hazards, rules, safety practices
	Clear delineation of work, responsibilities, hand-over
	See also Maintenance, Permits-to-work, Personal Protection, Site restrictions, etc.
First aid	Emergency showers (or equivalent, e.g. baths)
	Eye-wash bottles (or equivalent, e.g. fountains)
	Chemicals for decontamination
	Antidotes where relevant (e.g. cyanides)
	Usual first aid provisions
	Resuscitation equipment (location and provisions)
Inspection and testing (and cleaning/ maintenance where appropriate)	General ventilation provisions (note temporary obstructions)
	Local exhaust ventilation provisions (test and report on at regular intervals)
	Fire protection
	Alarm systems (HTA, HPA, fire, evacuation, etc.)
	Plant and equipment generally; portable tools; flexible hoses
	Safety devices, e.g. PSVs, explosion reliefs
	Monitoring and control instruments
	Protective clothing and equipment, emergency equipment
	Drains and floor drainage
	Bund walls
	Electrical equipment; earthing and bonding
Maintenance	Arrangements for issue, control, testing, repair of lifting gear, ladders, scaffolding, etc.
	Scheduled maintenance for key plant items
	Use of job cards/log book to identify tasks precisely
	Permit-to-work systems:[21]
	Flame-cutting/welding (or soldering, brazing):
	On vessels, piping, drums which have contained flammable materials[22]
	In an area in which flammable vapours/gases could be present
	In an area from which all combustible material has not been removed
	Where non-flammable vapour subject to degradation may be present (e.g. trichloroethylene) or toxic fumes/vapours may be volatilised
	In confined spaces (i.e. consider NO_x, CO, etc.)
	Line-breaking
	Electrical work
	Equipment removal, e.g. to workshop
	Work on roofs
	Maintenance of guards on machinery, open vessels, handrails; screens at sampling/drumming-up points, etc., and on glass equipment
	Use of sparkproof tools where appropriate (e.g. where hydrogen or acetylene may be present)
	Restriction on employees permitted to perform electrical maintenance
Management training	Refresher courses on fundamentals of safety, hazard recognition, procedures
	Participation in hazard and operability studies on existing operations and procedures

Table 19.6 (*Cont'd*)

Manning levels	Advisability/otherwise of lone working in specific areas Adequacy of emergency assistance—particularly on shift Adequacy of immediate supervision—particularly on shift

Materials handling	Adequacy of procedure for receipt of materials:
	    In bulk, e.g. checks on tanker contents, earthing, bonding,
	        identification of receiving vessel
	    In small containers, e.g. carboy handling, cylinder unloading
	Adequacy of procedure for despatch of materials:
	    Inspection of tankers, carboys, cylinders, etc., prior to filling
	    Identification and labelling of materials; driver instructions
	Use of earthing clips on portable containers of flammable liquids
	Stacking practice

Monitoring (and follow-up)	Working environments:
	    Toxic contaminants
	    Temperature
	    Noise[23]
	    Lighting
	    Vibration
	    Ionising radiation
	Appropriate medical supervision:
	    Pre-employment medical (for selection, establishing base levels)
	    Working conditions in specific areas
	    Employees' routine or statutory medicals, exposure profiles

Operating procedures	Clearly written operating instructions accessible to operators
	    (preferably with reference to numbered plant items):
	        Start-up/shutdown
	        Normal operation
	        Emergency shutdown
	        Procedures for non-routine operations, e.g. clearance of blockages,
	          reprocessing of materials, temporary process alteration
	Established procedures for draining, purging, venting, isolating,
	    testing, inspection, prior to opening/entering/maintaining plant
	    (see also Permit-to-work systems, Maintenance)
	Quality control on raw materials, materials in process, products,
	    wastes
	Materials control to enable losses, over-use, under-use, accumulations
	    of materials to be detected; control of quantities in store

Operator training	Formal training programme; refresher courses Instruction in hazards associated with work and safe procedures[24] Instruction and practice in emergency procedures Encourage/enforce use of personal protection Special training needs, e.g. first aid, emergency rescue, fire-fighting

Permit-to-work systems	See under Maintenance
	Entry into confined spaces (e.g. vat, vessel, flue, sewer, boiler,
	    etc.)[25]
	Use of non-flameproof electrical equipment or vehicles where flammable
	    liquids, vapours, dusts may arise

Table 19.6(*Cont'd*)

Personal hygiene	Adequate washing/showering facilities (location and provisions)[15] Skin-cleansing, barrier and condition cream provision Double locker system
Personal protection	Overalls, special requirements (e.g. nylon for asbestos workers; flame-retardant or antistatic); frequency of laundering Protective clothing: suits, spats, armlets, helmets, gloves for specific applications; helmets; footwear (industrial/antistatic); hearing protectors Eye-protection; specific provision for various duties[26] Respirators; specific types for different applications, e.g. full face mask, ori-nasal, frame and pad, air-supplied types[27]

Safety management	Safety audit system[28,29]
	 Adequacy and location of fire-fighting, emergency rescue, alarm equipment
	 Emergency procedures (particularly with low manning-levels, e.g. at weekends), following:
	     Fire/explosion
	     Toxic release
	     Serious accident
	 Major emergency procedures:
	     Internal (evacuation, communications, damage control)
	     External liaison (fire, police, hospitals, neighbours)

Site restrictions	Prohibition of eating/drinking except in designated areas Prohibition of smoking, carrying matches/cigarette lighters except in designated areas; enforcement arrangements Restriction on employees permitted to drive factory transport[30]
Storage	Segregation of incompatible materials (e.g. nitrates/chlorates from carbonaceous materials, oxidising acids from organic materials) Good housekeeping Compliance with limits set for stocks of potentially hazardous chemicals Storage, segregation, handling of gas cylinders; supporting of cylinders

The benefits of established operating procedures are not restricted to occupational safety; they encourage efficient operation and reduce the likelihood of 'pollution incidents' due to maloperation.

Regulations proposed in the UK for the labelling of road tankers carrying dangerous substances would require the marking of tankers carrying either single or multi-loads. Under the proposals, the Hazardous Substances (Conveyance by Road) Tank Labelling Regulations 1977, tankers carrying a prescribed dangerous substance would display a hazard-warning panel of the type shown in Figure 19.3. This is intended to warn the public of the presence of a dangerous substance and that in the event of an incident involving the tanker they should alert the emergency services and keep clear. It is also to advise the emergency services by coded information of the proper immediate action in an incident involving fire or spillage and to enable them to obtain detailed information. The label comprises four main sections:

(i) *Emergency action code:* numbers and letters providing coded information, to be interpreted using a pocket card. This covers which firefighting medium to use, whether spillage should be contained or washed away, whether evacuation of the area may be necessary, whether protective clothing or breathing apparatus should be worn and whether there is risk of violent reaction.

(ii) *Diamond warning sign:* an internationally recognised warning, of which there are 13.

(iii) *Substance identification number:* together, optionally, with the name of the substance. With multi-loads the identification number would be replaced by 'multi-load'.

(iv) *Specialist advice:* further advice would be obtainable from the telephone number given.

A fifth section may show the manufacturer's or company house name or symbol. For single loads the panels would be securely attached to the rear and both sides of the tanker; for multi-loads a panel would be securely attached to the rear with compartment labels attached to both sides of every compartment.

A schedule of prescribed hazardous substances, including hazardous waste, would be published in conjunction with the proposed regulations.

Fig. 19.3 Tanker warning panel for single loads (basic colours: orange, black, white)

Accidental Pollution

Even when proper measures have been incorporated into a process, and a system of work introduced, to recover wastes and minimise pollution there remains the question of accidental gaseous emissions and potential pollution due to spillage, seepage or run-off of liquid wastes or of the leachate from solid wastes.

Attempts are now being made to assess potential danger to local residents from airborne pollution associated with waste deposition.[31] Predictions take into account factors such as:

Topography of site
Strength and direction of winds
Location of nearest residential properties
Wastes generated on site, together with their potential for harm
Likelihood of incidents, including reactions with any wastes coming on to site
    in a tanker or skip serving the complex.

For example, when a gas similar in density to air is generated, transfer is by diffusion which can be correlated by the simplified equation[32]

$$X = \frac{Q}{\pi \, \sigma_y \, \sigma_z \, U}$$

where X = concentration (g/s) at downwind distance x
        Q = generation rate (g/s)
    σ_y, σ_z = values obtained from tables which take account of downwind distance x
        U = wind speed (m/s).

It is thus possible, by adopting an appropriate value for permissible short-term exposure to the public, to calculate the critical generation rate for toxic gas generation up-wind of a residential area. The appropriate concentration may be taken, albeit with caution, as the appropriate Threshold Limit Value–Short-Term Exposure Limit (TLV–STEL); this is essentially the maximum concentration to which 15 minutes' continuous occupational exposure is currently believed to be permissible.[33]

With regard to solid waste, the potential for accidental pollution is one factor to be investigated by Waste Disposal Authorities, of which there are 46 in England, when providing a site licence required by the Control of Pollution Act 1974. In addition to considering the possible effects on the inhabitants, wildlife and amenities of the area arising from normal operation, they should, in the case of a landfill site, have regard to the type and quantity of waste delivered to the site in relation to its capacity and the possibility of ground- or surface-water pollution. This requires an assessment of the physical, chemical and biological barriers to leachates and their likely interactions. In some cases existing sites may need to be modified, by sealing and/or by leachate treatment.

It is relevant to note here that, in addition to the duty under Section 5 to prevent dangerous emissions from places of work, Section 3 of the Health and Safety at Work, etc., Act 1974 requires every employer to conduct his undertaking to ensure, so far as is reasonably practicable, that persons (not in his employment) who may be affected thereby are not exposed to risks to their health or safety. This covers the potential hazard associated with equipment or plant to which the public have access and also the conveyance of dangerous substances.

Safety precautions may in themselves add a measure of pollution; for example, the flares which are an essential safety device in handling flammable gases from petrochemical works can produce black smoke unless steam injection is practised, which is a noisy procedure.

Where inconvenience and minor damage to property are the only foreseeable results of pollution, the costs of prevention have to be balanced against the probable accident frequency and the loss likely to be incurred. As with normal pollution control measures, the nature of the pollutant and the location of the factory are important considerations. Thus failure of bag filters on extraction plant associated with shot-blasting operations might result in characteristic damage, for example rust spotting on the horizontal surfaces of any number of motor vehicles parked in the vicinity. This is an example where regular inspection and maintenance is essential and could result in failure being foreseen and avoided.

Liabilities and Insurance

Insurance of buildings, plant and equipment against loss due to fire is normal business practice. However, cover should also be taken out against liabilities involving the public and employees. If a product is marketed, it is also advisable to be covered against potential losses arising from its use.

Of particular relevance to waste collection and treatment, and to pollution control generally in English law, is the Rule of Rylands v. Fletcher[34] which established that where an occupier brings on to land and collects and keeps there anything likely to do harm if it escapes, he is prima facie responsible for all the damage which is a natural consequence of any escape. This is 'strict liability' and it exists irrespective of whether the occupier has taken careful precautions to prevent escape of the 'thing' causing the damage. The Rule has been held in the past to apply to fire, 'things' likely to give off noxious gas and fumes, slag heaps, spoil heaps,[35] explosives, gas and electricity. As an example, when acid smuts escaped from the chimney of an oil depot on the edge of a residential area and caused damage to a resident's car which was standing outside his house, and to laundry on the line, the occupiers of the refinery were held liable for both forms of damage.[36]

It is normal to insure against the potential costs, that is damages and expenses arising from accidental injury to any person or accidental damage to property, associated with strict liability. This will generally cover the occupier for claims which arise from emissions due to specific breakdown of plant or accidental maloperation or isolated, definable acts of 'negligence'.

An employer may also be liable for damages for bodily injury sustained by an employee during the course of his work. The injury may be caused by an 'accident' or may be the result of occupational short-term exposure to a toxic material, or of long-term exposure to a material or noise. As a general rule, under the Employer's Liability (Compulsory Insurance) Act, every company in the UK must be insured against this liability.

Special environmental problems are posed by 'major hazards', i.e. chemical and process plants in which operation is on such a scale that the consequences of an 'accident' may extend well beyond the site in the form of (a) a confined or unconfined explosion of a vapour or dust cloud, (b) a major leakage of toxic fumes and their dispersal over a wide area or (c) a major fire. For example, at Flixborough in 1974 a vapour cloud of about 25 tonnes of cyclohexane exploded resulting in 28 deaths and damage extending over many square kilometres.[37] At Seveso in Italy in 1976 an emission of TCDD (2,3,7,8-tetrachloro-dibenzo-p-dioxine), less by a factor of 10^4 than the Flixborough cloud, not only resulted in the deaths of domestic animals and the contraction by many people of chloracne but also caused long-term damage to all vegetation and posed a severe hazard to the unborn. In the UK a system of 'notifiable installations' has been proposed to cover, for instance, any installation from which 15 tonnes of flammable gas or 'equivalent' to 10 tonnes of chlorine could be released. The complete list (Table 19.7) takes no account of long-term hazards due to emissions.[38]

TABLE 19.7 PROPOSED INSTALLATIONS FOR NOTIFICATION AS MAJOR HAZARDS[38]

Installations storing or processing toxic material where, if containment is lost, there can be an emission of toxic gases or vapours equivalent in effect to more than 10 tonnes of chlorine

Installations storing or processing flammable materials where, if containment is lost, there can be rapid emission of flammable gases or vapours of more than 15 tonnes

Installations storing or processing materials which are intrinsically unstable or of very high exothermic reactivity where the total inventory is more than 5 tonnes. Examples are ethylene oxide, acetylenes, organic peroxides

Installations with a large inventory of stored pressure energy, typically process operations at 100 bar or above using gas phase reactions

Installations storing or processing flammable materials which have a flashpoint of less than 73°F (22·8°C) where the total inventory is more than 10 000 tonnes

Installations storing or processing liquid oxygen where the total inventory is more than 135 tonnes

Installations storing or processing ammonium nitrate where the total inventory is more than 5000 tonnes

Installations storing or processing materials which, in a fire, can cause an emission of toxic gases or vapours equivalent in effect to more than 10 tonnes of chlorine

Such plants and manufacturing operations require even more stringent and elaborate safeguards than are normal in the process industries. However, on plant of any scale, maloperation or malfunctioning of equipment may result in an escape of toxic or flammable dust, vapour or liquid. There have been numerous examples: a heavy emission of coal-tar volatiles from a tar works was caused by a faulty after-burner;[39] on another occasion, blockage of a caustic soda solution pipeline to a scrubber caused waste gas containing bromine, a dangerous vapour with a TLV of only 0·7 mg/m³, to escape unscrubbed.[39] A minor operator error at one works permitted the release of a few pounds of thionyl chloride which hydrolysed rapidly in the atmosphere to produce a small dense cloud of sulphur dioxide and hydrochloric acid which drifted for some distance without rapid dispersion.[39]

Plant failure can have similar consequences. For example, at a works manufacturing and using chlorine, two instances of cast iron pipe fracture in frosty weather culminated in releases of chlorine; over 30 workpeople on the site and adjoining sites were affected by the dense gas cloud.[39] However, on suitably located chemical and process plants the consequences of accidental escapes are generally confined within the site. This should ideally always be the case with non-volatile liquid spills provided the drains are segregated and storage and processing areas are bunded.

Modelling

Mathematical modelling is a relatively new science evolved from the need for the rigorous analysis of the behaviour of systems. It developed rapidly with the introduction of advanced computer technology in the 1960s.

Modelling broadly involves the representation of a relationship between two or more variables as a mathematical expression, often in the form of an equation or a series of equations. Some simple examples are given in Chapter 20 where the capital costs of processes or equipment are expressed as a function of capacity, throughput or size.

The relationships, causal or otherwise, between the various social, economic, technical and political factors that affect society may be integrated into one model to predict the effects which changes in any one or more of these factors will have on future patterns and standards of living; early examples of complex world models are given by Meadows et al.[40] and Forrester.[41]

The methodology is often used for prediction in a broad sense, either to forecast what may happen in the future or to predict consequences, where a variable is changed or where variables interact. Forecasting is outside the scope of this book, although valuable for marketing of plant, equipment or recovered products. A physical analogy of predictive modelling is the construction of a scale model of a chimney to assess the flow patterns of emitted smoke in relationship to local buildings and the effects, for example, of wind direction, wind speed and chimney height.

Construction of a scale model and a study of its performance over a whole range of operating parameters, covering every forseeable permutation, is relatively inexpensive and may avoid costly alterations to the final equipment. Wind tunnels are widely used in this way for the investigation of airborne pollution. Scale models are also widely used in three-dimensional plant design and location studies.

The world model depicted in Figure 19.4 was employed to predict food

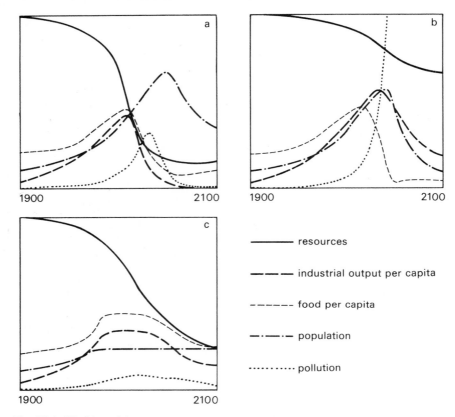

Fig. 19.4 World model
 a Standard run
 b With 'unlimited' resources
 c With stabilised population and capital

resources, industrial output, population growth and pollution levels under varying conditions of resource consumption rate.[40] Figure 19.4a shows the 'standard' run with no major changes in the physical, economic or social relationships which have historically governed the development of the world system. Food, industrial output and population continue to grow exponentially until the diminished resource base forces down industrial output. There is a delayed effect on population and pollution, and the growth rate of the former is halted by a rise in death rate due to decreased food and medical services. A wide range of scenarios were considered and two are selected to illustrate some of the results of the exercise.

Figure 19.4b shows the result of removing the limited resource base assumption of the 'standard' case. It is assumed that unlimited nuclear power will double the resource reserves and that nuclear energy will permit extensive recycling and substitution. With only these assumptions, growth is stopped by rising pollution. A similar effect occurs if the initial resource base is doubled.

Solutions to the pollution problem by assumed advances in the control of pollution creates a food crisis which only has the effect of delaying the decline in growth. With the solution to each problem come undesirable effects on the other constraints, always resulting in a similar conclusion.

Figure 19.4c shows how temporary relative stability is achieved by adopting a population stabilisation policy by equating births with deaths, and restricting capital growth. Longer term stability is achieved by a changed emphasis from industrial output to food and services, and improved technological policies on conservation, recycling, and pollution control.

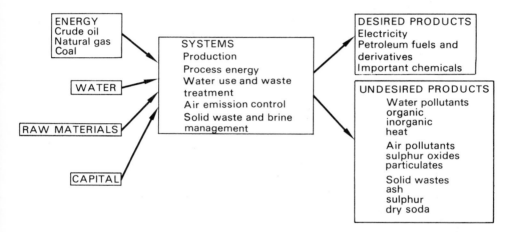

Fig. 19.5 Fundamental components of representative industry models

In 1974 nine major global modelling projects were reported with over 30 institutions involved in world models and world issue modelling.[42] The numbers have probably doubled since then, research being directed towards establishing more 'acceptable' modelling parameters such as the classical economic basis of the SARUM project.[43]

A model predicting the pollution control investment requirements of the US chemical industry up to 1985,[41] required 10 individual industry models as shown in Figure 19.5, which covered 48 major final and intermediate products. The general interrelationships of the ten industries are shown in Figure 19.6. The model is basically a process economic model, and employs linear programming for solution. The effect of different levels of pollution control specification is shown in Table 19.8 for waste-water discharge and in Table 19.9 for sulphur dioxide control in addition to waste-water control. The figures surprisingly suggest that the costs are largely independent of the standards required, and only a small extra cost is required for minimum discharge compared with current practice and requirements. Considerable additional information was obtained from the study.[44]

TABLE 19.8 PRODUCTION COSTS AND CAPITAL REQUIREMENTS OF THE INTEGRATED
INDUSTRY MODEL FOR DIFFERENT WASTE-WATER STANDARDS IN USA[44]

	Waste-water treatment level				
	SWT	BPT	BAT	ZOD	ZD
Processing costs, 1985	31·79	33·45	33·66	34·20	34·74
Fuel and materials costs, 1985	98·32	98·55	98·53	98·80	98·83
Total costs, 1985	130·11	132·00	132·19	133·00	133·57
Capital requirements from 1975 to 1985	63·37	64·57	64·89	64·95	65·11

All costs in 1974 US dollars $\times 10^9$

    SWT = secondary water treatment (approximates to current standards)
    BPT = best practicable technology
    BAT = best available technology
    ZOD = zero organics discharge
    ZD = zero discharge (total)

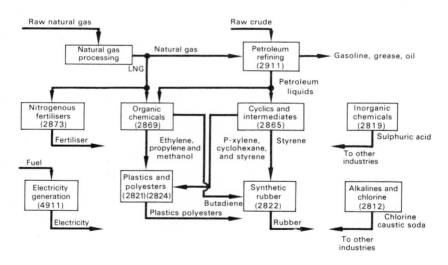

Fig. 19.6 General interrelationships among ten four-digit standard industrial
classifications in the integrated industry model

Many examples of modelling, such as recycling of metals, pollution in rivers
and estuaries, seepage from landfill and a wide range of environmental
problems, are to be found in the literature, which also includes texts on the
theory and practice of modelling.

TABLE 19.9 CAPITAL REQUIREMENTS OF THE INTEGRATED INDUSTRY MODEL FOR DIFFERENT LEVELS OF SULPHUR DIOXIDE REMOVAL AND WASTE-WATER TREATMENT, USA, PARTICULATE CONTROL ASSUMED, FROM 1975 TO 1985[44]

| | BPT | | | ZD | | |
| | Sulphur dioxide removal | | | Sulphur dioxide removal | | |
	0%	50%	90%	0%	50%	90%
All industries	64·87	64·22	78·65	66·43	65·86	82·37
Electric power	60·93	60·09	74·12	61·68	61·00	77·02

All costs in 1974 US dollars × 10^9

References

1. FISHLOCK, D., *Financial Times*, 2 October 1970.
2. WALKER, A., *Law of Industrial Pollution Control*, Godwin, 1979.
3. KEEN, R. C., private communication re European Council of Environmental Law, 1978.
4. CHALMERS, R. K., in *Progress in Water Technology*, Vol. 3, JENKINS, S. H. (Ed.), Pergamon, 1973.
5. PAVONI, J. K., HEER, J. E. and HAGERTY, D. J., *Handbook of Solid Waste Disposal—Materials and Energy Recovery*, Van Nostrand Reinhold, 1975.
6. KEEN, R. C., *Public Cleansing*, **LXI**(2), 65, 1971.
7. CHANLETT, E. T., *Environmental Protection*, McGraw-Hill, 1973, p. 199.
8. COPE, C. B. and KEEN, R. C., *Municipal Engineering*, 46, 9 January 1976.
9. KEEN, R. C., *Surveyor*, 22, 13 May 1974.
10. Department of Employment, *Asbestos: Health Precautions in Industry*, HSW 44, HMSO, 1971.
11. *Recommended Code of Practice for the Handling and Disposal of Asbestos Waste Materials*, Asbestosis Research Council, 1973.
12. Health and Safety at Work, etc., Act, 1974.
13. REDGRAVE, A., *Factories Acts*, Part II, *The Factories Act 1961 and Regulations and Orders for Safety and Health and Welfare in Miscellaneous Industries*, 22nd edn, Butterworth, 1972.
14. KEEN, R. C., *Solid Wastes*, **65**, 101 and 205, 1975.
15. KEEN, R. C. and MUMFORD, C. J., *Annals of Occupational Hygiene*, **18**, 213, 1975.
16. Health and Safety Executive Guidance Notes: Environmental Hygiene No. 11, *Arsine* and No. 12, *Stibine*, HMSO, 1977.
17. Department of Employment, *Cloakroom Accommodation and Washing Facilities*, HSW 18, HMSO, 1968.
18. Department of Employment, *Industrial Dermatitis: Precautionary Measures*, HSW 18, HMSO, 1972.
19. LA BENZ, P., COHEN, A. and PEARSON, B., *American Industrial Hygiene Association Journal*, **28**, 117, 1967.
20. *Anthrax*, Technical Data Note 20 (rev.), Health and Safety Executive, 1976.
21. *Safety in Inspection and Maintenance of Chemical Plant*, British Chemical Industry Safety Council, 1959.
22. *The Safe Cleaning, Repair and Demolition of Large Tanks for Storing Flammable Liquids*, Technical Data Note 18 (rev.), HM Factory Inspectorate, 1973.
23. Department of Employment, *Noise and the Worker*, HSW 25, HMSO, 1971.
24. *Safety Training—a Guide for the Chemical Industry*, Chemical Industries Association, 1972.
25. *Entry into Confined Spaces: Hazards and Precautions*, Technical Data Note 47, HM Factory Inspectorate, 1974.

26. The Protection of Eyes Regulations, 1974.
27. BS 4275: 1974, *The Selection, Use and Maintenance of Respiratory Protective Equipment,* British Standards Institution, 1974.
28. *Safety Audits—a Guide for the Chemical Industry,* Chemical Industries Association.
29. WILLIAMS, D., *Symposium Series No. 34,* Institution of Chemical Engineers, 1971, p. 220.
30. *Road Transport in Factories,* Technical Data Note 44, Health and Safety Executive, 1973.
31. KEEN, R. C., unpublished work, 1978.
32. TURNER, D. B. V., *Workbook of Atmospheric Dispersion Estimates,* US Department of Health, Education and Welfare.
33. *Threshold Limit Values for 1976,* Guidance Data EH15/76, Health and Safety Executive, 1976.
34. Rylands *v.* Fletcher, 1878, L.R. 3HL 330; 37 L.J. Ex 161.
35. *Report of the Tribunal—The Disaster at Aberfan 21 October 1966,* HMSO, 1967.
36. Halsey *v.* Esso Petroleum Co. Ltd, 1961, 2 All. E.R. 145.
37. *The Flixborough Disaster, Report of the Court of Enquiry,* HMSO, 1975.
38. *First Report, Advisory Committee on Major Hazards,* HMSO, 1976.
39. Department of the Environment, *111th Annual Report on Alkali, etc., Works,* HMSO, 1974.
40. MEADOWS, D. H., MEADOWS, D. L., RANDERS, J. and BEHRENS, W. W. III, *The Limits to Growth,* Earth Island, 1972.
41. FORRESTER, J. W., *World Dynamics,* MIT, 1971.
42. COLE, H. S. D., *Futures,* 201, June 1974.
43. ROBERTS, P. C., *Futures,* 3, February 1977.
44. CALLOWAY, J. A. and THOMPSON, R. G., *Engineering and Process Economics,* **1,** 199, 1976.

CHAPTER 20

Technical Economics for Waste Treatment and Recycling Processes

The provision of a new or replacement waste treatment facility requires consideration of both the initial capital cost and the operating cost, as well as the technical requirements of producing a consistently satisfactory effluent or discharge under all conditions of operation.

In this chapter methods are presented for estimating costs and evaluating proposals for effluent treatment plants and for waste recovery/recycling. The technology for such operations is rarely a limiting factor and it is primarily on the economics that a recovery proposal will stand or fall. Economics also mainly determines the best treatment plant for a given situation.

Economic Factors

In any waste-handling system for recovery, treatment or disposal there is:

(a) the cost of installing the facility, termed the capital or fixed cost, or investment;

(b) the cost of running or operating the facility, termed the operating or variable cost;

(c) potential income from recovered materials, or reduced costs by treatment.

These are combined and quantified in the evaluation or assessment of profitability of the project.

The capital cost may be simply broken down into (i) equipment and (ii) installation which includes site preparation. More sophisticated analyses consider each element of direct and indirect capital cost such as equipment, instrumentation, services, site, electricals, and apportion to each an approximate percentage of the total capital cost. Newly developed 'short-cut' or rapid methods provide rough estimates without the necessity of complex and detailed procedures. In addition, working capital is needed before start-up to finance raw material stocks, replacements and initial operating costs. At the end of the life of the facility the plant has a scrap value and the working capital is recovered. In practical terms the useful life is rarely more than ten years without major alterations and the scrap value is often insignificant.

Operating costs may be broken down in a variety of ways but the most generally applicable and useful analysis is: raw materials, direct labour and labour-related costs, energy, and capital or fixed investment-related costs. The last can include depreciation as part of the total operating cost, but depreciation is essentially a book transaction for accounting purposes, and is not a true cost. This is discussed further when considering profitability criteria. Operating cost may refer to the total cost of processing a material, by including an allowance for the capital employed, or it may just refer to the variable elements involved in running the plant. It is important to understand and specify which definition is used.

Where there is a possibility of recycling it is necessary to predict the market size and price obtainable for each recoverable material. These are perhaps the most difficult cost components to assess as so many factors are involved (see Chapter 2), and they can fluctuate rapidly and widely and may be highly susceptible to market forces. Considerable experience, business contacts and good fortune are probably required to obtain valid forecasts. These are unlikely to be necessary either when recycling internally or returning waste/scrap to the original manufacturer as established practice when price structures are agreed. In the case of treatment and/or disposal, there may be an incremental income arising from reduced costs. For example, installation of a filter press may considerably reduce disposal costs.

One aspect of evaluation is the payoff between relatively high capital expenditure on a high level of automation and hence lower operating cost, and relatively low-capital-cost plant with inherently higher operating costs. Factors which influence the choice include availability of capital, market conditions, economic conditions, access to site, availability and cost of labour, legislative and other constraints and the extent of equipment and services available. It is important therefore to consider each case on its merits and ensure that sufficient information is available to make a realistic and sensible decision.

The viability of most investments in new projects is assessed by their profitability. This attempts to relate the amount of money made by manufacturing a product or providing a service to the size of the investment required to set up the initial facility. For this purpose techniques based on rates of return, time for capital recovery or net profits may be employed for evaluating recovery schemes, but waste treatment plants are difficult to analyse as there is no saleable product or service, only a net cost; hence many of the profitability criteria may become meaningless.

The contribution of expenditure and income to the cash flow of an enterprise is conveniently depicted on a cash flow diagram (Figure 20.1). Expenditure is denoted as a negative cash flow and income as a positive cash flow.

Typically, for a chemical process such as a commercial waste recovery scheme, the cash flow curve would be expected to follow line A. For waste treatment or disposal there is a constant negative cash flow for operating costs after the initial capital expenditure and this would be represented by line B.

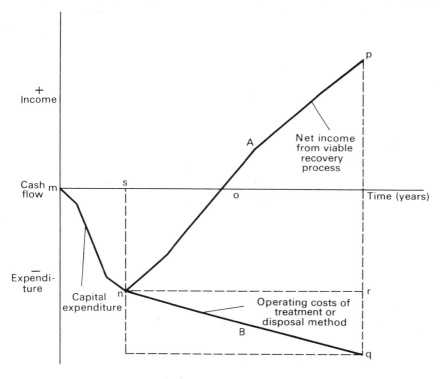

Fig. 20.1 Cash-flow curve

Evaluation

Economic evaluation of a proposal is essential to ensure that adequate returns are obtained from the capital employed. The level or degree of return may be assessed as a percentage rate of return, in money or cash terms, or in time units.

When profitability is expressed as a rate of return, this must be compared with the minimum acceptable rate of return. Investment in a project must at least cover the interest charge on borrowed money, termed the cost of capital, and should be at least as attractive as investment in securities or gilt edged. It should also take account of inflation in considering replacement. The minimum acceptable commercial rate of return can be approximated to the cost of capital plus the inflation rate. This is currently around 20% for the UK, ranges from 10% to 30% and changes with time and location. A further factor that affects the minimum acceptable rate of return is the risk or uncertainty associated with the venture, which increases the return necessary. Assessment is largely subjective. For a waste recovery proposal, which might be considered a relatively greater risk than a chemical manufacturing process, the minimum return necessary might be set at anything from 30 to 50%, or even more in exceptional cases. Local government may, however, accept a return equivalent to the cost of capital or the return on municipal bonds when participating in 'social' ventures.

Project evaluation in terms of the overall cash surplus that results from operation is clearly unrealistic as it is necessary to pay interest on borrowed capital and, moreover, money depreciates as a result of inflation. There is, however, a very good method of overcoming these difficulties in the 'net present worth' technique, described later. This principle is valuable in assessing and comparing waste treatment proposals where there is no income to compare with investment.

Assessment of profitability in terms of time is based on, for instance, payback time as described below.

There are a great many techniques for assessing profitability based on the above three general criteria.[1,2,3,4] The more useful and common methods are described below.

Return on Investment (ROI)

This is usually defined as the average annual net cash flow, that is the surplus left over after meeting all operating expenses out of income, either before or after tax, divided by the total fixed investment, and expressed as a percentage. In terms of the cash flow diagram (Figure 20.1) it can be represented approximately by

$$\frac{(pr)/(rn)}{sn} \times 100\%$$

It is necessary to define clearly what is meant by the expression 'return on investment' as this is widely interpreted and may, for example, include or exclude depreciation and/or tax. The result is compared with a notional minimum acceptable rate of return as described earlier. If the return on investment is greater than the minimum acceptable rate of return, then the project is considered economically attractive. If it is about equal, re-examination is necessary, and if it is less the venture is probably not viable. If there is a range of alternatives, the higher the rate of return, the greater the attraction.

This is perhaps the most widely used method of assessing the viability of both a project and a company, but it must be clearly understood what is included in the calculation and what is excluded. Furthermore, this method does not allow comparison of the effects of rapid recovery of costs and delayed recovery, and this can be an important factor for the operating company, particularly in situations of high risk. Similarly, changes in the fixed investment and project life cannot be included, and there are various other minor disadvantages. In its favour, however, is the widespread practice and familiarity of expressing profitability as a rate of return.

In waste treatment, however, no money or profit is being made by the producer (excluding that from the operations by which the waste is generated). Hence rate of return becomes a meaningless concept, unless it is considered in the context of overall profitability of the company or production facility, which it will reduce. Ability to assess the 'profitability' of an effluent treatment plant is of considerable importance when evaluating, for example, the payoff between high capital cost and high operating cost.

Example 1: Calculation of ROI

It is required to ascertain the profitability of a proposal to recover up to 200 tonnes per year of copper from waste electrolysis solutions. The total capital cost is esimated to be £110 000 and the plant will take one year to build, with an estimated life of five years and a scrap value of £10 000. The value of the reclaimed copper is assumed to be £800 per tonne and there are fixed operating costs of £10 000 per year plus variable operating costs of £370 per tonne. For marketing and technical reasons the process is assumed to operate at 70% capacity for the first year, 85% for the second year and full capacity for the remainder of its life. The cost of capital may be assumed to be 13% and corporation tax to be 50%.

A cash flow table (Table 20.1) should first be constructed to show the expenditure and income in each year of the project.

ROI before tax

$$= \frac{(33\ 000\ +\ 45\ 750\ +\ 58\ 500\ +\ 58\ 500\ +\ 58\ 500) \div 5}{110\ 000} \times 100\%$$

$$= \frac{50\ 850}{110\ 000} \times 100\%$$

$$= 46 \cdot 2\%$$

Assuming, for tax calculations, straight-line depreciation of plant at £20 000 per year (initial cost of £110 000 less scrap value of £10 000), the return after tax may be estimated (Table 20.2). This is only an estimate as there is sufficient flexibility in tax legislation to permit a company to minimise its overall tax bill. Depreciation and taxation are covered in more detail later in this chapter. Inclusion of some provision for taxation allows a more realistic assessment:

$$\text{ROI after tax} = \frac{(33\ 000\ +\ 39\ 250\ +\ 45\ 625\ +\ 39\ 250\ +\ 39\ 250) \div 5}{110\ 000} \times 100\%$$

$$= 35 \cdot 7\%$$

TABLE 20.1 CALCULATION OF NET CASH FLOW BEFORE TAX (EXAMPLE 1)

Year	Capital cost (£)	Fixed operating cost (£)	Output (tonnes copper p.a.)	Variable operating cost (£)	Interest on loan at 15%* (£)	Income (£)	Net cash flow (before tax) (£)
0	−110 000						−110 000
1		−10 000	140	−52 500	−16 500	+112 000	+33 000
2		−10 000	170	−63 750	−16 500	+136 000	+45 750
3		−10 000	200	−75 000	−16 500	+160 000	+58 500
4		−10 000	200	−75 000	−16 500	+160 000	+58 500
5		−10 000	200	−75 000	−16 500	+160 000	+58 500
6	+10 000						+10 000†

* Assuming the capital is borrowed at 15% interest for the duration of the project. This represents the worst situation since it is likely that in practice some of the initial borrowed investment will be repaid out of receipts during operation of the project.
† Recovery of scrap value of plant in year after project terminates.

With the cost of capital at around 13% and inflation at about 10% (1979 rates), giving a minimum acceptable rate of return of about 23%, the ROI after tax of 35·7% seems quite attractive, allowing a reasonable margin for risk and profit-taking.

One of the inherent problems of ROI is the lack of precise definition; for example, the ROI after tax in the above example could be calculated over a six year period, including tax in Year 6 and excluding scrap, to be 26·8%.

Incremental Return on Investment

Although projects may be compared in terms of size of return, it is often very helpful to examine the differences in costs and incomes between the alternatives. Consideration of the possibilities of additional income arising out of additional expenditure, known as incremental return on investment, assists in choosing between otherwise similarly attractive projects (see Example 2) and may be extended to look at a range of discrete increments, such as the profitability of adding extra effects to a multi-effect evaporator.[1]

This technique may also be applied to operations such as effluent treatment where there is no income, but where additional capital cost may be offset by savings in operating costs. This is illustrated in Example 3.

Example 2: Calculation of Incremental ROI

Compare the proposal of Example 1 with a more expensive process to recover a higher grade of metal, of which the fixed capital cost is 10% higher, but the product is worth 5% more (Table 20.3).

ROI before tax

$$= \frac{(36\,950 + 50\,900 + 64\,850 + 64\,850 + 64\,850) \div 5}{121\,000} \times 100\%$$

$$= \frac{56\,480}{121\,000} \times 100\%$$

$$= 46\cdot7\%$$

This appears to be as attractive as the first proposal, but no more so:

$$\text{Incremental ROI (before tax)} = \frac{\text{average additional annual income}}{\text{additional capital cost}}$$

$$= \frac{56\,480 - 50\,850}{121\,000 - 110\,000} \times 100\%$$

$$= \frac{5630}{11\,000} \times 100\%$$

$$= 51\cdot2\%$$

TABLE 20.2 CALCULATION OF NET CASH FLOW AFTER TAX (EXAMPLE 1)

Year	Net cash flow before tax (£)	Tax allowance (£)	Taxable profit (£)	Corporation tax at 50%* (£)	Net cash flow after tax (£)
0	−110 000				−110 000
1	+33 000	20 000	13 000		+33 000
2	+45 750	20 000	25 750	(−) 6 600	+39 250
3	+58 500	20 000	38 500	(−)12 875	+45 625
4	+58 500	20 000	38 500	(−)19 250	+39 250
5	+58 500	20 000	38 500	(−)19 250	+39 250
6	+10 000			(−)19 250	−9 250

* Corporation tax is usually paid the year after liability is incurred

TABLE 20.3 CALCULATION OF NET CASH FLOW BEFORE TAX (EXAMPLE 2)

Year	Capital cost (£)	Fixed operating cost (£)	Variable operating cost (£)	Interest on loan at 15% (£)	Income (£)	Net cash flow before tax (£)
0	−121 000					−121 000
1		−10 000	−52 500	−18 150	+117 600	+36 950
2		−10 000	−63 750	−18 150	+142 800	+50 900
3		−10 000	−75 000	−18 150	+168 000	+64 850
4		−10 000	−75 000	−18 150	+168 000	+64 850
5		−10 000	−75 000	−18 150	+168 000	+64 850
6	+11 000					+11 000

Compared with 46·2% and 46·7% for the individual projects, this demonstrates that the return on the additional capital is well justified. A return of less than about 25% would have indicated that the additional capital cost was not justified.

Example 3: Calculation of Incremental ROI
Neutralisation of acid-bearing aqueous effluents is usually carried out with caustic soda (NaOH) or lime (CaO). The economics of the alternatives are dependent on the scale of operation, as for caustic soda neutralisation the capital costs are lower but the operating costs are higher than for lime neutralisation.

Which system would be preferred for an effluent treatment plant to treat 22·5 m³/h (5000 gal/h) waste sulphuric acid containing an average of 3% free acid? Assume 2500 hours per year operation. Data are given in Table 20.4.

TABLE 20.4 NEUTRALISATION PLANT DATA

	Caustic soda plant	Lime plant
Reagent requirement per tonne acid	0·8 tonnes	1·1 tonnes
Reagent cost per tonne	£40	£10
Plant capital cost	£44 000	£60 000
Operating costs: labour per year	£3000	£4000
energy per year	£200	£400
Sludge disposal costs	nil	£15 per tonne lime used

Annual cost of running caustic soda plant:

	£
Labour	3 000
Energy	200
Reagent (22·5 m³ × 1 t/m³ × 0·8 t/t × £40/t × 2500 h/yr × 0·03 kg/kg effluent)	54 000
	57 200

Annual cost of running lime plant:

	£
Labour	4 000
Energy	400
Reagent (22·5 m³ × 1 t/m³ × 1·1 t/t × £10/t × 2500 h/yr × 0·03 kg/kg effluent)	18 563
Tipping sludge	27 844
	50 807

The additional cost of the lime plant is £16 000, and the saving by use of the lime plant is £6393, therefore

$$\text{incremental ROI} = \frac{6393}{16\ 000} \times 100\% = 40\%$$

Thus the additional expenditure on the lime plant is justified.

If the additional capital cost of the lime plant had been £32 000 the incremental ROI would be $(6393/32\ 000) \times 100\% = 19\cdot9\%$, which would not be acceptable so that in this case the additional expenditure would not be justified.

Payback Time

The time to recover the total investment is known as payback time and is represented usually by *so* or sometimes by *mo* in Figure 20.1. It represents the period of time that the investment is at risk, but does not consider any cash flow after recovery of the fixed investment. There are variations such as payback time with interest, and equivalent maximum investment period.[2]

Again this cannot be used when there is no income (Case B, Figure 20.1), as in an effluent treatment plant. This method is most useful in assessing the value of relatively minor expenditures such as plant modifications: the most attractive alternative is that with the shortest payback time.

In Example 2 above the payback time (before tax) is just over $2\frac{1}{2}$ years from the commencement of operation, or more accurately $2\cdot53$ years. This represents the length of time that the investment is at risk before being completely recovered, but ignores the interest payable on the borrowed capital. In the same example the payback time after tax is $2\cdot83$ years.

Net Present Worth (Net Present Value)

Return on investment and payback time compare the net income with the capital expenditure and take no account of the shape of the cash flow curve (Figure 20.1) or the timing of the cash flows. This can be a very important factor in assessing profitability as interest needs to be charged on borrowed capital and surplus income may, at least theoretically, be invested to secure additional income until cessation of the project.

Money has a time value which can be significant when interest rates are high. For example, £100 invested at 10% interest now will be worth £110 in one year's time and £121 in two years' time. £100 is the *present value* and £110 the *future value* of £100 at 10% interest for one year. Similarly, at 10% interest, an amount of £121 two years in the future has a *present value* of £100. This may be expressed as

$$F = P(1 + i)^n$$

where F = future value or worth
   P = present value or worth
   i = fractional rate of interest
   n = number of years

and gives the future value or worth F of an investment P now, at interest rate $100i\%$ for n years.

This may be turned round to calculate the present worth or value of a future income or expense:

$$P = F \ \frac{1}{(1 + i)^n}$$

where $1/(1 + i)^n$ is known as the discount factor, with i the discount rate. Tables of discount factors for a range of years and discount or interest rates are available,[1,2] and some values are given in Table 20.5. Discount factors are always less than unity and the present worth is thus always less than the future worth.

TABLE 20.5 DISCOUNT FACTORS

Year	Discount rate %						
	10	15	20	25	30	35	40
1	0·9091	0·8696	0·8333	0·8000	0·7692	0·7407	0·7143
2	0·8264	0·7561	0·6944	0·6400	0·5917	0·5487	0·5103
3	0·7513	0·6575	0·5787	0·5120	0·4552	0·4064	0·3644
4	0·6830	0·5718	0·4823	0·4096	0·3501	0·3011	0·2603
5	0·6209	0·4972	0·4019	0·3277	0·2693	0·2230	0·1859
6	0·5645	0·4323	0·3349	0·2621	0·2072	0·1652	0·1328
7	0·5132	0·3759	0·2791	0·2097	0·1594	0·1224	0·0949
8	0·4665	0·3269	0·2326	0·1678	0·1226	0·0906	0·0678
9	0·4241	0·2843	0·1938	0·1342	0·0943	0·0671	0·0484
10	0·3855	0·2472	0·1615	0·1074	0·0725	0·0497	0·0346
11	0·3505	0·2149	0·1346	0·0859	0·0558	0·0368	0·0247
12	0·3186	0·1869	0·1122	0·0687	0·0429	0·0273	0·0176
13	0·2897	0·1625	0·0935	0·0550	0·0330	0·0202	0·0126
14	0·2633	0·1413	0·0779	0·0440	0·0254	0·0150	0·0090
15	0·2394	0·1229	0·0649	0·0352	0·0195	0·0111	0·0064
16	0·2176	0·1069	0·0541	0·0281	0·0150	0·0082	0·0046
17	0·1978	0·0929	0·0451	0·0225	0·0116	0·0061	0·0033
18	0·1799	0·0808	0·0376	0·0180	0·0089	0·0045	0·0023
19	0·1635	0·0703	0·0313	0·0144	0·0068	0·0033	0·0017
20	0·1486	0·0611	0·0261	0·0115	0·0058	0·0025	0·0012

The process of calculating all the present worths of incomes and expenditures during the lifetime of a project is known as discounting, and the algebraic sum of the present worths of income (positive) and expenditure (negative) is known as the Net Present Worth (NPW). The choice of discount rate is important and should represent at least the cost of capital, i.e. the interest rate charged on money borrowed for investment, which is around 13% (1979); or, more usually, the minimum acceptable rate of return. As explained earlier this can be approximated to the cost of capital plus the inflation rate plus an allowance for risk, and is around 23% (1979) for a low-risk venture.

The result may be positive, indicating that the project overall will make a useful contribution to the viability of the company, or negative, representing a potential overall loss. The size of the contribution or loss is given by the amount of the NPW. Thus alternative projects may be compared, but if the capital investments are significantly different, care must be taken that this does not distort the answer. This technique is particularly valuable for evaluating effluent treatment plants as the alternative with the highest or least negative (i.e. nearest to zero) NPW will cost the company the least amount of money over the life of the plant. This approach enables comparisons to be made between high capital/low operating cost and low capital/high operating cost proposals. It is the only common economic evaluation technique that is applicable to non-profitmaking ventures, and gives a particularly useful answer in that all cash flows are properly considered at the time they occur. This method should not be used to compare projects of different capital investment.

TABLE 20.6 NET PRESENT WORTH CALCULATIONS

	Net cash flow, excluding interest, after tax				
Year	Net cash flow before tax (excl. interest) (£)	Tax allowance (£)	Taxable profit (£)	Corporation tax at 50% (£)	Net cash flow after tax (£)
0	−110 000				−110 000
1	+49 500	20 000	29 500		+49 500
2	+62 250	20 000	42 250	−14 750	+47 500
3	+75 000	20 000	55 000	−21 125	+53 875
4	+75 000	20 000	55 000	−27 500	+47 500
5	+75 000	20 000	55 000	−27 500	+47 500
6	+10 000			−27 500	−17 500

	Net Present Worth				
Year	Net cash flow after tax (£)	15% discount factors	Present worth (£)	30% discount factor	Present worth (£)
0	−110 000	1·0	−110 000	1·0	−110 000
1	+49 500	0·870	+43 065	0·769	+38 070
2	+47 500	0·756	+35 910	0·592	+28 120
3	+53 875	0·658	+35 450	0·455	+24 510
4	+47 500	0·572	+27 170	0·350	+16 625
5	+47 500	0·497	+23 610	0·269	+12 780
6	−17 500	0·432	−7 560	0·207	−3 620

Net Present Worth = +£47 645   Net Present Worth = +£6485

Example 4: Calculation of NPW

The copper recovery process proposal described in Example 1 is re-evaluated by the NPW method. Discount rates of 15% to represent the cost of capital, and 30% to represent the minimum acceptable rate of return, are selected for calculations (Table 20.6). As the principle of discounting takes into account the time value of money and thus the need to pay interest on borrowed money, the interest payments in the next cash flow calculations performed for the ROI calculations must not be included. The calculations are shown in Table 20.6.

That a positive value is obtained for the NPW at 30% discount suggests that the project is attractive and most likely to be viable. A small negative value at 30% discount rate would indicate that re-examination was necessary. A large positive figure at 15% discount rate indicates attractiveness but only in a qualitative sense. A low positive or negative value would only be acceptable in exceptional circumstances, while a large negative value at 15% discount rate would almost certainly cause the proposal to be rejected.

Discounted Cash Flow Rate of Return (Internal Rate of Return)

This is defined as the rate of return that makes the NPW zero, and is calculated on this basis. It represents the rate of interest that all income would have to earn together with that income over the life of the project to pay back all costs and the interest accrued on those costs over the life of the project. It is the value of r, rate of interest, that satisfies the equation

$$\Sigma_1^n \text{ income} + \Sigma_1^n \text{ interest on income at } r\%$$

$$= \Sigma_1^n \text{ costs} + \Sigma_1^n \text{ interest on costs at } r\%$$

where n is the life of the project.

The value of r must be compared either with the cost of capital, i.e. cost of borrowing money from a bank (about 13%, early 1979) or with the minimum acceptable rate of return (about 23%). This is an arbitrary return below which a company would not wish to invest and reflects the nature of the investment and the risks involved as well as other factors. For a 'normal' industrial venture, a return of 25% after tax would be considered the minimum acceptable. For higher-risk ventures such as waste recovery schemes a return in excess of 30% or even 50% might be considered reasonable. This method should not be used for comparison of ventures of different lives.

These discounting techniques are the most valuable evaluation methods available; all costs and incomes are properly considered at the time of occurrence and the result is immediately useful. Application of this method to a waste treatment operation where there is no income is not possible without the concept of a negative rate of interest or rate of return. In this case the most attractive alternative is that with the least negative rate of return (Example 5).

Example 5: Calculation of DCF Rate of Return

The copper recovery process of Examples 1 and 4 is again used. The NPW after tax of this venture at 15% discount rate is +£47 645 and at 30% discount rate it is +£6485. Calculation at 40% discount rate gives the NPW as −£11 920. The DCF rate of return thus lies between 30% and 40%. Graphical interpolation (Figure 20.2) gives the DCF rate of return after tax as 33%.

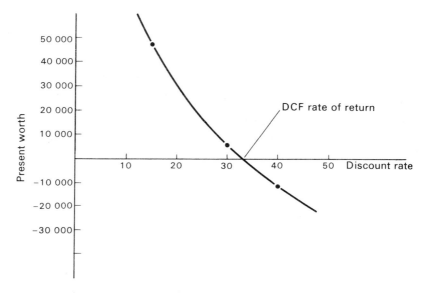

Fig. 20.2 Graphical estimation of DCF rate of return

Uncertainty

Unfortunately, estimates and forecasts of cash flows are rarely accurate and hence predicted profitabilities are uncertain. There are several ways of taking account of uncertainties in data, of which the most widely employed are sensitivity analysis and risk analysis.

Sensitivity analysis[2,5] is carried out by examining the effect of changes in each cost element on the profitability of the project. For example, NPW and DCF rate of return would be recalculated for a 10% increase in capital cost, 10% increase in operating cost, 10% reduction in realisation (income unit price), 10% reduction in market size, and combinations of these changes. This identifies the cost areas which most affect profitability. Alternative percentage changes and combinations in predicted costs and incomes may also be explored. The cost area most sensitive in chemical process proposal evaluation is often total income, made up of market size and price, which is also often the area of greatest uncertainty in forecasting (see also Chapter 2).

A more thorough examination is carried out by risk analysis[2,4,5] where each cost is recognised to be only an estimate and hence uncertain, and this uncertainty is quantified as a probability distribution. Assignation of a distribution to each cost may be arbitrary, or based on experience or a consensus of informed opinion. Each cost/income distribution is combined in a technique known as Monte Carlo simulation to give a probability distribution of profitability, usually NPW or DCF rate of return. The result might, for example, indicate that a proposal had a 90% chance of achieving a DCF rate of return in excess of 30%, and thus a 10% chance of achieving a return of less than 30%. In this case the project would probably be considered an acceptable risk.

Both these techniques and others are widely documented and illustrated by, for example, Allen[2] and ICI;[5] see also de la Mare.[4] Even with this information, decisions are often based additionally on other data and are affected by factors such as political or public pressure and availability of money. Most waste treatment and disposal ventures do not require sophisticated analysis, which is more useful for more complex or larger enterprises such as recycling which may also be regarded as more speculative.

Principles of Capital Cost Estimation

The capital cost of a plant usually assumes major significance as it occurs early in the life of the project, and is often a single or several large sums. Considerable research has been carried out into ways of improving the accuracy and/or reducing the cost and time of producing an estimate. A number of useful standard texts are available.[1,2,3,4,6] The various techniques of capital cost estimation are almost all based on the principles of ratios, factors and/or step counting. In their simplest form, these may be employed for less accurate but more rapid estimates in preliminary assessment of a proposal. As the accuracy demanded of an estimate increases, the cost rises as a result of the additional time and information required.[1,6]

Only the simpler and more rapid methods of capital cost estimation are explained here, with reference to more comprehensive sources of information. These methods will be found useful (a) in carrying out a fairly rapid evaluation of a proposed waste recovery or disposal scheme; (b) in comparing a range of alternatives to select the most economic; (c) to study the payoff between low capital cost/high operating cost versus high capital cost/low operating cost; (d) in checking the plausibility or accuracy of other estimates. Detailed cost estimates employ similar principles but require much more information and, particularly, specialist data often only accessible to and held by the contractor.

Capital Cost Analysis

The total capital cost of a plant installed and ready to operate is made up of many elements.[1,4] A simplified breakdown is shown in Table 20.7 which lists some of the important generalised contributions to total capital cost.[1] The significance of each of the 13 elements is given in Table 20.8, where a typical range of values and a median is given for substantial chemical process installations.[1]

Usually capital costs are either quoted as equipment costs (costs of buying the main plant items such as pumps, tanks—delivered or purchased equipment cost) or refer to the total installed capital cost which includes all expenditure on equipment, materials, labour and other costs to provide a plant ready for operation. The total installed capital cost may represent the cost of setting up a plant on an established site with all services and utilities readily available; this is known as the 'battery limits' cost. Alternatively, it includes all costs necessary to provide both the plant and all the necessary services such as utilities and access. This is known as the 'greenfield' or 'grass roots' site cost, which is generally about 35–40% more than the battery limits cost.

TABLE 20.7 BREAKDOWN OF FIXED-CAPITAL INVESTMENT ITEMS FOR A CHEMICAL PROCESS PLANT (based on PETERS and TIMMERHAUS[1])

Direct Costs
1. Purchased equipment
    All equipment listed on a complete flow sheet
        Plus: Spare parts and non-installed equipment spares
            Surplus equipment, supplies, and equipment allowance
            Inflation cost allowance
            Carriage charges
            Taxes, insurance, duties
            Allowance for modifications during start-up

2. Purchased-equipment installation
    Installation of all equipment listed on complete flow sheet
        Plus: Structural supports, insulation, paint

3. Instrumentation and controls
    Purchase, installation, calibration

4. Piping
    Process piping (carbon steel, alloy, cast iron, lead, lined, aluminium, copper, asbestos-cement, ceramic, plastic, rubber, reinforced concrete)
        Plus: Pipe hangers, fittings, valves
            Insulation (piping, equipment)

5. Electrical equipment and materials
    Electrical equipment (switches, motors, conduit, wire, fittings, feeders, grounding, instrument and control wiring, lighting, panels)

    Electrical materials and labour

6. Buildings (including services)
    Process buildings (substructures, superstructures, platforms, supports, stairways, ladders, access ways, cranes, monorails, hoists, elevators)

    Auxiliary buildings (administration and office, medical or dispensary, cafeteria, garage, product warehouse, parts warehouse, security and safety, fire station, changing rooms, personnel building, shipping office and loading bay, research laboratory, control laboratory)

Table 20.7(*Cont'd*)

Maintenance shops (electric, piping, sheet metal, machine, welding, carpentry, instrument)

Building services (plumbing, heating, ventilation, dust collection, air conditioning, building lighting, elevators, escalators, telephones, intercommunication systems, painting, sprinkler systems, fire alarm)

7. Site improvements

Site development (site clearing, grading, roads, walkways, railways, fences, parking areas, wharves and piers, recreational facilities, landscaping)

8. Service facilities

Utilities (steam, water, power, refrigeration, compressed air, fuel, waste disposal)

Facilities (boiler plant, incinerator, wells, river intake, water treatment, cooling towers, water storage, electric substation, refrigeration plant, air plant, fuel storage, waste disposal plant, fire protection)

Non-process equipment (office furniture and equipment, cafeteria equipment, safety and medical equipment, automotive equipment, yard material-handling equipment, laboratory equipment, locker-room equipment, garage equipment, shelves, bins, pallets, hand trucks, housekeeping equipment, fire extinguishers, hoses, fire engines, loading stations)

Distribution and packaging (raw material and product storage and handling equipment, product packaging equipment, blending facilities, loading stations)

9. Land

Surveys and fees
Property purchase

Indirect Costs

10. Engineering and supervision

Engineering costs (administrative, process, design and general engineering, drafting, cost engineering, procuring, expediting, reproduction, communications, scale models, consultant fees, travel)

Engineering supervision and inspection

11. Construction Expenses

Construction, operation and maintenance of temporary facilities, offices, roads, parking areas, railroads, electrical, piping, communications, fencing

Plus: Construction tools and equipment
Construction supervision, accounting, timekeeping, purchasing, expediting
Warehouse personnel and expense, guards
Safety, medical fringe benefits
Permits, field tests, special licences
Taxes, insurance, interest

12. Contractor's fee

13. Contingency

TABLE 20.8 TYPICAL VARIATIONS IN CONTRIBUTION OF EACH CAPITAL COST ELEMENT TO TOTAL INSTALLED CAPITAL COST IN THE CHEMICAL AND ALLIED PROCESS INDUSTRIES[1]

Component	Range %	Median %
Direct costs		
Purchased equipment	20–40	32·5
Purchased-equipment installation	7·3–26·0	12·5
Instrumentation and controls (installed)	2·5–7·0	4·3
Piping (installed)	3·5–15·0	9·3
Electrical (installed)	2·5–9·0	5·8
Buildings (including services)	6·0–20·0	11·5
Site improvements	1·5–5·0	3·2
Service facilities (installed)	8·1–35·0	18·3
Land	1·0–2·0	1·5
Indirect costs		
Engineering and supervision	4·0–21·0	13·0
Construction expense	4·8–32·0	14·5
Contractor's fee	1·5–5·0	3·0
Contingency	6·0–18·0	12·3

Companies engaged in the construction and installation of pollution control plants and recycling processes will of course have their own established methods of estimating costs using their accumulated experience and information. The contents of this chapter provide some short cuts or alternative procedures. For others interested in estimating capital costs, for example waste producers assessing alternatives before going out to tender, some easy and workable techniques are presented together with sufficient information to enable a reasonable cost estimate to be obtained.

Cost Index

Costs change with time for several reasons of which inflation is perhaps the most significant. Technological advance leading to process design improvement can, however, make a beneficial contribution. The last few years have seen very high inflation rates worldwide and thus increases in costs with time have assumed much greater significance, while the benefits of technological progress have been relatively reduced.

Changes in costs are usually accounted for by a cost index of which there are at least 17 for the chemical and allied process industries alone. One of the most recent and wide-ranging, published by *Engineering and Process Economics*,[7] is currently available for 16 countries. This is a non-specific cost index, base 100 in January 1970, which may be appropriately used in the chemical industries generally including effluent treatment, pollution control, recycling and similar processes (see Table 20.19, page 664).

To calculate, for example, the cost in December 1978 of an effluent treatment plant in the UK that was estimated to cost £30 000 in August 1975, the index is used thus:

$$\text{Present cost} = \text{previous cost} \times \frac{\text{present index value}}{\text{previous index value}}$$

therefore

$$\text{Cost in December 1978} = £30\ 000 \times \frac{318}{230}$$

$$= £41\ 480$$

where 318 = EPE(UK) cost index value December 1978
       230 = EPE(UK) cost index value August 1975.

It must be emphasised that a cost index can only provide an approximation to the change of costs with time, as other factors such as the national economy, changes in legislation, and market forces can introduce errors of up to 30%. At best, therefore, use of a cost index provides only a guide to the effect of inflation. In substantial contracts a price-adjustment clause may be inserted to take account of inflation. This will often incorporate one of the recognised cost indices by agreement between contractor and client.

Location Index

Costs also vary according to location. Such differences may be negligible within one country, but the translation of costs for one country into those for another by simple application of exchange rate conversion is not necessarily valid. As a general guide, basic equipment costs in industrialised countries are comparable; the cost of specialised equipment, however, follows similar rules as for complete plant. Approximate ratios related to unit UK cost are given in Table 20.9.

TABLE 20.9 LOCATION FACTORS (BASE UK = 1·0)

UK	1·0	Japan	1·0
Australia	1·4–1·5	Portugal	0·9
Belgium	1·1	Scandinavia	1·2
Canada	1·3	South Africa	1·3
France	1·1	South America	2·0–3·0
W. Germany	1·1	Spain	0·9
Holland	1·1	Switzerland	1·2
Italy	1·0	USA	1·1

For chemical plant and specialised equipment of comparable performance, the UK cost should be multiplied by the appropriate coefficient and then converted at the ruling exchange rate to give the cost in the required country.

It is important to note that account is taken of special local factors in this list, which applies to function or performance and not to a specific design. If a cost index is necessary also, it must be an index related to the country concerned.

This is explained largely by differences in overall labour costs which are derived from unit wages and productivity. The latter is very difficult to assess and the ratios suggested have been derived empirically.

Cost/Capacity Ratio Estimating Techniques

Scale Effects

Capital costs of equipment and plants do not normally vary proportionally with size or capacity. An increase in process capacity of 100%, for example, causes capital costs to increase by about 50%. This is known as economy of scale, and is usually represented by the equation:

$$\frac{C_1}{C_2} = \left(\frac{Q_1}{Q_2}\right)^x$$

where C_1 is the capital cost of plant 1

C_2 is the capital cost of plant 2

Q_1 is the size, capacity or throughput of plant 1

Q_2 is the size, capacity or throughput of plant 2

x is a scale factor that varies from $0 \cdot 2$ to $1 \cdot 0$; a typical figure for chemical processes is $0 \cdot 6$ or $0 \cdot 67$ (i.e. $\frac{2}{3}$). Data are available for specific processes or types of equipment (Table 20.10).

If the capital cost and size of a given plant or piece of equipment is known, it is possible to estimate the capital cost of any other size of the same plant or equipment using the appropriate scale factor.

One risk in cost estimation is the use of data for one process to estimate costs of another. It would be unreasonable to expect a high level of accuracy in such a case. A second risk is that the accuracy of a scale factor is often assumed constant which is not true for extremes of size. At relatively low capacities, for example, economy of scale increases and the scale factor approaches zero, while at relatively very high capacities duplication of equipment causes loss of economy of scale and the scale factor approaches $1 \cdot 0$ (Figure 20.3). Only the portion of curve C–D may be satisfactorily used with this technique. Unfortunately there are no rigid rules as to these limits: a rough general guideline is to limit its use to an increase or decrease in capacity of not more than a factor of 5 to avoid losing too much accuracy. A cost index may be necessary to up-date cost estimates.

Cost Estimation

This principle may be extended to obtain absolute estimates of capital cost if some base data are available. Information may be presented graphically[1] or in the form of cost models, as given at the end of this chapter for a range of relevant processes and equipment. These ratio estimating techniques are the simplest method of cost estimation but should only be expected to give a rough cost to within ± 30–40%.

TABLE 20.10 SCALE FACTORS (see also section on *functional units* and TABLE 20.14)

	Scale factor
Processes generally	
Chemical processes generally	0·60–0·67
Chemical processes involving mostly gaseous reagents	0·60
Chemical processes involving mostly liquid reagents	0·65
Chemical processes involving mostly solid reagents	0·75–0·80
Specific processes	
Household refuse disposal processes	
Composting	
<about 500 tonnes/day	0·65
>about 500 tonnes/day	0·95
Incineration	
<about 10 tonnes/h throughput	0·78
>about 10 tonnes/h throughput	0·90–0·95
Landfill	0·93
Pyrolysis	0·78
RDF recovery	0·70
Biological (sewage) effluent treatment	0·78
Non-biological effluent treatment	
>4·5 m³/h (1000 gal/h)	0·40
4·5–45 m³/h throughput	0·59
<45 m³/h (10 000 gal/h) throughput	0·80
Miscellaneous processes (see also Refs. 8 and 9)	
Aluminium	0·76
Ammonium sulphate or phosphate (fertiliser)	0·68
Coke oven gas separation	0·82
Electricity generating plant (steam)	0·79
Organic solvent manufacture (general)	0·70
Solid materials separation	0·70
Sulphuric acid	0·67
Water treatment	0·91
Specific operations	
Biological effluent treatment	
Activated sludge	0·85
Anaerobic sludge treatment: heated primary	0·97
cold secondary	0·50
Biological filters: once through	0·82
recirculation	0·77
Sedimentation: rectangular tanks	0·56
circular tanks	0·66
all types, low capacity	0·44
Non-biological effluent treatment	
Agitated mixing tanks/reactors (0·45–91 m³; 100–20 000 gal)	0·50
Aqueous chrome reduction (9·1–91 m³/h; 2000–20 000 gal/h)	0·38
Aqueous cyanide oxidation (9·1–91 m³/h; 2000–20 000 gal/h) (single-stage)	0·38

Table 20.10(*Cont'd*)

	Scale factor
Deep well drilling	1·38
Filter press (22·7–91 m³/h; 5000–20 000 gal/h)	0·55–0·60
Flotation: low-capacity, <3 m³ cell capacity	0·37
high-capacity, >3 m³ cell capacity	0·74
Filter, pressure-leaf	0·49
Air pollution control	
Cyclones, dry 0·1–1·0 tonnes/h	0·75
Dust collection—bag	0·71
Electrostatic precipitators: low voltage	0·61
high voltage	0·83
Chimney stacks	1·0
Scrubbers	0·85–0·95
Incinerator for combustible gases	0·40
Miscellaneous and equipment	
Classifier, rake	0·35
Cooling tower	0·69
Distillation: flash	0·64
vacuum	0·80
Drum dryers: atmospheric	0·40
vacuum	0·65
Pulverisers	0·79
Furnace	0·85
Rotary dryers	0·80–0·95
Screen vibrating: heavy duty	0·90–0·99
medium-duty, single-deck	0·62
medium-duty, double-deck	0·67
fines, single-deck	0·87
fines, double-deck	0·69
Silo	0·90
Solvent extractors	0·67
Spray dryers	0·23
Conveyors: belt	0·78
vibrating	1·0
screw	0·80
Crystallisers	0·60
Evaporators	0·5–0·55
Boilers: low-pressure	0·50
high-pressure	0·60
Pumps, centrifugal with motor	
Process vessels generally	0·66
Hoppers	0·68
Hammermills	0·67
Heat-exchangers: air-cooled	0·66
shell-and-tube	0·60
Heavy media separator	0·33
Leaching equipment	0·60
Magnetic separators: permanent dry	0·83
permanent wet	1·0

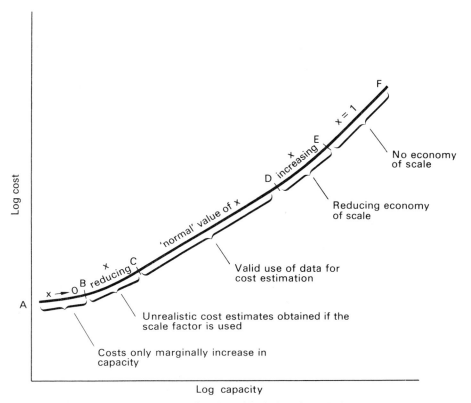

Fig. 20.3 Economy of scale and variations in scale factors

Factor Estimating

In general, more accurate estimation of capital cost requires more information. One of the most widely established methods of estimation that is used both at a preliminary stage and for more detailed estimates is based on multiplying the cost of the main plant items in a process by factors to take account of all the additional costs outlined earlier in Table 20.7, such as installation, instrumentation, electricals, civil engineering and supervision.

Detailed studies of a wide range of chemical processes have shown that equipment cost is invariably the largest single item and all other costs may be related to it. The total of the individual factors for each element of capital cost is known as the Lang factor. The construction of the Lang factor for three types of chemical process is shown in Table 20.11. The delivered-equipment cost of a process multiplied by the factor appropriate to the type of process gives the total installed capital cost.

The generalisations implicit in the Lang factor approach may easily be modified for specific situations using the same basis but permitting flexibility in the individual cost element factors. This is shown in Table 20.12, based on Tables 20.8 and 20.11 above.

TABLE 20.11 DERIVATION OF LANG FACTORS FOR CHEMICAL PROCESS PLANTS ON A BATTERY LIMITS BASIS[1]

	Percentage of delivered-equipment cost for		
	Solid-processing plant	Solid–fluid-processing plant	Fluid-processing plant
Direct costs			
Purchased equipment—delivered (included fabricated equipment and process machinery)	100	100	100
Purchased-equipment installation	45	39	47
Instrumentation and controls (installed)	9	13	18
Piping (installed)	16	31	66
Electrical (installed)	10	10	11
Buildings (including services)	25	29	18
Site improvements	13	10	10
Service facilities (installed)	40	55	70
Land (if purchase is required)	6	6	6
Total direct plant cost	264	293	346
Indirect costs			
Engineering and supervision	33	32	33
Construction expenses	39	34	41
Total direct and indirect plant costs	336	359	420
Contractor's fee (about 5% of direct and indirect plant costs)	17	18	21
Contingency (about 10% of direct and indirect plant costs)	34	36	42
Fixed capital investment	387	413	483
Lang factor	3·87	4·13	4·83

Example 6: Calculation of Overall Factor for Effluent Treatment Plant
Calculate the overall factor for an automated non-biological effluent treatment plant sited in the open, on an existing unprepared site. Use this factor to calculate the total capital cost of an effluent treatment plant if the delivered equipment cost of the main plant items is £14 750.

Delivered equipment cost	1·00
Installation	0·40
Instrumentation	0·10
Piping	0·10

Electricals	0·10
Buildings	0·20
Site	0·05
Services	0·15
Land	—
Engineering and supervision	0·20
Construction expenses	0·20
	2·50
Contractors fee @ 10% (typically)	0·25
Contingency @ 5%	0·125

Therefore overall factor (analogous to Lang factor) = 2·875

Total installed capital cost = £14 750 × 2·875 = £42 406

This derived overall factor agrees well with other information relating to relatively small-scale inorganic effluent treatment plants.

A problem arises with the Lang factor method when using more expensive materials of construction such as stainless steel. Although the equipment cost of stainless steel items may be between two and three times that of mild steel, the cost of installation, instrumentation and many of the other costs are usually relatively unaffected. Straightforward use of the Lang factor can give rise to a serious overestimate in such situations. This may be overcome by estimating the cost of equivalent mild steel equipment, using the Lang factor, then adding on the incremental cost of employing stainless steel, both in the equipment and ancillary costs.

TABLE 20.12 GENERALISED FACTOR APPROACH

Delivered-equipment cost	E
Equipment installation	0·18–1·00 E
Instrumentation and controls (installed)	0·06–0·20 E
Piping (installed)	0·09–0·60 E
Electricals (installed)	0·06–0·35 E
Buildings	0·15–1·20 E
Site improvements	0·04–0·25 E
Services (installed)	0·10–1·00 E
Land	0·02–0·10 E
Engineering and supervision	0·15–0·60 E
Construction expenses	0·15–0·60 E
Subtotal	
Contractor's fee	5–15% Subtotal
Contingency	5–15% Subtotal
Total	

Many modifications of the Lang approach have been made to overcome problems and/or improve accuracy. One example of this is illustrated in Table 20.13 in which individual factors for each item of equipment are proposed. The total capital cost is found by multiplying the cost of each item of equipment by the appropriate factor, to give the total installed cost of that item, and then summing the individual total installed costs.

A more sophisticated development considers the effect of more expensive materials of construction, different factors for direct and indirect costs, the relationship between different types of equipment, and the overall labour and material cost elements.[10]

The simple factor approach has, in fact, been developed extensively to devise better and/or more accurate and/or less costly ways of improving capital cost estimates. For example, factors covering each element of capital cost for a range of equipment sizes may be developed. Ultimately this will become a set of subfactors for each item of equipment in every situation. Such complexity needs to be computerised to be effective. Many of the larger companies have sophisticated computerised in-house systems to take account of the high level of complexity and tight financial margins in a competitive and modern industry,[11] based on independent and interdependent factors derived from accumulated knowledge and experience.

TABLE 20.13 SOME PROCESS COST FACTORS FOR INDIVIDUAL EQUIPMENT[1]

Equipment	Factor
Blender	2·0
Blowers and fans (including motor)	2·5
Centrifuges (process)	2·0
Compressors:	
Centrifugals, motor-driven (less motor)	2·0
Steam turbine (including turbine)	2·0
Reciprocating, steam and gas	2·3
Motor-driven (less motor)	2·3
Ejectors (vacuum units)	2·5
Furnaces (package units)	2·0
Heat-exchangers	4·8
Instruments	4·1
Motors, electric	8·5
Pumps:	
Centrifugal, motor-driven (less motor)	7·0
Steam turbine (including turbine)	6·5
Positive displacement (less motor)	5·0
Reactors—factor as approximate equivalent type of equipment	
Refrigeration (package unit)	2·5
Tanks:	
Process	4·1
Storage	3·5
Fabricated and field-erected (>227 m^3 ($>50\,000$ gal))	2·0
Towers (columns)	4·0

The more complex the estimating system, the more information is required, and the more accurate the answer is likely to be.

For recycling processes, detailed cost estimates are likely to be expensive in time and money and require extensive data not normally available. Even highly detailed estimates of new processes may be grossly in error due to unforeseen design problems.[12] Effluent treatment and pollution abatement, however, is usually based on relatively simple and proven technology and the simple factor approach described earlier can often provide an acceptable level of accuracy.

Delivered-equipment Cost Estimation

The factor method of estimating requires firstly an estimate of the delivered-equipment cost of the main items of equipment. By implication, therefore, a detailed mass balance and equipment schedule is required. This cost information may be derived from such sources as quotations, in-company information, proprietary data banks and published information. In preliminary design work and for many simple pollution control processes, satisfactory estimates may be obtained by using published information and the cost-capacity scaling procedure described earlier. A representative selection of the costs of the more common equipment likely to be encountered in pollution control and, to a lesser extent, recycling is given in Table 20.16 later in this chapter. This is presented as cost models for simplicity, with a suggested range of application of the data. In some cases minor simplifications have been incorporated for ease of use, but without significant effect on accuracy.

Short-cut Methods of Capital Cost Estimation

Where the more traditional methods of capital cost estimation are either impracticable or too costly in time or money, perhaps due to novelty, lack of information or significant differences from conventional practice, one of a number of rapid methods of cost estimation which overcome the need for detailed information may be used to obtain a realistic estimate.

Approximations to Delivered-equipment Cost

One group of techniques derives an estimate for the delivered-equipment cost and then employs the traditional factors approach to obtain a total installed capital cost. The methods are based on the concept of the average cost of a main plant item being a function of several variables. The delivered-equipment cost is then the number of main plant items (main items of equipment) × average cost. A simple example of such a calculation is:[13]

$$C = f . N . (21 . V^{0.675}) . F_m . F_p . F_T$$

where C = total capital cost of plant (£) 1971

f = investment factor—obtained graphically and dependent on the phases being processed and the average unit cost of main plant items (equivalent to Lang factor)

N = number of main plant items, excluding pumps

$(21 \cdot V^{0.675})$ = average unit cost of main plant items, where V = average throughput of the main plant items (tonnes p.a.), which may be satisfactorily approximated to plant capacity (tonnes p.a.)

F_m = materials-of-construction factor—obtained from a table. Values range from 1·0 for carbon steel through 1·1 for aluminium and 1·3 for stainless steel to 2·0 for titanium

F_p = factor for design pressure if below 1 atmosphere or above 7 atmospheres—obtained graphically. A weighted mean is used if pressure varies

F_T = factor for design temperature if below 0°C or above 100°C— obtained graphically. A weighted mean is used if temperatures change in different items of equipment.

A cost index needs to be incorporated to update the estimate to the present.

This procedure is only valid for continuous chemical manufacturing processes and will not give reasonable results with effluent treatment or pollution control plants.

Another, more complex method overcomes some of the simplifications of other procedures to give a better estimate.[14] As this is only strictly valid for fluid processes in the petrochemical industry, it has only limited usefulness in waste recovery or pollution control processes.

Functional Unit or Step-counting Approach

The other group of techniques is based on the functional unit or step-counting approach and is quite different from any of the techniques already described.

A functional unit is a significant step in a process and includes all equipment and ancillaries necessary for operation of that unit. Thus the sum of the costs of all functional units in a process gives the total capital cost.

Generally a functional unit may be characterised as a unit operation, unit process or separation method that has energy transfer, moving parts and/or a high level of 'internals'. Main process stream, recycle and side streams are all considered. Examples include a reactor, leaching operation, filter press, distillation column. The following are ignored: pumping and heat-exchange, which are considered to be part of a functional unit unless substantial loads (e.g. gas compressors) or unusual circumstances (e.g. refrigeration) are involved; storage, unless mechanical handling is involved (i.e. for solids), as the cost is relatively low and tends to be a constant function of the process; multi-stage operation; 'mechanical' separation (e.g. cyclone, gravity settler), as the cost is usually relatively insignificant. The correlation implicitly includes allowances for a certain level of the items ignored.

The average cost of a functional unit is a function of the process parameters, such as throughput or capacity, temperature and pressure conditions, and materials of construction.

A number of correlations and procedures have been devised (e.g. Zevnik and

Buchanan[15]), mostly for gas-phase processes in the petrochemical field.[16]

One correlation has, however, been developed for liquid–solid phase processes which tends to be much more applicable to waste recovery. This has been derived from metal extraction processes but is applicable to any chemical process where liquids, solids or liquids + solids undergo a conversion process to give a finished product:

$$C = K.N. \left(\frac{Q}{S^{0.5}}\right)^{0.85} \left(\frac{T.n_1}{N}\right)^{-0.17} \left(\frac{P.n_2}{N}\right)^{0.14} F_m . \frac{EPE(UK)}{100}$$

where

C = total installed capital cost (£) excluding working capital, on a greenfield (grassroots) site basis; battery limits basis may be obtained by dividing by 1·4 to allow for existence of services, access, etc

K = correlation constant, a function of plant capacity (see Figure 20.4). Some fixed costs associated with capital investment, not covered by the usual scale factors, become significant at low plant capacities and are covered by the 'variable constant' K

N = number of functional units

Q = plant capacity (tonnes p.a.)

S = (weight desired reactor product)/(weight total reactor feed). Size of plant, hence its cost, is related to throughput rather than capacity or output. As these are not related, and throughput can vary considerably, it is advantageous to approximate throughput rather than rely on capacity. This is done by dividing capacity by a conversion factor to give throughput: square-rooting effectively averages it over the plant

T = maximum temperature of any functional unit in the main process stream (°C)

n_1 = number of functional units operating on the main process stream at $> T/2$. This is an arbitrary attempt to relate the extent to which high temperature is employed as the fraction n/N of units operating at above half the maximum. Fractions of $\frac{1}{2}$ may be satisfactorily used in doubtful cases

P = maximum pressure of any functional unit (atmospheres)

n_2 = number of functional units operating at $> P/2$. The same methodology applies as for temperature. (The effect for liquids and solids is significantly less than for gases, due to their incompressibility)

F_m = materials-of-construction factor, taken as:

0·7 for non-corrosive/organic systems

0·9 for mildly corrosive systems

1·1 for corrosive/inorganic/acid systems

1·3 for exeptional conditions

Intermediate values may be used

EPE (UK) = EPE Cost Index (see page 664).

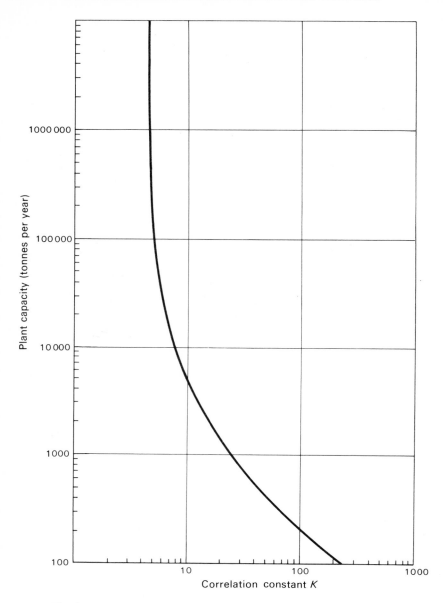

Fig. 20.4 Variation of correlation constant K with plant capacity

The accuracy of the correlation should lie within ±25% of the actual cost, which is a most acceptable level of accuracy at this level of process design. The equation has been used with considerable success for processes ranging from a few hundred tonnes per year capacity to several hundred million tonnes per year.

Other correlations have been developed for chemical processes generally and for more specific processes:

(a) *Continuous gas phase processes only*, in the chemical process industries.

$$C = 1040N \cdot Q^{0.616} F_m \frac{\text{EPE (UK)}}{300}$$

where C = battery limits fixed capital cost (£)
N = number of functional units or steps
Q = plant capacity, or average plant capacity if more than one product (tonnes p.a.)
F_m = materials of construction factor = 1·0 for mild steel, 1·3 for stainless steel

Range of applicability: $5000 < Q < 100\,000$.

(b) *Continuous liquid–solid phase processes only*, in the chemical process industries.

Throughputs > 60 000 tonnes p.a.:

$$C = 77N \left(\frac{Q}{S}\right)^{0.675} \frac{\text{EPE (UK)}}{100}$$

Throughputs < 60 000 tonnes p.a.:

$$C = 6750N \left(\frac{Q}{S}\right)^{0.30} \frac{\text{EPE (UK)}}{100}$$

where Q = plant capacity (tonnes p.a.)
S = reactor 'conversion' = (weight desired reactor product)/(weight reactor input)
Q/S = throughput
Other notation as (a).

(c) *Refuse sorting and separation processes*.

$$C = N(426\,000 + 612Q) \frac{\text{EPE (UK)}}{300}$$

where Q = plant capacity (tonnes refuse feed/day)
Other notation as (a).

(d) *Non-biological effluent treatment:* This is described below.

The principles may be readily applied to any specific or general situation where historical data are available from which a correlation may be obtained by regression analysis.

This functional unit approach is also attractive in the ease with which large numbers of related alternatives may be readily compared on grounds of capital cost, when the actual cost may be irrelevant. In this situation the process with fewest steps will cost the least. This facilitates sensitivity analyses on the range of parameters employed and enables the pay-off between alternatives to be explored: for example, a low efficiency process of 15 steps can be compared with a high efficiency process of 11 steps.

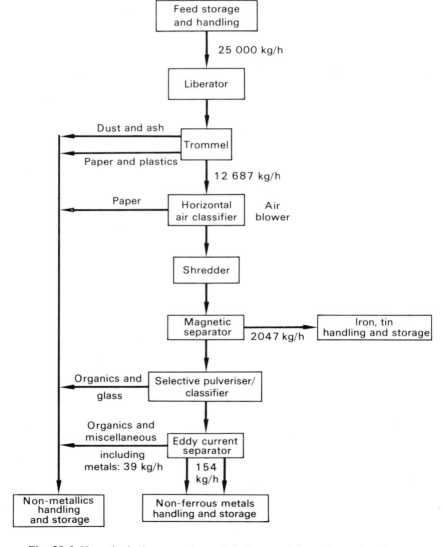

Fig. 20.5 Hypothetical process for reclaiming metal from domestic refuse

Example 7: Calculation of Capital Cost by Functional Unit Approach
A hypothetical process for reclaiming metal from domestic refuse is shown in
Figure 20.5, with an outline mass balance. There are two possible
products—all metals (17 608 tonnes per year) or non-ferrous metals only
(1232 tonnes/year)—and hence two capacities to use as a basis for cost estimation. The capital cost of both alternatives is calculated in Table 20.14,
which demonstrates reasonable agreement between the two estimates. The only
alternative calculation method, since no historical data are available, would be
a relatively detailed estimate which would consume much more money, man-
power and time and require substantial effort for changes in process scope and
design.

TABLE 20.14 CAPITAL COST ESTIMATE OF METAL-SORTING PROCESS (FIGURE 20.5)

	Capacity 17 608 tonnes p.a. total metals	Capacity 1232 tonnes p.a. non-ferrous metals
Constant K	62	200
No. of functional units N	11	11
Conversion factor S based on horizontal air classifier	$2240/12\,687 = 0\cdot177$	$193/12\,687 = 0\cdot0152$
$S^{0.5}$	$0\cdot42$	$0\cdot123$
Temperature, ambient, 20°C $\left(\dfrac{T_n}{N}\right)^{-0.17}$	$\left(\dfrac{20\times11}{11}\right)^{-0.17} = 0\cdot60$	$\left(\dfrac{20\times11}{11}\right)^{-0.17} = 0\cdot60$
Pressure, ambient, 1 atm	1	1
Materials-of-construction factor, F_m	$0\cdot9$	$0\cdot9$
EPE cost index value (January 1978)	300	300
Capital cost:		
Greenfield site basis	£9 384 100	£8 964 700
Battery limits basis (greenfield site cost/$1\cdot4$)	£6 703 000	£6 403 400
Mean battery limits cost	\multicolumn{2}{c}{$= £6\,553\,200$}

One of the problems in assessing the validity of the result lies in the inconsistent
and occasionally suspect figures quoted for other solid waste resource recovery
schemes. In any newly developing technology the uncertainties are considerable and proponents are likely to take an optimistic view. These initial
uncertainties in the design of new processes are sometimes referred to as the
'learning factor', which can often double or triple the estimated cost. As more
experience is gained in constructing and operating plants, the learning factor
will reduce to unity. The correlation proposed above includes only a relatively
small element for 'learning'.

Effluent Treatment

The above expressions are only valid as defined, and will not give satisfactory results for effluent treatment processes. The following equation has been derived for non-biological effluent treatment plants and is illustrated in Example 8:

$$C = 312 . N' . Q^{0.453} . \frac{EPE(UK)}{260}$$

or

$$C = 3591 . N' . M^{0.453} . \frac{EPE(UK)}{260}$$

where $C =$ total installed capital cost (£) battery limits basis, fully automated plant. Basic civil engineering included but buildings excluded

$N' =$ number of effluent treatment steps. Effluent treatment steps are:

Acid/alkali neutralisation

Chrome reduction, aqueous (if gaseous sulphur dioxide is used, add a half step)

Cyanide oxidations to cyanate, aqueous (if gaseous chlorine is used, add a half step)

Demulsification

Filter press

Ion exchange

Lime reagent preparation

Settlement

Water recycle system

$Q =$ design throughput (gal/h)

$M =$ design throughput (m³/h).

The capital cost includes all equipment, materials, labour, civil engineering, installation, commissioning and cubicle for the control panel. Reagent warehousing would cost about 20% more, and complete enclosure up to 100% more. Piping, sumps and work outside the plant perimeter would cost extra (see Example 9).

Example 8: Calculation of Capital Cost of Effluent Treatment Plant

Estimate the capital cost of 18·2 m³h (4000 gal/h) effluent plant to handle effluent from a chrome plating works in January 1979.

The plant consists of:

chrome reduction
neutralisation
settlement
filtration

$$£ \text{ capital cost (Jan. 1979)} = 3591 \times 4 \times (18·2)^{0.453} \times \frac{319}{260}$$

$$= £65\ 600$$

The additional cost of using a gaseous chrome reduction system would be approximately £8200.

Example 9: Comparison of Cost Estimation Methods
This example compares the effluent treatment plant correlation with the detailed factor cost estimate.

An effluent treatment plant to handle $9 \cdot 1$ m³/h (2000 gal/h) waste acid requires the following equipment:

    Alkali make-up tank, agitated, mild steel, $2 \cdot 27$ m³ (500 gal)
    Neutralisation tank, agitated, lined steel, $3 \cdot 63$ m³ (800 gal)
    Sump pump, stainless steel, $9 \cdot 1$ m³/h (2000 gal/h)
    Transfer pump, cast iron, $9 \cdot 1$ m³/h (2000 gal/h)
    Settling tank, mild steel, $45 \cdot 4$ m³ (10 000 gal)

What is the equipment cost and the total installed capital cost on a January 1978 basis?

Capital cost models (see Table 20.16):

Agitated tank, mild steel	$£C = 799 \text{ (volume, m}^3)^{0.48}$
Factor for lining: $1 \cdot 8$	
Settling tank, mild steel	$£C = 478 \text{ (volume, m}^3)^{0.52}$
Pump, cast iron	$£C = 148 \cdot 0 \text{ (capacity, m}^3/\text{h})^{0.4}$
Pump, stainless steel	$£C = 266 \cdot 7 \text{ (capacity, m}^3/\text{h})^{0.4}$

Factor to give total installed capital cost $= 2 \cdot 875$ (see Example 6).

(a) Detailed factor cost estimate:

Alkali make-up tank	£1184
Neutralisation tank	£1484 × $1 \cdot 8$ = £2670
Settling tank	£3476
Pumps	£358 + £645 = £1003
	Total equipment cost = £8333

Total installed capital cost $= 8333 \times 2 \cdot 875 = £23\ 957$.

(b) Short-cut method using correlation for effluent treatment plant:

$$£C = 3591 \cdot N' \cdot (M)^{0.453} \frac{\text{EPE (UK)}}{260}$$

$$(N' = 2 : \text{neutralisation and settlement})$$

$$= 3591 \cdot 2 \cdot (9 \cdot 1)^{0.453} \cdot \frac{300}{260}$$

$$= £22\ 534$$

Total installed capital cost by approximation $= £22\ 534$.

Data

The information in this section may be employed with the techniques described earlier to obtain capital cost estimates, but can only be regarded as a rough, although reasonable, guide to capital costs.

Processes and Operations

Table 20.15 gives models for estimating costs of processes and operations. In some cases economy of scale is not known or information is limited and only a single cost is quoted, but wherever possible at a stated capacity. Cost data for new processes employing unproven technology are likely to be optimistic, i.e. probably low. This is certainly true in the field of resource recovery from domestic refuse where published capital cost estimates have increased considerably more than the prevalent inflation rate.[12] In addition to cost data for specific processes, information is also provided for some readily identified processes, also on a total installed capital cost basis. Some indication of the reliability and accuracy of the cost models is also included. Wherever possible data have been normalised and crosschecked; sometimes, however, there is such a spread of data that only a rough guide can be provided at a lower reliability, and occasionally crosschecks were not possible.

The total capital cost of a process employing a mix of any of these operations may be obtained by adding the costs of the individual operations. Even if there are gaps in the available information for a specific process the principle of the functional unit approach may be employed by taking the average cost per functional unit and multiplying by the total number of steps in the process.

All costs are quoted as battery limits cost on a January 1978 basis (EPE(UK) cost index value 300) for consistency and may be easily updated using a cost index.

Equipment

Table 20.16 provides equivalent data for equipment on the basis of delivered-equipment cost. Again, cost models are quoted with suggested limits where possible, otherwise the best available data are given. At this level of detail, the models and information should be regarded only as a guide. Quotations, tenders and manufacturers' published costs are likely to be much more accurate.

Most industries operate on a competitive basis and costs of some items, particularly basic fabrications such as tanks, can vary widely between firms in different locations and at different times, but such price differentials are less likely with more complex, sophisticated and/or expensive items.

The data refer to likely UK costs as at January 1978. The cost of imported equipment or the use of cost data from outside Europe may increase costs or estimates by up to 30% or occasionally more for specialised hardware.

TABLE 20.15 CAPITAL COST MODELS FOR PROCESS AND OPERATIONS

Bases: Total installed capital cost
Battery limits
Fully instrumented plant
January 1978 costs (EPE(UK) cost index value 300)

Notation: C = total capital cost (£)
E = equipment cost (£)
F = volumetric throughput (scfm)
G = volumetric throughput (UK gal/h)
M = volumetric throughput (m³/h)
N = volumetric throughput (Nm³/h)
S = hourly throughput (tonnes)
T = daily throughput (tonnes)
V = volume (UK gal)
W = volume (m³)

* indicates only a rough guide due to wide spread of information.
† indicates limited source of data and hence possible lower reliability and/or accuracy.

Liquid effluent treatment
Non-biological
Non-biological aqueous effluent treatment
$(G = 1000\text{--}10\,000; M = 4.5\text{--}45.5)$ $C = 381(G)^{0.59} = 9183(M)^{0.59}$
$(G \geqslant 10\,000; M \geqslant 45.5)$ $C = 55.1(G)^{0.8} = 4118(M)^{0.8}$
$(G < 1000; M < 4.5)$ $C = 1415(G)^{0.4} = 12\,242(M)^{0.4}$
Demulsification and oil separation $†C = 379(G)^{0.5} = 5621(M)^{0.5}$
Cyanide oxidation, single-stage $(G = 2000\text{--}10\,000; M = 9.1\text{--}45.5)$
   manual operation $C = 455(G)^{0.38} = 3530(M)^{0.38}$
   automatic operation $C = 765(G)^{0.38} = 5942(M)^{0.38}$
Chrome reduction $(G = 2000\text{--}10\,000; M = 9.1\text{--}45.5)$
   manual operation $C = 641(G)^{0.38} = 4978(M)^{0.38}$
   automatic operation $C = 881(G)^{0.38} = 6841(M)^{0.38}$
Neutralisation $(G = 2000\text{--}10\,000; M = 9.1\text{--}45.5)$
   manual operation $C = 544(G)^{0.38} = 4225(M)^{0.38}$
   automatic operation $C = 693(G)^{0.38} = 5378(M)^{0.38}$

Table 20.15 (*Cont'd*)

Filtration ($G = 2000-10\,000$; $M = 9 \cdot 1 - 45 \cdot 5$)

manual operation	$\dagger C = 419(G)^{0.55} = 8138(M)^{0.55}$
automatic operation	$\dagger C = 465(G)^{0.55} = 9037(M)^{0.55}$

Biological

Deep Shaft (ICI) sewage treatment	$C = 29 \cdot 1(G)^{0.8} = 2174(M)^{0.8}$
Sewage treatment, conventional	$C = 80 \cdot 1(G)^{0.78} = 5379(M)^{0.78}$
($X =$ design population)	$C = 142(X)^{0.78}$
Biological filter once through (installed cost)	$C = 2 \cdot 21(V)^{0.82} = 184(\cdot\cdot)^{0.82}$
Biological filter, recirculation (installed cost)	$C = 3 \cdot 44(V)^{0.77} = 219(W)^{0.77}$
Activated sludge (installed cost)	$C = 3 \cdot 16(V)^{0.85} = 309(W)^{0.85}$
Anaerobic sludge treatment, heated primary digester (installed cost)	$C = 0 \cdot 65(V)^{0.97} = 122(W)^{0.97}$
Anaerobic sludge treatment, cold secondary digester (installed cost)	$C = 86 \cdot 6(V)^{0.50} = 1347(W)^{0.50}$
Sedimentation tank, rectangular (installed cost)	$C = 55 \cdot 7(V)^{0.56} = 1142(W)^{0.56}$
Sedimentation tank, circular (installed cost)	$C = 30 \cdot 2(V)^{0.66} = 1061(W)^{0.66}$
Sludge dewatering, continuous belt pressing	$C = 842(G)^{0.66} = 21\,368(M)^{0.66}$

Solid Waste

Pyrolysis of household refuse including some materials recovery ($T = 500-1500$)	*£21\,000 per tonne per day capacity $C = 84\,000(T)^{0.8}$
Pyrolysis of industrial organic waste including some materials recovery ($T = 100-500$)	*£32\,000 per tonne per day capacity $C = £92\,000(T)^{0.8}$
Materials recovery from household refuse ($T = 500-1500$)	*£8000 per tonne per day capacity $C = 63\,000(T)^{0.7}$
RDF recovery from household refuse including some materials recovery ($T = 500-1500$)	*£8000 per tonne per day capacity $C = 63\,000(T)^{0.7}$
Incineration including pollution control ($T = 500-1500$)	*£8480 per tonne per day capacity $C = 33\,800(T)^{0.8}$
Incineration with heat recovery including pollution control ($T = 500-1500$)	*£11\,700 per tonne per day capacity $C = 46\,600(T)^{0.8}$

Landfill   *£780 per tonne per day capacity

Transfer station (household refuse)   *$C = 1260(T)^{0.93}$
   *£1160 per tonne per day capacity

Pulverisation of household refuse   *$C = 1890(T)^{0.93}$

Composting of household refuse
fully mechanised ($T > 400$)   *$C = 350(T)^{0.8}$
   †£14 210 per tonne per day capacity

Copper recovery from cable by granulation   †$C = 26\,420(T)^{0.9}$

Copper recovery from cable by burning including wet scrubber   £26 per tonne throughput per year
   £10 per tonne throughput per year

Gaseous Emissions

Carbon adsorption of solvents   †£65 000–105 000

Miscellaneous

Deep well injection excluding any surface facilities
(X = depth of well (ft): ≤ 15 000) $C = 0 \cdot 78(X)^{1.38}$
(X = depth of well (m): ≤ 5000) $C = 4 \cdot 01(X)^{1.38}$

Chimney stack, 1·5–4·5 m, 5–15 ft diameter

(X = height of chimney (ft): ≥ 500)   †$C = 768(X)$
(X = height of chimney (m): ≥ 150)   †$C = 235(X)$

Lagoon or reservoir
(V ≥ 5 million) $C = 8 \cdot 72(V)^{0.72}$
(W ≥ 20 000) $C = 423(W)^{0.72}$

TABLE 20.16 SOME EQUIPMENT COSTS

Bases: Total installed capital cost
    Battery limits
    Fully instrumented plant
    January 1978 costs (EPE(UK) cost index value 300)

Notation and constraints as for Table 20.15

Tanks, storage, mixing and reaction
  Storage tanks, general purpose, mild steel
    ($V \leqslant 25\,000; W \leqslant 115$) $C = 8.69(V)^{0.61} = 234(W)^{0.61}$
    ($V = 25\,000{-}175\,000; W = 115 - 800$) $C = 58.7(V)^{0.44} = 632(W)^{0.44}$
    ($V > 175\,000; W > 800$) $C = 0.972(V)^{0.78} = 65.3(W)^{0.78}$
    304 stainless steel multiply above costs by   2·0
    Copper, multiply above cost by   †2·3
    Aluminium, multiply above costs by   †2·5
    316 stainless steel, multiply above costs by   4·2
    Titanium, multiply above costs by   †10·6
  Heated storage tanks, mild steel, multiply above costs by   †1·25
  Clad/lined steel tanks
    Lead-lined, multiply above costs by   1·8
    Plastic-lined, multiply above costs by   1·8
    Rubber-lined, multiply above costs by   1·8
    Nickel or stainless steel cladding, multiply above costs by   2·5
    Titanium-lined, multiply above costs by   †4·9
  Silo, for powdered lime (complete)   £17 000.
  Agitated, mixing or reaction tank
    Mild steel ($V = 100{-}17\,000; W = 5{-}75$) $*C = 60.0(V)^{0.48} = 799(W)^{0.48}$
    304 stainless steel ($V = 100{-}17\,000; W = 5{-}75$) $*C = 114.3(V)^{0.48} = 1522(W)^{0.48}$
    For other materials, solid or clad, use factors for storage tanks.

Solid–liquid separation
  Rotary disc filter
    (X = filter area (ft²) = 22–1800)   †$C = 2024(X)^{0.44}$
    (X = filter area (m²) = 6·7–550)   †$C = 5758(X)^{0.44}$
  Rotary drum filter
    (X = filter area, ft² = 12–720)   †$C = 3526(X)^{0.33}$
    (X = filter area, m² = 3·7–220)   †$C = 7724(X)^{0.33}$
  Thickener, tank and mechanism
    (X = tank diameter (ft) = 10–225)   †$C = 120(X)^{1.38}$
    (X = tank diameter (m) = 3–70)   †$C = 618(X)^{1.38}$
  Sedimentation tanks, mild steel
    ($V \leqslant 25\,000$; $W \leqslant 115$) $C = 28·9(V)^{0.52} = 478(W)^{0.52}$
    ($V = 25\,000$–$60\,000$; $W = 115$–275) $C = 26·5(V)^{0.55} = 515(W)^{0.55}$
  Filter press, cast iron
    manual ($G = 1000$–$10\,000$; $M = 4·5$–45) $C = 80(G)^{0.6} \quad = 2035(M)^{0.6}$
    semi-automatic ($G = 5000$–$20\,000$; $M = 22·7$–91) $C = 101(G)^{0.6} = 2571(M)^{0.6}$

Solids handling and processing
  Hammermill
    (X = area of feed opening (in²) = 24–2760)   †$C = 177(X)^{0.67}$
    (X = area of feed opening (mm²) = 15·5 × 10³ – 1780 × 10³)   †$C = 2·32(X)^{0.67}$
  Pulveriser
    (X = area of feed opening (in²) = 150–300)   †$C = 43·7(X)^{0.79}$
    (X = area of feed opening (mm²) = 96·8 × 10³ – 194 × 10³) ($S = 1$–20) †$C = 0·26(X)^{0.79}$
  Cyclone, dry: ($S = 0·1$–1·0)   †$C = 6800(S)^{0.06}$
                ($S = 1·0$–10)   †$C = 6800(S)^{0.42}$
                ($S = 10$–70)   †$C = 2632(S)^{0.82}$
  Screen, vibrating (heavy-duty, large particle size)
    single-deck (X = area of screen (ft²) = 80–160)   †$C = 135(X)^{0.99}$
    double-deck (X = area of screen (ft²) = 70–160 each)   †$C = 242(X)^{0.9}$
  Screen, vibrating (fines screening)
    single-deck (X = area of screen (ft²) = 30–100)   †$C = 177(X)^{0.87}$
    double-deck (X = area of screen (ft²) = 30–100 each)   †$C = 421(X)^{0.69}$

Table 20.16(*Cont'd*)

Heavy media separator complete ($S = 22$–180)

$\dagger C = 20\,000(S)^{0.33}$

Jigs: ($T = 40$–360)

$\dagger C = 928(S)^{0.17}$

($T = 725$–1420)

$\dagger C = 0.17(S)^{1.56}$

Magnetic separator, electromagnetic, dry ($S = 0.65$–10.5)

$\dagger C = 64.7(S)^{0.6}$

Dust collection/removal

Cyclone, dry ($F = 900$–20 000; $N = 1529$–33 975)

$\dagger C = 0.74(F)^{0.79} = 0.49(N)^{0.79}$

Cloth bag filter ($F = 2000$–10 000; $N = 3397$–16 987)

$\dagger C = 8.6(F)^{0.72} = 5.87(N)^{0.72}$

Electrostatic separator, high voltage ($F = 7000$–19 000; $N = 11\,890$–32 276)

$\dagger C = 65.7(F)^{0.61} = 47.6(N)^{0.61}$

Electrostatic separator, low voltage ($F = 1000$–19 000; $M = 1699$–32 276)

$\dagger C = 4.8(F)^{0.83} = 3.1(N)^{0.83}$

Scrubbers, with precleaners ($F = 1000$–15 000; $N = 1699$–25 480)

$\dagger C = 0.62(F)^{0.98} = 0.37(N)^{0.98}$

without precleaners ($F = 1000$–15 000; $N = 1699$–25 480)

$\dagger C = 0.45(F)^{0.98} = 0.27(N)^{0.98}$

Pumps and Blowers

General purpose centrifugal pump, including motor

cast iron

$* C = 17.2(G)^{0.4} = 148.0(M)^{0.4}$

stainless steel

$* C = 30.8(G)^{0.4} = 266.7(M)^{0.4}$

Centrifugal slurry pump, rubber lined

open impeller ($G = 70$–700: $M = 0.32$–3.2)

$\dagger C = 387(G)^{0.36} = 2698(M)^{0.36}$

closed impeller ($G = 200$–4000; $M = 0.91$–18.2)

$\dagger C = 308(G)^{0.64} = 9721(M)^{0.64}$

Centrifugal blower, excluding motor

($F = 800$–17 000; $N = 1359$–28 880)

$\dagger C = 86.6(F)^{0.62} = 62.4(N)^{0.62}$

Miscellaneous

Incinerator for combustible gases

$\dagger C = 462(F)^{0.375} = 378(N)^{0.375}$

Cooling tower ($G = 60\,000$–6 000 000; $M = 273$–27 300)

$\dagger C = 8.34(G)^{0.69} = 345(M)^{0.69}$

Heat exchangers, shell and tube, carbon steel

($X = $ heat transfer surface (m²) = 15–1000)

$C = 561(X)^{0.57}$

($X = $ heat transfer surface (ft²) = 150–1000)

$C = 145(X)^{0.57}$

Heat exchangers, air cooled

($X = $ finned heat transfer surface area (m²) = 1000–50 000)

$C = 124(X)^{0.66}$

($X = $ finned heat transfer surface area (ft²) = 10 000–500 000)

$C = 25.9(X)^{0.66}$

Total Disposal and Treatment Costs

Table 20.17 gives approximate overall disposal and treatment costs for a variety of methods and processes. Both capital and operating costs are incorporated into these figures, which may be used for comparison and preliminary evaluation of alternatives. These figures should not be used outside the context of rough estimates, as there are many factors, including scale of operation, that can significantly affect the overall cost.

TABLE 20.17 APPROXIMATE OVERALL COSTS OF DISPOSAL AND TREATMENT OPERATIONS (1978)

Solid waste	
Baling, self-sustaining	£4–8/tonne
Baling, wired	£3–6/tonne
Composting	£10–15/tonne
Hand sorting	£2–4/tonne
Incineration	£6–9/tonne
Landfill, tipping	£1–2/tonne
Magnetic separation	£2–4/tonne
Packaging and sealing solid cyanide for disposal (inclusive)	£100/tonne approx.
Pulverisation/size reduction	£2–4/tonne
Tipping	£1–2/tonne
Transfer	£1–2/tonne
Liquid waste	
Acid/alkaline neutralisation	£0·08/m³; £0·35/1000 gal
Chemical sealing toxic waste	£8–17/tonne
Chrome reduction	£0·13/m³; £0·60/1000 gal
Cyanide oxidation	£0·17/m³; £0·75/1000 gal
Demulsification, chemicals for	£0·45–1·55/m³; £2–7/1000 gal
Discharge to sewer	£0·08–0·16/m³; £0·35–0·7/1000 gal
Distillation of solvents	£80–160/tonne
Dumping to landfill	£3·1–4·4/m³; £14–20/1000 gal
Packaging and sealing low level radioactive waste	£200/tonne approx.
Purification of spent lubricating oil	£0·22–0·44/m³; £1–2/ gal
Stripping, air, hydrocarbons	£0·44–0·88/m³; £2–4/1000 gal
Vacuum distillation	£150–300/tonne

Operating Cost

Operating or variable costs comprise all the recurrent costs directly or indirectly incurred in manufacturing the product or running the pollution control process. The constituent elements (Figure 20.6) are all conventionally estimated as functions of the following:

raw materials (including process chemicals)
labour (direct operating)
energy (or utilities, services)
fixed investment related costs
selling price of product

The following overall equation for operating cost has been derived by averaging many results:[17]

$$O = 1 \cdot 13R + 2 \cdot 6L + 1 \cdot 13E + 0 \cdot 13I$$

where O = total operating cost
R = raw material cost
L = direct labour cost
E = energy (or utilities) cost
I = fixed capital cost

Any consistent money units per unit produced or per unit time may be used.

This represents a generalised expression for the total operating or variable cost of a typical chemical process based on orthodox practice. It does, however, lack flexibility for dealing with, for example, raw material conversions or labour requirements outside the normal range for chemical processes; a more comprehensive model that considers all reasonable variations is given in Table 20.18, where S = selling price.[17] Hence, for a typical process,

$$\text{total cost} = 1 \cdot 05R + 2 \cdot 195L + 1 \cdot 05E + 0 \cdot 133I + 0 \cdot 134S$$

which, by elimination[17] of S, reduces to

$$\text{total cost} = 1 \cdot 225R + 2 \cdot 562L + 1 \cdot 225E + 0 \cdot 172I$$

Raw Materials

In a waste recovery process the cost of the waste as a raw material is often zero, and may be ascribed a negative cost when the cost of alternative treatment is reduced or removed. This may either be included on the credit side of operating cost as income, or included as a negative raw material cost if it may be adequately expressed in this way. If disposal costs of the waste are significant, then their discontinuance will make a significant contribution to reducing the operating cost.

In pollution control, the chemical reagents required to treat the effluent may be an appreciable part of the total cost. It is important therefore that the correct process is installed to minimise the overall cost, and also that the chemicals are bought in the optimum quantity and at the optimum quality: for example, purchase of dilute sulphuric acid in large quantities means paying for unnecessary transportation of water; the use of concentrated acid may represent a significant saving. Another example is in purchasing caustic soda liquor by the tanker load, when it becomes very much cheaper than having it delivered in

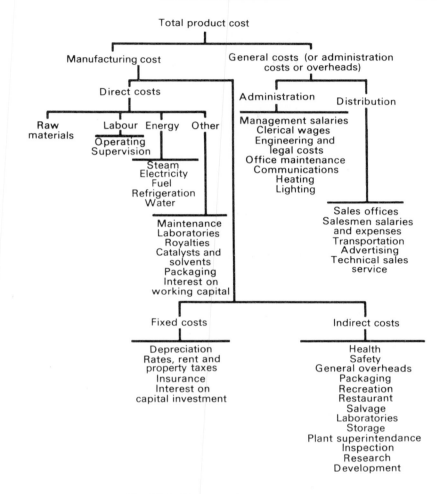

Fig. 20.6 Elements of operating cost

drums. In general, materials should be purchased at the minimum purity for satisfactory operation of the process. It is frequently possible to reduce significantly feedstock and chemical costs by careful consideration of the alternatives, both at the initial design stage of a new plant and in reassessing existing facilities. Purchasing on long-term contracts can also be advantageous.

Prices of materials constantly change, and while a number of publications such as *European Chemical News* and *Chemical Marketing Reporter* provide current price lists, they are probably not a very reliable guide to the actual costs due to rapidly changing market conditions and discounts allowed on long-term or bulk orders. Quotations are the best way to obtain current prices.

Labour

The direct operating labour costs for a continuous chemical process may be expressed (basis UK, 1978) as:[17,18]

$$L = 2600N \cdot Q^{-0.87} \quad \text{£ per tonne product}$$

or $\quad\quad\quad L = 2600N \cdot Q^{0.13} \quad$ £ per year

where L = direct labour cost
$\quad\quad N$ = number of steps or functional units
$\quad\quad Q$ = plant capacity (tonnes p.a.)

Updating requires a labour cost index, and conversion for other countries requires a knowledge of labour rates and productivity as well as exchange rates.

This technique is well established and is a traditional method of estimating labour costs for continuous chemical processes.

In effluent treatment plants the above correlation will be incorrect if 24 hour operation is not practised, and allowance must be made for this. Moreover, effluent treatment steps are much less labour-demanding. The following equation is suggested (1978 basis):

$$L, \text{£ per shift per year} = 260N' \cdot Q^{0.13}$$

where N' = number of effluent steps (page 646).

An alternative technique is to allocate men or fractions of men to specific operations.[1] In orthodox pollution control practice, where plants are usually well instrumented, one man is probably adequate for up to $22 \cdot 7 \text{ m}^3/\text{h}$ (5000 gal/h) throughput and two men for larger throughputs. Extra manning is required for less well automated plants and for work beyond the plant boundary such as drain inspection, sampling, and maintenance other than routine.

Energy

The energy or utility requirements of a process can usually only be estimated by detailed heat balances. Pollution control other than by incineration or thermal treatment does not usually involve significant energy consumption and this can often be ignored when estimating operating costs.

For a continuous chemical process such as a recycling operation the alternative to a detailed calculation is either to assess energy cost very roughly as 10% of the product value, or to use the following correlation (1978 basis):

$$E = 0 \cdot 39 I^{0.75} Q^{0.25} N^{0.77}$$

where E = total energy cost (£ per year)
$$I = \frac{\text{capital cost (£)}}{\text{EPE index, base 100 in 1970}}$$

Q = plant capacity (tonnes p.a.)
N = number of steps or functional units.

An energy cost index is required for updating. Conversion to other currencies is complicated by money units appearing on both sides of the equation, as well as different energy prices related to exchange rates.

This equation, derived from a study of a range of processes,[18] has not been widely tested and should therefore be used with discretion. In the absence of any other information it provides a useful guide. In-plant fuel utilisation and exceptional processing conditions may give unrealistic estimates. As total energy cost rarely exceeds 20% of total product cost[18] significant errors can be tolerated at this level of estimating.

Capital Investment

Procedures for estimating capital cost have been described earlier.

Total Operating Cost

Total operating cost is calculated using the overall equation or procedure for operating cost given on page 656.

Example 10

The estimated operating cost of the process described in Example 7 (Figure 20.5) is calculated (basis mid-1978):

	£
raw materials cost R assumed	0
labour cost $L = 2600 \times (17\ 608)^{0.13} =$	101 930
energy cost $E = 0.39 \times (11)^{0.77} \times (17\ 608)^{0.25}$	
$\times \dfrac{(6\ 553\ 200)^{0.75}}{300} =$	51 150
fixed investment I (from Table 20.14) =	6 553 200

Therefore

$$\text{Annual operating cost} = 0 + (2.6 \times 101\ 930)$$
$$+ (1.13 \times 51\ 150)$$
$$+ (0.13 \times 6\ 553\ 200)$$
$$= £1\ 174\ 700$$
$$(= £66.7 \text{ per tonne product, average})$$

(N.B. Note that the total operating cost is about double the likely income from sales of scrap, so the proposal would not be viable.)

TABLE 20.18 OPERATING COST ESTIMATION[17]

	Typical	Minimum	Maximum
Direct costs			
(a) Raw material	R		
(b) Energy	E		
(c) Labour	L		
(d) Supervision	0·20L	0·10L low level technology, high labour level	0·25L high level technology, low labour level
(e) Payroll	0·25 × |(c) + (d)|	0·15|(c) + (d)| developing country	0·50|(c) + (d)| Europe
(f) Maintenance	0·06I	0·02I mild conditions low utilisation	0·15I very corrosive, very abrasive, high utilisation
(g) Operating supplies	0·0075I	0·005I simple process	0·01I complex process
(h) Laboratory	0·10L	0·03L well established or bulk product	0·20L new product, high specification, specialist product
(j) Royalty		0·0 own process	0·06S new process
(k) Contingency	0·05 × |(a) − (j)|	0·01|(a)—(j)| low uncertainty	0·10|(a)—(j)| high uncertainty
Indirect costs			
(l) Rates	0·03I	0·02I undeveloped area	0·04I developed area
(m) Insurance	0·01I	0·004I low risk/hazard	0·02I high risk/hazard
(n) Overhead/ Administration	0·50L +0·02I	0·40L large plant, few variations, large orders +0·01I	0·80L small plant, many variations, small orders +0·04I
(p) Research	0·03S	0·015S old chemical, old process	0·055S new chemical, new process
(q) Distribution and selling	0·10S	0·02S old product, contract sales, large orders	0·20S new product, small orders, many variations
(r) Contingency	0·03 × |(l) − (n)|	0·01|(l)—(n)| low uncertainty	0·05|(l)—(n)| high uncertainty

Operating Cost Data

There is a dearth of information on operating costs of both recycling and waste disposal processes. Where data are available, as for example in resource recovery from household refuse[12] or aqueous effluent treatment processes[19] they cannot be relied on as accurate since there may be no indication as to whether they are complete. Interest and depreciation of capital may or may not be included and there are often so many uncertainties, for example the quantity of neutralisation reagents required for a specific process, that any data available should be treated with great caution. Estimation of operating costs is neither difficult nor time-consuming, and is likely to provide a more complete and accurate figure than published information. This is particularly true when reagents or chemicals have to be purchased, as raw material costs may be a significant part of the total operating costs and cannot be generalised.

However, total cost per unit weight can often be useful information. This total cost represents the elements of capital repayment or depreciation and interest on borrowed money, together with all operating costs and profit to the operator. It is particularly useful in allocating overall costs to relatively minor but complex processes, such as transport costs (for which published data are available), and also overall disposal costs, for example when choosing the cheapest method from a range available. These overall costs are usually quoted for established, existing and freely available processes (see Table 20.17). It must again be emphasised that such costs represent order of magnitude only and can change significantly for many reasons including particularly scale of operation, location and characteristics of waste.

Depreciation, Grants and Taxation

Depreciation, grants and taxation are interrelated and affect costs and profitability of any venture. It is impossible to do more than mention them as each is complex and needs expert attention.

Depreciation

There is a variety of methods for depreciating plant, machinery and buildings, or processes generally, which may be used to calculate taxation or total cost. Depreciation is essentially an artificial concept as it rarely represents a real cash flow, but rather an arbitrary allocation of change in value for calculation of other cash flows, particularly taxation. Example 1 used the simplest method of depreciation known as straight-line, which is calculated by subtracting the scrap value from the initial cost and dividing by the life in years. There is sufficient flexibility built into the rules and laws on taxation to permit optimisation of a company's liabilities by adjusting depreciation allowances year by year for the whole portfolio of projects, rather than each separately; this exercise is usually left to the accountants. Allowances for inflation and the introduction of current cost accounting may affect the above simplifications.

A depreciation element is sometimes included in operating cost to give an approximation to total manufacturing cost. Since capital investments often change due, for example, to modification or expansion, in addition to the significant effect of inflation and other factors on capital value, this method of producing a total cost can give misleading results unless used with caution. This approach has been used in calculating the overall disposal and treatment costs in Table 20.17.

Investment Grant

In order to attract industry to selected areas of a country, usually where unemployment is high, governments may offer an incentive in the form of a cash refund of a specified percentage of capital expenditure, usually 20–25%, sometimes restricted to certain classes of expenditure. An alternative incentive sometimes offered outside the UK is a tax 'holiday' for a specified period of years, which avoids the need for a government to pay out money while encouraging industry to move, operate successfully and help reduce unemployment. This is a complex subject and needs careful and expert attention as the grant may, for example, affect cash flows and tax allowances.

Taxation

The rules of taxation are complex and change frequently, and it is left to the accountants to minimise companies' overall tax liability. Basically, tax must be paid on any surplus of income over permitted expenditure including allowances or permitted investments. Examples 1 and 4 are simple illustrations of how the taxable profit is derived by subtracting allowances from net cash flow. The taxable profit is multiplied by the tax rate to give the tax liability, which is usually paid the year after being incurred because the necessary information is not available until the end of the company's financial year. The tax liability is subtracted from the net cash flow to give the profit after tax for that year. In waste treatment or disposal schemes, a tax credit should ideally be included when comparing alternatives.

Further elaboration is beyond the scope of this book but information is usually readily available if required from accountants and finance departments within an organisation, or specialist texts.

Markets

In assessing the viability of a waste recovery proposal, probably the most important single factor affecting the venture is the market for the recovered materials in terms of total revenue. The revenue is dependent on size or extent of market and realisations or price obtained. This aspect of recycling is not only the most important and probably the most neglected; it also presents the most problems, which are focused on finding a buyer for the recovered material and obtaining or agreeing a price.

A buyer may be found by advertising,[20] personal contact, direct approach or waste exchange service.[21] The buyer may agree to purchase all the product either for resale or reprocessing in an established operation (e.g. scrap iron and steel; waste solvents); alternatively, the reclaimed material may be 'retailed' in small parcels to a range of buyers rather than to a captured market.

Prices can change frequently and widely due to market forces and cannot normally be expected to remain constant. A typical example of the problems in finding a market for recovered materials is the household refuse materials recovery industry. The potentially most valuable materials to recover are the metal fractions, but as these are frequently relatively impure, not only are the prices obtainable well below the usual levels but the impurities may render the scrap unsuitable for recycling in the usual way. The price can also fluctuate widely over very short periods of time with changing market forces, economic conditions and buying policies of the scrap merchants and the secondary iron and steel metal industries. Similar problems face recovery of paper, glass and plastics. Conversion to heat and fuel creates further but related problems which are discussed in Chapter 17.

Guidance is therefore difficult, as recovering materials in a free market situation can be a very risky business. Some of the more successful ventures have resulted from close co-operation between producer and recycling agent, as outlined in Chapter 3, resulting in greater stability and less uncertainty for both. This is perhaps one of the safer alternatives, but every situation needs careful examination to optimise opportunity and profitability.

TABLE 20.19 EPE COST INDEXES

Date	UK	Australia	Austria	Belgium	Canada	Denmark	France
1970 Jan	100	100	100	100	100	100	100
Jul	106	103	103	102	105	105	104
1971 Jan	113	106	107	105	110	110	109
Jul	120	110	111	111	112	113	115
1972 Jan	126	116	114	117	115	116	120
Jul	131	120	138	120	119	125	125
1973 Jan	132	125	126	133	123	138	130
Jul	143	132	158	144	129	152	146
1974 Jan	150	143	156	154	135	170	168
Jul	176	167	176	166	150	187	182
1975 Jan	205	186	199	188	165	204	197
Jul	229	199	230	192	175	203	207
1976 Jan	245	214	195	201	189	211	219
Jul	276	237	228	212	198	233	242
1977 Jan	285	245	217	211	208	240	256
Feb	284	246	211	212	210	242	255
Mar	286	253	213	214	210	243	255
Apr	286	254	215	215	210	245	257
May	287	257	217	216	211	247	258
Jun	288	258	219	218	214	249	259
Jul	288	260	221	219	217	250	262
Aug	288	265	223	220	217	252	265
Sep	289	265	225	222	220	254	267
Oct	289	265	227	223	221	255	268
Nov	298	267	229	225	222	257	269
Dec	298	269	231	226	223	259	271
1978 Jan	302	271	233	227	225	260	272
Feb	303	274	235	229	226	262	274
Mar	305	275	237	230	228	264	275
Apr	306	276	239	231	229	266	276
May	308	278	241	233	230	267	277
Jun	309	280	243	234	232	269	278
Jul	311	283	245	235	233	271	280
Aug	312	285	247	237	235	272	281
Sep	314	287	249	238	236	274	282
Oct	315	289	251	239	237	276	283
Nov	317	291	253	241	239	277	284
Dec	318	294	255	242	240	279	286

Date		W. Germany	Ireland	Netherlands	S. Africa	Spain	Sweden	USA
1970	Jan	100	100	100	100	100	100	100
	Jul	105	106	104	107	106	100	102
1971	Jan	110	113	108	112	112	99	104
	Jul	114	122	116	114	118	101	106
1972	Jan	118	131	123	115	124	103	107
	Jul	123	132	127	122	136	104	109
1973	Jan	124	145	130	128	142	106	113
	Jul	131	163	137	138	164	107	116
1974	Jan	137	176	154	147	175	108	119
	Jul	150	204	163	168	193	132	140
1975	Jan	176	240	173	188	217	154	149
	Jul	172	267	182	215	267	161	144
1976	Jan	174	287	191	219	267	171	149
	Jul	191	315	195	246	297	185	152
1977	Jan	186	344	195	263	337	182	163
	Feb	187	349	196	264	342	183	163
	Mar	188	353	197	265	347	185	164
	Apr	189	357	198	266	352	186	165
	May	190	361	199	264	357	187	166
	Jun	191	366	200	264	362	188	169
	Jul	192	370	201	264	367	190	169
	Aug	191	374	202	264	372	191	170
	Sep	191	379	203	270	377	192	171
	Oct	191	383	204	270	382	193	173
	Nov	192	387	205	272	387	195	173
	Dec	193	392	206	272	392	196	175
1978	Jan	194	396	207	284	397	197	176
	Feb	194	400	208	284	402	198	178
	Mar	195	404	209	284	407	200	179
	Apr	195	408	210	284	412	201	181
	May	195	413	211	286	417	202	182
	Jun	195	417	212	288	422	203	183
	Jul	196	422	213	289	427	205	185
	Aug	196	426	214	291	432	206	186
	Sep	197	430	215	293	437	207	187
	Oct	197	435	216	295	442	208	189
	Nov	197	438	217	296	447	210	190
	Dec	198	443	218	298	452	211	191

References

1. PETERS, M. S. and TIMMERHAUS, K. D. *Plant Design and Economics for Chemical Engineers,* McGraw-Hill, 1968.
2. ALLEN, D. H., *A Guide to the Economic Evaluation of Projects,* Institution of Chemical Engineers, 1972.
3. JELEN, F. C. *Cost and Optimization Engineering,* McGraw-Hill, 1973.
4. DE LA MARE, R., Books for Engineering Economics Education (occasional series of reviews), *Engineering and Process Economics,* **1–3,** 1976–78.
5. Imperial Chemical Industries, *Assessing Projects,* Methuen, 1968.
6. PARK, W. R., *Cost Engineering Analysis,* Wiley, 1973.
7. CRAN, J., EPE International Cost Indices, *Engineering and Process Economics* **1**(1), 15, 1976, quarterly thereafter.
8. HASELBARTH, J. E. and BERK, J. M., *Chemical Engineering,* **67,** 158, 1960.
9. GUTHRIE, K. M., *Process Plant Estimating, Evaluation and Control,* Craftsman Book Co., 1974.
10. HIRSCH, J. H. and GLAZIER, E. M., *Chemical Engineering Progress,* **56**(12), 37, 1960.
11. LIDDLE, C. J. and GERRARD, A. M., *The Application of Computers to Capital Cost Estimation,* Institution of Chemical Engineers, 1975.
12. WILSON, D. C., *Engineering and Process Economics,* **2**(4) 35, 1977.
13. WILSON, G. T., *British Chemical Engineering and Process Technology,* **16**(10), 931, 1971.
14. ALLEN, D. H. and PAGE, R. C., *Chemical Engineering,* 142, 3 March 1975.
15. ZEVNIK, F. C. and BUCHANAN, R. L., *Chemical Engineering Progress,* **59**(2), 70, 1968.
16. BRIDGWATER, A. V., *Cost Engineer,* 1, September 1974.
17. BRIDGWATER, A. V., *Proceedings of Design Congress, Birmingham,* Symposium Series No. 45, Institution of Chemical Engineers, 1976.
18. BRIDGWATER, A. V., *Chemical Engineer,* 583, November 1973.
19. ZIEVERS, J. F., CRAIN, R. W. and BARCLAY, F. G., *Plating,* 1171, November 1968.
20. *Reclamation Industries Journal,* (bimonthly).
21. POLL, A. and ALLEN, J., *Chemistry and Industry,* 238, 20 March 1976. (See also Chapter 12.)

CHAPTER 21

Sources of Information

'The environment' continues to attract an increasing share of attention with the creation of new journals and the continued publication of books and papers. This is perhaps best illustrated by the annual literature review published by the *Journal of the Water Pollution Control Federation*, which in June 1976 listed 6369 references in 52 sections relating just to water pollution control over a 12 month period. It is claimed that the number of references in this area increases by 12% each year, so that about 20 000 references arise each year in the broad areas of waste, pollution, environment, resources and conservation, and probably over 100 000 have been published since 1970. A number of professional abstracting services provide a regular and up to date service; details of these and their coverage are given in Table 21.1.

A list of specialist journals is given in Table 21.2, grouped under broad subject headings. Most scientific and technical journals, including those published by learned societies, publish articles dealing with problems relating to the environment, and many symposia and conferences are held each year. Unless directly relevant, these are omitted from Table 21.2. It is not difficult for any scientist, technologist or manager to keep in touch with activities in his field by following the appropriate scientific press. Subscriptions to journals and the establishment or development of a company or works library can be a highly rewarding investment in encouraging employees to follow progress and apply new ideas.

Table 21.3 provides a classified bibliography of relevant books published since 1970. While this is intended as a comprehensive and authoritative selection, its completeness cannot be guaranteed.

TABLE 21.1 ABSTRACTING SERVICES

Abstracts of Air and Water Conservation Literature
    American Petroleum Institute, 275 Madison Avenue, 1271 Avenue of the Americas, New York, NY 10016, USA.

Abstracts on Health Effects of Environmental Pollutants
    Biosciences Information Service of Biological Abstracts (BIOSIS), 2100 Arch Street, Philadelphia, PA 19103, USA.

Air Pollution Abstracts
    US Environmental Protection Agency, Air Pollution Technical Information Center, Research Triangle Park, NC 27711, USA.

Air Pollution Titles
    Pennsylvania State University for Air Environment Studies, 266 Fenske Laboratory, 266 Chemical Engineering Building, University Park, USA.

Applied Science and Technology Index (general coverage)
    H. W. Wilson Co., 950 University Avenue, Bronx, NY 10452, USA.

Belgian Environmental Research Index,
    Centre National de Documentation Scientifique et Technique, Kiezerslaan 4 Boulevard d l'Empereur, 1000 Brussels, Belgium.

Biodeterioration Research Titles,
    Biodeterioration Information Centre, University of Aston in Birmingham, 80 Coleshill Street, Birmingham B4 7PF, UK.

British Technology Index (general coverage)
    Library Association, 7 Ridgmount Street, Store Street, London, WC1E 7AE, UK.

Bulletin Signalétique, Port 885 Nuisances
    Centre National de la Recherche Scientifique, Centre de Documentation, 26 Rue Boyer, 75791 Paris 20, France.

Chemical Abstracts (general coverage)
    American Chemical Society, Ohio State University, Columbus, OH 43210, USA.

Copper Abstracts
    International Copper Development Council, Orchard House, Mutton Lane, Potters Bar, Herts, EN6 3AP, UK.

Current Contents–Agriculture, Biology, Environmental Sciences (general coverage)
                Engineering, Technology and Applied Sciences (general coverage)
    Institute for Scientific Information, 325 Chestnut Avenue, Philadelphia, PA 19106, USA; and 132 High Street, Uxbridge, Middlesex, UK.

Engineering Index (general coverage)
    Engineering Index Inc., 345 East 47th Street, New York, NY 10017, USA.

Environmental Abstracts
    Environment Information Center Inc., 124 East 39th Street, New York, NY 10016, USA.

Lead Abstracts
    Lead Development Association, Zinc-Lead Library and Abstracts Service, 34 Berkeley Square, London W1X 6AJ, UK.

Table 21.1 (*Cont'd*)

Marine Pollution Research Titles
Citadel Hill, Plymouth, Devon PL1 2PB, UK.

Metals Abstracts
American Society for Metals, Metals Park, OH 44073, USA; *and* Metals Society, 1 Carlton House Terrace, London, SW1Y 5DB, UK.

Noise and Vibration Bulletin
Multiscience Publishing Co. Ltd., The Old Mill, Dorset Place, London E15, UK.

Pollution Abstracts
Pollution Abstracts Inc., 620 S. Fifth Street, Louisville, KY 40202, USA.

Selected Water Resources Abstracts
Water Resources Scientific Information Center, Office of Water Resources Research, National Technical Information Service, US Department of Commerce, Springfield, VA 22161, USA.

Water Pollution Abstracts
Department of the Environment, HMSO Box 569, London SE1 9NH, UK.

Water Resources Abstracts
American Water Resources Association, St Anthony Falls Hydraulic Laboratory, Mississippi River at Third Avenue SE, Minneapolis, MN 55414, USA.

World Aluminium Abstracts
European Primary Aluminium Association, Königsallee 30, Box 1207, D-4000 Dusseldorf 1, W. Germany.

Zinc Abstract
Zinc Development Association, 34 Berkeley Square, London W1X 6AJ, UK.

TABLE 21.2 JOURNALS

Air Pollution
Air Pollution Control Association Journal (US) (monthly)
Air Pollution Control Association, 4400 Fifth Avenue, Pittsburgh, PA 15213, USA.

Atmospheric Environment (UK, US) (monthly)
Pergamon Press, Headington Hill Hall, Oxford OX3 0BW, UK.

Clean Air (UK) (quarterly)
National Society for Clean Air, 136 North Street, Brighton BN1 1RG, UK.

Pollution Atmosphérique (France) (quarterly)
Société de la Revue, 21 Rue Murillo, 75008 Paris, France.

General
American Society of Civil Engineers Environmental Engineering Division Journal (US) (bimonthly)
American Society of Civil Engineers, 345 East 47th Street, New York, NY 10017, USA.

Table 21.2 (*Cont'd*)

Biodeterioration Research Titles (UK) (quarterly)
Biodeterioration Information Centre, University of Aston in Birmingham, 80 Coleshill Street, Birmingham B4 7PF, UK.

Bulletin of Environmental Contamination and Toxicology (Germany) (monthly)
Springer-Verlag, Heidelberger Platz 3, 1000 Berlin 3, W. Germany.

Catalyst for Environmental Quality (US) (quarterly)
274 Madison Avenue, New York, NY 10016, USA.

Chemosphere (UK, US) (bimonthly)
Pergamon Press, Headington Hill Hall, Oxford OX3 0BW, UK.

Environment (US) (10 per year)
Scientists' Institute for Public Information, 438 N. Skinker Boulevard, St Louis, MO 63130, USA.

Environmental Reporter (US) (weekly)
Bureau of National Affairs Inc., 1231 25th Street NW, Washington DC 20037, USA.

Environmental Pollution (UK) (8 per year)
Applied Science Publishers, Ripple Road, Barking, Essex, UK.

Environmental Pollution Control Journal (US) (monthly)
Environmental Publications, 87 Christian Street, Box 230, Oxford, CT 06483.

Environmental Pollution Management (UK) (bimonthly)
McDonald Publications, 268 High Street, Uxbridge, Middlesex, UK.

Environmental Science and Technology (US) (monthly)
American Chemical Society, 1155, 16th Street, NW, Washington DC 20036, USA.

International Biodeterioration Bulletin (UK) (quarterly)
Biodeterioration Information Centre, University of Aston in Birmingham, 80 Coleshill Street, Birmingham B4 7PF, UK.

International Journal of Environmental Studies (UK) (bimonthly)
Gordon and Breach Science Publishers, 41–42 William IV Street, London WC2, UK.

Journal of Environmental Systems (US) (quarterly)
Baywood Publishing Co., 43 Central Avenue, Farmingdale, NY 11735, USA.

Journal of the Society of Environmental Engineers (UK) (formerly Environmental Engineering) (quarterly)
Modino Press, 50 Pine Grove, London N20 8LA, UK.

Municipal Engineering (UK) (weekly)
Municipal Publications, 178–202 Great Portland Street, London W1N 6NH, UK.

Nuisance et Environment (France) (monthly)
Compagnie Francaise d'Editions, 40 Rue du Colisée, 75008 Paris, France.

Phoenix Quarterly (US) (quarterly)
Institute of Scrap, Iron and Steel Inc., 1729 H Street NW, Washington DC 20006, USA.

Table 21.2 (*Cont'd*)

Pollution Engineering (USA) (monthly)
    Technical Publishing Co., 1301 S Grove Avenue, Barrington, IL 60010, USA.

Pollution Monitor (UK) (bimonthly)
    Wealden Press, South Park Lodge, Mayfield Lane, Wadhurst, Sussex TN5 6JE, UK.

Prospect (UK) (quarterly)
    Redland Purle Ltd, 48a Burbage Road, London SE24 9HE.

Waste Age (US) (monthly)
    Three Sons Publishing Co., 6311 Gross Point Road, Niles, IL 60648, USA.

Waste Treatment Research Highlights (US) (semiannual)
    US Environmental Protection Agency, 200 SW 35th Street, Corvallis, OR 97330, USA.

Water, Air and Soil Pollution (Holland) (quarterly)
    D. Reidel Publishing Co., POB 17, 38 Papeterspad, Dordrecht, Netherlands.

Environmental Affairs (US) (quarterly)
    Boston College Law School, Environmental Law Center, Brighton, MA 02135, USA.

Environmental Law (US) (3 per year)
    Lewis and Clark Law School, North Western School of Law, 10015 SW Terwilliger Boulevard, Portland, OR 97219, USA.

Journal of Planning and Environment Law (UK) (monthly)
    Sweet and Maxwell Ltd., 11 New Fetter Lane, London EC4P 4EE, UK.

Recycling and Conservation
    Conservation and Recycling (UK) (quarterly)
        Pergamon Press, Headington Hill Hall, Oxford OX3 0BW, UK.

Industrial Recovery (UK) (monthly)
    National Industrial Materials Recovery Association, McDonald Publications, 268 High Street, Uxbridge, Middlesex UB8 1UA, UK.

Materials Reclamation Weekly (UK) (weekly)
    Maclaren Publishers, PO Box 109, Davis House, 69–77 High Street, Croydon, Surrey CR9 1QH, UK.

NCRR Bulletin (USA) (quarterly)
    National Center for Resource Recovery, 1211 Connecticut Avenue NW, Washington DC 20036, USA.

Reclamation Industries International (UK) (monthly)
    Maclaren Publishers, PO Box 109, 69–77 High Street, Croydon, Surrey CR9 1QH, UK.

Recycling and Waste Disposal (UK) (formerly Pollution Technology International) (monthly)
    Marylebone Press, 25–27 Cross Street, Manchester M2 1WL, UK.

Resource Recovery (US) (bimonthly)
    Wakeman-Walworth Inc., PO Box 1144, Darien, CT 06820, USA.

Table 21.2 (*Cont'd*)

Resource Recovery and Conservation (Holland) (quarterly)
Elsevier Scientific Publishing Co., PO Box 211, Amsterdam, Netherlands.

Resources (US) (3 per year)
Resources for the Future Inc., 1755 Massachusetts Avenue NW, Washington DC 20036, USA.

Resources Policy (UK) (quarterly)
IPC Science and Technology Press, 32 High Street, Guildford, Surrey GU2 5BH.

Reuse/Recycle (US) (monthly)
Technomic Publishing Co., 265 W State Street, Westport, CT 06880, USA.

Solid Wastes Management (USA) (monthly)
Communication Channels Inc., 461 Eighth Avenue, New York, NY 10001, USA.

Waste (Supplement to Materials Handling News) (monthly) (UK)
IPC Industrial Press, Dorset House, Stamford Street, London SE1 9LU, UK.

Noise

Journal of Sound and Vibration (UK) (24 per year)
Academic Press, 24 Oval Road, London NW1 7DX, UK.

Noise Control and Vibration Isolation (UK) (9 per year)
Trade and Technical Press, Crown House, Morden, Surrey SM4 5EW.

Solid Wastes

Compost Science (US) (bimonthly)
Rodale Press, 33E Minor Street, Emmans, PA 18049, USA.

Municipal Engineering (UK) (weekly)
Municipal Publications, 178–202 Great Portland Street, London W1N 6NH, UK.

NCRR Bulletin (USA) (quarterly)
National Center for Resource Recovery, 1211 Connecticut Avenue NW, Washington DC 20036, USA.

Solid Wastes Management (UK) (monthly)
Institute of Solid Wastes Management, 28 Portland Place, London W1N 4DE, UK.

Solid Wastes Management (USA) (monthly)
Communication Channels Inc., 461 Eighth Avenue, New York, NY 10001, USA.

Water Pollution

California Water Pollution Control Association Bulletin (US) (quarterly)
California Water Pollution Control Association, 127 N Madison Avenue, NO 304, Pasadena, CA 91101, USA

Table 21.2 (*Cont'd*)

Desalination (Holland) (bimonthly)
Elsevier Scientific Publishing Co., Box 211, Amsterdam, Netherlands.

Effluent and Water Treatment Journal (UK) (monthly)
Thunderbird Enterprises, 102 College Road, Harrow, Middlesex HA1 1BQ.

Industrial Water Engineering (US) (monthly)
Publicom Inc., 17 Sherwood Place, Greenwich, CT 06830, USA.

Journal of the Institution of Water Engineers (UK) (8 per year)
Institution of Water Engineers, 6–8 Sackville Street, London W1X 1DD.

Marine Pollution Bulletin (UK) (monthly)
Macmillan Journals, 4 Little Essex Street, London WC2R 3LF, UK.

Progress in Water Technology (UK, US) (bimonthly)
Pergamon Press, Headington Hill Hall, Oxford OX3 0BW, UK.

Rockwell Water Journal (US) (quarterly)
Rockwell International, 400 N Lexington Avenue, Pittsburgh, PA 15208, USA.

Wasser, Luft und Betrieb (Germany) (monthly)
Krauss Kopf-Verlag fuer Wirtschaft Gmbh, Lessingstrasse 12–14, D-6500 Mainz, West Germany.

Water Examination and Treatment (UK) (quarterly)
Society for Water Treatment and Examination, North Derbyshire Water-board, West Street, Chesterfield, Derbyshire S40 4TZ, UK.

Water Pollution Control (UK) (quarterly)
Institute of Water Pollution Control, 53 London Road, Maidstone, Kent ME16 8JH, UK.

Water and Pollution Control (Canada) (monthly)
Southam Business Publications, 1450 Don Mills Road, Don Mills, Ontario, Canada.

Water Pollution Control Federation Journal (US) (monthly)
Water Pollution Control Federation, 3900 Wisconsin Avenue NW, Washington DC 20016, USA.

Water Research (UK) (monthly)
Pergamon Press, Headington Hill Hall, Oxford OX3 0BW, UK.

Water Service (UK) (monthly)
Fuel and Metallurgical Journals, Queensway House, 2 Queensway, Redhill, Surrey RH1 1QS, UK.

Water and Sewage Works (US) (monthly)
Scranton Publishing Co., 434 S Wabash Avenue, Chicago, IL 60605, USA.

Water and Wastes Engineering (US) (monthly)
Dun Donnelley Publishing Co., 666 Fifth Avenue, New York, NY 10019, USA.

Water and Waste Treatment (UK) (monthly)
D. R. Publications, 111, St James Road, Croydon, Surrey CR9 2TH, UK.

TABLE 21.3 BIBLIOGRAPHY

Air and Gaseous Wastes and Pollution (General)

Air Pollution, V. Brodine, Harcourt, 1973.
Air Pollution, V. Cantinti, Butterworth, 1971.
Air Pollution, W. L. Faith and A. A. Atkisson, Wiley, 1972.
Air Pollution, J. O. Leadbetter, Dekker, 1972.
Air Pollution, H. C. Perkins, McGraw-Hill, 1974.
Air Pollution, A. C. Stern (Ed.), multivolume, Academic Press, 1976, 1967.
Air Pollution Abatement and Regional Economic Development, W. H. Miernyk and J. T. Sears, Lexington, 1974.
Air Pollution Control and Clean Energy, S-156, A. I. Chem E., 1976.
Air Pollution Control: Guidebook for Management, A. T. Rossano, McGraw-Hill, 1974.
Air Pollution and Industry, R. D. Ross, Van Nostrand, 1972.
Air Pollution and its Control, American Institute of Chemical Engineers, 2.
Air Pollution Control, R. E. Kohn, Lexington, 1975.
Air Pollution Control, A. T. Rossano (Ed.), Environmental Science Services Corp., 1970.
Air Pollution Control, W. Strauss (Ed.), Wiley, 1972.
Air Pollution Control and Industrial Energy Production, K. E. Noll, W. T. Davis and J. R. Duncan, Wiley, 1975.
Air Pollution Control: Techniques for Industrial Processes and Power Generation, K. E. Noll and J. Duncan, Ann Arbor, 1973.
Air Pollution Control Technology, R. M. Bethea, Van Nostrand, 1977.
Air Pollution Control Theory, M. Crawford, McGraw-Hill, 1976.
Air Pollution Damage to Vegetation, American Chemical Society, 1973.
Air Pollution: Physical and Chemical Fundamentals, J. H. Seinfeld, McGraw-Hill, 1974.
(The) Analysis of Air Pollutants, W. Leithe, Ann Arbor, 1972.
Chlorofluorocarbons and their Effect on Stratospheric Ozone, Pollution Paper No 5, HMSO, 1975.
Clean Air—Law and Practice, J. F. Garner and R. K. Crow, D. R. Publications, 1975.
Clearing the Air: The Impact of the Clean Air Act on Technology, C. J. Redmond, J. C. Cook and A. A. J. Hoffman, IEEE/Wiley, 1972.
Control of Air Pollution in the USSR, N. F. Izmerov, World Health Organisation Public Health Papers No. 54, 1973.
Disposition and Control of Atmospheric Emissions, S-165, A. I. Chem. E., 1977.
Dust Control and Air Cleaning, R. G. Dorman, Pergamon, 1974.
Fundamentals of Air Pollution, A. C. Stern, H. C. Wohlers, R. W. Boubel and W. P. Lowry, Academic Press, 1973.
Fundamentals of Air Pollution, S. J. Williamson, Addison-Wesley, 1973.
Gas Purification, A. Kohl and F. Riesenfeld, 2nd edn., Gulf, 1974.
Gas Purification Processes for Air Pollution Control, G. Nonhebel, 2nd edn., Newnes-Butterworth, 1972.
Handbook on Air Pollution Control, F. L. Cross, Technomic, 1973.
Important Chemical Reactions in Air Pollution Control, American Institute of Chemical Engineers, 1971.
Industrial Air Pollution Control, K. Noll and J. Duncan (Ed.), Ann Arbor Science, 1973.
Industrial Gas Cleaning, Vol. 8, W. Strauss, Pergamon, 1974.
Industrial Odour Technology Assessment, P. N. Cheremisinoff, Wiley, 1975.
Medical Aspects of Air Pollution, Society of Automotive Engineers Inc., New York, 1971.
Methods for the Detection of Toxic Substances in Air, H.M. Factory Inspectorate, HMSO, 1971.
Notes on Air Pollution Control, C. R. Cresswell, H. K. Lewis, 1974.
Photochemical Smog and Ozone Reactions, American Chemical Society, 1972.
Pollution in the Air: Problems, Policies and Priorities, R. S. Scorren, Routledge, 1974.
Quantitative Analysis of Gaseous Pollutants, W. Ruch, Ann Arbor, 1973.
Recent Advances in Air Pollution Control, S-137. A. I. Chem. E., 1974.
Source Testing for Air Pollution Control, H. R. L. Cooper and A. T. Rossano, McGraw-Hill, 1974.
Systems Approach to Air Pollution Control, R. J. Bibbero and I. G. Young, Wiley, 1974.

Trace Elements in the Atmosphere, H. Israel and G. Israel, Ann Arbor, 1974.
Understanding and Controlling Air Pollution, H. E. Hesketh, Ann Arbor, 1972.

Liquid Wastes and Pollution (General)

Advanced Wastewater Treatment, G. Culp and L. Russel, Van Nostrand, 1971.
Advances in Water Pollution Research: Proceedings of the 6th International Conference held in Jerusalem, S. H. Jenkins (Ed.), Pergamon, 1973.
Aeration of Activated Sludge in Sewage Treatment, D. L. Gibbon, Pergamon, 1974.
Aerobic Treatment of Waste Waters, A. W. Busch, Gulf Publishing, 1971.
Anaerobic Biological Treatment Processes, American Chemical Society, 1971.
Analysis of Industrial Wastewaters, K. H. Mancy and W. J. Weber, Wiley, 1972.
Analysis of Raw Potable and Waste Waters, HMSO, 1972.
Application of New Concepts of Physico-chemical Wastewater Treatment, W. W. Eckefelder and L. K. Cecil, Pergamon, 1973.
Biochemical Ecology of Water Pollution, P. R. Dugan, Planum Press, 1972.
Biological Waste Treatment, P. R. Canale, Wiley, 1972.
Biology and Water Pollution Control, C. E. Warren and P. Doudoroff, Saunders, 1971.
Community Adoption of Water Reuse Systems in the United States, R. E. Kasperson, Clark University, 1974.
Complete Water Reuse: Industry's Opportunities, American Institute of Chemical Engineers, 1973.
(The) Control of Oil Pollution on the Sea and Inland Waters, J. Wardley-Smith, Graham and Trotman D. R. Publications, 1976.
(The) Design and Operation of Small Sewage Works, D. Barnes and F. Wilson, Spon, 1976.
(The) Design of Sewers and Sewage Treatment Works, J. B. White, Arnold, 1970.
Disposal of Community Wastewater: Report of a WHO Expert Committee on Disposal of Community Wastewater, World Health Organisation, 1974.
Developments in Water Quality Research, Jerusalem International Conference on Water Quality and Pollution Research, Ann Arbor—Humphrey Science, 1969.
Discharge of Industrial Effluent to Municipal Sewerage Systems: Symposium, 29–30 November 1971, London, Institute of Water Pollution Control, 1971.
Discharge of Sewage from Sea Outfalls, A. L. H. Gameson, Pergamon, 1975.
Disposal of Sewage and Other Water-Borne Wastes, K. Imhoff, W. J. Muller and D. K. B. Thistlethwayte (2nd edn rev.), Butterworth, 1971.
Economic and Institutional Analysis of Wastewater Reclamation and Reuse Projects, H. O. Banks *et al.*, Leeds, Hill and Jewett, Report PB 206522, 1971.
Economics of Water Collection and Waste Recycling, G. Smith, Cambridge University Architecture Dept., 1973.
(The) Effect of Las Vegas Wash Effluent Upon the Water Quality in Lake Mead, D. A. Hoffman, P. R. Tramutt and F. C. Heller, US Bureau of Reclamation, Engineering and Research Center, Denver, Colorado, 1971.
Efficient Pricing for Urban Waste Water Renovation, R. Laak, R. Leonard and H. Kardestuncer, Connecticut University, Report PB 231353, 1973.
Elements of Water Supply and Wastewater Disposal, G. N. Fair, J. C. Geyer and D. A. Okun, Wiley, 1971.
Evaluating Water Reuse Alternatives in Water Resources Planning, A. Bruce Bishop *et al.*, Utah Water Research Lab., Report PB 232996, 1974.
Fresh Water Pollution Papers, C. W. Hendricks *et al.*, MSS Information Corp., 1973.
Ground Water Pollution, W. K. Summers and Z. Spiegal, Wiley, 1974.
Impingement of Man on the Oceans, D. W. Hood, Wiley, 1971.
Industrial Waste Water—Stockholm 1970, B. Goronsson, Butterworth, 1972.
Industrial Waste Water and Wastes—2, B. Goransson, Pergamon/IUPAC, 1976.
Industrial Waste Water Management, H. S. Azad, McGraw-Hill, 1976.
Industrial Water Purification, L. F. Martin, Noyes Data Corp., 1974.
Influence of Liquid Waste Disposal on the Geochemistry of Water at the National Reactor Testing Station, Idaho: 1952–1970, J. B. Robertson, R. Schoer and J. T. Barraclough, US Geological Survey, 1974.

Instrumentation, Control and Automation for Waste Water Treatment Systems, J. F. Andrews, R. Briggs and S. H. Jenkins, Pergamon, 1974.

International Congress on Industrial Waste Water Symposium Proceedings—Stockholm 2–6 November, IWPAC, 1970.

Introduction to Waste Waster Treatment Processes, R. S. Ramalho, Academic Press, 1977.

Investigations on the Subsurface Disposal of Waste Effluents at Inland Sites, L. G. Wilson, US Office of Saline Water, 1971.

Levels of Sewage Treatment for Sewage Effluent Discharge into Offshore Waters, J. P. Craven, Conference on the matter of pollution on the navigable waters of Pearl Harbor and its Tributaries in the State of Hawaii, 1971.

Lime in Waste Water Treatment, British Quarrying and Slag Federation Ltd, 1974.

Liquid Waste of Industry: Theories, Practices and Treatment, N. L. Nemerow, Addison-Wesley, 1971.

(The) Management of Water Quality and the Environment, J. G. Rothenberg and I. G. Heggie, Macmillan, 1974.

(The) Marine Disposal of Sewage Sludge and Dredge Spoil in the Waters of the New York Bight, R. A. Horne, A. J. Mahler and R. C. Rosello, Woods Hole Oceanographic Institution, 1971.

Marine Pollution and Marine Waste Disposal, E. A. Pearson and E. de Fraja Frangipane, Pergamon, 1974.

Metallic Effluents of Industrial Origin in the Marine Environment, Graham and Trotman, 1977.

Missouri Effluent Guidelines, Missouri Water Pollution Board, 1971.

Ocean Outfalls and other Methods of Treated Waste Water Disposal in Southeast Florida, Environmental Protection Agency, 1973.

Ocean Waste Disposal. A Bibliography with Abstracts, E. J. Lehmann, National Technical Information Service, 1974.

Oil Spill Prevention and Removal Handbook, M. Sittig, Noyes Data Corp., 1974.

Optimal Expansion of a Water Resources System, D. T. O'Laoghaire and D. M. Himmelblau, Academic Press, 1974.

pH and pIon Control in Process and Waste Streams, F. G. Shinskey, Wiley, 1973.

Physicochemical Processes for Water Quality Control, W. J. Weber, Wiley, 1972.

Potable Water from Polluted Sources, Symposium Sponsored by Society for Water Treatment Journal, 1972.

Principles of Water Quality Management, H. Fish, Thunderbird, 1976.

Principles of Water Quality Control, T. H. Y. Tebbutt, Pergamon, 1976.

Proceedings of Conference on Land Disposal of Municipal Effluents and Sludges Held at Rutgers—The State University of New Jersey, Environmental Protection Agency, Report PB 227115, 1973.

Proceedings—Workshop on Land Disposal of Wastewaters, J. M. Stewart, North Carolina Water Resources Research Inst., 1973.

Proposed Municipal Waste Water–Groundwater Exchange, City of Tucson: Arra-Marana Valley, Arizona Water Resources Research Center, Report PB 226910, 1971

Public Health Engineering—Design in Metric: Waste Water Treatment, R. E. Bartlett, Applied Science, 1971.

Recreational Reuse of Municipal Wastewater, M. Headstream *et al.*, Texas Tech. Univ. Lubback, Water Resources Center, 1974.

Recycling Treated Municipal Wastewater and Sludge through Forest and Cropland, W. E. Sopper and L. T. Kandos (Eds), Pennsylvania State University Press, 1973.

Renovated Waste Water: An Alternative Source of Municipal Water Supply in the United States, J. F. Johnson, University of Chicago, Department of Geography Research Paper, 1971.

Renovating Secondary Sewage by Ground Water Recharge with Infiltration Basins, H. Bouwer, R. C. Rice, E. D. Escarcega and M. S. Riggs, US Environmental Protection Agency, 1972.

Renovation of Secondary Effluent for Reuse as a Water Resource, L. T. Kandos *et al.*, Pennsylvania State Univ., 1974.

Reuse of Effluents: Methods of Wastewater Treatment and Health Safeguards, Report of a WHO meeting of Experts on the Reuse of Effluents, WHO Technical Report, 1973.

River Pollution—3 vols, L. Klein, Butterworth, 1969–71.

Scientific Stream Pollution Analysis, N. L. Nenerow, McGraw-Hill, 1974.

Second International Conference on Waste Water and Wastes, Stockholm, Institute of Water

Pollution Control, 1975.

Select List of References on Electrical Methods of Treating Sewage and Industrial Effluents 1965 onwards, Electricity Council, 1970.

Seminar on Methods of Detection, Measurement and Monitoring of Pollutants in the Marine Environment, 1970. A Guide to Marine Pollution, Gordon and Breach, 1972.

Sewage Sludge Treatment, R. W. James, Noyes Data Corp., 1972.

Sewage Treatment: Basic Principles and Trends, R. L. Bolton and L. Klein, Ann Arbor, 1971.

Slurry Handling and Disposal, North of Scotland College of Agriculture, 1973.

Social, Economic, Environmental and Technical Factors Influencing Water Reuse, A. B. Bishop *et al.,* Utah Centre for Water Resources Research, 1973.

A Special Report on the Pollution of River Waters, J. P. Kirkwood, Arno Press, 1970.

Survey of Wastewater Treatment and Disposal—Laughlin AFB TX, C. R. Williams, Environmental Health Lab., Report AD 785 372, 1974.

Systems Analysis and Water Quality Control, R. V. Thomann, McGraw-Hill, 1974.

Treatment and Disposal of Waste Water from Homes by Soil Infiltration and Evapotranspiration, Vol. I, Univ. Toronto Press, 1973.

Treatment and Disposal of Wastewater Sludges, P. A. Vesilind, Wiley, 1974.

Treatment of Industrial Effluents, A. G. Callely, C. F. Forster and D. A. Stafford, Hodder and Stoughton, 1977.

Waste Treatment Lagoons, International Symposium Proceedings, Kansas City, R. E. McKinney (Ed.), 1970.

Waste Water Treatment Technology, J. W. Patterson, Ann Arbor Science, 1975.

Wastewater Engineering: Collection, Treatment, Disposal, Metcalf and Eddy International, McGraw-Hill, 1972.

Wastewater Reclamation: Socio-Economics, Technology and Public Acceptance, Stone (Ralph) and Co., Report PB 233 675, 1974.

Wastewater Reuse, J. Gavis, National Water Commission, Arlington, Report PB 201 535, 1971.

Wastewater Treatment, R. E. Bartlett, Applied Science, 1971.

Wastewater Treatment Technology, J. W. Patterson and R. A. Minear, Illinois Institute of Technology, 1971.

Water, M. Overman, Open University, 1977.

Water, American Institute of Chemical Engineers, 1970, 1971, 1972, *et seq.*

Water and Wastewater Technology, J. Hammer, Wiley, 1975.

Water and Wastewater Treatment, E. D. Schroeder, McGraw-Hill, 1977.

Water and Water Pollution Handbook (4 vols), L. L. Ciaccio (Ed.), Dekker, 1972.

Water Borne Wastes, V. C. Marshall, Institution of Chemical Engineers, 1974.

Water Pollution, J. McCaull and J. Crossland, Harcourt, 1974.

Water Pollution Control, G. W. Graves, California University, Western Management Science Institute, 1972.

Water Pollution, G. Newsom and J. G. Sherratt, Sherratt & Sons, 1972.

Water Pollution Control Engineering, Central Office of Information, HMSO, 1970.

Water Pollution Control in New Jersey, P. H. Burch, Rutgers University, Bureau of Government Research, 1973.

Water Pollution: Disposal and Reuse (2 vols), J. E. Zajic, Dekker, 1971.

Water Pollution in the Greater New York Area, A. A. Johnson (Ed.), Gordon and Breach, 1970.

Water Pollution Manual 1972, J. R. Fuller, Thunderbird Enterprises, 1972.

Water Pollution Microbiology, R. Mitchell (Ed.), Wiley, 1972.

Water Renovation and Reuse, H. I. Shuval, Academic Press, 1976.

Water Reuse, American Institute of Chemical Engineers, 1971.

Water Supply and Water Pollution Control, J. W. Clark, W. Viewssman and M. J. Hammer, International Textbook, 1971.

Water Treatment Handbook, Degremont, 1973.

Solid Wastes and Pollution (General) see also *Specific Areas—Refuse*

Advances in Solid Waste Treatment Technology, A. Hershaft, Grumman Aerospace Corp., Bathpage N.Y. Research Dept., Report AO 749 409, 1972.

(The) Chemical Conversion of Solid Wastes to Useful Products, D. Barbour *et al.,* Report PB 233 178, 1974.

Chemical Engineering Applications of Solid Waste Treatment, American Institute of Chemical Engineers, 1972.
(The) Disposal of Solid Waste, F. L. D. Flinthoff, British Plastics Federation, Hutchinson, 1973.
Environmental Problems Arising from the Storage, Collection and Disposal of Solid Wastes, D. E. Lawrence, Institution of Municipal Engineers, 1972.
Evaluation, Extraction and Recycling of Certain Solid Waste Components, Great Lakes Research Inst., Report PB 208 674, 1972.
Handbook of Solid Waste Disposal: Materials and Energy Recovery, J. L. Pavoni, J. E. Heer, J. D. L. Hagerty, Van Nostrand, 1976.
Incineration of Solid Wastes, F. N. Rubel, Noyes Data Corp., 1974.
Large Scale Composting, M. J. Satriana, Noyes Data Corp., 1974.
Managing Solid Wastes, H. C. Goddard, Praeger, 1975.
Recycling and Disposal of Solid Waste, T. F. Yen, Ann Arbor, 1974.
Resource Recovery and Utilization, H. Alter and E. Horowitz, ASTM Special Technical Publication, 1974.
Sanitary Landfill, National Center for Resource Recovery, Lexington, 1975.
Sanitary Landfill Technology, S. Weiss, Noyes Data Corp., 1974.
Solid Waste Disposal, B. Baum *et al.*, Ann Arbor, 1973.
Solid Waste Management, D. J. Hagerty, J. L. Pavoni and J. E. Heer, Van Nostrand Reinhold, 1974.
Solid Waste Management Criteria: Objectives, Premises, Principles, Standards, Denver Regional Council of Governments, Report PB 218 991, 1972.
Solid Waste Management in the Denver Region: Recycling, Resource Recovery, Disposal, Regional Management, Situation, Alternatives, Program, Strategy, Denver Regional Council of Governments, Report PB 218 992, 1972.
Solid Waste Management: Technology Assessment, General Electric Company, McGraw-Hill, 1976.
Solid Waste Management. Selected Abstracts Rept., W. A. Ryerson, National Technical Information Service, 1973.
Solid Waste Treatment and Disposal, N.Y. Kirov (Ed.), Ann Arbor, 1972.
Solid Wastes, C. L. Mantell, Wiley, 1975.
Solid Wastes Disposal and Control, Report of WHO Expert Committee on Solid Wastes Disposal and Control, 1971.
Solid Wastes: Engineering Principles and Management Issues, G. Tchobanoglous, R. Eliassen and H. Theisen, McGraw-Hill, 1977.
Solid Wastes Management—A Regional Solution, K. C. Clayton and J. M. Huie, Wiley, 1974.
Study to Identify Opportunities for Increased Solid Waste Utilisation, National Technical Information Service, Report PB 212 730, 1972.
Survey of the Locations, Disposal and Prospective Uses of the Major Industrial By-Products and Waste Materials, E. Gutt and P. J. Nixon, Building Research Establishment, 1974.
Technical Evaluation Study, Solid Waste Generation and Disposal, Watervliet Arsenal, H. G. Rigo, Construction Engineering Research Lab., 1974.
Utilisation of Waste Materials, Building Research Station, 1972.

Specific Areas

Agriculture and Food

Agricultural Waste Management, R. C. Loehr, Academic Press, 1974.
An Agricultural Treatment, A. Howard, Rodale, 1972.
Animal Waste Management. Symposium Proceedings, US Environmental Protection Agency, 1971.
Combined Cooling and Bio-Treatment of Beet Sugar Factory Condenser Water Effluent, G. O. G. Loef, J. C. Ward and O. J. Has, Colorado State University, Environmental Resources Center, 1971.
(The) Disposal and Utilisation of Abattoir Waste in the European Communities, W. Weiers and R. Fische, Graham and Trotman, 1978.
Farm Wastes Management, J. B. Weller and S. L. Willetts, Crosby Lockwood Staples, 1977.
Feasibility Study of Waste Water Recovery in Shrimp Processing, Gibbs and Hill, 1972.

Forage Crop Irrigation with Oxidation Pond Effluent, J. B. Allen and J. C. McWhorter, Mississippi State University, Water Resources Research Institute, 1970.

Irrigation of Citrus with Citrus Processing Waste Water, R. C. J. Koo, Florida Univ., Gainesville, Water Resources Research Center, Report PB 232 046, 1974.

Pollution Abatement and By-Product Recovery in Shellfish and Fisheries Processing, CRESA, Report PB 208 214, 1971.

Pollution Control in Meat, Poultry and Seafood Processing, H. R. Jones, Noyes Data Corp., 1974.

Poultry Processing Wastewater Treatment and Reuse, J. D. Clise, Maryland Dept. of Health of Mental Hygiene, Baltimore, Report PB 237 185, 1974.

Slurry and Farm Waste Disposal, D. Gowan, Farming Press, 1972.

Solid Waste Management in the Food Processing Industry, A. M. Katsuyarma, N. A. Olson, R. L. Quirk and W. A. Mercer, National Carriers Association, Report PB 219 019, 1973.

Utilisation and Disposal of Crab and Shrimp Wastes, V. Mendenhall, Alaska Univ., 1971.

Waste Disposal Control in the Fruit and Vegetable Industry, H. R. Jones, Noyes Data Corp., 1973.

Chemicals

Aqueous Wastes from Petroleum and Petrochemical Plants, M. R. Beychok, Wiley, 1967.

(The) Chemical Industry and Pollution Control, National Industrial Pollution Control Council, 1971.

Disposal/Recycle Management System Development for Airforce Waste Petroleum Oils and Lubricants, M. Lieverman, Esso Research and Engineering Co., Report AD 779 723, 1974.

Environmental Control in the Organic and Petrochemical Industries, H. R. Jones, Noyes Data Corp., 1971.

Hydrocarbon Oils, Reclamation and Recycling Digest No. 2, Industrial Aids Ltd, 1975.

Mineral Oil Wastes, Waste Management Paper No. 7, HMSO, 1976.

Pollution Control in the Organic Chemical Industry, M. Sittig, Noyes Data Corp., 1974.

Pollution Control in the Petroleum Industry, H. R. Jones, Noyes Data Corp., 1973.

Polychlorinated Biphenyl (PCB) Wastes, Waste Management Paper No. 6., HMSO, 1976.

Sulphuric Acid Manufacture and Effluent Control, Chemical Progress Review No. 55, Noyes Data Corp., 1971.

Waste Oil: Headache or Resource, Proceedings 2nd Intl. Conference on Waste Oil Recovery and Reuse; Association Petroleum Re-refiners, 1975.

Desalination

A Study of Deep-Well Disposal of Desalination Brine Waste, P. G. LeGros *et al.*, Dow Chemical Co., Report PB 203 268, 1969.

A Study of the Disposal of the Effluent from a Large Desalination Plant, P. G. LeGros *et al.*, Dow Chemical Co., Report PB 206 020, 1968.

Brine Disposal Pond Manual, M. E. Day *et al.*, Bureau of Reclamation, Denver, Report PB 198 938, 1970.

Disposal of Brine Effluents, R. R. Grinstead and T. E. Lingafelter, Dow Chemical Co., Report PB 215 037, 1972.

Disposal of Brine Effluents from Inland Desalting Plants: Review and Bibliography, G. W. DePuy, US Bureau of Reclamation, Denver, Report PB 208 835, 1969.

Disposal of Brines Produced in Renovation of Municipal Waste Water, Burmot Roc, Report PB 197 597, 1970.

Disposal of the Effluents from Desalination Plants into Estuarine Waters, M. A. Zeitoun, E. F. Mandelli and W. F. McIlhenney, Dow Chemical Co., Report PB 203 841, 1969.

Disposal of the Effluents from Desalination Plants: the Effects of Copper Content, Heat and Salinity, M. A. Zeitoun, E. F. Mandelli and W. F. McIlhenny, Dow Chemical Co., Report PB 203 857, 1969.

Final Disposal of Effluent Brines from Inland Desalting Plants, J. R. Booth, B. P. Shepherd and W. F. McIlhenny, Dow Chemical Co., Report PB 218 432, 1972.

Mineral Recovery from Concentrated Brines, J. M. Glassett, C. M. Wong, W. S. Gillam and L. Leiserson, Brigham Young Univ., Report PB 198 942, 1970.

Systems Analysis of Brine Disposal from Reverse Osmosis Plants, P. G. LeGros, C. E. Gustafson, B. P. Shepherd and W. F. McIlhenny, Dow Chemical Co., Report PB 198 937, 1970.

Energy

Combustion Disposal of Manure Wastes and Utilization of Residue, E. G. Davis, I. L. Field and J. H. Brown, US Bureau of Mines, Report PB 206 892, 1972.
Disposal of Solid Wastes by Incineration, E. J. Ostte, Combustion Engineering Association, 1974.
(The) Efficient use of Energy, HMSO, 1974.
Energy from Solid Waste, F. R. Jackson, Noyes Data Corp., 1974.
Energy Recovery from Waste. A Municipal Utility Joint Venture, St Louis City and Union Electric Co., Report PB 213 534, 1972.
Incineration, National Center for Resource Recovery, Inc., Lexington, 1974.
Incineration of Solid Waste, F. N. Rubel, Noyes Data Corp., 1974.
Incineration of Waste Material with Special Reference to Plastics and the Recovery or Treatment of Associated Gaseous Products, C. A. M. Robertson, University of Manchester Institute of Science and Technology, 1972.
Physical and Engineering Aspects of Thermal Pollution, P. A. Krenkel, Butterworth, 1970.
Pollution Control and Energy Needs, American Chemical Society, 1973.
Principles and Practice of Incineration, R. C. Corey, Wiley, 1969.
Reducing Pollution from Selected Energy Transformation Sources, Systems International Ltd, Graham and Trotman, 1976.
Thermal Processing of Municipal Solid Waste for Resource and Energy Recovery, N. J. Weinstein and R. F. Toro, Ann Arbor, 1976.

Law

Concepts in Environmental Law for Managers, J. Bockrath, McGraw-Hill, 1977.
(The) Law of Rivers and Watercourses, A. S. Wisdon, D. R. Publications, 1976.
(The) Law and Practice Relating to Pollution Control in the Member States of the European Communities, Graham and Trotman, 1976.
Law of Industrial Pollution Control, A. Walker, Godwin, 1979.
(The) Law of Rivers and Drains, J. F. Garner, D. R. Publications, 1975.

Metal (see also Chapter 15, Further Reading)

Automotive Scrap Recycling, J. W. Sawyer, Resources for the Future, 1974.
Cycling and Control of Metals, M. G. Curvy and G. M. Grigliotti, National Environmental Research Centre, Report PB 216 184, 1973.
Development and Application of the Waste-plus-waste Process for Recovering Metals from Electroplating and other Wastes, A. A. Cockban and L. C. George, US Bureau of Mines, 1974.
Effective Technology for Recycling Metal, National Association of Secondary Material Industries, 1971.
Effluent Treatment in the Copper and Copper Alloy Industries, D. J. Whistance and E. C. Mantle, BNFMRA, 1965.
Identification of Opportunities for Increased Recycling of Ferrous Solid Waste, US Environmental Protection Agency/National Technical Information Service, 1972.
In Support of Clean Water—Disposing of Effluents from Film Processing, L. E. West, Kodak Publication No. J-44, 1973.
Lead in the Environment and its Significance to Man, Pollution Paper No. 2, HMSO, 1974.
Management of Water in the Iron and Steel Industry, Annual General Meeting Proceedings, ISI Publication, 1970.
Metal Processing Wastes. A Bibliography with Abstracts, E. J. Lehmann, National Technical Information Service, 1973.
Non-ferrous Metals, Reclamation and Recycling Digest No. 1, Industrial Aids Ltd, 1975.
Pollution Abatement in the Electroplating Industry, J. W. Funke, S. Africa National Institute for Water Research, 1973.
Pollution Control in Metal Finishing, M. R. Watson, Noyes Data Corp., 1973.
Pollution Control in the Non-Ferrous Metals Industry, H. R. Jones, Noyes Data Corp., 1972.

Prevention of Air Pollution in the Non-Ferrous Metals Industries, E. C. Mantle, BNFMRA, 1974.
Recovery of Phosphates and Metals from Phosphates Sludge by Solvent Extraction, H. E. Powell and L. L. Smith, US Bureau of Mines, 1972.
Removal of Heavy Metals from Mine Drainage by Precipitation, L. W. Ross, US Environmental Protection Agency, Report PB 228 584, 1973.
Review of Literature Concerning the Steel Industry and Pollution, Pt. 1, *The Background to Pollution*, D. G. Brinn, British Steel Corporation, 1974.
Silver Recovery from Waste Photographic Solutions by Metallic Displacement, R. O. Dannenberg and G. M. Potter, US Bureau of Mines, 1968.
Toxicity of Industrial Metals, E. Browning, Butterworth, 1969.

Noise

Code of Practice for Reducing the Exposure of Employed Persons to Noise, HMSO, 1972.
Noise Abatement, C. Duerden, Butterworth, 1972.
Noise Control, Process Plant Association, 1973.
Noise and the Worker, HMSO, 1971.
Noise Pollution, D. E. Anthrop, Lexington, 1973.
Noise Reduction Manual, P. M. Reynolds, BNFMRA.
Notes for the Guidance of Designers on the Reduction of Machinery Noise, HMSO, 1975.
Our Acoustic Environment, F. A. White, Wiley, 1976.
(The) Protection Handbook of Industrial Noise, Alan Osborne and Associates, 1974.

Paper

Colour Removal and Sludge Disposal Process for Kraft Mill Effluents, E. L. Spruill, US Environmental Protection Agency, 1974.
Detoxification of Kraft Pulp Mill Effluent by an Aerated Lagoon, J. A. Serviri and R. W. Gordon, International Pacific Salmon Fisheries Commission, 1972.
Pollution by the Pulp and Paper Industry: Present Situation and Trends, OECD, 1973.
Pollution Control and Chemical Recovery in the Pulp and Paper Industry, H. R. Jones, Noyes Data Corp., 1973.
Recycle of Papermill Waste Waters and Application of Reverse Osmosis, D. C. Morris, W. R. Nelson and G. O. Walraven, Green Bay Packaging, Report PB 211 021, 1972.
Studies on Waste Water from Pulp Mills, J. Refelt, Chalmers University of Technology, 1974.

Refuse

Analysis of Urban Solid Waste Services, R. M. Clark, Wiley, 1977.
Case Studies of Municipal Waste Disposal Systems, H. W. Sheffer, E. C. Baker and G. C. Evans, US Bureau of Mines, Report PB 199 073, 1971.
Disposal of Refuse and Other Waste, J. Skitt, Knight, 1972.
Municipal Refuse Disposal, American Public Works Association and Institute for Solid Wastes, 1970.
Municipal Waste Disposal: Problem or Opportunity, R. H. Clark and J. H. Brown, Ontario Economic Council, 1971.
Recovery and Utilisation of Municipal Solid Waste, N. L. Drobny, H. E. Hull and R. F. Testin, Battelle Memorial Inst., Report PB 204 922, 1971.
Recycling and Reclaiming of Municipal Solid Wastes, F. R. Jackson, Noyes Data Corp., 1975.
Recycling of Municipal Solid Wastes, G. A. Zerlaut and A. M. Stake, Illinois Institute of Technology, 1974.
Recycling Resources Refuse, A. Porteous, Longman, 1977.
Refuse Disposal, HMSO, 1971.
Resource Recovery from Municipal Solid Waste, National Center for Resource Recovery, Lexington, 1974.
State of the Art Review of Municipal Refuse Collection, National Center for Resource Recovery, Lexington, 1973.
Thermal Processing of Municipal Solid Waste for Resource and Energy Recovery, N. J. Weinstein and R. F. Toro, Ann Arbor, 1976.

Miscellaneous

Disposal of Plastics Wastes and Litter, J. J. P. Staudinger, Society of Chemical Industry, 1970.
Disposal of Radioactive Waste: Proceedings of the Information Meeting Organised by the Nuclear Energy Agency, OECD, 1972.
Effluent Treatment and Water Conservation, Committee of Directors of Textile Research Associations, Effluent and Water Conservation Sub-Committee, 1973.
Environmental Control, R. A. Leone, Lexington, 1976.
Forest Products Pollution Control, M. E. Johnson, Western Forest Products Lab., Reports PB 210 728 and 222 173, 1972–1973.
Incentives for Recycling and Reuse of Plastics, T. Milgram, Report PB 214 045, 1974.
Pesticides and Pollution, K. Mellanby, Collins, 1970.
Pollution Control in the Dairy Industry, H. R. Jones, Noyes Data Corp., 1974.
Pollution Control in the Plastics and Rubber Industry, M. Sittig, Noyes Data Corp., 1975.
Pollution Control in the Textile Industry, H. R. Jones, Noyes Data Corp., 1973.
Pollution in the Electric Power Industry, D. L. Scott, Lexington, 1973.
Study of the Reclamation and Reuse of Waste Tyres, Rubber and Plastics Research Association of Great Britain, 1976.
Survey of Effluent Disposal in the Glass Industry, S. E. Bedford, British Glass Industry Research Association, 1973.
Waste Disposal Problems in Selected Industries, J. E. Ullman, Hofstra University, School of Business, 1969.

General Texts

Advances in Environmental Science and Technology, Vol. 1 et seq., J. N. Pitts and R. L. Metcalf (eds), Wiley, 1970 onwards.
Air and Water Pollution, W. E. Brittin, R. West and R. Williams, Hilger, 1972.
Air Pollution and Water Conservation, Industrial Newspapers Ltd., 1970.
An Introduction to Environmental Sciences, J. M. Moran, M. D. Morgan and J. H. Wiersman, Brown and Co, 1973.
Application of a Large Scale Nonlinear Programming Algorithm to Pollution Control, G. Graves and D. Pingry, Purdue University, 1971.
Aspects of Environmental Protection, I.P. Environmental Ltd., 1972.
Beyond the Age of Waste, D. Gabor, V. Colombo, A. King and R. Galli, Pergamon, 1978.
Chemical Control of the Human Environment, Butterworth, 1970.
Chemistry for Environmental Engineers, C. Sawyer and P. McCarty, McGraw-Hill, 1976.
Conservation of Materials, UKAEA, Harwell, 1974.
Conservation of Resources, The Chemical Society, 1977.
Controlling Pollution, Department of the Environment, HMSO, 1974.
(The) Cost of Energy and a Clean Environment, R. G. Thompson and J. A. Calloway, Gulf, 1978.
Dangerous Properties of Industrial Materials, N.I. Sax, Van Nostrand, 1975.
Design of Environmental Information Systems, R. A. Deininger, Wiley, 1974.
Development of a State Effluent Charge System, US Environmental Protection Agency, 1972.
Directory of Pollution Control Equipment Companies in Western Europe, R. Whiteside, Graham and Trotman, 1977.
Directory of Waste Disposal and Recovery, A. Pratt, Godwin, 1978.
(The) Diseases of Occupations, 5th edn, D. Hunter, English Universities Press, 1975.
Ecology and Economics: Controlling Pollution in the 70's, M. I. Goldman (Ed.), Prentice-Hall, 1972.
Ecology, Pollution, Environment, A. Turk et al., Saunders, 1972.
(The) Economics of Recycling, Environment Resources Ltd, Graham and Trotman, 1978.
Encyclopaedia of Environmental Control, N. I. Sax, Van Nostrand, 1976.
Environment and Pollution, F. H. V. Lek and R. K. C. Lak, Thomas, 1974.
Environmental Chemistry, J. O'M. Bockris, Plenum, 1976.
Environmental Chemistry, G. Eglinton, Chemical Society, 1975.
Environmental Chemistry, J. W. Moore and E. A. Moore, Academic Press, 1976.
Environmental Economics Bibliography, Vols. 1 and 2, B. O. Pettman and D. Pearce, NKB Journals, 1975.

Environmental Engineering, G. Lindner and K. Nyberg, Reidel, 1973.
Environmental Pollution: Awareness and Control, E. I. Shakeen, Eng. Technology, 1974.
Environmental Pollution, L. Hodges, Holt, 1973.
Environmental Pollution Control: Technical, Economic and Legal Aspects, A. D. McKnight *et al.*, Allen and Unwin, 1974.
Environmental Protection, E. T. Chanlett, McGraw-Hill, 1973.
Environmental Sources and Emissions Handbook, M. Sittig, Noyes Data Corp., 1975.
Environmental Systems Engineering, L. G. Rich, McGraw-Hill, 1973.
(The) Estimation of Pollution Damage, P. J. W. Saunders, Manchester University Press, 1976.
Federal Pollution Control Programs: Water, Air and Solid Wastes, US Bureau of National Affairs, 1971.
Flow Studies in Air and Water Pollution, R. E. A. Arndt *et al.*, American Society of Mechanical Engineers, 1973.
Industrial Pollution. A Guide to Assessment and Control, D. C. Murphy, Industrial and Commercial Techniques Ltd., 1972.
Industrial Pollution, N. I. Sax, Van Nostrand, 1975.
Industrial Pollution Control, K. Tearle (Ed.), Business Books, 1973.
Industrial Pollution Control Handbook, H. F. Lund, McGraw-Hill, 1971.
Industrial Pollution Control Yearbook, Fuel and Metallurgical Journals, 1974.
Industrial Pollution Control Yearbook, B. Laverick, Industrial Newspapers Ltd, 1974.
Industrial Waste, A. W. Neal, Business Books, 1971.
Industrial Waste Disposal, B. Koziorowski and J. Kucharski, Pergamon, 1972.
Industrial Waste Disposal, R. D. Ross, Van Nostrand, 1968.
Introduction to Environmental Sciences, J. M. Moran, M. D. Morgan and J. H. Wiersma, Little Brown, 1974.
Kaiser Refractories Environmental Studies Final Report, J. P. Harville (Ed.), Technical Pub. No. 71–3, California State Colleges/Moss Landing Marine Laboratories, 1971.
(The) Limits to Growth, D. H. Meadows *et al.*, Earth Island, 1972.
Methods for Chemical Analysis of Water and Waste, Environmental Protection Agency, 1971.
Models for Environmental Pollution Control, R. A. Deininger, Wiley, 1974.
(The) Natural Environment: Wastes and Control, Goodyear Publishing, 1973.
Persistent Pesticides in the Environment, C. A. Edwards, Butterworth, 1970.
Pollutant Removal Handbook, M. Sittig, Noyes Data Corp., 1973.
Pollution, L. K. Hamblin, Stacey, 1971.
Pollution, L. Stewart and W. Clarke, Day, 1971.
Pollution and its Control: the Role of Instrumentation to 1980: A Study of the UK Situation, British Scientific Instrument Research Association, 1971.
Pollution Control and Management, New England Commission, 1969.
(The) Pollution Crisis, E. H. Rabin and M. D. Schwartz, Oceana, 1972.
Pollution Detection and Monitoring Handbook, M. Sittig, Noyes Data Corp., 1974.
Pollution Engineering Techniques, IPEC, Ann Arbor, 1974.
Pollution Profits and Progress, H. A. Schroeder, Stephen Greane, 1971.
Pollution: The Professionals and the Public, K. Attenborough, C. Pollitt and A. Porteous, Open University, 1977.
Practical Waste Treatment and Disposal, D. Dickinson (Ed.), Applied Science, 1974.
Problems of our Physical Environment: Energy, Transportation, Pollution, J. Priest, Addison-Wesley, 1973.
Proceedings of 31st Industrial Waste Conference, 1976, J. M. Bell, Wiley, 1977.
Provisional Code of Practice for Disposal of Wastes, Institution of Chemical Engineers, 1971.
Purity or Pollution, P. Rondiere, Collins, 1971.
Recycling Activity Description: Transfer, Intermediate Storage, Processing, Recycling, Denver Regional Council of Governments, Report PB 218 990, 1972.
Recycling and Ecosystem Response, H. K. Stevens, T. C. Bahr and R. A. Cole, Michigan State University, Report PB 208 669, 1972.
Recycling Assessment and Prospects for Success, A. Darnay, Environmental Protection Agency, Report PB 213 961, 1972.
Recycling Day in New York 1971, US National Association of Secondary Materials Industries and New York Board of Trade, 1971.
Recycling Resources, Report, US National Association of Secondary Materials Industries, April 1971.

Research in Environmental Economics in the UK 1974, D. W. Pearce and B. O. Pettrian, MCB Journals, 1975.

Resource Conservation: Social and Economic Dimensions of Recycling, D. W. Pearce and I. Walter (eds), Longman, 1977.

Sourcebook on the Environment, C. S. Revelle and P. L. Revelle, Houghton Mifflin, 1974.

Study of Water Recovery and Solid Waste Processing for Aerospace and Domestic Applications, Vols. 1 and 2. *Final Report*, C. A. Guarneri, A. Reed and R. E. Renman, Grumman Aerospace Corp., 1972.

Symposium on the Global Effects of Environmental Pollution, Springer, 1970.

Technology and Management of the Environment: Seminar, Oregon State University, Water Resources Research Institute, Corvallus, 1971.

(The) Treatment of Industrial Wastes, E. B. Besselievre and M. Schwartz, McGraw-Hill, 1976.

Underground Waste Management and Environmental Implications, T. D. Cook, American Association of Petroleum Geologists, 1972.

Urban Environmental Management Planning for Pollution Control, B. J. L. Berry and F. E. Horton, Prentice-Hall, 1974.

Waste Disposal and Treatment in Permafrost Areas, M. P. Snodgrass, US Dept. of the Interior, Report PB 198 988, 1971.

Waste Management, Control, Recovery and Reuse, N. Y. Kirov, Ann Arbor, 1975.

Waste Management Research, Cornell Argricultural Waste Management Conference, 1972.

Water Quality Improvement by Physical and Chemical Processes. Water Resources Symposium, E. F. Gloyna and W. W. Eckenfelder, University of Texas Center for Research in Water Resources, 1970.

Water Recovery and Solid Waste Processing for Aerospace and Domestic Applications, Vols. 1 and 2, R. W. Murray, General Electric Co., Philadelphia, 1973.

World Dynamics, J. W. Forrester, MIT, 1971.

Index